NATIONAL LEAGUE GREEN BOOK—1996

THE NATIONAL LEAGUE OF PROFESSIONAL BASEBALL CLUBS
350 Park Avenue, New York, New York 10022

TABLE OF CONTENTS

All-Star Game	46
Attendance Data	89, 104
Awards, 1995	
Batting Champion	87
Cy Young Award	86
ERA Leader	86
Gold Gloves	84
Lou Brock Award (Stolen Bases)	88
Manager of the Year	86
Mel Ott Award (Home Runs)	85
Most Valuable Player	84
Players, Pitchers of the Month	87
Players of the Week	87
Rookie of the Year	85
RBI Champion	84
Batting	
All-Time Top Ten, by Club	58-61
Club, 1995	97
Individual, 1995	94-97
Leaders, All-Time by Dept. (1876-1995)	55
Lifetime	56-57
National League Champs (1876-1995)	87
RBI Leaders, All-Time by Position	62-63
RBI Leaders, by Years	84
RBI Leaders, Yearly by Club	64-65
Top Ten, 1995 (Average, Games, Runs, Hits, etc.)	93
Championship Series, 1995	48
Club Officials Directory	2-6
Clubs' Top Marks Since 1900	77-79
Commissioners	Inside Front Cover
Dates to Remember, 1996	102
Division Series, 1995	47
Farm Clubs	9
Fielding, Club, 1995	97
Fielding, Individual, 1995	98-99
Franchises, N.L.	Inside Front Cover
Free Agents, Unsigned	88
Ground Rules, 1996	6-7
Hall of Fame, National League	90
Highs & Lows, 1995	92
Home Runs	
At Each Park, 1995	52
Grand Slams (Lifetime, 1995, All-Time Leaders)	53
Leaders, All-Time by Position	62-63
Leaders, by Years	85
Pitchers' Home Runs	57
30 or More Per Season	54
How They Finished (1900-1995)	80-83
Inter-Club Totals	83
Managers, 1876-1996	41
Managers, 1996	39-40
Park Data and Club Addresses, 1996	2-6
Pitching	
All-Time Leaders, by Club	74
Club, 1995	103
ERA Leaders, by Years	86
Individual, 1995	100-103
Lifetime Records	70-71
Lifetime Records Against Opposing Clubs	68-69
Low-Run Complete Games, 1995	75
Low-Run Games by Pitching Staff, 1995	75
No-Hit & One-Hit Pitchers	76
Records vs. Opposing Clubs, 1995	66-67
Shutouts, 1995	76
Shutouts, 1995, by Staff	75
Shutouts, Lifetime	76
Strikeout Leaders, by Years	89
Top Ten, 1995 (ERA, Wins, Saves, Innings Pitched, etc.)	93
Twenty-Game Winners, by Years	72-73
Won-Lost Percentage Leaders, by Years	75
Presidents, National League	Inside Front Cover
Qualifications (Batting Champ, ERA, Rookie)	8
Records Set and Tied, M.L. & N.L., 1995	100
Retired Uniforms	9
Rookie Prospects, 1996	42
Rosters	
Atlanta	10-11
Chicago	12-13
Cincinnati	14-15
Colorado	16-17
Florida	18-19
Houston	20-21
Los Angeles	22-23
Montreal	24-25
New York	26-27
Philadelphia	28-29
Pittsburgh	30-31
St. Louis	32-33
San Diego	34-35
San Francisco	36-37
Rules, National League for 1996	8
Schedule, 1996, Official League	Back Cover
Standings (Doubleheaders, Extra-Inning, Night Games, One-Run Shutouts)	51
Standings (Final, Home-Road, Monthly, Inter- and Intra-Divisional)	50
Stolen Base Leaders, by Years	88
Stolen Base N.L. Career Leaders	88
Streaks, Club and Player, 1995	91
Ten Top Control Artists, 1995	103
Ten Toughest to Double, 1995	103
Ten Toughest to Fan, 1995	103
Ticket Prices, 1996	104
Time of Games, 1995	82
Transactions, National League, 1995-96	38
Umpires, National League	43-45
World Series, 1995	49

© 1996 The National League of Professional Baseball Clubs. Published by The Sporting News Publishing Co.

ATLANTA BRAVES
Atlanta National League Baseball Club, Inc.

P.O. Box 4064
Atlanta, GA 30302
(404) 522-7630
FAX: (404) 614-1391

Owner	R.E. Turner III
Chairman of the Board of Directors	William C. Bartholomay
Directors	Henry L. Aaron, Stanley H. Kasten, Rubye M. Lucas, Terence F. McGuirk, John Schuerholz, M.B. Seretean, Allison Thornwell, Jr., R.E. Turner III
President	Stanley H. Kasten
Executive Vice President & General Manager	John Schuerholz
Senior Vice President & Assistant to the President	Henry L. Aaron
Senior Vice President Administration	Bob Wolfe
Vice President, Director of Marketing & Broadcasting	Wayne Long
Vice President	Lee Douglas
Assistant General Manager	Dean Taylor
Director of Scouting & Player Development	Paul Snyder
Director of Minor League Operations	Rod Gilbreath
Assistant Director of Scouting and Player Development	Deric Ladnier
Special Assistants/Player Personnel	Willie Stargell, Jose Martinez
Director of Team Travel & Equipment Manager	Bill Acree
Senior Director of Promotions & Civic Affairs	Miles McRea
Controller	Chip Moore
Director of Ticket Sales	Paul Adams
Director of Stadium Operations & Security	Larry Bowman
Director of Braves Foundation	Danny Goodwin
Field Director	Ed Mangan
Director of Ticket Operations	Ed Newman
Director of Advertising	Amy Richter
Director of Community Relations and Fan Development	Dexter Santos
Director of Public Relations	Jim Schultz
Director of Sports Human Resources	Lisa Stricklin

Games At: Atlanta-Fulton County Stadium
521 Capitol Avenue, SW
Atlanta, GA 30312

Capacity: 52,769   Surface: Natural Grass
Playing Field Distances:
Left Field Fence	330 feet
Center Field Fence	402 feet
Right Field Fence	330 feet
Plate to Grandstand	60 feet
Power Alleys (Left and Right)	385 feet

Height of Walls:
All	10 feet

CHICAGO CUBS
Chicago National League Ball Club, Inc.

1060 West Addison St.
Chicago, IL 60613-4397
(312) 404-2827
FAX: (312) 404-4129

BOARD OF DIRECTORS
Jim Dowdle, Andrew B. MacPhail, Andrew J. McKenna

President and Chief Executive Officer	Andrew B. MacPhail

BASEBALL OPERATIONS
General Manager	Ed Lynch
Director, Scouting	Jim Hendry
Director, Baseball Administration	Scott Nelson
Director, Minor Leagues	David Wilder
Director, Arizona Operations/Special Assignment Scout	Larry Himes
Special Assistants to the G.M.	Al Goldis, John Young
Director, Media Relations	Sharon Pannozzo
Special Player Consultant	Hugh Alexander
Major League Advance Scout	Keith Champion
Traveling Secretary	Jimmy Bank

BUSINESS OPERATIONS
Executive Vice President, Business Operations	Mark McGuire
Vice President, Marketing and Broadcasting	John McDonough
Director, Stadium Operations	Tom Cooper
Director, Minor League Business Operations	Connie Kowal
Director, Human Resources	Janice Maltby
Director, Ticket Operations	Frank Maloney
Director, Publications/Special Projects	Ernie Roth
Assistant Director, Ticket Sales	Jim Coffey
Assistant Director, Ticket Services	Joe Kirchen
Assistant Director, Stadium Operations	Paul Rathje
Senior Legal Counsel	Crane Kenney
Corporate Secretary	Stanley Gradowski

Games At: Wrigley Field

Capacity: 38,765   Surface: Natural Grass
Playing Field Distances:
Left Field Fence	355 feet
Center Field Fence	400 feet
Right Field Fence	353 feet
Plate to Grandstand	60½ feet
Power Alleys (Left and Right)	368 feet

Height of Walls:
Left and Right Field	11½ feet

CINCINNATI REDS
The Cincinnati Reds

100 Riverfront Stadium
Cincinnati, OH 45202
(513) 421-4510
FAX: (513) 421-7342

President & Chief Executive Officer	Marge Schott

BASEBALL OPERATIONS
General Manager	James G. Bowden IV
Director of Scouting	Julian Mock
Director of Player Development	Sheldon (Chief) Bender
Special Assistant to the General Manager	Gene Bennett
Senior Advisor/Baseball Operations	Larry Barton, Jr.
Senior Advisor/Player Personnel	Jack McKeon
Traveling Secretary	Gary Wahoff
Administrative Assistant to the G.M.	Lois Schneider
Administrative Assistant/Scouting	Wilma Mann
Secretary/Player Development	Lois Hudson

BUSINESS ADMINISTRATION
Controller	John Allen
Director of Stadium Operations	Joanne Pettyjohn
Director of Ticket Department	John O'Brien
Director of Season Ticket Sales	Pat McCaffrey
Director of Group Sales	Barb McManus
Director of Marketing	Chip Baker
Director of Publicity	Mike Ringering
Assistant Ticket Director	Ken Ayer
Manager Gift Shop	Roberta Moore
Administrative Assistant/Business	Ginny Kamp
Payroll Supervisor	Cathy Secor

Games At: Riverfront Stadium

Capacity: 52,952   Surface: Artificial
Playing Field Distances:
Left Field Fence	330 feet
Center Field Fence	404 feet
Right Field Fence	330 feet
Plate to Grandstand	51 feet
Power Alleys (Left and Right)	375 feet

Height of Walls:
Outfield Fence	8 feet

COLORADO ROCKIES
Colorado Rockies Baseball Club

Coors Field
2001 Blake St.
Denver, CO 80205
(303) 292-0200
(303) 312-2325 (PR)
(303) 312-2398 (Press Box)
FAX: (303) 312-2319

Chairman, President, Chief Executive Officer	Jerry McMorris
Executive Vice President/General Manager	Bob Gebhard
Senior Vice President/Business Operations	Keli McGregor
Senior Vice President/Chief Financial Officer	Hal Roth
Senior Vice President/Secretary & Corporate Counsel	Clark Weaver
Vice President/Finance	Michael Kent
Vice President/Player Personnel	Dick Balderson
Vice President/Sales & Marketing	Greg Feasel
Vice President/Ticket Operations	Sue Ann McClaren
Assistant General Manager	Tony Siegle
Director, Broadcasting	Eric Brummond
Director, Charitable and Community Affairs	Roger Kinney
Director, Corporate Marketing	Michael Arthur
Director, Corporate Sales	Marcy English
Director, Management Information Systems	Mary Burns
Director, Merchandising	Jim Kellogg
Director, Promotions and Special Events	Alan Bossart
Director, Publications	Jimmy Oldham
Director, Public Relations	Mike Swanson
Director, Scouting	Pat Daugherty
Director, Stadium Services	Kevin Kahn
Director, Team Travel	Peter Durso
Director, Ticket Operations	Chuck Javernick
Assistant Director, Player Personnel	Paul Egins
Assistant Director, Public Relations	Coley Brannon
Assistant Director, Scouting	Jay Darnell
Manager, Advertising	Lisa Cisneros
Manager, Broadcast Services	Angie Gebhard
Manager, Client Services and Communications	Jan Giovino
Manager, Group Party Facilities/Special Programs	Jill Campbell
Manager, In-Game Entertainment	Jennifer Berger
Head Groundskeeper	Mark Razum
Coordinator of Instruction	Rick Mathews
National Cross-Checkers	Dave Holliday, Jeff Schugel
Regional Cross-Checkers	Bruce Andrew, Bill Gayton, Robyn Lynch

Games At: Coors Field

2001 Blake St.
Denver, CO 80205-2010
(303) 292-2000

Capacity: 50,200 Surface: Natural Grass

Playing Field Distances:	
Left Field Fence	347 feet
Center Field Fence	415 feet
Right Field Fence	350 feet
Plate to Grandstand	56'4"
Power Alleys (Left)	390 feet
(Right)	375 feet
Height of Walls:	
(rf foul pole to rf power alley)	14 feet
(lf foul pole to rf power alley)	8 feet

FLORIDA MARLINS
Florida Marlins Baseball Club

Joe Robbie Stadium
2267 NW 199th St.
Miami, FL 33056
(305) 626-7400

Chairman	H. Wayne Huizenga
Partners	Steven R. Berrard, Harris W. Hudson, Harry Huizenga, Wayne Huizenga, Jr.

EXECUTIVE

President	Donald A. Smiley
Executive Vice President & General Manager	David Dombrowski
Vice President of Broadcasting	Dean Jordan
Vice President of Sales and Marketing	Bob Kramm
Vice President and Assistant General Manager	Frank Wren
Vice President of Player Personnel	Gary Hughes
Vice President of Player Development	John Boles
Special Counsel	James J. Blosser
Special Consultant	Richard C. Rochon
Executive Assistant to the President	Lori McCarron

BASEBALL OPERATIONS

Executive Vice President and General Manager	David Dombrowski
Vice President and Assistant General Manager	Frank Wren
Vice President of Player Personnel	Gary Hughes
Vice President of Player Development	John Boles
Director of Scouting	Orrin Freeman
Director of Latin American Operations	Al Avila
Senior Advisor, Player Personnel	Whitey Lockman
Director of Minor League Administration	Dan Lunetta
Assistant, Baseball Operations	DeJon Watson
Director of Team Travel	Bill Beck
Director of Media Relations	Chuck Pool
Assistant Directors of Media Relations	Ron Colangelo, Adolfo Salgueiro
Media Services Coordinator	Margo Allen Malone
Latin American Operations Assistant	Louis Eljaua

BROADCASTING

Vice President of Broadcasting	Dean Jordan

FINANCE AND ADMINISTRATION

Vice President of Finance and Administration	Jonathan D. Mariner
Director of Information Systems	David Hunter
Accounting Manager	Susan Jaison
Senior Staff Accountants	David Kuan, Donna Hancock
Staff Accountant	Nancy Hernandez

SALES AND MARKETING

Vice President of Sales and Marketing	Bob Kramm
Director of Season and Group Sales	Frank Gernert
Director of Corporate Sponsorships and Promotions	Ben Creed
Director of Marketing Communications	Mark Geddis
Director of International Relations	Tony Perez
Director of Community Relations	Jose Sotolongo
Corporate Sales Manager	Pat McNamara
Publications Manager	Leslie Riguero

Games At: Joe Robbie Stadium

2267 N.W. 199th St.
Miami, FL 33056

Capacity: 40,585 Surface: Natural Grass

Playing Field Distances:	
Left Field Fence	335 feet
Center Field Fence	410 feet
Right Field Fence	345 feet
Plate to Grandstand	60 feet
Power Alleys (Left and Right)	380 feet

HOUSTON ASTROS
Houston Astros Baseball Club

The Astrodome
P.O. Box 288
Houston, TX 77001-0288
(713) 799-9500
FAX:
(713) 799-9562 (Accounting & BB Admin.)
(713) 799-9794 (Bus. Operations)
(713) 799-9812 (Group & Season Sales)
(713) 799-9881 (Media Relations)

BOARD OF DIRECTORS

Chairman & CEO	Drayton McLane, Jr.
Directors	Drayton McLane, Jr., Sandy Sanford, Jr., Bob McClaren

BASEBALL ADMINISTRATION

President	Tal Smith
General Manager	Gerry Hunsicker
Special Assistant to the General Manager	Fred Nelson
Director of Player Development & Scouting	Dan O'Brien
Director of Major League Player Relations	Tim Purpura
Director of Baseball Administration	Barry Waters
Assistant Director of Scouting & Director of International Development	David Rawnsley
Assistant to the Director of Player Development	Trey Wilkinson
Administrative Assistant, Major League Operations	Beverly Rains
Administrative Assistant, Scouting	Traci Franklin
Administrative Assistant, Player Development	Carol Wogsland
Equipment Manager	Dennis Liborio
Assistant Equipment Manager	Dan O'Rourke
Visiting Clubhouse Manger	Steve Perry
Head Athletic Trainer	Dave Labossiere
Assistant Athletic Trainer	Rex Jones
Strength & Conditioning Coach	Dr. Gene Coleman
Senior Team Physician	Dr. Bill Bryan
Co-Team Physician	Dr. David Lintner
Internist/Coordiantor of Physical Examinations	Dr. Mike Feltovich
Consultant/Hand & Wrist Injuries	Dr. Tom Mehlhoff

BUSINESS OPERATIONS

Senior Vice President	Bob McClaren
Controller	Robert McBurnett
Director of Marketing	Pam Gardner
Director of Broadcasting & Promotions	Jamie Hildreth
Director of Community Development	Gene Pemberton
Director of Advertising	Amy Kress
Director of Ticket Sales & Services	Rich Fromstein
Director of Media Relations	Rob Matwick
Assistant Director of Media Relations	Tyler Barnes
Assistant Director of Advertising	Erin Skelley
Youth Programs Coordinator	Heather Cox
Advertising Sales	Jim Ballweg
Advertising Sales Assistant	Marian Harper
Producer/Engineer	Mike Cannon
Program Executive—Community Outreach	Robert Reid
Mascot Program Coordinator	Steve Amaya
Program Manager—Premium Sales	John Sorrentino
Accounts Receivable	Mary Ann Bell
Accounts Payable	Irene Dumenil
Payroll	Marla Rodgers
General Accounting	Mary Duvernay, Rita Suchma
Administrative Assistant, Broadcasting	Anna Cardinale
Administrative Assistant, Community Development	Natalie Hart
Administrative Assistant, Group & Season Sales	Joannie Cobb
Administrative Assistant, Media Relations/Receptionist	Monica Gardner

Games At: The Astrodome
8400 Kirby Dr.
Receiving #3, Level 9
Houston, TX 77054-1599

Capacity: 54,370 Surface: Artificial

Playing Field Distances:	
Left Field Fence	325 feet
Center Field Fence	400 feet
Right Field Fence	325 feet
Power Alleys (left and right)	375 feet
Plate to Grandstand	52 feet
Height of Walls:	
(foul line to scoreboards)	8 feet
(left field and right field scoreboards)	16 feet
(scoreboard to scoreboard)	10 feet

LOS ANGELES DODGERS
Los Angeles Dodgers, Inc.

1000 Elysian Park Avenue
Los Angeles, CA 90012
(213) 224-1500
FAX: (213) 224-1459

President	Peter O'Malley
Executive Vice President	Fred Claire
Vice President, Campo Las Palmas	Ralph Avila
Vice President, Communications	Tommy Hawkins
Vice President, Finance	Bob Graziano
Vice President, Marketing	Barry Stockhamer
Vice President, Treasurer	Roland Seidler
Vice President, Minor League Operations	Charlie Blaney
Asst. Sec. & General Counsel	Santiago Fernandez
Director, Accounting & Finance	Bill Foltz
Director, Advertising & Special Events	Paul Kalil
Director, Broadcasting & Publications	Brent Shyer
Director, Community Relations	Don Newcombe
Director, Community Affairs	Monique Brandon
Director, Human Resources & Administration	Irene Tanji
Director, Management Information Services	Mike Mularky
Director, Scouting	Terry Reynolds
Director, Ticket Marketing	Allan Erselius
Director, Publicity	Jay Lucas
Traveling Secretary	Bill DeLury
Director, Ticket Operations	Debra Duncan
Administrator, Baseball Operations	Robert Schweppe
Assistant Director, Publicity	Derrick Hall

Games At: Dodger Stadium

Capacity: 56,000   Surface: Natural Grass
Playing Field Distances:

Left Field Fence	330 feet
Center Field Fence	395 feet
Right Field Fence	330 feet
Plate to Grandstand	75 feet
Power Alleys (Left and Right)	385 feet

Height of Walls:

Outfield Fence	8 feet

MONTREAL EXPOS
Montreal Baseball Club, Inc.

P.O. Box 500, Station M
Montreal, Quebec
Canada H1V 3P2
(514) 253-3434
FAX: (514) 253-8282

President and General Partner	Claude R. Brochu
Chairman of the Partnership Committee	L. Jacques Menard
Vice Chairmen of the Partnership Committee	Claude Blanchet, Jocelyn Proteau, Louis A. Tanguay

BASEBALL MANAGEMENT

Vice President, Baseball Operations	Bill Stoneman
Vice President & General Manager	Jim Beattie
Director, Scouting	Ed Creech
Director, Player Development	Bill Geivett
Director, International Operations	Fred Ferreira
Assistant Director, Scouting	Gregg Leonard
Assistant Director, Player Development	Neal Huntington

BUSINESS MANAGEMENT

Vice President, Finance	Laurier Carpentier
Director, Financial Planning & Administration	Michel Bussiere
Director, Accounting Services	Constance Jodoin

MARKETING & COMMUNICATIONS

Vice President, Marketing & Communications	Richard Morency
Directors, Advertising Sales	Luigi Carola, Pierre Dicaire, John Di Terlizzi, Danielle La Roche
Director, Media Services	Monique Giroux
Director, Advertising	Johanne Heroux
Director, Media Relations	P.J. Loyello

OPERATIONS

Vice President, Stadium Operations	Claude Delorme
Director, Ticket Office	Chantal Dalpe
Director, Merchandising & Licensing	Susan LeBlanc
Director, Operations	Pierre Touzin

SALES

Vice President, Sales	Lucien Baril
Director, Season Ticket Sales	Gilles Beauregard
Director, Group Sales	Anne Dion

Games At: Olympic Stadium
4549 Pierre De Coubertin Ave.
Montreal, Quebec H1V 3P2

Capacity: 46,500   Surface: Artificial
Playing Field Distances:

Left Field Fence	325 feet
Center Field Fence	404 feet
Right Field Fence	325 feet
Plate to Grandstand	53 feet
Power Alleys (Left and Right)	375 feet

Height of Walls:

All	12 feet

NEW YORK METS
Sterling Doubleday Enterprises, L.P.

123-01 Roosevelt Ave.
Flushing, NY 11368
(718) 565-4330
FAX: (718) 565-4382

Chairman of the Board	Nelson Doubleday
President & Chief Executive Officer	Fred Wilpon
Directors	Nelson Doubleday, Fred Wilpon, Saul B. Katz, Joe McIlvaine, Marvin B. Tepper
Special Advisor to the Board of Directors	Richard Cummins

BASEBALL OPERATIONS

Executive Vice President, Baseball Operations	Joe McIlvaine
Assistant General Manager	Steve Phillips
Vice President & Consultant	Frank Cashen
Director of Scouting	John Barr
Director of Minor League Operations	Jack Zduriencik
Assistant Director of Minor Leagues & Scouting	Jim Duquette
Baseball Administrator	Maureen Cooke
Administrative Assistant, Scouting	Tom Allison
Administrative Assistant, Minor Leagues	Tom Hutchinson

BUSINESS OPERATIONS

Senior Vice President & Treasurer	Harold W. O'Shaughnessy
Vice President, Business Affairs & General Counsel	Dave Howard
Vice President, Marketing & Broadcasting	Mark Bingham
Vice President, Stadium Operations	Bob Mandt
Vice President, Ticket Sales & Services	Bill Ianniciello
Controller	Lennie Labita
Legal Counsel	David Cohen
Director, Administration & Data Processing	Russ Richardson
Director, Amateur Baseball Relations	Tommy Holmes
Director, Community Outreach	Jill Knee
Community Outreach Representative	Mookie Wilson
Director, Customer Relations	Joanne Galardy
Director, Media Relations	Jay Horwitz
Director, Promotions	James Plummer
Director, Ticket Operations	Dan DeMato

Games At: Shea Stadium

Capacity: 55,777   Surface: Natural Grass
Playing Field Distances:

Left Field Fence	338 feet
Center Field Fence	410 feet
Right Field Fence	338 feet
Plate to Grandstand	80 feet
Power Alleys (Left and Right)	371 feet

Height of Walls:

All	8 feet

PHILADELPHIA PHILLIES
The Phillies

P.O. Box 7575
Philadelphia, PA 19101
(215) 463-6000
FAX:
(215) 755-9324 (BB Ops)
(215) 389-3050 (PR/Admin./Fin.)
(215) 463-8765 (Com Rel/TravSec/Stad Ops/Merch)
(215) 463-6025 (Mktg/Prom/Tix)
(215) 463-9434 (Exec. Office)

President, CEO and Managing General Partner	Bill Giles
Executive Vice President, Chief Operating Officer and Co-General Partner	David Montgomery
Partners	Claire S. Betz, Tri-Play Associates (Alexander K. Buck, J. Mahlon Buck, Jr., William C. Buck), Double Play, Inc., (Herbert H. Middleton, Jr.), Fitz Eugene Dixon, Jr.
ADMINISTRATION	
President, CEO and Managing General Partner	Bill Giles
Exec. Vice President, COO and Co-General Partner	David Montgomery
Secretary & General Counsel	Bill Webb
Executive Secretary	Nancy Nolan
Director, Planning/Development	Tom Hudson
Director, Business Development	Joseph Giles
BASEBALL ADMINISTRATION	
Senior Vice President & General Manager	Lee Thomas
Assistant General Manager	Ed Wade
Director, Player Development	Del Unser
Director, Scouting	Mike Arbuckle
Assistant to the President	Paul Owens
Administrator, Baseball Operations	Susan Ingersoll
Traveling Secretary	Eddie Ferenz
Conditioning Coordinator	Scott Hoffman
FINANCE/ACCOUNTING	
Senior Vice President, Finance & Planning	Jerry Clothier
Secretary, Finance	JoAnn Marano
Controller	Lou Perez
PUBLIC RELATIONS/COMMUNITY RELATIONS	
Vice President, Public Relations	Larry Shenk
Manager, Print/Creative Services	Tina Urban
Manager, Publicity	Leigh Tobin
Manager, Media Relations	Gene Dias
Administrator, Public Relations	Karen Nocella
Director, Community Relations	Regina Castellani
MARKETING/PROMOTIONS	
Vice President, Marketing	Dennis Mannion
Assistant to VP Marketing	Debbie Nocito
Manager, Events	Kurt Funk
Manager, Advertising/Broadcasting	Jo-Anne Levy-Lamoreaux
Director, Advertising Sales	Dave Buck
Manager, Entertainment	Chris Legault
Manager, Fan Development	Rob Holiday
Manager, Merchandising	Mike Connor
Manager, Promotions	John Brazer
SALES/TICKETS	
Vice President, Ticket Operations	Richard Deats
Director, Sales	Rory McNeil
Director, Ticket Department	Dan Goroff
Director, Sales Operations	John Weber
Director, Group Sales	Kathy Killian
COMPUTER OPERATIONS	
Director, Information Systems	Brian Lamoreaux
Manager, Computer Operations	Christopher Pohl
Manager, Software & Analysis	Donna Underwood
STADIUM OPERATIONS	
Director, Stadium Operations	Mike DiMuzio
Secretary, Stadium Operations	Bernie Mansi
Receptionist	Kelly Addario-DiGiacomo
Supervisor, Field & Maintenance Operations	Ralph Frangipani

Games At: **Veterans Stadium**
3501 S. Broad St.
Philadelphia, PA 19148

Capacity: 62,136 Surface: Artificial

Playing Field Distances:	
Left Field Fence	330 feet
Center Field Fence	408 feet
Right Field Fence	330 feet
Plate to Grandstand	60 feet
Power Alleys (Left and Right)	371 feet
Height of Walls: All	12 feet

PITTSBURGH PIRATES
Pittsburgh Pirates Baseball Club

P.O. Box 7000
Pittsburgh, PA 15212
(412) 323-5000
FAX: (412) 323-9133 (P.R.)
(412) 323-5024

Chief Executive Officer	Kevin McClatchy
EXECUTIVE	
President	Mark Sauer
Executive Assistant & Support Staff Coordinator	June Schaut
BASEBALL OPERATIONS	
Senior Vice President and General Manager	Cam Bonifay
Assistant G.M./Director of Player Personnel	Pete Vuckovich
Secretary, Senior V.P. and General Manager	Jean Donatelli
Special Assistants to the General Manager	Leland Maddox, Ken Parker, Chet Montgomery, Lenny Yochim
Traveling Secretary	Greg Johnson
Director of Major League Baseball Administration	John Sirignano
Director of Scouting	Paul Tinnell
Director of Bradenton Baseball Operations	Jeff Podobnik
FINANCE/ADMINISTRATION	
Vice President, Finance & Administration	James D. Plake
Director of Accounting	Patti Mistick
Treasurer	Kenneth C. Curcio
Director of Information Systems	Dale Dressler
Personnel Administrator	Linda Zwergel
MEDIA RELATIONS	
Director of Media Relations	Jim Trdinich
Assistant Director of Media Relations	Ben Bouma
Assistant Director of Media Relations	Sally O'Leary
MARKETING/SALES	
Vice President, Marketing & Operations	Steven N. Greenberg
Director of Marketing & Communications	Mike Gordon
Secretary, VP, Marketing & Operations	Donna Beltz
Director of Community Services & Sales	Al Gordon
Director of Corporate Affairs	Nellie Briles
OPERATIONS/PROMOTIONS/MERCHANDISING	
Director of Operations	Dennis DaPra
Director of Community Relations & Special Events	Kathy Guy
Director of Merchandising	Joe Billetdeaux
Warehouse & Mini-Clubhouse Store Manager	Judy Gardner
TICKET OPERATIONS	
Director of Ticket Operations	Gary Remlinger
Customer Service Coordinator	David Jarosz
Ticket Operations Coordinator	Marc Garda
Ticket Processing Coordinator	Jeff Smith
Ticket Services Coordinator	Dave Wysocki
Ticket Service Representative	Dana Williams
BROADCASTING	
Vice President, Broadcasting & Advertising Sales	Mark Driscoll
Sales Manager, Broadcasting & Promotions	Mark Ferraco
Broadcasting Coordinator	Jon Mercurio
National Account Executive	Harold Balk

Games At: **Three Rivers Stadium**
600 Stadium Circle
Pittsburgh, PA 15212

Capacity: 47,972 Surface: Artificial

Playing Field Distances:	
Left Field Fence	335 feet
Center Field Fence	400 feet
Right Field Fence	335 feet
Plate to Grandstand	60 feet
Power Alleys (Left and Right)	375 feet
Height of Walls: All	10 feet

ST. LOUIS CARDINALS
St. Louis National Baseball Club, Inc.

250 Stadium Plaza
St. Louis, MO 63102
(314) 421-3060
FAX: (314) 425-0640

Chairman of the Board	August A. Busch, III
Vice Chairman	Fred L. Kuhlmann
President/CEO	Mark Lamping
Vice President, Business Operations	Mark Gorris
Controller	Brad Wood
Vice President, General Manager	Walt Jocketty
Sr. Administrative Assistant to President/CEO	Elaine Milo
Sr. Administrative Assistant to V.P.,G.M.	Judy Carpenter Barada
Administrative Assistant to V.P., Business Operations	Renee Garrett
Vice President, Community Relations	Marty Hendin
Administrative Assistant to V.P., Community Relations	Mary Ellen Edmiston
Director, Promotions & Player Promotions	Thane Van Breusegen
Director, Major League Personnel	Jerry Walker
Director, Player Development	Mike Jorgensen
Director, Scouting	Marty Maier
Assistant to Director, Player Development	Scott Smulczenski
Asst. to Player Dev. & Major League Operations	John Vuch
Director, Public Relations	Brian Bartow
Director, Broadcasting & Corporate Sales	Dan Farrell
Director, Group Sales	Joe Strohm
Director, Target Marketing	Ted Savage
Director, Ticket Operations	Josephine Arnold
Director, Human Resources & Office Services	Marian Rhodes
Director, Ticket Sales	Kevin Wade
Group Director, Facility Operations	Joe Abernethy
Manager, Customer Service & Telephone Operations	Patti McCormick
Traveling Secretary	C.J. Cherre
Director, Facility Operations	Mike Bertani
Head Groundskeeper	Steve Peeler
Director, Special Projects	Vicki Bryant
Director, Secutiry and Special Services	Joe Walsh
Director, Quality Assurance and Guest Services	Pat Breihan

Games At: Busch Stadium

Capacity: 57,673 Surface: Grass

Playing Field Distances:	
Left Field Fence	330 feet
Center Field Fence	402 feet
Right Field Fence	330 feet
Plate to Grandstand	64 feet
Power Alleys (Left and Right)	375 feet
Height of Walls: All	8 feet

SAN DIEGO PADRES
San Diego Padres Baseball Partnership

P.O. Box 2000
San Diego, CA 92112-2000
(619) 283-4494
FAX: (619) 282-8886 (Media Rel.)
(619) 282-2228 (BB Op.)

Chairman	John Moores
President & Chief Executive Officer	Larry Lucchino
Executive Vice President	Bill Adams
V.P./Baseball Operations & General Manager	Kevin Towers
Vice President/Marketing	Don Johnson
Vice President/Public Affairs	Charles Steinberg
Vice President/Special Projects	Andy Strasberg
Vice President/Finance	Bob Wells
Assistant General Manager	Fred Uhlman Jr.
Director/Community Relations	Michele Anderson
Director/Merchandising	Michael Babida
Director/Corporate Development	Michael Dee
Director/Baseball Operations	Eddie Epstein
Controller	Steve Fitch
Director/Administrative Services	Lucy Freeman
Director/Ticket Operations & Services	Dave Gilmore
Director/Stadium Operations	Mark Guglielmo
Director/Hispanic Marketing	Enrique Morones
Director/Padres Foundation	Jennifer Moores
Director/Player Development	Russ Nixon
Director/Minor League Administration	Priscilla Oppenheimer
Club Counsel	Alan Ostfield
Director/Media Relations and Team Travel	Roger Riley
Director/Sales	Louis Ruvane
Director/Scouting	Brad Sloan
Trainer	Larry Duensing
Assistant Trainer	Todd Hutcheson
Strength and Conditioning Coach	Dean Armitage
Club Physicians	Cliff Colwell, Jan Fronek, Paul Hirshman, Blaine Phillips

Games At: San Diego/Jack Murphy Stadium
9449 Friars Road
San Diego, CA 92108

Capacity: 46,510   Surface: Natural Grass
Playing Field Distances:
- Left Field Fence .... 327 feet
- Center Field Fence .... 405 feet
- Right Field Fence .... 327 feet
- Plate to Grandstand .... 75 feet
- Power Alleys (Left and Right) .... 370 feet

Height of Walls:
- All .... 8½ feet

SAN FRANCISCO GIANTS
San Francisco Baseball Associates L.P.

Candlestick Park
San Francisco, CA 94124
(415) 468-3700
FAX: (415) 467-0485

Managing General Partner	Peter A. Magowan
Senior General Partner	Harmon E. Burns

Limited Partners S. Daniel Abraham, Laurence M. Baer, Phillip J. Buchanan, Alex B. Byer, Allan G. Byer, George Drysdale, John J. Fisher, Daniel Geller, Richard N. Goldman, Philip Greer, William Hewlett, David Jenkins, Charles B. Johnson, KNBR Inc., KTVU Inc., Robert A. Lurie, Philip D. Morais, William Neukom, Lawrence Nibbi, Sergio Nibbi, Arthur Rock, Sydney Rosenberg, Theodore Rosenberg, Robert Sockolov

ADMINISTRATION
President	Peter A. Magowan
Executive Vice President	Laurence M. Baer
Senior Vice President and General Manager	Robert E. Quinn
Senior Vice President, Business Operations	Patrick J. Gallagher
Vice President and Chief Financial Officer	John F. Yee
Director of Legal and Government Affairs	Jack F. Bair, Esq.

BASEBALL OPERATIONS
Senior Vice President, Player Personnel	Brian Sabean
Director of Major League Administration	Ned Colletti
Director of Player Development	Jack Hiatt
Director of Travel	Reggie Younger Jr.
Coordinator of Scouting	Bob Hartsfield
Coordinator of Latin American Operations	Luis Rosa
Special Assistant to the General Manager	Dick Tidrow

BUSINESS OPERATIONS
Vice President, Stadium Operations/Security	Jorge Costa
Director of Marketing/Sales	Mario Alioto
Director of Public Relations and Community Development	Bob Rose
Director of Stadium Operations	Gene Telucci
Director of Ticket Services	Russ Stanley
General Manager, Retail/Internet	Connie Kullberg
Controller	Larry Dodd
Media Relations Manager	Jim Moorehead

Games At: Candlestick Park

Capacity: 63,000   Surface: Natural Grass
Playing Field Distances:
- Left Field Fence .... 335 feet
- Center Field Fence .... 400 feet
- Right Field Fence .... 328 feet
- Plate to Grandstand .... 57 feet
- Power Alleys (Left and Right) .... 365 feet

Height of Walls:
- All .... 8 feet

ATLANTA BRAVES
ATLANTA FULTON COUNTY STADIUM

GROUND RULES

DUGOUTS—Dugouts are bounded by guard rails and any ball hitting guard rail is IN PLAY. Ball hitting netting on home plate side of either dugout is IN PLAY. Ball hitting facing on or over either dugout is IN PLAY. Ball hitting front ledge of lip in front of dugout is IN PLAY.
BACKSTOP—Ball lodging in padding or on top of camera booth is dead—ONE BASE on pitch and TWO BASES on throw by a fielder. Ball thrown into stands under fence going from dugout to dugout—ONE BASE on pitch and TWO BASES on throw by a fielder.
CANVAS—Catch may be made off of canvas. Ball lodged behind or under canvas is dead—ONE BASE on pitch and TWO BASES on throw by a fielder. Batted ball lodging behind or under canvas—TWO BASES.
FOUL POLES—Ball hitting any part of screen area supported by poles down left or right field line—HOME RUN. Ball going over outfield fence into open space directly below screen area—HOME RUN.

CHICAGO CUBS
WRIGLEY FIELD

GROUND RULES

WHEN BALL:
Hits railing or screen above bleacher wall, and bounces back on playing field—IN PLAY.
Sticks in screen in front of bleachers—TWO BASES.
Sticks in vines on bleacher walls—TWO BASES. If ball comes out—IN PLAY.
Hits left field or right field foul markers above painted mark—HOME RUN.
Hits foul markers below painted mark, and bounces back on playing field—IN PLAY.
Goes in or under grates in left or right field and remains there—TWO BASES.
Goes in or under grates, on either side of home plate, and remains there—ONE BASE on pitched ball. TWO BASES on thrown ball.

CINCINNATI REDS
RIVERFRONT STADIUM

GROUND RULES

FOUL SCREEN—Any ball hitting foul screen in left or right field—HOME RUN.
THE OUTFIELD—Any ball bouncing over fence—TWO BASE HIT. Any ball hit down right or left field line and bouncing into box seats in stands—TWO BASES. Batted ball must clear (not strike) yellow line atop outfield fence to be considered a home run.
CANVAS (TARP)—Ball remaining behind or underneath canvas—ONE BASE on pitch and TWO BASES on throw by fielder. TWO BASES on batted ball, otherwise in play. Fielder may make catch standing on canvas.
DUGOUTS—Everything in play unless the ball goes into the dugout.

COLORADO ROCKIES
COORS FIELD

GROUND RULES

DUGOUTS—Everything IN PLAY unless ball goes into the dugout. Photographers' areas are considered part of the dugout.
FOUL POLES—Ball hitting any part of screen area supported by poles down left or right field lines—HOME RUN.
Ball hitting net in left field and bouncing back onto playing field—IN PLAY.
CANVAS (TARP)—Ball remaining behind or underneath canvas—ONE BASE on pitch and TWO BASES on throw by fielder. TWO BASES on batted ball, otherwise in play. Fielder may make catch standing on canvas.
SCOREBOARD IN RIGHTFIELD—Ball going through the scoreboard, either on the bound or the fly—TWO BASES.

NATIONAL LEAGUE STADIUMS' GROUND RULES

FLORIDA MARLINS
JOE ROBBIE STADIUM
GROUND RULES

WHEN:
Ball bounds off of any portion of railing around photographer's booths—IN PLAY.
Ball strikes any portion of left field scoreboard below the upper most edge—IN PLAY.
Ball strikes any portion of foul poles:
1. In left field above any edge of the scoreboard—HOME RUN.
2. In right field above top of wall—HOME RUN.

HOUSTON ASTROS
ASTRODOME
GROUND RULES

DUGOUTS—The ball remains in play unless it enters the dugout. ONE BASE on throw by pitcher; TWO BASES on throw by a fielder.
BEHIND HOME PLATE—Any thrown ball hitting above, on or below padding behind home plate remains IN PLAY if it rebounds onto field. If ball lodges in the padding or behind plexiglass camera shield—ONE BASE on pitch; TWO BASES on throw by a fielder.
HITTING ROOF OR SPEAKERS—Ball hitting roof or speakers in fair territory is playable if caught by fielder—batter is out. Ball hitting roof or speakers in fair territory shall be judged fair or foul in relation to where it hits the ground or is touched by a fielder. Any ball that hits speakers or roof in foul territory is a foul ball and the ball is dead.
OUTFIELD AREA—Fairly batted ball in left, center and right field hitting ABOVE yellow line—HOME RUN. Any ball bouncing above line is considered to have left the playing field and should be ruled a TWO BASE hit.

LOS ANGELES DODGERS
DODGER STADIUM
GROUND RULES

LEFT- AND RIGHT-FIELD FOUL POLES—Ball IN PLAY when it hits below railing (white section of foul pole). HOME RUN on ball hitting foul pole above railing (yellow section).
DUGOUTS—All Television and Photography booths, as well as Dugouts, considered bench. Ball striking any forward facing of Dugouts—IN PLAY.
BACKSTOP SCREEN—Screen Roof of Fans' Dugout Boxes considered same as sloping area of a Backstop. Ball striking guide wire supporting Backstop—OUT OF PLAY.

MONTREAL EXPOS
OLYMPIC STADIUM
GROUND RULES

Ball hitting roof on outside side of orange line is a HOME RUN.
Everything in play—
  EXCEPT: Ball going into the dugouts and camera pits—BOOK RULE.
    Popup or fly ball hit into any one of four designated camera areas is out of play.
    If ball hits overhanging speakers in fair territory, it is a HOME RUN.
    If ball hits overhanging speakers in foul territory, it is a DEAD BALL.
    Ball caught in padding of outfield fence is GROUND RULE DOUBLE.

NEW YORK METS
SHEA STADIUM
GROUND RULES

Ball rolling under any part of field boxes and staying out of sight—ONE BASE on throw by pitcher from rubber—TWO BASES on throw by infielder.
Ball hitting side of facing of dugout considered IN DUGOUT.
Ball going into dugout—ONE BASE on throw by pitcher from rubber—TWO BASES from field.
Fair ball bouncing over fence—TWO BASES.
Fair ball bouncing over temporary fence in foul territory in left and right field—TWO BASES.

PHILADELPHIA PHILLIES
VETERANS STADIUM
GROUND RULES

DUGOUTS—Ball has to actually enter dugout area or hit the yellow bars or yellow line to be considered out of play. Ball entering open area above end of dugout inside yellow line is considered OUT OF PLAY.
FOUL POLES—Are outside playing area and balls hitting them are to be considered HOME RUN.
FENCES—Glass areas have openings at top. If ball sticks in opening it is a GROUND RULE DOUBLE. Ball sticking underneath padding in outfield fence is IN PLAY. In left and right field the stands protrude to a point near the foul lines. If ball lands in fair territory and bounces over the points and lands in the playing area, it is considered to be in the stands and ruled a GROUND RULE DOUBLE.
Ball off screen behind home plate is IN PLAY. Ball hitting pipe to right of right field foul pole is IN PLAY.

PITTSBURGH PIRATES
THREE RIVERS STADIUM
GROUND RULES

Ball hitting any part of foul-line screen above top of outfield fence—HOME RUN.
For purpose of Ground Rules photographers' benches which abut outfield ends of home and visiting clubs' benches are considered to be part of player's bench.
Fair hit ball striking screen in front of right or left field bullpen is IN PLAY.
Fair hit ball sticking in screen in front of right or left field bullpen—TWO BASES.
Fair hit ball going through or under screen in front of right or left field bullpen—TWO BASES.

ST. LOUIS CARDINALS
BUSCH STADIUM
GROUND RULES

OUTFIELD AREA—Fair ball hitting above yellow line on outfield wall—HOME RUN. Ball hitting on or below yellow line is IN PLAY. Fair ball bounding into field boxes, bleachers, over fence in outfield, or enclosed area in left or right field corners or going through or under fences—TWO BASES.
DUGOUTS—Ball rolling onto top step of dugouts (which are at ground level) is IN PLAY. Photographer's area of each dugout shall be regarded as part of the dugout. Ball thrown by pitcher from the rubber to catch base-runner off first or third base that goes into stand or dugout—ONE BASE. A pitched, thrown or batted ball that hits anyone on the playing field, except as otherwise provided for in the Official Playing Rules is IN PLAY. Ball going through wire behind plate or lodging in it—ONE BASE on throw by a pitcher—TWO BASES on throw by fielder.

SAN DIEGO PADRES
SAN DIEGO/JACK MURPHY STADIUM
GROUND RULES

Photographers' areas adjacent to first base and third base dugouts are considered part of dugouts. Ball out of play, same as both dugouts (Field Level).
Bullpens are IN PLAY.
Everything else is standard ground rules.

SAN FRANCISCO GIANTS
CANDLESTICK PARK
GROUND RULES

1. Ball hitting either foul pole (or screen attached) *above* black ring painted on foul pole—HOME RUN. Hitting black ring or below on foul pole or hitting top of fence and bounding onto playing field—IN PLAY. If bounding into stands or over fence—TWO BASES.
2. Thrown ball going behind backstop screen—ONE BASE, if thrown by pitcher from rubber. Other overthrows—TWO BASES.
3. Ball going over fence under screen attached to foul poles—HOME RUN.
4. Ball hitting face of dugouts or face of bat racks—IN PLAY. Must go *into* dugouts to be out of play.
5. Ball IN PLAY in bullpens.
6. Ball hitting any portion of right field stands above the top of the outfield fence and bounding onto playing field—HOME RUN.

DISABLED LIST NUMBERS IN THE 90'S

The following are the numbers of placements/players on the disabled lists during the 1990's:

1990—121/109	1993—153/124
1991—135/117	1994—143/118
1992—170/142	1995—180/142

NATIONAL LEAGUE RULES & POINTS OF INFORMATION

LIMITATIONS ON VISITORS

UMPIRES' ROOM—No visitors shall be permitted at any time in the umpires' dressing room. The term "visitors" shall include club officials and employees, newspaper, radio and television representatives, photographers, friends and relatives. No one except the umpires, League officers and the clubhouse attendant assigned to the umpires' room shall be permitted in these rooms before, during, or after a ball game. **There are no exceptions to this rule.** The Umpire-in-Chief shall be responsible for its enforcement, and for reporting any violation to the President.

CLUBHOUSE AND BENCH—No persons shall be admitted to the team clubhouse or permitted to enter or visit the bench except accredited photographers and accredited representatives of the press, radio and television. Such authorized visitors shall not be permitted in the dugout during a game, nor shall they enter the clubhouse except at times authorized by the manager.

Photographers shall not be permitted on the playing field at any time during the progress of a championship game. Photographers may take pictures on the field during spring training games because vantage points are not available to them in most spring training parks.

RIGHT TO POSTPONE GAMES

The right to postpone the playing of a game shall be vested in the home club. Once a game has started, the Umpire-in-Chief shall have sole right to determine whether the game shall be terminated because of bad weather or unfit playing conditions. Under the provisions of the Official Playing Rules, the Umpire-in-Chief shall have the sole and unquestioned authority to determine whether and when play shall be halted during a game; whether and when play shall be resumed; and whether and when a game shall be terminated because of bad weather or unfit playing conditions. The Official Playing Rules provide that when a game is temporarily suspended for rain, umpires must wait 30 minutes before calling the game. However, National League umpires have been instructed to wait at least 1 hour and 15 minutes before calling the game. Should there be a second suspension, umpires shall wait at least 45 minutes before calling a game. For third and any subsequent rain delays umpires are to wait at least 30 minutes.

NIGHT GAME

According to National League rules, a night game "shall be any game with the official starting time fixed after 5 p.m. All games, with official starting times fixed for 5 p.m., prevailing time, or earlier, shall be 'day games.'"

WAIVERS

WAIVERS—Major League waivers must be secured for all Major League trades from August 1st until the day after the regular season concludes. NO WAIVERS are required to trade a Major League player at any other time.

DISABLED LISTS

15-day . . . . . No limit on number of players per club
60-day (Emergency)—No limit on number of players, but may only be used when a club is at the maximum limit of 40 players.
(Players carried on this list do not count against 40-man under control limit. If placed or transferred here after August 1, player must remain through end of season and post-season.)

Day 1 is day following player's last game appearance.

Reinstatements may be made beginning Day 16 or 61, respectively; after minimum period has expired player may be reinstated at any time (except in certain "Emergency" cases. . .see above).

There shall be no assignment of a player by a Major League Club to a National Association Club while such player is on a Major League Disabled List; provided, however, that with the Player's written consent, a copy of which shall be forwarded to the Player's Association, and with the approval of the League President, a player on the disabled list may be assigned to a National Association Club for up to a maximum of twenty days (thirty days for pitchers) for the purpose of rehabilitation.

Note: the 21-day and 30-day disabled lists were eliminated late in the 1990 season.

MAJOR LEAGUE SERVICE...

... is credited for each day the player appears on an active roster **or** major league disabled list or suspended list.

... in the case of a player called up from the minor leagues, is credited beginning with the date he physically reports.

... in the case of a major league player who is traded and reports in the normal course, service is not interrupted.

... in the case of a player sent down to the minor leagues, is credited through the date of the assignment.

... in the case of a player who is unconditionally released, is credited through the date waivers were requested.

... for a player who appears on his club's opening day roster, is credited as of the earliest scheduled opener, without regard to the actual opening date of his own club.

... is credited at the rate of 172 days per "year", though the season is actually 183 days long.

... is not credited during any period or periods of optional assignment totalling 20 days or more during a single season.

QUALIFICATIONS

QUALIFICATIONS FOR BATTING CHAMPIONSHIP: Highest batting average based on a minimum of 502 appearances at the plate, which may include walks, sacrifices, hit by pitcher, etc.

QUALIFICATIONS FOR PITCHING CHAMPIONSHIP: Lowest earned run average with a minimum of 162 innings pitched.

QUALIFICATIONS FOR A ROOKIE: Not more than 130 at bats or 50 innings pitched in the major leagues during a previous season or seasons, nor more than 45 days on a major league roster during the 25-player limit (excluding time in military service, or on the disabled list).

GUIDELINES FOR CUMULATIVE PERFORMANCE RECORDS

10.24 CONSECUTIVE HITTING STREAKS
(a) A consecutive hitting streak shall not be terminated if the plate appearance results in a base on balls, hit batsman, defensive interference or a sacrifice bunt. A sacrifice fly shall terminate the streak.

(b) CONSECUTIVE-GAME HITTING STREAKS
A consecutive-game hitting streak shall not be terminated if all the player's plate appearances (one or more) result in a base on balls, hit batsman, defensive interference or a sacrifice bunt. The streak shall terminate if the player has a sacrifice fly and no hit.

The player's individual consecutive-game hitting streak shall be determined by the consecutive games in which the player appears and is not determined by his club's games.

(c) CONSECUTIVE PLAYING STREAK
A consecutive-game playing streak shall be extended if the player plays one half-inning on defense, or if he completes a time at bat by reaching base or being put out. A pinch-running appearance only shall not extend the streak. If a player is ejected from a game by an umpire before he can comply with the requirements of this rule, his streak shall continue.

(d) SUSPENDED GAMES
For the purpose of this rule, all performances in the completion of a suspended game shall be considered as occurring on the original date of the game.

HOW TO FIGURE

MAGIC NUMBER: Determine the number of games yet to be played, add one, then subtract the number of games ahead in the lost column of the standings from the closest opponent.

BATTING AVERAGE: Divide the number of hits by the number of at bats.

EARNED RUN AVERAGE: Multiply the number of earned runs by nine, then divide the result by the number of innings pitched.

SLUGGING PERCENTAGE: Divide the total bases of all safe hits by the total times at bat as defined by Rule 10.02 (a).

FIELDING AVERAGE: Divide the total putouts and assists by the total of putouts, assists and errors.

ON-BASE PERCENTAGE: Divide hits plus total bases on balls plus hit-by-pitch by at bats plus total bases on balls plus hit-by-pitch and sacrifice flies (for purposes of this percentage ignore being awarded first base on interference or obstruction).

FARM CLUB AFFILIATIONS

ATLANTA
Richmond, International (AAA)	O
Greenville, Southern (AA)	O
Durham, Carolina (A)	PDC
Macon, South Atlantic (A)	O
Eugene, Northwest (Short A)	PDC
Danville, Appalachian (Rookie)	O
West Palm Beach, Gulf Coast (Rookie)	O
San Pedro de Macoris, Dominican Summer League (Rookie)	O

CHICAGO
Iowa, American Association (AAA)	PDC
Orlando, Southern (AA)	O
DAYTONA, FLORIDA STATE (A)	PDC
Rockford, Midwest (A)	O
Williamsport, NY-Penn (A)	PDC
Fort Myers Cubs, Gulf Coast (Rookie)	O

CINCINNATI
Indianapolis, American Association (AAA)	PDC
Chattanooga, Southern (AA)	PDC
Winston-Salem, Carolina (A)	PDC
Charleston, WV, South Atlantic (A)	PDC
Billings, Pioneer (Rookie)	PDC
Princeton, WV, Appalachian (Rookie)	O

COLORADO
Colorado Springs, Pacific Coast (AAA)	PDC
New Haven, Eastern (AA)	PDC
Salem, VA, Carolina (A)	PDC
Asheville, South Atlantic (A)	PDC
Portland, OR, Northwest (A)	PDC
Mesa, (Rookie)	PDC

FLORIDA
Charlotte, International (AAA)	PDC
Portland, ME, Eastern League (AA)	PDC
Brevard County, Florida State (A)	O
Kane County, Midwest League (A)	PDC
Uitca, New York-Penn League (A)	PDC
Viera, Gulf Coast League (Rookie)	O
Santo Domingo, Dominican Summer League (Rookie)	O

HOUSTON
Tucson, Pacific Coast (AAA)	PDC
Jackson, Texas (AA)	PDC
Quad City, Midwest (A)	PDC
Kissimmee, FL, Florida State (A)	O
Auburn, NY-Penn (Short Season A)	PDC
KISSIMMEE, GULF COAST (Rookie)	O

LOS ANGELES
ALBUQUERQUE, PACIFIC COAST (AAA)	PDC
San Antonio, Texas (AA)	PDC
SAN BERNARDINO, CALIFORNIA (A)	PDC
Vero Beach, Florida State (A)	O
Savannah, GA, South Atlantic (A)	PDC
Yakima, WA, Northwest (A)	PDC
Great Falls, Pioneer (Rookie)	PDC
Santo Domingo, Dominican Summer (Rookie)	O
La Romana, Dominican Summer (Rookie)	O

MONTREAL
OTTAWA, INTERNATIONAL (AAA)	PDC
Harrisburg, Eastern (AA)	PDC
West Palm Beach, Florida State (A)	O
Delmarva, South Atlantic (A)	PDC
VERMONT, NY-PENN (A)	PDC
Gulf Coast, Gulf Coast (Rookie)	O
Mendoza, Dominican Summer League (Rookie)	PDC

NEW YORK
Norfolk, VA, International (AAA)	PDC
Binghamton, Eastern (AA)	PDC
St. Lucie, Florida State (A)	O
Pittsfield, NY-Penn (A)	PDC
Columbia, South Atlantic (A)	PDC
KINGSPORT, APPALACHIAN (Rookie)	O
St. Lucie, Gulf Coast (Rookie)	O

PHILADELPHIA
Scranton/Wilkes-Barre, International (AAA)	PDC
READING, EASTERN (AA)	PDC
Clearwater, Florida State (A)	O
Piedmont, South Atlantic (A)	PDC
Batavia, NY-Penn (A)	PDC
Martinsville, Appalachian (Rookie)	O

PITTSBURGH
Calgary, Pacific Coast (AAA)	PDC
CAROLINA, SOUTHERN (AA)	PDC
Lynchburg, Carolina (A)	PDC
AUGUSTA, SOUTH ATLANTIC (A)	PDC
Erie, NY-Penn (A)	PDC
Bradenton, Gulf Coast (Rookie)	O

ST. LOUIS
LOUISVILLE, AMERICAN ASSOCIATION (AAA)	PDC
Arkansas, Texas (AA)	PDC
St. Petersburg, Florida State (A)	PDC
Peoria, Midwest (A)	PDC
New Jersey, NY-Penn (Short Season A)	PDC
Johnson City, Appalachian (Rookie)	O

SAN DIEGO
Las Vegas, Pacific Coast (AAA)	PDC
Memphis, Southern (AA)	PDC
Rancho Cucamonga, California (A)	PDC
Clinton, Midwest (A)	PDC
Peoria, Arizona (Rookie)	PDC
Idaho Falls, Pioneer (Rookie)	PDC

SAN FRANCISCO
Phoenix, Pacific Coast (AAA)	PDC
Shreveport, Texas (AA)	PDC
San Jose, California (A)	PDC
Burlington, Midwest (A)	PDC
Bellingham, WA, Northwest (Rookie)	PDC
San Pedro de Macoris, Dominican Summer (Rookie)	PDC

PDC—Player Development Contract   O—Owned

ALL CAPS—WON LEAGUE CHAMPIONSHIP

RETIRED UNIFORM NUMBERS

ATLANTA
3	Dale Murphy
21	Warren Spahn
35	Phil Niekro
41	Eddie Mathews
44	Henry Aaron

CHICAGO
14	Ernie Banks
26	Billy Williams

CINCINNATI
1	Fred Hutchinson
5	Johnny Bench

COLORADO
None

FLORIDA
None

HOUSTON
25	Jose Cruz
32	Jim Umbricht
33	Mike Scott
40	Don Wilson

LOS ANGELES
1	Pee Wee Reese
4	Duke Snider
19	Jim Gilliam
24	Walt Alston
32	Sandy Koufax
39	Roy Campanella
42	Jackie Robinson
53	Don Drysdale

MONTREAL
8	Gary Carter
10	Rusty Staub

NEW YORK
14	Gil Hodges
37	Casey Stengel
41	Tom Seaver

PHILADELPHIA
1	Richie Ashburn
20	Mike Schmidt
32	Steve Carlton
36	Robin Roberts

PITTSBURGH
1	Billy Meyer
4	Ralph Kiner
8	Willie Stargell
9	Bill Mazeroski
20	Pie Traynor
21	Roberto Clemente
33	Honus Wagner
40	Danny Murtaugh

ST. LOUIS
6	Stan Musial
14	Ken Boyer
17	Dizzy Dean
20	Lou Brock
45	Bob Gibson

SAN DIEGO
6	Steve Garvey

SAN FRANCISCO
	Christy Mathewson
	John McGraw
3	Bill Terry
4	Mel Ott
11	Carl Hubbell
24	Willie Mays
27	Juan Marichal
44	Willie McCovey

Atlanta Braves (EAST)

MANAGER: BOBBY COX (6)

Coaches:
JIM BEAUCHAMP (37)
PAT CORRALES (39)
CLARENCE JONES (28)
LEO MAZZONE (54)
JIMY WILLIAMS (22)
NED YOST (42) - bullpen

Team Physician—DR. DAVID T. WATSON
Trainer—DAVE PURSLEY
Assistant Trainer—JEFF PORTER

Director of Public Relations—JIM SCHULTZ
Director of Team Travel—BILL ACREE

No.	PITCHERS (18)	B	T	Ht.	Wt.	Born	Birthplace	Residence	1995 Club	W-L	ERA	G	GS	CG	SV	IP	H	R	ER	BB	SO	M.L. Service
33	AVERY, STEVE	L	L	6-4	205	4-14-70	Trenton, MI	Taylor, MI	Atlanta	7-13	4.67	29	29	3	0	173.1	165	92	90	52	141	5.060
51	BORBON, PEDRO	L	L	6-1	205	11-15-67	Mao, D.R.	Texas City, TX	Atlanta	2-2	3.09	41	0	0	2	32.0	29	12	11	17	33	1.033
50	BOROWSKI, JOE*	R	R	6-2	225	5-4-71	Bayonne, NJ	Bayonne, NJ	Rochester	1-3	4.04	28	0	0	6	35.2	32	16	16	18	32	
									Bowie	2-2	3.92	16	0	0	7	20.2	16	9	9	7	32	
									Baltimore	0-0	1.23	6	0	0	0	7.1	5	1	1	4	3	0.048
52	CLONTZ, BRAD	R	R	6-1	180	4-25-71	Stuart, VA	Patrick Spring, VA	Atlanta	8-1	3.65	59	0	0	4	69.0	71	29	28	22	55	0.160
64	DANIELS, LEE*	R	R	6-4	190	3-31-71	Rochelle, GA	Rochelle, GA	Durham	1-4	4.24	21	0	0	4	23.1	26	13	11	14	24	0.000
45	FOX, CHAD*	R	R	6-3	175	9-3-70	Coronado, TX	Houston, TX	Chattanooga	4-5	5.06	20	17	0	0	80.0	76	49	45	52	56	0.000
47	GLAVINE, TOM	L	L	6-1	185	3-25-66	Concord, MA	Alpharetta, GA	Atlanta	16-7	3.08	29	29	3	0	198.2	182	76	68	66	127	7.171
65	JACOBS, RYAN*	R	L	6-2	175	2-3-74	Richmond, VA	Winston-Salem, NC	Durham	11-6	3.51	29	25	1	0	148.2	145	72	58	57	99	0.000
31	MADDUX, GREG	R	R	6-0	175	4-14-66	San Angelo, TX	Las Vegas, NV	Atlanta	19-2	1.63	28	28	10	0	209.2	147	39	38	23	181	8.140
34	MAY, DARRELL*	L	L	6-2	170	6-13-72	San Bernardino, CA	Rogue River, OR	Greenville	2-8	3.55	15	15	0	0	91.1	81	44	36	20	79	
									Richmond	4-2	3.71	9	9	0	0	51.0	53	21	21	16	42	
									Atlanta	0-0	11.25	2	0	0	0	4.0	10	5	5	0	1	0.029
38	McMICHAEL, GREG	R	R	6-3	215	12-1-66	Knoxville, TN	Alpharetta, GA	Atlanta	7-2	2.79	67	0	0	2	80.2	64	27	25	32	74	2.119
46	SCHMIDT, JASON*	R	R	6-5	185	1-29-73	Kelso, WA	Kelso, WA	Atlanta	2-2	5.76	9	2	0	0	25.0	27	17	16	18	19	0.052
									Richmond	8-6	2.25	19	19	0	0	116.0	97	40	29	48	95	
62	SCHUTZ, CARL*	L	L	5-11	200	8-22-71	Hammond, LA	Gramercy, LA	Greenville	3-7	4.94	51	0	0	26	58.1	53	36	32	36	56	0.000
29	SMOLTZ, JOHN	R	R	6-3	185	5-15-67	Warren, MI	Duluth, GA	Atlanta	12-7	3.18	29	29	2	0	192.2	166	76	68	72	193	7.019
49	THOBE, TOM*	L	L	6-6	195	9-3-69	Covington, KY	Huntington Beach, CA	Richmond	7-0	1.84	48	2	1	5	88.0	65	27	18	26	57	
									Atlanta	0-0	10.80	3	0	0	0	3.1	7	4	4	0	2	0.022
36	WADE, TERRELL*	L	L	6-3	205	1-25-73	Rembert, SC	Rembert, SC	Richmond	10-9	4.56	24	23	1	0	142.0	137	76	72	63	124	
									Atlanta	0-1	4.50	3	0	0	0	4.0	3	2	2	4	3	0.023
43	WOHLERS, MARK	R	R	6-4	207	1-23-70	Holyoke, MA	Alpharetta, GA	Atlanta	7-3	2.09	65	0	0	25	64.2	51	16	15	24	90	3.054
48	WOODALL, BRAD*	B	L	6-0	175	6-25-69	Atlanta, GA	Blythewood, SC	Atlanta	1-1	6.10	9	0	0	0	10.1	13	10	7	8	5	0.045
									Richmond	4-4	5.10	13	11	0	0	65.1	70	39	37	17	44	

No.	CATCHERS (4)	B	T	Ht.	Wt.	Born	Birthplace	Residence	1995 Club	AVG.	G	AB	R	H	2B	3B	HR	RBI	BB	SO	SB	M.L. Service
60	AYRAULT, JOE*	R	R	6-3	190	10-8-71	Rochester, MI	Sarasota, FL	Greenville	.245	89	302	27	74	20	0	7	42	13	70	2	0.000
55	HOUSTON, TYLER*	L	R	6-2	210	1-17-71	Las Vegas, NV	Henderson, NV	Richmond	.255	103	349	41	89	10	3	12	42	18	62	3	0.000
8	LOPEZ, JAVIER	R	R	6-3	185	11-5-70	Ponce, P.R.	Ponce, P.R.	Atlanta	.315	100	333	37	105	11	4	14	51	14	57	0	2.013
12	PEREZ, EDUARDO	R	R	6-1	175	5-4-68	Cuidad Ojeda, Ven.	Zulia, Ven.	Richmond	.265	92	324	31	86	19	0	5	40	12	58	1	
									Atlanta	.308	7	13	1	4	1	0	1	4	0	2	0	0.032

No.	INFIELDERS (10)	B	T	Ht.	Wt.	Born	Birthplace	Residence	1995 Club	AVG.	G	AB	R	H	2B	3B	HR	RBI	BB	SO	SB	M.L. Service
2	BELLIARD, RAFAEL	R	R	5-6	160	10-24-61	Pueblo Nuevo, D.R.	Boca Raton, FL	Atlanta	.222	75	180	12	40	2	1	0	7	6	28	2	11.027
4	BLAUSER, JEFF	R	R	6-0	180	11-8-65	Los Gatos, CA	Alpharetta, GA	Atlanta	.211	115	431	60	91	16	2	12	31	57	107	8	7.047
17	GIOVANOLA, ED*	L	R	5-10	170	3-4-69	Los Gatos, CA	San Jose, CA	Richmond	.321	99	321	45	103	18	2	4	36	55	37	8	
									Atlanta	.071	13	14	2	1	0	0	0	0	3	5	0	0.022
57	GRAFFANINO, TONY*	R	R	6-1	175	6-6-72	Amityville, NY	Seneca, SC	Richmond	.190	50	179	20	34	6	0	4	17	15	49	2	0.000
10	JONES, CHIPPER	S	R	6-3	195	4-24-72	DeLand, FL	Marietta, GA	Atlanta	.265	140	524	87	139	22	3	23	86	73	99	8	1.143
20	LEMKE, MARK	S	R	5-9	167	8-13-65	Utica, NY	Marietta, GA	Atlanta	.253	116	399	42	101	16	5	5	38	44	40	2	5.155
68	MALLOY, MARTY*	L	R	5-10	160	4-6-72	Gainesville, FL	Trenton, FL	Greenville	.278	124	461	73	128	20	3	10	59	39	58	11	0.000
27	McGRIFF, FRED	L	L	6-3	215	10-31-63	Tampa, FL	Tampa, FL	Atlanta	.280	144	528	85	148	27	1	27	93	65	99	3	8.128
16	MORDECAI, MIKE	R	R	5-11	175	12-13-67	Birmingham, AL	Pinson, AL	Atlanta	.280	69	75	10	21	6	0	3	11	9	16	0	1.009
61	SMITH, ROBERT*	R	R	6-3	190	5-10-74	Oakland, CA	Oakland, CA	Greenville	.261	127	444	75	116	27	3	14	58	40	109	12	0.000

No.	OUTFIELDERS (8)	B	T	Ht.	Wt.	Born	Birthplace	Residence	1995 Club	AVG.	G	AB	R	H	2B	3B	HR	RBI	BB	SO	SB	M.L. Service
67	DYE, JERMAINE*	R	R	6-0	195	1-28-74	Oakland, CA	Vacaville, CA	Greenville	.285	104	403	50	115	26	4	15	71	27	74	4	0.000
9	GRISSOM, MARQUIS	R	R	5-11	190	4-17-67	Atlanta, GA	Fairburn, GA	Atlanta	.258	139	551	80	142	23	3	12	42	47	61	29	5.161
66	HOLLINS, DAMON*	R	L	5-11	180	6-12-74	Fairfield, CA	Vallejo, CA	Greenville	.247	129	466	64	115	26	2	18	77	44	120	6	0.000
23	JUSTICE, DAVID	L	L	6-3	200	4-14-66	Cincinnati, OH	Los Angeles, CA	Atlanta	.253	120	411	73	104	17	2	24	78	73	68	4	5.119
18	KLESKO, RYAN	L	L	6-3	220	6-12-71	Westminster, CA	Boynton Beach, FL	Atlanta	.310	107	329	48	102	25	2	23	70	47	72	5	2.025
									#Greenville	.231	4	13	1	3	0	0	1	4	2	1	0	
63	MONDS, WONDERFUL*	R	R	6-3	190	1-11-73	Fort Pierce, FL	Fort Pierce, FL	Gulf C. Braves	.133	4	15	1	2	0	0	1	1	8	2		
									Durham	.279	81	297	44	83	17	0	6	33	17	63	28	0.000
7	SMITH, DWIGHT	L	R	5-11	195	11-8-63	Tallahassee, FL	Fairburn, GA	Atlanta	.252	103	131	16	33	8	2	3	21	13	35	0	6.101
19	WALTON, JEROME	R	R	6-1	185	7-8-65	Newnan, GA	Fairburn, GA	Cincinnati	.290	102	162	32	47	12	1	8	22	17	25	10	5.042

*Rookie
#Rehabilitation Assignment

FULL NAMES AND PHONETICS

Avery, Steven Thomas
Ayrault, Joseph Alan (AY-ralt)
Belliard, Rafael Leonidas (BELL-ee-ard)
Blauser, Jeffrey Michael (BLAU-zer)
Borbon, Pedro Felix (bore-BONE)
Borowski, Joseph Thomas
Clontz, John Bradley
Daniels, Lee Andrew
Dye, Jermaine Terrell
Fox, Chad Douglas
Giovanola, Edward Thomas (gee-oh-va-NO-la)
Glavine, Thomas Michael (GLA-vin)

Graffanino, Anthony Joseph (graf-a-NEEN-oh)
Grissom, Marquis (mar-KEESE)
Houston, Tyler Sam
Jacobs, Ryan Christopher
Jones, Larry Wayne
Justice, David Christopher
Klesko, Ryan Anthony
Lemke, Mark Alan (LEM-kee)
Lopez, Javier Torres
Maddux, Gregory Alan (MADD-ucks)
Malloy, Marty Thomas
May, Darrell Kevin

McGriff, Frederick Stanley
McMichael, Gregory Winston
Monds, Wonderful Terrific III
Mordecai, Michael Howard, Jr. (more-dah-KYE)
Perez, Eduardo
Schmidt, Jason David
Schutz, Carl James
Smith, John Dwight
Smith, Robert Eugene
Smoltz, John Andrew
Thobe, Thomas Neal (TOE-bee)
Wade, Hawatha Terrell (tur-RELL)

Walton, Jerome O'Terrell
Wohlers, Mark Edward (WOE-lers)
Woodall, David Bradley

MANAGER AND COACHES

Robert J. Cox
James Edward Beauchamp (BEE-chum)
Patrick Corrales
Clarence Woodrow Jones
Leo O. Mazzone (mah-ZOE-nee)
James F. Williams
Edgar Frederick Yost

Chicago Cubs (CENTRAL)

MANAGER JIM RIGGLEMAN (5)

Coaches:
DAVE BIALAS (43) - bullpen
FERGIE JENKINS (31)
TONY MUSER (40)
MAKO OLIVERAS (3)
DAN RADISON (42)
BILLY WILLIAMS (26)

Team Physicians—JOHN MARQUARDT, M.D.
MICHAEL SCHAFER, M.D.
Trainer—JOHN FIERRO
Assistant Trainer—BRIAN McCANN

Media Relations Director—SHARON PANNOZZO
Traveling Secretary—JIMMY BANK

No.	PITCHERS (17)	B	T	Ht.	Wt.	Born	Birthplace	Residence	1995 Club	W-L	ERA	G	GS	CG	SV	IP	H	R	ER	BB	SO	M.L. Service
51	ADAMS, TERRY*	R	R	6-3	205	3-6-73	Mobile, AL	Semmes, AL	Orlando	2-3	1.43	37	0	0	19	37.2	23	9	6	16	26	
									Iowa	0-0	0.00	7	0	0	5	6.1	3	0	0	2	10	
									Chicago N.L.	1-1	6.50	18	0	0	1	18.0	22	15	13	10	15	0.049
52	BULLINGER, JIM	R	R	6-2	190	8-21-65	New Orleans, LA	Sarasota, FL	Chicago N.L.	12-8	4.14	24	24	1	0	150.0	152	80	69	65	93	2.113
									Orlando	0-0	0.00	1	1	0	0	4.0	3	0	0	1	2	
55	CASIAN, LARRY	R	L	6-0	175	10-28-65	Lynwood, CA	Salem, OR	#Iowa	0-0	2.13	13	0	0	1	12.2	9	3	3	2	9	
									Chicago N.L.	1-0	1.93	42	0	0	0	23.1	23	6	5	15	11	3.044
49	CASTILLO, FRANK	R	R	6-1	200	4-1-69	El Paso, TX	Cave Creek, AZ	Chicago N.L.	11-10	3.21	29	29	2	0	188.0	179	75	67	52	135	3.156
32	FOSTER, KEVIN	R	R	6-1	170	1-13-69	Evanston, IL	Bradenton, FL	Chicago N.L.	12-11	4.51	30	28	0	0	167.2	149	90	84	65	146	1.093
29	GUZMAN, JOSE	R	R	6-3	200	4-9-63	Santa Isabel, P.R.	Austin, TX	Fort Myers	0-0	1.50	2	2	0	0	6.0	5	1	1	0	3	9.074
27	JONES, DOUG	R	R	6-2	225	6-24-57	Covina, CA	Tucson, AZ	Baltimore	0-4	5.01	52	0	0	22	46.2	55	30	26	16	42	8.085
59	MYERS, RODNEY*	R	R	6-1	200	6-26-69	Rockford, IL	Rockford, IL	Omaha	4-5	4.10	38	0	0	2	48.1	52	26	22	19	38	0.000
38	NAVARRO, JAIME	R	R	6-4	230	3-27-68	Bayamon, P.R.	Milwaukee, WI	Chicago N.L.	14-6	3.28	29	29	1	0	200.1	194	79	73	56	128	6.025
35	PATTERSON, BOB	R	L	6-1	195	5-16-59	Jacksonville, FL	Hickory, NC	California	5-2	3.04	62	0	0	0	53.1	48	18	18	13	41	6.138
47	PEREZ, MIKE	R	R	6-0	200	10-19-64	Yauco, P.R.	Ellisville, MO	Chicago N.L.	2-6	3.66	68	0	0	2	71.1	72	30	29	27	49	4.013
41	RIVERA, ROBERTO*	L	L	6-0	200	1-1-69	Bayamon, P.R.	Bayamon, P.R.	Orlando	6-2	2.38	49	0	0	6	68.0	50	18	18	11	34	
									Chicago N.L.	0-0	5.40	7	0	0	0	5.0	8	3	3	2	2	0.031
36	SWARTZBAUGH, DAVE*	R	R	6-2	210	2-11-68	Middletown, OH	Middletown, OH	Iowa	3-0	1.53	30	0	0	0	47.0	33	10	8	18	38	
									Orlando	4-0	2.48	16	0	0	0	29.0	18	10	8	7	37	
									Chicago N.L.	0-0	0.00	7	0	0	0	7.1	5	2	0	3	5	0.030
44	TELEMACO, AMAURY*	R	R	6-3	210	1-19-74	Higuey, D.R.	La Romana, D.R.	Orlando	8-8	3.29	22	22	3	0	147.2	112	60	54	42	151	0.000
46	TRACHSEL, STEVE	R	R	6-4	205	10-31-70	Oxnard, CA	Anaheim, CA	Chicago N.L.	7-13	5.15	30	29	2	0	160.2	174	104	92	76	117	1.136
58	WALKER, WADE*	R	R	6-1	190	9-18-71	Baton Rouge, LA	Gonzalez, LA	Daytona	8-6	2.53	25	24	2	0	135.0	113	50	38	36	117	0.000
13	WENDELL, TURK	L	R	6-2	195	5-19-67	Pittsfield, MA	Dalton, MA	#Orlando	1-0	3.86	5	0	0	1	7.0	6	3	3	4	7	
									#Daytona	0-0	1.17	4	2	0	0	7.2	5	2	1	1	8	
									Chicago N.L.	3-1	4.92	43	0	0	0	60.1	71	35	33	24	50	1.051

No.	CATCHERS (2)	B	T	Ht.	Wt.	Born	Birthplace	Residence	1995 Club	AVG.	G	AB	R	H	2B	3B	HR	RBI	BB	SO	SB	M.L. Service
6	HUBBARD, MIKE*	R	R	6-1	195	2-16-71	Lynchburg, VA	Madison Heights, VA	Iowa	.260	75	254	28	66	6	3	5	23	26	60	6	
									Chicago N.L.	.174	15	23	2	4	0	0	1	2	2	0	0.052
9	SERVAIS, SCOTT	R	R	6-2	205	6-4-67	LaCrosse, WI	Sugar Land, TX	Houston	.225	28	89	7	20	10	0	1	12	9	15	0	
									Chicago N.L.	.286	52	175	31	50	12	0	12	35	23	37	2	4.035

No.	INFIELDERS (11)	B	T	Ht.	Wt.	Born	Birthplace	Residence	1995 Club	AVG.	G	AB	R	H	2B	3B	HR	RBI	BB	SO	SB	M.L. Service
37	BROWN, BRANT*	L	L	6-3	205	6-22-71	Porterville, CA	Porterville, CA	Orlando	.271	121	446	67	121	27	4	6	53	39	77	8	0.000
15	FRANCO, MATT*	L	R	6-2	210	8-19-69	Santa Monica, CA	Thousand Oaks, CA	Iowa	.281	121	455	51	128	28	5	6	58	37	44	1	
									Chicago N.L.	.294	16	17	3	5	1	0	0	1	0	4	0	0.034
17	GRACE, MARK	L	L	6-2	190	6-28-64	Winston-Salem, NC	Chicago, IL	Chicago N.L.	.326	143	552	97	180	51	3	16	92	65	46	6	7.101
24	HANEY, TODD	R	R	5-9	165	7-30-65	Galveston, TX	San Antonio, TX	Iowa	.313	90	326	38	102	20	2	4	30	28	21	2	
									Chicago N.L.	.411	25	73	11	30	8	0	2	6	7	11	0	0.128
18	HERNANDEZ, JOSE	R	R	6-1	180	7-14-69	Vega Alta, P.R.	Vega Alta, P.R.	Chicago N.L.	.245	93	245	37	60	11	4	13	40	13	69	1	2.016
16	MAGADAN, DAVE	L	R	6-4	210	9-30-62	Tampa, FL	Tampa, FL	Houston	.313	127	348	44	109	24	0	2	51	71	56	2	8.148
50	MAXWELL, JASON*	R	R	6-1	175	3-26-72	Lewisburg, TN	Lewisburg, TN	Daytona	.263	117	388	66	102	13	3	10	58	63	68	12	0.000
54	MORRIS, BOBBY*	L	R	6-0	190	11-22-72	Hammond, IN	Munster, IN	Daytona	.308	95	344	44	106	18	2	2	55	38	46	22	0.000
57	ORIE, KEVIN*	R	R	6-4	210	9-1-72	West Chester, PA	West Chester, PA	Daytona	.244	119	409	54	100	17	4	9	51	42	71	5	0.000
11	SANCHEZ, REY	R	R	5-9	175	10-5-67	Rio Piedras, P.R.	Carolina, P.R.	Chicago N.L.	.278	114	428	57	119	22	2	3	27	14	48	6	3.140
23	SANDBERG, RYNE	R	R	6-2	190	9-18-59	Spokane, WA	Phoenix, AZ		DID NOT PLAY												12.106

No.	OUTFIELDERS (10)	B	T	Ht.	Wt.	Born	Birthplace	Residence	1995 Club	AVG.	G	AB	R	H	2B	3B	HR	RBI	BB	SO	SB	M.L. Service
10	BULLETT, SCOTT	L	L	6-2	220	12-25-68	Martinsburg, WV	Welland, Ont.	Chicago N.L.	.273	104	150	19	41	5	7	3	22	12	30	8	1.054
1	GLANVILLE, DOUG*	R	R	6-2	170	8-25-70	Hackensack, NJ	Teaneck NJ	Iowa	.270	112	419	48	113	16	2	4	37	16	64	13	0.000
25	GONZALEZ, LUIS	L	R	6-2	185	9-3-67	Tampa, FL	Houston, TX	Houston	.258	56	209	35	54	10	4	6	35	18	30	1	
									Chicago N.L.	.290	77	262	34	76	19	4	7	34	39	33	5	4.151
53	HIGHTOWER, VEE*	S	R	6-5	215	4-26-72	Pittsburgh, PA	Pittsburgh, PA	Rockford	.265	64	238	51	63	11	1	7	36	39	52	23	0.000
39	JENNINGS, ROBIN*	L	L	6-2	205	4-11-72	Singapore	Springfield, VA	Orlando	.296	132	490	71	145	27	7	17	79	44	61	7	0.000
19	KIESCHNICK, BROOKS*	L	R	6-4	225	6-6-72	Robstown, TX	Caldwell, TX	Iowa	.295	138	505	61	149	30	1	23	73	58	91	2	0.000
56	McRAE, BRIAN	S	R	6-0	190	8-27-67	Bradenton, FL	Leawood, KS	Chicago N.L.	.288	137	580	92	167	38	7	12	48	47	92	27	5.005
21	SOSA, SAMMY	R	R	6-0	190	11-12-68	S.P. de Macoris, D.R.	S.P. de Macoris, D.R.	Chicago N.L.	.268	144	564	89	151	17	3	36	119	58	134	34	5.168
30	TIMMONS, OZZIE	R	R	6-2	220	9-18-70	Tampa, FL	Tampa, FL	Chicago N.L.	.263	77	171	30	45	10	1	8	28	13	32	3	0.160
28	VALDES, PEDRO*	L	L	6-1	180	6-29-73	Fajardo, P.R.	Loiza, P.R.	Orlando	.300	114	426	57	128	28	3	7	68	37	77	3	0.000

*Rookie
#Rehabilitation Assignment

FULL NAMES AND PHONETICS

Adams, Terry Wayne
Brown, Brant Michael
Bullett, Scott Douglas
Bullinger, James Eric (BULL-in-jer)
Casian, Lawrence Paul (CASS-ee-un)
Castillo, Frank Anthony (cas-TEE-yoh)
Foster, Kevin Christopher
Franco, Matthew Neil
Glanville, Douglas Metunwa
Gonzalez, Luis Emilio   Grace, Mark Eugene
Guzman, Jose Alberto Mirabel (GOOZ-min)
Haney, Todd Michael
Hernandez, Jose Antonio

Hightower, Vegrin Joseph
Hubbard, Michael Wayne
Jennings, Robin Christopher
Kieschnick, Michael Brooks (KEE-shnik)
Magadan, David Joseph (MAG-ah-din)
Maxwell, Jason Ramond
McRae, Brian Wesley
Morris, Robert David
Moten, Christopher Scott (MOE-ten)
Myers, Rodney Luther
Navarro, Jaime (nah-VAR-ro, JAY-mee)   Orie,
Kevin Leonard

Perez, Michael Irvin
Rivera, Roberto Diaz
Sanchez, Rey Francisco Guadalupe (SAN-chez)
Sandberg, Ryne Dee
Servais, Scott Daniel (SER-viss)
Sosa, Samuel
Sturtze, Tanyon James (STURTS, TAN-yin)
Swartzbaugh, David Theodore (SWORTS-baw)
Telemaco, Amaury Regalado
 (tel-ah-MAH-ko, AH-mer-ee)
Timmons, Osborne Llewellyn
Trachsel, Stephen Christopher (TRACK-s'l)

Valdes, Pedro Jose Manzo (val-DEZ)
Walker, Michael Charles
Wendell, Steven John (WEN-d'l)

MANAGER AND COACHES
James David Riggleman
David Bruce Bialis (bee-AL-is)
Ferguson Arthur Jenkins
Anthony Joseph Muser (MYEW-ser)
Max Oliveras
Daniel John Radison
Billy Leo Williams

Cincinnati Reds (CENTRAL)

MANAGER
RAY KNIGHT (25)

Coaches:
MARC BOMBARD (50)
DON GULLETT (35)
TOM HUME (72) - bullpen
JIM LETT (55)
HAL McRAE (4)
JOEL YOUNGBLOOD (2)

Head Trainer—GREG LYNN
Assistant Trainer—MARK MANN
Traveling Secretary—GARY WAHOFF
Equipment Manager—BERNIE STOWE
Publicity Director—MIKE RINGERING

No.	PITCHERS (17)	B	T	Ht.	Wt.	Born	Birthplace	Residence	1995 Club	W-L	ERA	G	GS	CG	SV	IP	H	R	ER	BB	SO	M.L. Service
45	BRANTLEY, JEFF	R	R	5-10	180	9-5-63	Florence, AL	Clinton, MS	Cincinnati	3-2	2.82	56	0	0	28	70.1	53	22	22	20	62	7.008
34	BURBA, DAVE	R	R	6-4	240	7-7-66	Dayton, OH	Gilbert, AZ	San Francisco	4-2	4.98	37	0	0	0	43.1	38	26	24	25	46	
									Cincinnati	6-2	3.27	15	9	1	0	63.1	52	24	23	26	50	4.006
58	CARRASCO, HECTOR	R	R	6-2	180	10-22-69	S.P. de Macoris, D.R.	San Diego, CA	Cincinnati	2-7	4.12	64	0	0	5	87.1	86	45	40	46	64	1.119
37	HERNANDEZ, XAVIER	L	R	6-2	195	8-16-65	Port Arthur, TX	Missouri City, TX	Cincinnati	7-2	4.60	59	0	0	3	90.0	95	47	46	31	84	5.134
32	JARVIS, KEVIN	L	R	6-2	200	8-1-69	Lexington, KY	Lexington, KY	Indianapolis	4-2	4.45	10	10	2	0	60.2	62	33	30	18	37	
									Cincinnati	3-4	5.70	19	11	1	0	79.0	91	56	50	32	33	0.137
31	McELROY, CHUCK	L	L	6-0	195	10-1-67	Port Arthur, TX	Friendswood, TX	Cincinnati	3-4	6.02	44	0	0	0	40.1	46	29	27	15	27	5.020
53	MOORE, MARCUS	B	R	6-5	195	11-2-70	Oakland, CA	Oakland, CA	Indianapolis	1-0	4.97	7	1	0	1	12.2	13	8	7	14	6	0.164
									Chattanooga	6-1	4.98	36	0	0	2	43.1	31	24	24	34	57	
21	PORTUGAL, MARK	R	R	6-0	190	10-30-62	Los Angeles, CA	Barrington, RI	San Francisco	5-5	4.15	17	17	1	0	104.0	106	56	48	34	63	
									Cincinnati	6-5	3.82	14	14	0	0	77.2	79	35	33	22	33	8.112
40	PUGH, TIM	R	R	6-6	225	1-26-67	Lake Tahoe, CA	Florence, KY	Indianapolis	2-4	4.68	6	6	1	0	42.1	42	24	22	14	20	
									Cincinnati	6-5	3.84	28	12	0	0	98.1	100	46	42	32	38	2.051
27	RIJO, JOSE	R	R	6-3	215	5-13-65	San Cristobal, D.R.	San Cristobal, D.R.	Cincinnati	5-4	4.17	14	14	0	0	69.0	76	33	32	22	62	10.065
48	ROPER, JOHN	R	R	6-0	175	11-21-71	Southern Pines, NC	Raeford, NC	Cincinnati	0-0	10.29	2	2	0	0	7.0	13	9	8	4	6	1.093
									#Chattanooga	0-0	1.00	3	3	0	0	9.0	5	1	1	1	6	
									#Indianapolis	2-5	4.97	8	8	0	0	41.2	47	26	23	16	23	
									Phoenix	0-1	9.00	1	1	0	0	3.0	5	3	3	0	2	
									San Francisco	0-0	27.00	1	0	0	0	1.0	2	3	3	2	0	
26	RUFFIN, JOHNNY	R	R	6-3	170	7-29-71	Butler, AL	Lisman, AL	Cincinnati	0-0	1.35	10	0	0	0	13.1	4	3	2	11	11	1.085
									Indianapolis	3-1	2.90	36	1	0	0	49.2	27	19	16	37	58	
42	SALKELD, ROGER	R	R	6-5	215	3-6-71	Burbank, CA	Saugus, CA	Tacoma	1-0	1.80	4	3	0	1	15.0	8	4	3	7	11	0.103
									Indianapolis	12-2	4.22	20	20	1	0	119.1	96	60	56	57	86	
46	SCHOUREK, PETE	L	L	6-5	205	5-10-69	Austin, TX	Clifton, VA	Cincinnati	18-7	3.22	29	29	2	0	190.1	158	72	68	45	160	4.065
57	SMILEY, JOHN	L	L	6-4	210	3-17-65	Phoenixville, PA	Baden, PA	Cincinnati	12-5	3.46	28	27	1	0	176.2	173	72	68	39	124	8.154
56	SULLIVAN, SCOTT*	R	R	6-4	210	3-13-71	Tuscaloosa, AL	Carrollton, AL	Indianapolis	4-3	3.53	44	0	0	1	58.2	51	31	23	24	54	
									Cincinnati	0-0	4.91	3	0	0	0	3.2	4	2	2	2	2	0.011
38	WHITE, GABE	L	L	6-2	200	11-20-71	Sebring, FL	Sebring, FL	Ottawa	2-3	3.90	12	12	0	0	62.1	58	31	27	17	37	
									Montreal	1-2	7.01	19	1	0	0	25.2	26	21	20	9	25	

No.	CATCHERS (2)	B	T	Ht.	Wt.	Born	Birthplace	Residence	1995 Club	AVG.	G	AB	R	H	2B	3B	HR	RBI	BB	SO	SB	M.L. Service
6	BERRYHILL, DAMON	S	R	6-0	205	12-3-63	South Laguna, CA	Laguna Niguel, CA	Cincinnati	.183	34	82	6	15	3	0	2	11	10	19	0	7.106
10	TAUBENSEE, EDDIE	L	R	6-4	205	10-31-68	Beeville, TX	Windermere, FL	Cincinnati	.284	80	218	32	62	14	2	9	44	22	52	2	3.164

No.	INFIELDERS (10)	B	T	Ht.	Wt.	Born	Birthplace	Residence	1995 Club	AVG.	G	AB	R	H	2B	3B	HR	RBI	BB	SO	SB	M.L. Service
69	BELK, TIM*	R	R	6-3	200	4-6-70	Cincinnati, OH	Houston, TX	Indianapolis	.301	57	193	30	58	11	0	4	18	16	30	2	0.000
29	BOONE, BRET	R	R	5-10	180	4-6-69	El Cajon, CA	Orlando, FL	Cincinnati	.267	138	513	63	137	34	2	15	68	41	84	5	2.092
20	BRANSON, JEFF	L	R	6-0	180	1-26-67	Waynesboro, MS	Union, KY	Cincinnati	.260	122	331	43	86	18	2	12	45	44	69	2	3.088
12	GREENE, WILLIE	L	R	5-11	185	9-23-71	Milledgeville, GA	Haddock, GA	Cincinnati / Indianapolis	.105 / .243	8 / 91	19 / 325	1 / 57	2 / 79	0 / 12	0 / 2	0 / 19	0 / 45	3 / 38	7 / 67	0 / 3	0.140
28	HARRIS, LENNY	L	R	5-10	210	10-28-64	Miami, FL	Miami, FL	Cincinnati	.208	101	197	32	41	8	3	2	16	14	20	10	6.150
30	HUNTER, BRIAN R.	R	L	6-0	195	3-4-68	El Toro, CA	Anaheim, CA	Cincinnati / #Indianapolis	.215 / .361	40 / 9	79 / 36	9 / 7	17 / 13	6 / 5	0 / 0	1 / 4	9 / 11	11 / 6	21 / 11	2 / 0	4.035
11	LARKIN, BARRY	R	R	6-0	195	4-28-64	Cincinnati, OH	Cincinnati, OH	Cincinnati	.319	131	496	98	158	29	6	15	66	61	49	51	9.001
23	MORRIS, HAL	L	L	6-4	210	4-9-65	Fort Rucker, AL	Union, KY	Cincinnati / #Indianapolis	.279 / .400	101 / 2	359 / 5	53 / 2	100 / 2	25 / 0	2 / 0	11 / 0	51 / 1	29 / 1	58 / 0	1 / 0	6.036
18	OWENS, ERIC*	R	R	6-1	185	2-3-71	Danville, VA	Danville, VA	Indianapolis / Cincinnati	.314 / 1.000	108 / 2	427 / 2	86 / 0	134 / 2	24 / 0	8 / 0	12 / 0	63 / 1	52 / 0	61 / 0	33 / 0	0.003
3	REESE, POKEY*	R	R	5-11	180	6-10-73	Columbia, SC	Columbia, SC	Indianapolis	.239	89	343	51	82	21	1	10	46	36	81	8	0.000

No.	OUTFIELDERS (11)	B	T	Ht.	Wt.	Born	Birthplace	Residence	1995 Club	AVG.	G	AB	R	H	2B	3B	HR	RBI	BB	SO	SB	M.L. Service
9	ANTHONY, ERIC	L	L	6-2	195	11-8-67	San Diego, CA	Sugar Land, TX	Cincinnati / #Indianapolis	.269 / .292	47 / 7	134 / 24	19 / 7	36 / 7	6 / 0	0 / 0	5 / 4	23 / 8	13 / 6	30 / 4	2 / 2	5.014
33	GIBRALTER, STEVE*	R	R	6-0	190	10-9-72	Dallas, TX	Duncanville, TX	Indianapolis / Cincinnati	.316 / .333	79 / 4	263 / 3	49 / 0	83 / 1	19 / 0	3 / 0	18 / 0	63 / 0	25 / 0	70 / 0	0 / 0	0.005
7	GOODWIN, CURTIS	L	L	5-11	180	9-30-72	Oakland, CA	San Leandro, CA	Rochester / Baltimore	.264 / .263	36 / 87	140 / 289	24 / 40	37 / 76	3 / 11	3 / 3	0 / 1	7 / 24	12 / 15	15 / 53	17 / 22	0.122
22	HOWARD, THOMAS	S	R	6-2	205	12-11-64	Middletown, OH	Elk Grove, CA	Cincinnati	.302	113	281	42	85	15	2	3	26	20	37	17	4.133
15	KELLY, MIKE	R	R	6-4	195	6-2-70	Los Angeles, CA	Phoenix, AZ	Richmond / Atlanta	.289 / .190	15 / 97	45 / 137	5 / 26	13 / 26	1 / 6	0 / 1	2 / 3	8 / 17	5 / 11	17 / 49	0 / 7	1.018
61	KING, ANDRE*	R	R	6-1	180	11-26-73	Kingston, Jamaica	Fort Lauderdale, FL	Durham / Prince William	.252 / .156	111 / 9	421 / 32	59 / 4	106 / 5	22 / 1	3 / 1	9 / 0	33 / 3	39 / 6	126 / 9	15 / 1	0.000
67	LADELL, CLEVELAND*	R	R	5-11	170	9-19-70	Paris, TX	Dallas, TX	Chattanooga	.292	135	517	76	151	28	7	5	43	39	88	28	0.000
54	MOTTOLA, CHAD*	R	R	6-3	220	10-15-71	Augusta, GA	Fort Lauderdale, FL	Chattanooga / Indianapolis	.293 / .259	51 / 69	181 / 239	32 / 40	53 / 62	13 / 11	1 / 1	10 / 8	39 / 37	13 / 20	32 / 50	1 / 8	0.000
16	SANDERS, REGGIE	R	R	6-1	185	12-1-67	Florence, SC	Tampa, FL	Cincinnati	.306	133	484	91	148	36	6	28	99	69	122	36	3.165
68	WATKINS, PAT*	R	R	6-2	185	9-2-72	Raleigh, NC	Garner, NC	Winston-Salem / Chattanooga	.206 / .291	27 / 105	107 / 358	14 / 57	22 / 104	3 / 26	1 / 2	4 / 12	13 / 57	10 / 33	24 / 53	1 / 5	0.000
51	WILSON, NIGEL*	L	L	6-1	185	1-12-70	Oshawa, Ont.	Ajax, Ont.	Indianapolis / Cincinnati	.313 / .000	82 / 5	304 / 7	53 / 0	95 / 0	27 / 0	3 / 0	17 / 0	51 / 0	13 / 0	95 / 4	5 / 0	0.049

*Rookie
#Rehabilitation Assignment

FULL NAMES AND PHONETICS

Anthony, Eric Todd
Belk, Timothy William
Berryhill, Damon Scott
Boone, Bret Robert
Branson, Jeffery Glenn
Brantley, Jeffrey Hoke
Burba, David Allen
Carrasco, Hector Pacheco Pipo (Car-roscoe)
Gibralter, Stephan Benson
Goodwin, Curtis LaMar
Greene, Willie Louis
Harris, Leonard Anthony
Hernandez, Francis Xavier

Howard, Thomas Sylvester, Jr.
Hunter, Brian Ronald
Jarvis, Kevin Thomas
Kelly, Michael Raymond
King, Andre Omar
Ladell, Cleveland Marquis (La-DELL)
Larkin, Barry Louis
McElroy, Charles Dwayne, Sr. (MACK-ilroy)
Moore, Marcus Braymont
Morris, William Harold, III
Mottola, Charles Edward (Muh-TOE-lah)
Owens, Eric Blake
Portugal, Mark Steven

Pugh, Timothy Dean (PEW)
Reese Jr., Calvin "Pokey"
Rijo, Jose Antonio (REE-ho)
Roper, John Christopher
Ruffin, Johnny Renando
Salkeld, Roger W.
Sanders, Reggie Laverne
Schourek, Peter Alan (SHORE-eck)
Smiley, John Patrick
Sullivan, Scott
Taubensee, Edward Kenneth (TAW-ben-see)
Watkins, William Patrick

White, Gabriel Allen
Wilson, Nigel Edward

MANAGER AND COACHES

Charles Ray Knight
Marc Stephen Bombard
Donald Edward Gullett
Thomas Hubert Hume
James Curtis Lett
Harold Abraham McRae
Joel Randolph Youngblood

Colorado Rockies (WEST)

MANAGER DON BAYLOR (25)

Coaches:
FRANK FUNK (45)
GENE GLYNN (2)
KEN GRIFFEY (24)
JACKIE MOORE (47)
PAUL ZUVELLA (46)

Team Physician—DR. WAYNE GERSOFF
Trainer—DAVE CILLADI
Assistant Trainer—TOM PROBST

Director of Public Relations—MIKE SWANSON
Director of Travel—PETER DURSO

No.	PITCHERS (23)	B	T	Ht.	Wt.	Born	Birthplace	Residence	1995 Club	W-L	ERA	G	GS	CG	SV	IP	H	R	ER	BB	SO	M.L. Service
50	ALSTON, GARVIN*	R	R	6-1	185	12-8-71	Mount Vernon, NY	Mount Vernon, NY	New Haven	4-4	2.84	47	0	0	6	66.2	47	24	21	26	73	
									Colorado	0-0	0.00	0	0	0	0	0.0	0	0	0	0	0	0.012
51	ARTEAGA, IVAN*	L	R	6-2	227	7-20-72	Puerto Cabello, Ven.	Puerto Cabello, Ven.	New Haven	2-4	5.56	14	11	0	0	34.0	36	26	21	21	18	0.000
38	BAILEY, ROGER	R	R	6-1	180	10-3-70	Chattahoochee, FL	Englewood, CO	Colorado	7-6	4.98	39	6	0	0	81.1	88	49	45	39	33	
									Colorado Spr.	0-0	2.70	3	3	0	0	16.2	15	9	5	8	7	0.130
37	BURKE, JOHN*	B	R	6-4	215	2-9-70	Durango, CO	Highlands Ranch, CO	Colorado Spr.	7-1	4.55	19	17	0	1	87.0	79	46	44	48	65	0.000
41	DeJEAN, MIKE*	R	R	6-2	205	9-28-70	Baton Rouge, LA	Denham Springs, LA	Norwich	5-5	2.99	59	0	0	20	78.1	58	29	26	34	57	0.000
36	FARMER, MIKE*	B	L	6-1	193	7-3-68	Gary, IN	Gary, IN	New Haven	10-5	4.89	40	12	0	0	110.1	117	63	60	35	77	0.000
44	FREEMAN, MARVIN	R	R	6-7	222	4-10-63	Chicago, IL	Country Club Hills, IL	Colorado	3-7	5.89	22	18	0	0	94.2	122	64	62	41	61	6.134
40	HOLMES, DARREN	R	R	6-0	202	4-25-66	Asheville, NC	Fletcher, NC	Colorado	6-1	3.24	68	0	0	14	66.2	59	26	24	28	61	4.122
57	JONES, BOBBY*	R	L	6-0	175	4-11-72	Orange, NJ	Rutherford, NJ	New Haven	5-2	2.61	26	8	0	4	72.1	60	27	21	36	70	
									Colorado Spr.	1-2	7.30	11	8	0	0	40.2	50	38	33	33	48	0.000
16	LESKANIC, CURTIS	R	R	6-0	180	4-2-68	Homestead, PA	Littleton, CO	Colorado	6-3	3.40	76	0	0	10	98.0	83	38	37	33	107	1.118
43	MUNOZ, MIKE	L	L	6-2	192	7-12-65	Baldwin Park, CA	South Lake, TX	Colorado	2-4	7.42	64	0	0	2	43.2	54	38	36	27	37	3.138
17	NIED, DAVID	R	R	6-2	185	12-22-68	Dallas, TX	Englewood, CO	#Portland	0-0	0.00	1	1	0	0	3.0	1	0	0	1	5	
									#New Haven	0-0	8.10	1	1	0	0	3.1	4	3	3	0	0	
									Colorado Spr.	1-1	4.99	7	7	0	0	30.2	31	18	17	25	21	
									Colorado	0-0	20.77	2	0	0	0	4.1	11	10	10	3	3	2.103
28	PAINTER, LANCE	L	L	6-1	197	7-21-67	Bedford, England	Littleton, CO	Colorado	3-0	4.37	33	1	0	0	45.1	55	23	22	10	36	
									Colorado Spr.	0-3	5.96	11	4	0	0	25.2	32	20	17	11	12	1.075
39	REED, STEVE	R	R	6-2	212	3-11-66	Los Angeles, CA	Arvada, CO	Colorado	5-2	2.14	71	0	0	3	84.0	61	24	20	21	79	2.133
23	REKAR, BRYAN	R	R	6-3	210	6-3-72	Oak Lawn, IL	Orland Park, IL	New Haven	6-3	2.13	12	12	1	0	80.1	65	28	19	16	80	
									Colorado Spr.	4-2	1.49	7	7	2	0	48.1	29	10	8	13	39	
									Colorado	4-6	4.98	15	14	1	0	85.0	95	51	47	24	60	0.077
42	REYNOSO, ARMANDO	R	R	6-0	204	5-1-66	San Luis Potosi, Mex.	Jalisco, Mex.	#Colorado Spr.	2-1	1.57	5	5	0	0	23.0	14	4	4	6	17	
									Colorado	7-7	5.32	20	18	0	0	93.0	116	61	55	36	40	3.019
30	RITZ, KEVIN	R	R	6-4	222	6-8-65	Eatonstown, NJ	Byesville, OH	Colorado	11-11	4.21	31	28	0	2	173.1	171	91	81	65	120	4.070
18	RUFFIN, BRUCE	B	L	6-2	215	10-4-63	Lubbock, TX	Austin, TX	Colorado	0-1	2.12	37	0	0	11	34.0	26	8	8	19	23	
									#New Haven	0-0	0.00	2	2	0	0	2.0	1	0	0	0	2	8.124
31	SABERHAGEN, BRET	R	R	6-1	200	4-11-64	Chicago Heights, IL	Port St. Lucie, FL	New York N.L.	5-5	3.35	16	16	3	0	110.0	105	45	41	20	71	
									Colorado	2-1	6.28	9	9	0	0	43.0	60	33	30	13	29	11.119
20	SWIFT, BILL	R	R	6-0	197	10-27-61	South Portland, ME	Paradise Valley, AZ	Colorado	9-3	4.94	19	19	0	0	105.2	122	62	58	43	68	9.040
32	THOMPSON, MARK	R	R	6-2	205	4-7-71	Russellville, KY	Russellville, KY	Colorado	2-3	6.53	21	5	0	0	51.0	73	42	37	22	30	
									Colorado Spr.	5-3	6.10	11	10	0	0	62.0	73	43	42	25	38	0.093
48	THOMSON, JOHN*	R	R	6-3	175	10-1-73	Vicksburg, MS	Sulpher, LA	New Haven	7-8	4.18	26	24	0	0	131.1	132	69	61	56	82	0.000
53	VIANO, JAKE*	R	R	5-10	177	9-4-73	Los Altos, CA	Long Beach, CA	New Haven	3-6	3.38	57	0	0	19	72.0	51	31	27	38	85	0.000

No.	CATCHERS (3)	B	T	Ht.	Wt.	Born	Birthplace	Residence	1995 Club	AVG.	G	AB	R	H	2B	3B	HR	RBI	BB	SO	SB	M.L. Service
27	BRITO, JORGE	R	R	6-1	190	6-22-66	Moncion, D.R.	Athens, AL	Colorado Colorado Spr.	.216 .229	18 32	51 96	5 9	11 22	3 4	0 1	0 2	7 15	2 2	17 20	1 0	0.086
34	OWENS, JAYHAWK	R	R	6-1	213	2-10-69	Cincinnati, OH	Castle Rock, CO	Colorado Spr. Colorado	.294 .244	70 18	221 45	47 7	65 11	13 2	5 0	12 4	48 12	20 2	61 15	2 0	0.169
15	REED, JEFF	L	R	6-2	190	11-12-62	Joliet, IL	Elizabethton, TN	San Francisco	.265	66	113	12	30	2	0	0	9	20	17	0	10.021

No.	INFIELDERS (7)	B	T	Ht.	Wt.	Born	Birthplace	Residence	1995 Club	AVG.	G	AB	R	H	2B	3B	HR	RBI	BB	SO	SB	M.L. Service
6	BATES, JASON	S	R	5-11	181	1-5-71	Downey, CA	Engelwood, CO	Colorado	.267	116	322	42	86	17	4	8	46	42	70	3	0.160
9	CASTILLA, VINNY	R	R	6-1	200	7-4-67	Oaxaca, Mex.	Littleton, CO	Colorado	.309	139	527	82	163	34	2	32	90	30	87	2	2.164
4	COUNSELL, CRAIG*	L	R	6-0	170	8-21-70	South Bend, IN	Fort Myers Beach, FL	Colorado Spr. Colorado	.281 .000	118 3	399 1	60 0	112 0	22 0	6 0	0 0	53 0	34 1	47 0	10 0	0.016
14	GALARRAGA, ANDRES	R	R	6-3	235	6-18-61	Caracas, Venezuela	Caracas, Venezuela	Colorado	.280	143	554	89	155	29	3	31	106	32	146	12	9.165
35	VANDER WAL, JOHN	L	L	6-2	198	4-29-66	Grand Rapids, MI	Royal Palm Beach, FL	Colorado	.347	105	101	15	35	8	1	5	21	16	23	1	3.150
22	WEISS, WALT	S	R	6-0	178	11-28-63	Tuxedo, NY	Aurora, CO	Colorado	.260	137	427	65	111	17	3	1	25	98	57	15	7.151
21	YOUNG, ERIC	R	R	5-9	170	5-18-67	New Brunswick, NJ	New Brunswick, NJ	Colorado	.317	120	366	68	116	21	9	6	36	49	29	35	3.014

No.	OUTFIELDERS (7)	B	T	Ht.	Wt.	Born	Birthplace	Residence	1995 Club	AVG.	G	AB	R	H	2B	3B	HR	RBI	BB	SO	SB	M.L. Service
10	BICHETTE, DANTE	R	R	6-3	235	11-18-63	W. Palm Beach, FL	Palm Bch Gardens, FL	Colorado	.340	139	579	102	197	38	2	40	128	22	96	13	6.080
26	BURKS, ELLIS	R	R	6-2	198	9-11-64	Vicksburg, MS	Englewood, CO	#Colorado Spr. Colorado	.310 .266	8 103	29 278	9 41	9 74	2 10	1 6	2 14	6 49	4 39	8 72	0 7	8.105
1	HUBBARD, TRENIDAD*	R	R	5-8	183	5-11-66	Chicago, IL	Houston, TX	Colorado Spr. Colorado	.340 .310	123 24	480 58	102 13	163 18	29 4	7 0	12 3	66 9	61 8	59 6	37 2	0.077
52	JONES, TERRY*	S	R	5-10	165	2-15-71	Birmingham, AL	Pinson, AL	New Haven	.269	125	472	78	127	12	1	1	26	39	104	51	0.000
3	McCRACKEN, QUINTON*	S	R	5-7	173	3-16-70	Wilmington, NC	Southport, NC	New Haven Colorado Spr. Colorado	.357 .361 .000	55 61 3	221 244 1	33 55 0	79 88 0	11 14 0	4 6 0	1 3 0	26 28 0	21 23 0	32 30 1	26 17 0	0.016
29	PULLIAM, HARVEY	R	R	6-0	218	10-20-67	San Francisco, CA	Altamonte Springs, FL	Colorado Spr. Colorado	.327 .400	115 5	407 5	90 1	133 2	30 1	6 0	25 1	91 3	49 0	59 2	6 0	1.019
33	WALKER, LARRY	L	R	6-3	225	12-1-66	Maple Ridge, B.C.	West Palm Beach, FL	Colorado	.306	131	494	96	151	31	5	36	101	49	72	16	6.164

*Rookie
#Rehabilitation Assignment

FULL NAMES AND PHONETICS

Alston, Garvin James (ALL-stun, GAR-vin)
Arteaga, Ivan Jose (ar-tee-AH-gah)
Bailey, Charles Roger
Bates, Jason Charles
Bichette, Alphonse Dante
 (bih-SHET, DAHN-tay)
Brito, Jorge (BREE-toe, HOR-hay)
Burke, John C.
Burks, Ellis Rena
Castellano, Pedro Orlando
 (cass-ta-YAH-no)
Castilla, Vinicio Soria (cass-TEE-yah)
Counsell, Craig John (COWN-sel)
DeJean, John (DE-zshonn)

Farmer, Mike
Freeman, Marvin
Galarraga, Andres Jose
 (gahl-la-RAH-gah, ON-dress)
Habyan, John Gabriel (HAY-bee-un)
Holmes, Darren Lee
Hubbard, Trenidad (HUB-ard, TREHN-i-dad)
Jones, Bobby
Jones, Terry
Leskanic, Curtis John (les-CAN-ik)
McCracken, Quinton Antoine
Munoz, Michael Anthony (MOON-yoze)
Nied, David Glen (NEED)
Owens, Claude J.

Painter, Lance T.
Pullman, Harvey
Reed, Jeffrey Scott
Reed, Steven Vincent
Rekar, Bryan (REE-car)
Reynoso, Martia Armando Gutierrez
 (ray-NO-so, are-MAHN-do)
Ritz, Kevin D.
Ruffin, Bruce Wayne
Saberhagen, Bret William (SAY-ber-hay-gun)
Swift, William Charles
Thompson, Mark Radford
Thomson, John
Vander Wal, John Henry (VAN-derr-wall)

Viano, Jake (VEE-ah-no)
Voisard, Mark Allen (VOY-sard)
Walker, Larry Kenneth Robert
Weiss, Walter William (WICE)
Young, Eric Orlando

MANAGER AND COACHES

Don Edward Baylor
Frank Funk
Gene Glynn
George Kenneth Griffey Sr.
Jackie Spencer Moore
Paul Zuvella

Florida Marlins (EAST)

MANAGER
RENE LACHEMANN (15)

Coaches:
JOE BREEDEN (12) - bullpen
RUSTY KUNTZ (22)
JOSE MORALES (34)
COOKIE ROJAS (1)
LARRY ROTHSCHILD (47)
RICK WILLIAMS (30)

Team Physician—DR. DAN KANELL
Trainer—LARRY STARR
Assistant Trainer—KEVIN RAND

Media Relations Director—CHUCK POOL
Director of Travel—JOHN PANAGAKIS

No.	PITCHERS (25)	B	T	Ht.	Wt.	Born	Birthplace	Residence	1995 Club	W-L	ERA	G	GS	CG	SV	IP	H	R	ER	BB	SO	M.L. Service
56	ADAMSON, JOEL*	L	L	6-4	185	7-2-71	Lakewood, CA	Lakewood, CA	Charlotte	8-4	3.29	19	18	2	0	115.0	113	51	42	20	80	0.000
57	ALFONSECA, ANTONIO*	R	R	6-4	180	4-16-72	La Romano, D.R.	La Romano, D.R.	Portland	9-3	3.64	19	17	1	0	96.1	81	43	39	42	75	0.000
43	BATISTA, MIGUEL*	R	R	6-0	180	2-19-71	Santo Domingo, D.R.	S.P. de Macoris, D.R.	Charlotte	6-12	4.80	34	18	0	0	116.1	118	79	62	60	58	0.018
46	BOWEN, RYAN	R	R	6-0	185	2-10-68	Hanford, CA	Plantation, FL	#Brevard County	0-2	2.45	3	3	0	0	11.0	6	3	3	6	10	
									#Charlotte	0-1	9.64	1	1	0	0	4.2	5	5	5	4	3	
									Florida	2-0	3.78	4	3	0	0	16.2	23	11	7	12	15	3.091
27	BROWN, KEVIN	R	R	6-4	195	3-14-65	McIntyre, GA	Macon, GA	Baltimore	10-9	3.60	26	26	3	0	172.1	155	73	69	48	117	6.170
33	BURKETT, JOHN	R	R	6-2	211	11-28-64	New Brighton, PA	Scottsdale, AZ	Florida	14-14	4.30	30	30	4	0	188.1	208	95	90	57	126	5.149
11	HAMMOND, CHRIS	L	L	6-1	195	1-21-66	Atlanta, GA	Hallandale, FL	#Brevard County	0-0	0.00	1	1	0	0	4.0	3	1	0	0	4	
									#Charlotte	0-0	0.00	1	1	0	0	4.0	3	1	0	2	3	
									Florida	9-6	3.80	25	24	3	0	161.0	157	73	68	47	126	4.159
24	HEREDIA, WILSON*	R	R	6-0	175	3-30-72	La Romana, D.R.	La Romana, D.R.	Texas	0-1	3.75	6	0	0	0	12.0	9	5	5	15	6	0.021
									Oklahoma City	1-4	6.82	8	7	0	0	31.2	40	26	24	25	21	
									Tulsa	4-2	3.18	8	7	1	1	45.1	42	19	16	21	34	
									Portland	4-0	2.00	4	4	0	0	27.0	22	7	6	14	19	
	HERNANDEZ, LIVAN	R	R	6-2	220	2-20-75	Villaclara, Cuba	Miami, FL	Cuban Natl' Team	..	..	..	..	..	..	..	..	..	..	..	..	0.000
50	HURST, BILL*	R	R	6-7	215	4-28-70	Miami Beach, FL	Miami, FL	Brevard County	1-4	3.02	39	4	0	12	50.2	33	20	17	41	35	0.000
55	JUELSGAARD, JAROD*	R	R	6-3	195	6-27-68	Harlan, IA	Elk Horn, IA	Portland	3-1	3.89	48	0	0	2	71.2	65	35	31	44	44	0.000
36	LARKIN, ANDY*	R	R	6-4	175	6-27-74	Chelan, WA	Medford, OR	Portland	1-2	3.38	9	9	0	0	40.0	29	16	15	11	23	0.000
25	LEITER, AL	L	L	6-3	215	10-23-65	Toms River, NJ	Plantation, FL	Toronto	11-11	3.64	28	28	2	0	183.0	162	80	74	108	153	6.014
18	MANTEI, MATT*	R	R	6-1	181	7-7-73	Tampa, FL	Sawyer, MI	#Portland	1-0	2.38	8	0	0	1	11.1	10	3	3	5	15	
									#Charlotte	0-1	2.57	6	0	0	0	7.0	1	3	2	5	10	
									Florida	0-1	4.73	12	0	0	0	13.1	12	8	7	13	15	0.160
51	MATHEWS, TERRY	L	R	6-2	225	10-5-64	Alexandria, LA	Alexandria, LA	Florida	4-4	3.38	57	0	0	3	82.2	70	32	31	27	72	2.141
									#Charlotte	0-0	4.91	2	0	0	0	3.2	5	2	2	0	5	
53	MILLER, KURT*	R	R	6-5	205	8-24-72	Tucson, AZ	Bakersfield, CA	Charlotte	8-11	4.62	22	22	0	0	126.2	143	76	65	55	83	0.019
31	NEN, ROBB	R	R	6-4	200	11-28-69	San Pedro, CA	Seal Beach, CA	Florida	0-7	3.29	62	0	0	23	65.2	62	26	24	23	68	2.119
58	PEREZ, YORKIS	L	L	6-0	180	9-30-67	Bajos de Haina, D.R.	Bajos de Haina, D.R.	Florida	2-6	5.21	69	0	0	1	46.2	35	29	27	28	47	1.154
59	POWELL, JAY*	R	R	6-4	225	1-19-72	Meridian, MS	Collinsville, TN	Portland	5-4	1.87	50	0	0	24	53.0	42	12	11	15	53	
									Florida	0-0	2.18	9	0	0	0	8.1	7	2	1	6	4	0.023
48	RAPP, PAT	R	R	6-3	215	7-13-67	Jennings, LA	Sunrise, FL	Charlotte	0-1	6.00	1	1	0	0	6.0	6	4	4	1	5	
									Florida	14-7	3.44	28	28	3	0	167.1	158	72	64	76	102	2.055
41	SEELBACH, CHRIS*	R	R	6-4	180	12-18-72	Lufkin, TX	Lufkin, TX	Richmond	4-6	4.66	14	14	1	0	73.1	64	39	38	39	65	
									Greenville	6-0	1.64	9	9	1	0	60.1	38	15	11	30	65	0.000
44	VALDES, MARC*	R	R	6-0	187	12-20-71	Dayton, OH	Tampa, FL	Charlotte	9-13	4.86	27	27	3	0	170.1	189	98	92	59	104	
									Florida	0-0	14.14	3	3	0	0	7.0	17	13	11	9	2	0.035
52	VERES, RANDY	R	R	6-3	210	11-25-65	San Francisco, CA	Folsom, CA	Charlotte	1-0	2.70	6	0	0	1	6.2	3	2	2	5	5	
									Florida	4-4	3.88	47	0	0	1	48.2	46	25	21	22	31	1.154
42	WARD, BRYAN*	L	L	6-2	210	1-28-72	Bristol, PA	Mt. Holly, NJ	Brevard County	5-1	2.88	11	11	0	0	72.0	68	27	23	17	65	
									Portland	7-3	4.50	20	11	1	2	72.0	70	42	36	31	71	0.000
35	WEATHERS, DAVE	R	R	6-3	220	9-25-69	Lawrenceburg, TN	Loretto, TN	Florida	4-5	5.98	28	15	0	0	90.1	104	68	60	52	60	2.104
									#Brevard County	0-0	0.00	1	1	0	0	4.0	4	0	0	1	3	
									#Charlotte	0-1	9.00	1	1	0	0	5.0	10	5	5	5	0	
30	WHISENANT, MATT*	B	L	6-3	215	6-8-71	Los Angeles, CA	La Canada, CA	Portland	10-6	3.50	23	22	2	0	128.2	106	57	50	65	107	0.000

No.	CATCHERS (2)	B	T	Ht.	Wt.	Born	Birthplace	Residence	1995 Club	AVG.	G	AB	R	H	2B	3B	HR	RBI	BB	SO	SB	M.L. Service
23	JOHNSON, CHARLES	R	R	6-2	215	7-20-71	Fort Pierce, FL	Pembroke Pines, FL	Florida	.251	97	315	40	79	15	1	11	39	46	71	0	0.165
									#Portland	.000	2	7	0	0	0	0	0	0	1	3	0	
13	NATAL, BOB	R	R	5-11	190	11-13-65	Long Beach, CA	Chula Vista, CA	Florida	.233	16	43	2	10	2	1	2	6	1	9	0	1.159
									Charlotte	.314	53	191	23	60	14	0	3	24	11	23	0	

No.	INFIELDERS (6)	B	T	Ht.	Wt.	Born	Birthplace	Residence	1995 Club	AVG.	G	AB	R	H	2B	3B	HR	RBI	BB	SO	SB	M.L. Service
7	ABBOTT, KURT	R	R	6-0	185	6-2-69	Zanesville, OH	Davie, FL	#Charlotte	.278	5	18	3	5	0	0	1	3	1	3	1	1.146
									Florida	.255	120	420	60	107	18	7	17	60	36	110	4	
26	ARIAS, ALEX	R	R	6-3	185	11-20-67	New York, NY	Hollywood, FL	Florida	.269	94	216	22	58	9	2	3	26	22	20	1	3.000
4	COLBRUNN, GREG	R	R	6-0	200	7-26-69	Fontana, CA	Weston, FL	Florida	.277	138	528	70	146	22	1	23	89	22	69	11	3.035
9	PENDLETON, TERRY	S	R	5-9	195	7-16-60	Los Angeles, CA	Duluth, GA	Florida	.290	133	513	70	149	32	1	14	78	38	84	1	11.022
16	RENTERIA, EDGAR*	R	R	6-1	172	8-7-75	Barranquilla, Col.	Barranquilla, Col.	Portland	.289	135	508	70	147	15	7	7	68	32	85	30	0.000
3	VERAS, QUILVIO	S	R	5-9	166	4-3-71	Santo Domingo, D.R.	Santo Domingo, D.R.	Florida	.261	124	440	86	115	20	7	5	32	80	68	56	0.160

No.	OUTFIELDERS (6)	B	T	Ht.	Wt.	Born	Birthplace	Residence	1995 Club	AVG.	G	AB	R	H	2B	3B	HR	RBI	BB	SO	SB	M.L. Service
19	CONINE, JEFF	R	R	6-1	220	6-27-66	Tacoma, WA	Weston, FL	Florida	.302	133	483	72	146	26	2	25	105	66	94	2	3.026
27	McMILLON, BILL*	L	L	5-11	172	11-17-71	Otero, NM	Sumter, SC	Portland	.313	141	518	92	162	29	3	14	93	96	90	15	0.000
6	ORSULAK, JOE	L	L	6-1	205	5-31-62	Glen Ridge, NJ	Cockeysville, MD	New York N.L.	.283	108	290	41	82	19	2	1	37	19	35	1	10.097
10	SHEFFIELD, GARY	R	R	5-11	190	11-18-68	Tampa, FL	St. Petersburg, FL	Florida	.324	63	213	46	69	8	0	16	46	55	45	19	6.150
20	TAVAREZ, JESUS	S	R	6-0	170	3-26-71	Santo Domingo, D.R.	Santo Domingo, D.R.	Charlotte	.300	39	140	15	42	6	2	1	8	9	19	7	0.137
									Florida	.289	63	190	31	55	6	2	2	13	16	27	7	
2	WHITE, DEVON	S	R	6-2	190	12-29-62	Kingston, Jamaica	Mesa, AZ	Toronto	.283	101	427	61	121	23	5	10	53	29	97	11	9.008

*Rookie
#Rehabilitation Assignment

FULL NAMES AND PHONETICS

Abbott, Kurt Thomas
Adamson, Joel Lee
Alfonseca, Antonio (AL-fon-say-ka)
Arias, Alejandro (AIR-ee-us)
Batista, Miguel Descartes (Bah-TEE-sta)
Bowen, Ryan Eugene
Brown, James Kevin
Burkett, John David (BURK-it)
Colbrunn, Gregory Joseph (COAL-brun)
Conine, Jeffery Guy
Hammond, Christopher Andrew

Heredia, Wilson
Hernandez, Eisler Livan
Hurst, William Hansel
Juelsgaard, Jarod Del (JEWLS-guard)
Larkin, Andrew Dane
Leiter, Alois Terry (LIGHTER)
Mantei, Matthew Bruce (MAN-tie)
Mathews, Terry Alan
Miller, Kurt Everett
Natal, Robert Marcel (NAY-tul)
Nen, Robert Allen

Orsulak, Joseph Michael (OR-soo-lack)
Pendleton, Terry Lee
Perez, Yorkis Miguel
Powell, James Willard
Rapp, Patrick Leland
Renteria, Edgar Enrique (Ren-ter-ree-ah)
Seelbach, Christopher Don (SEAL-back)
Sheffield, Gary Antonian
Weathers, John David
Whisenant, Matthew Michael (WIZ-eh-nant)
White, Devon Markes

MANAGER AND COACHES
Rene George Lachemann (ruh-NAY LATCH-men)
Russell J. Kuntz
Jose Manuel Morales
Octavio Victor Rojas
Larry L. Rothschild
Richard Anthony Williams

Houston Astros (CENTRAL)

MANAGER TERRY COLLINS (2)

Coaches:
MATT GALANTE (48)
STEVE HENDERSON (55)
JULIO LINARES (1)
BRENT STROM (42)
RICK SWEET (18)

Team Physician—DR. WILLIAM BRYAN
Trainer—DAVE LABOSSIERE
Assistant Trainer—REX JONES

Director of Media Relations—ROB MATWICK
Dir. of Baseball Administration—BARRY WATERS

No.	PITCHERS (22)	B	T	Ht.	Wt.	Born	Birthplace	Residence	1995 Club	W-L	ERA	G	GS	CG	SV	IP	H	R	ER	BB	SO	M.L. Service
46	BROCAIL, DOUG	L	R	6-5	235	5-16-67	Clearfield, PA	Missouri City, TX	Houston	6-4	4.19	36	7	0	1	77.1	87	40	36	22	39	2.082
									Tucson	1-0	3.86	3	3	0	0	16.1	18	9	7	4	16	
38	CREEK, RYAN*	R	R	6-1	180	9-24-72	Winchester, VA	Martinsburg, WV	Jackson	9-7	3.63	26	24	1	0	143.2	137	74	58	64	120	0.000
49	DOUGHERTY, JIM	R	R	6-0	210	3-8-68	Brentwood, NY	Kitty Hawk, NC	Houston	8-4	4.92	56	0	0	0	67.2	76	37	37	25	49	0.139
									Tucson	1-0	3.27	8	0	0	1	11.0	11	4	4	5	12	
15	DRABEK, DOUG	R	R	6-1	185	7-25-62	Victoria, TX	The Woodlands, TX	Houston	10-9	4.77	31	31	2	0	185.0	205	104	98	54	143	9.079
44	GALLAHER, KEVIN*	R	R	6-3	190	8-1-68	Fairfax, VA	Vienna, VA	Kissimmee	1-1	5.71	7	7	0	0	17.1	8	11	11	24	21	
									Tucson	1-1	6.43	3	3	0	0	14.0	19	11	10	9	11	
									Jackson	2-2	3.40	6	6	1	0	42.1	31	18	16	23	28	0.000
43	GRZANICH, MIKE*	R	R	6-1	180	8-24-72	Canton, IL	Champagne, IL	Jackson	5-3	2.74	50	0	0	8	65.2	55	22	20	38	44	0.000
10	HAMPTON, MIKE	R	L	5-10	180	9-9-72	Brooksville, FL	Homosassa, FL	Houston	9-8	3.35	24	24	0	0	150.2	141	73	56	49	115	2.020
58	HARTGRAVES, DEAN	R	L	6-0	185	8-12-66	Bakersfield, CA	Salem, OR	Tucson	3-2	2.11	14	0	0	5	21.1	21	6	5	5	15	
									Houston	2-0	3.22	40	0	0	0	36.1	30	14	13	16	24	0.138
53	HENRIQUEZ, OSCAR*	R	R	6-6	220	1-28-74	LaGuaria, Ven.	LaGuaria, Ven.	Kissimmee	3-4	5.04	20	0	0	1	44.2	40	29	25	30	36	0.000
45	HOLT, CHRIS*	R	R	6-4	205	9-18-71	Dallas, TX	Dallas, TX	Jackson	2-2	1.67	5	5	1	0	32.1	27	8	6	5	24	
									Tucson	5-8	4.10	20	19	0	0	118.2	155	65	54	32	69	0.000
35	HUDEK, JOHN	B	R	6-1	200	8-8-66	Tampa, FL	Sugar Land, TX	Houston	2-2	5.40	19	0	0	7	20.0	19	12	12	5	29	1.119
59	JONES, TODD	L	R	6-3	200	4-24-68	Marietta, GA	Pell City, AL	Houston	6-5	3.07	68	0	0	15	99.2	89	38	34	52	96	2.036
57	KILE, DARRYL	R	R	6-5	185	12-2-68	Garden Grove, CA	Sugar Land, TX	Houston	4-12	4.96	25	21	0	0	127.0	114	81	70	73	113	4.048
									Tucson	2-1	8.51	4	4	0	0	24.1	29	23	23	12	15	
54	LOISELLE, RICH*	R	R	6-5	225	1-12-72	Neenah, WI	Oshkosh, WI	Memphis	6-3	3.55	13	13	1	0	78.2	82	46	31	33	48	
									Las Vegas	2-2	7.24	8	7	1	0	27.1	36	27	22	9	16	
									Tucson	0-0	2.61	2	1	0	0	10.1	8	4	3	4	4	0.000
50	MLICKI, DOUG*	R	R	6-3	175	4-12-71	Cleveland, OH	Galloway, OH	Jackson	8-3	2.79	16	16	2	0	96.2	73	41	30	33	72	
									Tucson	1-2	5.56	6	6	0	0	34.0	44	27	21	6	22	0.000
51	MORMAN, ALVIN*	L	L	6-3	210	1-6-69	Rockingham, NC	Rockingham, NC	Tucson	5-1	3.91	45	0	0	3	48.1	50	26	21	20	36	0.000
37	REYNOLDS, SHANE	R	R	6-3	210	3-26-68	Bastrop, LA	Houston, TX	Houston	10-11	3.47	30	30	3	0	189.1	196	87	73	37	175	2.017
36	SMALL, MARK*	R	R	6-3	205	11-12-67	Portland, OR	Seattle, WA	Tucson	3-3	4.09	51	0	0	19	66.0	74	32	30	19	51	0.000
21	SWINDELL, GREG	R	L	6-3	225	1-2-65	Fort Worth, TX	Houston, TX	Houston	10-9	4.47	33	26	1	0	153.0	180	86	76	39	96	8.165
31	TABAKA, JEFF	R	L	6-2	195	1-17-64	Barberton, OH	Clinton, OH	Las Vegas	0-1	1.99	19	0	0	6	22.2	16	6	5	14	27	
									San Diego	0-0	7.11	10	0	0	0	6.1	10	5	5	5	6	
									Houston	1-0	2.22	24	0	0	0	24.1	17	6	6	12	19	1.051
13	WAGNER, BILLY*	L	L	5-11	180	6-25-71	Tannersville, VA	Dublin, VA	Jackson	2-2	2.57	12	12	0	0	70.0	49	25	20	36	77	
									Tucson	5-3	3.18	13	13	0	0	76.1	70	28	27	32	80	
									Houston	0-0	0.00	1	0	0	0	0.1	0	0	0	0	0	0.021
56	WALL, DONNE*	R	R	6-1	180	7-11-67	Potosi, MO	Festus, MO	Tucson	17-6	3.30	28	28	0	0	177.1	190	72	65	32	119	
									Houston	3-1	5.55	6	5	0	0	24.1	33	19	15	5	16	0.031

No.	CATCHERS (2)	B	T	Ht.	Wt.	Born	Birthplace	Residence	1995 Club	AVG.	G	AB	R	H	2B	3B	HR	RBI	BB	SO	SB	M.L. Service
20	EUSEBIO, TONY	R	R	6-2	210	4-27-67	S.J. de Los Llamos, D.R.	Kissimmee, FL	Houston	.299	113	368	46	110	21	1	6	58	31	59	0	2.011
3	WILKINS, RICK	L	R	6-2	215	6-4-67	Jacksonville, FL	Jacksonville, FL	Chicago N.L.	.191	50	162	24	31	2	0	6	14	36	51	0	4.023
									Houston	.250	15	40	6	10	1	0	1	5	10	10	0	
									#Jackson	.000	4	11	0	0	0	0	0	0	3	2	0	
									#Tucson	.333	4	12	0	4	0	0	0	4	2	0	0	

No.	INFIELDERS (7)	B	T	Ht.	Wt.	Born	Birthplace	Residence	1995 Club	AVG.	G	AB	R	H	2B	3B	HR	RBI	BB	SO	SB	M.L. Service
5	BAGWELL, JEFF	R	R	6-0	195	5-27-68	Boston, MA	Houston, TX	Houston	.290	114	448	88	130	29	0	21	87	79	102	12	4.119
									#Jackson	.167	4	12	0	2	0	0	0	0	3	2	0	
17	BERRY, SEAN	R	R	5-11	200	3-22-66	Santa Monica, CA	Torrance, CA	Montreal	.318	103	314	38	100	22	1	14	55	25	53	3	3.065
7	BIGGIO, CRAIG	R	R	5-11	180	12-14-65	Smithtown, NY	Spring Lake, NJ	Houston	.302	141	553	123	167	30	2	22	77	80	85	33	7.046
12	GUTIERREZ, RICKY	R	R	6-1	175	5-23-70	Miami, FL	Miami, FL	Houston	.276	52	156	22	43	6	0	0	12	10	33	5	2.040
									Tucson	.301	64	236	46	71	12	4	1	26	28	28	9	
30	HAJEK, DAVE*	R	R	5-10	165	10-14-67	Roseville, CA	Colorado Springs, CO	Tucson	.327	131	502	99	164	37	4	4	78	39	27	12	0.020
									Houston	.000	5	2	0	0	0	0	0	0	1	1	1	
29	HOLBERT, RAY	R	R	6-0	175	9-25-70	Torrance, CA	Glendale, AZ	San Diego	.178	63	73	11	13	2	1	2	5	8	20	4	1.003
									#Las Vegas	.115	9	26	3	3	1	0	0	3	5	10	1	
24	MILLER, ORLANDO	R	R	6-1	180	1-13-69	Changuinola, Pan.	Estafeta el Dorado, Pan	Houston	.262	92	324	36	85	20	1	5	36	22	71	3	1.025

No.	OUTFIELDERS (7)	B	T	Ht.	Wt.	Born	Birthplace	Residence	1995 Club	AVG.	G	AB	R	H	2B	3B	HR	RBI	BB	SO	SB	M.L. Service
63	ABREU, BOB*	L	R	6-0	160	3-11-74	Aragua, Ven.	Aragua, Ven.	Tucson	.304	114	415	72	126	24	17	10	75	67	120	16	0.000
14	BELL, DEREK	R	R	6-2	215	12-11-68	Tampa, FL	Tampa, FL	Houston	.334	112	452	63	151	21	2	8	86	33	71	27	4.000
60	HIDALGO, RICHARD*	R	R	6-3	190	7-2-75	Caracas, Ven.	Caracas, Ven.	Jackson	.266	133	489	59	130	28	6	14	59	32	76	8	0.000
19	HUNTER, BRIAN L.	R	R	6-4	180	3-5-71	Portland, OR	Vancouver, WA	Tucson	.329	38	155	28	51	5	1	1	16	17	13	11	0.118
									Houston	.302	78	321	52	97	14	5	2	28	15	52	24	
									#Jackson	.500	2	6	1	3	0	0	0	0	1	0	0	
16	MAY, DERRICK	L	R	6-4	225	7-14-68	Rochester, NY	Newark, DE	Milwaukee	.248	32	113	15	28	3	1	1	9	5	18	0	4.007
									Houston	.301	78	206	29	62	15	1	8	41	19	24	5	
6	MOUTON, JAMES	R	R	5-9	175	12-29-68	Denver, CO	Missouri City, TX	Houston	.262	104	298	42	78	18	2	4	27	25	59	25	1.119
									#Tucson	.455	3	11	1	5	0	0	1	1	0	2	0	
23	SIMMS, MIKE	R	R	6-4	200	1-12-67	Orange, CA	Villa Park, CA	Houston	.256	50	121	14	31	4	0	9	24	13	28	1	1.063
									Tucson	.295	85	319	56	94	26	8	13	66	35	65	10	

*Rookie
#Rehabilitation Assignment

FULL NAMES AND PHONETICS

Abreu, Bob Kelly (a-BREW)
Bagwell, Jeffery Robert (BAG-well)
Bell, Derek Nathaniel
Berry, Sean Robert
Biggio, Craig Alan (BIDG-jee-oh)
Brocail, Douglas Keith (broh-KALE)
Creek, Ryan Matthew
Dougherty, James E. (DOR-a-tee)
Drabek, Douglas Dean (DRAY-beck)
Eusebio, Raul Antonio (you-SAY-bee-oh)
Gallaher, Kevin John (GAL-a-her)
Grzanich, Michael Edward (gra-ZAN-ich)
Gutierrez, Ricardo (GOO-tier-uhz)

Hampton, Michael William
Hartgraves, Dean Charles
Henriquez, Oscar Eduardo (en-REE-kay)
Hidalgo, Richard Jose
Holbert, Ray Arthur
Holt, Christopher Michael
Hudek, John Raymond (WHO-deck)
Hunter, Brian Lee
Jones, Todd Barton
Kile, Darryl Andrew
Loiselle, Richard Frank (loy-ZELL)
May, Derrick Brant

Miller, Orlando Salmon
Mlicki, Douglas James (ma-LICK-ee)
Morman, Alvin (MORE-mun)
Mouton, James Raleigh (MOO-tawn)
Reynolds, Richard Shane
Simms, Michael Howard
Small, Mark Allen
Swindell, Forest Gregory (swin-DELL)
Tabaka, Jeffery Jon (ta-BAW-ka)
Wagner, William Edward
Wall, Donne Lee
Wilkins, Richard David

MANAGER AND COACHES

Terry Lee Collins
Matthew J. Galante (ga-LAHN-tee)
Stephen Curtis Henderson
Julio Linares
Brent Terry Strom
Ricky Joe Sweet

Los Angeles Dodgers (WEST)

MANAGER TOM LASORDA (2)

Coaches:
JOE AMALFITANO (8)
MARK CRESSE (58)
BILL RUSSELL (18)
REGGIE SMITH (9)
DAVE WALLACE (17)

Team Physicians—FRANK W. JOBE, M.D., MICHAEL F. MELLMAN, M.D.
Trainer—CHARLIE STRASSER
Assistant Trainer—STAN JOHNSTON
Director of Publicity—JAY LUCAS
Traveling Secretary—BILL DeLURY

No.	PITCHERS (21)	B	T	Ht.	Wt.	Born	Birthplace	Residence	1995 Club	W-L	ERA	G	GS	CG	SV	IP	H	R	ER	BB	SO	M.L. Service
56	ASTACIO, PEDRO	R	R	6-2	195	11-28-69	Hato Mayor, D.R.	Miami, FL	Los Angeles	7-8	4.24	48	11	1	0	104.0	103	53	49	29	80	2.171
	BREWER, BILLY	L	L	6-1	175	4-15-68	Fort Worth, TX	Waco, TX	Kansas City	2-4	5.56	48	0	0	0	45.1	54	28	28	20	31	2.119
									Springfield	0-0	0.00	1	0	0	1	2.0	2	1	0	1	2	
									Omaha	0-0	0.00	6	0	0	0	7.0	1	0	0	7	5	
49	CANDIOTTI, TOM	R	R	6-2	215	8-31-57	Walnut Creek, CA	Danville, CA	Los Angeles	7-14	3.50	30	30	1	0	190.1	187	93	74	58	141	10.085
64	CORREA, RAMSER	R	R	6-5	200	11-13-70	Carolina, P.R.	Carolina, P.R.	San Antonio	1-4	4.53	42	0	0	17	49.2	54	29	25	21	34	
									Albuquerque	0-0	0.00	2	0	0	0	4.0	5	0	0	1	3	0.000
41	CUMMINGS, JOHN	L	L	6-3	200	5-10-69	Torrance, CA	Laguna Niguel, CA	Seattle	0-0	11.81	4	0	0	0	5.1	8	8	7	7	4	
									Tacoma	0-1	7.71	1	1	0	0	2.1	6	4	2	3	3	
									San Antonio	0-2	3.95	6	5	0	0	27.1	28	13	12	7	13	
									Los Angeles	3-1	3.00	35	0	0	0	39.0	38	16	13	10	21	1.126
37	DREIFORT, DARREN	R	R	6-2	205	5-18-72	Wichita, KS	Wichita, KS	Los Angeles						DID NOT PLAY							0.082
63	DURAN, ROBERTO*	L	L	6-0	167	3-6-73	Moca, D.R.	Moca, D.R.	Vero Beach	7-4	3.38	23	22	0	0	101.1	82	42	38	70	114	0.000
51	EISCHEN, JOEY	L	L	6-1	190	5-25-70	West Covina, CA	West Covina, CA	Ottawa	2-1	1.72	11	0	0	0	15.2	9	4	3	8	13	
									Los Angeles	0-0	3.10	17	0	0	0	20.1	19	9	7	11	15	0.106
									Albuquerque	3-0	0.00	13	0	0	2	16.1	8	0	0	3	14	
35	GORECKI, RICK*	R	R	6-3	167	8-27-73	Evergreen Park, IL	Oak Forest, IL	#Vero Beach	1-2	0.67	6	5	0	0	27.0	19	6	2	9	24	0.160
52	GUTHRIE, MARK	R	L	6-4	207	9-22-65	Buffalo, NY	Bradenton, FL	Minnesota	5-3	4.46	36	0	0	0	42.1	47	22	21	16	48	
									Los Angeles	0-2	3.66	24	0	0	0	19.2	19	11	8	9	19	5.151
52	HALL, DARREN	R	R	6-3	205	7-14-64	Marysville, OH	Irving, TX	Toronto	0-2	4.41	17	0	0	3	16.1	21	9	8	9	11	1.100
47	MARTINEZ, JESUS*	L	L	6-2	145	3-13-74	Santo Domingo, D.R.	Santo Domingo, D.R.	San Antonio	6-9	3.54	24	24	1	0	139.2	129	64	55	71	83	
									Albuquerque	1-1	4.50	2	0	0	0	4.0	4	2	2	4	5	0.000
48	MARTINEZ, RAMON J.	B	R	6-4	186	3-22-68	Santo Domingo, D.R.	Santo Domingo, D.R.	Los Angeles	17-7	3.66	30	30	4	0	206.1	176	95	84	81	138	6.080
16	NOMO, HIDEO	R	R	6-2	210	8-31-68	Osaka, Japan	Kobe, Japan	Bakersfield	0-1	3.38	1	1	0	0	5.1	6	2	2	1	6	
									Los Angeles	13-6	2.54	28	28	4	0	191.1	124	63	54	78	236	0.154
13	OSUNA, ANTONIO	R	R	5-11	160	4-12-73	Sinaloa, Mexico	El Tigre, Ven.	Los Angeles	2-4	4.43	39	0	0	0	44.2	39	22	22	20	46	0.121
									#San Bernardino	0-0	1.29	5	0	0	0	7.0	3	1	1	5	11	
									#Albuquerque	0-1	4.42	19	0	0	11	18.1	15	9	9	9	19	
61	PARK, CHAN HO*	R	R	6-2	195	6-30-73	Kong Ju City, Korea	Los Angeles, CA	Albuquerque	6-7	4.91	23	22	0	0	110.0	93	64	60	76	101	
									Los Angeles	0-0	4.50	2	1	0	0	4.0	2	2	2	2	7	0.045
50	RODRIGUEZ, FELIX*	R	R	6-1	180	12-5-72	Monte Cristi, D.R.	Monte Cristi, D.R.	Albuquerque	3-2	4.24	14	11	0	0	51.0	52	29	24	26	46	
									Los Angeles	1-1	2.53	11	0	0	0	10.2	11	3	3	5	5	0.029
59	VALDES, ISMAEL	R	R	6-3	207	8-21-73	Victoria, Mex.	Victoria, Mex.	Los Angeles	13-11	3.05	33	27	6	1	197.2	168	76	67	51	150	1.052
68	WATTS, BRANDON*	L	L	6-3	195	9-13-72	Ruston, LA	Ruston, LA	Vero Beach	5-3	4.04	13	8	0	0	49.0	46	29	22	22	42	0.000
65	WEAVER, ERIC*	R	R	6-5	230	8-4-73	Springfield, IL	Illiopolis, IL	San Antonio	8-11	4.07	27	26	1	0	141.2	147	83	64	72	105	0.000
38	WORRELL, TODD	R	R	6-5	222	9-28-59	Arcadia, CA	St. Louis, MO	Los Angeles	4-1	2.02	59	0	0	32	62.1	50	15	14	19	61	9.160

No.	CATCHERS (3)	B	T	Ht.	Wt.	Born	Birthplace	Residence	1995 Club	AVG.	G	AB	R	H	2B	3B	HR	RBI	BB	SO	SB	M.L. Service
26	HERNANDEZ, CARLOS	R	R	5-11	215	5-24-67	San Felix, Bol., Ven.	Santa Monica, CA	Los Angeles	.149	45	94	3	14	1	0	2	8	7	25	0	4.046
10	HUCKABY, KENNETH*	R	R	6-1	205	1-27-71	San Leandro, CA	Philadelphia, PA	Albuquerque	.324	89	278	30	90	16	2	1	40	12	26	3	0.000
31	PIAZZA, MIKE	R	R	6-3	215	9-4-68	Norristown, PA	Valley Forge, PA	Los Angeles	.346	112	434	82	150	17	0	32	93	39	80	1	2.153

No.	INFIELDERS (10)	B	T	Ht.	Wt.	Born	Birthplace	Residence	1995 Club	AVG.	G	AB	R	H	2B	3B	HR	RBI	BB	SO	SB	M.L. Service
20	BLOWERS, MIKE	R	R	6-2	210	4-24-65	Wurzburg, W. Germany	Tacoma, WA	Seattle	.257	134	439	59	113	24	1	23	96	53	128	2	4.038
25	BUSCH, MIKE*	R	R	6-5	220	7-7-68	Davenport, IA	Donahue, IA	Albuquerque	.269	121	443	68	119	32	1	18	62	42	103	2	
									Los Angeles	.235	13	17	3	4	0	0	3	6	0	7	0	0.034
60	CASTRO, JUAN*	R	R	5-10	163	6-20-72	Los Mochis, Mex.	Los Mochis, Mex.	Albuquerque	.267	104	341	51	91	18	4	3	43	20	42	4	
									Los Angeles	.250	11	4	0	1	0	0	0	0	1	1	0	0.031
14	DeSHIELDS, DELINO	L	R	6-1	175	1-15-69	Seaford, DE	West Palm Beach, FL	Los Angeles	.256	127	425	66	109	18	3	8	37	63	83	39	5.119
3	FONVILLE, CHAD	S	R	5-6	155	3-5-71	Jacksonville, NC	Midway Park, NC	Montreal	.333	14	12	2	4	0	0	0	0	0	3	0	
									Los Angeles	.276	88	308	41	85	6	1	0	16	23	39	20	0.160
21	GAGNE, GREG	R	R	5-11	180	11-12-61	Fall River, MA	Somerset, MA	Kansas City	.256	120	430	58	110	25	4	6	49	38	60	3	11.009
62	GUERRERO, WILTON*	R	R	5-11	145	10-24-74	Don Gregorio, D.R.	Nizau, D.R.	San Antonio	.348	95	382	53	133	13	6	0	26	26	63	21	
									Albuquerque	.327	14	49	10	16	1	1	0	2	1	7	2	0.000
5	HANSEN, DAVE	L	R	6-0	195	11-24-68	Long Beach, CA	Long Beach, CA	Los Angeles	.287	100	181	19	52	10	0	1	14	28	28	0	4.072
33	INGRAM, GAREY	R	R	5-11	185	7-25-70	Columbus, GA	Columbus, GA	Los Angeles	.200	44	55	5	11	2	0	0	3	9	8	3	0.124
									Albuquerque	.246	63	232	28	57	11	4	1	30	21	40	10	
23	KARROS, ERIC	R	R	6-4	222	11-4-67	Hackensack, NJ	Manhattan Beach, CA	Los Angeles	.298	143	551	83	164	29	3	32	105	61	115	4	3.155

No.	OUTFIELDERS (6)	B	T	Ht.	Wt.	Born	Birthplace	Residence	1995 Club	AVG.	G	AB	R	H	2B	3B	HR	RBI	BB	SO	SB	M.L. Service
7	ASHLEY, BILLY	R	R	6-7	235	7-11-70	Taylor, MI	Glendale, AZ	Los Angeles	.237	81	215	17	51	5	0	8	27	25	88	0	1.060
22	BUTLER, BRETT	L	L	5-10	161	6-15-57	Los Angeles, CA	Atlanta, GA	New York N.L.	.311	90	367	54	114	13	7	1	25	43	42	21	
									Los Angeles	.274	39	146	24	40	5	2	0	13	24	9	11	13.128
27	CEDENO, ROGER*	S	R	6-1	165	8-16-74	Valencia, Ven.	Valencia, Ven.	Albuquerque	.305	99	367	67	112	19	9	2	44	53	56	23	
									Los Angeles	.238	40	42	4	10	2	0	0	3	3	10	1	0.058
12	GARCIA, KARIM*	L	L	6-0	172	10-29-75	Ciudad Obregon, Mexico	Ciudad Obregon, Mexico	Albuquerque	.319	124	474	88	151	26	10	20	91	38	102	12	
									Los Angeles	.200	13	20	1	4	0	0	0	0	0	4	0	0.032
28	HOLLANDSWORTH, TODD*	L	L	6-2	193	4-20-73	Dayton, OH	San Ramon, CA	Los Angeles	.233	41	103	16	24	2	0	5	13	10	29	2	0.160
									#San Bernardino	.500	1	2	0	1	0	0	0	0	0	1	0	
									#Albuquerque	.237	10	38	9	9	2	0	2	4	6	8	1	
43	MONDESI, RAUL	R	R	5-11	212	3-12-71	San Cristobal, D.R.	New York, NY	Los Angeles	.285	139	536	91	153	23	6	26	88	33	96	27	2.002

*Rookie
#Rehabilitation Assignment

FULL NAMES AND PHONETICS

Ashley, Billy Manuel
Astacio, Pedro Julio (ah-STA-see-oh)
Blowers, Michael Roy
Brewer, William Robert
Busch, Michael Anthony
Butler, Brett Morgan
Candiotti, Thomas Cesar (kan-dee-AH-tee)
Castro, Juan (KASS-tro)
Cedeno, Roger (said-DANE-yo)
Correa, Ramser Andino (KO-ray-ah, RAM-zer)
Cummings, John Russell
DeShields, Delino Lamont (duh-LYNE-oh)
Dreifort, Darren (DRY-fort)

Duran, Roberto (DER-an)
Eischen, Joseph Raymond (EYE-shen)
Fonville, Chad Everette
Gagne, Gregory Carpenter (GAG-nee)
Garcia, Gustavo "Karim" (KA-reem)
Gorecki, Rick (GORE-eck-ee)
Guerrero, Wilton
Guthrie, Mark Andrew
Hall, Michael Dean
Hansen, David Andrew
Hernandez, Carlos Alberto
Hollandsworth, Todd (HAHL-enz-worth)
Huckaby, Kenneth Paul (HUCK-a-bee)

Ingram, Garey Lamar
Karros, Eric Peter (CARE-ose)
Martinez, Jesus (mar-TEE-nez)
Martinez, Ramon Jaime (mar-TEE-nez)
Mondesi, Raul (MON-de-see)
Nomo, Hideo (NO-mo, hee-DAY-oh)
Osuna, Antonio (OH-soo-na)
Park, Chan Ho (CHAN HO)
Piazza, Michael Joseph (PEE-ah-za)
Rodriguez, Felix Antonio
Valdez, Ismael (val-DEZ, ISH-male)
Watts, Brandon

Weaver, James Eric
Worrell, Todd Roland (wor-RELL)

MANAGER AND COACHES

Thomas Charles Lasorda
John Joseph Amalfitano (uh-mahl-fuh-TAWN-oh)
Mark Emory Cresse (CRESS-ee)
William Ellis Russell
Reginald Carl Smith
Dave Wallace

Montreal Expos (EAST)

MANAGER FELIPE ALOU (17)

Coaches:
PIERRE ARSENAULT (67) - bullpen
TOMMY HARPER (21)
JOE KERRIGAN (32)
JERRY MANUEL (6)
LUIS PUJOLS (56)
JIM TRACY (23)

Team Orthopedist — DR. LARRY COUGHLIN
Trainers — RON McCLAIN, MIKE KOZAK

Director, Media Services — MONIQUE GIROUX
Director, Media Relations — PETER LOYELLO

No.	PITCHERS (21)	B	T	Ht.	Wt.	Born	Birthplace	Residence	1995 Club	W-L	ERA	G	GS	CG	SV	IP	H	R	ER	BB	SO	M.L. Service
48	ALVAREZ, TAVO*	R	R	6-3	235	11-25-71	Obregon, Mex.	Obregon, Mex.	Harrisburg	2-1	2.25	3	3	0	0	16.0	17	8	4	5	14	
									Ottawa	2-1	2.49	3	3	0	0	21.2	17	6	6	5	11	
									Montreal	1-5	6.75	8	8	0	0	37.1	46	30	28	14	17	0.045
34	CORMIER, RHEAL	L	L	5-10	187	4-23-67	Moncton, N.B.	Shediac, N.B.	Boston	7-5	4.07	48	12	0	0	115.0	131	60	52	31	69	4.001
	DAAL, OMAR	L	L	6-3	185	3-1-72	Maracaibo, Ven.	Valencia, Ven.	Albuquerque	2-3	4.05	17	9	0	1	53.1	56	28	24	26	46	
									Los Angeles	4-0	7.20	28	0	0	0	20.0	29	16	16	15	11	2.003
53	FALTEISEK, STEVE*	R	R	6-2	200	1-28-72	Mineola, NY	Floral Park, NY	Harrisburg	9-6	2.95	25	25	5	0	168.0	152	74	55	64	112	
									Ottawa	2-0	1.17	3	3	1	0	23.0	17	4	3	5	18	0.000
13	FASSERO, JEFF	L	L	6-1	195	1-5-63	Springfield, IL	Brownsburg, IN	Montreal	13-14	4.33	30	30	1	0	189.0	207	102	91	74	164	4.082
61	GENTILE, SCOTT*	R	R	5-10	205	12-21-70	New Britain, CT	Kensington, CT	Harrisburg	2-2	3.44	37	0	0	11	49.2	36	19	19	15	48	0.000
20	HENDERSON, ROD*	R	R	6-4	193	3-11-71	Greensburg, KY	Lexington, KY	Harrisburg	3-6	4.31	12	12	0	0	56.1	51	28	27	18	53	0.091
45	MARTINEZ, PEDRO J.	R	R	5-11	170	7-25-71	Manoguayabo, D.R.	Santo Domingo, D.R.	Montreal	14-10	3.51	30	30	2	0	194.2	158	79	76	66	174	2.145
59	PACHECO, ALEX*	R	R	6-3	200	7-19-73	Caracas, Ven.	Caracas, Ven.	Harrisburg	9-7	4.27	45	0	0	4	86.1	76	45	41	31	88	
									Ottawa	1-0	6.23	4	0	0	0	8.2	8	6	6	5	4	0.000
62	PANIAGUA, JOSE*	R	R	6-2	185	8-20-73	S.J. De Ocoa, D.R.	Santo Domingo, D.R.	Harrisburg	7-12	5.34	25	25	2	0	126.1	140	84	75	62	89	0.000
33	PEREZ, CARLOS	L	L	6-3	195	1-14-71	Nigua, D.R.	Nigua, D.R.	Montreal	10-8	3.69	28	23	2	0	141.1	142	61	58	28	106	0.160
51	ROJAS, MEL	R	R	5-11	195	12-10-66	Haina, D.R.	Santo Domingo, D.R.	Montreal	1-4	4.12	59	0	0	30	67.2	69	32	31	29	61	4.127
42	RUETER, KIRK	L	L	6-3	195	12-1-70	Centralia, IL	Hoyleton, IL	Montreal	5-3	3.23	9	9	1	0	47.1	38	17	17	9	28	1.097
									Ottawa	9-7	3.06	20	20	3	0	120.2	120	50	41	25	67	
54	SCOTT, TIM	R	R	6-2	205	11-16-66	Hanford, CA	Hanford, CA	Montreal	2-0	3.98	62	0	0	2	63.1	52	30	28	23	57	3.080
64	STULL, EVERETT*	R	R	6-3	200	8-24-71	Fort Riley, KS	Stone Mountain, GA	Harrisburg	3-12	5.54	24	24	0	0	126.2	114	88	78	79	132	0.000
41	URBINA, UGUETH*	R	R	6-2	185	2-15-74	Caracas, Ven.	Caracas, Ven.	W. Palm Beach	1-0	0.00	2	2	0	0	9.0	4	0	0	1	11	
									Ottawa	6-2	3.04	13	11	2	0	68.0	46	26	23	26	55	
									Montreal	2-2	6.17	7	4	0	0	23.1	26	17	16	14	15	0.027
	VERES, DAVE	R	R	6-2	195	10-19-66	Montgomery, AL	Gresham, OR	Houston	5-1	2.26	72	0	0	1	103.1	89	29	26	30	94	1.082
57	WEBER, NEIL*	L	L	6-5	215	12-6-72	Newport Beach, CA	Newport Beach, CA	Harrisburg	6-11	5.01	28	28	0	0	152.2	157	98	85	90	119	0.000
	WITTE, TREY*	R	R	6-1	190	1-15-70	Houston, TX	Houston, TX	Port City	3-2	1.73	48	0	0	11	62.1	48	17	12	14	39	0.000
58	YAN, ESTEBAN*	R	R	6-4	230	6-22-74	C. Deleseybo, D.R.	S.P. de Macoris, D.R.	W. Palm Beach	6-8	3.07	24	21	1	1	137.2	139	63	47	33	89	0.000

No.	CATCHERS (3)	B	T	Ht.	Wt.	Born	Birthplace	Residence	1995 Club	AVG.	G	AB	R	H	2B	3B	HR	RBI	BB	SO	SB	M.L. Service
24	FLETCHER, DARRIN	L	R	6-1	200	10-3-66	Elmhurst, IL	Oakwood, IL	Montreal	.286	110	350	42	100	21	1	11	45	32	23	0	4.087
19	LAKER, TIM	R	R	6-3	200	11-27-69	Encino, CA	Simi Valley, CA	Montreal	.234	64	141	17	33	8	1	3	20	14	38	0	1.105
2	SPEHR, TIM	R	R	6-2	200	7-2-66	Excelsior Springs, MO	Waco, TX	Montreal	.257	41	35	4	9	5	0	1	3	6	7	0	2.152

No.	INFIELDERS (10)	B	T	Ht.	Wt.	Born	Birthplace	Residence	1995 Club	AVG.	G	AB	R	H	2B	3B	HR	RBI	BB	SO	SB	M.L. Service
56	ALCANTARA, ISRAEL*	R	R	6-2	180	5-6-73	Santo Domingo, D.R.	Santo Domingo, D.R.	Harrisburg	.211	71	237	25	50	12	2	10	29	21	81	1	
									W. Palm Beach	.276	39	134	16	37	7	2	3	22	9	35	3	0.000
11	ANDREWS, SHANE	R	R	6-1	215	8-28-71	Dallas, TX	Carlsbad, NM	Montreal	.214	84	220	27	47	10	1	8	31	17	68	1	0.160
30	FLOYD, CLIFF	L	R	6-4	235	12-5-72	Chicago, IL	Markham, IL	Montreal	.130	29	69	6	9	1	0	1	8	7	22	3	1.135
4	GRUDZIELANEK, MARK	R	R	6-1	185	6-30-70	Milwaukee, WI	Milwaukee, WI	Montreal	.245	78	269	27	66	12	2	1	20	14	47	8	0.106
									Ottawa	.298	49	181	26	54	9	1	1	22	10	17	12	
3	LANSING, MIKE	R	R	6-0	185	4-3-68	Rawlins, WY	Casper, WY	Montreal	.255	127	467	47	119	30	2	10	62	28	65	27	2.119
	McGUIRE, RYAN*	L	L	6-1	195	11-23-71	Wilson, NC	Woodland Hills, CA	Trenton	.333	109	414	59	138	29	1	7	59	58	51	11	0.000
25	SEGUI, DAVID	S	L	6-1	202	7-19-66	Kansas City, KS	Kansas City, KS	New York N.L.	.329	33	73	9	24	3	1	2	11	12	9	1	
									Montreal	.305	97	383	59	117	22	3	10	57	28	38	1	4.158
9	SILVESTRI, DAVE	R	R	6-0	196	9-29-67	St. Louis, MO	St. Louis, MO	New York A.L.	.095	17	21	4	2	0	0	1	4	4	9	0	
									Montreal	.264	39	72	12	19	6	0	2	7	9	27	2	1.061

No.	OUTFIELDERS (7)	B	T	Ht.	Wt.	Born	Birthplace	Residence	1995 Club	AVG.	G	AB	R	H	2B	3B	HR	RBI	BB	SO	SB	M.L. Service
18	ALOU, MOISES	R	R	6-3	195	7-3-66	Atlanta, GA	Santo Domingo, D.R.	Montreal	.273	93	344	48	94	22	0	14	58	29	56	4	4.156
15	BENITEZ, YAMIL*	R	R	6-2	195	5-10-72	San Juan, P.R.	Rio Piedras, P.R.	Ottawa	.259	127	474	66	123	24	6	18	69	44	128	14	
									Montreal	.385	14	39	8	15	2	1	2	7	1	7	0	0.017
20	McDAVID, RAY*	L	R	6-2	200	7-20-71	San Diego, CA	San Diego, CA	Las Vegas	.271	52	166	28	45	8	1	5	27	30	35	7	
									Arizona Padres	.464	9	28	13	13	2	1	1	6	8	7	3	
									San Diego	.176	11	17	2	3	0	0	0	0	2	6	1	0.043
40	RODRIGUEZ, HENRY	L	L	6-1	205	11-8-67	Santo Domingo, D.R.	New York, NY	Los Angeles	.263	21	80	6	21	4	1	1	10	5	17	0	
									Montreal	.207	24	58	7	12	0	0	1	5	6	11	0	2.150
									#Ottawa	.200	4	15	0	3	1	0	0	2	1	4	0	
50	STOVALL, DAROND*	S	L	6-1	185	1-3-73	St. Louis, MO	East St. Louis, IL	W. Palm Beach	.232	121	461	52	107	22	2	4	51	44	117	18	0.000
44	TARASCO, TONY	L	R	6-1	205	12-9-70	New York, NY	Santa Monica, CA	Montreal	.249	126	438	64	109	18	4	14	40	51	78	24	2.011
22	WHITE, RONDELL	R	R	6-1	205	2-23-72	Milledgeville, GA	Gray, GA	Montreal	.295	130	474	87	140	33	4	13	57	41	87	25	1.098

*Rookie
#Rehabilitation Assignment

FULL NAMES AND PHONETICS

Alcantara, Israel Crisostomo (AL-can-tarr-uh)
Alou, Moises Rojas (ah-LOO) (MOY-sezz)
Alvarez, Cesar Octavio
Andrews, Darrell Shane
Aucoin, Derek Alfred (OH-coin)
Benitez, Yamil Antonio
Berry, Sean Robert
Daal, Omar Jose
Eversgerd, Bryan David (evers-GURD)
Falteisek, Steven James (FALT-e-seck)
Fassero, Jeffrey Joseph (fuh-SAIR-oh)
Fletcher, Darrin Glen
Floyd, Cornelius Clifford

Gentile, Scott Patrick (JEN-teel)
Grudzielanek, Mark James
 (gruzz-ELL-uh-neck)
Henderson, Rodney Wood
Laker, Timothy John
Lansing, Michael Thomas
Martinez, Pedro Jaime (mar-TEE-nezz)
McDavid, Ray Darnell
Pacheco, Alexander Melchor (pa-CHE-coh)
Paniagua, Jose Luis (pan-ee-AH-gwah)
Perez, Carlos Gross
Pride, Curtis John

Rodriguez, Henry Anderson
Rojas, Melquiades (ROH-hoss)
Rueter, Kirk Wesley (REE-ter)
Scott, Timothy Dale
Segui, David Vincent (soh-GHEE)
Silvestri, David Joseph (SIL-VES-tree)
Spehr, Timothy Joseph (SPEER)
Stovall, Darond (dah-ROND)
Stull, Everett James
Tarasco, Anthony Giacinto
Urbina, Ugueth Urtain (ooo-GETT)
Veres, David Scott (VEER-z)
Weber, Neil Aaron

White, Rondell Bernard
Witte, Laurence Joseph III (WITT-ay)
Yan, Esteban Luis

MANAGER AND COACHES

Felipe Rojas Alou (feh-LEE-pay) (ah-LOO)
Pierre Jean Arsenault
Thomas Harper
Joseph Thomas Kerrigan
Jerry Manuel
Luis Pujols (POO-holes)
James Edwin Tracy

New York Mets (EAST)

MANAGER DALLAS GREEN (46)

Coaches:
MIKE CUBBAGE (4)
FRANK HOWARD (55)
TOM McCRAW (10)
GREG PAVLICK (52)
STEVE SWISHER (8) - bullpen
BOBBY WINE (7)

Team Physicians—DR. DAVID ALTCHEK, DR. DAVID DINES
Trainer—FRED HINA
Assistant Trainer—SAM McCRARY
Director, Media Relations—JAY HORWITZ
Directors of Travel—CHARLIE SAMUELS, JAY HORWITZ

No.	PITCHERS (21)	B	T	Ht.	Wt.	Born	Birthplace	Residence	1995 Club	W-L	ERA	G	GS	CG	SV	IP	H	R	ER	BB	SO	M.L. Service
39	ACEVEDO, JUAN	R	R	6-2	195	5-5-70	Juarez, Mex.	Carpentersville, IL	Colorado	4-6	6.44	17	11	0	0	65.2	82	53	47	20	40	0.083
									Colorado Spr.	1-1	6.14	3	3	0	0	14.2	18	11	10	7	7	
									Norfolk	0-0	0.00	2	2	0	0	3.0	0	0	0	1	2	
43	BYRD, PAUL*	R	R	6-1	185	12-3-70	Louisville, KY	Baton Rouge, LA	Norfolk	3-5	2.79	22	10	1	6	87.0	71	29	27	21	61	
									New York N.L.	2-0	2.05	17	0	0	0	22.0	18	6	5	7	26	0.066
36	CARTER, JOHN*	R	R	6-1	195	2-16-72	Chicago, IL	Chicago, IL	Canton/Akron	1-2	3.95	5	5	0	0	27.1	27	13	12	13	14	0.000
47	CORNELIUS, REID	R	R	6-0	200	6-2-70	Thomasville, AL	W. Palm Beach, FL	Montreal	0-0	8.00	8	0	0	0	9.0	11	8	8	5	4	
									Ottawa	1-1	6.75	4	3	0	0	10.2	16	12	8	5	7	
									Norfolk	7-0	0.90	10	10	1	0	70.1	57	10	7	19	43	
									New York N.L.	3-7	5.15	10	10	0	0	57.2	64	36	33	25	35	0.089
45	DiPOTO, JERRY	R	R	6-2	200	5-24-68	Jersey City, NJ	Kansas City, MO	New York N.L.	4-6	3.78	58	0	0	2	78.2	77	41	33	29	49	2.025
62	EDMONDSON, BRIAN*	R	R	6-2	185	1-29-73	Fontana, CA	Plant City, FL	Binghamton	7-11	4.76	23	22	2	0	134.1	150	82	71	59	69	0.000
31	FRANCO, JOHN	L	L	5-10	185	9-17-60	Brooklyn, NY	Staten Island, NY	New York N.L.	5-3	2.44	48	0	0	29	51.2	48	17	14	17	41	11.107
27	HARNISCH, PETE	R	R	6-0	207	9-23-66	Commack, NY	Lake Mary, FL	New York N.L.	2-8	3.68	18	18	0	0	110.0	111	55	45	24	82	6.082
35	HENRY, DOUG	R	R	6-4	205	12-10-63	Sacramento, CA	Hartland, WI	New York N.L.	3-6	2.96	51	0	0	4	67.0	48	23	22	25	62	4.012
44	ISRINGHAUSEN, JASON	R	R	6-3	195	9-7-72	Brighton, IL	Brighton, IL	Binghamton	2-1	2.85	6	6	1	0	41.0	26	15	13	12	59	
									Norfolk	9-1	1.55	12	12	3	0	87.0	64	17	15	24	75	
									New York N.L.	9-2	2.81	14	14	1	0	93.0	88	29	29	31	55	0.081
28	JONES, BOBBY	R	R	6-4	225	2-10-70	Fresno, CA	Fresno, CA	New York N.L.	10-10	4.19	30	30	3	0	195.2	209	107	91	53	127	2.001
41	MARTINEZ, PEDRO A.	R	L	6-2	185	11-29-68	Santo Domingo, D.R.	Santo Domingo, D.R.	Houston	0-0	7.40	25	0	0	0	20.2	29	18	17	16	17	1.149
									Tucson	1-1	6.62	20	3	0	2	34.0	44	28	25	13	21	
34	MINOR, BLAS	R	R	6-3	203	3-20-66	Merced, CA	Gilbert, AZ	New York N.L.	4-2	3.66	35	0	0	1	46.2	44	21	19	13	43	2.065
38	MLICKI, DAVE	R	R	6-4	190	6-8-68	Cleveland, OH	Phoenix, AZ	New York N.L.	9-7	4.26	29	25	0	0	160.2	160	82	76	54	123	1.151
40	NABHOLZ, CHRIS	L	L	6-5	217	1-5-67	Harrisburg, PA	Pottsville, PA	#Iowa	0-2	6.41	6	5	0	0	19.2	27	17	14	12	16	
									Chicago N.L.	0-1	5.40	34	0	0	0	23.1	22	15	14	14	21	4.113
29	PERSON, ROBERT*	R	R	5-11	180	10-6-69	St. Louis, MO	St. Louis, MO	Binghamton	5-4	3.11	26	7	1	7	66.2	46	27	23	25	65	
									Norfolk	2-1	4.50	5	4	0	0	32.0	30	17	16	13	33	
									New York N.L.	1-0	0.75	3	1	0	0	12.0	5	1	1	2	10	0.018
21	PULSIPHER, BILL	L	L	6-3	200	10-9-73	Fort Benning, GA	Clifton, VA	Norfolk	6-4	3.14	13	13	4	0	91.2	84	36	32	33	63	
									New York N.L.	5-7	3.98	17	17	2	0	126.2	122	58	56	45	81	0.110
65	RAMIREZ, HECTOR*	R	R	6-3	218	12-15-71	El Seybo, D.R.	El Seybo, D.R.	Binghamton	4-12	4.60	20	20	2	0	123.1	127	69	63	48	63	0.000
64	ROGERS, BRYAN*	R	R	5-11	178	10-30-67	Hollister, CA	Gilroy, CA	Norfolk	8-3	2.21	56	0	0	10	77.1	58	22	19	22	50	0.000
49	WALKER, PETE*	R	R	6-2	195	4-8-69	Beverly, MA	East Lyme, CT	Norfolk	5-2	3.91	34	1	0	8	48.1	51	24	21	16	39	
									New York N.L.	1-0	4.58	13	0	0	0	17.2	24	9	9	5	5	0.053
63	WALLACE, DEREK*	R	R	6-3	185	9-1-71	Van Nuys, CA	Chatsworth, CA	Wichita	4-3	4.40	26	0	0	6	43.0	51	23	21	13	24	
									Binghamton	0-1	5.28	15	0	0	2	15.1	11	9	9	9	8	0.000

No.	CATCHERS (4)	B	T	Ht.	Wt.	Born	Birthplace	Residence	1995 Club	AVG.	G	AB	R	H	2B	3B	HR	RBI	BB	SO	SB	M.L. Service
30	CASTILLO, ALBERTO	R	R	6-0	184	2-10-70	San Juan de la Maguana, D.R.	Las Matas de Far Fan, D.R.	Norfolk New York N.L.	.267 .103	69 13	217 29	23 2	58 3	13 0	1 0	4 0	31 0	26 3	32 9	2 1	0.078
66	GREENE, CHARLIE*	R	R	6-1	177	1-23-71	Miami, FL	Miami, FL	Binghamton Norfolk	.237 .193	100 27	346 88	26 6	82 17	13 3	0 0	2 0	34 4	15 3	47 28	2 0	0.000
9	HUNDLEY, TODD	S	R	5-11	185	5-27-69	Martinsville, VA	Palatine, IL	New York N.L.	.280	90	275	39	77	11	0	15	51	42	64	1	4.045
17	MAYNE, BRENT	L	R	6-1	190	4-19-68	Loma Linda, CA	Corona Del Mar, CA	Kansas City	.251	110	307	23	77	18	1	1	27	25	41	0	4.137

No.	INFIELDERS (6)	B	T	Ht.	Wt.	Born	Birthplace	Residence	1995 Club	AVG.	G	AB	R	H	2B	3B	HR	RBI	BB	SO	SB	M.L. Service
13	ALFONZO, EDGARDO	R	R	5-11	187	8-11-73	St. Teresa, Ven.	St. Teresa, Ven.	New York N.L.	.278	101	335	26	93	13	5	4	41	12	37	1	0.160
23	BOGAR, TIM	R	R	6-2	198	10-28-66	Indianapolis, IL	Arlington Heights, IL	New York N.L.	.290	78	145	17	42	7	0	1	21	9	25	1	2.119
26	BROGNA, RICO	L	L	6-2	200	4-18-70	Turner Falls, MA	Watertown, CT	New York N.L.	.289	134	495	72	143	27	2	22	76	39	111	0	1.058
42	HUSKEY, BUTCH*	R	R	6-3	244	11-10-71	Anadarko, OK	Lawton, OK	Norfolk New York N.L.	.284 .189	109 28	394 90	66 8	112 17	18 1	1 0	28 3	87 11	39 10	88 16	8 1	0.071
12	KENT, JEFF	R	R	6-1	185	3-7-68	Bellflower, CA	Springwood, TX	New York N.L.	.278	125	472	65	131	22	3	20	65	29	89	3	3.119
15	VIZCAINO, JOSE	S	R	6-1	180	3-26-68	San Cristobal, D.R.	El Cajon, CA	New York N.L.	.287	135	509	66	146	21	5	3	56	35	76	8	5.062

No.	OUTFIELDERS (7)	B	T	Ht.	Wt.	Born	Birthplace	Residence	1995 Club	AVG.	G	AB	R	H	2B	3B	HR	RBI	BB	SO	SB	M.L. Service
3	EVERETT, CARL	S	R	6-0	190	6-3-71	Tampa, FL	Tampa, FL	New York N.L. Norfolk	.260 .300	79 67	289 260	48 52	75 78	13 16	1 4	12 6	54 35	39 20	67 47	2 12	0.148
33	GILKEY, BERNARD	R	R	6-0	190	9-24-66	St. Louis, MO	St. Louis, MO	St. Louis Louisville	.298 .333	121 2	480 6	73 3	143 2	33 1	4 0	17 1	69 1	42 1	70 0	12 0	4.149
1	JOHNSON, LANCE	L	L	5-11	160	7-6-63	Lincoln Heights, OH	Mobile, AL	Chicago A.L.	.306	142	607	98	186	18	12	10	57	32	31	40	6.121
8	JONES, CHRIS	R	R	6-2	205	12-16-65	Utica, NY	Cedar Rapids, IA	Norfolk New York N.L.	.333 .280	33 79	114 182	20 33	38 51	12 6	1 2	3 8	19 31	1 13	20 45	5 2	2.170
75	LOWERY, TERRELL	R	R	6-3	180	10-25-70	Oakland, CA	Vallejo, CA	Gulf C. Rangers Charlotte	.265 .257	10 11	34 35	10 4	9 9	3 2	1 2	3 0	7 4	6 6	7 6	1 1	
22	OCHOA, ALEX*	R	R	6-0	185	3-29-72	Miami Lakes, FL	Miami Lakes, FL	Rochester Norfolk New York N.L.	.274 .309 .297	91 34 11	336 123 37	41 17 7	92 38 11	18 6 1	2 2 0	8 2 0	46 15 0	26 14 2	50 12 10	17 7 1	0.018
20	THOMPSON, RYAN	R	R	6-3	215	11-4-67	Chestertown, MD	Edesville, MD	#Norfolk New York N.L. #Binghamton	.340 .251 .500	15 75 2	53 267 8	7 39 2	18 67 4	3 13 0	0 0 0	2 7 1	11 31 4	4 19 1	15 77 2	4 3 0	2.079

*Rookie
#Rehabilitation Assignment

FULL NAMES AND PHONETICS

Acevedo, Juan Carlos (Ahs-a-VA-do)
Alfonzo, Edgardo Antonio
Bogar, Timothy Paul
Brogna, Rico Joseph (BRONE-yah)
Byrd, Paul Gregory
Carter, John Christopher
Castillo, Alberto Terrero
Cornelius, Reid Jonathan
DiPoto, Gerard Peter (da-POE-toe)
Edmondson, Brian Christopher
Everett, Carl Edward
Franco, John Anthony

Gilkey, Otis Bernard
Harnisch, Peter Thomas (HARN-ish)
Henry, Richard Douglas
Hundley, Todd Randolph
Huskey, Robert Leon
Isringhausen, Jason Derek (IS-ring-how-zin)
Johnson, Kenneth Lance
Jones, Christopher Carlos
Jones, Robert Joseph
Kent, Jeffrey Franklin
Lowery, Quenton Terrell (LAOW-er-ee)
Martinez, Pedro (Aquino)

Mayne, Brent Danem (MAIN)
Minor Jr., Blas (Bloss)
Mlicki, David John (Mah-LICK-ee)
Nabholz, Christopher William
Ochoa, Alex (OH-Cho-a)
Person, Robert Alan
Pulsipher, William Thomas (PUL-sif-her)
Ramirez, Hector Benevenido
Rivera, Luis Antonio
Rogers, Bryan Alan
Thompson, Ryan Orlando
Vizcaino, Jose Luis (Pimental) (VIZ-kai-een-nyo)

Walker, Peter Brian
Wallace, Derek Robert

MANAGER AND COACHES

George Dallas Green
Michael Lee Cubbage
Frank Oliver Howard
Thomas McCraw
Gregory Pavlick
Steven Eugene Swisher
Robert Paul Wine Sr.

Philadelphia Phillies (EAST)

MANAGER JIM FREGOSI (11)

Coaches:
LARRY BOWA (2)
DAVE CASH (30)
DENIS MENKE (14)
JOHNNY PODRES (46)
JOHN VUKOVICH (3)

Team Physician—DR. PHILLIP MARONE
Trainer—JEFF COOPER
Assistant Trainer—MARK ANDERSEN

Vice President, Public Relations—LARRY SHENK
Travelling Secretary—EDDIE FERENZ

No.	PITCHERS (19)	B	T	Ht.	Wt.	Born	Birthplace	Residence	1995 Club	W-L	ERA	G	GS	CG	SV	IP	H	R	ER	BB	SO	M.L. Service
29	BANKS, WILLIE	R	R	6-1	195	2-27-69	Jersey City, NJ	Miami, FL	Chicago N.L.	0-1	15.43	10	0	0	0	11.2	27	23	20	12	9	
									Los Angeles	0-2	4.03	6	6	0	0	29.0	36	21	13	16	23	
									Florida	2-3	4.32	9	9	0	0	50.0	43	27	24	30	30	3.105
61	BLAZIER, RON*	R	R	6-5	205	7-30-71	Altoona, PA	Bellwood, PA	Reading	4-5	3.29	56	3	0	1	106.2	93	44	39	31	102	0.000
42	BORLAND, TOBY	R	R	6-6	193	5-29-69	Quitman, LA	Quitman, LA	Philadelphia	1-3	3.77	50	0	0	6	74.0	81	37	30	37	59	1.046
									#Scr./W.-B.	0-0	0.00	8	0	0	1	11.1	5	0	0	6	15	
52	BOTTALICO, RICKY	L	R	6-1	208	8-26-69	New Britain, CT	Newington, CT	Philadelphia	5-3	2.46	62	0	0	1	87.2	50	25	24	42	87	0.171
54	CRAWFORD, CARLOS*	R	R	6-1	190	10-4-71	Charlotte, NC	Charlotte, NC	Buffalo	0-1	5.64	13	3	0	1	30.1	36	22	19	12	15	0.000
									Canton/Akron	2-2	2.61	8	8	2	0	51.2	47	19	15	15	36	
50	FERNANDEZ, SID	L	L	6-1	230	10-12-62	Honolulu, HA	Kailua, HA	Baltimore	0-4	7.39	8	7	0	0	28.0	36	26	23	17	31	11.032
									Bowie	1-0	0.75	2	2	1	0	12.0	4	2	1	3	10	
									Philadelphia	6-1	3.34	11	11	0	0	64.2	48	25	24	21	79	
55	GOMES, WAYNE*	R	R	6-2	205	1-15-73	Langley A.F.B., VA	Nashville, TN	Reading	7-4	3.96	22	22	1	0	104.2	89	54	46	70	102	0.000
44	GRACE, MIKE*	R	R	6-4	220	6-20-70	Joliet, IL	Clearwater, FL	Reading	13-6	3.54	24	24	2	0	147.1	137	65	58	35	118	
									Scranton/W.-B.	2-0	1.59	2	2	0	0	17.0	17	3	3	2	13	
									Philadelphia	1-1	3.18	2	2	0	0	11.1	10	4	4	4	7	0.035
28	GREEN, TYLER	R	R	6-5	211	2-18-70	Springfield, OH	Englewood, CO	Philadelphia	8-9	5.31	26	25	4	0	140.2	157	86	83	66	85	1.009
48	JORDAN, RICARDO*	L	L	6-0	180	6-27-70	Delray Beach, FL	Delray Beach, FL	Syracuse	0-0	6.57	13	0	0	0	12.1	15	9	9	7	17	
									Toronto	1-0	6.60	15	0	0	1	15.0	18	11	11	13	10	0.057
53	KARP, RYAN*	L	L	6-4	214	4-5-70	Los Angeles, CA	Coral Gables, FL	Reading	1-2	3.06	7	7	0	0	47.0	44	18	16	15	37	
									Philadelphia	0-0	4.50	1	0	0	0	2.0	1	1	1	3	2	0.005
									Scranton/W.-B.	7-1	4.20	13	13	0	0	81.1	81	43	38	31	73	
45	MIMBS, MICHAEL	L	L	6-2	190	2-13-69	Macon, GA	Macon, GA	Philadelphia	9-7	4.15	35	19	2	1	136.2	127	70	63	75	93	0.160
57	MITCHELL, LARRY*	R	R	6-1	219	10-16-71	Flint, MI	Charlottesville, VA	Reading	6-11	5.54	25	24	1	0	128.1	136	85	79	72	107	0.000
35	MUNOZ, BOBBY	R	R	6-7	259	3-3-68	Rio Piedras, P.R.	Odessa, TX	#Reading	0-4	10.80	4	4	0	0	15.0	28	19	18	3	8	
									#Scr./W.-B.	1-0	0.56	2	2	1	0	16.0	8	2	1	3	10	
									Philadelphia	0-2	5.74	3	3	0	0	15.2	15	13	10	9	6	2.037
51	RYAN, KEN	R	R	6-3	230	10-24-68	Pawtucket, RI	Attleboro, MA	Boston	0-4	4.96	28	0	0	7	32.2	34	20	18	24	34	
									Trenton	0-2	5.82	11	0	0	2	17.0	23	13	11	5	16	
									Pawtucket	0-1	6.30	9	0	0	0	10.0	12	7	7	4	6	
38	SCHILLING, CURT	R	R	6-4	226	11-14-66	Anchorage, AK	Philadelphia, PA	Philadelphia	7-5	3.57	17	17	1	0	116.0	96	52	46	26	114	5.081
33	SPRINGER, RUSS	R	R	6-4	205	11-7-68	Alexandria, LA	Pollock, LA	Vancouver	2-0	3.44	6	6	0	0	34.0	24	16	13	23	23	
									California	1-2	6.10	19	6	0	1	51.2	60	37	35	25	38	
									Philadelphia	0-0	3.71	14	0	0	0	26.2	22	11	11	10	32	2.015
63	WALLACE, B.J.*	R	L	6-3	195	5-18-71	Mobile, AL	Monroeville, AL	Montreal					DID NOT PLAY								
40	WEST, DAVID	L	L	6-6	247	9-1-64	Memphis, TN	Palm City, FL	Philadelphia	3-2	3.79	8	8	0	0	38.0	34	17	16	19	25	5.155
									#Scr./W.-B.	1-0	0.00	1	1	1	0	7.0	2	0	0	0	6	
									#Reading	0-0	1.50	1	1	0	0	6.0	2	1	1	3	8	
41	WILLIAMS, MIKE	R	R	6-2	195	7-29-68	Radford, VA	Newport, VA	Philadelphia	3-3	3.29	33	8	0	0	87.2	78	37	32	29	57	2.014
									Scranton/W.-B.	0-1	4.66	3	3	1	0	9.2	8	5	5	2	8	

No.	CATCHERS (3)	B	T	Ht.	Wt.	Born	Birthplace	Residence	1995 Club	AVG.	G	AB	R	H	2B	3B	HR	RBI	BB	SO	SB	M.L. Service
24	LIEBERTHAL, MIKE	R	R	6-0	178	1-18-72	Glendale, CA	Westlake Village, CA	Philadelphia	.255	16	47	1	12	2	0	0	4	5	5	0	0.102
									Scranton/W.-B.	.281	85	278	44	78	20	2	6	42	44	26	1	
18	SANTIAGO, BENITO	R	R	6-1	185	3-9-65	Ponce, P.R.	Davie, FL	Cincinnati	.286	81	266	40	76	20	0	11	44	24	48	2	
27	WEBSTER, LENNY	R	R	5-9	202	2-10-65	New Orleans, LA	Charlotte, NC	Philadelphia	.267	49	150	18	40	9	0	4	14	16	27	0	4.047

No.	INFIELDERS (10)	B	T	Ht.	Wt.	Born	Birthplace	Residence	1995 Club	AVG.	G	AB	R	H	2B	3B	HR	RBI	BB	SO	SB	M.L. Service
60	BATTLE, HOWARD*	R	R	6-0	197	3-25-72	Biloxi, MS	Biloxi, MS	Syracuse	.251	118	443	43	111	17	4	8	48	39	73	10	
									Toronto	.200	9	15	3	3	0	0	0	0	4	8	1	0.029
5	BENJAMIN, MIKE	R	R	6-0	169	11-22-65	Euclid, OH	Chandler, AZ	San Francisco	.220	68	186	19	41	6	0	3	12	8	51	11	4.142
58	DOSTER, DAVE*	R	R	5-10	185	10-8-70	Fort Wayne, IN	Reading, PA	Reading	.265	139	551	84	146	39	3	21	79	51	61	11	0.000
25	JEFFERIES, GREGG	S	R	5-10	184	8-1-67	Burlingame, CA	Pleasonton, CA	Philadelphia	.306	114	480	69	147	31	2	11	56	35	26	9	7.017
23	JORDAN, KEVIN*	R	R	6-1	193	10-9-69	San Francisco, CA	San Francisco, CA	Scranton/W.-B.	.310	106	410	61	127	29	4	5	60	28	36	3	
									Philadelphia	.185	24	54	6	10	1	0	2	6	2	9	0	0.055
12	MORANDINI, MICKEY	L	R	5-11	176	4-22-66	Kittanning, PA	Valparaiso, IN	Philadelphia	.283	127	494	65	140	34	7	6	49	42	80	9	4.153
6	SCHALL, GENE*	R	R	6-3	206	6-5-70	Abington, PA	Willow Grove, PA	Scranton/W.-B.	.313	92	320	52	100	25	4	12	63	49	54	3	
									Philadelphia	.231	24	65	2	15	2	0	0	5	6	16	0	0.045
31	SEFCIK, KEVIN*	R	R	5-10	175	2-10-71	Oak Lawn, IL	Tinely Park, IL	Scranton/W.-B.	.346	7	26	5	9	6	1	0	6	3	1	0	
									Reading	.272	128	508	68	138	18	4	4	46	38	48	14	
									Philadelphia	.000	5	4	1	0	0	0	0	0	0	2	0	0.024
19	STOCKER, KEVIN	S	R	6-1	175	2-13-70	Spokane, WA	Philadelphia, PA	Philadelphia	.218	125	412	42	90	14	3	1	32	43	75	6	2.036
27	ZEILE, TODD	R	R	6-1	200	9-9-65	Van Nuys, CA	Newhall, CA	Louisville	.125	2	8	0	1	0	0	0	0	0	2	0	
									St. Louis	.291	34	127	16	37	6	0	5	22	18	23	1	
									Chicago N.L.	.227	79	299	34	68	16	0	9	30	16	53	0	5.155

No.	OUTFIELDERS (7)	B	T	Ht.	Wt.	Born	Birthplace	Residence	1995 Club	AVG.	G	AB	R	H	2B	3B	HR	RBI	BB	SO	SB	M.L. Service
10	DAULTON, DARREN	L	R	6-2	207	1-3-62	Arkansas City, KS	Philadelphia, PA	Philadelphia	.249	98	342	44	85	19	3	9	55	55	52	3	10.127
4	DYKSTRA, LENNY	L	L	5-10	188	2-10-63	Santa Ana, CA	Philadelphia, PA	Philadelphia	.264	62	254	37	67	15	1	2	18	33	28	10	10.063
8	EISENREICH, JIM	L	L	5-11	195	4-18-59	St. Cloud, MN	Blue Springs, MO	Philadelphia	.316	129	377	46	119	22	2	10	55	38	44	10	9.151
16	LONGMIRE, TONY	L	R	6-1	218	8-12-68	Vallejo, CA	Vallejo, CA	Philadelphia	.356	59	104	21	37	7	0	3	19	11	19	1	2.153
56	MURRAY, GLENN	R	R	6-2	225	11-23-70	Manning, SC	Manning, SC	Pawtucket	.244	104	336	66	82	15	0	25	66	34	109	5	
26	TINSLEY, LEE	S	R	5-10	196	3-4-69	Shelbyville, KY	Shelbyville, KY	Boston	.284	100	341	61	97	17	1	7	41	39	74	18	
									Trenton	.389	4	18	3	7	1	0	0	3	1	5	1	
22	WHITEN, MARK	S	R	6-3	235	11-25-66	Pensacola, FL	Clearwater, FL	Boston	.185	32	108	13	20	3	0	1	10	8	23	1	
									Pawtucket	.284	28	102	19	29	3	1	4	13	19	30	4	
									Philadelphia	.269	60	212	38	57	10	1	11	37	31	63	7	4.162

*Rookie
#Rehabilitation Assignment

FULL NAMES AND PHONETICS

Banks, Willie Anthony
Battle, Howard Dion
Benjamin, Michael Paul
Bennett, Gary David, Jr.
Blazier, Ronald Patrick (BLAZE-yer)
Borland, Toby Shawn
Bottalico, Richard Paul (Bo-TAL-e-koh)
Crawford, Carlos Lamonte
Daulton, Darren Arthur (DALL-tun)
Doster, David (DAH-ster)
Dykstra, Lenny Kyle (DIKE-struh)
Eisenreich, James Michael (EYE-zen-rike)
Fernandez, Charles Sidney

Gomes, Wayne M. (GOMES)
Grace, Michael James
Green, Tyler Scott
Greene, Ira Thomas
Holifield, Marshall Rickey (HOLE-lee-field)
Jefferies, Gregory Scott (JEFF-rees)
Jordan, Kevin Wayne
Jordan, Ricardo
Karp, Ryan Jason
Leiper, David Paul (LEEP-er)
Lieberthal, Michael Scott (LEE-ber-thal)
Longmire, Anthony Eugene
Marsh, Thomas Owen

Mimbs, Michael Randall (MIMS)
Mitchell, Larry Paul II
Morandini, Michael Robert (MOR-an-dee-nee)
Munoz, Roberto (MUN-yose)
Schall, Eugene David (SHAWL)
Schilling, Curtis Montague (SHILL-ing)
Sefcik, Kevin John (SEF-sik)
Springer, Russell Paul
Stocker, Kevin Douglas
Wallace, Billy Lyle, Jr.
Webster, Leonard Irell
West, David Lee
Whiten, Mark Anthony (WIT-en)

Williams, Micheal Darren
Zeile, Todd Edward (ZEAL)

MANAGER AND COACHES

James Louis Fregosi (Fre-GO-see)
Larry Bowa
Dave Cash
Denis John Menke (MEN-kee)
John Joseph Podres (POD-res)
John Christopher Vukovich (VU-ko-vitch)

Pittsburgh Pirates (CENTRAL)

MANAGER JIM LEYLAND (10)

Coaches:
GENE LAMONT (23)
MILT MAY (39)
RAY MILLER (31)
TOMMY SANDT (37)
SPIN WILLIAMS (54)

Team Physician—DR. JOSEPH COROSO
Team Orthopedist—DR. JACK FAILLA
Trainers—KENT BIGGERSTAFF, DAVE TUMBAS

Director of Media Relations—JIM TRDINICH
Traveling Secretary—GREG JOHNSON

No.	PITCHERS (18)	B	T	Ht.	Wt.	Born	Birthplace	Residence	1995 Club	W-L	ERA	G	GS	CG	SV	IP	H	R	ER	BB	SO	M.L. Service
41	CHRISTIANSEN, JASON	R	L	6-5	234	9-21-69	Omaha, NE	Elkhorn, NE	Pittsburgh	1-3	4.15	63	0	0	0	56.1	49	28	26	34	53	0.160
26	COOKE, STEVE	R	L	6-6	236	1-14-70	Kauai, HA	Tigard, OR	#Augusta	1-0	0.00	1	1	0	0	5.0	2	0	0	1	6	
									#Carolina	0-0	7.20	1	1	0	0	5.0	5	4	4	5	4	3.019
62	DYER, MIKE	R	R	6-3	200	9-8-66	Upland, CA	Fullerton, CA	Pittsburgh	4-5	4.34	55	0	0	0	74.2	81	40	36	30	53	1.160
57	ERICKS, JOHN	R	R	6-7	251	9-16-67	Oak Lawn, IL	Midlothian, IL	Calgary	2-1	2.48	5	5	0	0	29.0	20	8	8	13	25	
									Pittsburgh	3-9	4.58	19	18	1	0	106.0	108	59	54	50	80	0.102
42	HANCOCK, LEE*	L	L	6-4	220	6-27-67	Van Nuys, CA	Saratoga, CA	Calgary	6-10	5.07	34	17	1	0	113.2	146	78	64	27	49	
									Pittsburgh	0-0	1.93	11	0	0	0	14.0	10	3	3	2	6	0.031
47	LIEBER, JON	L	R	6-3	220	4-2-70	Council Bluffs, IA	Birmingham, AL	Pittsburgh	4-7	6.32	21	12	0	0	72.2	103	56	51	14	45	1.002
									Calgary	1-5	7.01	14	14	0	0	77.0	122	69	60	19	34	
34	LOAIZA, ESTEBAN	R	R	6-4	190	12-31-71	Tijuana, Mex.	Imperial Beach, CA	Pittsburgh	8-9	5.16	32	31	1	0	172.2	205	115	99	55	85	0.160
32	MICELI, DAN	R	R	6-0	216	9-9-70	Newark, NJ	Orlando, FL	Pittsburgh	4-4	4.66	58	0	0	21	58.0	61	30	30	28	56	1.098
55	MOREL, RAMON*	R	R	6-2	193	8-15-74	Villa Gonzalez, D.R.	Villa Gonzalez, D.R.	Lynchburg	3-7	3.47	12	12	1	0	72.2	80	35	28	13	44	
									Carolina	3-3	3.52	10	10	0	0	69.0	71	31	27	10	34	
									Pittsburgh	0-1	2.84	5	0	0	0	6.1	6	2	2	2	3	0.021
15	NEAGLE, DENNY	L	L	6-2	225	9-13-68	Gambrills, MD	Bradenton, FL	Pittsburgh	13-8	3.43	31	31	5	0	209.2	221	91	80	45	150	4.019
60	PARRIS, STEVE	R	R	6-0	190	12-17-67	Joliet, IL	Joliet, IL	Carolina	9-1	2.51	14	14	2	0	89.2	61	25	25	16	86	
									Pittsburgh	6-6	5.38	15	15	1	0	82.0	89	49	49	33	61	0.105
38	PETERS, CHRIS*	L	L	6-1	162	1-28-72	Ft. Thomas, KY	McMurray, PA	Lynchburg	11-5	2.43	24	24	3	0	144.2	126	57	39	35	132	
									Carolina	2-0	1.29	2	2	0	0	14.0	9	2	2	2	7	0.000
56	PISCIOTTA, MARC*	R	R	6-5	227	8-7-70	Edison, NJ	Charlotte, NC	Carolina	6-4	4.15	56	0	0	9	69.1	60	37	32	45	57	0.000
19	PLESAC, DAN	L	L	6-5	217	2-4-62	Gary, IN	St. Charles, IL	Pittsburgh	4-4	3.58	58	0	0	3	60.1	53	26	24	27	57	9.119
53	ROGERS, KEVIN	L	L	6-1	198	8-20-68	Cleveland, MS	Cleveland, MS	San Jose	0-2	1.80	4	4	0	0	10.0	10	2	2	1	5	
									Phoenix	0-0	4.15	3	1	0	0	4.1	9	2	2	2	1	2.150
49	RUEBEL, MATT*	L	L	6-2	180	10-16-69	Cincinnati, OH	Oklahoma City, OK	Carolina	13-5	2.76	27	27	4	0	169.1	150	68	52	45	136	0.000
50	RYAN, MATT*	R	R	6-5	187	3-30-72	Chattanooga, TN	Oxford, MS	Carolina	2-1	1.57	44	0	0	26	46.0	33	10	8	19	23	
									Calgary	0-0	1.93	5	0	0	1	4.2	5	1	1	1	2	0.000
43	WAGNER, PAUL	R	R	6-1	209	11-14-67	Milwaukee, WI	Germantown, WI	Pittsburgh	5-16	4.80	33	25	3	1	165.0	174	96	88	72	120	2.149

No.	CATCHERS (2)	B	T	Ht.	Wt.	Born	Birthplace	Residence	1995 Club	AVG.	G	AB	R	H	2B	3B	HR	RBI	BB	SO	SB	M.L. Service
2	ENCARNACION, ANGELO	R	R	5-8	177	4-18-73	Santo Domingo, D.R.	Santo Domingo, D.R.	Calgary	.250	21	80	8	20	3	0	1	6	1	12	1	
									Pittsburgh	.226	58	159	18	36	7	2	2	10	13	28	1	0.122
52	KENDALL, JASON*	R	R	6-0	181	6-26-74	San Diego, CA	Torrance, CA	Carolina	.326	117	429	87	140	26	1	8	71	56	22	10	0.000

No.	INFIELDERS (10)	B	T	Ht.	Wt.	Born	Birthplace	Residence	1995 Club	AVG.	G	AB	R	H	2B	3B	HR	RBI	BB	SO	SB	M.L. Service
48	AUDE, RICH	R	R	6-5	215	7-13-71	Van Nuys, CA	Chatsworth, CA	Pittsburgh	.248	42	109	10	27	8	0	2	19	6	20	1	0.121
									Calgary	.333	50	195	34	65	14	2	9	42	12	30	3	
3	BELL, JAY	R	R	6-0	182	12-11-65	Eglin A.F.B., FL	Valrico, FL	Pittsburgh	.262	138	530	79	139	28	4	13	55	55	110	2	7.057
13	GARCIA, CARLOS	R	R	6-1	205	10-15-67	Tachira, Ven.	Depew, NY	Pittsburgh	.294	104	367	41	108	24	2	6	50	25	55	8	3.069
22	GARCIA, FREDDY	R	R	6-2	205	8-1-72	La Romana, D.R.	La Romana, D.R.	Pittsburgh	.140	42	57	5	8	1	1	0	1	8	17	0	0.160
17	HAYES, CHARLIE	R	R	6-0	215	5-29-65	Hattiesburg, MS	Houston, TX	Philadelphia	.276	141	529	58	146	30	3	11	85	50	88	5	6.075
36	JOHNSON, MARK	L	L	6-4	230	10-17-67	Worcester, MA	Worcester, MA	Pittsburgh	.208	79	221	32	46	6	1	13	28	37	66	5	0.112
									Calgary	.304	9	23	7	7	4	0	2	8	6	4	1	
7	KING, JEFF	R	R	6-1	184	12-26-64	Marion, IN	Wexford, PA	Pittsburgh	.265	122	445	61	118	27	2	18	87	55	63	7	6.071
16	LIRIANO, NELSON	S	R	5-10	181	6-3-64	Puerto Plata, D.R.	Puerto Plata, D.R.	Pittsburgh	.286	107	259	29	74	12	1	5	38	24	34	2	5.072
12	WEHNER, JOHN	R	R	6-3	206	6-29-67	Pittsburgh, PA	Fombell, PA	Calgary	.329	40	158	30	52	12	2	4	24	12	16	8	
									Pittsburgh	.308	52	107	13	33	0	3	0	5	10	17	3	2.029
29	YOUNG, KEVIN	R	R	6-2	221	6-16-69	Alpena, MI	Kansas City, KS	Calgary	.356	45	163	24	58	23	1	8	34	15	21	6	
									Pittsburgh	.232	56	181	13	42	9	0	6	22	8	53	1	2.043

No.	OUTFIELDERS (10)	B	T	Ht.	Wt.	Born	Birthplace	Residence	1995 Club	AVG.	G	AB	R	H	2B	3B	HR	RBI	BB	SO	SB	M.L. Service
46	ALLENSWORTH, JERMAINE*	R	R	6-0	190	1-11-72	Anderson, IN	Anderson, IN	Carolina	.269	56	219	37	59	14	2	1	14	25	34	13	
									Calgary	.316	51	190	46	60	13	4	3	11	13	30	13	0.000
25	BEAMON, TREY*	L	R	6-3	195	2-11-74	Dallas, TX	Dallas, TX	Calgary	.334	118	452	74	151	29	5	5	62	39	55	18	0.000
5	BRUMFIELD, JACOB	R	R	6-0	186	5-27-65	Bogalusa, LA	Atlanta, GA	Pittsburgh	.271	116	402	64	109	23	2	4	26	37	71	22	2.141
									#Carolina	.417	3	12	2	5	0	0	2	2	1	2	0	
35	CLARK, DAVE	L	R	6-2	213	9-3-62	Tupelo, MS	Tupelo, MS	Pittsburgh	.281	77	196	30	55	6	0	4	24	24	38	3	6.089
61	CLAUDIO, PATRICIO*	S	R	6-0	160	4-12-72	Santiago, D.R.	Santiago, D.R.	Bakersfield	.281	32	128	19	36	9	3	1	9	13	26	5	
									Kinston	.265	89	298	37	79	7	4	5	27	26	73	27	0.000
30	CUMMINGS, MIDRE	L	R	6-0	203	10-14-71	St. Croix, V.I.	St. Croix, V.I.	Pittsburgh	.243	59	152	13	37	7	1	2	15	13	30	1	0.133
									Calgary	.277	45	159	19	44	9	1	1	16	6	27	1	
11	KINGERY, MIKE	L	L	6-0	185	3-29-61	St. James, MN	Atwater, MN	Colorado	.269	119	350	66	94	18	4	8	37	45	40	13	6.042
28	MARTIN, AL	L	L	6-2	210	11-24-67	West Covina, CA	Scottsdale, AZ	Pittsburgh	.282	124	439	70	124	25	3	13	41	44	92	20	2.147
6	MERCED, ORLANDO	L	R	5-11	183	11-2-66	San Juan, P.R.	Orlando, FL	Pittsburgh	.300	132	487	75	146	29	4	15	83	52	74	7	5.012
59	PETERSON, CHARLES*	R	R	6-3	203	5-8-74	Laurens, SC	Laurens, SC	Lynchburg	.274	107	391	61	107	9	4	7	51	43	73	31	
									Carolina	.329	20	70	13	23	3	1	0	7	9	15	2	0.000

*Rookie
#Rehabilitation Assignment

FULL NAMES AND PHONETICS

Allensworth, Jermaine LaMont
Aude, Richard Thomas (AW-day)
Beamon, Clifford
Bell, Jay Stuart
Brumfield, Jacob Donnell
Christiansen, Jason Samuel
Clark, David Earl
Claudio, Patricio Ortiz
Cooke, Stephen Montague
Cummings, Midre Almeric (MEE-dray)
Dyer, Michael Lawrence
Encarnacion, Angelo Benjamin
  (en-kar-NAH-see-ohn)

Ericks, John Edward
Garcia, Carlos Jesus
Garcia, Freddy Adrian Felix
Hancock, Leland David
Johnson, Mark Patrick
Kendall, Jason Daniel
King, Jeffrey Wayne
Lieber, Jonathan Ray (LEE-ber)
Liriano, Nelson (leer-ee-AH-no)
Loaiza, Esteban Antonio (low-EYE-zah)
Martin, Albert Lee
Merced, Orlando Luis (mer-SED)
Miceli, Daniel (mah-SELL-ee)

Morel, Ramon Rafael
Neagle, Dennis Edward, Jr. (NAY-gul)
Parris, Steven Michael
Peters, Christopher Michael
Peterson, Charles Edward
Pisciotta, Marc George (pah-SHOW-tah)
Plesac, Daniel Thomas (PLEE-sack)
Rogers, Charles Kevin
Ruebel, Matthew Alexander (ROO-bul)
Ryan, William Matthew
Wagner, Paul Alan
Wehner, John Paul (WAIN-er)

Womack, Anthony Darrell
Young, Kevin Stacey

MANAGER AND COACHES

James Richard Leyland (LEE-land)
Gene William Lamont
Milton S. May
Raymond Roger Miller
Thomas James Sandt
Donald Ray Williams

St. Louis Cardinals (CENTRAL)

MANAGER TONY LA RUSSA (10)

Coaches:
MARK DeJOHN (9)
DAVE DUNCAN (18)
RON HASSEY (28) - bullpen
GEORGE HENDRICK (25)
DAVE McKAY (39)
TOMMIE REYNOLDS (15)

Team Physician—DR. STAN LONDON
Trainer—GENE GIESELMANN
Assistant Trainer—BRAD HENDERSON

Media Relations Director—BRIAN BARTOW
Traveling Secretary—C.J. CHERRE

No.	PITCHERS (19)	B	T	Ht.	Wt.	Born	Birthplace	Residence	1995 Club	W-L	ERA	G	GS	CG	SV	IP	H	R	ER	BB	SO	M.L. Service
65	AYBAR, MANUEL*	R	R	6-1	165	10-5-74	Bani, D.R.	Bani, D.R.	Savannah	3-8	3.04	18	18	2	0	112.2	82	46	38	36	99	0.000
									St. Petersburg	2-5	3.35	9	9	0	0	48.1	42	27	18	16	43	
59	BAILEY, CORY*	R	R	6-1	208	1-24-71	Herrin, IL	Marion, IL	Louisville	5-3	4.55	55	0	0	25	59.1	51	30	30	30	49	0.063
									St. Louis	0-0	7.36	3	0	0	0	3.2	2	3	3	2	5	
52	BARBER, BRIAN*	R	R	6-1	175	3-4-73	Hamilton, OH	Orlando, FL	Louisville	6-5	4.70	20	19	0	0	107.1	105	67	56	40	94	0.048
									St. Louis	2-1	5.22	9	4	0	0	29.1	31	17	17	16	27	
41	BENES, ALAN*	R	R	6-5	215	1-21-72	Evansville, IN	Lake Forest, IL	Louisville	4-2	2.41	11	11	0	0	56.0	37	16	15	14	54	0.016
									St. Louis	1-2	8.44	3	3	0	0	16.0	24	15	15	4	20	
40	BENES, ANDY	R	R	6-6	245	8-20-67	Evansville, IN	St. Louis, MO	San Diego	4-7	4.17	19	19	1	0	118.2	121	65	55	45	126	6.001
									Seattle	7-2	5.86	12	12	0	0	63.0	72	42	41	33	45	
62	BUSBY, MIKE*	R	R	6-4	210	12-27-72	Lomita, CA	Wilmington, CA	Arkansas	7-6	3.29	20	20	1	0	134.0	125	63	49	35	95	0.000
									Louisville	2-2	3.29	6	6	1	0	38.1	28	18	14	11	26	
43	ECKERSLEY, DENNIS	R	R	6-2	195	10-3-54	Oakland, CA	Sudbury, MA	Oakland	4-6	4.83	52	0	0	29	50.1	53	29	27	11	40	20.119
48	FOSSAS, TONY	L	L	6-0	200	9-23-57	Havana, Cuba	Fort Lauderdale, FL	St. Louis	3-0	1.47	58	0	0	0	36.2	28	6	6	10	40	5.168
60	FRASCATORE, JOHN*	R	R	6-1	210	2-4-70	Queens, NY	Oceanside, NY	Louisville	2-8	3.95	28	10	1	5	82.0	89	54	36	34	55	0.054
									St. Louis	1-1	4.41	14	4	0	0	32.2	39	19	16	16	21	
32	HONEYCUTT, RICK	L	L	6-1	191	6-29-54	Chattanooga, TN	Signal Mountain, TN	Oakland	5-1	2.42	49	0	0	2	44.2	37	13	12	9	21	17.161
									New York A.L.	0-0	27.00	3	0	0	0	1.0	2	3	3	1	0	
29	JACKSON, DANNY	R	L	6-0	220	1-5-62	San Antonio, TX	Overland Park, KS	St. Louis	2-12	5.90	19	19	2	0	100.2	120	82	66	48	52	11.078
									#Louisville	1-0	1.29	1	1	1	0	7.0	8	1	1	2	2	
54	LUDWICK, ERIC*	R	R	6-5	220	12-14-71	Whiteman A.F.B., MO	Las Vegas, NV	Binghamton	12-5	2.95	23	22	3	0	143.1	108	52	47	68	131	0.000
									Norfolk	1-1	5.85	4	3	0	0	20.0	22	15	13	7	9	
33	MATHEWS, T.J.*	R	R	6-2	200	1-19-70	Belleville, IL	Henderson, NV	Louisville	9-4	2.70	32	7	0	1	66.2	60	35	20	27	50	0.066
									St. Louis	1-1	1.52	23	0	0	2	29.2	21	7	5	11	28	
36	MORGAN, MIKE	R	R	6-2	220	10-8-59	Tulare, CA	Las Vegas, NV	#Orlando	0-2	7.59	2	2	0	0	10.2	13	9	9	7	5	13.058
									St. Louis	5-6	3.88	17	17	1	0	106.2	114	48	46	25	46	
									Chicago N.L.	2-1	2.19	4	4	0	0	24.2	19	8	6	9	15	
31	OSBORNE, DONOVAN	L	L	6-2	195	6-21-69	Roseville, CA	Tierra Verde, FL	St. Louis	4-6	3.81	19	19	0	0	113.1	112	58	48	34	82	3.119
									#Arkansas	0-1	2.45	2	2	0	0	11.0	12	4	3	2	6	
									Louisville	0-1	3.86	1	1	0	0	7.0	8	3	3	0	3	
49	PARRETT, JEFF*	R	R	6-3	205	8-26-61	Indianapolis, IN	Lexington, KY	St. Louis	4-7	3.64	59	0	0	0	76.2	71	33	31	28	71	7.081
46	PETKOVSEK, MARK	R	R	6-0	185	11-18-65	Beaumont, TX	Beaumont, TX	Louisville	4-1	2.32	8	8	2	0	54.1	38	16	14	8	30	1.071
									St. Louis	6-6	4.00	26	21	1	0	137.1	136	71	61	35	71	
30	STOTTLEMYRE, TODD	L	R	6-3	200	5-20-65	Yakima, WA	Yakima, WA	Oakland	14-7	4.55	31	31	2	0	209.2	228	117	106	80	205	7.058
24	URBANI, TOM	L	L	6-1	190	1-21-68	Santa Cruz, CA	St. Louis, MO	Louisville	1-1	2.93	2	2	0	0	15.1	16	6	5	5	11	1.168
									St. Louis	3-5	3.70	24	13	0	0	82.2	99	40	34	21	52	

No.	CATCHERS (3)	B	T	Ht.	Wt.	Born	Birthplace	Residence	1995 Club	AVG.	G	AB	R	H	2B	3B	HR	RBI	BB	SO	SB	M.L. Service
71	MARRERO, ELIESER*	R	R	6-1	180	11-17-73	Havana, Cuba	Miami, FL	St. Petersburg	.211	107	383	43	81	16	1	10	55	23	55	9	0.000
19	PAGNOZZI, TOM	R	R	6-1	190	7-30-62	Tucson, AZ	Gilbert, AZ	St. Louis	.215	62	219	17	47	14	1	2	15	11	31	0	8.034
									#Louisville	.500	5	16	4	8	2	0	1	3	1	0	0	
4	SHEAFFER, DANNY	R	R	6-0	195	8-2-61	Jacksonville, FL	Mount Airy, NC	St. Louis	.231	76	208	24	48	10	1	5	30	23	38	0	3.054

No.	INFIELDERS (12)	B	T	Ht.	Wt.	Born	Birthplace	Residence	1995 Club	AVG.	G	AB	R	H	2B	3B	HR	RBI	BB	SO	SB	M.L. Service
27	BELL, DAVID	R	R	5-10	175	9-14-72	Cincinnati, OH	Cincinnati, OH	Buffalo	.272	70	254	34	69	11	1	8	34	22	37	0	
									Cleveland	.000	2	2	0	0	0	0	0	0	0	0	0	
									Louisville	.276	18	76	9	21	3	1	1	9	2	10	4	
									St. Louis	.250	39	144	13	36	7	2	2	19	4	25	1	0.065
12	CLAYTON, ROYCE	R	R	6-0	183	1-2-70	Burbank, CA	Redwood Shores, CA	San Francisco	.244	138	509	56	124	29	3	5	58	38	109	24	3.088
7	CROMER, TRIPP	R	R	6-2	165	11-21-67	Lake City, SC	Murrells Inlet, SC	St. Louis	.226	105	345	36	78	19	0	5	18	14	66	0	1.023
8	GAETTI, GARY	R	R	6-0	205	8-19-58	Centralia, IL	Raleigh, NC	Kansas City	.261	137	514	76	134	27	0	35	96	47	91	3	13.131
2	GALLEGO, MIKE	R	R	5-8	175	10-31-60	Whittier, CA	Scottsdale, AZ	Oakland	.233	43	120	11	28	0	0	0	8	9	24	0	
									#Edmonton	.278	6	18	1	5	1	0	0	1	0	4	0	9.159
53	GULAN, MIKE*	R	R	6-1	192	12-18-70	Steubenville, OH	Steubenville, OH	Arkansas	.314	64	242	47	76	16	3	12	48	11	52	4	
									Louisville	.236	58	195	21	46	10	4	5	27	10	53	2	0.000
68	HOLBERT, AARON*	R	R	6-0	160	1-9-73	Torrance, CA	Fontana, CA	Louisville	.257	112	401	57	103	16	4	9	40	20	60	14	0.000
64	JOHNS, KEITH*	R	R	6-1	175	7-19-71	Jacksonville, FL	Chesterfield, MO	Arkansas	.280	111	396	69	111	13	2	2	28	55	53	14	
									Louisville	.000	5	10	0	0	0	0	0	0	0	2	0	0.000
47	MABRY, JOHN	L	R	6-4	195	10-17-70	Wilmington, DE	Warwick, MD	St. Louis	.307	129	388	35	119	21	1	5	41	24	45	0	
									Louisville	.083	4	12	0	1	0	0	0	0	0	0	0	1.002
42	OLIVA, JOSE	R	R	6-3	215	3-3-71	San Pedro de Macoris, D.R.	San Pedro de Macoris, D.R.	Atlanta	.156	48	109	7	17	4	0	5	12	7	22	0	
									St. Louis	.122	22	74	8	9	1	0	2	8	5	24	0	1.022
1	SMITH, OZZIE	S	R	5-10	180	12-26-54	Mobile, AL	St. Louis, MO	St. Louis	.199	44	156	16	31	5	1	0	11	17	12	4	17.119
63	YOUNG, DMITRI*	S	R	6-2	240	10-11-73	Vicksburg, MS	Camarillo, CA	Arkansas	.292	97	367	54	107	18	6	10	62	30	46	2	
									Louisville	.286	2	7	3	2	0	0	0	0	1	1	0	0.000

No.	OUTFIELDERS (6)	B	T	Ht.	Wt.	Born	Birthplace	Residence	1995 Club	AVG.	G	AB	R	H	2B	3B	HR	RBI	BB	SO	SB	M.L. Service
55	BRADSHAW, TERRY*	L	R	6-0	180	2-3-69	Franklin, VA	Zuni, VA	Louisville	.283	111	389	65	110	24	8	8	42	53	60	20	
									St. Louis	.227	19	44	6	10	1	1	0	2	2	10	1	0.028
5	GANT, RON	R	R	6-0	200	3-2-65	Victoria, TX	Smyrna, GA	Cincinnati	.276	119	410	79	113	19	4	29	88	74	108	23	7.001
3	JORDAN, BRIAN	R	R	6-1	205	3-29-67	Baltimore, MD	Stone Mountain, GA	St. Louis	.296	131	490	83	145	20	4	22	81	22	79	24	2.167
16	LANKFORD, RAY	L	L	5-11	198	6-5-67	Modesto, CA	Chesterfield, MO	St. Louis	.277	132	483	81	134	35	2	25	82	63	110	24	4.163
70	MEJIA, MIGUEL*	R	R	6-1	155	3-25-75	San Pedro de Macoris, D.R.	San Pedro de Macoris, D.R.	Bluefield	.298	51	181	50	54	6	3	3	30	18	30	36	
									High Desert	.269	37	119	14	32	6	1	0	12	14	17	16	0.000
23	SWEENEY, MARK*	L	L	6-1	195	10-26-69	Framingham, MA	Holliston, MA	Vancouver	.345	69	226	48	78	14	2	7	59	43	33	3	
									Louisville	.368	22	76	15	28	8	0	2	22	14	8	2	
									St. Louis	.273	37	77	5	21	2	0	2	13	10	15	1	0.059

*Rookie
#Rehabilitation Assignment

FULL NAMES AND PHONETICS

Aybar, Manuel (I-bar)
Bailey, Philip Cory
Barber, Brian Scott
Benes, Alan Paul (ben-es)
Benes, Andrew Charles (ben-es)
Busby, Michael J.
Bell, David Michael
Bradshaw, Terry Leon
Clayton, Royce Spencer
Cromer, Roy Bunyan III (CROW-mur)
Eckersley, Dennis Lee
Fossas, Emilio Anthony
Frascatore, John Vincent (fras-ka-TOR-ee)

Gaetti, Gary Joseph (guy-ET-ee)
Gallego, Michael Anthony (guy-eggo)
Gant, Ronald Edwin
Gulan, Michael W. (GOO-lan)
Holbert, Aaron Keith
Honeycutt, Frederick Wayne
Jackson, Danny Lynn
Johns, Robert Keith
Jordan, Brian O'Neal
Lankford, Raymond Lewis
Ludwick, Eric D.
Mabry, John Steven
Marrero, Elieser (ma-rare-o e-le-ser)

Mathews, Timothy J.
Mejia, Miguel (mi-hia)
Morgan, Michael Thomas
Oliva, Jose Galvez
Osborne, Donovan Alan
Pagnozzi, Thomas Alan (pag-NOHZ-ee)
Parrett, Jeffrey Dale
Petkovsek, Mark Joseph (pet-ky-zik)
Sheaffer, Danny Todd
Smith, Osborne Earl
Stottlemyre, Todd Vernon
Sweeney, Mark Patrick

Urbani, Thomas James
Young, Dmitri Dell

MANAGER AND COACHES

Tony La Russa
Mark DeJohn
Dave Duncan
Ron Hassey
George Hendrick
Dave McKay
Tommie Reynolds

San Diego Padres (WEST)

MANAGER BRUCE BOCHY (15)

Coaches:
TIM FLANNERY (4)
GRADY LITTLE (22) - bullpen
DAVEY LOPES (42)
ROB PICCIOLO (5)
MERV RETTENMUND (16)
DAN WARTHEN (37)

Team Physician—SCRIPPS CLINIC MEDICAL STAFF
Trainer—LARRY DUENSING
Assistant Trainer—TODD HUTCHESON

Director of Media Relations—ROGER RILEY
Team Travel—ROGER RILEY

No.	PITCHERS (19)	B	T	Ht.	Wt.	Born	Birthplace	Residence	1995 Club	W-L	ERA	G	GS	CG	SV	IP	H	R	ER	BB	SO	M.L. Service
43	ASHBY, ANDY	R	R	6-5	190	7-11-67	Kansas City, MO	Pittston, PA	San Diego	12-10	2.94	31	31	2	0	192.2	180	79	63	62	150	3.140
35	BECKETT, ROBBIE*	R	L	6-5	240	7-16-72	Austin, TX	Austin, TX	Memphis	3-4	4.80	36	8	2	0	86.1	65	57	46	73	98	0.000
55	BERUMEN, ANDRES	R	R	6-2	205	4-5-71	Tijuana, Mex.	Banning, CA	San Diego	2-3	5.68	37	0	0	1	44.1	37	29	28	36	42	0.160
									Las Vegas	0-0	5.40	3	0	0	0	3.1	4	2	2	2	3	
									#R. Cucamonga	0-0	2.45	4	0	0	1	7.1	6	2	2	1	11	
47	BLAIR, WILLIE	R	R	6-1	185	12-18-65	Paintsville, KY	Lexington, KY	San Diego	7-5	4.34	40	12	0	0	114.0	112	60	55	45	83	4.108
45	BOCHTLER, DOUG	R	R	6-3	200	7-5-70	W. Palm Beach, FL	W. Palm Beach, FL	Las Vegas	2-3	4.25	18	2	0	1	36.0	31	18	17	26	32	
									San Diego	4-4	3.57	34	0	0	1	45.1	38	18	18	19	45	0.096
33	DISHMAN, GLENN	R	L	6-1	195	11-5-70	Baltimore, MD	Fort Worth, TX	Las Vegas	6-3	2.55	14	14	3	0	106.0	91	37	30	20	64	
									San Diego	4-8	5.01	19	16	0	0	97.0	104	60	54	34	43	0.102
39	FLORIE, BRYCE	R	R	5-11	190	5-21-70	Charleston, SC	Hanahan, SC	San Diego	2-2	3.01	47	0	0	1	68.2	49	30	23	38	68	1.014
50	HAMILTON, JOEY	R	R	6-4	230	9-9-70	Statesboro, GA	Statesboro, GA	San Diego	6-9	3.08	31	30	2	0	204.1	189	89	70	56	123	1.068
38	HARRIGER, DENNY*	R	R	5-11	185	7-21-69	Kittanning, PA	Ford City, PA	Las Vegas	9-9	4.07	29	28	7	0	177.0	187	94	80	60	97	0.000
48	HERMANSON, DUSTIN	R	R	6-2	195	12-21-72	Springfield, OH	Phoenix, AZ	Las Vegas	0-1	3.50	31	0	0	11	36.0	35	23	14	29	42	
									San Diego	3-1	6.82	26	0	0	0	31.2	35	26	24	22	19	0.084
51	HOFFMAN, TREVOR	R	R	6-0	205	10-13-67	Bellflower, CA	San Diego, CA	San Diego	7-4	3.88	55	0	0	31	53.1	48	25	23	14	52	2.119
56	KAUFMAN, BRAD*	R	R	6-2	210	4-26-72	Marshalltown, IA	Traer, IA	Memphis	11-10	5.76	27	27	0	0	148.1	142	112	95	90	119	0.000
54	KROON, MARC*	R	R	6-2	195	4-2-73	Bronx, NY	Phoenix, AZ	Memphis	7-5	3.51	22	19	0	2	115.1	90	49	45	61	123	
									San Diego	0-1	10.80	2	0	0	0	1.2	1	2	2	2	2	0.003
52	LONG, JOEY*	R	L	6-2	220	7-15-70	Sidney, OH	Conover, OH	Las Vegas	1-3	4.60	25	0	0	0	31.1	38	22	16	16	13	0.000
									Memphis	0-2	3.32	25	0	0	0	21.2	28	15	8	10	18	
27	SANDERS, SCOTT	R	R	6-4	220	3-25-69	Hannibal, MO	San Diego, CA	San Diego	5-5	4.30	17	15	1	0	90.0	79	46	43	31	88	1.166
									#Las Vegas	0-0	0.00	1	1	0	0	3.0	3	0	0	1	2	
31	TEWKSBURY, BOB	R	R	6-4	205	11-30-60	Concord, NH	Concord, NH	Texas	8-7	4.58	21	21	4	0	129.2	169	75	66	20	53	7.067
									Charlotte	1-0	0.00	1	1	0	0	6.0	3	0	0	0	4	
34	VALENZUELA, FERNANDO	L	L	5-11	202	11-1-60	Sonora, Mex.	Los Angeles, CA	San Diego	8-3	4.98	29	15	0	0	90.1	101	53	50	34	57	12.090
49	VILLONE, RON	L	L	6-3	235	1-16-70	Englewood, NJ	Bergenfield, NJ	Seattle	0-2	7.91	19	0	0	0	19.1	20	19	17	23	26	
									Tacoma	1-0	0.61	22	0	0	13	29.2	9	6	2	19	43	
									San Diego	2-1	4.21	19	0	0	1	25.2	24	12	12	11	37	0.116
36	WORRELL, TIM	R	R	6-4	220	7-5-67	Pasadena, CA	Glendale, AZ	#R. Cucamonga	0-2	5.16	9	3	0	1	22.2	25	17	13	6	17	
									#Las Vegas	0-2	6.00	10	3	0	0	24.0	27	21	16	17	18	
									San Diego	1-0	4.73	9	0	0	0	13.1	16	7	7	6	13	2.049

No.	CATCHERS (4)	B	T	Ht.	Wt.	Born	Birthplace	Residence	1995 Club	AVG.	G	AB	R	H	2B	3B	HR	RBI	BB	SO	SB	M.L. Service
11	AUSMUS, BRAD	R	R	5-11	190	4-14-69	New Haven, CT	Carlsbad, CA	San Diego	.293	103	328	44	96	16	4	5	34	31	56	16	2.017
53	CASANOVA, RAUL*	S	R	5-11	200	8-23-72	Humacao, P.R.	Ponce, P.R.	Memphis	.271	89	306	42	83	18	0	12	44	25	51	4	0.000
25	JOHNSON, BRIAN	R	R	6-2	200	1-8-68	Oakland, CA	Chicago, IL	San Diego	.251	68	207	20	52	9	0	3	29	11	39	0	1.100
59	MULLIGAN, SEAN*	R	R	6-2	210	4-25-70	Lynwood, CA	Diamond Bar, CA	Las Vegas	.274	101	339	34	93	20	1	7	43	27	61	0	0.000

No.	INFIELDERS (11)	B	T	Ht.	Wt.	Born	Birthplace	Residence	1995 Club	AVG.	G	AB	R	H	2B	3B	HR	RBI	BB	SO	SB	M.L. Service
7	BUSH, HOMER*	R	R	5-10	175	11-12-72	East St. Louis, IL	East St. Louis, IL	Memphis	.280	108	432	53	121	12	5	5	37	15	83	34	0.000
21	CAMINITI, KEN	S	R	6-0	200	4-21-63	Hanford, CA	Richmond, TX	San Diego	.302	143	526	74	159	33	0	26	94	69	94	12	7.084
10	CEDENO, ANDUJAR	R	R	6-1	170	8-21-69	La Romana, D.R.	La Romana, D.R.	San Diego	.210	120	390	42	82	16	2	6	31	28	92	5	3.151
29	CIANFROCCO, ARCHI	R	R	6-5	215	10-6-66	Rome, NY	Rome, NY	Las Vegas	.311	89	322	51	100	20	2	10	58	16	61	5	
									San Diego	.263	51	118	22	31	7	0	5	31	9	28	0	2.078
20	JOYNER, WALLY	L	L	6-2	200	6-16-62	Atlanta, GA	Lee's Summit, MO	Kansas City	.310	131	465	69	144	28	0	12	83	69	65	3	9.119
8	LIVINGSTONE, SCOTT	L	R	6-0	190	7-15-65	Dallas, TX	Southlake, TX	San Diego	.337	99	196	26	66	15	0	5	32	15	22	2	4.017
1	LOPEZ, LUIS	S	R	5-11	175	9-4-70	Cidra, P.R.	Cidra, P.R.	San Diego					DID NOT PLAY								1.147
23	PETAGINE, ROBERTO	L	L	6-1	170	6-2-71	Nueva Esparita, Venezuela	Caracas, Ven.	San Diego	.234	89	124	15	29	8	0	3	17	26	41	0	
									Las Vegas	.214	19	56	8	12	2	1	1	5	13	17	1	0.163
2	REED, JODY	R	R	5-9	165	7-26-62	Tampa, FL	Tampa, FL	San Diego	.256	131	445	58	114	18	1	4	40	59	38	6	7.148
18	SHIPLEY, CRAIG	R	R	6-1	190	1-7-63	Sydney, Australia	Jupiter, FL	Houston	.263	92	232	23	61	8	1	3	24	8	28	6	4.123
57	VELANDIA, JORGE*	R	R	5-9	160	1-12-75	Miranda, Ven.	Caracas, Ven.	Memphis	.204	63	186	23	38	10	2	4	17	14	37	0	
									Las Vegas	.262	66	206	25	54	12	3	0	25	13	37	0	0.000

No.	OUTFIELDERS (6)	B	T	Ht.	Wt.	Born	Birthplace	Residence	1995 Club	AVG.	G	AB	R	H	2B	3B	HR	RBI	BB	SO	SB	M.L. Service
12	FINLEY, STEVE	L	L	6-2	180	3-12-65	Union City, TN	Del Mar, CA	San Diego	.297	139	562	104	167	23	8	10	44	59	62	36	6.119
19	GWYNN, TONY	L	L	5-11	215	5-9-60	Los Angeles, CA	Poway, CA	San Diego	.368	135	535	82	197	33	1	9	90	35	15	17	13.024
24	HENDERSON, RICKEY	R	L	5-10	190	12-25-58	Chicago, IL	Phoenix, AZ	Oakland	.300	112	407	67	122	31	1	9	54	72	66	32	16.048
58	JOHNSON, EARL*	S	R	5-10	165	10-3-71	Detroit, MI	Detroit, MI	R. Cucamonga	.293	81	341	51	100	11	3	0	25	25	51	34	
									Memphis	.200	2	10	0	2	0	0	0	0	1	0	0	0.000
14	NEWFIELD, MARC	R	R	6-4	205	10-19-72	Sacramento, CA	Huntington Beach, CA	Tacoma	.278	53	198	30	55	11	0	5	30	19	30	1	
									Seattle	.188	24	85	7	16	3	0	3	14	3	16	0	
									Las Vegas	.343	20	70	10	24	5	1	3	12	3	11	2	
									San Diego	.309	21	55	6	17	5	1	1	7	2	8	0	0.149
3	NIEVES, MELVIN	S	R	6-2	210	12-28-71	San Juan, P.R.	Parkland, FL	San Diego	.205	98	234	32	48	6	1	14	38	19	88	2	1.064

*Rookie
#Rehabilitation Assignment

FULL NAMES AND PHONETICS

Ashby, Andrew Jason
Ausmus, Bradley David (AHHS-muss)
Barry, Jeff
Beckett, Robert Joseph
Berumen, Andres (Buh-ROOM-un)
Blair, Willie
Bochtler, Douglas Eugene (BOCK-ler)
Bush, Homer Giles
Caminiti, Kenneth Gene (kam-un-NET-ee)
Casanova, Raul
Cedeno, Andujar (sa-DAYN-yo)
Cianfrocco, Archi (SIN-frock-oh), R-key)
Dishman, Glenn
Finley, Steven Allen (FIN-lee)

Florie, Bryce Bettencourt (FLOOR-ee)
Gwynn, Anthony Keith (GWIN)
Gwynn, Christopher Karlton (GWIN)
Hamilton, Johns Joseph
Harriger, Denny (HAIR-i-ger)
Henderson, Rickey Henley
Hermanson, Dustin
Hoffman, Trevor William
Ingram, Riccardo Benay
Johnson, Brian David
Johnson, Earl Ramon
Joyner, Wallace Keith
Kaufman, Brad
Kroon, Marc Jason (CROON)

Livingstone, Scott Louis
Long, Joey
Lopez, Luis Santos
Mulligan, Sean Patrick
Murphy, Robert Albert, Jr.
Newfield, Marc Alexander
Nieves, Melvin Ramos (nee-EV-uhz)
Petagine, Roberto Antonio (pet-a-GEE-nee)
Reed, Jody Eric
Sanders, Scott Gerald
Sharperson, Mike
Shipley, Craig Barry
Tewksbury, Robert Alan
Valenzuela, Fernando Anguamea

Velandia, Jorge (Va-lan-dea)
Villone, Ron (VA-lone)
Worrell, Timothy Howard

MANAGER AND COACHES

Bruce Douglas Bochy (BOW-chee)
Tim Flannery
David Earl Lopes
Robert Michael Picciolo (PEACH-ah-low)
Mervin Weldon Rettenmund (RETT-un-mund)
Dan Warthen

San Francisco Giants (WEST)

MANAGER DUSTY BAKER (12)

Coaches:
BOBBY BONDS (16)
BOB BRENLY (15)
WENDELL KIM (20)
BOB LILLIS (5)
DICK POLE (48)

Team Physician—DR. GORDON CAMPBELL
Trainer—MARK LETENDRE
Assistant Trainer—BARNEY NUGENT

Director of Media Relations—BOB ROSE
Director of Travel—REGGIE YOUNGER, JR.

No.	PITCHERS (18)	B	T	Ht.	Wt.	Born	Birthplace	Residence	1995 Club	W-L	ERA	G	GS	CG	SV	IP	H	R	ER	BB	SO	M.L. Service
14	BARTON, SHAWN	R	L	6-3	195	5-14-63	Los Angeles, CA	Reading, PA	Phoenix	2-0	1.80	15	0	0	0	25.0	20	5	5	5	25	
									San Francisco	4-1	4.26	52	0	0	1	44.1	37	22	21	19	22	1.023
38	BAUTISTA, JOSE	R	R	6-2	205	7-25-64	Bani, D.R.	Cooper City, FL	San Francisco	3-8	6.44	52	6	0	0	100.2	120	77	72	26	45	4.157
47	BECK, ROD	R	R	6-1	236	8-3-68	Burbank, CA	Scottsdale, AZ	San Francisco	5-6	4.45	60	0	0	33	58.2	60	31	29	21	42	4.051
55	BOURGEOIS, STEVE*	R	R	6-1	220	8-4-72	Lutcher, LA	Paulina, LA	Shreveport	12-3	2.85	22	22	2	0	145.1	140	50	46	53	91	
									Phoenix	1-1	3.38	6	5	0	0	34.2	38	18	13	13	23	0.000
30	BREWINGTON, JAMIE*	R	R	6-4	180	9-28-71	Greenville, NC	Phoenix, AZ	Shreveport	8-3	3.06	16	16	1	0	88.1	72	39	30	55	74	
									San Francisco	6-4	4.54	13	13	0	0	75.1	68	38	38	45	45	0.071
51	CREEK, DOUG*	L	L	5-10	205	3-1-69	Winchester, VA	Martinsburg, WV	Louisville	3-2	3.23	26	0	0	0	30.2	20	12	11	21	29	
									Arkansas	4-2	2.88	26	0	0	1	34.1	24	12	11	16	50	
									St. Louis	0-0	0.00	6	0	0	0	6.2	2	0	0	3	10	0.016
46	DeLUCIA, RICH	R	R	6-0	185	10-7-64	Reading, PA	Columbia, SC	St. Louis	8-7	3.39	56	1	0	0	82.1	63	38	31	36	76	3.161
40	DEWEY, MARK	R	R	6-0	216	1-3-65	Grand Rapids, MI	Jenison, MI	San Francisco	1-0	3.13	27	0	0	0	31.2	30	12	11	17	32	2.127
36	ESTES, SHAWN*	R	L	6-2	185	2-18-73	San Bernardino, CA	Gardnerville, NV	Wisconsin Rapids	0-0	0.90	2	2	0	0	10.0	5	1	1	5	11	
									Burlington	0-0	4.11	4	4	0	0	15.1	13	8	7	12	22	
									San Jose	5-2	2.17	9	8	0	0	49.2	32	13	12	17	61	
									Shreveport	2-0	2.01	4	4	0	0	22.1	14	5	5	10	18	
									San Francisco	0-3	6.75	3	3	0	0	17.1	16	14	13	5	14	0.019
22	FERNANDEZ, OSVALDO	R	R	6-2	190	11-4-68	Holguin, Cuba	Santo Domingo, D.R.	Cuban Natl' Team	..	..	..	..	..	..	..	..	..	..	..	..	0.000
43	JUDEN, JEFF	R	R	6-8	265	1-19-71	Salem, MA	Salem, MA	Scranton/W.-B.	6-4	4.10	14	13	0	0	83.1	73	43	38	33	65	
									Philadelphia	2-4	4.02	13	10	1	0	62.2	53	31	28	31	47	0.158
31	LEITER, MARK	R	R	6-3	210	4-13-63	Joliet, IL	Lanoka Harbor, NJ	San Francisco	10-12	3.82	30	29	7	0	195.2	185	91	83	55	129	5.124
52	PICKETT, RICKY*	L	L	6-1	200	1-19-70	Fort Worth, TX	Fort Worth, TX	Chattanooga	4-5	3.28	40	0	0	9	46.2	22	20	17	44	69	
									Shreveport	2-0	1.71	14	0	0	3	21.0	9	5	4	9	23	0.000
34	SERVICE, SCOTT	R	R	6-6	226	2-26-67	Cincinnati, OH	Cincinnati, OH	Indianapolis	4-1	2.18	36	0	0	18	41.1	33	13	10	15	48	
									San Francisco	3-1	3.19	28	0	0	0	31.0	18	11	11	20	30	1.077
35	VALDEZ, CARLOS*	R	R	5-11	175	12-26-71	Nizao Bani, D.R.	Nizao Bani, D.R.	Shreveport	3-2	1.27	22	3	0	5	64.0	40	11	9	14	51	
									Phoenix	1-0	2.76	18	0	0	2	29.1	29	10	9	13	30	
									San Francisco	0-1	6.14	11	0	0	0	14.2	19	10	10	8	7	0.039
41	VALDEZ, SERGIO	R	R	6-1	190	9-7-65	Elias Pina, D.R.	Santo Domingo, D.R.	Phoenix	6-7	4.45	18	18	2	0	109.1	117	58	54	25	64	
									San Francisco	4-5	4.75	13	11	1	0	66.1	78	43	35	17	29	3.001
50	VanLANDINGHAM, WILLIAM	R	R	6-2	210	7-16-70	Columbia, TN	San Francisco, CA	San Jose	1-0	0.00	1	1	0	0	6.2	4	0	0	2	5	
									San Francisco	6-3	3.67	18	18	1	0	122.2	124	58	50	40	95	1.073
39	WATSON, ALLEN	L	L	6-3	190	11-18-70	Jamaica, NY	Middle Village, NY	St. Louis	7-9	4.96	21	19	0	0	114.1	126	68	63	41	49	
									Louisville	2-2	2.63	4	4	1	0	24.0	20	10	7	6	19	
									Arkansas	1-0	0.00	1	1	0	0	5.0	4	1	0	0	7	2.036

No.	CATCHERS (3)	B	T	Ht.	Wt.	Born	Birthplace	Residence	1995 Club	AVG.	G	AB	R	H	2B	3B	HR	RBI	BB	SO	SB	M.L. Service
54	JENSEN, MARCUS*	S	R	6-4	195	12-14-72	Oakland, CA	Oakland, CA	Shreveport	.283	95	321	55	91	22	8	4	45	41	68	0	0.000
49	LAMPKIN, TOM	L	R	5-11	185	3-4-64	Cincinnati, OH	Camas, WA	San Francisco	.276	65	76	8	21	2	0	1	9	9	8	2	3.032
8	MANWARING, KIRT	R	R	5-11	203	7-15-65	Elmira, NY	Scottsdale, AZ	San Francisco	.251	118	379	21	95	15	2	4	36	27	72	1	6.087

No.	INFIELDERS (10)	B	T	Ht.	Wt.	Born	Birthplace	Residence	1995 Club	AVG.	G	AB	R	H	2B	3B	HR	RBI	BB	SO	SB	M.L. Service
26	AURILIA, RICH*	R	R	6-1	170	9-2-71	Brooklyn, NY	Scottsdale, AZ	Shreveport	.327	64	226	29	74	17	1	4	42	27	26	10	
									Phoenix	.279	71	258	42	72	12	0	5	34	35	29	2	
									San Francisco	.474	9	19	4	9	3	0	2	4	1	2	1	0.027
18	BATISTE, KIM	R	R	6-0	200	3-15-68	New Orleans, LA	Prairieville, LA	Scranton/W.-B.	.230	32	122	10	28	4	1	4	18	2	14	1	
									Bowie	.358	24	95	16	34	5	0	4	27	6	14	2	
									Rochester	.281	66	260	31	73	13	1	3	29	8	27	4	2.065
19	CANIZARO, JAY*	R	R	5-9	170	7-4-73	Beaumont, TX	Orange, TX	Shreveport	.293	126	440	83	129	25	7	12	60	58	98	16	0.000
21	DUNSTON, SHAWON	R	R	6-1	180	3-21-63	Brooklyn, NY	Fremont, CA	Chicago N.L.	.296	127	477	58	141	30	6	14	69	10	75	10	10.040
32	KING, BRETT*	R	R	6-1	190	7-20-72	Orlando, FL	Apopka, FL	San Jose	.274	107	394	61	108	29	4	3	41	41	86	28	0.000
33	MUELLER, BILL*	S	R	5-11	175	3-17-71	Maryland Hts, MO	Maryland Hts, MO	Shreveport	.309	88	330	56	102	16	2	1	39	53	36	6	
									Phoenix	.297	41	172	23	51	13	6	2	19	19	31	0	0.000
17	PHILLIPS, J.R.	L	L	6-1	185	4-29-70	West Covina, CA	Scottsdale, AZ	San Francisco	.195	92	231	27	45	9	0	9	28	19	69	1	1.045
23	SCARSONE, STEVE	R	R	6-2	195	4-11-66	Anaheim, CA	Scottsdale, AZ	San Francisco	.266	80	233	33	62	10	3	11	29	18	82	3	2.156
6	THOMPSON, ROBBY	R	R	5-11	173	5-10-62	West Palm Beach, FL	Tequesta, FL	San Francisco	.223	95	336	51	75	15	0	8	23	42	76	1	9.119
9	WILLIAMS, MATT	R	R	6-2	216	11-28-65	Bishop, CA	Scottsdale, AZ	San Francisco	.336	76	283	53	95	17	1	23	65	30	58	2	
									#San Jose	.182	4	11	2	2	0	0	1	2	0	3	0	7.060

No.	OUTFIELDERS (9)	B	T	Ht.	Wt.	Born	Birthplace	Residence	1995 Club	AVG.	G	AB	R	H	2B	3B	HR	RBI	BB	SO	SB	M.L. Service
7	BENARD, MARVIN*	L	L	5-9	180	1-20-70	Bluefields, Nicaragua	Mesa, AZ	Phoenix	.304	111	378	70	115	14	6	6	32	50	66	10	
									San Francisco	.382	13	34	5	13	2	0	1	4	1	7	1	0.027
25	BONDS, BARRY	L	L	6-1	185	7-24-64	Riverside, CA	Murrieta, CA	San Francisco	.294	144	506	109	149	30	7	33	104	120	83	31	9.076
45	CARREON, MARK	R	L	6-0	195	7-9-63	Chicago, IL	Tucson, AZ	San Francisco	.301	117	396	53	119	24	0	17	65	23	37	0	7.025
1	HILL, GLENALLEN	R	R	6-2	220	3-22-65	Santa Cruz, CA	San Diego, CA	San Francisco	.264	132	497	71	131	29	4	24	86	39	98	25	5.153
28	JAVIER, STAN	S	R	6-0	185	1-9-64	S.F. de Macoris, D.R.	Santiago, D.R.	Oakland	.278	130	442	81	123	20	2	8	56	49	63	36	9.063
2	LEONARD, MARK	L	R	6-0	212	8-14-64	Mountain View, CA	San Jose, CA	Phoenix	.296	112	392	73	116	25	3	14	79	81	63	3	
									San Francisco	.190	14	21	4	4	1	0	1	4	5	2	0	2.112
22	McCARTY, DAVID	R	L	6-5	207	11-23-69	Houston, TX	Minneapolis, MN	Minnesota	.218	25	55	10	12	3	1	0	4	4	18	0	
									Indianapolis	.336	37	140	31	47	10	1	8	32	15	30	0	
									Phoenix	.351	37	151	31	53	19	2	4	19	17	27	1	
									San Francisco	.250	12	20	1	5	1	0	0	2	2	4	1	1.133
60	SINGLETON, CHRIS*	L	L	6-2	195	8-15-72	Martinez, CA	Hercules, CA	San Jose	.277	94	405	55	112	13	5	2	31	17	49	33	0.000
42	WILLIAMS, KEITH*	R	R	6-0	190	4-21-72	Bedford, PA	Bedford, PA	Shreveport	.305	75	275	39	84	20	1	9	55	23	39	5	
									Phoenix	.301	24	83	7	25	4	1	2	14	5	11	0	0.000

*Rookie
#Rehabilitation Assignment

FULL NAMES AND PHONETICS

Barton, Shawn Edward
Batiste, Kimothy Emil (bah-TEEST)
Bautista, Jose Joaquin (bah-TEEST-uh)
Beck, Rodney Roy
Benard, Marvin Larry (buh-NARD)
Bonds, Barry Lamar
Bourgeois, Steven James (booj-WAH)
Brewington, Jamie Chancellor
Burgos, Enrique
Canizaro, Jason Kyle
Carreon, Mark Steven
Creek, Paul Douglas
Cruz, Jacob

DeLucia, Richard Anthony (duh-LOO-sha)
Dewey, Mark Alan
Dunston, Shawon Donnell (SHAWN)
Estes, Aaron Shawn (EST-us)
Hill, Glenallen
Jensen, Marcus C.
Jones, Dax Xenos
Juden, Jeffrey Daniel
King, Brett Alan
Lampkin, Thomas Michael
Leiter, Mark Edward (LITE-er)
Leonard, Mark David
Manwaring, Kirt Dean (man-WAR-ing)

McCarty, David Andrew
Mueller, William Richard (MIL-ler)
Phillips, Charles Gene
Pickett, Cecil Lee
Powell, LeJon Dante
Rosselli, Joseph Donald
Scarsone, Steven Wayne (scar-SONE-ee)
Service, Scott David
Singleton, Christopher Verdell
Thompson, Robert Randall
Valdez, Carlos Luis
Valdez, Sergio Sanchez

VanLandingham, William Joseph
Watson, Allen Kenneth
Williams, David Keith
Williams, Matthew Derrick

MANAGER AND COACHES

Johnnie B. Baker
Bobby Lee Bonds
Robert Earl Brenly
Wendell Kealohapauloe Kim
Robert Perry Lillis
Richard Henry Pole

1995-1996 DEALS MADE BY NATIONAL LEAGUE CLUBS

4/ 4/95 Phillies sign free agent (RHR) **Gene Harris**.

4/ 5/95 Cubs trade the contracts of (RHP) **Derek Wallace** and minor league player Eugenio Morones to Kansas City for the contract of (OF) **Brian McRae**.

4/ 5/95 Cardinals trade the contract of (LHP) **Bryan Eversgerd** and (OF) **Darond Stovall** to the Expos for the contract of (RHS) **Ken Hill** and minor league player Kurt Bollinger.

4/ 5/95 Mets sign free agent (LHR) **John Franco**.

4/ 5/95 Expos trade the contract of minor league player Fernando Seguignol and cash considerations to New York (AL) for the contract of (RHR) **John Wetteland**.

4/ 5/95 Reds sign free agent (OF) **Eric Anthony**.

4/ 6/95 Expos trade the contract of (OF) **Marquis Grissom** to Atlanta for the contracts of (OF) **Roberto Kelly**, (OF) **Tony Tarasco**, (RHR) **Esteban Yan** and cash considerations.

4/ 6/95 Phillies sign free agent (IF) **Charlie Hayes**.

4/ 6/95 Giants sign free agent (RHR) **Jose Bautista**.

4/ 7/95 Marlins sign free agents (IF) **Terry Pendleton**, (RHS) **Mark Gardner** and (IF) **Jerry Browne**.

4/ 7/95 Pirates sign free agent (RHR) **Jim Gott**.

4/ 7/95 Cardinals sign free agents (C) **Scott Hemond** and (IF) **Gerald Perry**.

4/ 7/95 Cubs sign free agent (IF) **Mark Grace**.

4/ 7/95 Giants sign free agent (LHS) **Trevor Wilson**.

4/ 8/95 Cardinals trade the contracts of (OF) **Mark Whiten** and (LHS) **Rheal Cormier** to Boston for the contracts of (IF) **Scott Cooper**, (RHR) **Phillip Bailey** and cash considerations or a player to be named.

4/ 8/95 Cardinals sign free agent (OF) **Bernard Gilkey**.

4/ 8/95 Reds sign free agent (RHR) **Mike Jackson**.

4/ 8/95 Rockies sign free agents (RHS) **Bill Swift** and (OF) **Larry Walker**.

4/ 8/95 Giants sign free agent (LHS) **Terry Mulholland**.

4/ 9/95 Rockies sign free agent (RHR) **Omar Olivares**.

4/ 9/95 Marlins sign free agents (RHS) **John Burkett** and (RHS) **Bobby Witt**.

4/ 9/95 Cubs sign free agent (RHS) **Jaime Navarro**.

4/ 9/95 Giants sign free agent (OF) **Glenallen Hill**.

4/10/95 Marlins sign free agent (OF) **Andre Dawson**.

4/10/95 Rockies trade the contract of (RHR) **Marcus Moore** to Cincinnati for the contract of minor league player Chris Sexton.

4/11/95 Mets sign free agent (OF) **Brett Butler**.

4/12/95 Braves sign free agent (SS) **Jeff Blauser**.

4/12/95 Cubs awarded the contract of (RHR) **Steve Dixon** from Cleveland on a waiver claim.

4/12/95 Braves sign free agent (OF) **Dwight Smith**.

4/15/95 Astros sign free agent (IF) **Dave Magadan**.

4/17/95 Braves awarded the contract of (RHR) **Lee Daniels** from Toronto on a waiver claim.

4/17/95 Reds sign free agent (C) **Benito Santiago**.

4/17/95 Padres sign free agent (IF) **Jody Reed**.

4/17/95 Return of Rule 5 Draftee (IF) **Craig Worthington** from Phillies to (AAA) Indianapolis.

4/22/95 Return of Rule 5 Draftee (IF) **Benji Simonton** from Boston to (A) San Jose.

4/22/95 Reds awarded the contract of (OF) **Nigel Wilson** from Marlins on waiver claim.

4/22/95 Return of Rule 5 Draftee (LHS) **Kevin Logsdon** from Rockies to (AAA) Buffalo.

4/22/95 Giants awarded the contract of (LHR) **Enrique Burgos** from Kansas City via trade for a player to be named.

4/24/95 Mets awarded the contracts of (RHR) **Phillip Stidham** and (RHS) **Brian Edmonson** from Detroit on a waiver claim.

4/24/95 Expos sign free agent (RHS) **Luis Aquino**.

4/26/95 Marlins awarded the contract of (RHS) **Aaron Small** from Toronto on a waiver claim.

4/26/95 Astros trade the contract of minor league player Buck McNabb to Cleveland for the contracts of (OF) **Antonio Mitchell** and minor league player Mitch Meluskey.

4/28/95 Return of Rule 5 Draftee (LHR) **Nathaniel Cromwell** from Astros to (AAA) Las Vegas.

5/9/95 Reds award the contract of (LHS) **Benjamin Vanryn** to California on a waiver claim.

5/11/95 Mets trade the contract of (IF) **Mike Remlinger** to Cincinnati for the contract of minor league player Cobi Cradle.

5/15/95 Mets award the contract of (C) **Brook Fordyce** to Cleveland on a waiver claim.

5/15/95 Astros award the contract of (C) **Eddie Tucker** to Cleveland on a waiver claim.

5/18/95 Astros trade the contract of (RHS) **Domingo Jean** to Texas for the contract of minor league player Roger Luce.

5/21/95 Giants trade the contracts of (RHS) **Salomon Torres** and (LHR) **Steve Frey** to Seattle for the contracts of (LHS) **Shawn Estes** and minor league player Wilson Delgado.

5/23/95 Expos trade the contracts of (OF) **Roberto Kelly** and (LHS) **Joseph Eischen** to the Dodgers for the contracts of (OF) **Henry Rodriguez** and (IF) **Jeff Treadway**.

5/24/95 Reds awarded the contract of (LHR) **Jimmy White** from the Astros on a waiver claim.

5/25/95 Dodgers awarded the contract of (LHR) **John Cummings** from Seattle on a waiver claim.

5/25/95 Return of rule 5 Draftee (LHR) **Matthew Dunbar** from Marlins to (AAA) Columbus.

5/26/95 Cubs award the contract of (OF) **Karl Rhodes** to Boston on a waiver claim.

5/30/95 Return of Rule 5 Draftee (RHS) **Kevin Lomon** from Mets to (AAA) Richmond.

5/31/95 Expos award the contract of (IF) **Chad Fonville** to Dodgers on a waiver claim.

6/ 2/95 Reds awarded the contract of (IF) **Brandon Wilson** from Chicago (A.L.) on a waiver claim.

6/ 5/95 Mets award the contract of (RHR) **Josias Manzanillo** to New York (A.L.) on a waiver claim.

6/ 8/95 Reds trade the contract of (LHS) **John Courtright** to Minnesota for the contract of (IF) **David McCarty**.

6/ 8/95 Mets trade the contract of (OF) **David Segui** to the Expos for the contract of (RHS) **Reid Cornelius**.

6/10/95 Astros trade the contract of (IF) **Chris Donnels** to Boston for a player to be named.

6/16/95 Cardinals trade the contract of (IF) **Todd Zeile** to the Cubs for the contracts of (RHS) **Mike Morgan**, minor league players Paul Torres and Francisco Morales and cash considerations.

6/16/95 Reds trade the contracts of minor league players Antonio Nieto and Danny Clyburn to Baltimore for the contract of (LHR) **Brad Pennington**.

6/16/95 Reds awarded the contract of (OF) **Darren Burton** from Kansas City on a waiver claim.

6/16/95 Cardinals release **Joe Torre** as manager and sign **Mike Jorgensen** as manager.

6/18/95 Phillies trade the contract of (RHR) **Gene Harris** to Baltimore for the contract of (OF) **Andy Van Slyke**.

6/19/95 Cubs trade the contract of (RHS) **Willie Banks** to the Dodgers for minor league player Dax Winslett.

6/21/95 Astros awarded the contract of (OF) **Derrick May** from Milwaukee via trade for a player to be named.

6/22/95 Cubs awarded the contract of (OF) **Darren Burton** from the Reds on a waiver claim.

6/28/95 Cubs trade the contract of (C) **Rick Wilkins** to the Astros for the contracts of (OF) **Luis Gonzalez** and (C) **Scott Servais**.

6/29/95 Braves awarded the contract of (C) **Eddie Tucker** from Cleveland on a waiver claim.

7/ 7/95 Cubs award the contract of (OF) **Kevin Roberson** to Seattle on a waiver claim.

7/11/95 Phillies awarded the contract of (RHR) **Omar Olivares** from the Rockies on a waiver claim.

7/15/95 Phillies sign free agent (LHP) **Sid Fernandez**.

7/16/95 Expos trade the contract of minor league player Tyrone Horne to New York (A.L.) for the contract of (IF) **Dave Silvestri**.

7/19/95 Astros trade the contract of (OF) **Phil Plantier** to the Padres for the contracts of (LHR) **Jeffrey Tabaka** and minor league player Richard Loiselle.

7/20/95 Astors awarded the contract of (RHS) **Erik Bennett** from California on a waiver claim.

7/21/95 Mets traded the contract of (LHS) **Jason Jacome** and minor league player Allen McDill to Kansas City for the contract of (RHS) **Derek Wallace** and minor league player Eugenio Morones.

7/21/95 Reds trade the contract of (OF) **Deion Sanders**, (RHS) **John Roper**, (OF) **David McCarty** and minor league players Scott Service and Ricky Pickett to the Giants for the contracts of (RHS) **Mark Portugal**, (RHR) **Dave Burba** and (OF) **Darren Lewis**.

7/24/95 Expos trade the contract of (RHS) **Luis Aquino** to the Giants for the contract of (RHS) **Louis Pote**.

7/24/95 Phillies trade the contract of (IF) **Dave Hollins** to Boston for the contract of (OF) **Mark Whiten** and cash considerations.

7/27/95 Cardinals trade the contract of (RHSP) **Ken Hill** to Cleveland for the contracts of (IF) **David Bell** and minor league players Rick Heiserman and Pepe McNeal.

7/28/95 Mets trade the contract of (OF) **Bobby Bonilla** to Baltimore for the contracts of (OF) **Damon Buford** and minor league player Alex Ochoa.

7/30/95 Expos trade the contract of (OF) **Lou Frazier** to Texas for a player to be named.

7/31/95 Reds trade the contracts of (LHS) **C.J. Nitkowski**, minor league player David Tuttle and (IF) **Mark Lewis** (who became the player to be named on 11/16/95) to Detroit for the contract of (LHS) **David Wells**.

7/31/95 Braves trade the contract of (LHR) **Mike Stanton** to Boston for a player to be named.

7/31/95 Dodgers trade the contract of (RHS) **Greg Hansell**, (RHS) **Jose Parra** and (IF) **Ron Coomer** to Minnesota for the contracts of (RHS) **Kevin Tapani** and (LHR) **Mark Guthrie**.

7/31/95 Padres trade the contract of (RHS) **Andy Benes** to Seattle for the contracts of (OF) **Marc Newfield** and (LHR) **Ron Villone**.

7/31/95 Mets trade the contract of (RHS) **Bret Saberhagen** to the Rockies for the contracts of (RHS) **Juan Acevedo** and minor league player Arnold Gooch.

7/31/95 Cubs trade the contract of (LHS) **Bryan Hickerson** to the Rockies for future considerations.

8/ 4/95 Mets award the contract of (LHS) **Eric Gunderson** to Seattle on a waiver claim.

8/ 7/95 Marlins trade the contract of (LHS) **Michael Myers** to Detroit for the contract of (LHS) **Buddy Groom**.

8/ 8/95 Marlins award the contract of (RHS) **Bobby Witt** to Texas on a waiver claim.

8/ 8/95 Reds awarded the contract of (IF) **Mariano Duncan** from the Phillies on a waiver claim.

8/ 9/95 Marlins awarded the contract of (RHP) **Richard Garces** from the Cubs on a waiver claim.

8/ 9/95 Phillies trade the contract of (OF) **Dave Gallagher** to California for the contract of (IF) **Kevin Flora**.

8/10/95 Marlins awarded the contract of (RHS) **Willie Banks** from the Dodgers on a waiver claim.

8/10/95 Astros awarded the contract of (RHR) **Mike Henneman** from Detroit for a player to be named (IF **Phil Nevin**).

8/11/95 Braves trade the contract of minor league player Troy Hughes to New York (A.L.) for the contract of (OF **Luis Polonia** and cash considerations.

8/12/95 Astros awarded the contract of (C) **Pat Borders** from Kansas City for a player to be named.

8/15/95 Astros award the contract of (IF) **Phil Nevin** to Detroit on a waiver claim.

8/15/95 Phillies awarded the contract of (RHS) **Russ Springer** from California on a waiver claim.

8/17/95 Astros award the contract of (RHS) **Richard Huisman** to Kansas City on a waiver claim.

8/18/95 Mets trade the contract of (OF) **Brett Butler** to the Dodgers for the contracts of minor league players Dwight Maness and Scott Hunter.

8/25/95 Braves trade the contract of (IF) **Jose Oliva** to the Cardinals for the contract of minor league player Anton French.

8/25/95 Braves trade the contract of minor league player Andre King to Chicago (A.L.) for the contract of (OF) **Mike Devereaux**.

8/28/95 Expos trade the contract of (RHR) **Jeffrey Shaw** to Chicago (A.L.) for the contract of (RHR) **Jose DeLeon**.

8/31/95 Reds awarded the contract of (RHS) **Domingo Jean** from Texas on a waiver claim.

8/31/95 Braves trade the contract of (RHS) **Matt Murray** to Boston for the contract of minor league player Michael Jacobs.

8/31/95 Marlins trade the contract of (RHR) **Alejandro Pena** to Atlanta for a player to be named (minor league player Chris Seelbach).

8/31/95 Pirates trade the contract of (C) **Mark Parent** to the Cubs for future considerations.

9/ 8/95 Dodgers trade the contract of (RHR) **Todd Williams** to Oakland for the contract of minor league player Matt McDonald.

10/ 4/95 Phillies awarded the contract of (RHS) **Willie Banks** from the Marlins on a waiver claim.

10/ 6/95 Phillies trade the contract of (RHS) **Jeff Juden** and minor league player S. Thomas Eason to the Giants for the contract of (IF) **Mike Benjamin**.

10/10/95 Padres trade the contract of (IF) **Ray Holbert** to the Astros for the contract of (LHS) **Pedro A. Martinez**.

10/12/95 Expos award the contract of (RHS) **John Thobe** to Boston on a waiver claim.

10/13/95 Expos award the contract of (LHS) **Butch Henry** to Boston on a waiver claim.

10/23/95 Cardinals release **Mike Jorgensen** as manager and sign **Tony La Russa** as manager.

10/26/95 Giants award the contract of (RHS) **John Roper** to the Reds on a waiver claim.

10/26/95 Giants award the contract of (LHR) **Kevin Rogers** to the Pirates on a waiver claim.

10/30/95 Reds release **Davey Johnson** as manager and sign **Ray Knight** as manager.

10/31/95 Cubs sign free agent (IF) **Ryne Sandberg**.

11/ 1/95 Dodgers sign free agent (RHR) **Michael Hall**.

11/ 3/95 Cubs awarded the contract of (RHS) **Christopher Moten** from Minnesota on a waiver claim.

11/ 9/95 Dodgers sign free agent (OF) **Brett Butler**.

11/14/95 Padres trade the contract of (IF) **Timothy Hyers** to Detroit for a player to be named.

11/16/95 Dodgers sign free agent (RHS) **Ramon Martinez**.

11/20/95 Pirates award to the contract of (OF) **Micah Franklin** to Detroit on a waiver claim.

11/20/95 Rockies award the contract of (OF) **Thomas Schmidt** to Detroit on a waiver claim.

11/20/95 Rockies trade the contract of (C) **Joe Girardi** to New York (A.L.) for the contract of minor league player Michael DeJean.

11/20/95 Mets sign free agent (LHS) **Chris Nabholz**.

11/21/95 Marlins sign free agent (OF) **Devon White**.

11/27/95 Cubs award the contract of (OF) **Darren Burton** to Kansas City on a waiver claim.

11/27/95 Phillies sign free agent (LHS) **Sid Fernandez**.

11/29/95 Dodgers trade the contracts of (IF) **Miguel Cairo** and (IF) **Willis Otanez** to Seattle for the contract of (IF) **Mike Blowers**.

12/ 1/95 Giants trade the contract of (OF) **Rikkert Faneyte** to Texas for a player to be named.

12/ 4/95 Marlins trade the contract of (OF) **Chuck Carr** to Milwaukee for the contract of minor league player Juan E. Gonzalez.

12/ 4/95 Braves sign free agent (IF) **Fred McGriff**.

12/ 4/95 Dodgers sign free agent (IF) **Greg Gagne**.

12/ 4/95 Cardinals awarded the of (OF) **Miguel Mejia** from Kansas City via trade for a player to be named or cash considerations.

12/ 4/95 Cardinals trade the contract of (OF) **Andre King** to the Reds for the contract of minor league player Luis Ordaz.

12/ 5/95 Marlins sign free agent (OF) **Joe Orsulak**.

12/ 6/95 Phillies trade the contract of (RHS) **Paul Quantrill** to Toronto for the contracts of (IF) **Howard Battle** and (LHR) **Ricardo Jordan**.

12/ 6/95 Rockies sign free agent (IF) **Walt Weiss**.

12/ 6/95 Reds sign free agent (IF) **Hal Morris**.

12/ 7/95 Phillies sign free agent (OF) **Jim Eisenreich**.

12/ 7/95 Padres sign free agent (LHS) **Fernando Valenzuela**.

12/ 7/95 Cardinals sign free agent (RHR) **Jeff Parrett**.

12/ 8/95 Giants sign free agent (OF) **Stan Javier**.

12/ 8/95 Cubs sign free agent (RHS) **Jaime Navarro**.

12/ 8/95 Cardinals sign free agent (RHS) **Mike Morgan**.

12/14/95 Astros sign free agent (IF) **Craig Biggio**.

12/14/95 Pirates sign free agent (OF) **Mike Kingery**.

12/14/95 Dodgers trade the contract of (LHR) **Omar Daal** to the Expos for the contract of minor league player Rick Clelland.

12/14/95 Marlins sign free agent (LHS) **Al Leiter**.

12/14/95 Giants trade the contracts of (IF) **Royce Clayton** and Minor League player Chris Wimmer to the Cardinals for the contracts of (LHS) **Allen Watson**, (LHS) **Paul Creek** and (RHR) **Rich DeLucia**.

12/15/95 Expos trade the contract of (LHS) **Gabe White** to the Reds for the contract of minor league player Jhonny Carvajal.

12/15/95 Mets sign free agent (OF) **Lance Johnson**.

12/15/95 Dodgers sign free agent (RHS) **Tom Candiotti**.

12/15/95 Padres trade the contract of (LHR) **Pedro A. Martinez** to the Mets for the contract of minor league player Jeff Barry.

12/17/95 Braves trade the contract of (LHS) **Kent Mercker** to Baltimore for the contracts of (RHR) **Joseph Borowski** and minor league player Rachaad Stewart.

12/17/95 Dodgers trade the contract of (IF) **Jose Offerman** to Kansas City for the contract of (LHR) **Billy Brewer**.

12/18/95 Padres sign free agent (RHS) **Bob Tewksbury**.

12/19/95 Padres sign free agent (IF) **Jody Reed**.

12/19/95 Mets trade the contract of minor league player Alfred Shirley to Kansas City for the contract of (C) **Brent Mayne**.

12/19/95 Cardinals sign free agent (IF) **Gary Gaetti**.

12/20/95 Expos trade the contract of (IF) **Sean Berry** to the Astros for the contracts of (RHR) **David Veres** and minor league player Raul Chavez.

12/21/95 Cubs sign free agent (IF) **Mark Grace**.

12/21/95 Padres trade the contracts of (IF) **Bip Roberts** and minor league player Bryan Wolff to Kansas City for the contracts of (IF) **Wally Joyner** and minor league player Aaron Dorlarque.

12/21/95 Rockies sign free agent (C) **Jeff Reed**.

12/21/95 Astros sign free agent (RHS) **Darryl Kile**.

12/21/95 Expos awarded the contract of (OF) **Ray McDavid** from the Padres on a waiver claim.

12/21/95 Phillies sign free agents (LHS) **David West**, (RHS) **Curt Schilling** and (OF) **Mark Whiten**.

12/21/95 Padres sign free agent (IF) **Andujar Cedeno**.

12/21/95 Cardinals awarded the contract of (LHR) **Rick Honeycutt** via trade from New York (A.L.) for cash considerations.

12/23/95 Cardinals sign free agents (OF) **Ron Gant** and (RHS) **Andy Benes**.

12/26/95 Padres sign free agent (RHR) **Willie Blair**.

12/26/95 Reds trade the contract of (LHS) **David Wells** to Baltimore for the contracts of (OF) **Curtis Goodwin** and minor league player Trovin Valdez.

12/28/95 Cubs sign free agent (RHR) **Doug Jones**.

1/ 2/96 Phillies sign free agent (IF) **Todd Zeile**.

1/ 2/96 Padres sign free agent (OF) **Rickey Henderson**.

1/ 3/96 Braves sign free agent (OF) **Jerome Walton**.

1/ 4/96 Marlins sign free agent (RHS) **Kevin Brown**.

1/ 5/96 Cubs sign free agent (IF) **Dave Magadan**.

1/ 5/96 Padres sign free agent (IF) **Craig Shipley**.

1/ 8/96 Braves sign free agent (OF) **Dwight Smith**.

1/ 9/96 Giants sign free agent (IF) **Shawon Dunston**.

1/ 9/96 Braves trade the contract of (OF) **Mike Kelly** to the Reds for the contracts of (RHS) **Chad Fox** and a minor league player to be named.

1/ 9/96 Cardinals trade the contracts of (OF) **Allen Battle**, (RHS) **Gerald Witasick** and minor league players Bret Wagner and Carl Dale to Oakland for the contract of (RHS) Todd Stottlemyre.

1/10/96 Expos trade the contracts of (IF) **Wil Cordero** and (LHR) **Bryan Eversgerd** to Boston for the contracts of (LHS) **Rheal Cormier** and minor league players Ryan McGuire and Shayne Bennett.

1/11/96 Pirates sign free agent (IF) **Charlie Hayes**.

1/11/96 Cardinals sign free agent (IF) **Mike Gallego**.

1/11/96 Braves award the contract of (LHS) **Michael Potts** to Milwaukee on a waiver claim.

1/16/96 Cubs sign free agent (LHR) **Bob Patterson**.

1/17/96 Mets trade the contract of (C) **Kelly Stinnett** to Milwaukee for the contract of minor league player Cory Fulton Lidle.

1/18/96 Mets trade the contract of (IF) **Aaron Ledesma** to California for the contract of (IF) **Kevin Flora**.

1/22/96 Cardinals trade the contract of (OF) **Bernard Gilkey** to the Mets for the contracts of minor league players Eric Ludwick, Erik Hiljus and Yudith Ozorio.

SINCE 1876 NATIONAL LEAGUE OF PROFESSIONAL BASEBALL CLUBS ™

NATIONAL LEAGUE MANAGERS 1996

ATLANTA—BOBBY COX

Born May 21, 1941, Tulsa, OK . . . Resides: Marietta, GA . . . 6'0" . . . 185 . . . Married Pam Boswell . . . Three children, Keisha, Kami, Skyla.

The Atlanta Braves, under the field leadership of Bobby Cox, have won more games (454) the past five years than any team in major league baseball. Excluding 1990, when he took over managing the Braves in June, Cox's teams have finished first in the last five complete seasons he has managed, winning five division titles (including one with Toronto), three pennant crowns and last year's World Championship.

The Braves, appreciative of his accomplishments, extended his contract two years through 1997 on July 21, 1995.

Cox, the Braves' winningest manager in the modern era with 760 victories, became the 41st skipper in major league history to win at least 1,000 games when Atlanta beat the Reds, 6-5, June 18, 1994. He finished the 1995 regular season with 1,115 major league wins.

In 1993 the Braves won a franchise-record 104 games and became the first National League West team to win three straight division titles. The Sporting News named Cox N.L. Manager of the Year for the second time in three seasons.

Cox, 54, managed the Braves from 1978-81, compiling a 266-323 record and laying the groundwork for the club's National League West title in 1982. Cox began a four-year tenure as Toronto's manager that season, lifting an habitual seventh-place team to within one game of attaining a 1985 World Series berth.

In 1982, Cox led the Blue Jays to a 78-84 mark, the best record in their six-year existence. Toronto improved to 89-73 each of the next two seasons and then won the American League East crown by going 99-62 in 1985.

Cox returned to the Braves as General Manager in October of 1985 and oversaw a farm system which produced many of the team's current standouts. He added the field managing responsibilities on June 22, 1990, then devoted all his time to those duties when the Braves named John Schuerholz General Manager in October of that year.

Cox spent seven years in the Dodgers' farm system before being acquired by Atlanta late in 1966. After playing in 1967 for AAA Richmond, he was traded to the New York Yankees and beat out Mike Ferraro, the Yankees' outstanding spring training rookie, for the third base job in 1968. Cox made the Topps Rookie All-Star team that season, but lost his position to roommate Bobby Murcer in 1969.

Bad knees forced Cox to retire at the age of 30. He was appointed manager of the Yankees' Class A Fort Lauderdale club in 1971. His teams never finished lower than fourth in his six seasons in the Yankees' system. He won the Eastern League pennant and championship with West Haven in 1972 and placed second and third twice in four years at Syracuse, winning the International League's Governor's Cup in 1976. After serving as New York's first base coach in 1977, Cox moved south to manage the Braves.

CHICAGO—JIM RIGGLEMAN

Born November 9, 1952, Fort Dix, NJ . . . Resides: Madeira Beach, FL . . . One son, Jon.

Jim Riggleman is in his second season as the Cubs' manager. He brought an overall major league managerial record of 185-250 into the campaign.

Riggleman was named the 45th manager in Cubs history October 21, 1994. In his first year with the Cubs, he led the club to a 73-71 record. In the process, he was named to National League manager Felipe Alou's coaching staff for the 1995 All-Star Game.

He joined the Cubs after spending two-plus seasons as the manager of the San Diego Padres, compiling a 112-179 record. He also recorded a 558-554 record in nine years as a minor league manager in the St. Louis and San Diego farm systems.

He began his professional career in 1974 after being selected by the Los Angeles Dodgers in the fourth round of the June draft. An infielder/outfielder, he played in the minors for eight seasons in the Los Angeles (1974-1976) and St. Louis (1976-1981) farm systems.

His coaching career began in 1981 when, after being released by the Cardinals' Arkansas (AA) affiliate May 25, he promptly joined that club's coaching staff. After opening the 1982 season as a coach for St. Louis' Louisville (AAA) club, he received his first managerial opportunity later that year when he took over the Cardinals' St. Petersburg (A) affiliate June 4.

Riggleman was at the helm at St. Petersburg through the 1984 season and at Arkansas from 1985 through June 21, 1988, before taking over as St. Louis' director of player development. He reached the majors for the first time in 1989, serving as the Cardinals' first base coach for two seasons.

He returned to the managerial ranks in 1991 with San Diego's Las Vegas (AAA) affiliate, spending two years with that club before his late-September promotion to the Padres in 1992.

CINCINNATI—RAY KNIGHT

Born December 28, 1952, Albany, GA . . . Resides: Albany, GA . . . 6'2" . . . 190 . . . Married Nancy Lopez . . . Four children, Brooks, Ashley, Erinn, Terri.

Ray Knight was named manager of the Reds on October 30, 1995, replacing Davey Johnson. Ray was first named to the Reds' coaching staff on May 24, 1993, serving as bench and hitting coach in 1993, third base and hitting coach in 1994 and assistant manager in 1995.

Knight played 13 seasons in the major leagues as a third baseman and first baseman, including six years with the Reds . . . A 10th-round draft choice of Cincinnati in the June 1970 free-agent draft, Ray first reached the majors with the Reds in 1974 . . . Followed Pete Rose as the club's regular third baseman in 1979 and earned team MVP honors that season as he hit .318 (third best in the National League) . . . Hit .286 (4-for-14) in the 1979 National League Championship Series vs. Pittsburgh . . . Named to the National League All-Star Team in 1980 . . . Hit two homers in an inning, including a grand slam, May 13, 1980 vs. the Mets at Riverfront Stadium (5th inning) . . . Tied a single-season team record with three grand slams in 1980 . . . Traded to Houston for Cesar Cedeno in December 1981 . . . Hit .294 in 1982 and .304 in 1983 for the Astros . . . Named to the National League All-Star team in 1982 . . . Traded to the Mets August 28, 1984 for three players to be named (outfielder Gerald Young, infielder Manny Lee and pitcher Mitch Cook) . . . Named National League Comeback Player of the Year by The Sporting News in 1986, when he hit .298 in 137 games for the Mets . . . Voted MVP of the 1986 World Series vs. Boston, hitting .391 . . . Drove in a run and scored the winning run in New York's memorable three-run 10th-inning rally in Game 6 . . . Had three hits, including a tie-breaking home run in the seventh inning in the Mets' Game 7 win . . . Played his final two seasons in the American League . . . Signed with Baltimore as a free agent in 1987 . . . Traded to Detroit for pitcher Mark Thurmond in 1988 . . . Was a broadcaster for ESPN from 1989 until becoming a Reds coach in 1993.

COLORADO—DON BAYLOR

Born June 28, 1949, Austin, TX . . . Resides: La Quinta, CA . . . 6'1" . . . 220 . . . Married, Becky . . . One child, Don Jr.

The Colorado Rockies' meteoric rise to contention was characterized by winning the 1995 wild-card championship and the club's first appearance in postseason play. Rockies Manager Don Baylor has been at the helm for every step of the team's unprecedented trajectory to success. In recognition of that, the BBWAA awarded him their 1995 National League Manager of the Year Award.

On October 27, 1992, Baylor was named to his first managerial assignment, after serving as a major league hitting instructor for the Brewers in 1990 and '91, and for the Cardinals in 1992. As a manager, Don Baylor has guided the Colorado Rockies to many records. In his first season as a manager he led the team to a 67-95 record, setting the mark for the most wins ever by a National League expansion team. With their 33rd win in 1994, the Rockies became the fastest expansion team to 100 wins in Major League history. The 1995 season saw Baylor captain the club to the fastest playoff berth in expansion history, shattering the old mark by four years, held by the 1969 Miracle Mets.

Baylor's 22-year professional baseball playing career was characterized by winning from beginning to end. Drafted by the Orioles in 1967, his first professional club won the Appalachian League title. In 1988, Baylor's final season as a player, culminated with an appearance in the World Series with the Oakland A's. All told, he appeared in seven American League Championship Series and three World Series with five different clubs. He earned a championship ring in the 1987 Series as a Minnesota Twin, hitting .387 against the Cardinals.

Awards and honors were also mixed into Don Baylor's 19-year Major League career. In 1979, while with California, he had his best overall season, hitting .296 with 36 home runs and he led the league with 120 runs and 139 RBI. The effort earned him the American League MVP award. In 1985 he was awarded the Roberto Clemente award, for the player who best exemplifies the qualities of the late Pittsburgh outfielder, both on and off the field.

An all-round team player, Baylor saw action as an outfielder, a first baseman and designated hitter. Known for his grit and determination, he would do whatever it took to get on base. Baylor holds the major league record for hit by pitches in a career with 267. He also set the American League record for most times hit by a pitch in a single season when he was struck 35 times in 1986.

FLORIDA—RENE LACHEMANN

Born May 4, 1945, Los Angeles, CA . . . Resides: Mesa, AZ . . . 6-0 . . . 200 . . . Married Lauri Thomas . . . Two children, Jim and Britt.

Under Rene Lachemann's guidance, the Marlins improved their record for the third straight season in 1995, becoming just the fourth expansion team to improve its record in each of its first three seasons. Rene and Marcel Lachemann of the California Angels are the first brothers to hold managerial jobs simultaneously in the Major Leagues since the turn of the century.

Prior to becoming Florida's first manager in 1993, Lachemann spent the previous eight years as a major league coach, with stops in Boston (1985-86) and Oakland (1987-92). He was the Red Sox third base coach for both years in Boston and the last four years with the Athletics. During his coaching tenure, Lachemann was involved as a coach in five of the last seven American League Championship Series and four of the last seven World Series.

Two days after his 36th birthday, Lachemann made his major league debut as a manager when he replaced Maury Wills at the helm of the Seattle Mariners, becoming the youngest manager in the majors at the time. He led them to a 38-47 record (15-18 before the strike, 23-29 after) in his rookie season as manager. Led the Mariners to a club record 76 wins in 1982 and a fourth-place finish in his first full season. Was replaced by Del Crandall as Mariners' manager on June 25, 1983 after struggling to a 26-47 start.

Hired to replace Harvey Kuenn at Milwaukee in 1984, Lachemann saw his defending American League champs decimated by injuries and struggle to a 67-94 record.

Lachemann followed his brother Marcel to USC after graduation from Dorsey High in Los Angeles. After one season of college baseball, Rene signed a contract as a catcher with the Kansas City Athletics in 1964 and reached the majors the following season. He hit .227 with nine homers as a rookie in 92 games, but saw action in only 26 additional major league games. He retired as a player in 1972 and began his managerial career at Burlington in 1973.

In addition to his minor league experience, Lachemann also managed for six seasons during the winter and earned Manager of the Year honors in 1976 after leading Mayaguez to the Caribbean World Series title.

STADIUMS OF NATIONAL LEAGUE FRANCHISES

BRAVES

Park	Date Opened	Capacity
South End Grounds*	April 29, 1876	3,000
South End Grounds*‡	July 20, 1894	7,000
Braves Field*	Aug. 18, 1915	44,500
Milwaukee County Stadium†	April 14, 1953	44,091
Atlanta Stadium	April 12, 1966	52,870

*Boston †Milwaukee ‡Park destroyed by fire May 16, 1894; rebuilt and reopened 1894

CUBS

Park	Date Opened	Capacity
23rd Street Park	May 10, 1876	2,500
Lake Park	May 14, 1878	3,000
Loomis Street Park	June 5, 1885	10,300
West Side Park	May 13, 1893	13,000
Cubs' Park	April 20, 1916	14,000
Wrigley Field*		37,741

*Cubs' Park renamed Wrigley Field and capacity expanded

REDS

Park	Date Opened	Capacity
Avenue Grounds	April 25, 1876	3,000
Bank Street Grounds	May 1, 1880	2,000
League Park	April 19, 1890	6,000
Palace of the Fans	April 17, 1902	12,000
Crosley Field*		29,488
Riverfront Stadium	June 30, 1970	51,786

*Palace of the Fans renamed Crosley Field and capacity expanded

ROCKIES

Park	Date Opened	Capacity
Mile High Stadium	April 9, 1993	76,100
Coors Field	April 26, 1995	50,200

MARLINS

Park	Date Opened	Capacity
Joe Robbie Stadium	April 5, 1993	47,226

ASTROS

Park	Date Opened	Capacity
Colt Stadium	April 10, 1962	25,000
Astrodome	April 12, 1965	45,000

DODGERS

Park	Date Opened	Capacity
Washington Park*	April 28, 1890	8,000
Eastern Park*	April 27, 1891	12,000
Washington Park*	April 30, 1898	18,000
Ebbets Field	April 9, 1913	24,000
		†31,903
Memorial Coliseum	April 18, 1958	94,600
Dodger Stadium	April 10, 1962	56,000

*Brooklyn †Capacity expanded

EXPOS

Park	Date Opened	Capacity
Jarry Park	April 14, 1969	28,000
Olympic Stadium	April 15, 1977	58,215

METS

Park	Date Opened	Capacity
Polo Grounds	April 13, 1962	55,000
Shea Stadium	April 17, 1964	55,300

PHILLIES

Park	Date Opened	Capacity
Athletic Baseball Grounds	April 22, 1876	3,000
Recreation Park	May 1, 1883	2,000
Philadelphia Baseball Grounds (Baker Bowl)	April 28, 1887	12,500
Shibe Park	July 4, 1938	33,000
Connie Mack Stadium*		
Veterans Stadium	April 10, 1971	55,581

*Shibe Park renamed Connie Mack Stadium

PIRATES

Park	Date Opened	Capacity
Recreation Park	April 30, 1887	9,000
Exposition Park	April 22, 1889	6,500
Forbes Field	June 30, 1909	24,000
		*35,000
Three Rivers Stadium	July 16, 1970	50,235

*Capacity expanded

CARDINALS

Park	Date Opened	Capacity
Grand Avenue Grounds	May 5, 1876	3,000
Robison Field	June 6, 1885	10,300
Sportsman's Park	July 1, 1920	17,600
Busch Stadium*		30,500
Busch Memorial Stadium	May 12, 1966	50,100

*Sportsman's Park renamed Busch Stadium and capacity expanded

PADRES

Park	Date Opened	Capacity
San Diego Stadium	April 8, 1969	47,634
Jack Murphy Stadium†		*58,000

*Capacity expanded †San Diego Stadium renamed Jack Murphy Stadium

GIANTS

Park	Date Opened	Capacity
Union Grounds*	April 25, 1876	2,000
Polo Grounds*	May 1, 1883	12,000
Manhattan Field*	July 8, 1889	15,000
Polo Grounds*	April 22, 1891	15,000
		†55,131
Polo Grounds*‡	June 28, 1911	30,000
Seals Stadium	April 15, 1958	23,750
Candlestick Park	April 12, 1960	42,500
		†58,000

*New York city †Capacity expanded ‡Polo Grounds' stands destroyed by fire, April, 1911; rebuilt and opened, June 28

NATIONAL LEAGUE MANAGERS 1996

HOUSTON—TERRY COLLINS

Born May 27, 1949, Midland, MI . . . Resides: Houston, TX . . . 5'8" . . . 160 . . . Married Linda . . . Two children, Kim and Eric.

Returns for his third season at the helm of the Astros after leading the club to a 66-49 mark and second-place finish in the N.L. Central in his rookie campaign in 1994 and a 76-68 mark and second-place finish in 1995.

Named the 11th manager in franchise history on November 17, 1993, after spending the 1992 and 1993 seasons as bullpen coach of the Pittsburgh Pirates.

Enters his 25th year in professional baseball in 1996, which included nine years as a minor league player, 11 as a minor league manager and two as a major league coach. His minor league managing record was 824-736, a .528 winning percentage. On the Triple A level, he was 634-578, a .523 winning mark.

In three seasons as skipper of the Buffalo Bisons from 1989-91, Collins led the team to three straight 80-win seasons. His 1990 team finished tied for first before losing an 18-inning, one-game playoff for the division title, while the 1991 squad won the American Association's Eastern Division title before falling in the championship series.

Collins managed in the Los Angeles organization for eight seasons before moving to Buffalo. In 1988, he was named Pacific Coast League Manager of the Year after leading Albuquerque to an 85-56 record. He was also named the NL manager in the first-ever Triple A All-Star Game on July 13 that season.

He led the Dukes to their first championship in five seasons in 1987, and was named minor league Manager of the Year by The Sporting News.

Collins played four seasons of college baseball at Eastern Michigan and was twice named to the NAIA World Series All-Tournament team. In the fall of 1994, he was inducted into the university's sports Hall of Fame. He was a 14th round pick by the Pirates in the 1971 June free agent draft and started his playing career at Niagara Falls.

LOS ANGELES—TOM LASORDA

Born September 22, 1927, Norristown, PA . . . Resides: Fullerton, CA . . . 5'9" . . . 185 . . . Married Jo . . . One child, Laura.

The "dean" of Major League managers, Tom Lasorda enters his 20th season as manager of the Los Angeles Dodgers. Only one man has managed the Dodgers longer—Walter Alston (23 years). Only Alston has won more games than Lasorda (Alston 2,042-Lasorda 1,558).

Lasorda, who took over the Dodgers upon Alston's retirement on Sept. 29, 1976, has a 1,558-1,404 record and has been with his club longer than any other active manager in the majors.

In Lasorda's 19-plus seasons, he has guided the Dodgers to two World Championships (1981, '88) and four National League pennants (1977, '78, '81 and '88). His 1980 club tied for the division title, only to lose to Houston in a one-game playoff.

The 1996 season marks Lasorda's 47th year in the Dodger organization. His Dodger career began in 1949 after he signed his first professional contract with the Philadelphia Phillies in 1945. He played 11 years in the Dodger organization, mostly in Montreal. He played parts of the 1954 and '55 seasons with Brooklyn. He played the 1956 season with Kansas City. Lasorda ended his playing career in 1960 and became a scout in the Dodger organization for five years. He managed for seven years in the Dodgers' minor league system, winning five pennants during that span. Lasorda was selected The Sporting News' Minor League Manager of the Year in 1970. He served as the Dodgers' third base coach from 1972-76 before being named manager.

Lasorda has earned Manager of the Year honors from the BBWAA (1983 and '88), AP (1977, '81 and '83) and UPI (1977, '83 and '88). While guiding the Dodgers to the 1977 pennant, Lasorda became only the 19th manager in league history to win a league title in his first year of managing in the majors. He also became only the second manager in N.L. history to win league titles in his first two full years of managing in the majors.

MONTREAL—FELIPE ALOU

Born May 12, 1935, Haina, Dominican Republic . . . Resides: Lake Worth, FL . . . 5'9" . . . 195 . . . Married Lucie Gagnon . . . Felipe and Lucie have two children, Valerie and Felipe, Jr.

Alou completed his fourth season at the helm of the Expos and despite the club's losing record last season, his winning percentage stands at .558 (304-241) since he took over as skipper in May 1992 . . . as 1994 Manager of the Year, he directed the National League squad at the All-Star Game at Arlington, TX . . . the National League defeated the American by a 3-2 score . . . celebrated his 60th birthday on May 12th with a 9-6 win at New York . . . collected his 250th career managerial win at the major league level on May 16 at Cincinnati, raising his winning percentage to .594 (250-171) . . . celebrated his third anniversary as the Expos manager on May 22 with a 5-2 win over the Marlins . . . won his 300th game against Cincinnati on September 19 by a 4-1 score . . . was selected by Major League Baseball to overlook a series of baseball clinics in his home country at the conclusion of the season.

Alou was named AP's Major League Manager of the Year in 1994 ahead of the Yankees' Buck Showalter and N.L. Manager of the Year by the BBWAA, in a near-unanimous result, capturing 27 of 28 first-place votes . . . was named the 1994 N.L. Manager of the Year award by The Sporting News, leading a team with the second-lowest payroll in the N.L. and with just two active players of 30 years old, to the best record in major-league baseball . . . Reds' Davey Johnson was second . . . ranked third in 1993 in N.L. Manager of the Year voting to Dusty Baker (Giants) and Jim Fregosi (Phils) tied with Bobby Cox of the Braves . . . finished second in the same award to Jim Leyland (Pirates) in his first, partial season in 1992.

He finished his third complete season as a major-league manager in 1995, having taken over from Tom Runnells on May 22, 1992 . . . has a record of 304-241-1 (.558) in 546 games as Expos manager . . . his 304 Expos wins combined with a total of 884 minor league victories in 12 seasons give him 1,188 victories as a manager in North American professional baseball (541 in A-Florida State League; 71 in the AA-Southern League and 272 in the AAA-American Association) . . . recorded his 200th ML win on June 10, 1994 at New York, with son Moises leading the way with a homer and three RBI . . . fastest 200 in Expos history . . . already had fastest 100, in his 178th game as Expos manager, June 4, 1993 vs. the Cubs.

Alou has been a member of the Montreal organization for 18 years. He was an instructor at spring training 1976, managed A West Palm Beach 1977 and 1986-91, AA Memphis 1978, AAA Wichita 1982-83, and AAA Indianapolis 1985. Also managed in the winter leagues for 12 seasons, winning the Caribbean World Series in 1990. Was a coach for the Expos 1978-80, 1984 and beginning of 1992.

Played 17 years in the majors for the Giants, Braves, A's, Yankees, Expos and Brewers. Alou played on three All-Star teams and played all seven games in the 1962 World Series with the Giants. Had a career .286 average, 2,101 hits, 206 home runs, 852 RBIs. Made history in September 1963, appearing in same Giants' outfield with brothers Matty and Jesus.

NEW YORK METS—DALLAS GREEN

Born August 4, 1934, Newport DE . . . Resides: West Grove, PA . . . 6-5 . . . 260 . . . Married Sylvia Taylor . . . Four children, Dana, Kim, John, Douglas.

Was appointed the 15th manager in New York Mets history on May 19, 1993. Has a 170-206 record with the Mets. Last year he guided his club to a 44-31 record after the All-Star break to finish with a 69-75 mark and a second-place tie with the Phillies in the East Division.

In 1994, Dallas led the Mets to a third-place finish in the N.L. East with a 55-58 record. New York improved 20.5 games in the standings from 1993, the best turnaround in club history.

Has also served as manager with the Philadelphia Phillies (1979-81) and New York Yankees (1989). Compiled a winning record in each of his three seasons with Philadelphia and was 56-65 with the Yankees before being replaced by Bucky Dent on August 18, 1989. Had been appointed as Yankees manager on October 7, 1988. Has a career .498 winning percentage (271-273) as a manager in the majors.

Was a member of the Phillies organization following his retirement as an active player in 1967 until culminating his career by guiding the Phillies to their first-ever World Championship in 1980. First named as Phillies manager on August 31, 1979, replacing Danny Ozark, and led the Phils to a 19-11 mark to close out the 1979 campaign.

Became the 17th rookie major league manager to guide his club into the World Series when he skippered the Phillies to a 91-71 mark in 1980 and a five-game triumph over the Houston Astros in the NLCS. Then became just the fourth rookie manager to lead his club to a World Series Championship when the Phillies defeated the Kansas City Royals in six games.

In 1981, Dallas led the Phillies to a first-half Eastern Division Championship with a record of 34-24 and a berth in the Division Championship (the Phillies lost to Montreal, three games to two). Was 59-48 with Philadelphia during that strike year, the third-best overall record in the N.L. East.

Spent six years (1982-87) as Cubs General Manager, also holding the team's President's role during the 1985-87 seasons. Named Baseball Executive of the Year in 1984 by The Sporting News, United Press International and ESPN as he helped mold the first Cubs club since 1945 to compete in post-season play.

Pitched parts of eight seasons in the majors, compiling a 20-22 lifetime record in 185 games, the majority of that action (175 games) with the Phillies.

Becomes just the third person in baseball history to serve as manager of both the New York Mets and Yankees, joining Yogi Berra (Mets, 1972-75; Yankees, 1964 & '84-85) and Casey Stengel (Mets, 1962-65; Yankees, 1949-60). Also becomes the seventh manager in Mets history to have played for the club (Gil Hodges, Berra, Roy McMillan, Joe Torre, Buddy Harrelson & Mike Cubbage).

Attended the University of Delaware, where he received a bachelor's degree in 1981.

PHILADELPHIA—JIM FREGOSI

Born April 4, 1942, San Francisco, CA . . . Resides: Tarpon Springs, FL . . . 6'2" . . . 210 . . . Married Joni Dunn. . . Five children, Jim Jr., Jennifer, Nicole, Robert and Lexi.

Jim Fregosi enters his sixth season as Phillies manager, which is the fourth-longest current tenure in the National League. He has held his position longer than any other Phils skipper since Danny Ozark's eight-year stint (1973-79). Also, Fregosi moved into eighth place on the Phillies' all-time list for games managed with 732 and enters the '96 season just 86 games behind Eddie Sawyer (818) for fifth place on that list.

During his Phillies tenure, Fregosi was named the AP's Manager of the Year for 1993 after leading the Phillies from last place the previous season to capturing the NL championship by defeating the Braves in six games. The Phillies remain as the only NL club to top Atlanta in the last four playoffs.

In 1994, Fregosi managed the NL All-Star team to an 8-7, 10-inning win in one of the most exciting midsummer classics in recent history.

After joining the Phillies organization as a Special Assignments Scout May 29, 1989, Fregosi took over as manager on April 23, 1991, just 13 games into that season. He ended up guiding the club to a third-place finish, its best since 1986.

After an 18-year major league playing career, during which he was a six-time All-Star and a Gold Glove-winning shortstop, Fregosi retired in 1978 and managed the California Angels from 1978-81, which included an AL West title in '79. He also managed the Louisville Redbirds (AAA) from 1983-86 and later returned to the majors where he skippered the Chicago White Sox from mid-June 1986 through 1988.

PITTSBURGH—JIM LEYLAND

Born December 15, 1944, Toledo, OH . . . Resides: Pittsburgh, PA. . . . 6'0" . . . 180 . . . Married Katie O'Connor . . . Two children, Patrick and Kellie.

Jim Leyland is in his 11th season as manager of the Pittsburgh Pirates. Only two other managers in club history have skippered the Bucs for 10 seasons or more (Fred Clarke for 16 years and Danny Murtaugh for 15).

During his first 10 seasons with the club, Leyland has compiled a record of 776-771 (.502 winning percentage) and established himself as one of the finest managers in the game of baseball.

In terms of seniority in Major League Baseball, only Los Angeles' Tommy Lasorda (20 years) has been with his team longer than Jim Leyland. On October 17, 1995, Leyland signed a contract extension which will keep him in a Pirates' uniform through the year 2000.

Leyland picked up his 712th win in a Pittsburgh uniform on July 25, 1994, and surpassed Chuck Tanner (711 wins) to become the third-winningest manager in the 109-year history of the Pirates. Only Clarke (1,422) and Murtaugh (1,115) have won more games as skipper of the Bucs.

During the 1992 season, Leyland guided the Pirates to a 96-66 record and a third straight National League Eastern Division championship. His efforts did not go unnoticed as he was named National League Manager of the Year by both The Sporting News and the Baseball Writers' Association of America. It marked the third time he has won The Sporting News award (also 1988 and 1990) and the second time he has been honored by the BBWAA (also 1990).

Following more than 22 years of professional baseball experience, including 11 as a manager in the Detroit Tigers' farm system, Leyland became manager of the Pirates on November 20, 1985. Just prior to joining the Bucs, Jim spent four seasons as the Chicago White Sox's third-base coach and outfield instructor.

In 1971, at the age of 26, Leyland received his first managerial assignment, taking over the Tigers' Bristol club in the Appalachian Rookie League. The former catcher capped off his 11-year minor league managerial career with three seasons with the Triple-A Evansville club. His teams advanced to the playoffs in five of his last six seasons, winning three league titles. For these accomplishments, he was named Manager of the Year in the Class A Florida State League in 1977 and 1978 and also for the Triple-A American Association in 1979.

ST. LOUIS—TONY LA RUSSA

Born October 4, 1944, Tampa, FL . . . Resides: Danville, CA . . . 6'0" . . . 185 . . . Married Elaine . . . Two children, Bianca Tai and Devon Kai.

Tony LaRussa is entering his first season as the Cardinals' manager. LaRussa, who was hired by the Cardinals on October 23, 1995, begins his first season of managing in the National League after spending the past 17 years managing in the American League with Oakland and Chicago.

LaRussa began the 1996 season ranked second to the Dodgers' Tom Lasorda in career wins among active managers with 1,320 and ranks fifth in winning percentage (.527) among active major league skippers.

Regarded by his peers as one of the game's top managers, LaRussa's honors include three Manager of the Year awards, five American League West Division titles, three American League championships and one World Series championship.

LaRussa began his professional managing career in 1978 with Knoxville of the Double-A Southern League, before taking his first major league managing job on August 2, 1979, with the Chicago White Sox.

In seven-plus seasons (1979-86) with the White Sox, Tony quickly established himself as one of the game's top managers, and he saw his efforts pay off in 1983 when he guided the White Sox to an American League West title with baseball's best record, 99-63. He was rewarded that year with the first of his three Manager of the Year Awards, drawing accolades from The Sporting News, The Associated Press and the Baseball Writers Association of America.

In 1984, Tony had the White Sox tied for first place at the All-Star break before finishing fifth that year with a 74-88 record. He was relieved of his duties on June 19, 1986, and assumed the manager's role with Oakland on July 7, 1986.

In just his second full season with the A's, 1988, Tony managed the club to an American League West record 104 wins and the A.L. pennant. He once again earned Manager of the Year honors from the BBWAA and The Sporting News.

For three straight seasons, 1988-90, the A's led the major leagues in victories, only the 11th time in baseball history that a team had accomplished such a feat. During that span, LaRussa's A's became the first team to win three consecutive A.L. pennants since the 1976-78 New York Yankees.

In 1989, Tony guided the Athletics to their fourth World Series title since moving to Oakland, sweeping the Giants in four games during the earthquake-interrupted Bay Bridge Series.

On July 14, 1991, LaRussa became the 40th manager in major league history to win 1,000 games. He earned a third Manager of the Year Award in 1992 after steering the A's to their fourth A.L. West title in five years. He is the Oakland A's all-time leader in games managed (1,471) and victories (798).

A former infielder, LaRussa signed his first pro contract with the Kansas City A's on the night he graduated from high school in 1962. He made his major league debut one year later with the A's. Tony went on to play professionally for 16 season but never once spent an entire season in the majors. Following his stint with Kansas City in 1963, Tony didn't make it to the majors again until 1968, this time with the A's of Oakland. He went on to play parts of four years in Oakland before finishing out his playing career with Atlanta and the Chicago Cubs.

LaRussa, who becomes the Cardinals' 48th manager, was actually employed by the Cardinals once previously, serving as a player and coach for the club's Triple-A New Orleans affiliate in 1977.

A graduate of Florida State University's School of Law in 1978, Tony passed the bar exam in December 1979, making him one of five lawyer/managers in baseball history. The others, all Hall of Famers, are Monte Ward (New York Giants and Brooklyn Dodgers, late 1880s), Hughie Jennings (Detroit, 1907-20), Miller Huggins (St. Louis Cardinals and New York Yankees, 1913-29) and Branch Rickey (St. Louis Browns, 1914-15).

LaRussa also holds a degree in incustrial management from the University of South Florida in Tampa.

SAN DIEGO—BRUCE BOCHY

Born April 16, 1955, in Landes de Boussac, France . . . Resides: San Diego, CA . . . 6'4" . . . 215 . . . Married Kim . . . Two sons, Greg and Brett.

In 1995, his first year as a Major League manager, Bochy led the Padres to a 70-74 mark (.488), making the club the most improved in the National League (47-70, .402 in '94) . . . recorded the best record by a first-year Padres manager since the club went 67-48 under Jack McKeon in 1988 . . . managed 40 different Padres in 1995, including five who made their Major League debut . . . Bruce became the 15th manager in Padres' history on October 21, 1994 . . . he is the youngest active manager in the Majors (Buck Showalter, manager of the expansion Arizona Diamondbacks, is younger) . . . won three league championships and posted a .507 winning percentage in four seasons managing in the Padres' minor league system (1989-92) . . . served as the Padres' third-base coach in 1993 and '94 . . . is the only Padres manager to have also played for the club.

As a minor league manager, Bruce's Spokane Indians posted a 41-34 mark to place second overall in the Northwest League in 1989 and earn a spot in postseason play. The team then won the league championship by defeating Southern Oregon in the playoff final . . . he moved up to the California League in 1990 and recorded a 64-78 record with the Riverside Red Waves . . . he moved with the club to High Desert in 1991, where the team compiled a 73-63 mark and a new California League attendance record. Bochy and his High Desert Mavericks marched through the playoffs to capture the league crown . . . Bochy was promoted to Class AA Wichita in 1992 and continued his winning ways, posting a 70-66 mark and winning his third championship as the Wranglers swept Shreveport in a best-of-seven series.

As a player, Bruce spent parts of nine seasons in the big leagues as a catcher with the Astros, Mets and Padres . . . finished his career with a .239 average . . . his best season was 1986, when he set personal bests in home runs (8), RBIs (22), games played (63) and starts behind the plate (29) . . . hit a pair of game-winning pinch home runs . . . also third in the National League that year in home runs per at-bat (one every 15.9 ABs) . . . in 1986, he batted 7-for-20 (.350) with 6 RBIs as a pinch-hitter . . . was a member of the Padres during their N.L. pennant-winning season of 1984. He had one at-bat in the World Series, delivering a pinch-hit single in Game 5 at Detroit . . . made his major league debut on July 19, 1978 for the Houston Astros against the New York Mets, going 2-for-3 in Shea Stadium . . . blasted first big-league homer the following day off Kevin Kobel . . . came to the Padres February 23, 1983, signing a minor league contract before contract was purchased by the major league club June 29 of that year . . . coaching career started in 1988, serving the dual role of player/coach for Las Vegas.

SAN FRANCISCO—DUSTY BAKER

Born June 15, 1949, Riverside, CA . . . Resides: San Bruno, CA . . . 6'2" . . . Married Melissa Espiana . . . One daughter, Natosha.

Dusty Baker returns for his fourth year as manager of the San Francisco Giants sporting a 225-196 career mark. Many called the 1995 campaign his finest season as a manager, keeping a club plagued by injuries in the National League playoff hunt until the final weeks of the season.

The 34th manager in Giants franchise history and 14th in San Francisco annals, Baker registered his 200th career victory as manager in the Giants' 3-1 victory over the Dodgers August 6, 1995. With that victory, it was the fourth quickest a San Francisco manager had reached the 200-victory plateau, in terms of games. He accomplished that feat over 370 contests to trail only Alvin Dark (1961-64, 340 games), Herman Franks (1965-68, 349) and Roger Craig (1985-92, 363).

Baker's clubs emphasize power, speed and defense, as the Giants have ranked among the National League leaders in each of those categories over the last three years.

A two-time National League All-Star, Baker began his career as the Braves' 26th pick in June, 1967 and made his ML debut the following year. He enjoyed a prestigious playing career spanning nearly 16 full seasons in the Majors.

His only previous managerial experience was in the winter of 1992-93, when he led the Scottsdale Scorpions to a 25-28 mark in the first year of the Arizona Fall League. Prior to being named the Giants' skipper, he served under previous manager Roger Craig as first base coach in 1988 and as hitting instructor from 1989-92.

NATIONAL LEAGUE MANAGERS, 1876 TO 1996

BRAVES
1876-1881 Harry Wright
1882-1888 John F. Morrill
1889 Jim Hart
1890-1901 Frank Selee
1902-1904 Al Buckenberger
1905-1907 Fred Tenney
1908 Joe Kelley
1909 Frank Bowerman & Harry Smith
1910 Fred Lake
1911 Fred Tenney
1912 John Kling
1913-1920 George Stallings
1921-1923 Fred Mitchell
1924-1927 Dave Bancroft
1928 Jack Slattery & Rogers Hornsby
1929 Emil Fuchs & Rabbit Maranville
1930-1937 Bill McKechnie
1938-1943 Casey Stengel
1944 Bob Coleman
1945 Coleman & Del Bissonette
1946-1950 Billy Southworth
1951 Southworth & Tommy Holmes
1952 Holmes & Charlie Grimm
1953-1955 Charlie Grimm
1956 Grimm & Fred Haney
1957-1959 Fred Haney
1960 Charlie Dressen
1961 Dressen & Birdie Tebbetts
1962 Birdie Tebbetts
1963-1965 Bobby Bragan
1966 Bragan & Billy Hitchcock
1967 Hitchcock & Ken Silvestri
1968-1971 Luman Harris
1972 Harris & Eddie Mathews
1973 Eddie Mathews
1974 Mathews & Clyde King
1975 King & Connie Ryan
1976-1977 Dave Bristol
1978-1981 Bobby Cox
1982-1984 Joe Torre
1985 Eddie Haas & Bobby Wine
1986-1987 Chuck Tanner
1988 Tanner & Russ Nixon
1989 Russ Nixon
1990 Nixon & Bobby Cox
1991-1996 Bobby Cox

CUBS
1876-1877 Al Spalding
1878 Bob Ferguson
1879-1897 Cap Anson
1898-1899 Tom Burns
1900-1901 Tom Loftus
1902-1904 Frank Selee
1905 Selee & Frank Chance
1906-1912 Frank Chance
1913 John Evers
1914 Hank O'Day
1915 Roger Bresnahan
1916 Joe Tinker
1917-1920 Fred Mitchell
1921 John Evers & Bill Killefer
1922-1924 Bill Killefer
1925 Killefer, Rabbit Maranville & George Gibson
1926-1929 Joe McCarthy
1930 McCarthy & Rogers Hornsby
1931 Rogers Hornsby
1932 Hornsby & Charlie Grimm
1933-1937 Charlie Grimm
1938 Grimm & Gabby Hartnett
1939-1940 Gabby Hartnett
1941-1943 Jimmy Wilson
1944 Wilson & Charlie Grimm
1945-1948 Charlie Grimm
1949 Grimm & Frank Frisch
1950 Frank Frisch
1951 Frisch & Phil Cavarretta
1952-1953 Phil Cavarretta
1954-1956 Stan Hack
1957-1959 Bob Scheffing
1960 Charlie Grimm & Lou Boudreau
1961-1965 None
1966-1971 Leo Durocher
1972 Durocher & Whitey Lockman
1973 Whitey Lockman
1974 Lockman & Jim Marshall
1975-1976 Jim Marshall
1977-1979 Herman Franks
1980 Preston Gomez & Joe Amalfitano
1981 Joe Amalfitano
1982 Lee Elia
1983 Elia & Charlie Fox
1984-1985 Jim Frey
1986 Frey & Gene Michael
1987 Michael & Frank Lucchesi
1988-1990 Don Zimmer
1991 Zimmer & Jim Essian
1992-1993 Jim Lefebvre
1994 Tom Trebelhorn
1995-1996 Jim Riggleman

REDS
1876 Charles Gould
1877 Gould & Lipman Pike
1878 Calvin McVey
1879 McVey & James "Deacon" White
1880 John Clapp
1881-1889 Not in league
1890-1891 Tom Loftus
1892-1894 Charles Comiskey
1895-1899 Buck Ewing
1900 Robert Allen
1901 John McPhee
1902 McPhee, Frank Bancroft & Joe Kelley
1903-1905 Joe Kelley
1906-1907 Ned Hanlon
1908 John Ganzel
1909-1911 Clark Griffith
1912 Hank O'Day
1913 Joe Tinker
1914-1915 Buck Herzog
1916 Herzog & Christy Mathewson
1917 Christy Mathewson
1918 Mathewson & Heinie Groh
1919-1923 Pat Moran
1924-1929 Jack Hendricks
1930-1932 Dan Howley
1933 Donie Bush
1934 Bob O'Farrell & Chuck Dressen
1935-1936 Chuck Dressen
1937 Dressen & Bobby Wallace
1938-1946 Bill McKechnie
1947 Johnny Neun
1948 Neun & Bucky Walters
1949 Bucky Walters
1950-1951 Luke Sewell
1952 Sewell & Rogers Hornsby
1953 Rogers Hornsby
1954-1957 Birdie Tebbetts
1958 Tebbetts & Jimmy Dykes
1959 Mayo Smith & Fred Hutchinson
1960-1964 Fred Hutchinson
1965 Dick Sisler
1966 Don Heffner & Dave Bristol
1967-1969 Dave Bristol
1970-1978 George "Sparky" Anderson
1979-1981 John McNamara
1982 McNamara & Russ Nixon
1983 Russ Nixon
1984 Vern Rapp & Pete Rose
1985-1988 Pete Rose
1989 Rose & Tommy Helms
1990-1992 Lou Piniella
1993 Tony Perez & Davey Johnson
1994-1995 Davey Johnson
1996 Ray Knight

ROCKIES
1993-1996 Don Baylor

MARLINS
1993-1996 Rene Lachemann

ASTROS
1962-1963 Harry Craft
1964 Craft & Lum Harris
1965 Lum Harris
1966-1967 Grady Hatton
1968 Hatton & Harry Walker
1969-1971 Harry Walker
1972 Walker & Leo Durocher
1973 Leo Durocher
1974 Preston Gomez
1975 Gomez & Bill Virdon
1976-1981 Bill Virdon
1982 Virdon & Bob Lillis
1983-1985 Bob Lillis
1986-1988 Hal Lanier
1989-1993 Art Howe
1994-1996 Terry Collins

DODGERS
1890 William McGunnigle
1891-1892 John Montgomery Ward
1893-1896 Dave Foutz
1897 William Barnie
1898 Barnie, Mike Griffin & C.H. Ebbets
1899-1905 Ned Hanlon
1906-1908 Patsy Donovan
1909 Harry Lumley
1910-1913 Bill Dahlen
1914-1931 Wilbert Robinson
1932-1933 Max Carey
1934-1936 Casey Stengel
1937-1938 Burleigh Grimes
1939-1946 Leo Durocher
1947 Burt Shotton
1948 Leo Durocher & Burt Shotton
1949-1950 Burt Shotton
1951-1953 Chuck Dressen
1954-1976 Walter Alston
1977-1996 Tom Lasorda

EXPOS
1969-1975 Gene Mauch
1976 Karl Kuehl & Charlie Fox
1977-1980 Dick Williams
1981 Williams & Jim Fanning
1982 Jim Fanning
1983 Bill Virdon
1984 Virdon & Jim Fanning
1985-1990 Buck Rodgers
1991 Rodgers & Tom Runnells
1992 Runnells & Felipe Alou
1993-1996 Felipe Alou

METS
1962-1964 Casey Stengel
1965 Stengel & Wes Westrum
1966 Wes Westrum
1967 Westrum & Salty Parker
1968-1971 Gil Hodges
1972-1974 Yogi Berra
1975 Berra & Roy McMillan
1976 Joe Frazier
1977 Frazier & Joe Torre
1978-1981 Joe Torre
1982 George Bamberger
1983 Bamberger & Frank Howard
1984-1989 Dave Johnson
1990 Johnson & Bud Harrelson
1991 Harrelson & Mike Cubbage
1992 Jeff Torborg
1993 Torborg & Dallas Green
1994-1996 Dallas Green

PHILLIES
1876 A.L.H. Wright
1877-1882 Not in league
1883 Horace Phillips
1884-1893 Harry Wright
1894-1895 Arthur Irwin
1896 Billy Nash
1897 George Stallings
1898 Stallings & Bill Shettsline
1899-1902 Bill Shettsline
1903 Chief Zimmer
1904-1906 Hugh Duffy
1907-1909 Billy Murray
1910-1914 Charlie Dooin
1915-1918 Pat Moran
1919 Jack Coombs & Gavvy Cravath
1920 Gavvy Cravath
1921 Wild Bill Donovan & Irvin Wilhelm
1922 Irvin Wilhelm
1923-1926 Art Fletcher
1927 Stuffy McInnis
1928-1933 Burt Shotton
1934-1937 Jimmy Wilson
1938 Wilson & Hans Lobert
1939-1941 Doc Prothro
1942 Hans Lobert
1943 Bucky Harris & Fred Fitzsimmons
1944 Fred Fitzsimmons
1945 Fitzsimmons & Ben Chapman
1946-1947 Ben Chapman
1948 Chapman & Eddie Sawyer
1949-1951 Eddie Sawyer
1952 Sawyer & Steve O'Neill
1953 Steve O'Neill
1954 O'Neill & Terry Moore
1955-1957 Mayo Smith
1958 Smith & Eddie Sawyer
1959 Eddie Sawyer
1960 Sawyer & Gene Mauch
1961-1967 Gene Mauch
1968 Mauch & Bob Skinner
1969 Skinner & George Myatt
1970-1971 Frank Lucchesi
1972 Lucchesi & Paul Owens
1973-1978 Danny Ozark
1979 Ozark & Dallas Green
1980-1981 Dallas Green
1982 Pat Corrales
1983 Corrales & Paul Owens
1984 Paul Owens
1985-1986 John Felske
1987 John Felske & Lee Elia
1988 Elia & John Vukovich
1989-1990 Nick Leyva
1991 Leyva & Jim Fregosi
1992-1996 Jim Fregosi

PIRATES
1887-1888 Horace B. Phillips
1889 Phillips, Fred Dunlap & Ned Hanlon
1890 Guy Hecker
1891 Ned Hanlon & Bill McGunnigle
1892 Tommy Burns & Al Buckenberger
1893 Al Buckenberger
1894 Buckenberger & Connie Mack
1895-1896 Connie Mack
1897 Patsy Donovan
1898 W.H. Watkins
1899 Watkins & Patsy Donovan
1900-1915 Fred Clarke
1916 Jimmy Callahan
1917 Callahan, Hans Wagner & Hugo Bezdek
1918-1919 Hugo Bezdek
1920-1921 George Gibson
1922 Gibson & Bill McKechnie
1923-1926 Bill McKechnie
1927-1928 Donie Bush
1929 Bush & Jewel Ens
1930-1931 Jewel Ens
1932-1933 George Gibson
1934 Gibson & Pie Traynor
1935-1939 Pie Traynor
1940-1946 Frank Frisch
1947 Billy Herman
1948-1952 Bill Meyer
1953-1955 Fred Haney
1956 Bobby Bragan
1957 Bragan & Danny Murtaugh
1958-1964 Danny Murtaugh
1965-1966 Harry Walker
1967 Walker & Danny Murtaugh
1968-1969 Larry Shepard
1970-1971 Danny Murtaugh
1972 Bill Virdon
1973 Virdon & Danny Murtaugh
1974-1976 Danny Murtaugh
1977-1985 Chuck Tanner
1986-1996 Jim Leyland

CARDINALS
1876 S.M. Graffen
1877 J.R. Lucas & George McManus
1878-1884 Not in league
1885 Fred Dunlap, Benjamin Fine & H.V. Lucas
1886 Gus Schmelz
1887-1891 Not in league
1892 Chris Von Der Ahe
1893 W.H. Watkins
1894 George Miller & H.B. Martin
1895 Al Buckenberger, Joe Quinn, Lewis Phelan & Chris Von Der Ahe
1896 Harry Diddledock, Arlie Latham, Roger Connor & Tom Dowd
1897 Dowd, Hugh Nicol, Billy Hallman & Chris Von Der Ahe
1898 Tim Hurst
1899 Oliver Tebeau
1900 Tebeau & Louis Heilbroner
1901-1903 Patsy Donovan
1904 Charles "Kid" Nichols
1905 Nichols, Jimmy Burke & Matthew Robison
1906-1908 John J. McCloskey
1909-1912 Roger Bresnahan
1913-1917 Miller Huggins
1918 Jack Hendricks
1919-1924 Branch Rickey
1925 Rickey & Rogers Hornsby
1926 Rogers Hornsby
1927 Bob O'Farrell
1928 Bill McKechnie
1929 McKechnie & Billy Southworth
1930-1932 Gabby Street
1933 Street & Frank Frisch
1934-1937 Frank Frisch
1938 Frisch & Mike Gonzalez
1939 Ray Blades
1940 Blades, Gonzalez & Billy Southworth
1941-1945 Billy Southworth
1946-1950 Eddie Dyer
1951 Marty Marion
1952-1954 Eddie Stanky
1955 Stanky & Harry Walker
1956-1957 Fred Hutchinson
1958 Hutchinson & Stan Hack
1959-1960 Solly Hemus
1961 Hemus & Johnny Keane
1962-1964 Johnny Keane
1965-1976 Red Schoendienst
1977 Vern Rapp
1978 Rapp & Ken Boyer
1979 Ken Boyer
1980 Boyer & Whitey Herzog
1981-1989 Whitey Herzog
1990 Herzog & Joe Torre
1991-1994 Joe Torre
1995 Torre & Mike Jorgensen
1996 Tony La Russa

PADRES
1969-1971 Preston Gomez
1972 Gomez & Don Zimmer
1973 Don Zimmer
1974-1976 John McNamara
1977 McNamara & Alvin Dark
1978-1979 Roger Craig
1980 Jerry Coleman
1981 Frank Howard
1982-1985 Dick Williams
1986 Steve Boros
1987 Larry Bowa
1988 Bowa & Jack McKeon
1989 Jack McKeon
1990 McKeon & Greg Riddoch
1991 Greg Riddoch
1992 Riddoch & Jim Riggleman
1993-1994 Jim Riggleman
1995-1996 Bruce Bochy

GIANTS
1876 W.H. Cammeyer
1877-1882 Not in league
1883 John Clapp
1884 James L. Price
1885-1891 Jim Mutrie
1892 Pat Powers
1893-1894 John Montgomery Ward
1895 George Davis, Jack Doyle & Harvey Watkins
1896 Arthur Irwin & Bill Joyce
1897 Bill Joyce
1898 Joyce & Cap Anson
1899 John B. Day & Fred Hoey
1900 Buck Ewing & George Davis
1901 George Davis
1902 Horace Fogel, George Smith & John McGraw
1903-1931 John J. McGraw
1932 McGraw & Bill Terry
1933-1941 Bill Terry
1942-1947 Mel Ott
1948 Ott & Leo Durocher
1949-1955 Leo Durocher
1956-1959 Bill Rigney
1960 Rigney & Tom Sheehan
1961-1964 Alvin Dark
1965-1968 Herman Franks
1969 Clyde King
1970 King & Charlie Fox
1971-1973 Charlie Fox
1974 Fox & Wes Westrum
1975 Wes Westrum
1976 Bill Rigney
1977-1978 Joe Altobelli
1979 Altobelli & Dave Bristol
1980 Dave Bristol
1981-1983 Frank Robinson
1984 Robinson & Danny Ozark
1985 Jim Davenport & Roger Craig
1986-1992 Roger Craig
1993-1996 Dusty Baker

MEET THE ROOKIES 1996

for Atlanta—

JASON SCHMIDT (RHP), 23, led the Class AAA International League with a 2.25 ERA in 1995. A strikeout pitcher with a fastball consistently in the mid-90s and an above-average fastball, he is the leading candidate to be the Braves' fifth starter in '96. He won his first major league start, 2-0, vs. the Chicago Cubs on September 3, 1995.

EDDIE PEREZ (C), 27, is slated to be Javy Lopez's backup in 1996. He hit .308—including a home run off the Cincinnati Reds' Mike Jackson in his first major league at-bat September 15—in a seven-game stint with Atlanta last season. Always strong defensively, he threw out 39 percent of opposing baserunners in the International League in '95.

TERRELL WADE (LHP), 23, could make Atlanta's pitching staff this year. He has always thrown hard (low-90s fastball) and has an effective changeup. He seemed to find his control in the Arizona Fall League, where he walked 14 and struck out 46 in 44 innings.

for Chicago—

TERRY ADAMS (RHP), 23, made a rapid ascension to the majors in 1995 in just his second professional season as a bullpen closer. After stops at Orlando (AA) and Iowa (AAA), he was called up to the major leagues August 9 and went 1-1 with one save in 18 appearances. He went 24-for-27 in his save opportunities at Orlando and Iowa, combining to go 2-3 with a 1.23 ERA in 44 games. Adams was 2-3 with 19 saves and a 1.43 ERA in 37 appearances at Orlando, allowing 23 hits in 37.2 innings and holding opposing batters to a .177 average. In seven Triple-A outings with Iowa, he was 0-0 with five saves and a 0.00 ERA.

BROOKS KIESCHNICK (OF), 23, was an American Association midseason and postseason All-Star at Iowa (AAA), batting .295 with a league-high 23 homers and 73 RBIs. He led the league in hits (149), extra-base hits (54) and total bases (250) and was second in at-bats (505) and games (138), third in slugging percentage (.495) and fifth in RBIs. He was selected to Baseball America's Triple-A All-Star team. Baseball America also named him the Cubs organization's Player of the Year and the fifth-best prospect in the league. Kieschnick was named to the Topps/National Association Class AAA All-Star team after the season.

for Cincinnati—

STEVE GIBRALTER (OF), 23, a tremendous hustler, Gibralter was leading the American Association in home runs and RBIs when his season ended July 16 due to torn thumb ligaments. His .616 slugging percentage earned him a spot on the league's postseason All-Star team . . . A fine defensive outfielder, he was the 1992 Midwest League MVP at Cedar Rapids.

ERIC OWENS (2B), 25, is a base-stealing threat who, in his first year in AAA, had the best season of his career, winning MVP honors in the American Association. He hit .314, scored 86 runs, stole 33 bases and was the sparkplug on hiş team. He was strong defensively at second base and shortstop as well.

SCOTT SULLIVAN (RHP), 25, made it to the major leagues in 1995 after spending less than two full years in the minors. A reliever who jumped from rookie league in 1993 to AA in '94 and still excelled, Sullivan has struck out 244 batters in 234 innings as a pro. His deceptive sidearm delivery helped him post a 3.53 ERA at AAA Indianapolis last season.

for Colorado—

JOHN BURKE (RHP), 26, was the Rockies' first-ever June draft selection (in 1992). Burke led the Pacific Coast League champion Colorado Springs Sky Sox with a .875 winning percentage, going 7-1 in 19 games (17 starts) with one save and 65 strikeouts in 87.0 innings.

CRAIG COUNSELL (IF), 25, is another member of Colorado's draft class of 1992. Counsell has progressed through the Rockies' farm system on an exacting pace, moving up the affiliate ladder one step each year. Craig turned in his third consecutive solid year in 1995, hitting .281 with 112 hits, 22 doubles, six triples, 53 RBIs and 60 runs scored for AAA Colorado Springs.

QUINTON McCRACKEN (OF), 26, tore up the AA Eastern League and the AAA Pacific Coast League in 1995, culminating in his first September callup. Beginning the year at AA New Haven, McCracken led the Eastern League with a .357 average in 55 games with a .419 on-base percentage and 26 stolen bases before getting called to AAA Colorado Springs. Showing no signs of slowing, he continued to be a hot hitter with a .361 average in 61 games with a .418 on-base percentage and 17 stolen bases. Quinton was the only organizational player to be named Minor League Player of the Month twice in 1995 (May and August).

for Florida—

MATT MANTEI (RHP), 22, missed part of the 1995 season while battling injuries but showed a live fastball in 12 appearances and went on to pitch a healthy winter campaign with Ponce in Puerto Rico. He has fanned 177 batters in 148.1 innings in the minors and averaged better than a strikeout per inning in his big-league stint (15 in 13.1 innings) last year.

EDGAR RENTERIA (SS), 20, was selected as the Marlins' Minor League Player of the Year after hitting .289 with seven homers, 30 steals and 68 RBIs at AA Portland. He followed that up by hitting .318 during the winter at Ponce. A member of the Marlins' organization since the team began play in 1992, Renteria will try in 1996 to become the fourth native of Colombia to reach the majors.

for Houston

BOB ABREU (OF), 21, spent his first year at Triple A in 1995 and hit over .300 for the second straight season. He led all professional players with 17 triples and also ranked among Pacific Coast League leaders with 18 outfield assists, 51 extra-base hits and 67 walks. His .304 average ranked seventh in the Houston system and his 75 RBIs were third-best among all Astro minor league players.

BILLY WAGNER (LHP), 24, reached the majors for the first time in September 1995 after being selected by the Astros in the first round of the 1993 June draft. He was a Texas League All-Star after going 2-2 with a 2.57 ERA in 12 games. He had 77 strikeouts in 70.0 innings and allowed only 6.3 hits per nine innings. After a promotion to Tucson, he had a 5-3 mark with a 3.18 ERA in 13 starts. He has averaged 10.8 strikeouts per nine innings in his pro career.

DONNE WALL (RHP), 28, became professional baseball's first 20-game winner of 1995 when he beat St. Louis, 7-3, in the Astrodome on September 23. Earned Player of the Year honors in the Pacific Coast League after going 17-6 with a 3.30 ERA in 28 starts. He led the league in wins, ERA, innings and strikeouts. He was the first pitcher to win PCL Player of the Year honors since 1987. He compiled a 3-1 record in six games with Houston.

for Los Angeles—

KARIM GARCIA (OF), 19, ranked among the Pacific Coast League leaders in eight offensive categories while playing at Albuquerque last season, including first in total bases (257) and second in RBIs (90). He was named The Sporting News Minor League Player of the Year.

TODD HOLLANDSWORTH (OF), 23, batted .233 (24-for-103) with two doubles, five home runs and 13 RBIs in 41 games. He was troubled by a few key injuries last season, including a fractured hamate bone and a fractured right thumb.

CHAN HO PARK (RHP), 22, went 6-7 with a 4.91 ERA and a club-high 101 strikeouts at Class AAA Albuquerque. His 110 innings pitched was the third highest on the Dukes team.

for Montreal—

DEREK AUCOIN (RHP), 25, pitched for two pennant-winning teams in 1995—at AAA Ottawa in the International League and Mesa in the Arizona Fall League. The 6-7, 235-pound Quebec-born reliever spent the regular season at AA Harrisburg but joined AAA Lynx in time for the International League playoffs (he was the winning pitcher in the clinching game against Norfolk for the league championship). He tied for the Arizona Fall League lead in saves at Mesa and was voted the AFL's top pitching prospect by league managers.

YAMIL BENITEZ (OF), 23, has the power and speed to be a 20-20 player in the big leagues. He led the AAA Ottawa Lynx in extra-base hits (48, 4th in the International League), at-bats (474), runs (66), doubles (24) and triples (6). He finished third in the Expos' minor league system in home runs and RBIs and was fifth in the I.L. with 217 total bases. He had 39 impressive September at-bats with the Expos. The first of his two home runs was off Pete Schourek, which gave him three hits in his first three at-bats in the majors.

UGUETH URBINA (RHP), 22, was 6-2 with a 3.04 ERA at AAA Ottawa and won six straight decisions (in 10 starts) from May 20 through July 7. He set a team record with a streak of 26.1 scoreless innings. He threw a one-hitter on June 21 at Norfolk, retiring the last 21 batters he faced. He was selected Ottawa's Player of the Month and the Expos organization's Pitcher of the Month in June (4-0, 0.74 ERA). He was recalled twice by the Expos and got a win in his first start. He pitched in seven games in the big leagues—four starts—and was 2-2. Bothered by a sore shoulder, he was successfully scoped in September.

for New York—

PAUL WILSON (RHP), 23, led all minor league pitchers last season with 194 strikeouts in 186.2 innings . . . Had a combined 11-6 record with Class AA Binghamton of the Eastern League and Class AAA Norfolk of the International League . . . A former All-America at Florida State, Wilson was the No. 1 pick in the country in the June 1994 free-agent draft.

REY ORDONEZ (SS), 24, paced Norfolk of the International League in games (125), at-bats (439) and tied for the team lead in doubles (21) . . . Finished fourth on the team with 50 RBIs and hit .214 . . . Ordonez defected from the Cuban National Team after the World University Games in Buffalo, N.Y., in July 1993 and was acquired by the Mets in a lottery of Cuban defectors on October 29, 1993.

JAY PAYTON (OF), 24, was named Most Valuable Player of the Eastern League in 1995 . . . Playing for Binghamton, he led the league with a .345 batting average and had 20 doubles, three triples, 14 homers, 54 RBIs and 16 stolen bases . . . Promoted to Norfolk of the International League on July 3 . . . In 50 games there, he hit .240 with 11 doubles, four triples, four homers, 30 RBIs and 11 stolen bases . . . Earned All-America honors at Georgia Tech . . . Was the 29th overall pick in the June 1994 free-agent draft.

ALEX OCHOA (OF), 24, was selected to the International League All-Star team in 1995 for his play with the Orioles' Rochester team and the Mets' Norfolk club . . . For the two teams, he hit a combined .283 (130-for-459) with 24 doubles, four triples, 10 homers, 61 RBIs and 24 stolen bases . . . Made nine starts for New York after his recall from Norfolk on September 15 . . . Acquired by the Mets on July 28, 1995 with outfielder Damon Buford from the Orioles in exchange for infielder/outfielder Bobby Bonilla and a player to be named later (pitcher Jimmy Williams).

for Philadelphia

HOWARD BATTLE (3B), 24, was International League All-Star Game MVP in 1995 while playing at Syracuse . . . Also was the league's Player of the Week May 22-28 (.444, 8-for-18, one home run, 2 RBIs) . . . Voted the best defensive third baseman in Baseball's America's Tools of the Trade evaluation . . . Made major league debut on September 5 and appeared in nine games for Toronto . . . Has decent power and good speed to go along with a strong throwing arm . . . Has reached 20-home run mark and 80-plus RBIs twice in the minors . . . In '94 at Class AAA Syracuse, he stole 26 bases in 28 attempts . . . Acquired by the Phillies on December 6 as part of a trade that sent pitcher Paul Quantrill to Toronto.

KEVIN JORDAN (2B), 26, was a Class AAA All-Star at Scranton/Wilkes-Barre after hitting .310 with 29 doubles, five home runs and 60 RBIs and finishing second in the International League in fielding percentage (.976) . . . Was named the Phillies' Minor League Player of the Month for July (.347, 19 RBIs) . . . Called up August 8 and made his major league debut that night . . . Hit two home runs with six RBIs in 24 games for the Phillies . . . 6-1, 194 pounds . . . Has good, productive bat, especially for his position . . . Has good power.

GENE SCHALL (1B-OF), 25, while playing at Scranton/Wilkes-Barre, he finished second in the International League in on-base percentage (.415), third in slugging percentage (.528) and fifth in average (.317) . . . Called up to the Phillies for two weeks in June, hitting .417 in five games before being sent back down . . . Recalled on August 31 and started the Phils' last 10 games in place of an injured Gregg Jefferies . . . Was Phillies Minor League Player of the Year in '94 (.285, 35 doubles, 16 homers, 89 RBIs) . . . Has potential to be a legitimate power hitter . . . Improved defense at first base . . . Also learned to play left field in 1995.

B.J. WALLACE (LHP), 24, shoulder surgery has kept him sidelined since May 1994 . . . Expos' first pick in the 1992 June draft and third pick overall . . . Member of the 1992 U.S. Olympic team in Barcelona (1-1, 2.87 ERA) . . . In first pro season in '93, he was 11-8 with a 3.28 ERA for Class A West Palm Beach and ranked in the top 10 in wins, ERA and strikeouts (137) . . . Promoted to Class AA Harrisburg in '94, but season was cut short due to shoulder injury . . . 21-9 in three-year career at Mississippi State with 271 strikeouts in 265 innings . . . Selected by Phillies in the 1995 Rule 5 draft.

for Pittsburgh—

TREY BEAMON (OF), 21, ranked third in the Pacific Coast League with a .334 batting average in 1995. He led Calgary in hitting and was named the club's Most Valuable Player. The Pirates' second-round supplemental selection in the 1992 June draft, Beamon led the Southern League with a .323 average in 1994 and has a career average of .317 in four minor league seasons.

JASON KENDALL (C), 21, the Pirates' first-round selection (23rd overall) in the 1992 June draft, Kendall was named the Southern League's Most Valuable Player in 1995. He set club records with a .326 batting average and 87 runs scored. In addition, Jason set a career high with eight home runs and his 140 hits tied the club record. Behind the plate, he threw out 24 of 59 (41 percent) of runners attempting to steal. His father, Fred, played 12 seasons in the major leagues with San Diego, Cleveland and Boston.

MATT RYAN (RHP), 23, saved 26 games in 1995 which tied him for second in the Southern League and established a single-season club record for Carolina. Ryan was Pittsburgh's 25th-round selection in the 1993 June draft. He has saved a total of 46 games the past two seasons and has posted a career ERA of 1.67 in 133 minor league games.

for St. Louis

ALAN BENES (RHP), 24, missed a substantial portion of the 1995 season due to soreness in his right forearm. He recovered in time to throw a pair of three-hit complete games in the postseason, helping to lead Louisville to the American Association championship. Promoted to St. Louis, Benes made three starts in September. He pitched in the Arizona Fall League and was the league's top pitcher, leading the league in wins (six), ERA (1.78) and strikeouts (62).

MIKE GULAN (3B), 25, was named the Cardinals' minor league player of the year after finishing among the organization's leaders in homers, RBIs, doubles, runs and hits. He started the year at Class AA Arkansas, where he batted .314 with 12 homers and 48 RBIs in 64 games. Promoted to Class AAA Louisville, he batted .236 with five homers in 58 games there.

for San Diego

MARC KROON (RHP), 22, struck out 123 batters in 115.0 innings at Double-A Memphis, where he was used as both a starter and as a reliever before being recalled by the Padres July 7. He lost in his Major League debut the following day against Houston but pitched effectively in his second outing two days later.

JOEY LONG (LHP), 25, split last season between Double-A Memphis and Triple-A Las Vegas and was used exclusively out of the bullpen. In the Southern League playoffs for Memphis, he pitched 2.0 scoreless innings and struck out three batters. In '94, he averaged a strikeout per inning at Single-A Rancho Cucamonga.

for San Francisco

RICH AURILIA (IF), 24, rose through the ranks in his first year in the Giants' organization, seeing action at three different levels. Named the starting shortstop on the Texas League mid-season All-Star team with Shreveport. Played 71 games at shortstop for Phoenix and committed just nine errors for a .975 fielding percentage. Started the final four games of the season at Colorado and went 9-for-15 (.600) with two homers and 4 RBIs.

DOUG CREEK (LHP), 26, acquired in an off-season trade, Creek enjoyed a banner year in the Cardinals' farm system in 1995 with a combined record of 7-4 and 3.05 ERA at Arkansas and Louisville. In 52 relief appearances, he muzzled minor league foes to the tune of 44 hits and 79 strikeouts in only 65.0 innings. He ranked first in strikeouts per nine innings (13.11) and third in batting average against (.198) among Texas League relievers while at Arkansas. His .182 average-against figure with Louisville ranked second in the American Association. A September call-up by the Cardinals last year, he was nearly flawless in the first major league action of his career: 0-0 record, 0.00 ERA, two hits, 10 strikeouts and three walks over 6.2 innings and six appearances.

SHAWN ESTES (RHP), 22, made the formidable climb from Class A to the majors last year. Compiled a 7-1 mark with a 2.14 ERA over 18 appearances (including one playoff start) for four minor league clubs last year. Held opponents to a .186 average (60-for-322) while yielding only four home runs in 92.1 innings of work.

BILLY WAGNER

UGUETH URBINA

PAUL WILSON

JASON KENDALL

ALAN BENES

1996 NATIONAL LEAGUE UMPIRES

DIRECTOR OF UMPIRE SUPERVISION—Ed Vargo

36 WALLY BELL
Born January 10, 1965, in Ravenna, OH . . . Resides in Canfield, OH . . . 6'2" . . . 225 lbs . . . Single . . . Worked first National League game June 16, 1992 . . . Became regular member of N.L. staff in April, 1993 . . . Previously umpired in NY-Penn League, South Atlantic League, Carolina League, Southern League, Dominican Republic League, Triple Alliance and International League . . . Hobbies include golf and fishing.

34 GREGORY BONIN
Born June 15, 1955 in Lafayette, LA . . . Resides in Broussard, LA. . . . 5'10" . . . 160 lbs . . . Single . . . Two children, Samuel and Benjamin . . . Played Colt League and American Legion Baseball . . . Graduate of Southwestern Louisiana University . . . Worked first National League game on April 25, 1984 . . . Became regular member of N.L. staff in April, 1986 . . . Previously umpired in Florida State League, Texas League, International League, Colombian Winter League, and Dominican Republic Winter League . . . Works in family business during off-season . . . Hobbies include fishing, golf and hunting.

40 GERALD JOSEPH (JERRY) CRAWFORD
Born August 13, 1947 in Philadelphia, PA . . . Resides in Havertown, PA . . . 6' . . . 194 lbs . . . Married Carol Alessi February 24, 1968 . . . Two children, Christopher and Alyson . . . Played American Legion and Connie Mack baseball . . . Worked first National League game in 1975 . . . Became regular member of N.L. staff May 15, 1976 . . . Previously umpired in Florida State League, Carolina League, Eastern League and International League . . . Hobbies include HO trains and music.

35 GARY RICHARD DARLING
Born October 9, 1957 in San Francisco, CA . . . Resides in Phoenix, AZ . . . 6'3" . . . 208 lbs . . . Married Cheryl Hellmann December 19, 1987 . . . Two children, Cameron and Courtney . . . Graduated from Cosumnes River Junior College . . . Played high school, college and American Legion baseball . . . Worked first National League game on June 6, 1986 . . . Became regular member of N.L. staff in April 1988 . . . Previously umpired in Northwest League. California League, Arizona Instructional League, Colombian Winter League, Puerto Rico Winter League and Pacific Coast League . . . Hobbies include golf and basketball.

31 ROBERT ALLAN (BOB) DAVIDSON
Born August 3, 1952 in Chicago, Ill . . . Resides in Littleton, CO . . . 6'2" . . . 224 lbs . . . Married Denise Nesheim September 27, 1980 . . . Two children, Amber Adelle and Andrea Lynn . . . Attended University of Minnesota, where he played baseball . . . Also played high school baseball . . . Worked first National League game May 31, 1982 . . . Became regular member of N.L. staff for 1983 season . . . Previously umpired in Midwest League, Florida State League, Florida Instructional League, Southern League, Dominican Republic Winter League and the American Association . . . During off-season Bob is a high school basketball official.

12 GERALD (GERRY) DAVIS
Born February 22, 1953 in St. Louis, MO . . . Resides in Appleton, WI . . . 6'2" . . . 236 lbs . . . Married Lynn Mentzel October 9, 1980 . . . One child, Jeremy Joseph . . . Played semi-pro baseball as a pitcher, first baseman in St. Louis . . . Worked first National League game June 9, 1982 . . . Became regular member of staff for 1985 season . . . Previously umpired in Midwest League, Eastern League, American Association, Florida Instructional League, and Puerto Rico Winter League . . . During the off-season Gerry coaches the University of Wisconsin-Fox Valley Junior College basketball team . . . His hobby is golf.

32 DANA ANDREW DeMUTH
Born May 30, 1956 in Fremont, OH . . . Resides in Gilbert, AZ . . . 6' . . . 216 lbs . . . Married Marjorie Whitaker December 2, 1978 . . . One child, Dane . . . Worked first National League game June 3, 1983 . . . Became a regular member of the N.L. staff in April, 1985 . . . Previously umpired in California League, Texas League, and Pacific Coast League . . . Also worked in Colombia and Dominican Republic Winter League.

6 BRUCE NEAL FROEMMING*
Born September 28, 1939 in Milwaukee, WI . . . Resides in Vero Beach, FL . . . 5'8" . . . 238 lbs . . . Married Rose Marie Loch May 2, 1959 . . . Two children, Kevin and Steven . . . Played high school and semi-pro baseball . . . Worked first National League game in April, 1971, when he became regular member of the staff . . . Previously umpired in Nebraska State League, Midwest League, Northern League, Northwest League, Texas League and Pacific Coast League . . . Began umpiring professionally when he was 18 years old, which made him the youngest professional umpire . . . Partner in umpire school in Cocoa, Fla . . . His hobby is golf.

9 BRIAN GORMAN
Born June 11, 1959, in Whitestone, NY . . . Resides in Camarillo, CA . . . 6'1" . . . 190 lbs . . . Married Marsha Traeger November 3, 1990 . . . Worked first National League game April 24, 1991 . . . Became regular member os staff in April, 1993 . . . Previously umpired in NY-Penn League, Florida State League, Southern League Triple Alliance and American Association.

7 ERIC EUGENE GREGG
Born May 18, 1951 in Philadelphia, PA . . . Resides in Philadelphia . . . 6'3" . . . 325 lbs . . . Married Ramona Camilo December 31, 1974 . . . Four children, Eric, Kevin, Ashley and Jamie . . . Played high school baseball . . . Worked first National League game September 26, 1975 . . . Became regular member of N.L. staff in 1978 . . . Previously umpired in New York-Penn League, Florida State League, Eastern League, Dominican Republic League and Pacific Coast League.

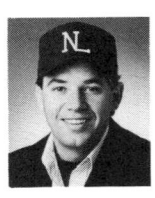

20 THOMAS FRANCIS (TOM) HALLION
Born September 5, 1956 in Saugerties, NY . . . Resides in Louisville, KY . . . 5'10" . . . 168 lbs . . . Married Elizabeth Carnright September 11, 1983 . . . Three children, Corey, Kyle and Jacob . . . Lettered in football, basketball and baseball in high school . . . Attended University of Buffalo . . . Worked first National League game on June 10, 1985 . . . Became regular member of N.L. staff in April, 1986 . . . Previously umpired in New York-Penn League, Carolina League, Eastern League and American Association . . . Hobbies include golf, tennis and antiques.

5 ANGEL HERNANDEZ
Born August 26, 1961 in Havana, Cuba . . . Resides in Hollywood, FL . . . 6'2" . . . 200 lbs . . . Married Mireya Lopez November 10, 1984 . . . Two children, Jennifer and Melissa . . . Played high school baseball . . . Worked first National League game May 23, 1991 . . . Became regular member of N.L. staff in April, 1993 . . . Previously umpired in Florida State League, Carolina League, Southern League Venezuelan League, Florida Instructional League, Triple Alliance and American Association . . . Hobbies include hunting, motorcycles and Khoury League youth baseball and Pony League.

4 MARK HIRSCHBECK
Born September 22, 1960 in Bridgeport, CT . . . Resides in Stratford, CT . . . 5'9" . . . 189 lbs . . . Married Mary Frances Mallon November 20, 1982 . . . Four children, Jaclyn, Nikki, Monica and Mark, Jr. . . . Played football in high school . . . Worked first National League game on June 19, 1987 . . . Became regular member of N.L. staff in April, 1988 . . . Previously umpired in Gulf Coast League, Florida State League, Midwest League, Eastern League, Dominican Republic League, Florida Instructional League and American Association . . . Hobbies include hunting, fishing and golf.

29 WILLIAM JOHN (BILL) HOHN
Born June 29, 1955 in Butler, PA . . . Resides in Collegeville, PA . . . 6' . . . 180 lbs . . . Married Grace Grippo December 26, 1983 . . . One child, Meredith . . . Played high school and amateur baseball . . . Worked first National League game on May 29, 1987 . . . Became regular member of N.L. staff in April, 1989 . . . Previously umpired in Gulf Coast League, Florida Instructional League, Florida State League, Southern League, Puerto Rico Winter League and Pacific Coast League . . . Hobbies include hunting, archery and reading.

NATIONAL LEAGUE UMPIRES

8 JEFFREY KELLOGG
Born August 29, 1961, in Coldwater, MI... Resides in Ypsilanti Township, MI... 6'... 190 lbs... Married Roxine Tackett September 14, 1990... One child, Trenton... Received Bachelor of Science degree in criminal justice from Ferris State... Played high school football, baseball and participated in wrestling... Worked first National League game June 11, 1991... Became regular member of N.L. staff in April, 1993... Previously umpired in Appalachian League, Midwest League, Eastern League, Triple Alliance, Florida Instructional League and International League... Hobbies include golf, weight training and aerobics.

24 JERRY BLAKE LAYNE
Born September 28, 1958 in Pikeville, KY... Resides in Winter Haven, FL... 6'4"... 249 lbs... Married Jacqueline Heck September 19, 1982... Two children, Brittany and Monica... Became regular member of N.L. staff in April, 1989... Previously umpired in Appalachian League, Florida State League, Florida Instructional League, Southern League and Pacific Coast League... Hobbies include golf.

30 RANDALL GILBERT (RANDY) MARSH
Born April 8, 1949 in Covington, KY... Resides in Edgewood, KY... 6'... 210 lbs... Married Roxanne McFarland October 7, 1978... One child, Lauren... Attended University of Kentucky... Worked first National League game in May, 1981... Became regular member of N.L. staff for 1982 season... Previously umpired in Appalachian League, Florida State League, Eastern League, Florida Instructional League, Dominican Republic League and Pacific Coast League... Was Umpire-in-Chief of Pacific Coast League... Hobbies include photography and golf.

10 JOHN PATRICK McSHERRY*
Born September 11, 1944 in New York, NY... Resides in Dobbs Ferry, NY... 6'2½"... 328 lbs... Single... Attended St. John's University... Umpired sandlot and high school baseball... Worked first National League game June 1, 1971, when he became regular member of staff... Previously umpired in Carolina League, International League and Florida Instructional League.

11 EDWARD MICHAEL (ED) MONTAGUE
Born November 3, 1948 in San Francisco, CA... Resides in San Mateo, CA... 5'10"... 184 lbs... Married Marcia Simons October 14, 1978... Three children, Edward Michael, Brooke and Brett... Attended San Francisco City College, where he played baseball... Worked first National League games last two days of 1974 season... Became regular member of N.L. staff in April, 1976... Previously umpired in California League, Arizona Instructional League, Pacific Coast League and Puerto Rico Winter League... Hobbies include magic, guitar, running, golf and fitness.

13 LARRY PONCINO
Born February 3, 1957, in Los Angeles, CA... Resides in Tucson, AZ... 5'10"... 210 lbs... Married Jo Ann Thibert October 24, 1992... Worked first National League game July 11, 1985... Became regular member of staff in April, 1993... Previously umpired in California League, Texas League, Dominican Republic Winter League and Pacific Coast League... Hobbies include golf and Ditto's.

14 FRANK VICTOR PULLI*
Born March 22, 1935 in Easton, PA... Resides in Palm Harbor, FL... 5'11"... 194 lbs... Married Kim Hale December 29, 1984... Six children, Vicky, Michelle, Frank, Jr., Michael, Candice and Nikki... Played high school baseball and basketball... Worked first National League game in April, 1972, when he became regular member of staff... Previously umpired in Midwest League, Eastern League and International League.

15 JAMES EDWARD (JIM) QUICK*
Born September 6, 1943 in Sacramento, CA... Resides in Scottsdale, AZ... 6'... 229 lbs... Married Sandra Smith July 6, 1985... Three children, Kresten, Kimberly and Kara... Has AA degree from Yuba Junior College, where he played football and baseball... Worked first National League game in August, 1974... Became regular member of N.L. staff in 1976... Previously umpired in Northwest League, California League, Texas League and Pacific Coast League... During off-season Jim helps his wife in their group tour business... Hobbies include golf, skiing and hunting.

23 EDWARD RAPUANO, JR.
Born September 30, 1957 in New Haven, CT... Resides in North Haven, CT... 5'10"... 185 lbs... Married Valerie Funaro October 12, 1984... Three children, Eddie III, Rosalie Ann and Nicholas... Graduate of Technical Careers Institute... Played high school baseball... Worked first National League game May 11, 1990... Became regular member of N.L. staff April 8, 1991... Previously umpired in NY-Penn League, Florida State League, Southern League and Triple Alliance... Hobbies include youth basketball and golf.

18 CHARLES HAROLD RELIFORD
Born September 19, 1956 in Ashland, KY... Resides in Tampa, FL... 5'9"... 180 lbs... Single... Attended University of Kentucky and Ohio University... Worked first National League game May 29, 1989... Became regular member of N.L. staff April 8, 1991... Previously umpired in Appalachian League, Florida State League, Southern League, American Association and Triple Alliance... In the off-season Charlie is a high school basketball referee.

27 THOMAS STEVEN (STEVE) RIPPLEY
Born May 2, 1954 in St. Petersburg, FL... Resides in Seminole, FL... 6'... 196 lbs... Married Marie Allen November 5, 1994... One child, Tiffany Marie... Lettered in football, basketball and baseball in high school... Worked first National League game on May 30, 1983... Became regular member of N.L. staff for 1984 season... Previously umpired in Gulf Coast League, Florida State League, Eastern League, Southern League, American Association, Dominican Republic Winter League, and Puerto Rico Winter League... Steve's hobbies include golf, racquetball and running.

17 PAUL EDWARD RUNGE*
Born October 20, 1940 in St. Catharines, Ontario, Canada... Resides in El Cajon, CA... 6'1"... 206 lbs... Married Anastasia Mouzas October 17, 1965... Two children, Brian and Renee... Graduate of Arizona State University... Played minor league ball for Houston and California... Worked first National League game in September, 1973... Became regular member of N.L. umpire staff in April, 1974... Previously umpired in California League, Eastern League and Pacific Coast League... During off-season Paul is a real estate broker in El Cajon... Hobbies include golf, bowling, racquetball, fishing, swimming and camping.

19 TERRY ANTHONY TATA*
Born April 24, 1940 in Waterbury, CT... Resides in Cheshire, CT... 5'10"... 200 lbs... Married Janice Membrino October 5, 1973... One child, Lisa... Was very active in amateur sports, baseball, basketball and football on sandlot level... Worked first National League game April 5, 1973, when he became regular member of staff... Previously umpired in Midwest League, Northern League, Texas League and International League... Hobbies include reading, aerobics, wood splitting and he is a fine wine collector.

28 LARRY VANOVER
Born August 22, 1955, in Owensboro, KY... Resides in Antioch, TN... 6'... 200 lbs... Married Dianne Jo Baird September 23, 1989... Worked first National League game June 24, 1991... Became regular member of staff in April, 1993... Previously umpired in South Atlantic League, Midwest League, Southern League, Venezuelan Winter League, Pacific Coast League and American Association.

NATIONAL LEAGUE UMPIRES

21 HARRY HUNTER WENDELSTEDT, JR*
Born July 27, 1938 in Baltimore, MD . . . Resides in Ormond Beach, FL . . . 6'2" . . . 248 lbs . . . Single . . . Two children, Harry, III and Amy . . . Attended Essex Community College and University of Maryland where he played basketball and baseball . . . Also played high school and American Legion baseball and professional soccer . . . Became regular member of N.L. umpire staff in April, 1966 . . . Previously umpired in Georgia-Florida League, Northwest League, Texas League and International League . . . During off-season Harry is owner-operator of umpire school in Florida . . . Served four terms as President of Major League Umpire Association . . . Hobbies include fishing.

22 JOSEPH HENRY (JOE) WEST
Born October 31, 1952 in Asheville, NC . . . Resides in Ft. Lauderdale, FL and Kilby Island, NC . . . 6'1" . . . 275 lbs . . . Married Jean Jo Mason December 25, 1988 . . . Quarterbacked Elon College to three conference championships . . . Elected to Elon Sports Hall of Fame in '86 . . . Worked first National League game in September, 1976 . . . Became regular member of N.L. staff in April, 1978 . . . Previously umpired in Western Carolinas League, Carolina League, Southern League, American Association and Puerto Rico Winter League . . . Invented patented hard shell chest protector worn by a majority of Major League umpires . . . Singer and songwriter . . . Has performed at Grand Ole Opry . . . Does charity work for Adam Walsh Children's Foundation.

25 CHARLES HERMAN (CHARLIE) WILLIAMS
Born December 20, 1943, in Denver, CO . . . Resides in Chicago, IL . . . 5'9" . . . 211 lbs . . . Married Diana Gilkes June 20, 1979 . . . Two children, Charles and Gaberial . . . Attended Long Beach City College and Cal State, Los Angeles . . . Worked first National League game April 26, 1978 . . . Became regular member of N.L. staff for 1982 season . . . Previously umpired in California League, Texas League and Pacific Coast League . . . During the off-season Charlie is a salesman . . . His hobbies include golf, bowling and reading.

33 MICHAEL JOHN (MIKE) WINTERS
Born November 19, 1958, in Oceanside, CA . . . Resides in Poway, CA . . . 6' . . . 193 lbs . . . Married Cindy Livingston January 7, 1989 . . . Two children, Sean and Erin . . . Received associate degree from San Diego Mesa College . . . Also attended San Diego State . . . Worked first National League game July 9, 1988 . . . Became regular member of NL staff April 9, 1990 . . . Previously umpired in Northwest League, California League, Arizona Instructional League, Texas League, Dominican Republic Winter League and Pacific Coast League . . . Hobbies include golf and racquetball.

*Crew Chief

ED VARGO—Begins his 10th year as Director of Umpire Supervision. Umpired in the NL from 1960-1983. Became an umpire consultant in 1984. Ed worked 4 All-Star Games, 4 League Championships and 4 World Series.

RETIRED UNIFORM NUMBERS
In 1995 the National League retired the uniform numbers of the three National League umpires who are members of the Hall of Fame.
- #1—Bill Klem, inducted 1953
- #2—Jocko Conlan, inducted 1974
- #3—Al Barlick, inducted 1989

In 1996 the following minor league umpires will be used by the National League in spring training and the regular season as the need arises. They are Ron Barnes, Mark Barron, C.B. Bucknor, Kerwin Danley, Bruce Dreckman, Brian Gibbons, Jerry Meals, Paul Nauert, Scott Potter and Rich Rieker.

UMPIRES' UNIFORMS
National League umpires, beginning with the 1996 season, will be sporting new uniforms and caps, made by Logo Athletic, Inc. and New Era Cap Company, respectively. The new navy caps will feature an N.L. insignia superimposed over a red "N". The umpires wear gray slacks, navy blue blazers, navy blue short-sleeve collared shirts, or navy blue full turtlenecks with an embroidered National League logo on the left neck. The home plate and base shirts will feature two color sleeve stripes; a knit collar with two color striping; and a two button placket. The umpires are also issued: navy blue ribbed crew neck sweaters; navy blue pullover windbreaker-jackets featuring a half zip front, striped knit rib cuffs and bottom band. National League logos are worn on the left chest of the sweaters and windbreakers; and on the left chest pocket of the blazers, home plate and base shirts. Umpire's numbers will be worn on the right sleeves of shirts, blazers, windbreakers and sweaters.

In Memoriam
ALBERT J. BARLICK
1915-1995

UMPIRES' SERVICE

	Years Service Thru 1995	All-Star Games	Division Series	Championship Series	World Series
Harry Wendelstedt	30	1968, '76, '83, '92	1995	1970, '72, '77, '81, '82, '84, '88, '90	1973, '80, '86, '91, '95
Bruce Froemming	25	1975, '86	1995	1973, '77, '80, '82, '85, '89, '91, '93	1976, '84, '88, '95
John McSherry	25	1975, '82, '91	1995	1974, '78, '83, '85, '88, '90, '92	1977, '87
Frank Pulli	24	1977, '88	1995	1975, '79, '84, '86, '91, '93	1978, '83, '90, '95
Terry Tata	23	1978, '88	1995	1976, '80, '83, '85, '89, '93	1979, '87, '91
Paul Runge	22	1978, '86, '94	—	1977, '81, '82, '85, '88, '90, '95	1979, '84, '89, '93
Jim Quick	20	1981, '83, '91	—	1979, '87, '89, '93, '95	1985, '90
Ed Montague	20	1982, '90	1995	1979, '84, '87, '92	1986, '91
Jerry Crawford	19	1989	—	1980, '83, '85, '90, '93, '95	1988, '92
Eric Gregg	18½	1986	1995	1981, '87, '91	1989
Joe West	18	1987	1995	1981, '86, '88, '93	1992
Charlie Williams	15	1985, '95	—	1989	1993
Randy Marsh	14	1985, '88	—	1989, '92, '95	1990
Bob Davidson	14	1987, '93	1995	1988, '91	1992
Steve Rippley	12½	1990	—	1992	—
Gerry Davis	12	1989	—	1990, '92, '95	—
Dana DeMuth	12	1990	—	1991, '95	1993
Greg Bonin	10	1991	—	—	—
Tom Hallion	10	1992	—	—	—
Gary Darling	9	1993	1995	1992	—
Mark Hirschbeck	8	1993	—	—	—
Bill Hohn	7	1994	—	—	—
Jerry Layne	7	1994	1995	—	—
Mike Winters	6	1995	—	—	—
Charlie Reliford	6	—	1995	—	—
Ed Rapuano	5½	1995	—	—	—
Brian Gorman	4	—	—	—	—
Larry Poncino	4	—	—	—	—
Jeffrey Kellogg	3½	—	—	—	—
Wally Bell	3	—	—	—	—
Angel Hernandez	3	—	—	—	—
Larry Vanover	3	—	—	—	—

ALL-STAR GAME SCORES

1933	AL 4	NL 2
1934	AL 9	NL 7
1935	AL 4	NL 3
1936	NL 4	AL 3
1937	AL 8	NL 3
1938	NL 4	AL 1
1939	AL 3	NL 1
1940	NL 4	AL 0
1941	AL 7	NL 5
1942	AL 3	NL 1
1943	AL 5	NL 3
1944	NL 7	AL 1
1946	AL 12	NL 0
1947	AL 2	NL 1
1948	AL 5	NL 2
1949	AL 11	NL 7
1950	NL 4	AL 3
1951	NL 8	AL 3
1952	NL 3	AL 2
1953	NL 5	AL 1
1954	AL 11	NL 9
1955	NL 6	AL 5
1956	NL 7	AL 3
1957	AL 6	NL 5
1958	AL 4	NL 3
1959	NL 5	AL 4
1959	AL 5	NL 3
1960	NL 5	AL 3
1960	NL 6	AL 0
1961	NL 5	AL 4
1961	NL 1	AL 1
1962	NL 3	AL 1
1962	AL 9	NL 4
1963	NL 5	AL 3
1964	NL 7	AL 4
1965	NL 6	AL 5
1966	NL 2	AL 1
1967	NL 2	AL 1
1968	NL 1	AL 0
1969	NL 9	AL 3
1970	NL 5	AL 4
1971	AL 6	NL 4
1972	NL 4	AL 3
1973	NL 7	AL 1
1974	NL 7	AL 2
1975	NL 6	AL 3
1976	NL 7	AL 1
1977	NL 7	AL 5
1978	NL 7	AL 3
1979	NL 7	AL 6
1980	NL 4	AL 2
1981	NL 5	AL 4
1982	NL 4	AL 1
1983	AL 13	NL 3
1984	NL 3	AL 1
1985	NL 6	AL 1
1986	AL 3	NL 2
1987	NL 2	AL 0
1988	AL 2	NL 1
1989	AL 5	NL 3
1990	AL 2	NL 0
1991	AL 4	NL 2
1992	AL 13	NL 6
1993	AL 9	NL 3
1994	NL 8	AL 7
1995	NL 3	AL 2

ALL-STAR MVP's

1962 (1)	Maury Wills, Los Angeles	N.L.
1962 (2)	Leon Wagner, Los Angeles	A.L.
1963	Willie Mays, San Francisco	N.L.
1964	Johnny Callison, Philadelphia	N.L.
1965	Juan Marichal, San Francisco	N.L.
1966	Brooks Robinson, Baltimore	A.L.
1967	Tony Perez, Cincinnati	N.L.
1968	Willie Mays, San Francisco	N.L.
1969	Willie McCovey, San Francisco	N.L.
1970	Carl Yastrzemski, Boston	A.L.
1971	Frank Robinson, Baltimore	A.L.
1972	Joe Morgan, Cincinnati	N.L.
1973	Bobby Bonds, San Francisco	N.L.
1974	Steve Garvey, Los Angeles	N.L.
1975	Bill Matlock, Chicago	N.L.
	Jon Matlack, New York	N.L.
1976	George Foster, Cincinnati	N.L.
1977	Don Sutton, Los Angeles	N.L.
1978	Steve Garvey, Los Angeles	N.L.
1979	Dave Parker, Pittsburgh	N.L.
1980	Ken Griffey Sr., Cincinnati	N.L.
1981	Gary Carter, Montreal	N.L.
1982	Dave Concepcion, Cincinnati	N.L.
1983	Fred Lynn, California	A.L.
1984	Gary Carter, Montreal	N.L.
1985	LaMarr Hoyt, San Diego	N.L.
1986	Roger Clemens, Boston	A.L.
1987	Tim Raines, Montreal	N.L.
1988	Terry Steinbach, Oakland	A.L.
1989	Bo Jackson, Kansas City	A.L.
1990	Julio Franco, Texas	A.L.
1991	Cal Ripken Jr., Baltimore	A.L.
1992	Ken Griffey Jr., Seattle	A.L.
1993	Kirby Puckett, Minnesota	A.L.
1994	Fred McGriff, Atlanta	N.L.
1995	Jeff Conine, Florida	N.L.

1995 NATIONAL LEAGUE ALL-STARS BY CLUB

Atlanta (2)
Greg Maddux
Fred McGriff*

Chicago (3)
Mark Grace
Randy Myers
Sammy Sosa

Cincinnati (3)
Ron Gant
Barry Larkin
Reggie Sanders

Colorado (2)
Dante Bichette
Vinny Castilla

Florida (1)
Jeff Conine

Houston (1)
Craig Biggio*

Los Angeles (5)
Raul Mondesi
Hideo Nomo
Jose Offerman
Mike Piazza*
Todd Worrell

Montreal (1)
Carlos Perez

New York (1)
Bobby Bonilla

Philadelphia (5)
Darren Daulton*
Lenny Dykstra*
Tyler Green
Mickey Morandini
Heathcliff Slocumb

Pittsburgh (1)
Denny Neagle

St. Louis (2)
Tom Henke
Ozzie Smith*†

San Diego (1)
Tony Gwynn*

San Francisco (2)
Barry Bonds
Matt Williams*†

*Elected starter
†Injured, unable to play

The 1996 All-Star Game will be played on Tuesday, July 9, at Veterans Stadium in Philadelphia.

The 1996 game will be the fourth All-Star Game played in Philadelphia. The previous Midsummer Classics in Philadelphia were played at Shibe Park in 1943 and 1952, and at Veterans Stadium in 1976. The 1997 All-Star Game will be played at Jacobs Field in Cleveland.

NATIONAL LEAGUE HONORARY CAPTAINS

1975	Stan Musial
1976	Robin Roberts
1977	Willie Mays
1978	Eddie Mathews
1979	Carl Hubbell
1980	Roy Campanella
1981	Warren Spahn
1982	Duke Snider
1983	Ernie Banks
1984	Willie McCovey
1985	Sandy Koufax
1986	Rusty Staub
1987	Billy Williams
1988	Willie Stargell
1989	Don Drysdale
1990	Juan Marichal
1991	Henry Aaron
1992	Willie Mays
1993	Bob Gibson
1994	Buck Leonard
1995	Ferguson Jenkins

1995 ALL-STAR GAME BOX SCORE

NATIONAL (3)

	AB	R	H	BI
Dykstra, cf	2	0	0	0
Sosa, cf	1	0	0	0
Gwynn, rf	2	0	0	0
Sanders, rf	1	0	0	0
Mondesi, rf	1	0	0	0
Bonds, lf	3	0	0	0
Bichette, lf	1	0	0	0
Piazza, c	3	1	1	1
Daulton, c	0	0	0	0
McGriff, 1b	3	0	0	0
Grace, 1b	0	0	0	0
Gant, dh	2	0	0	0
Conine, ph	1	1	1	1
Larkin, ss	3	0	0	0
Offerman, ss	0	0	0	0
Castilla, 3b	2	0	0	0
Bonilla, 3b	1	0	0	0
Biggio, 2b	2	1	1	1
Morandini, 2b	1	0	0	0
Nomo, p	0	0	0	0
Smiley, p	0	0	0	0
Green, p	0	0	0	0
Neagle, p	0	0	0	0
Perez, p	0	0	0	0
Slocumb, p	0	0	0	0
Henke, p	0	0	0	0
Myers, p	0	0	0	0
TOTALS	29	3	3	3

AMERICAN (2)

	AB	R	H	BI
Lofton, cf	3	0	0	0
Edmonds, ph-cf	1	0	0	0
Baerga, 2b	3	1	3	0
Alomar, pr-2b	1	0	0	0
E. Martinez, dh	3	0	0	0
T. Martinez, ph	1	0	1	0
Thomas, 1b	2	1	1	2
Vaughn, 1b	2	0	0	0
Belle, lf	3	0	0	0
O'Neill, lf	1	0	0	0
Ripken, ss	3	0	2	0
DiSarcina, pr-ss	1	0	0	0
Boggs, 3b	2	0	1	0
Seitzer, ph-3b	2	0	0	0
Puckett, rf	2	0	0	0
Ramirez, ph-rf	0	0	0	0
Rodriguez, c	3	0	0	0
Stanley, c	1	0	0	0
Johnson, p	0	0	0	0
Appier, p	0	0	0	0
D. Martinez, p	0	0	0	0
Rogers, p	0	0	0	0
Ontiveros, p	0	0	0	0
Wells, p	0	0	0	0
Mesa, p	0	0	0	0
TOTALS	34	2	8	2

E—None. LOB—National 0, American 7. 2B—Baerga. HR—Thomas, Biggio, Piazza, Conine. SB—Alomar. CS—Dykstra, Baerga. BB—National 1 (Dykstra); American 2 (Ramirez 2). SO—National 9 (McGriff 2, Bichette, Bonds, Bonilla, Castilla, Gant, Morandini, Sanders); American 8 (Vaughn 2, Belle, Edmonds, Lofton, E. Martinez, Puckett, Rodriguez). T—2:40. A—50,920. Umpires: HP—Durwood Merrill (AL); 1B—Charlie Williams (NL); 2B—Al Clark (AL); 3B—Mike Winters (NL); LF—Ted Hendry (AL); RF—Ed Rapuano (NL). Official scorers—Burt Hawkins, Paul Meyer, Jim Reeves.

NATIONAL

	IP	H	R	ER	BB	SO
Nomo	2	1	0	0	0	3
Smiley	2	2	2	2	0	0
Green	1	2	0	0	0	1
Neagle	1	1	0	0	0	1
Perez	1/3	1	0	0	0	1
Slocumb (W)	1	1	0	0	0	2
Henke	2/3	0	0	0	0	1
Myers (S)	1	0	0	0	1	0

AMERICAN

	IP	H	R	ER	BB	SO
Johnson	2	0	0	0	1	3
Appier	2	0	0	0	0	1
D. Martinez	2	1	1	1	0	0
Rogers	1	1	1	1	0	2
Ontiveros (L)	2/3	2	1	1	0	1
Wells	1/3	0	0	0	0	1
Mesa	1	0	0	0	0	1

National .... 0 0 0 0 0 1 1 1 0—3
American .... 0 0 0 2 0 0 0 0 0—2

1995 NATIONAL LEAGUE DIVISION SERIES

ATLANTA BRAVES

PLAYER	AVG	G	AB	R	H	2B	3B	HR	RBI	BB	SO	SB
Belliard, R.	.000	4	5	1	0	0	0	0	0	0	1	0
Blauser, J.	.000	3	6	0	0	0	0	0	0	1	3	0
Devereaux, M.	.200	4	5	1	1	0	0	0	0	0	1	0
Grissom, M.	.524	4	21	5	11	2	0	3	4	0	3	2
Jones, C.	.389	4	18	4	7	2	0	2	4	2	2	0
Justice, D.	.231	4	13	2	3	0	0	0	5	2	0	0
Klesko, R.	.467	4	15	5	7	1	0	0	1	0	3	0
Lemke, M.	.211	4	19	3	4	1	0	0	1	1	3	0
Lopez, J.	.444	3	9	0	4	0	0	0	3	0	2	0
McGriff, F.	.333	4	18	4	6	0	0	2	6	2	3	0
Mordecai, M.	.667	2	3	1	2	1	0	0	2	0	0	0
O'Brien, C.	.200	2	5	0	1	0	0	0	0	1	1	0
Polonia, L.	.333	3	3	0	1	0	0	0	2	0	1	0
Smith, D.	.667	4	3	0	2	1	0	0	1	0	0	0
Glavine, T.	.333	1	3	0	1	0	0	0	0	0	1	0
Maddux, G.	.167	2	6	1	1	0	0	0	0	0	1	0
Smoltz, J.	.000	1	2	0	0	0	0	0	0	0	0	0
BRAVES	.331	4	154	27	51	8	0	7	24	12	27	3

PITCHER	W	L	ERA	G	GS	CG	IP	H	R	ER	BB	SO
Avery, S.	0	0	13.50	1	0	0	0.2	1	1	1	0	1
Borbon, P.	0	0	0.00	1	0	0	1.0	1	0	0	1	3
Clontz, B.	0	0	0.00	1	0	0	1.1	0	0	0	0	2
Glavine, T.	0	0	2.57	1	1	0	7.0	5	3	2	1	3
Maddux, G.	1	0	4.50	2	2	0	14.0	19	7	7	2	7
McMichael, G.	0	0	6.75	2	0	0	1.1	1	1	1	2	1
Mercker, K.	0	0	0.00	1	0	0	0.1	0	0	0	0	0
Pena, A.	2	0	0.00	3	0	0	3.0	3	0	0	1	2
Smoltz, J.	0	0	7.94	1	1	0	5.2	5	5	5	1	6
Wohlers, M.	0	1	6.75	3	0	0	2.2	6	2	2	2	4
BRAVES	3	1	4.38	4	4	0	37.0	41	19	18	9	29

COLORADO ROCKIES

PLAYER	AVG	G	AB	R	H	2B	3B	HR	RBI	BB	SO	SB
Bates, J.	.250	4	4	0	1	0	0	0	0	0	0	0
Bichette, D.	.588	4	17	6	10	3	0	1	3	1	3	0
Burks, E.	.333	2	6	1	2	1	0	0	2	0	1	0
Castilla, V.	.467	4	15	3	7	1	0	3	6	0	1	0
Galarraga, A.	.278	4	18	1	5	1	0	0	0	0	6	0
Girardi, J.	.125	4	16	0	2	0	0	0	0	0	2	0
Hubbard, T.	.000	3	2	0	0	0	0	0	0	0	1	0
Kingery, M.	.200	4	10	1	2	0	0	0	0	0	1	0
Owens, J.	.000	1	1	0	0	0	0	0	0	0	0	0
Vander Wal, J.	.000	4	4	0	0	0	0	0	0	0	2	0
Walker, L.	.214	4	14	3	3	0	0	1	3	3	4	1
Weiss, W.	.167	4	12	1	2	0	0	0	0	3	3	1
Young, E.	.438	4	16	3	7	1	0	1	2	2	2	1
Painter, L.	.000	2	2	0	0	0	0	0	0	0	1	0
Ritz, K.	.000	2	2	0	0	0	0	0	0	0	0	0
Saberhagen, B.	.000	1	1	0	0	0	0	0	0	0	0	0
Swift, B.	.000	1	3	0	0	0	0	0	0	0	2	0
ROCKIES	.287	4	143	19	41	7	0	6	18	9	29	3

PITCHER	W	L	ERA	G	GS	CG	IP	H	R	ER	BB	SO
Holmes, D.	1	0	0.00	3	0	0	1.2	6	2	0	0	2
Leskanic, C.	0	1	6.00	3	0	0	3.0	3	2	2	0	4
Munoz, M.	0	1	13.50	4	0	0	1.1	4	2	2	1	1
Painter, L.	0	0	5.40	1	1	0	5.0	5	3	3	2	4
Reed, S.	0	0	0.00	3	0	0	2.2	2	0	0	1	3
Reynoso, A.	0	0	0.00	1	0	0	1.0	2	0	0	0	0
Ritz, K.	0	0	7.71	2	1	0	7.0	12	7	6	3	5
Ruffin, B.	0	0	2.70	4	0	0	3.1	3	1	1	2	2
Saberhagen, B.	0	1	11.25	1	1	0	4.0	7	6	5	1	3
Swift, B.	0	0	6.00	1	1	0	6.0	7	4	4	2	3
Thompson, M.	0	0	0.00	1	0	0	1.0	0	0	0	0	0
ROCKIES	1	3	5.75	4	4	0	36.0	51	27	23	12	27

Game 1
At COLORADO
Tuesday, October 3 (night)

Atlanta 0 0 1 0 0 2 0 1 1   5 12 1
Colorado 0 0 0 3 0 0 0 1 0   4 13 4

W—Pena, L—Leskanic, S—Wohlers, T—3:19, A—50,040

Game 2
At COLORADO
Wednesday, October 4 (night)

Atlanta 1 0 1 2 0 0 0 3 0   7 13 1
Colorado 0 0 0 0 0 3 0 1 0   4 8 2

W—Pena, L—Munoz, S—Wohlers, T—3:08, A—50,063

Game 3
At ATLANTA
Friday, October 6 (night)

Colorado 1 0 2 0 0 2 0 0 0 2   7 9 0
Atlanta 0 0 0 3 0 0 1 0 1 0   5 11 0

W—Holmes, L—Wohlers, S—Thompson, T—3:16, A—51,300

Game 4
At ATLANTA
Saturday, October 7 (night)

Colorado 0 0 3 0 0 1 0 0 0   4 11 1
Atlanta .... 0 0 4 2 1 3 0 0 x   10 15 0

W—Maddux, L—Saberhagen, T—2:38, A—50,027

SCORE BY INNINGS

Atlanta 1 0 6 6 1 5 1 1 6 0   27 51 2
Colorado 1 0 5 3 0 6 0 2 0 2   19 41 7

CINCINNATI REDS

PLAYER	AVG	G	AB	R	H	2B	3B	HR	RBI	BB	SO	SB
Boone, B.	.300	3	10	4	3	1	0	1	1	1	3	1
Branson, J.	.286	3	7	0	2	1	0	0	2	2	0	0
Duncan, M.	.667	2	3	1	2	0	0	0	1	0	0	1
Gant, R.	.231	3	13	3	3	0	0	1	2	0	3	0
Howard, T.	.100	3	10	0	1	1	0	0	0	0	2	0
Larkin, B.	.385	3	13	2	5	0	0	0	1	1	2	4
Lewis, D.	.000	3	3	0	0	0	0	0	0	0	1	0
Lewis, M.	.500	3	2	2	1	0	0	1	5	1	0	0
Morris, H.	.500	2	10	5	5	1	0	0	2	3	1	1
Sanders, R.	.154	3	13	3	2	1	0	1	2	1	9	2
Santiago, B.	.333	3	9	2	3	0	0	1	3	3	3	0
Walton, J.	.000	3	3	0	0	0	0	0	0	1	1	0
Jackson, M.	1.000	1	1	0	1	1	0	0	3	0	0	0
Schourek, P.	.000	1	2	0	0	0	0	0	0	0	1	0
Smiley, J.	.000	1	2	0	0	0	0	0	0	0	1	0
Wells, D.	.333	1	3	0	1	0	0	0	0	0	1	0
REDS	.279	3	104	22	29	6	0	5	22	13	28	9

PITCHER	W	L	ERA	G	GS	CG	IP	H	R	ER	BB	SO
Brantley, J.	0	0	6.00	3	0	0	3.0	5	2	2	0	2
Burba, D.	1	0	0.00	1	0	0	1.0	2	0	0	1	0
Jackson, M.	0	0	0.00	3	0	0	3.2	4	0	0	0	1
Schourek, P.	1	0	2.57	1	1	0	7.0	5	2	2	3	5
Smiley, J.	0	0	3.00	1	1	0	6.0	9	2	2	0	1
Wells, D.	1	0	0.00	1	1	0	6.1	6	1	0	1	8
REDS	3	0	2.00	3	3	0	27.0	31	7	6	5	17

LOS ANGELES DODGERS

PLAYER	AVG	G	AB	R	H	2B	3B	HR	RBI	BB	SO	SB
Ashley, B.	.000	1	0	0	0	0	0	0	0	1	0	0
Butler, B.	.267	3	15	1	4	0	0	0	1	0	3	0
DeShields, D.	.250	3	12	1	3	0	0	0	0	1	3	0
Fonville, C.	.500	3	12	1	6	0	0	0	0	0	1	0
Gwynn, C.	.000	1	1	0	0	0	0	0	0	0	1	0
Hansen, D.	.667	3	3	0	2	0	0	0	0	0	0	0
Hollandsworth, T.	.000	2	2	0	0	0	0	0	0	0	1	0
Karros, E.	.500	3	12	3	6	1	0	2	4	1	0	0
Kelly, R.	.364	3	11	0	4	0	0	0	1	0	1	0
Mondesi, R.	.222	3	9	2	2	0	0	0	0	0	2	0
Offerman, J.	.000	1	0	0	0	0	0	0	0	0	0	0
Osuna, A.	.000	3	0	0	0	0	0	0	0	0	0	0
Piazza, M.	.214	3	14	1	3	1	0	1	1	0	2	0
Wallach, T.	.083	3	12	0	1	0	0	0	0	1	3	0
Webster, M.	.000	2	2	0	0	0	0	0	0	0	0	0
Martinez, R.	.000	1	1	0	0	0	0	0	0	0	1	0
Nomo, H.	.000	1	2	0	0	0	0	0	0	0	2	0
Valdes, I.	.000	1	3	0	0	0	0	0	0	0	1	0
DODGERS	.279	3	111	7	31	2	0	3	7	5	17	0

PITCHER	W	L	ERA	G	GS	CG	IP	H	R	ER	BB	SO
Astacio, P.	0	0	0.00	3	0	0	3.1	1	0	0	0	5
Cummings, J.	0	0	20.25	2	0	0	1.1	3	3	3	2	3
Guthrie, M.	0	0	6.75	3	0	0	1.1	2	1	1	1	1
Martinez, R.	0	1	14.54	1	1	0	4.1	10	7	7	2	3
Nomo, H.	0	1	9.00	1	1	0	5.0	7	5	5	2	6
Osuna, A.	0	0	2.70	3	0	0	3.1	3	1	1	1	3
Tapani, K.	0	0	81.00	2	0	0	0.1	3	3	3	4	1
Valdes, I.	0	1	0.00	1	1	0	7.0	3	2	0	1	6
DODGERS	0	3	6.92	3	3	0	26.0	29	22	20	13	28

Game 1
At LOS ANGELES
Tuesday, October 3 (night)

Cincinnati 4 0 0 0 3 0 0 0 0   7 12 0
Los Angeles 0 0 0 0 1 1 0 0 0   2 8 0

W—Schourek, L—Martinez, T—3:15, A—44,199

Game 2
At LOS ANGELES
Wednesday, October 4 (night)

Cincinnati 0 0 0 2 0 0 0 1 2   5 6 0
Los Angeles 1 0 0 1 0 0 0 0 2   4 14 2

W—Burba, L—Osuna, T—3:21, A—46,051

Game 3
At CINCINNATI
Friday, October 6 (night)

Los Angeles 0 0 0 1 0 0 0 0 0   1 9 1
Cincinnati .... 0 0 2 2 1 0 4 3 0 x   10 11 2

W—Wells, L—Nomo, T—3:27, A—53,276

SCORE BY INNINGS

Cincinnati 4 0 2 3 3 4 3 1 2   22 29 2
Los Angeles 1 0 0 2 1 1 0 0 2   7 31 3

47

1995 NATIONAL LEAGUE CHAMPIONSHIP SERIES

ATLANTA BRAVES

PLAYER	AVG	G	AB	R	H	2B	3B	HR	RBI	BB	SO	SB
Belliard, R	.273	4	11	1	3	0	0	0	0	0	3	0
Blauser, J	.000	1	4	0	0	0	0	0	0	1	2	0
Devereaux, M	.308	4	13	2	4	1	0	1	5	1	2	0
Grissom, M	.263	4	19	2	5	0	1	0	0	1	4	0
Jones, C	.438	4	16	3	7	0	0	1	3	3	1	1
Justice, D	.273	3	11	1	3	0	0	0	1	2	1	0
Klesko, R	.000	4	7	0	0	0	0	0	0	3	4	0
Lemke, M	.167	4	18	2	3	0	0	0	1	1	0	0
Lopez, J	.357	3	14	2	5	1	0	1	3	0	1	0
McGriff, F	.438	4	16	5	7	4	0	0	3	0	0	0
Mordecai, M	.000	2	0	0	0	0	0	0	0	0	0	0
O'Brien, C	.400	2	5	1	2	0	0	1	3	0	1	0
Polonia, L	.500	3	2	0	1	0	0	0	1	0	0	0
Smith, D	.000	2	2	0	0	0	0	0	0	0	0	0
Avery, S	.500	2	2	0	1	0	0	0	0	0	0	0
Glavine, T	.000	1	1	0	0	0	0	0	0	1	0	0
Maddux, G	.000	1	3	0	0	0	0	0	0	0	1	0
Smoltz, J	.333	1	3	0	1	0	0	0	0	0	1	1
BRAVES	.282	4	149	19	42	6	1	4	17	16	22	2

PITCHER	W	L	ERA	G	GS	CG	IP	H	R	ER	BB	SO
Avery, S	1	0	0.00	2	1	0	6.0	2	0	0	4	6
Clontz, B	0	0	0.00	1	0	0	0.1	1	0	0	0	0
Glavine, T	0	0	1.29	1	1	0	7.0	7	1	1	2	5
Maddux, G	1	0	1.13	1	1	0	8.0	7	1	1	2	4
McMichael, G	1	0	0.00	3	0	0	2.2	0	0	0	1	2
Pena, A	0	0	0.00	3	0	0	3.0	2	0	0	1	4
Smoltz, J	0	0	2.57	1	1	0	7.0	7	2	2	2	2
Wohlers, M	1	0	1.80	4	0	0	5.0	2	1	1	0	8
BRAVES	4	0	1.15	4	4	0	39.0	28	5	5	12	31

CINCINNATI REDS

PLAYER	AVG	G	AB	R	H	2B	3B	HR	RBI	BB	SO	SB
Anthony, E	.000	2	1	0	0	0	0	0	0	1	1	0
Boone, B	.214	4	14	1	3	0	0	0	0	1	2	0
Branson, J	.111	4	9	2	1	1	0	0	0	2	1	0
Duncan, M	.000	3	3	0	0	0	0	0	0	1	1	0
Gant, R	.188	4	16	1	3	0	0	1	0	3	0	0
Harris, L	1.000	3	2	0	2	0	0	0	1	0	0	1
Howard, T	.250	4	8	0	2	1	0	0	1	2	0	0
Larkin, B	.389	4	18	1	7	2	1	0	1	1	1	1
Lewis, D	.000	2	1	0	0	0	0	0	0	0	0	0
Lewis, M	.250	2	4	0	1	0	0	0	0	1	1	0
Morris, H	.167	4	12	0	2	1	0	0	1	1	1	1
Sanders, R	.125	4	16	0	2	0	0	0	0	2	10	0
Santiago, B	.231	4	13	0	3	0	0	0	0	2	3	0
Taubensee, E	.500	2	2	0	1	0	0	0	0	0	0	0
Walton, J	.000	2	7	0	0	0	0	0	0	0	2	0
Schourek, P	.000	2	5	0	0	0	0	0	0	0	4	0
Smiley, J	.000	1	1	0	0	0	0	0	0	0	0	0
Wells, D	.500	1	2	0	1	0	0	0	0	0	0	0
REDS	.209	4	134	5	28	5	1	0	4	12	31	4

PITCHER	W	L	ERA	G	GS	CG	IP	H	R	ER	BB	SO
Brantley, J	0	0	0.00	2	0	0	2.2	0	0	0	2	1
Burba, D	0	0	0.00	2	0	0	3.2	0	0	0	4	0
Carrasco, H	0	0	0.00	1	0	0	1.1	1	0	0	0	3
Hernandez, X	0	0	27.00	1	0	0	0.2	3	2	2	0	0
Jackson, M	0	1	23.14	3	0	0	2.1	5	6	6	4	1
Portugal, M	0	1	36.00	1	0	0	1.0	3	4	4	1	0
Schourek, P	0	1	1.26	2	2	0	14.1	14	2	2	3	13
Smiley, J	0	0	3.60	1	1	0	5.0	5	2	2	0	1
Wells, D	0	1	4.50	1	1	0	6.0	8	3	3	2	3
REDS	0	4	4.62	4	4	0	37.0	42	19	19	16	22

Game 1
At CINCINNATI
Tuesday, October 10 (night)

Atlanta 0 0 0 0 0 0 0 0 1 0 1   2 7 0
Cincinnati 0 0 0 1 0 0 0 0 0 0 0   1 8 0

W—Wohlers, L—Jackson, S—McMichael, T—3:18, A—40,382

Game 2
At CINCINNATI
Wednesday, October 11 (night)

Atlanta 1 0 0 1 0 0 0 0 4   6 11 1
Cincinnati 0 0 0 0 2 0 0 0 0   2 9 1

W—McMichael, L—Portugal, T—3:26, A—44,624

Game 3
At ATLANTA
Friday, October 13 (night)

Cincinnati 0 0 0 0 0 0 0 1 1   2 8 0
Atlanta .... 0 0 0 0 0 3 2 0 x   5 12 1

W—Maddux, L—Wells, T—2:42, A—51,424

Game 4
At ATLANTA
Saturday, October 14 (night)

Cincinnati 0 0 0 0 0 0 0 0 0   0 3 1
Atlanta .... 0 0 1 0 0 0 5 0 x   6 12 1

W—Avery, L—Schourek, T—2:54, A—52,067

SCORE BY INNINGS

Atlanta 1 0 1 1 0 3 7 0 1 4 1   19 42 3
Cincinnati 0 0 0 1 2 0 0 1 1 0 0   5 28 2

NATIONAL LEAGUE CHAMPIONSHIP SERIES RESULTS

Year—Winner (Div.), Loser (Div.)
1969—New York (E) 3—Atlanta (W) 0
1970—Cincinnati (W) 3—Pittsburgh (E) 0
1971—Pittsburgh (E) 3—San Francisco (W) 1
1972—Cincinnati (W) 3—Pittsburgh (E) 2
1973—New York (E) 3—Cincinnati (W) 2
1974—Los Angeles (W) 3—Pittsburgh (E) 1
1975—Cincinnati (W) 3—Pittsburgh (E) 0
1976—Cincinnati (W) 3—Philadelphia (E) 0
1977—Los Angeles (W) 3—Philadelphia (E) 1
1978—Los Angeles (W) 3—Philadelphia (E) 1
1979—Pittsburgh (E) 3—Cincinnati (W) 0
1980—Philadelphia (E) 3—Houston (W) 2
1981—Los Angeles (W) 3—Montreal (E) 2
1982—St. Louis (E) 3—Atlanta (W) 0
1983—Philadelphia (E) 3—Los Angeles (W) 1
1984—San Diego (W) 3—Chicago (E) 2

Year—Winner (Div.), Loser (Div.)
1985—St. Louis (E) 4—Los Angeles (W) 2
1986—New York (E) 4—Houston (W) 2
1987—St. Louis (E) 4—San Francisco (W) 3
1988—Los Angeles (W) 4—New York (E) 3
1989—San Francisco (W) 4—Chicago (E) 1
1990—Cincinnati (W) 4—Pittsburgh (E) 2
1991—Atlanta (W) 4—Pittsburgh (E) 3
1992—Atlanta (W) 4—Pittsburgh (E) 3
1993—Philadelphia (E) 4—Atlanta (W) 2
1994—No Series
1995—Atlanta (E) 4—Cincinnati (C) 0

East Division has won 12 series,
West Division has won 14 series,
Central Division has won 0 series.

NATIONAL LEAGUE CHAMPIONSHIP SERIES MVP AWARD WINNERS

1977—Dusty Baker, Los Angeles Dodgers
1978—Steve Garvey, Los Angeles Dodgers
1979—Willie Stargell, Pittsburgh Pirates
1980—Manny Trillo, Philadelphia Phillies
1981—Burt Hooton, Los Angeles Dodgers
1982—Darrell Porter, St. Louis Cardinals
1983—Gary Matthews, Philadelphia Phillies
1984—Steve Garvey, San Diego Padres
1985—Ozzie Smith, St. Louis Cardinals
1986—Mike Scott, Houston Astros
1987—Jeffrey Leonard, San Francisco Giants
1988—Orel Hershiser, Los Angeles Dodgers
1989—Will Clark, San Francisco Giants
1990—Rob Dibble, Cincinnati Reds
      Randy Myers, Cincinnati Reds
1991—Steve Avery, Atlanta Braves
1992—John Smoltz, Atlanta Braves
1993—Curt Schilling, Philadelphia Phillies
1994—No Series
1995—Mike Devereaux, Atlanta Braves

1995 WORLD SERIES

ATLANTA BRAVES

PLAYER	AVG	G	AB	R	H	2B	3B	HR	RBI	BB	SO	SB
Belliard, R	.000	6	16	0	0	0	0	0	0	1	4	0
Devereaux, M	.250	5	4	0	1	0	0	0	1	2	1	0
Grissom, M	.360	6	25	3	9	1	0	1	1	3	3	0
Jones, C	.286	6	21	3	6	3	0	0	4	3	0	0
Justice, D	.250	6	20	3	5	1	0	1	5	5	1	0
Klesko, R	.313	6	16	4	5	0	0	3	4	3	4	0
Lemke, M	.273	6	22	1	6	0	0	0	3	3	2	0
Lopez, J	.176	6	17	1	3	2	0	1	3	1	1	0
McGriff, F	.261	6	23	5	6	2	0	2	3	3	7	1
Mordecai, M	.333	3	3	0	1	0	0	0	0	0	0	0
O'Brien, C	.000	2	3	0	0	0	0	0	0	0	1	0
Polonia, L	.286	6	14	3	4	1	0	1	4	1	3	1
Smith, D	.500	3	2	0	1	0	0	0	0	0	1	0
Glavine, T	.000	3	2	4	0	0	0	0	0	1	2	0
Maddux, G	.000	2	3	0	0	0	0	0	0	0	1	0
BRAVES	.244	6	193	23	47	10	0	8	23	25	34	5

PITCHER	W	L	ERA	G	GS	CG	IP	H	R	ER	BB	SO
Avery, S	1	0	1.50	1	1	0	6.0	3	1	1	5	3
Borbon, P	0	0	0.00	1	0	0	1.0	0	0	0	0	2
Clontz, B	0	0	2.70	2	0	0	3.1	2	1	1	0	2
Glavine, T	2	0	1.29	2	2	0	14.0	4	2	2	6	11
Maddux, G	1	1	2.25	2	2	1	16.0	9	6	4	3	8
McMichael, G	0	0	2.70	3	0	0	3.1	3	2	1	2	2
Mercker, K	0	0	4.50	1	0	0	2.0	1	1	1	2	2
Pena, A	0	1	9.00	2	0	0	1.0	3	1	1	2	0
Smoltz, J	0	0	15.43	1	1	0	2.1	6	4	4	2	4
Wohlers, M	0	0	1.80	4	0	0	5.0	4	1	1	3	3
BRAVES	4	2	2.67	6	6	1	54.0	35	19	16	25	37

CLEVELAND INDIANS

PLAYER	AVG	G	AB	R	H	2B	3B	HR	RBI	BB	SO	SB
Alomar, S	.200	5	15	3	3	2	0	0	1	0	2	0
Amaro, R	.000	2	2	0	0	0	0	0	0	0	1	0
Baerga, C	.192	6	26	1	5	2	0	0	4	1	1	0
Belle, A	.235	6	17	4	4	0	0	2	4	7	5	0
Espinoza, A	.500	2	2	1	1	0	0	0	0	0	0	0
Kirby, W	.000	3	1	0	0	0	0	0	0	0	1	0
Lofton, K	.200	6	25	6	5	1	0	0	0	3	1	6
Murray, E	.105	6	19	1	2	0	0	1	3	5	4	0
Pena, T	.167	2	6	0	1	0	0	0	0	0	0	0
Perry, H	.000	3	5	0	0	0	0	0	0	0	2	0
Ramirez, M	.222	6	18	2	4	0	0	1	2	4	5	1
Sorrento, P	.182	6	11	0	2	0	0	0	0	0	2	0
Thome, J	.211	6	19	1	4	1	0	0	1	3	5	0
Vizquel, O	.174	6	23	4	4	3	1	0	1	1	3	1
Hershiser, O	.000	2	2	0	0	0	0	0	0	0	1	0
Martinez, D	.000	2	2	0	0	0	0	0	0	0	0	0
Poole, J	.000	2	1	0	0	0	0	0	0	0	0	0
INDIANS	.179	6	195	19	35	7	1	5	17	25	37	8

PITCHER	W	L	ERA	G	GS	CG	IP	H	R	ER	BB	SO
Assenmacher, P	0	0	6.75	4	0	0	1.1	1	2	1	3	3
Embree, A	0	0	2.70	4	0	0	3.1	2	1	1	2	2
Hershiser, O	1	1	2.57	2	2	0	14.0	8	5	4	4	13
Hill, K	0	1	4.26	2	1	0	6.1	7	3	3	4	1
Martinez, D	0	1	3.48	2	2	0	10.1	12	4	4	8	5
Mesa, J	1	0	4.50	2	0	0	4.0	5	2	2	1	4
Nagy, C	0	0	6.43	2	2	0	7.0	8	5	5	1	4
Poole, J	0	1	3.86	2	0	0	2.1	1	1	1	0	1
Tavarez, J	0	0	0.00	5	0	0	4.1	3	0	0	2	1
INDIANS	2	4	3.57	6	6	0	53.0	47	23	21	25	34

Game 1
At ATLANTA
Saturday, October 21 (night)

```
Cleveland........... 1 0 0  0 0 0  0 0 1    2 2 0
Atlanta............. 1 1 0  0 0 0  2 0 x    3 3 2
```
W—Maddux, L—Hershiser, T—2:37, A—51,876

Game 2
At ATLANTA
Sunday, October 22 (night)

```
Cleveland........... 0 2 0  0 0 0  1 0 0    3 6 2
Atlanta............. 0 0 2  0 0 2  0 0 x    4 8 2
```
W—Glavine, L—Martinez, S—Wohlers, T—3:17, A—51,877

Game 3
At CLEVELAND
Tuesday, October 24 (night)

```
Atlanta............. 1 0 0  0 0 1  1 3 0 0 0    6 12 1
Cleveland........... 2 0 2  0 0 0  1 1 0 0 1    7 12 2
```
W—Mesa, L—Pena, T—4:09, A—43,584

Game 4
At CLEVELAND
Wednesday, October 25 (night)

```
Atlanta............. 0 0 0  0 0 1  3 0 1    5 11 1
Cleveland........... 0 0 0  0 0 1  0 0 1    2 6 0
```
W—Avery, L—Hill, S—Borbon, T—3:14, A—43,578

Game 5
At CLEVELAND
Thursday, October 26 (night)

```
Atlanta............. 0 0 0  1 1 0  0 0 2    4 7 0
Cleveland........... 2 0 0  0 0 2  0 1 x    5 8 1
```
W—Hershiser, L—Maddux, S—Mesa, T—2:33, A—43,595

Game 6
At ATLANTA
Saturday, October 28 (night)

```
Cleveland........... 0 0 0  0 0 0  0 0 0    0 1 1
Atlanta............. 0 0 0  0 0 1  0 0 x    1 6 0
```
W—Glavine, L—Poole, S—Wohlers, T—3:02, A—51,875

SCORE BY INNINGS
```
Atlanta......... 1 1 2  1 1 5  6 3 3 0 0    23 47 6
Cleveland....... 5 2 2  0 0 3  2 2 2 0 1    19 35 6
```

WORLD SERIES RESULTS

Year—Winner (Lg.), Loser (Lg.)
1903—Boston (A) 5—Pittsburgh (N) 3
1904—No Series
1905—New York (N) 4—Philadelphia (A) 1
1906—Chicago (A) 4—Chicago (N) 2
1907—Chicago (N) 4—Detroit (A) 0; 1 tie
1908—Chicago (N) 4—Detroit (A) 1
1909—Pittsburgh (N) 4—Detroit (A) 3
1910—Philadelphia (A) 4—Chicago (N) 1
1911—Philadelphia (A) 4—New York (N) 2
1912—Boston (A) 4—New York (N) 3; 1 tie
1913—Philadelphia (A) 4—New York (N) 1
1914—Boston (N) 4—Philadelphia (A) 0
1915—Boston (A) 4—Philadelphia (N) 1
1916—Boston (A) 4—Brooklyn (N) 1
1917—Chicago (A) 4—New York (N) 2
1918—Boston (A) 4—Chicago (N) 2
1919—Cincinnati (N) 5—Chicago (A) 3
1920—Cleveland (A) 5—Brooklyn (N) 2
1921—New York (N) 5—New York (A) 3
1922—New York (N) 4—New York (A) 0; 1 tie
1923—New York (A) 4—New York (N) 2
1924—Washington (A) 4—New York (N) 3
1925—Pittsburgh (N) 4—Washington (A) 3
1926—St. Louis (N) 4—New York (A) 3
1927—New York (A) 4—Pittsburgh (N) 0
1928—New York (A) 4—St. Louis (N) 0
1929—Philadelphia (A) 4—Chicago (N) 1
1930—Philadelphia (A) 4—St. Louis (N) 2
1931—St. Louis (N) 4—Philadelphia (A) 3
1932—New York (A) 4—Chicago (N) 0
1933—New York (N) 4—Washington (A) 1
1934—St. Louis (N) 4—Detroit (A) 3
1935—Detroit (A) 4—Chicago (N) 2
1936—New York (A) 4—New York (N) 2
1937—New York (A) 4—New York (N) 1
1938—New York (A) 4—Chicago (N) 0
1939—New York (A) 4—Cincinnati (N) 0
1940—Cincinnati (N) 4—Detroit (A) 3
1941—New York (A) 4—Brooklyn (N) 1
1942—St. Louis (N) 4—New York (A) 1
1943—New York (A) 4—St. Louis (N) 1
1944—St. Louis (N) 4—St. Louis (A) 2
1945—Detroit (A) 4—Chicago (N) 3
1946—St. Louis (N) 4—Boston (A) 3
1947—New York (A) 4—Brooklyn (N) 3
1948—Cleveland (A) 4—Boston (N) 2
1949—New York (A) 4—Brooklyn (N) 1
1950—New York (A) 4—Philadelphia (N) 0
1951—New York (A) 4—New York (N) 2
1952—New York (A) 4—Brooklyn (N) 3
1953—New York (A) 4—Brooklyn (N) 2
1954—New York (N) 4—Cleveland (A) 0
1955—Brooklyn (N) 4—New York (A) 3
1956—New York (A) 4—Brooklyn (N) 3
1957—Milwaukee (N) 4—New York (A) 3
1958—New York (A) 4—Milwaukee (N) 3
1959—Los Angeles (N) 4—Chicago (A) 2
1960—Pittsburgh (N) 4—New York (A) 3
1961—New York (A) 4—Cincinnati (N) 1
1962—New York (A) 4—San Francisco (N) 3
1963—Los Angeles (N) 4—New York (A) 0
1964—St. Louis (N) 4—New York (A) 3
1965—Los Angeles (N) 4—Minnesota (A) 3
1966—Baltimore (A) 4—Los Angeles (N) 0
1967—St. Louis (N) 4—Boston (A) 3
1968—Detroit (A) 4—St. Louis (N) 3
1969—New York (N) 4—Baltimore (A) 1
1970—Baltimore (A) 4—Cincinnati (N) 1
1971—Pittsburgh (N) 4—Baltimore (A) 3
1972—Oakland (A) 4—Cincinnati (N) 3
1973—Oakland (A) 4—New York (N) 3
1974—Oakland (A) 4—Los Angeles (N) 1
1975—Cincinnati (N) 4—Boston (A) 3
1976—Cincinnati (N) 4—New York (A) 0
1977—New York (A) 4—Los Angeles (N) 2
1978—New York (A) 4—Los Angeles (N) 2
1979—Pittsburgh (N) 4—Baltimore (A) 3
1980—Philadelphia (N) 4—Kansas City (A) 2
1981—Los Angeles (N) 4—New York (A) 2
1982—St. Louis (N) 4—Milwaukee (A) 3
1983—Baltimore (A) 4—Philadelphia (N) 1
1984—Detroit (A) 4—San Diego (N) 1
1985—Kansas City (A) 4—St. Louis (N) 3
1986—New York (N) 4—Boston (A) 3
1987—Minnesota (A) 4—St. Louis (N) 3
1988—Los Angeles (N) 4—Oakland (A) 1
1989—Oakland (A) 4—San Francisco (N) 0
1990—Cincinnati (N) 4—Oakland (A) 0
1991—Minnesota (A) 4—Atlanta (N) 3
1992—Toronto (A) 4—Atlanta (N) 2
1993—Toronto (A) 4—Philadelphia (N) 2
1994—No Series
1995—Atlanta (N) 4—Cleveland (A) 2

American League has won 53 series,
National League has won 38 series.

WORLD SERIES MVP AWARD WINNERS

1955—Johnny Podres, Brooklyn Dodgers
1956—Don Larsen, New York Yankees
1957—Lew Burdette, Milwaukee Braves
1958—Bob Turley, New York Yankees
1959—Larry Sherry, Los Angeles Dodgers
1960—Bobby Richardson, New York Yankees
1961—Whitey Ford, New York Yankees
1962—Ralph Terry, New York Yankees
1963—Sandy Koufax, Los Angeles Dodgers
1964—Bob Gibson, St. Louis Cardinals
1965—Sandy Koufax, Los Angeles Dodgers
1966—Frank Robinson, Baltimore Orioles
1967—Bob Gibson, St. Louis Cardinals
1968—Mickey Lolich, Detroit Tigers
1969—Donn Clendenon, New York Mets
1970—Brooks Robinson, Baltimore Orioles
1971—Roberto Clemente, Pittsburgh Pirates
1972—Gene Tenace, Oakland A's
1973—Reggie Jackson, Oakland A's
1974—Rollie Fingers, Oakland A's
1975—Pete Rose, Cincinnati Reds
1976—Johnny Bench, Cincinnati Reds
1977—Reggie Jackson, New York Yankees
1978—Bucky Dent, New York Yankees
1979—Willie Stargell, Pittsburgh Pirates
1980—Mike Schmidt, Philadelphia Phillies
1981—Ron Cey, Los Angeles Dodgers
       Pedro Guerrero, Los Angeles Dodgers
       Steve Yeager, Los Angeles Dodgers
1982—Darrell Porter, St. Louis Cardinals
1983—Rick Dempsey, Baltimore Orioles
1984—Alan Trammell, Detroit Tigers
1985—Bret Saberhagen, Kansas City Royals
1986—Ray Knight, New York Mets
1987—Frank Viola, Minnesota Twins
1988—Orel Hershiser, Los Angeles Dodgers
1989—Dave Stewart, Oakland Athletics
1990—Jose Rijo, Cincinnati Reds
1991—Jack Morris, Minnesota Twins
1992—Pat Borders, Toronto Blue Jays
1993—Paul Molitor, Toronto Blue Jays
1994—No Series
1995—Tom Glavine, Atlanta Braves

1995 FINAL STANDINGS

EASTERN DIVISION

	W	L	PCT.	GB	Atl.	Phi.	N.Y.	Fla.	Mon.	Cin.	Hou.	Chi.	St.L.	Pit.	L.A.	Col.	S.D.	S.F.
Atlanta	90	54	.625	—	—	7	5	10	9	8	6	8	7	4	5	9	5	7
Philadelphia	69	75	.479	21.0	6	—	6	7	9	5	3	7	1	5	6	9	2	6
New York	69	75	.479	21.0	8	7	—	6	6	5	6	3	3	4	6	4	9	8
Florida	67	76	.469	22.5	3	6	7	—	6	6	8	4	4	5	3	7	3	5
Montreal	66	78	.458	24.0	4	4	8	7	—	4	3	5	4	4	5	1	7	7

CENTRAL DIVISION

	W	L	PCT.	GB	Atl.	Phi.	N.Y.	Fla.	Mon.	Cin.	Hou.	Chi.	St.L.	Pit.	L.A.	Col.	S.D.	S.F.
Cincinnati	85	59	.590	—	5	9	7	6	8	—	12	7	5	8	4	5	3	6
Houston	76	68	.528	9.0	6	5	6	4	9	1	—	8	9	3	4	7	3	5
Chicago	73	71	.507	12.0	4	6	4	8	3	6	4	—	5	9	8	7	6	5
St. Louis	62	81	.434	22.5	5	4	4	3	3	5	4	7	—	9	5	7	5	6
Pittsburgh	58	86	.403	27.0	2	3	3	4	5	4	5	4	4	—	4	4	4	6

WESTERN DIVISION

	W	L	PCT.	GB	Atl.	Phi.	N.Y.	Fla.	Mon.	Cin.	Hou.	Chi.	St.L.	Pit.	L.A.	Col.	S.D.	S.F.
Los Angeles	78	66	.542	—	4	4	6	7	7	3	2	5	7	9	—	9	7	8
Colorado	77	67	.535	1.0	4	4	5	7	4	3	5	7	8	4	8	—	9	8
San Diego	70	74	.486	8.0	2	6	7	2	5	6	4	7	7	8	6	4	—	6
San Francisco	67	77	.465	11.0	1	6	8	3	6	3	3	7	7	6	5	5	7	—

Forfeit game—St. Louis at Los Angeles, August 10

STANDINGS OF NATIONAL LEAGUE CLUBS AT HOME AND ROAD FOR 1995

HOME GAMES

	W	L	PCT.	ATL W-L	CIN W-L	COL W-L	NY W-L	SD W-L	LA W-L	STL W-L	FLA W-L	SF W-L	HOU W-L	PHI W-L	CHI W-L	MON W-L	PIT W-L	EAST W-L	CENTRAL W-L	WEST W-L
Atlanta	44	28	.611	—	3 3	5 2	4 3	4 2	2 1	3 1	4 2	5 1	5 0	1 5	2 5	4 2	2 1	15 11	14 13	15 4
Cincinnati	44	28	.611	2 5	—	4 2	5 1	1 2	3 1	3 1	3 3	4 3	6 0	3 2	3 2	4 2	3 2	18 13	16 8	10 7
Colorado	44	28	.611	2 4	5 1	—	5 1	5 1	3 4	3 1	2 2	3 3	2 1	3 4	3 4	4 0	4 2	14 12	13 10	17 6
New York	40	32	.556	5 1	4 2	3 1	—	4 1	1 2	—	5 2	3 3	2 1	4 2	3 4	2 4	1 3	14 15	13 10	13 7
San Diego	40	32	.556	1 3	4 2	3 4	5 1	—	3 3	3 3	6 0	0 0	2 5	3 3	4 3	3 3	3 2	14 16	15 9	11 7
Los Angeles	39	33	.542	3 2	2 1	2 2	4 3	3 3	—	4 3	1 2	2 2	3 4	2 2	4 1	4 3	5 4	14 12	18 11	7 10
St. Louis	39	33	.542	3 3	3 3	2 3	3 1	5 1	3 4	—	3 1	4 2	3 5	2 1	4 1	2 1	2 3	13 9	12 14	14 10
Florida	37	34	.521	2 5	3 3	4 2	2 4	2 1	2 1	5 3	—	3 0	2 5	1 1	3 1	5 2	3 1	18 14	10 13	9 7
San Francisco	37	35	.514	1 2	1 1	3 3	4 2	3 2	2 4	4 3	5 2	—	2 4	—	4 2	2 2	2 3	13 9	11 14	13 12
Houston	36	36	.500	1 5	5 6	3 3	4 1	1 1	2 0	4 3	5 1	3 3	—	—	3 2	2 4	2 4	13 10	12 13	11 13
Philadelphia	35	37	.486	1 5	1 5	1 1	1 1	2 4	1 2	2 4	5 2	2 2	5 1	—	—	4 3	4 2	10 16	14 14	11 7
Chicago	34	38	.472	1 4	2 4	1 2	1 2	3 3	3 3	5 2	2 4	1 5	2 4	3 2	—	3 2	7 2	11 13	12 13	11 12
Montreal	31	41	.431	2 5	2 4	3 3	3 3	4 3	3 3	3 1	3 4	4 3	0 6	2 4	2 3	—	0 2	12 15	9 17	10 9
Pittsburgh	31	41	.431	1 2	1 5	3 3	2 1	4 1	2 2	5 2	1 5	2 2	2 4	3 3	4 3	2 3	—	13 9	11 15	9 15

ROAD GAMES

	W	L	PCT.	ATL W-L	CIN W-L	HOU W-L	CHI W-L	LA W-L	MON W-L	PHI W-L	COL W-L	FLA W-L	SD W-L	SF W-L	NY W-L	PIT W-L	STL W-L	EAST W-L	CENTRAL W-L	WEST W-L
Atlanta	46	26	.639	—	—	5 2	5 1	4 2	5 2	4 1	5 2	3 1	2 1	1 5	2 1	5 2	3 3	16 10	19 9	11 7
Cincinnati	41	31	.569	3 3	—	6 1	4 1	1 2	4 2	4 2	5 3	3 3	5 1	1 1	2 4	5 1	3 3	17 13	19 6	5 12
Houston	40	32	.556	5 1	0 6	—	4 2	2 1	6 0	4 2	1 2	2 1	1 3	4 2	3 1	3 2	5 4	19 11	13 8	8 13
Chicago	39	33	.542	2 4	2 3	3 4	—	4 2	0 3	3 1	4 2	2 5	3 1	3 2	5 1	4 2	4 3	19 11	13 13	7 9
Los Angeles	39	33	.542	1 3	1 3	1 1	3 3	—	3 2	2 5	5 1	2 1	3 4	3 4	3 3	4 5	3 1	15 18	13 13	11 2
Montreal	35	37	.486	2 4	2 4	2 3	2 3	2 4	—	4 3	0 4	4 2	3 2	3 3	6 1	2 1	3 2	16 19	10 15	9 3
Philadelphia	34	38	.472	5 2	2 4	2 4	2 3	2 3	5 3	—	1 3	2 3	2 4	1 5	5 3	3 2	2 1	15 17	12 12	8 14
Colorado	33	39	.458	2 4	2 4	2 3	4 2	4 3	3 1	3 1	—	1 1	4 5	5 2	2 2	1 4	0 4	11 13	12 15	10 10
Florida	30	42	.417	1 5	3 3	1 5	3 2	2 3	4 3	3 3	—	—	4 3	1 4	3 3	3 3	1 3	9 14	14 15	10 10
San Diego	30	42	.417	1 2	2 1	1 4	3 3	3 3	3 3	4 1	2 4	1 5	—	4 2	4 2	3 5	1 5	10 19	12 17	8 11
San Francisco	30	42	.417	0 5	2 2	1 3	5 1	1 5	3 3	5 3	1 5	2 3	3 3	—	4 2	2 4	2 4	10 21	12 14	8 12
New York	29	43	.403	3 4	1 4	1 5	2 1	2 4	4 2	4 2	1 4	1 5	5 2	2 4	—	2 4	2 1	10 16	12 14	8 12
Pittsburgh	27	45	.375	1 2	4 3	3 2	2 4	3 4	2 3	3 4	2 1	4 2	1 4	4 2	1 3	—	2 4	7 14	11 15	9 16
St. Louis	23	48	.324	2 4	2 4	1 5	2 5	1 3	2 2	1 3	2 2	4 2	0 6	2 5	1 2	3 4	—	6 18	8 18	9 16

EASTERN CLUBS vs. EAST

	W	L	PCT.
Atlanta	31	21	.596
New York	27	25	.519
Montreal	26	26	.500
Philadelphia	24	28	.462
Florida	22	30	.423

CENTRAL CLUBS vs. EAST

	W	L	PCT.
Cincinnati	35	26	.574
Chicago	25	21	.543
Houston	30	30	.500
Pittsburgh	20	23	.465
St. Louis	19	23	.452

WESTERN CLUBS vs. EAST

	W	L	PCT.
Colorado	25	23	.521
Los Angeles	28	28	.500
San Diego	22	27	.449
San Francisco	24	30	.444

EASTERN CLUBS vs. CENTRAL

	W	L	PCT.
Atlanta	33	22	.600
Florida	27	29	.482
New York	21	24	.467
Philadelphia	22	27	.449
Montreal	20	27	.426

CENTRAL CLUBS vs. CENTRAL

	W	L	PCT.
Cincinnati	35	14	.714
Houston	27	25	.519
Chicago	25	24	.510
Pittsburgh	20	32	.385
St. Louis	20	32	.385

WESTERN CLUBS vs. CENTRAL

	W	L	PCT.
San Diego	32	24	.571
Colorado	31	26	.544
Los Angeles	26	23	.531
San Francisco	26	25	.510

EASTERN CLUBS vs. WEST

	W	L	PCT.
Atlanta	26	11	.703
Philadelphia	23	20	.535
Florida	18	17	.514
New York	21	26	.447
Montreal	20	25	.444

CENTRAL CLUBS vs. WEST

	W	L	PCT.
Houston	19	13	.594
Chicago	23	26	.469
St. Louis	23	26	.469
Cincinnati	15	19	.441
Pittsburgh	18	31	.367

WESTERN CLUBS vs. WEST

	W	L	PCT.
Los Angeles	24	15	.615
Colorado	21	18	.538
San Francisco	17	22	.436
San Diego	16	23	.410

MONTHLY STANDINGS—1995

THROUGH APRIL 30

EAST
	W	L	GB
Atlanta	4	1	—
Montreal	3	2	1
Philadelphia	2	3	1½
New York	2	3	2
Florida	1	4	3

CENTRAL
	W	L	GB
Chicago	4	1	—
Houston	2	3	2
St. Louis	2	3	2
Pittsburgh	1	3	2½
Cincinnati	0	5	4

WEST
	W	L	GB
Colorado	4	1	—
San Diego	4	1	—
Los Angeles	3	2	1
San Francisco	2	3	2

THROUGH MAY 31

EAST
	W	L	GB
Philadelphia	23	9	—
Atlanta	19	13	4
Montreal	19	15	5
New York	13	20	10½
Florida	8	23	14½

CENTRAL
	W	L	GB
Chicago	20	11	—
Cincinnati	20	11	—
Houston	15	16	5
St. Louis	14	20	7½
Pittsburgh	12	18	7½

WEST
	W	L	GB
San Francisco	18	16	—
Colorado	17	16	½
Los Angeles	14	19	3½
San Diego	14	19	3½

THROUGH JUNE 30

EAST
	W	L	GB
Philadelphia	38	21	—
Atlanta	34	25	4
Montreal	29	31	9½
New York	23	37	15½
Florida	21	36	16

CENTRAL
	W	L	GB
Cincinnati	37	22	—
Houston	31	27	5½
Chicago	29	31	8½
Pittsburgh	24	33	12
St. Louis	25	36	13

WEST
	W	L	GB
Colorado	32	28	—
Los Angeles	32	29	½
San Diego	30	29	1½
San Francisco	30	30	2

THROUGH JULY 31

EAST
	W	L	GB
Atlanta	54	32	—
Philadelphia	47	41	8
Montreal	43	45	12
Florida	35	49	18
New York	35	52	19½

CENTRAL
	W	L	GB
Cincinnati	53	32	—
Houston	50	37	4
Chicago	43	44	11
Pittsburgh	36	49	17
St. Louis	37	51	17½

WEST
	W	L	GB
Colorado	49	39	—
Los Angeles	45	42	3½
San Diego	41	46	7½
San Francisco	39	48	9½

THROUGH AUGUST 31

EAST
	W	L	GB
Atlanta	73	42	—
Philadelphia	60	57	14
Montreal	56	60	17½
Florida	52	62	20½
New York	51	63	21½

CENTRAL
	W	L	GB
Cincinnati	72	43	—
Houston	59	57	13½
Chicago	58	58	14½
Pittsburgh	49	67	23½
St. Louis	49	67	23½

WEST
	W	L	GB
Los Angeles	61	56	—
Colorado	60	56	½
San Diego	56	59	4
San Francisco	54	62	6½

THROUGH SEPTEMBER 30

EAST
	W	L	GB
Atlanta	90	53	—
Philadelphia	69	74	21
New York	68	75	22
Florida	66	76	23½
Montreal	66	77	24

CENTRAL
	W	L	GB
Cincinnati	84	59	—
Houston	75	68	9
Chicago	73	70	11
St. Louis	62	80	21½
Pittsburgh	57	86	27

WEST
	W	L	GB
Los Angeles	77	66	—
Colorado	76	67	1
San Diego	70	73	7
San Francisco	67	76	10

50

1995 SHUTOUT GAMES

Club	Cin	Atl	Chi	Hou	SD	NY	Mon	LA	Phi	Pit	Fla	SF	StL	Col	Won	Lost	Pct.
Cincinnati	—	0	0	1	0	0	0	1	2	0	2	1	1	2	10	3	.769
Atlanta	1	—	1	0	0	1	1	1	1	0	1	0	2	2	11	4	.733
Chicago	0	0	—	0	1	1	0	1	2	0	0	2	3	2	12	5	.706
Houston	0	1	1	—	0	0	0	1	0	2	0	0	3	0	8	4	.667
San Diego	0	0	1	0	—	0	1	0	1	2	0	1	3	1	10	6	.625
New York	1	1	0	1	2	—	2	0	1	0	1	0	0	0	9	8	.529
Montreal	0	1	1	1	1	1	—	0	0	1	1	1	0	1	9	8	.529
Los Angeles	0	1	1	0	0	2	1	—	0	1	1	2	1	1	11	12	.478
Philadelphia	1	0	0	0	1	0	0	4	—	0	0	1	1	0	8	9	.471
Pittsburgh	0	0	0	1	0	2	1	1	—	0	0	1	1	0	7	8	.467
Florida	0	0	0	0	2	0	2	0	0	—	0	3	1	0	7	9	.438
San Francisco	0	0	0	0	0	0	1	1	0	2	—	0	1	0	5	8	.385
St. Louis	0	0	0	1	0	1	1	0	1	1	0	0	—	0	6	19	.240
Colorado	0	0	0	0	0	0	0	1	0	0	0	—	0	1	11	.083
LOST	3	4	5	4	6	8	8	12	9	8	9	8	19	11	114	114	.500

1995 ONE-RUN MARGINS

Club	Atl	SF	Cin	Fla	StL	Col	SD	NY	Phi	Mon	Hou	Chi	LA	Pit	Won	Lost	Pct.
Atlanta	—	1	2	3	4	2	3	2	1	4	1	2	3	3	31	17	.646
San Francisco	1	—	1	1	2	1	3	4	0	3	2	3	1	4	26	15	.634
Cincinnati	2	0	—	1	1	1	3	4	1	3	3	1	3	3	23	15	.605
Florida	1	0	1	—	0	3	0	2	3	1	3	1	1	2	18	17	.514
St. Louis	2	1	2	2	—	3	2	2	2	1	2	1	4	1	25	25	.500
Colorado	2	1	1	1	2	—	2	3	0	1	2	2	1	1	19	19	.500
San Diego	0	0	2	0	3	1	—	3	3	2	1	2	1	2	20	22	.476
New York	1	1	3	1	2	1	2	—	0	2	1	1	3	3	21	24	.467
Philadelphia	3	3	1	1	1	1	2	0	—	2	2	0	3	1	20	23	.465
Montreal	0	2	0	2	1	0	4	3	—	1	2	3	1		20	23	.465
Houston	2	2	0	1	1	2	3	0	3	1	—	3	0	2	20	23	.465
Chicago	0	0	1	0	4	2	0	2	3	3	1	—	3	1	19	24	.442
Los Angeles	1	3	1	1	2	2	1	2	0	2	0	—		3	19	26	.422
Pittsburgh	2	1	0	3	2	0	2	1	2	0	4	2	—		19	27	.413
LOST	17	15	15	17	25	19	22	24	23	23	23	24	26	27	300	300	.500

1995 NIGHT GAME STANDINGS

	HOME W	L	ROAD W	L	SEASON W	L	Pct.
Atlanta	33	24	32	16	65	40	.619
Cincinnati	32	19	30	24	62	43	.590
Los Angeles	32	27	29	24	61	51	.545
Houston	26	27	30	21	56	48	.538
Chicago	5	13	31	20	36	33	.522
Philadelphia	29	28	24	22	53	50	.515
New York	28	23	24	29	52	52	.500
San Diego	29	21	17	29	46	50	.479
Colorado	26	20	19	29	45	49	.479
Florida	33	32	19	29	52	61	.460
St. Louis	30	21	15	33	45	54	.455
Montreal	23	33	22	25	45	58	.437
Pittsburgh	23	31	21	29	44	60	.423
San Francisco	10	14	20	29	30	43	.411
TOTALS	359	333	333	359	692	692	.500

1995 DOUBLEHEADER STANDINGS

	Won	Lost	Split	Total Games W	L	Pct.
Houston	2	0	0	4	0	1.000
New York	1	0	0	2	0	1.000
Atlanta	0	0	0	0	0	.000
Colorado	0	0	0	0	0	.000
Los Angeles	0	0	0	0	0	.000
Montreal	0	0	0	0	0	.000
San Francisco	0	0	0	0	0	.000
Chicago	0	0	1	1	1	.500
Cincinnati	1	1	0	2	2	.500
Philadelphia	1	1	0	2	2	.500
San Diego	1	1	2	3	3	.500
Pittsburgh	1	2	0	2	4	.333
Florida	0	1	1	1	3	.250
St. Louis	0	1	0	0	2	.000

1995 EXTRA-INNING GAMES (99)

	Won	Lost	Pct.
Cincinnati	10	3	.769
St. Louis	9	5	.643
Chicago	8	6	.571
New York	9	7	.563
San Francisco	8	7	.533
Philadelphia	9	8	.529
Houston	11	10	.524
Pittsburgh	6	7	.462
San Diego	6	7	.462
Los Angeles	5	6	.455
Colorado	5	7	.417
Florida	6	9	.400
Montreal	4	8	.333
Atlanta	3	9	.250

1995 STANDINGS ON GRASS (575)

	Won	Lost	Pct.
Atlanta	65	44	.596
Los Angeles	62	51	.549
Colorado	63	52	.548
Houston	21	19	.525
Chicago	57	56	.504
San Diego	56	56	.500
San Francisco	55	56	.495
Florida	52	54	.491
New York	55	57	.491
Montreal	22	23	.489
Philadelphia	20	25	.444
Cincinnati	17	23	.425
Pittsburgh	16	29	.356
St. Louis	14	30	.318

1995 STANDINGS ON ARTIFICIAL SURFACES (432)

	Won	Lost	Pct.
Atlanta	25	10	.714
Cincinnati	68	36	.654
Houston	55	49	.529
Chicago	16	15	.516
Los Angeles	16	15	.516
Philadelphia	49	50	.495
St. Louis	48	51	.485
Colorado	14	15	.483
Montreal	44	55	.444
New York	14	18	.438
San Diego	14	18	.438
Pittsburgh	42	57	.424
Florida	15	22	.405
San Francisco	12	21	.364

1995 STANDINGS VS. LEFT-HANDED STARTERS

	Won	Lost	Pct.
Cincinnati	23	12	.657
Atlanta	23	13	.639
Colorado	28	17	.622
Houston	24	17	.585
Los Angeles	22	18	.550
Chicago	24	20	.545
Montreal	18	19	.486
New York	21	24	.467
Florida	21	28	.429
Philadelphia	20	27	.426
San Diego	17	23	.425
St. Louis	13	23	.361
San Francisco	10	20	.333
Pittsburgh	13	28	.317

1995 STANDINGS VS. RIGHT-HANDED STARTERS

	Won	Lost	Pct.
Atlanta	67	41	.620
Cincinnati	62	47	.569
Los Angeles	56	48	.538
San Diego	53	51	.510
Houston	52	51	.505
Philadelphia	49	48	.505
San Francisco	57	57	.500
Colorado	49	50	.495
Chicago	49	51	.490
Florida	46	48	.489
New York	48	51	.485
St. Louis	49	58	.458
Montreal	48	59	.449
Pittsburgh	45	58	.437

1995 CLUB HOME RUNS AT EACH PARK

By	Atl	Chi	Cin	Col	Fla	Hou	LA	Mtl	NY	Phil	Pitt	StL	SD	SF	1995 Total	1994 Total	Opp. Total
Atlanta	94	5	13	8	6	6	4	4	7	5	2	5	5	4	168	137	107
Chicago	8	83	2	12	9	6	5	1	8	3	6	5	5	5	158	109	162
Cincinnati	8	7	76	6	3	9	4	6	9	9	6	7	6	5	161	124	131
Colorado	8	4	6	134	7	3	6	5	1	5	5	4	10	2	200	125	160
Florida	4	7	6	13	68	6	2	3	4	10	10	2	0	9	144	94	139
Houston	9	13	1	5	3	41	1	3	6	1	7	7	6	6	109	120	118
Los Angeles	2	11	1	11	6	0	62	8	6	9	8	7	6	3	140	115	125
Montreal	6	9	6	6	7	3	4	43	3	12	4	1	4	10	118	108	128
New York	3	2	6	5	6	3	4	7	63	4	3	7	5	7	125	117	133
Philadelphia	7	0	1	2	4	3	1	2	6	51	4	3	5	5	94	80	134
Pittsburgh	2	6	5	7	3	4	4	0	2	5	69	2	8	8	125	80	130
St. Louis	3	8	7	9	0	1	3	5	3	0	3	54	4	7	107	108	135
San Diego	1	6	1	9	5	2	8	4	5	6	3	4	55	7	116	92	142
San Francisco	5	5	3	14	1	2	2	7	8	9	6	6	8	76	152	123	173
1995 Totals	160	166	134	241	128	89	110	98	131	129	136	114	127	154	1917		1917
1994 Totals	98	118	124	120	116	113	96	89	113	85	106	116	108	130		1532	1532

AT ATLANTA (160)

Atlanta (94)—Jones 15, Justice 15, Klesko 15, McGriff 15, Lopez 8, Blauser 7, Grissom 5, O'Brien 4, Lemke 3, Avery 2, Devereaux, Mordecai, Oliva, Smith, Glavine.
Chicago (8)—Roberson 2, Sosa 2, Dunston, Hernandez, McRae, Wilkins.
Cincinnati (8)—Gant 3, Larkin 2, M. Lewis, R. Sanders, Santiago.
Colorado (8)—Burks 2, Galarraga 2, Walker 2, Castilla, Girardi.
Florida (4)—Dawson 2, Pendleton 2.
Houston (9)—Bell 2, Bagwell, Biggio, Eusebio, Gonzalez, Hunter, May, Simms.
Los Angeles (2)—Offerman, Wallach.
Montreal (6)—Cordero 2, Alou, Lansing, Segui, R. White.
New York (3)—Bogar, Brogna, Hundley.
Philadelphia (7)—Hayes 3, Daulton, Duncan, Jefferies, Whiten.
Pittsburgh (2)—Bell, Merced.
St. Louis (3)—Cromer, Gilkey, Lankford.
San Diego (1)—Cianfrocco.
San Francisco (5)—Bonds, Carreon, Clayton, Phillips, Thompson.

AT CHICAGO (166)

Atlanta (5)—Blauser, Grissom, Jones, Justice, Mordecai.
Chicago (83)—Sosa 19, Dunston 8, Servais 7, Hernandez 6, Johnson 6, McRae 6, Zeile 6, Gonzalez 5, Timmons 5, Grace 4, Wilkins 3, Bullett 2, Parent 2, Roberson 2, Haney, Kmak.
Cincinnati (7)—Boone 3, R. Sanders 2, Larkin, Taubensee.
Colorado (4)—Bates, Hubbard, Walker, Young.
Florida (7)—Abbott, Arias, Browne, Decker, Gregg, Johnson, Sheffield.
Houston (13)—Biggio 3, Bagwell 2, May 2, Brumley, Gonzalez, Mouton, Shipley, Thompson, Wilkins.
Los Angeles (11)—Karros 3, Ashley 2, Wallach 2, DeShields, Kelly, Mondesi, Piazza.
Montreal (9)—R. White 2, Alou, Andrews, Berry, Cordero, Kelly, Lansing, Tarasco.
New York (2)—Bonilla, Hundley.
Pittsburgh (6)—C. Garcia, King, Merced, Parent, Young, Neagle.
St. Louis (8)—Caraballo 2, Cooper 2, Gilkey, Jordan, Lankford, Urbani.
San Diego (6)—Cedeno 2, Caminiti, Cianfrocco, Johnson, Nieves.
San Francisco (5)—Hill 2, Benjamin, Carreon, Williams.

AT CINCINNATI (134)

Atlanta (13)—McGriff 3, Jones 2, Justice 2, Grissom, Klesko, Lemke, Mordecai, O'Brien, Perez.
Chicago (2)—Grace 2.
Cincinnati (76)—Gant 12, Branson 9, R. Sanders 9, Larkin 8, Santiago 7, Boone 6, Morris 6, Taubensee 4, Walton 4, Anthony 3, Berryhill 2, Duncan 2, Howard, M. Lewis, D. Sanders, Smiley.
Colorado (6)—Bichette 2, Castilla, Galarraga, Kingery, Vander Wal.
Florida (6)—Conine, Dawson, Johnson, Morman, Pendleton, Sheffield.
Houston (1)—Simms.
Los Angeles (1)—Hernandez.
Montreal (6)—Alou 2, Benitez, Fletcher, Tarasco, R. White.
New York (6)—Alfonzo, Bonilla, Brogna, Hundley, C. Jones, Vizcaino.
Philadelphia (1)—Duncan.
Pittsburgh (5)—Johnson 2, C. Garcia, King, Merced.
St. Louis (7)—Mabry 2, Bell, Gilkey, Jordan, Lankford, Oliva.
San Diego (1)—E. Williams.
San Francisco (3)—Bonds 2, Benjamin.

AT COLORADO (241)

Atlanta (8)—McGriff 2, Blauser, Grissom, Jones, Justice, Klesko, O'Brien.
Chicago (12)—Sosa 4, Grace 2, Gonzalez, Hernandez, McRae, Wilkins, Zeile, Foster.
Cincinnati (6)—Gant 2, R. Sanders 2, Branson, Taubensee.
Colorado (134)—Bichette 31, Walker 24, Castilla 23, Galarraga 18, Burks 8, Girardi 6, Young 5, Bates 4, Kingery 4, Owens 3, Hubbard 2, Vander Wal 2, Mejia, Pulliam, Freeman, Swift.
Florida (13)—Conine 2, Dawson 2, Johnson 2, Pendleton 2, Sheffield 2, Carr, Colbrunn, Tavarez.
Houston (5)—Biggio 2, Bagwell, Bell, Mouton.
Los Angeles (11)—Mondesi 3, Piazza 3, Karros 2, Hollandsworth, Kelly, Webster.
Montreal (6)—Andrews 2, Berry, Cordero, Fletcher, Lansing.
New York (5)—Bonilla, Brogna, Hundley, C. Jones, Kent.
Philadelphia (2)—Jefferies, Morandini.
Pittsburgh (7)—Bell 2, King 2, Martin, Merced, Parent.
St. Louis (9)—Gilkey 3, Sheaffer 2, Jordan, Lankford, Mabry, Sweeney.
San Diego (9)—Plantier 3, Caminiti 2, Ausmus, Cianfrocco, Finley, Nieves.
San Francisco (14)—Williams 5, Aurilia 2, Bonds 2, Carreon 2, Phillips 2, Benard.

AT FLORIDA (128)

Atlanta (6)—McGriff 2, Grissom, Klesko, Lopez, Oliva.
Chicago (9)—Hernandez 2, Sosa 2, Dunston, Grace, Johnson, Sanchez, Zeile.
Cincinnati (3)—Morris, R. Sanders, Santiago.
Colorado (7)—Castilla 3, Burks 2, Walker 2.
Florida (68)—Conine 13, Abbott 12, Colbrunn 12, Pendleton 8, Sheffield 4, Johnson 3, Arias 2, Decker 2, Gregg 2, Natal 2, Veras 2, Carr, Dawson, Morman, Tavarez, Whitmore, Hammond.
Houston (3)—Biggio, Gonzalez, Magadan.
Los Angeles (6)—Mondesi 2, Piazza 2, Hollandsworth, Kelly.
Montreal (7)—Cordero 3, Berry 2, Andrews, Tarasco.
New York (6)—Bonilla 2, Kent 2, C. Jones, Stinnett.
Philadelphia (4)—Eisenreich, Morandini, Van Slyke, Webster.
Pittsburgh (3)—Parent 2, Martin.
San Diego (5)—Caminiti, Clark, Nieves, Petagine, E. Williams.
San Francisco (1)—Hill.

AT HOUSTON (89)

Atlanta (6)—Blauser, Grissom, Jones, Justice, Kelly, McGriff.
Chicago (6)—Grace 2, McRae, Servais, Sosa, Timmons.
Cincinnati (9)—Gant 4, Boone, M. Lewis, R. Sanders, Santiago, Walton.
Colorado (3)—Bates 2, Bichette.
Florida (6)—Sheffield 3, Colbrunn 2, Conine.
Houston (41)—Bagwell 10, Biggio 6, Eusebio 5, Simms 5, Bell 3, May 3, Cangelosi 2, Mouton 2, Goff, Gonzalez, Miller, Servais, Shipley.
Montreal (3)—Alou 2, Fletcher.
New York (3)—Bonilla, Buford, Stinnett.
Philadelphia (3)—Whiten 2, Jefferies.
Pittsburgh (4)—Bell, Clark, Johnson, Liriano.
St. Louis (1)—Lankford.
San Diego (2)—Gwynn, E. Williams.
San Francisco (2)—Bonds, Hill.

AT LOS ANGELES (110)

Atlanta (4)—Lopez 2, Justice, Oliva.
Chicago (5)—Sosa 3, Dunston, Grace.
Cincinnati (4)—Boone 2, Branson, Morris.
Colorado (6)—Bichette 2, Galarraga 2, Walker 2.
Florida (2)—Colbrunn, Johnson.
Houston (1)—May.
Los Angeles (62)—Karros 19, Mondesi 13, Piazza 9, Ashley 6, Wallach 4, Hollandsworth 3, DeShields 2, Kelly 2, Offerman 2, Gwynn, Hernandez.
Montreal (4)—Berry, Fletcher, Segui, Tarasco.
New York (4)—Bonilla 2, Brogna, Kent.
Philadelphia (1)—Eisenreich.
Pittsburgh (4)—Aude, Clark, King, Liriano.
St. Louis (3)—Jordan 2, Sweeney.
San Diego (8)—Caminiti 3, Cedeno, Gwynn, Livingstone, Nieves, Plantier.
San Francisco (2)—Bonds 2.

AT MONTREAL (98)

Atlanta (4)—Kelly, Klesko, Lopez, O'Brien.
Chicago (1)—Dunston.
Cincinnati (6)—Walton 2, Boone, Morris, R. Sanders, Taubensee.
Colorado (5)—Bichette, Castilla, Galarraga, Kingery, Walker.
Florida (3)—Johnson, Sheffield, Veras.
Houston (3)—Bagwell, Biggio, Simms.
Los Angeles (8)—Piazza 4, Mondesi 2, DeShields, Wallach.
Montreal (43)—Tarasco 7, R. White 6, Berry 5, Alou 4, Lansing 4, Segui 4, Fletcher 3, Andrews 2, Cordero 2, Benitez, Floyd, Grudzielanek, Laker, Rodriguez, Santangelo.
New York (7)—Everett 2, Hundley 2, Kent 2, Thompson.
Philadelphia (2)—Hollins, Jefferies.
St. Louis (5)—Jordan, Lankford, Oquendo, Pagnozzi, Zeile.
San Diego (4)—Livingstone 2, Caminiti, Finley.
San Francisco (7)—Bonds 3, Scarsone 2, Williams 2.

AT NEW YORK (131)

Atlanta (7)—Jones 2, Klesko, McGriff, O'Brien, Oliva, Smith.
Chicago (8)—McRae 2, Dunston, Grace, Hernandez, Sanchez, Servais, Zeile.
Cincinnati (9)—Gant 2, Taubensee 2, Anthony, Harris, Howard, Morris, R. Sanders.
Colorado (1)—Galarraga.
Florida (4)—Conine 3, Colbrunn.
Houston (6)—Biggio 2, Bagwell, Hunter, May, Miller.
Los Angeles (6)—Karros 2, DeShields, Mondesi, Prince, Wallach.
Montreal (3)—Lansing 2, Segui.
New York (63)—Brogna 13, Kent 11, Everett 9, Bonilla 7, Hundley 6, C. Jones 4, Thompson 3, Buford 2, Huskey 2, Segui 2, Vizcaino 2, Orsulak, Stinnett.
Philadelphia (6)—Marsh 2, Hayes, Van Slyke, Webster, Whiten.
Pittsburgh (2)—Johnson, Merced.
St. Louis (3)—Jordan, Lankford, Sheaffer.
San Diego (5)—Finley 2, Nieves 2, E. Williams.
San Francisco (8)—Hill 2, Bonds, Clayton, Sanders, Scarsone, Thompson, Williams.

AT PHILADELPHIA (129)

Atlanta (5)—Grissom, Jones, Justice, Klesko, Lemke.
Chicago (3)—Grace, Sanchez, Servais.
Cincinnati (9)—R. Sanders 2, Anthony, Boone, Duncan, Gant, Harris, Worthington, Smiley.
Colorado (5)—Bates, Bichette, Galarraga, Girardi, Vander Wal.
Florida (10)—Dawson 2, Sheffield 2, Abbott, Colbrunn, Conine, Gregg, Johnson, Veras.
Houston (1)—Gonzalez.
Los Angeles (9)—Piazza 4, DeShields 2, Karros 2, Mondesi.
Montreal (12)—Alou 2, Laker 2, Andrews, Fletcher, Segui, Silvestri, Spehr, Tarasco, R. White, Perez.
New York (4)—Brogna 2, Everett, Stinnett.
Philadelphia (51)—Daulton 7, Hayes 6, Eisenreich 5, Hollins 5, Whiten 5, Jefferies 4, Morandini 3, Dykstra 2, Flora 2, Longmire 2, Duncan, Elster, Gallagher, Jordan, Marsh, Stocker, Webster, Green, Juden, Olivares.
Pittsburgh (5)—Johnson, Liriano, Martin, Merced, Parent.
San Diego (6)—Caminiti, Gwynn, Johnson, Livingstone, Nieves, E. Williams.
San Francisco (9)—Bonds 3, Thompson 2, Williams 2, Sanders, Mulholland.

AT PITTSBURGH (136)

Atlanta (2)—Klesko 2.
Chicago (6)—Hernandez 2, Bullett, Gonzalez, McRae, Wilkins.
Cincinnati (6)—R. Sanders 4, Branson, Gant.
Colorado (5)—Burks, Castilla, Kingery, Owens, Walker.
Florida (10)—Abbott 2, Colbrunn 2, Conine, Gregg, Morman, Pendleton, Sheffield, Veras.
Houston (7)—Miller 3, Bagwell, Bell, Gonzalez, Plantier.
Los Angeles (8)—Piazza 4, Busch 2, Kelly, Mondesi.
Montreal (4)—Alou, Andrews, Fletcher, Segui.
New York (3)—Hundley 2, Bonilla.
Philadelphia (4)—Eisenreich 2, Jefferies, West.
Pittsburgh (69)—Bell 8, Martin 8, Merced 8, Johnson 7, King 7, Parent 5, Pegues 5, Young 5, Brumfield 4, C. Garcia 4, Clark 2, Encarnacion 2, Liriano 2, Aude, Cummings.
St. Louis (3)—Gilkey 2, Lankford.
San Diego (3)—Finley, E. Williams, Valenzuela.
San Francisco (6)—Carreon 5, Hill.

AT ST. LOUIS (114)

Atlanta (5)—Justice 2, Blauser, Kelly, McGriff.
Chicago (5)—Buechele, Haney, Servais, Sosa, Timmons.
Cincinnati (7)—Gant 2, R. Sanders 2, Hunter, Morris, Walton.
Colorado (4)—Bichette, Castilla, Kingery, Walker.
Florida (2)—Gregg, Johnson.
Houston (7)—Biggio 3, Plantier 2, Simms, Tucker.
Los Angeles (7)—Piazza 3, DeShields, Hansen, Karros, Mondesi.
Montreal (1)—Berry.
New York (7)—Bonilla 2, Alfonzo, Brogna, Butler, C. Jones, Kent.
Philadelphia (3)—Hayes, Hollins, Longmire.
Pittsburgh (2)—King, Martin.
St. Louis (54)—Lankford 16, Jordan 14, Gilkey 5, Coles 3, Hemond 3, Cromer 2, Mabry 2, Sheaffer 2, Zeile 2, Bell, Cooper, Oliva, Pagnozzi, Pena.
San Diego (4)—Ausmus, Cianfrocco, Gwynn, E. Williams.
San Francisco (6)—Williams 2, Bonds, Carreon, Hill, Scarsone.

AT SAN DIEGO (127)

Atlanta (5)—Blauser, Lopez, McGriff, O'Brien, Smith.
Chicago (5)—Sosa 3, Parent, Timmons.
Cincinnati (6)—Larkin 2, R. Sanders 2, Boone, Gant.
Colorado (10)—Galarraga 5, Walker 2, Burks, Castilla, Weiss.
Houston (6)—Bagwell, Bell, Biggio, Magadan, Plantier, Thompson.
Los Angeles (6)—Piazza 2, Busch, Karros, Mondesi, H. Rodriguez.
Montreal (4)—Berry 2, Alou, Fletcher.
New York (5)—Brogna, Buford, Hundley, Kent, Thompson.
Philadelphia (5)—Daulton, Jefferies, Morandini, Van Slyke, Whiten.
Pittsburgh (8)—Parent 4, Bell, Johnson, King, Martin.
St. Louis (4)—Gilkey, Jordan, Oquendo, Zeile.
San Diego (55)—Caminiti 16, Gwynn 5, Nieves 5, Finley 4, Reed 4, E. Williams 4, Cedeno 3, Ausmus 2, Petagine 2, Roberts 2, Cianfrocco, Clark, Holbert, Johnson, Livingstone, Newfield, Plantier, Valenzuela.
San Francisco (8)—Hill 3, Bonds, Clayton, Phillips, Sanders, Williams.

AT SAN FRANCISCO (154)

Atlanta (4)—Grissom, Lopez, McGriff, Oliva.
Chicago (5)—Grace 2, Dunston, Servais, Sosa.
Cincinnati (5)—Larkin 2, Gant, Howard, Santiago.
Colorado (2)—Bichette, Vander Wal.
Florida (9)—Colbrunn 3, Conine 3, Abbott, Diaz, Sheffield.
Houston (6)—Bagwell 3, Biggio 2, Shipley.
Los Angeles (3)—Karros 2, Offerman.
Montreal (10)—Tarasco 2, R. White 2, Berry, Cordero, Fletcher, Lansing, Segui, Silvestri.
New York (7)—Alfonzo 2, Thompson 2, Brogna, Huskey, Kent.
Philadelphia (5)—Eisenreich, Jefferies, Jordan, Webster, Whiten.
Pittsburgh (8)—King 4, Cummings, Merced, Parent, Pegues.
St. Louis (7)—Gilkey 3, Cromer 2, Lankford, Zeile.
San Diego (7)—Nieves 2, Ausmus, Caminiti, Finley, Holbert, E. Williams.
San Francisco (76)—Bonds 16, Hill 13, Williams 9, Carreon 7, Scarsone 7, Phillips 5, Manwaring 4, Thompson 4, Clayton 2, Sanders 2, Benjamin, Benzinger, Lampkin, Leonard, Lewis, Patterson, VanLandingham.

LIFETIME GRAND SLAM HOMERS
(Active NL Players for 1996 and those hitting NL grand slams in 1995)
(AL grand slams in parentheses)

Player	Team	GS
Ellis Burks	Rockies (8)	8
Gary Gaetti	Cardinals (8)	8
Andre Dawson	Marlins	7
Andres Galarraga	Rockies	7
Howard Johnson	FREE AGENT (1)	7
Lance Parrish	Pirates (6)	7
Mike Blowers	Dodgers (6)	6
Darren Daulton	Phillies	5
Wally Joyner	Pirates (5)	5
Fred McGriff	Braves (1)	5
Matt Williams	Giants	5
Dante Bichette	Rockies (1)	4
Barry Bonds	Giants	4
Mike Piazza	Dodgers	4
Kurt Abbott	Marlins	3
Darnell Coles	Cardinals (2)	3
Jim Eisenreich	Phillies (1)	3
Glenallen Hill	Giants (2)	3
Todd Hundley	Mets	3
Jeff King	Pirates	3
Terry Pendleton	Marlins	3
Chris Sabo	Reds	3
Ryne Sandberg	Cubs	3
Benito Santiago	FREE AGENT	3
Gary Sheffield	Marlins	3
Mitch Webster	Dodgers (1)	3
Devon White	Marlins (3)	3
Todd Zeile	Phillies	3
Eric Anthony	Reds	2
Jay Bell	Pirates	2
Craig Biggio	Astros	2
Ken Caminiti	Padres	2
Jeff Conine	Marlins	2
Shawon Dunston	Giants	2
Tony Eusebio	Astros	2
Steve Finley	Padres (2)	2
Greg Gagne	Dodgers (2)	2
Ron Gant	Cardinals	2
Charlie Hayes	Pirates	2
Brian R. Hunter	Reds	2
Brian Johnson	Padres	2
Jeff Kent	Mets	2
Derrick May	Astros	2
Brian McRae	Cubs (1)	2
Melvin Nieves	Padres	2
Joe Orsulak	Marlins (1)	2
Tom Pagnozzi	Cardinals	2
Dwight Smith	Braves	2
Bill Spiers	Astros (2)	2
Robby Thompson	Giants	2
Mark Whiten	Phillies (1)	2
Eddie Williams	Tigers	2
Moises Alou	Expos	1
Shane Andrews	Expos	1
Billy Bean	Padres	1
Sean Berry	Astros	1
Damon Berryhill	Reds	1
Jeff Blauser	Braves	1
Pat Borders	Cardinals (1)	1
Rico Brogna	Mets	1
Brett Butler	Dodgers (1)	1
Archi Cianfrocco	Padres	1
Greg Colbrunn	Marlins	1
Scott Cooper	FREE AGENT (1)	1
Delino DeShields	Dodgers	1
Lenny Dykstra	Phillies	1
Carl Everett	Mets	1
Mike Gallego	Cardinals (1)	1
Craig Grebeck	Marlins (1)	1
Tommy Gregg	Marlins	1
Marquis Grissom	Braves	1
Tony Gwynn	Padres	1
Chris Gwynn	Padres	1
Chris Hammond	Marlins	1
Dave Hansen	Dodgers	1
Lenny Harris	Reds	1
Rickey Henderson	Padres (1)	1
Jose Hernandez	Cubs	1
Ray Holbert	Astros	1
Gregg Jefferies	Phillies (1)	1
Lance Johnson	Mets (1)	1
Brian Jordan	Cardinals	1
Jeff Juden	Giants	1
David Justice	Braves	1
Roberto Kelly	FREE AGENT	1
Mike Kingery	Pirates (1)	1
Ryan Klesko	Braves	1
Ray Lankford	Cardinals	1
Mike Lansing	Expos	1
Nelson Liriano	Pirates	1
Luis Lopez	Padres	1
Tom Marsh	Phillies	1
Brent Mayne	Mets (1)	1
Willie McGee	Cardinals	1
Orlando Merced	Pirates	1
Raul Mondesi	Dodgers	1
Mickey Morandini	Phillies	1
Hal Morris	Reds	1
James Mouton	Astros	1
Denny Neagle	Pirates	1
John Patterson	Giants	1
Gerald Perry	Cardinals (1)	1
Luis Polonia	FREE AGENT (1)	1
Randy Ready	Phillies (1)	1
Jeff Reed	Rockies	1
Bip Roberts	Royals	1
David Segui	Expos	1
Danny Sheaffer	Cardinals	1
Craig Shipley	Padres	1
Don Slaught	Reds (1)	1
Tim Spehr	Expos (1)	1
Ryan Thompson	Mets	1
Andy Van Slyke	FREE AGENT	1
Quilvio Veras	Marlins	1
Larry Walker	Rockies	1
Walt Weiss	Rockies (1)	1
Rondell White	Expos	1
Rick Wilkins	Astros	1

N.L. ALL-TIME GRAND-SLAM HOMER LEADERS, 1901-1995

Willie McCovey, Giants (16); Padres (2)	18
Hank Aaron, Braves	16
Gil Hodges, Dodgers	14
George Foster, Reds (9); Mets (4)	13
Ernie Banks, Cubs	12
Rogers Hornsby, Cardinals (7); Giants (1); Cubs (4)	12
Ralph Kiner, Pirates (11); Cubs (1)	12
Johnny Bench, Reds	11
Gary Carter, Expos (7); Mets (4)	11
Dave Kingman, Giants (3); Mets (3); Padres (2); Cubs (3)	11
Willie Stargell, Pirates	11
Joe Adcock, Reds (1); Braves (9)	10
John Milner, Mets (5); Pirates (5)	10
Walker Cooper, Cardinals (1); Giants (4); Reds (1); Braves (1); Cubs (2)	9
Stan Musial, Cardinals	9
Orlando Cepeda, Giants (4); Braves (4)	8
Carl Furillo, Dodgers	8
George Kelly, Giants (7); Reds (1)	8
Eddie Mathews, Braves	8
Willie Mays, Giants	8
Bill Nicholson, Cubs	8
Ron Northey, Phillies (2); Cardinals (5); Cubs (1)	8
Andy Seminick, Phillies (5); Reds (3)	8
Ted Simmons, Cardinals (7); Braves (1)	8
Bobby Thomson, Giants (4); Braves (4)	8
Billy Williams, Cubs	8
Dick Allen, Phillies (5); Cardinals (2)	7
Ed Bailey, Reds (3); Giants (2); Braves (1); Cubs (1)	7
Wally Berger, Braves (6); Reds (1)	7
Ken Boyer, Cardinals	7
Hubie Brooks, Expos (6); Mets (1)	7
Ron Cey, Dodgers (5); Cubs (2)	7
Jack Clark, Cardinals (5); Cardinals (1); Padres (1)	7
Roberto Clemente, Pirates	7
Andre Dawson, Expos (2); Cubs (4); Marlins (1)	7
Ron Fairly, Dodgers (2); Expos (4); Cardinals (1)	7
Andres Galarraga, Expos (2); Cardinals (1); Rockies (4)	7
Sid Gordon, Giants (3); Braves (4)	7
Keith Hernandez, Cardinals (5); Mets (2)	7
Willie Jones, Phillies (6); Reds (1)	7
Chuck Klein, Phillies (6); Cubs (1)	7
Mike Marshall, Dodgers (6); Mets (1)	7
Mel Ott, Giants	7
Dave Parker, Pirates (2); Reds (5)	7
Mike Schmidt, Phillies	7
Wally Westlake, Pirates	7
Bill White, Cardinals (6); Phillies (1)	7
Fred Williams, Cubs (1); Phillies (6)	7
Bob Aspromonte, Astros	6
Bob Bailey, Pirates (2); Expos (4)	6
Jim Bottomley, Cardinals	6
Roy Campanella, Dodgers	6
Dave Concepcion, Reds	6
Eric Davis, Reds (5); Dodgers (1)	6
Vince DiMaggio, Pirates (2); Phillies (4)	6
Del Ennis, Phillies (5); Cardinals (1)	6
Howard Johnson, Mets (5); Rockies (1)	6
Ernie Lombardi, Reds (3); Giants (3)	6
Lee May, Reds (4); Astros (2)	6
Tim McCarver, Cardinals (5); Phillies (1)	6
Kevin McReynolds, Padres (1); Mets (5)	6
Al Oliver, Pirates (4); Expos (2)	6
Andy Pafko, Cubs (5); Dodgers (1)	6
Vada Pinson, Reds	6
Pee Wee Reese, Dodgers	6
Rusty Staub, Expos (2); Mets (4)	6
Darryl Strawberry, Mets (4); Dodgers (1); Giants (1)	6
Gus Bell, Pirates (2); Reds (3)	5
Dolph Camilli, Phillies (2); Dodgers (3)	5
Cesar Cedeno, Astros (4); Cardinals (1)	5
Nate Colbert, Padres	5
Kal Daniels, Dodgers (4); Cubs (1)	5
Darren Daulton, Phillies	5
Jody Davis, Cubs	5
Nick Esasky, Reds	5
Darrell Evans, Braves (3); Giants (2)	5
Elbie Fletcher, Braves (1); Pirates (4)	5
Augie Galan, Cubs (3); Dodgers (1); Reds (1)	5
Steve Garvey, Dodgers (4); Padres (1)	5
Gabby Hartnett, Cubs	5
Jim Hickman, Mets (3); Cubs (2)	5
Hank Leiber, Giants (2); Cubs (3)	5
Greg Luzinski, Phillies	5
Johnny Mize, Cardinals (2); Giants (3)	5
Wally Moon, Cardinals (4); Dodgers (1)	5
Dale Murphy, Braves (4); Phillies (1)	5
Tony Perez, Reds	5
Tim Raines, Expos	5
Bill Robinson, Phillies (2); Pirates (3)	5
Frank Robinson, Reds	5
Ron Santo, Cubs	5
Duke Snider, Dodgers	5
Dick Stuart, Pirates (3); Phillies (2)	5
Tim Wallach, Expos	5
Bob Watson, Astros	5
Wes Westrum, Giants	5
Matt Williams, Giants	5
Hack Wilson, Cubs (3); Dodgers (2)	5

1995 GRAND SLAMS

Eusebio, Astros	2
Galarraga, Rockies	2
Hundley, Mets	2
Nieves, Padres	2
Piazza, Dodgers	2
Abbott, Marlins	1
Andrews, Expos	1
Berry, Expos	1
Bichette, Rockies	1
Brogna, Mets	1
Caminiti, Padres	1
Cianfrocco, Padres	1
Colbrunn, Marlins	1
Dawson, Marlins	1
DeShields, Dodgers	1
Eisenreich, Phillies	1
Everett, Mets	1
Gant, Reds	1
Gregg, Marlins	1
Gwynn, Padres	1
Hammond, Marlins	1
Hernandez, Cubs	1
Hill, Giants	1
Holbert, Padres	1
Johnson, Padres	1
Juden, Phillies	1
King, Pirates	1
Klesko, Braves	1
Lansing, Expos	1
Liriano, Pirates	1
May, Astros	1
McRae, Cubs	1
Mondesi, Dodgers	1
Neagle, Pirates	1
Roberts, Padres	1
Segui, Expos	1
Sheaffer, Cardinals	1
Sheffield, Marlins	1
Smith, Braves	1
Veras, Marlins	1
White, Expos	1
Williams, Padres	1
Williams, Giants	1

1995 CLUB TOTALS

Club	GS
San Diego	9
Florida	7
Montreal	5
Los Angeles	4
New York	4
Colorado	3
Houston	3
Pittsburgh	3
Atlanta	2
Chicago	2
Philadelphia	2
San Francisco	2
Cincinnati	1
St. Louis	1

CAREER FIRSTS

Player	Date	Opp.
Veras, Quilvio	5/5	Mon.
Eusebio, Tony	5/19	Mon.
Roberts, Bip	5/2	Pit.
Lansing, Mike	5/23	S.D.
White, Rondell	5/28	L.A.
Hammond, Chris	5/29	Hou.
Berry, Sean	6/2	S.D.
Klesko, Ryan	6/6	Chi.
DeShields, Delino	6/21	St.L.
Neagle, Denny	6/27	Chi.
Gregg, Tommy	7/9	St.L.
Holbert, Ray	7/17	Cin.
Colbrunn, Greg	7/18	S.F.
Cianfrocco, Archi	7/21	Atl.
Nieves, Melvin	8/2	S.F.
Mondesi, Raul	8/15	Chi.
Liriano, Nelson	8/18	Fla.
Gwynn, Tony	8/22	Phi.
Everett, Carl	8/25	S.D.
Juden, Jeff	8/25	L.A.
Sheaffer, Danny	8/26	Col.
Hernandez, Jose	8/31	Fla.
Segui, David	9/5	S.F.
Brogna, Rico	9/17	Phi.
Andrews, Shane	9/28	Cin.

30 OR MORE HOME RUNS—SEASON

Total Homers	Player and Club	Year
56	Hack Wilson, Chicago	1930
54	Ralph Kiner, Pittsburgh	1949
52	Willie Mays, San Francisco	1965
52	George Foster, Cincinnati	1977
51	Ralph Kiner, Pittsburgh	1947
51	Johnny Mize, New York	1947
51	Willie Mays, New York	1955
49	Ted Kluszewski, Cincinnati	1954
49	Willie Mays, San Francisco	1962
49	Andre Dawson, Chicago	1987
48	Willie Stargell, Pittsburgh	1971
48	Dave Kingman, Chicago	1979
48	Mike Schmidt, Philadelphia	1980
47	Ralph Kiner, Pittsburgh	1950
47	Ed Mathews, Milwaukee	1953
47	Ted Kluszewski, Cincinnati	1955
47	Ernie Banks, Chicago	1958
47	Willie Mays, San Francisco	1964
47	Hank Aaron, Atlanta	1971
47	Kevin Mitchell, San Francisco	1989
46	Ed Mathews, Milwaukee	1959
46	Orlando Cepeda, San Francisco	1961
46	Barry Bonds, San Francisco	1993
45	Ernie Banks, Chicago	1959
45	Hank Aaron, Milwaukee	1962
45	Willie McCovey, San Francisco	1969
45	Johnny Bench, Cincinnati	1970
45	Mike Schmidt, Philadelphia	1979
44	Ernie Banks, Chicago	1955
44	Hank Aaron, Milwaukee	1957, 1963
	Atlanta	1966, 1969
44	Willie McCovey, San Francisco	1963
44	Willie Stargell, Pittsburgh	1973
44	Dale Murphy, Atlanta	1987
43	Chuck Klein, Philadelphia	1929
43	Johnny Mize, St. Louis	1940
43	Duke Snider, Brooklyn	1956
43	Ernie Banks, Chicago	1957
43	Dave Johnson, Atlanta	1973
43	Matt Williams, San Francisco	1994
42	Rogers Hornsby, St. Louis	1922
42	Mel Ott, New York	1929
42	Ralph Kiner, Pittsburgh	1951
42	Duke Snider, Brooklyn	1953, 1955
42	Gil Hodges, Brooklyn	1954
42	Billy Williams, Chicago	1970
41	Fred Williams, Philadelphia	1923
41	Roy Campanella, Brooklyn	1953
41	Willie Mays, New York	1954
41	Hank Sauer, Chicago	1954
41	Ed Mathews, Milwaukee	1955
41	Ernie Banks, Chicago	1960
41	Darrell Evans, Atlanta	1973
41	Jeff Burroughs, Atlanta	1977
40	Rogers Hornsby, Chicago	1929
40	Chuck Klein, Philadelphia	1930
40	Ralph Kiner, Pittsburgh	1948
40	Johnny Mize, New York	1948
40	Gil Hodges, Brooklyn	1951
40	Ted Kluszewski, Cincinnati	1953
40	Ed Mathews, Milwaukee	1954
40	Duke Snider, Brooklyn	1954, 1957
40	Wally Post, Cincinnati	1955
40	Hank Aaron, Milwaukee	1960
	Atlanta	1973
40	Willie Mays, San Francisco	1961
40	Richie Allen, Philadelphia	1966
40	Tony Perez, Cincinnati	1970
40	Johnny Bench, Cincinnati	1972
40	George Foster, Cincinnati	1978
40	Mike Schmidt, Philadelphia	1983
40	Ryne Sandberg, Chicago	1990
40	David Justice, Atlanta	1993
40	Dante Bichette, Colorado	1995
39	Rogers Hornsby, St. Louis	1925
39	Hack Wilson, Chicago	1929
39	Wally Berger, Boston	1930
39	Stan Musial, St. Louis	1948
39	Hank Aaron, Milwaukee	1959
	Atlanta	1967
39	Ed Mathews, Milwaukee	1960
39	Frank Robinson, Cincinnati	1962
39	Willie McCovey, San Francisco	1965, 1970
39	Lee May, Cincinnati	1971
39	Bobby Bonds, San Francisco	1973
39	Greg Luzinski, Philadelphia	1977
39	Darryl Strawberry, New York	1987, 1988
39	Jeff Bagwell, Houston	1994
39	Chuck Klein, Philadelphia	1932
38	Mel Ott, New York	1932
38	Joe Adcock, Milwaukee	1956
38	Frank Robinson, Cincinnati	1956
38	Willie Mays, San Francisco	1963
38	Lee May, Cincinnati	1969
38	Hank Aaron, Atlanta	1970
38	Nate Colbert, San Diego	1970, 1972
38	Mike Schmidt, Philadelphia	1975, 1976, 1977
38	Howard Johnson, New York	1991
38	Matt Williams, San Francisco	1993
37	Gabby Hartnett, Chicago	1930
37	Ralph Kiner, Pittsburgh	1952
37	Hank Sauer, Chicago	1952
37	Ed Mathews, Milwaukee	1956
37	Frank Robinson, Cincinnati	1961
37	Ernie Banks, Chicago	1962
37	Willie Mays, San Francisco	1966
37	Jim Wynn, Houston	1967
37	Tony Perez, Cincinnati	1969
37	Billy Williams, Chicago	1972
37	Dave Kingman, New York	1976, 1982
37	Dale Murphy, Atlanta	1985
37	Mike Schmidt, Philadelphia	1986
37	Eric Davis, Cincinnati	1987
37	Darryl Strawberry, New York	1990
37	Fred McGriff, San Diego-Atlanta	1993
37	Barry Bonds, San Francisco	1994
36	Mel Ott, New York	1938
36	Willard Marshall, New York	1947
36	Stan Musial, St. Louis	1949
36	Andy Pafko, Chicago	1950
36	Willie Mays, New York	1956
36	Wally Post, Cincinnati	1956
36	Frank Robinson, Cincinnati	1959
36	Willie McCovey, San Francisco	1966, 1968
36	Joe Torre, Atlanta	1966
36	Mike Schmidt, Philadelphia	1974, 1984
36	Dave Kingman, New York	1975
36	Dale Murphy, Atlanta	1982, 1983, 1984
36	Howard Johnson, New York	1987, 1989
36	Ron Gant, Atlanta	1993
36	Sammy Sosa, Chicago	1995
36	Larry Walker, Colorado	1995
35	Babe Herman, Brooklyn	1930
35	Rip Collins, St. Louis	1934
35	Mel Ott, New York	1934
35	Walker Cooper, New York	1947
35	Hank Sauer, Cincinnati	1948
35	Ralph Kiner, Pittsburgh-Chicago	1953
35	Stan Musial, St. Louis	1954
35	Ted Kluszewski, Cincinnati	1956
35	Willie Mays, New York	1957
35	Frank Thomas, Pittsburgh	1958
35	Joe Adcock, Milwaukee	1961
35	Dick Stuart, Pittsburgh	1961
35	Orlando Cepeda, San Francisco	1962
35	Greg Luzinski, Philadelphia	1978
35	Bob Horner, Atlanta	1980
35	Mike Schmidt, Philadelphia	1982, 1987
35	Jack Clark, St. Louis	1987
35	Will Clark, San Francisco	1987
35	Kevin Mitchell, San Francisco	1990
35	Fred McGriff, San Diego	1992
35	Mike Piazza, Los Angeles	1993
34	Wally Berger, Boston	1934, 1935
34	Dolf Camilli, Brooklyn	1941
34	Willie Mays, San Francisco	1959
34	Hank Aaron, Milwaukee	1961
	Atlanta	1972
34	Frank Thomas, New York	1962
34	Orlando Cepeda, San Francisco	1963
34	Billy Williams, Chicago	1965
34	Richie Allen, St. Louis	1970
34	Orlando Cepeda, Atlanta	1970
34	Lee May, Cincinnati	1970
34	Deron Johnson, Philadelphia	1971
34	Greg Luzinski, Philadelphia	1975
34	Dave Winfield, San Diego	1979
34	Dave Parker, Cincinnati	1985
34	Eric Davis, Cincinnati	1989
34	Glenn Davis, Houston	1989
34	Matt Williams, San Francisco	1991
34	Barry Bonds, Pittsburgh	1992
34	Bobby Bonilla, New York	1993
34	Phil Plantier, San Diego	1993
34	Fred McGriff, Atlanta	1994
33	Mel Ott, New York	1936
33	Bill Nicholson, Chicago	1944
33	Roy Campanella, Brooklyn	1951
33	Stan Musial, St. Louis	1955
33	Billy Williams, Chicago	1964
33	Frank Robinson, Cincinnati	1965
33	Ron Santo, Chicago	1965
33	Jim Hart, San Francisco	1966
33	Willie Stargell, Pittsburgh	1966, 1972
33	Richie Allen, Philadelphia	1968
33	Jim Wynn, Houston	1969
33	Bobby Bonds, San Francisco	1971
33	Earl Williams, Atlanta	1971
33	Johnny Bench, Cincinnati	1974
33	Steve Garvey, Los Angeles	1977
33	Bob Horner, Atlanta	1979
33	Dale Murphy, Atlanta	1980
33	Pedro Guerrero, Los Angeles	1985
33	Mike Schmidt, Philadelphia	1985
33	Barry Bonds, Pittsburgh	1990
	San Francisco	1995
33	Matt Williams, San Francisco	1990
33	Gary Sheffield, San Diego	1992
33	Sammy Sosa, Chicago	1993
32	Lefty O'Doul, Philadelphia	1929
32	Hank Sauer, Chicago	1950
32	Gil Hodges, Brooklyn	1950, 1952, 1956
32	Stan Musial, St. Louis	1951
32	Bobby Thomson, New York	1951
32	Roy Campanella, Brooklyn	1955
32	Stan Lopata, Philadelphia	1956
32	Ed Mathews, Milwaukee	1957, 1961, 1965
32	Ken Boyer, St. Louis	1960
32	Hank Aaron, Milwaukee	1965
32	John Callison, Philadelphia	1965
32	Deron Johnson, Cincinnati	1965
32	Ernie Banks, Chicago	1968
32	Richie Allen, Philadelphia	1969
32	Bobby Bonds, San Francisco	1969
32	Jim Hickman, Chicago	1970
32	Jim Wynn, Los Angeles	1974
32	Rick Monday, Chicago	1976
32	Reggie Smith, Los Angeles	1977
32	Willie Stargell, Pittsburgh	1979
32	Pedro Guerrero, Los Angeles	1982, 1983
32	Bob Horner, Atlanta	1982
32	Andre Dawson, Montreal	1983
32	Gary Carter, New York	1985
32	Bobby Bonilla, Pittsburgh	1990
32	Ron Gant, Atlanta	1990, 1991
32	Vinny Castilla, Colorado	1995
32	Eric Karros, Los Angeles	1995
32	Mike Piazza, Los Angeles	1995
31	Jim Bottomley, St. Louis	1928
31	Hack Wilson, Chicago	1928
31	Don Hurst, Philadelphia	1929
31	Chuck Klein, Philadelphia	1931
31	Mel Ott, New York	1935, 1937
31	Joe Medwick, St. Louis	1937
31	Hank Sauer, Cincinnati-Chicago	1949
31	Roy Campanella, Brooklyn	1950
31	Del Ennis, Philadelphia	1950
31	Duke Snider, Brooklyn	1950
31	Gil Hodges, Brooklyn	1953
31	George Crowe, Cincinnati	1957
31	Ed Mathews, Milwaukee	1958
31	Frank Robinson, Cincinnati	1958, 1960
31	Frank Howard, Los Angeles	1962
31	John Callison, Philadelphia	1964
31	Orlando Cepeda, San Francisco	1964
31	Jim Hart, San Francisco	1964
31	Mack Jones, Milwaukee	1965
31	Felipe Alou, Atlanta	1966
31	Willie McCovey, San Francisco	1967
31	Ron Santo, Chicago	1967
31	Willie Stargell, Pittsburgh	1970
31	Johnny Bench, Cincinnati	1977
31	Gary Carter, Montreal	1977
31	Mike Schmidt, Philadelphia	1981
31	Jason Thompson, Pittsburgh	1982
31	Glenn Davis, Houston	1986
31	Dave Parker, Cincinnati	1986
31	Fred McGriff, San Diego	1991
31	Andre Dawson, Chicago	1991
31	Andres Galarraga, Colorado	1994, 1995
30	Fred Williams, Philadelphia	1927
30	Hack Wilson, Chicago	1927
30	Ival Goodman, Cincinnati	1938
30	Mel Ott, New York	1942
30	Del Ennis, Philadelphia	1948
30	Sid Gordon, New York	1948
30	Andy Pafko, Chicago-Brooklyn	1951
30	Hank Sauer, Chicago	1951
30	Gus Bell, Cincinnati	1953
30	Stan Musial, St. Louis	1953
30	Frank Thomas, Pittsburgh	1953
30	Hank Sauer, Chicago	1958
30	Hank Aaron, Milwaukee	1958
30	Ron Santo, Chicago	1964, 1966
30	Billy Williams, Chicago	1968
30	Rusty Staub, Montreal	1970
30	Willie Montanez, Philadelphia	1971
30	Dusty Baker, Los Angeles	1977
30	Ron Cey, Los Angeles	1977
30	Dave Parker, Pittsburgh	1978
30	George Foster, Cincinnati	1979
30	Larry Parrish, Montreal	1979
30	Darrell Evans, San Francisco	1983
30	Glenn Davis, Houston	1988
30	Ryne Sandberg, Chicago	1989
30	Rick Wilkins, Chicago	1993
30	Kevin Mitchell, Cincinnati	1994

54

ALL-TIME NATIONAL LEAGUE LEADERS IN EACH BATTING DEPARTMENT, 1876-1995
*In Hall of Fame, Players in CAPS active in 1995

GAMES
Pete Rose	3,562
*Hank Aaron	3,076
*Stan Musial	3,026
*Willie Mays	2,992
*Honus Wagner	2,785
*Mel Ott	2,730
*Rabbit Maranville	2,670
*Lou Brock	2,616
*Willie McCovey	2,577
*Paul Waner	2,539

AT BATS
Pete Rose	14,053
*Hank Aaron	11,628
*Stan Musial	10,972
*Willie Mays	10,881
*Honus Wagner	10,427
*Lou Brock	10,332
*Rabbit Maranville	10,078
*Mel Ott	9,456
*Roberto Clemente	9,454
*Paul Waner	9,452

RUNS
Pete Rose	2,165
*Hank Aaron	2,107
*Willie Mays	2,062
*Stan Musial	1,949
*Mel Ott	1,859
*Honus Wagner	1,740
*Cap Anson	1,712
*Paul Waner	1,625
*Fred Clarke	1,620
*Lou Brock	1,610

HITS
Pete Rose	4,256
*Stan Musial	3,630
*Hank Aaron	3,600
*Honus Wagner	3,430
*Willie Mays	3,283
*Paul Waner	3,151
*Cap Anson	3,081
*Lou Brock	3,023
*Roberto Clemente	3,000
*Rogers Hornsby	2,895

SINGLES
Pete Rose	3,215
*Honus Wagner	2,426
*Cap Anson	2,331
*Stan Musial	2,253
*Lou Brock	2,247
*Paul Waner	2,246
*Hank Aaron	2,171
*Frank Frisch	2,171
*Roberto Clemente	2,154
*Richie Ashburn	2,119

DOUBLES
Pete Rose	746
*Stan Musial	725
*Honus Wagner	651
*Paul Waner	603
*Hank Aaron	600
*Joe Medwick	540
*Rogers Hornsby	532
*Cap Anson	526
*Willie Mays	523
*Mel Ott	488

TRIPLES
*Honus Wagner	252
*Jake Beckley	227
*Fred Clarke	219
*Roger Connor	212
*Paul Waner	190
*Dan Brouthers	183
*Joe Kelley	182
*Rabbit Maranville	177
*Stan Musial	177
*Zack Wheat	171

HOME RUNS
*Hank Aaron	733
*Willie Mays	660
*Mike Schmidt	548
*Willie McCovey	521
*Ernie Banks	512
*Mel Ott	511
*Eddie Mathews	503
*Stan Musial	475
*Willie Stargell	475
*Duke Snider	407
ANDRE DAWSON	407

TOTAL BASES
*Hank Aaron	6,591
*Stan Musial	6,134
*Willie Mays	6,066
Pete Rose	5,752
*Mel Ott	5,041
*Honus Wagner	4,888
*Ernie Banks	4,706
*Rogers Hornsby	4,660
*Roberto Clemente	4,492
*Paul Waner	4,470

RUNS BATTED IN
(Since 1920)
*Hank Aaron	2,202
*Stan Musial	1,951
*Willie Mays	1,903
*Mel Ott	1,860
*Ernie Banks	1,636
*Mike Schmidt	1,595
*Willie McCovey	1,555
*Willie Stargell	1,540
Tony Perez	1,477
*Eddie Mathews	1,426

BATTING PERCENTAGE
(500 or More Games)
*Willie Keeler	.377
*Jesse Burkett	.364
*Rogers Hornsby	.359
Lefty O'Doul	.353
*Billy Hamilton	.351
*Dan Brouthers	.348
*Ed Delahanty	.348
*Elmer Flick	.345
*Bill Terry	.341
*Cap Anson	.339

SLUGGING PERCENTAGE
(500 or More Games)
*Rogers Hornsby	.578
*Johnny Mize	.577
*Hank Aaron	.567
*Stan Musial	.559
*Willie Mays	.557
*Ralph Kiner	.554
*Frank Robinson	.548
*Hack Wilson	.545
*Chuck Klein	.543
BARRY BONDS	.541

★ ★ ★ ★ ★

MAJOR LEAGUE BASEBALL PROPERTIES
350 Park Avenue
New York, N.Y. 10022
(212) 339-7900
Don Gibson, Vice President of Business Affairs

PLAYER RELATIONS COMMITTEE
350 Park Avenue
New York, N.Y. 10022
(212) 339-7400
Randy Levine, President
Louis Melendez, Associate Counsel
John Westhoff, Associate Counsel
Barbara Ernst, Contract Administrator

MAJOR LEAGUE BASEBALL PLAYERS ASSOCIATION
12 East 49th St.
New York, N.Y. 10017
(212) 826-0808
Donald M. Fehr,
Executive Director & General Counsel

MAJOR LEAGUE BASEBALL INTERNATIONAL PARTNERSHIP
1301 Avenue of the Americas, 39th Floor
New York, NY 10019
(212) 977-7301
Tim Brosnan, Chief Operating Officer

MAJOR LEAGUE SCOUTING BUREAU
23712 Birtcher Drive
El Toro, CA 92630
(714) 458-7600

NATIONAL ASSOCIATION OF PROFESSIONAL BASEBALL LEAGUES
P.O. Box A
St. Petersburg, FL 33731
(813) 822-6937
Mike Moore, President

LIFETIME BATTING AVERAGES—NATIONAL LEAGUE PLAYERS

(100 or more games—records compiled in National and American Leagues)

Player	AVG.	G	AB	R	H	TB	2B	3B	HR	RBI	SB
Abbott, Kurt	.252	241	826	112	208	351	36	10	29	102	9
Alfonzo, Edgardo	.278	101	335	26	93	128	13	5	4	41	1
Alou, Moises	.295	467	1609	256	475	802	110	14	63	277	44
Anthony, Eric	.229	556	1740	209	399	673	70	6	64	242	22
Arias, Alex	.267	281	677	67	181	227	25	3	5	68	2
Ashley, Billy	.235	126	353	23	83	124	11	0	10	33	0
Ausmus, Brad	.269	253	815	107	219	318	36	6	17	70	23
5 Bagwell, Jeff	.306	684	2523	434	771	1300	158	16	113	469	57
Bates, Jason	.267	116	322	42	86	135	17	4	8	46	3
Bean, Billy	.226	272	478	42	108	147	20	2	5	53	3
Bell, Derek	.291	449	1617	218	471	684	66	6	45	228	87
Bell, Jay	.267	1071	4002	598	1070	1586	220	43	70	390	58
Belliard, Rafael	.224	989	2068	198	464	540	45	14	1	135	40
Benjamin, Mike	.196	299	637	79	125	196	26	3	13	51	21
Berry, Sean	.279	391	1073	143	299	492	61	6	40	154	31
Berryhill, Damon	.239	610	1863	158	445	687	98	6	44	234	3
Bichette, Dante	.289	820	2966	413	858	1449	183	15	126	488	88
Biggio, Craig	.285	1055	3880	615	1105	1611	221	24	79	389	196
Blauser, Jeff	.263	950	3177	463	835	1283	156	23	82	356	50
Blowers, Mike	.258	453	1378	179	355	592	67	4	54	229	6
Bogar, Tim	.249	206	402	41	100	138	20	0	6	51	2
Bonds, Barry	.286	1425	5020	999	1436	2714	306	48	292	864	340
Boone, Bret	.272	355	1294	168	352	568	75	6	43	189	11
Borders, Pat	.252	804	2473	219	624	950	135	10	57	282	6
Branson, Jeff	.260	377	936	113	243	360	44	5	21	98	6
8 Brogna, Rico	.298	182	652	91	194	331	39	4	30	99	1
Browne, Jerry	.271	982	3190	431	866	1120	135	25	23	288	73
Brumfield, Jacob	.271	311	826	146	224	330	50	7	14	62	54
Brumley, Mike	.206	295	635	78	131	173	17	8	3	38	20
Buford, Damon	.213	125	249	50	53	81	10	0	6	23	12
Bullett, Scott	.249	138	209	23	52	84	5	9	3	26	12
Burks, Ellis	.281	1013	3720	589	1044	1737	202	40	137	534	109
Butler, Brett	.291	2074	7706	1285	2243	2927	268	127	54	552	535
Caminiti, Ken	.266	1091	3967	483	1055	1597	213	13	101	539	51
Cangelosi, John	.248	716	1373	232	341	435	45	11	9	96	130
Carreon, Mark	.276	619	1578	190	435	687	74	2	58	224	9
Castilla, Vinny	.293	317	1015	136	297	504	55	10	44	139	6
Cedeno, Andujar	.241	512	1716	191	414	637	92	10	37	185	21
Cianfrocco, Archi	.241	292	792	86	191	311	31	4	27	122	7
Clark, Dave	.264	603	1464	189	387	600	54	6	49	212	15
Clark, Phil	.278	261	540	62	150	231	30	0	17	65	4
Clayton, Royce	.249	506	1790	179	445	607	72	18	18	184	66
Colbrunn, Greg	.276	307	1004	114	277	433	49	1	35	161	19
Coles, Darnell	.245	936	2869	332	702	1093	141	14	74	366	20
7 Conine, Jeff	.300	447	1640	220	492	767	84	13	55	277	5
Cooper, Scott	.272	517	1642	185	446	646	88	11	30	196	6
Cromer, Tripp	.217	117	368	38	80	114	19	0	5	18	0
Daulton, Darren	.244	1020	3223	440	785	1364	176	17	123	525	44
Dawson, Andre	.279	2585	9869	1367	2758	4763	501	98	436	1577	314
Decker, Steve	.211	168	478	31	101	150	12	2	11	47	1
DeShields, Delino	.271	754	2818	426	764	1033	108	31	33	251	253
Dunston, Shawon	.265	1140	4151	506	1100	1690	208	44	98	448	146
Dykstra, Lenny	.285	1238	4425	781	1263	1852	275	40	78	391	282
Eisenreich, Jim	.288	1084	3173	390	915	1294	175	33	46	389	88
Elster, Kevin	.220	580	1674	177	368	567	80	7	35	183	10
Eusebio, Tony	.291	178	546	68	159	227	31	2	11	88	0
Everett, Carl	.245	106	359	55	88	146	14	1	14	60	7
Finley, Steve	.278	919	3364	486	935	1318	132	55	47	292	185
Fletcher, Darrin	.258	482	1420	125	367	557	78	5	34	203	0
Floyd, Cliff	.253	139	434	52	110	156	20	4	6	51	13
Fonville, Chad	.278	102	320	43	89	97	6	1	0	16	20
Gaetti, Gary	.254	1972	7203	914	1832	3121	349	32	292	1075	86
Gagne, Greg	.254	1526	4731	615	1202	1831	263	45	92	492	102
Galarraga, Andres	.283	1308	4848	669	1371	2284	267	23	200	761	81

Player	AVG.	G	AB	R	H	TB	2B	3B	HR	RBI	SB
Gallego, Mike	.242	1033	2745	356	663	920	107	12	42	277	24
Gant, Ron	.263	977	3602	594	949	1716	177	31	176	568	180
Garcia, Carlos	.277	381	1392	174	385	544	65	11	24	130	44
Gilkey, Bernard	.282	593	2133	319	602	920	126	18	52	250	80
Gonzalez, Luis	.270	670	2284	300	617	989	141	27	59	332	58
5 Grace, Mark	.306	1155	4356	608	1333	1896	261	28	82	589	55
Grebeck, Craig	.255	414	1071	129	273	383	62	6	12	110	2
Gregg, Tommy	.243	433	861	85	209	312	39	2	20	88	13
Grissom, Marquis	.275	837	3229	510	889	1292	153	26	66	318	295
Gutierrez, Ricky	.252	275	869	125	219	278	27	7	6	66	11
1 Gwynn, Tony	.336	1830	7144	1073	2401	3206	384	80	87	804	285
Gwynn, Chris	.269	518	917	111	247	349	32	11	16	108	2
Hansen, Dave	.264	414	734	68	194	261	31	0	12	77	1
Harris, Lenny	.271	822	2042	256	553	682	71	11	12	172	84
Hayes, Charlie	.268	941	3370	361	904	1387	175	13	94	452	32
Hemond, Scott	.217	298	607	79	132	198	30	0	12	58	23
Henderson, Rickey	.290	2192	8063	1719	2338	3552	395	57	235	858	1149
Hernandez, Carlos	.226	221	464	29	105	146	14	0	9	40	1
Hernandez, Jose	.230	197	479	63	110	183	15	8	14	53	3
Hill, Glenallen	.260	595	1929	270	501	881	90	13	88	284	77
Howard, Thomas	.270	556	1464	185	395	548	70	10	21	140	56
Hulett, Tim	.249	720	2128	245	529	789	90	13	48	220	14
Hundley, Todd	.230	491	1468	169	338	557	61	4	50	187	7
Hunter, Brian R.	.231	361	924	113	213	403	54	5	42	165	3
Javier, Stan	.258	1089	2896	439	748	1007	120	23	31	275	155
Jefferies, Gregg	.296	976	3738	522	1106	1629	214	18	91	474	149
Johnson, Brian	.250	104	300	27	75	108	13	1	6	45	0
Johnson, Charles	.258	101	326	45	84	138	16	1	12	43	0
Johnson, Howard	.249	1531	4940	760	1229	2204	247	22	228	760	231
Johnson, Lance	.285	979	3618	487	1031	1346	108	78	17	334	232
Jones, Chris	.271	292	583	89	158	251	22	10	17	74	16
Jones, Chipper	.268	148	527	89	141	239	23	3	23	86	8
Jordan, Brian	.277	306	1084	147	300	505	47	16	42	162	41
Joyner, Wally	.290	1364	5105	725	1481	2283	290	19	158	789	50
Justice, David	.273	777	2718	452	741	1353	118	16	154	497	32
Karros, Eric	.265	575	2135	271	566	955	108	7	89	320	8
Kelly, Mike	.220	127	214	40	47	82	16	2	5	26	7
Kelly, Roberto	.285	962	3535	495	1006	1462	173	20	81	395	210
Kent, Jeff	.272	474	1688	235	459	768	91	10	66	263	10
King, Jeff	.256	739	2570	328	657	1025	137	12	69	382	32
Kingery, Mike	.272	702	1758	260	478	703	96	24	27	192	43
Klesko, Ryan	.291	234	605	93	176	351	39	5	42	123	6
Laker, Tim	.220	135	273	28	60	86	13	2	3	31	3
Lampkin, Tom	.216	215	380	41	82	117	13	2	6	41	11
Lankford, Ray	.268	711	2596	416	695	1158	150	32	83	351	143
Lansing, Mike	.270	374	1352	155	365	509	80	5	18	142	62
8 Larkin, Barry	.298	1176	4429	711	1322	1938	222	44	102	537	239
Lee, Manuel	.255	922	2693	304	686	871	88	20	19	249	31
Lemke, Mark	.247	794	2290	242	565	755	87	14	25	200	4
Leonard, Mark	.227	168	321	37	73	119	18	2	8	41	0
Liriano, Nelson	.263	623	1894	263	498	696	85	25	21	199	57
Livingstone, Scott	.292	430	1184	138	346	461	64	3	15	139	8
Longmire, Tony	.285	139	256	32	73	100	18	0	3	37	3
Lopez, Javier	.288	197	642	68	185	302	23	5	28	90	0
4 Mabry, John	.307	135	411	37	126	167	24	1	5	44	0
Magadan, Dave	.290	1039	3102	398	901	1174	164	11	29	372	9
Manwaring, Kirt	.247	660	1990	165	492	638	77	12	15	193	8
Martin, Al	.282	361	1207	204	340	555	63	16	40	140	51
May, Derrick	.282	494	1563	194	441	642	78	6	37	237	24
Mayne, Brent	.247	399	1113	104	275	355	50	3	8	119	6
McCarty, David	.227	179	556	68	126	172	27	5	3	39	5
10 McGee, Willie	.297	1704	6500	877	1933	2610	299	87	68	723	325
McGriff, Fred	.285	1291	4512	788	1284	2414	229	17	289	803	48
McRae, Brian	.267	751	2973	411	794	1145	147	39	42	296	120

56

LIFETIME BATTING AVERAGES—NATIONAL LEAGUE PLAYERS

(100 or more games—records compiled in National and American Leagues)

Player	AVG.	G	AB	R	H	TB	2B	3B	HR	RBI	SB
Mejia, Roberto	.224	126	397	47	89	154	23	6	10	38	7
Merced, Orlando	.282	656	2160	327	609	911	122	18	48	314	27
Miller, Orlando	.269	108	364	39	98	143	20	2	7	45	4
Mondesi, Raul	.295	293	1056	167	311	532	53	15	46	154	42
Morandini, Mickey	.266	584	2019	256	537	743	92	33	16	161	56
Morman, Russ	.249	197	457	48	114	164	15	4	9	41	2
3 Morris, Hal	.308	702	2394	327	737	1077	149	13	55	330	34
Mouton, James	.253	203	608	85	154	205	29	2	6	43	49
Nieves, Melvin	.207	139	319	38	66	127	8	1	17	46	2
Oquendo, Jose	.256	1190	3202	339	821	1015	104	24	14	254	35
Orsulak, Joe	.278	1268	3926	523	1091	1491	168	35	54	379	92
Pagnozzi, Tom	.253	732	2279	188	577	804	118	11	29	247	14
Parker, Rick	.242	147	211	34	51	65	8	0	2	23	8
Parrish, Lance	.252	1988	7067	856	1782	3113	305	27	324	1070	28
Patterson, John	.215	228	564	74	121	162	16	5	5	52	22
Pena, Geronimo	.264	373	1001	161	264	427	60	8	29	122	54
Pendleton, Terry	.274	1611	6114	772	1673	2435	311	38	125	825	122
Perry, Gerald	.265	1193	3144	383	832	1181	150	11	59	396	142
Phillips, J.R.	.193	118	285	29	55	100	10	1	11	35	2
2 Piazza, Mike	.322	389	1455	232	469	811	62	2	92	304	5
Polonia, Luis	.293	1095	3957	606	1159	1472	150	56	17	327	283
Pratt, Todd	.224	102	295	27	66	110	15	1	9	36	0
Prince, Tom	.181	198	448	30	81	126	28	1	5	49	3
Ready, Randy	.259	777	2110	312	547	816	107	21	40	239	27
Reed, Jeff	.234	722	1760	136	411	554	71	6	20	147	2
Reed, Jody	.276	1086	3947	515	1088	1424	241	10	25	335	35
Roberson, Kevin	.194	138	273	36	53	115	9	1	17	42	0
Rodriguez, Henry	.243	278	766	77	186	290	35	3	21	101	1
Sabo, Chris	.268	857	3229	479	866	1444	207	16	113	410	118
Sanchez, Rey	.275	402	1341	143	369	457	60	8	4	100	11
Sandberg, Ryne	.289	1879	7384	1179	2133	3361	349	72	245	905	325
Sanders, Deion	.264	494	1583	249	418	646	57	36	33	141	127
Sanders, Reggie	.278	503	1805	315	501	881	98	24	78	283	101
Santiago, Benito	.262	1110	3944	436	1034	1617	177	23	120	510	75
Scarsone, Steve	.258	194	469	73	121	199	27	3	15	57	3
Segui, David	.271	609	1766	218	478	691	92	5	37	225	6
Servais, Scott	.233	336	1015	101	237	398	60	1	33	141	2
Sharperson, Mike	.280	557	1203	149	337	438	61	5	10	123	22
Sheaffer, Danny	.229	234	616	67	141	202	24	2	11	79	2
Sheffield, Gary	.287	730	2696	399	774	1288	139	12	117	430	96
Shipley, Craig	.268	409	967	102	259	347	42	5	12	95	25
Simms, Mike	.229	132	293	37	67	121	12	0	14	45	3
Slaught, Don	.283	1231	3800	388	1075	1569	225	28	71	440	18
Smith, Dwight	.282	712	1654	228	466	718	83	20	43	210	41
Smith, Ozzie	.261	2491	9169	1221	2396	3000	392	67	26	775	573
Sosa, Sammy	.256	802	2881	419	738	1295	110	27	131	423	159
Spehr, Tim	.224	183	232	33	52	91	19	1	6	32	5
Spiers, Bill	.254	620	1764	236	448	591	59	18	16	189	52
Stankiewicz, Andy	.247	212	515	73	127	166	26	2	3	37	14
Stinnett, Kelly	.234	124	346	43	81	119	14	3	6	32	4
Stocker, Kevin	.263	277	942	126	248	316	37	8	5	91	13
Tarasco, Tony	.253	237	605	86	153	244	26	4	19	61	29
Taubensee, Eddie	.255	370	1056	115	269	424	50	6	31	143	7
Thompson, Milt	.277	1297	3695	488	1022	1391	154	37	47	354	213
Thompson, Robby	.260	1241	4385	636	1139	1784	227	38	114	437	101
Thompson, Ryan	.239	283	997	127	238	416	53	4	39	126	8
Thurman, Gary	.244	413	792	121	193	238	27	6	2	64	65
Vander Wal, John	.251	428	700	86	176	284	30	9	20	94	12
Van Slyke, Andy	.274	1658	5711	835	1562	2529	293	91	164	792	245
Varsho, Gary	.244	571	837	101	204	297	41	11	10	84	27
Veras, Quilvio	.261	124	440	86	115	164	20	7	5	32	56
Vizcaino, Jose	.269	612	1961	224	527	663	69	17	11	172	27
Walker, Larry	.286	805	2860	464	817	1442	178	21	135	485	114
Walton, Jerome	.264	523	1424	220	376	523	68	8	21	116	58
Webster, Lenny	.262	242	577	66	151	230	35	1	14	67	1
Webster, Mitch	.263	1265	3419	504	900	1370	150	55	70	342	160
Wehner, John	.259	175	375	43	97	117	14	3	0	19	9
Weiss, Walt	.252	933	2958	351	745	912	102	16	11	226	66
White, Devon	.260	1268	4942	789	1284	2039	246	58	131	515	249
White, Rondell	.289	193	644	112	186	295	46	6	17	85	27
Whiten, Mark	.256	633	2219	320	569	902	82	19	71	294	55
Whitmore, Darrell	.203	112	330	31	67	97	11	2	5	21	4
Wilkins, Rick	.254	470	1408	193	358	609	69	4	58	175	9
Williams, Matt	.260	1015	3735	525	970	1856	163	24	225	647	28
Young, Eric	.283	403	1216	196	344	482	51	18	17	119	101
Young, Kevin	.233	266	759	68	177	266	40	5	13	84	4
Zeile, Todd	.263	836	2993	390	787	1230	165	13	84	424	33

HOME RUNS BY PITCHERS

(Pitchers active in 1995 who have hit Major League home runs)

PITCHER	HOME RUNS	LAST HOME RUN DATE	OPPONENT
F. Valenzuela	10	9/17/95	Chi., NL
Kevin Gross	6	5/23/94	Chi., NL
Andy Benes	4	5/12/93	Cin.
Jim Gott	4	6/20/87	S.D.
Tommy Greene	4	9/3/93	Cin.
Chris Hammond	4	5/29/95	Hou.
Omar Olivares	4	7/24/95	Col.
Rick Aguilera	3	9/4/87	L.A.
Dennis Eckersley	3	5/26/86	Cin.
John Smoltz	3	6/29/94	Mtl.
Steve Avery	2	7/8/95	S.F.
Tim Belcher	2	5/16/92	Phi.
Tom Browning	2	6/19/93	L.A.
Ron Darling	2	6/30/89	Cin.
Doug Drabek	2	5/16/93	L.A.
Marvin Freeman	2	5/23/95	Chi., NL
Derek Lilliquist	2	5/1/90	N.Y., NL
Greg Maddux	2	4/20/92	Phi.
Denny Neagle	2	6/27/95	Chi., NL
Mark Portugal	2	6/16/93	S.D.
Armando Reynoso	2	8/28/93	N.Y., NL
Jose Rijo	2	7/31/93	S.D.
Scott Sanderson	2	5/1/87	S.D.
John Smiley	2	6/27/95	Phi.
Trevor Wilson	2	6/5/93	Pit.
Shawn Boskie	1	4/27/91	Cin.
Jim Bullinger	1	6/8/92	St.L.
Dennis Cook	1	5/19/90	L.A.
Danny Darwin	1	9/15/88	Cin.
Dave Eiland	1	4/10/92	L.A.
Sid Fernandez	1	9/21/89	St.L.
Kevin Foster	1	5/23/95	Col.
Tom Glavine	1	8/10/95	Cin.
Tyler Green	1	8/23/95	S.D.
Butch Henry	1	5/8/92	Pit.
Ken Hill	1	6/24/92	Phi.
Jeff Juden	1	8/25/95	L.A.
Darryl Kile	1	7/3/93	St.L.
Ramon Martinez	1	9/22/91	Atl.
Bobby Munoz	1	6/25/94	Atl.
Alejandro Pena	1	7/23/83	St.L.
Jeff Russell	1	8/23/83	Chi., NL
Pete Schourek	1	6/13/94	L.A.
Lee Smith	1	7/5/82	Atl.
John Wetteland	1	5/27/90	St.L.
Mitch Williams	1	9/18/89	N.Y., NL
Terry Mulholland	1	8/18/95	Phi.
Carlos Perez	1	5/11/95	Phi.
Bill Swift	1	5/7/95	L.A.
Tom Urbani	1	6/30/95	Chi., NL
W. VanLandingham	1	8/4/95	L.A.
Tim Wakefield	1	7/7/93	Hou.
David West	1	7/6/95	Pit.

CLUBS' ALL-TIME TOP TEN IN BATTING DEPARTMENTS

(Batting percentage column includes only players in 500 or more games.)

BRAVES

GAMES	AT BATS	RUNS	HITS	DOUBLES	TRIPLES
H. Aaron 3,076	H. Aaron 11,628	H. Aaron 2,107	H. Aaron 3,600	H. Aaron 600	Maranville 103
E. Mathews 2,223	E. Mathews 8,049	E. Mathews 1,452	E. Mathews 2,201	E. Mathews 338	H. Aaron 96
Murphy 1,926	Murphy 7,098	H. Long 1,294	Tenney 2,002	Murphy 306	H. Long 89
Maranville 1,795	H. Long 6,767	Tenney 1,127	H. Long 1,911	T. Holmes 291	Bruton 79
Tenney 1,715	Maranville 6,724	Murphy 1,103	Murphy 1,901	H. Long 277	Tenney 77
H. Long 1,642	Tenney 6,629	Duffy 998	Maranville 1,696	Berger 248	W. Nash 76
R. Lowe 1,403	R. Lowe 5,580	R. Lowe 997	R. Lowe 1,606	Maranville 244	Morrill 75
Crandall 1,394	T. Holmes 4,956	W. Nash 857	Duffy 1,560	Tenney 236	Duffy 72
Logan 1,351	Logan 4,931	Maranville 801	T. Holmes 1,503	Morrill 226	R. Lowe 70
T. Holmes 1,289	Morrill 4,746	Morrill 796	W. Nash 1,345	Logan 207	E. Mathews 70

CUBS

GAMES	AT BATS	RUNS	HITS	DOUBLES	TRIPLES
Banks 2,528	Banks 9,421	Anson 1,712	Anson 3,081	Anson 530	Ryan 136
Anson 2,253	Anson 9,084	Ryan 1,406	Banks 2,583	Banks 407	Anson 129
B. Williams 2,213	B. Williams 8,479	B. Williams 1,306	B. Williams 2,510	B. Williams 402	Schulte 117
Santo 2,126	Santo 7,768	Banks 1,305	Hack 2,193	Hartnett 391	Dahlen 106
Cavarretta 1,953	Sandberg 7,378	Hack 1,239	Santo 2,171	Hack 363	Cavarretta 99
Hack 1,938	Hack 7,278	Sandberg 1,177	Ryan 2,153	Santo 353	Tinker 93
Hartnett 1,926	Ryan 6,803	Santo 1,109	Sandberg 2,132	Ryan 350	Banks 90
Sandberg 1,866	Cavarretta 6,592	Cavarretta 968	Cavarretta 1,927	Sandberg 349	B. Williams 87
Ryan 1,656	Kessinger 6,355	Dahlen 899	Hartnett 1,867	B. Herman 346	Lange 83
Kessinger 1,648	Hartnett 6,282	B. Herman 875	B. Herman 1,710	Cavarretta 341	Hack 81

REDS

GAMES	AT BATS	RUNS	HITS	DOUBLES	TRIPLES
Rose 2,722	Rose 10,934	Rose 1,741	Rose 3,358	Rose 601	Roush 153
Concepcion 2,488	Concepcion 8,723	Bench 1,091	Concepcion 2,326	Concepcion 389	Rose 115
Bench 2,158	Bench 7,658	F. Robinson 1,043	Bench 2,048	Bench 381	McPhee 111
Perez 1,948	Perez 6,846	Concepcion 993	Perez 1,934	Pinson 342	Pinson 96
Pinson 1,565	Pinson 6,335	Pinson 978	Pinson 1,881	Perez 339	W.C. Walker 94
F. Robinson 1,502	F. Robinson 5,527	Perez 936	Roush 1,784	F. Robinson 318	M.F. Mitchell 88
Driessen 1,480	Roush 5,384	McPhee 919	F. Robinson 1,673	F. McCormick 285	Beckley 80
Roush 1,399	Kluszewski 4,961	Morgan 816	Kluszewski 1,499	Roush 260	Goodman 79
McMillan 1,348	Corcoran 4,848	Roush 815	F. McCormick 1,439	Kluszewski 244	Daubert 78
Kluszewski 1,339	F. McCormick 4,787	Kluszewski 745	G. Bell 1,343	Driessen 240	Groh 75

ROCKIES

GAMES	AT BATS	RUNS	HITS	DOUBLES	TRIPLES
Bichette 396	Bichette 1,601	Bichette 269	Bichette 511	Bichette 114	E. Young 18
Galarraga 366	Galarraga 1,441	Galarraga 237	Galarraga 462	Galarraga 85	Kingery 12
E. Young 354	Girardi 1,102	E. Young 187	E. Young 310	Hayes 68	Girardi 11
Girardi 304	E. Young 1,084	Girardi 145	Girardi 302	Castilla 54	Castilla 10
Castilla 296	Hayes 996	Hayes 135	Hayes 297	E. Young 50	Bichette 9
Hayes 270	Castilla 994	Castilla 134	Castilla 292	Kingery 45	Burks 9
Weiss 247	Weiss 850	Weiss 123	Weiss 217	Girardi 40	Liriano 8
Kingery 224	Kingery 651	Kingery 122	Kingery 199	Walker 31	Galarraga 7
Reed 196	Walker 494	Walker 96	Walker 151	Weiss 28	Weiss 7
Vander Wal 196	Clark 478	Burks 74	Clark 135	Clark 26	Clark 6

MARLINS

GAMES	AT BATS	RUNS	HITS	DOUBLES	TRIPLES
Conine 410	Conine 1,529	Conine 207	Conine 464	Conine 77	Conine 11
Carr 353	Carr 1,292	Carr 190	Carr 331	Carr 58	Abbott 10
Arias 249	Santiago 806	Sheffield 140	Sheffield 227	Barberie 36	Santiago 8
Santiago 240	Sheffield 771	Abbott 101	Barberie 216	Abbott 35	Veras 7
Sheffield 222	Abbott 765	Colbrunn 87	Santiago 200	Santiago 33	Barberie 4
Abbott 221	Barberie 747	Veras 86	Abbott 193	Colbrunn 32	Browne 4
Barberie 206	Destrade 699	Barberie 85	Colbrunn 193	Pendleton 32	Carr 4
Destrade 192	Colbrunn 683	Santiago 84	Destrade 172	Sheffield 32	Sheffield 4
Colbrunn 185	Arias 578	Destrade 73	Arias 152	Destrade 24	Arias 3
Browne 178	Browne 513	Pendleton 70	Pendleton 149	Browne 21	Dawson 3
	Pendleton 513				Destrade 3

ASTROS

GAMES	AT BATS	RUNS	HITS	DOUBLES	TRIPLES
Cruz 1,870	Cruz 6,629	Cedeno 890	Cruz 1,937	Cedeno 343	Cruz 80
Puhl 1,516	Cedeno 5,732	Cruz 871	Cedeno 1,659	Cruz 335	Morgan 63
Cedeno 1,512	Wynn 5,063	Wynn 829	Watson 1,448	Watson 241	Metzger 62
Wynn 1,426	Watson 4,883	Puhl 676	Puhl 1,357	Wynn 228	Puhl 56
Watson 1,381	Puhl 4,837	Watson 640	Wynn 1,291	Puhl 226	Cedeno 55
Rader 1,178	Doran 4,264	Biggio 615	Doran 1,139	Biggio 221	Reynolds 55
Reynolds 1,170	Rader 4,232	Doran 611	Cabell 1,124	Rader 197	Cabell 45
Doran 1,165	Cabell 4,005	Morgan 597	Biggio 1,105	Bass 194	Finley 41
Bass 1,122	Biggio 3,880	Cabell 522	Rader 1,060	Caminiti 180	Doran 35
Walling 1,072	Morgan 3,729	Rader 520	Bass 990	Doran 180	Wynn 32

DODGERS

GAMES	AT BATS	RUNS	HITS	DOUBLES	TRIPLES
Wheat 2,318	Wheat 8,859	Reese 1,338	Wheat 2,804	Wheat 464	Wheat 171
Russell 2,181	Reese 8,058	Wheat 1,255	Reese 2,170	Snider 343	W. Davis 110
Reese 2,166	W. Davis 7,495	Snider 1,199	W. Davis 2,091	Garvey 333	H. Myers 97
Hodges 2,006	Russell 7,318	Gilliam 1,163	Snider 1,995	Reese 330	Daubert 87
Gilliam 1,956	Gilliam 7,119	Hodges 1,088	Garvey 1,968	Furillo 324	Hummel 82
W. Davis 1,952	Hodges 6,881	W. Davis 1,004	Russell 1,926	W. Davis 321	Snider 82
Snider 1,923	Snider 6,640	J. Robinson 947	Furillo 1,910	Gilliam 304	Reese 80
Furillo 1,806	Garvey 6,543	Furillo 895	Gilliam 1,889	Hodges 294	Sheckard 80
Garvey 1,727	Furillo 6,378	Griffin 886	Hodges 1,884	Russell 293	T.P. Daly 74
Wills 1,593	Wills 6,156	Wills 876	Wills 1,732	F. Walker 274	Johnston 73

CLUBS' ALL-TIME TOP TEN IN BATTING DEPARTMENTS

(Batting percentage column includes only players in 500 or more games.)

BRAVES

HOME RUNS	TOTAL BASES	RUNS BATTED IN	EXTRA BASE HITS	BATTING AVG.	STOLEN BASES (since 1898)
H. Aaron 733	H. Aaron 6,591	H. Aaron 2,202	H. Aaron 1,429	Hamilton .... .338	H. Aaron 240
E. Mathews 493	E. Mathews 4,158	E. Mathews 1,388	E. Mathews 901	Duffy .... .336	Tenney 196
Murphy 371	Murphy 3,394	Murphy 1,143	Murphy 714	C.S. Stahl .... .328	Maranville 194
Adcock 239	H. Long 2,630	H. Long 961	Berger 499	Garr .... .317	Royster 174
Horner 215	Tenney 2,440	Duffy 926	Adcock 458	Carty .... .317	Murphy 160
Berger 199	Maranville 2,215	R. Lowe 872	H. Long 454	Richbourg .... .311	Nixon 160
Crandall 170	Berger 2,212	Nash 809	T. Holmes 426	H. Aaron .... .310	Gant 157
Justice 154	Adcock 2,164	Adcock 760	Horner 382	J.J. Collins .... .310	Sweeney 153
Gant 147	T. Holmes 2,152	Berger 746	Maranville 370	Berger .... .304	Bruton 143
J. Torre 142	R. Lowe 2,113	Horner 652	Crandall 354	T. Holmes .... .303	Garr 137

CUBS

HOME RUNS	TOTAL BASES	RUNS BATTED IN	EXTRA BASE HITS	BATTING AVG.	STOLEN BASES
Banks 512	Banks 4,706	Anson 1,715	Banks 1,009	Anson .... .339	Chance 404
B. Williams 392	B. Williams 4,262	Banks 1,636	B. Williams 881	Stephenson .... .336	Sandberg 325
Santo 337	Anson 4,145	B. Williams 1,353	Santo 756	Lange .... .336	Tinker 304
Sandberg 245	Santo 3,667	Santo 1,290	Anson 751	Everett .... .326	Evers 281
Hartnett 231	Sandberg 3,360	Hartnett 1,153	Hartnett 686	Cuyler .... .325	Schulte 200
Nicholson 205	Hartnett 3,079	Ryan 914	Sandberg 666	H. Wilson .... .322	Slagle 198
Sauer 198	Ryan 3,054	Sandberg 905	Ryan 579	Ryan .... .316	Hack 165
H. Wilson 190	Hack 2,889	Cavarretta 896	Cavarretta 532	Gore .... .316	Sheckard 163
Dawson 174	Cavarretta 2,742	Nicholson 833	Nicholson 503	M.J. Kelly .... .314	DeJesus 154
Durham 138	Schulte 2,351	H. Wilson 768	Hack 501	Demaree .... .309	Cuyler 153
					Hofman 153

REDS

HOME RUNS	TOTAL BASES	RUNS BATTED IN	EXTRA BASE HITS	BATTING AVG.	STOLEN BASES
Bench 389	Rose 4,645	Bench 1,376	Rose 868	Seymour .... .333	Morgan 406
F. Robinson 324	Bench 3,644	Perez 1,192	Bench 794	Roush .... .331	Concepcion 321
Perez 287	Perez 3,246	Rose 1,036	F. Robinson 692	Beckley .... .324	Bescher 320
Kluszewski 251	Concepcion 3,114	F. Robinson 1,009	Perez 682	Holliday .... .315	Davis 247
Foster 244	F. Robinson 3,063	Concepcion 950	Pinson 624	Hargrave .... .314	Larkin 239
Pinson 186	Pinson 2,973	Kluszewski 886	Concepcion 538	Bressler .... .311	Pinson 221
Davis 177	Kluszewski 2,542	Foster 861	Kluszewski 518	Lombardi .... .311	Roush 199
Post 172	Roush 2,488	Pinson 814	Foster 488	Morris .... .310	Corcoran 171
G. Bell 160	Foster 2,289	F. McCormick 803	Roush 459	C.B. Miller .... .308	Lobert 168
Morgan 152	G. Bell 2,121	Roush 754	G. Bell 423	Rose .... .307	Mitchell 165
Rose 152					

ROCKIES

HOME RUNS	TOTAL BASES	RUNS BATTED IN	EXTRA BASE HITS	BATTING AVG.	STOLEN BASES
Bichette 88	Bichette 907	Bichette 312	Bichette 211	No qualifying batters	E. Young 95
Galarraga 84	Galarraga 813	Galarraga 289	Galarraga 176		Bichette 48
Castilla 44	Castilla 498	Hayes 148	Hayes 109		Cole 30
Walker 36	Hayes 482	Castilla 138	Castilla 108		Weiss 27
Hayes 35	E. Young 444	Girardi 120	E. Young 84		Galarraga 22
Burks 27	Girardi 409	E. Young 108	Walker 72		Kingery 18
E. Young 16	Kingery 304	Walker 101	Kingery 69		Walker 16
Girardi 15	Walker 300	Kingery 78	Girardi 66		Hayes 14
Boston 14	Weiss 265	Burks 73	Burks 54		Girardi 12
Clark 13	Burks 239	Clark 67	Clark 45		Johnson 11

MARLINS

HOME RUNS	TOTAL BASES	RUNS BATTED IN	EXTRA BASE HITS	BATTING AVG.	STOLEN BASES
Conine 55	Conine 728	Conine 266	Conine 143	No qualifying batters	Carr 115
Sheffield 53	Sheffield 426	Sheffield 161	Sheffield 89		Veras 56
Colbrunn 29	Carr 421	Colbrunn 120	Abbott 71		Sheffield 43
Abbott 26	Abbott 326	Destrade 102	Carr 70		Colbrunn 12
Destrade 25	Santiago 321	Abbott 93	Santiago 65		Cotto 11
Santiago 24	Colbrunn 314	Carr 91	Colbrunn 62		Santiago 11
Pendleton 14	Barberie 290	Santiago 91	Destrade 52		Tavarez 8
Johnson 12	Destrade 277	Pendleton 78	Barberie 50		Abbott 7
Barberie 10	Pendleton 225	Barberie 64	Pendleton 47		Weiss 7
Carr 8	Arias 192	Arias 61	Veras 32		Briley 6
Dawson 8					

ASTROS

HOME RUNS	TOTAL BASES	RUNS BATTED IN	EXTRA BASE HITS	BATTING AVG.	STOLEN BASES
Wynn 223	Cruz 2,846	Cruz 942	Cedeno 561	Bagwell .... .306	Cedeno 487
G. Davis 166	Cedeno 2,601	Watson 782	Cruz 553	Watson .... .297	Cruz 288
Cedeno 163	Wynn 2,252	Cedeno 778	Wynn 483	Cruz .... .292	Morgan 219
Watson 139	Watson 2,166	Wynn 719	Watson 410	Cedeno .... .289	Puhl 217
Cruz 138	Puhl 1,881	Rader 600	Rader 355	Biggio .... .285	Biggio 196
Rader 128	Rader 1,701	G. Davis 518	Puhl 344	J. Alou .... .282	Cabell 191
Bagwell 113	Biggio 1,611	Bagwell 469	G. Davis 326	Cabell .... .281	Doran 191
Bass 87	Doran 1,596	Bass 468	Bagwell 324	Puhl .... .281	Wynn 180
L. May 81	Cabell 1,524	Caminiti 445	Bass 311	Finley .... .281	Young 153
Biggio 79	Bass 1,505	Puhl 432	Morgan 288	Bass .... .278	Hatcher 145

DODGERS

HOME RUNS	TOTAL BASES	RUNS BATTED IN	EXTRA BASE HITS	BATTING AVG.	STOLEN BASES
Snider 389	Wheat 4,003	Snider 1,271	Snider 814	Keeler .... .360	Wills 490
Hodges 361	Snider 3,669	Hodges 1,254	Wheat 766	F. Herman .... .339	Lopes 418
Campanella 242	Hodges 3,357	Wheat 1,227	Hodges 703	Fournier .... .337	W. Davis 335
Cey 228	W. Davis 3,094	Furillo 1,058	W. Davis 585	Wheat .... .317	Sax 290
Garvey 211	Reese 3,038	Garvey 992	Garvey 579	Phelps .... .315	Reese 232
Furillo 192	Garvey 3,004	Reese 885	Furillo 572	F.A. Jones .... .315	Sheckard 207
Guerrero 171	Furillo 2,922	Campanella 856	Reese 536	Mota .... .315	Gilliam 203
W. Davis 154	Gilliam 2,530	W. Davis 849	Cey 469	J. Robinson .... .311	Wheat 203
Baker 144	Russell 2,471	Cey 842	J. Robinson 464	F. Walker .... .311	J. Robinson 197
Camilli 139	Cey 2,321	J. Robinson 734	Gilliam 440	Guerrero .... .309	Daubert 187

CLUBS' ALL-TIME TOP TEN IN BATTING DEPARTMENTS
(Batting percentage column includes only players in 500 or more games.)

GAMES	AT BATS	RUNS	HITS	DOUBLES	TRIPLES

EXPOS
GAMES	AT BATS	RUNS	HITS	DOUBLES	TRIPLES
Wallach 1,767	Wallach 6,529	Raines 934	Wallach 1,694	Wallach 360	Raines 81
Carter 1,503	Dawson 5,628	Dawson 828	Raines 1,598	Dawson 295	Dawson 67
Dawson 1,443	Raines 5,305	Wallach 737	Dawson 1,575	Carter 274	Wallach 31
Raines 1,405	Carter 5,303	Carter 707	Carter 1,427	Raines 273	Cromartie 30
Cromartie 1,038	Cromartie 3,796	Cromartie 446	Cromartie 1,063	Cromartie 222	DeShields 25
Parrish 967	Parrish 3,411	Grissom 430	Parrish 896	Parrish 208	Webster 25
Bailey 951	Galarraga 3,082	Parrish 421	Galarraga 830	Galarraga 168	Carter 24
Speier 895	Bailey 2,991	Bailey 412	Bailey 791	Walker 147	Parrish 25
Galarraga 847	Speier 2,902	Galarraga 394	Grissom 747	Brooks 139	Bailey 23
Fairly 718	Grissom 2,678	Walker 368	Speier 710	Valentine 136	Grissom 23

METS
GAMES	AT BATS	RUNS	HITS	DOUBLES	TRIPLES
Kranepool 1,853	Kranepool 5,436	Strawberry 662	Kranepool 1,418	Kranepool 225	Wilson 62
Harrelson 1,322	Harrelson 4,390	H. Johnson 627	C. Jones 1,188	H. Johnson 214	Harrelson 45
Grote 1,235	C. Jones 4,223	Wilson 592	Wilson 1,112	Strawberry 187	C. Jones 33
C. Jones 1,201	Wilson 4,027	C. Jones 563	Harrelson 1,029	C. Jones 182	S. Henderson 31
H. Johnson 1,154	H. Johnson 3,968	Kranepool 536	Strawberry 1,025	Wilson 170	Strawberry 30
Wilson 1,116	Strawberry 3,903	Harrelson 490	Grote 994	Hernandez 159	Flynn 26
Strawberry 1,109	Grote 3,881	Hernandez 455	H. Johnson 997	McReynolds 153	Kranepool 25
Mazzilli 979	Hernandez 3,164	McReynolds 405	Hernandez 939	Stearns 152	Mazzilli 22
Staub 942	Mazzilli 3,013	Mazzilli 404	Mazzilli 796	Mazzilli 148	Garrett 20
Garrett 883	McReynolds 2,910	Garrett 389	McReynolds 791	Grote 143	Swoboda 20

PHILLIES
GAMES	AT BATS	RUNS	HITS	DOUBLES	TRIPLES
Schmidt 2,404	Schmidt 8,352	Schmidt 1,506	Schmidt 2,234	Delahanty 432	Delahanty 151
Ashburn 1,794	Ashburn 7,122	Delahanty 1,365	Ashburn 2,217	Schmidt 408	Magee 127
Bowa 1,739	Bowa 6,815	Ashburn 1,114	Delahanty 2,211	Magee 337	S. Thompson 103
Taylor 1,669	Delahanty 6,352	Klein 963	Ennis 1,812	Klein 336	Ashburn 97
Ennis 1,630	Ennis 6,327	S. Thompson 928	Bowa 1,798	Ennis 310	Callison 84
Delahanty 1,544	Taylor 5,799	R. Thomas 916	Klein 1,705	Ashburn 287	Bowa 81
W. Jones 1,520	Hamner 5,772	Magee 898	Magee 1,647	Hamner 271	Cravath 72
Magee 1,518	Magee 5,505	Ennis 891	F. Williams 1,553	Callison 265	Samuel 71
Hamner 1,501	W. Jones 5,419	Hamilton 877	Hamner 1,518	S. Thompson 258	Ennis 65
F. Williams 1,463	Callison 5,306	F. Williams 825	Taylor 1,511	Luzinski 253	Allen 64
					Klein 64
					Lajoie 64
					Titus 64

PIRATES
GAMES	AT BATS	RUNS	HITS	DOUBLES	TRIPLES
Clemente 2,433	Clemente 9,454	Wagner 1,520	Clemente 3,000	Wagner 556	Wagner 231
Wagner 2,432	Wagner 9,046	P. Waner 1,492	Wagner 2,970	P. Waner 556	P. Waner 186
Stargell 2,360	P. Waner 8,429	Clemente 1,416	P. Waner 2,868	Clemente 440	Clemente 166
Carey 2,171	Carey 8,406	Carey 1,414	Traynor 2,416	Stargell 423	Traynor 166
Mazeroski 2,163	Stargell 7,927	Stargell 1,195	Stargell 2,232	Carey 375	Clarke 155
P. Waner 2,154	Mazeroski 7,755	Traynor 1,183	L. Waner 2,317	Traynor 371	Carey 148
Traynor 1,941	Traynor 7,559	L. Waner 1,151	Clarke 2,017	Parker 296	Leach 137
L. Waner 1,803	L. Waner 7,256	Clarke 1,017	Mazeroski 2,016	Mazeroski 294	Vaughan 116
Leach 1,548	Leach 5,909	Leach 1,007	Vaughan 1,709	Vaughan 291	Beckley 114
Clarke 1,442	Clarke 5,471	Vaughan 936	Clarke 1,638	Oliver 276	L. Waner 114
				Suhr 276	

CARDINALS
GAMES	AT BATS	RUNS	HITS	DOUBLES	TRIPLES
Musial 3,026	Musial 10,972	Musial 1,949	Musial 3,630	Musial 725	Musial 177
Brock 2,289	Brock 9,125	Brock 1,427	Brock 2,713	Brock 434	Hornsby 143
O. Smith 1,908	O. Smith 6,933	Hornsby 1,089	Medwick 2,110	Medwick 377	Slaughter 135
Slaughter 1,820	Schoendienst 6,841	Slaughter 1,071	Slaughter 2,064	Hornsby 367	Brock 121
Schoendienst 1,795	Slaughter 6,775	Schoendienst 1,025	Schoendienst 1,980	Slaughter 366	Bottomley 119
Flood 1,738	K. Boyer 6,334	K. Boyer 988	O. Smith 1,880	Schoendienst 352	Konetchy 93
K. Boyer 1,667	Flood 6,318	O. Smith 955	K. Boyer 1,855	Bottomley 344	Medwick 83
Hornsby 1,580	Hornsby 5,881	Bottomley 921	Flood 1,853	Simmons 332	McGee 76
Javier 1,578	Simmons 5,725	Flood 845	Bottomley 1,727	O. Smith 328	J. Martin 75
Simmons 1,564	Javier 5,631	Frisch 831	Simmons 1,704	Frisch 286	Templeton 69

PADRES
GAMES	AT BATS	RUNS	HITS	DOUBLES	TRIPLES
Gwynn 1,830	Gwynn 7,144	Gwynn 1,073	Gwynn 2,401	Gwynn 384	Gwynn 80
Templeton 1,286	Templeton 4,512	Winfield 599	Templeton 1,135	Templeton 195	Richards 63
Winfield 1,117	Winfield 3,997	Richards 484	Winfield 1,134	Winfield 179	Winfield 39
Flannery 972	Richards 3,414	Colbert 442	Richards 994	Kennedy 158	Templeton 36
Richards 939	Colbert 3,080	Templeton 430	Kennedy 817	Colbert 130	Gaston 25
Colbert 866	Kennedy 2,987	B. Roberts 378	Colbert 780	Santiago 124	Flannery 25
Kennedy 835	Santiago 2,872	Santiago 312	Santiago 758	Richards 123	Salazar 24
Santiago 789	Gaston 2,615	Kennedy 308	B. Roberts 673	Martinez 111	Colbert 22
Martinez 783	Flannery 2,473	Garvey 291	Gaston 672	Garvey 107	B. Roberts 21
Gaston 766	Martinez 2,325	Martinez 286	Flannery 631	Grubb 101	O. Smith 19
			Garvey 631		

GIANTS
GAMES	AT BATS	RUNS	HITS	DOUBLES	TRIPLES
Mays 2,857	Mays 10,477	Mays 2,011	Mays 3,187	Mays 504	Tiernan 159
Ott 2,730	Ott 9,456	Ott 1,859	Ott 2,876	Ott 488	Mays 139
McCovey 2,256	McCovey 7,214	Tiernan 1,312	Terry 2,193	Terry 374	Connor 129
Terry 1,721	Terry 6,428	Terry 1,120	McCovey 1,974	McCovey 308	L. Doyle 117
Jackson 1,656	Jackson 6,086	McCovey 1,113	Jackson 1,875	Jackson 291	Terry 112
L. Doyle 1,615	L. Doyle 5,995	Van Haltren 982	L. Doyle 1,768	L. Doyle 275	Ewing 108
Davenport 1,501	Tiernan 5,910	Connor 939	L. Doyle 1,751	G.J. Burns 267	G.S. Davis 97
Lockman 1,485	Lockman 5,584	L. Doyle 906	J. Moore 1,615	J. Moore 258	Youngs 92
Tiernan 1,474	J. Moore 5,427	G.J. Burns 877	Van Haltren 1,592	W. Clark 249	Van Haltren 90
G.J. Burns 1,362	G.J. Burns 5,311	G.S. Davis 844	Lockman 1,571	Tiernan 248	Jackson 86

CLUBS' ALL-TIME TOP TEN IN BATTING DEPARTMENTS

(Batting percentage column includes only players in 500 or more games.)

EXPOS

HOME RUNS	TOTAL BASES	RUNS BATTED IN	EXTRA BASE HITS	BATTING AVG.	STOLEN BASES (Since 1898)
Dawson 225	Wallach 2,728	Wallach 905	Wallach 595	Raines .... .301	Raines 634
Carter 220	Dawson 2,679	Dawson 838	Dawson 587	Staub .... .295	Grissom 266
Wallach 204	Carter 2,409	Carter 823	Carter 518	Valentine .... .288	Dawson 253
Bailey 118	Raines 2,321	Raines 552	Raines 450	Walker .... .281	DeShields 187
Galarraga 106	Cromartie 1,525	Bailey 466	Parrish 332	Cromartie .... .280	Scott 139
Parrish 100	Parrish 1,452	Parrish 444	Cromartie 312	Dawson .... .280	Nixon 133
Walker 99	Galarraga 1,344	Galarraga 433	Galarraga 288	Grissom .... .279	Walker 98
Raines 96	Bailey 1,307	Brooks 390	Walker 262	Brooks .... .279	LeFlore 97
Valentine 95	Walker 1,142	Walker 384	Bailey 257	DeShields .... .277	Webster 96
Fairly 86	Valentine 1,119	Cromartie 371	Valentine 242	Hunt .... .277	Lintz 79

METS

HOME RUNS	TOTAL BASES	RUNS BATTED IN	EXTRA BASE HITS	BATTING AVG.	STOLEN BASES
Strawberry 252	Kranepool 2,047	Strawberry 733	Strawberry 469	Hernandez .... .297	Wilson 281
H. Johnson 192	Strawberry 2,028	H. Johnson 629	H. Johnson 424	Magadan .... .292	H. Johnson 202
Kingman 154	H. Johnson 1,823	Kranepool 614	Kranepool 368	Backman .... .283	Strawberry 191
McReynolds 122	C. Jones 1,715	C. Jones 521	C. Jones 308	C. Jones .... .281	Mazzilli 152
Kranepool 118	Wilson 1,586	Hernandez 468	Wilson 292	Dykstra .... .278	Dykstra 116
Foster 99	Hernandez 1,358	McReynolds 456	McReynolds 289	Millan .... .278	Harrelson 115
Milner 94	McReynolds 1,338	Staub 399	Hernandez 249	Wilson .... .276	Backman 106
C. Jones 93	Grote 1,278	Kingman 389	Mazzilli 238	Staub .... .276	Coleman 99
Bonilla 91	Harrelson 1,260	Foster 361	Kingman 230	Youngblood .... .274	Agee 92
Carter 89	Mazzilli 1,192	Grote 357	Staub 212	McReynolds .... .272	C. Jones 91
					Stearns 91

PHILLIES

HOME RUNS	TOTAL BASES	RUNS BATTED IN	EXTRA BASE HITS	BATTING AVG.	STOLEN BASES
Schmidt 548	Schmidt 4,404	Schmidt 1,595	Schmidt 1,015	Hamilton .... .362	Magee 387
Ennis 259	Delahanty 3,197	Delahanty 1,286	Delahanty 667	Delahanty .... .348	Bowa 288
Klein 243	Ennis 3,029	Ennis 1,124	Klein 643	Flick .... .345	Samuel 249
Luzinski 223	Klein 2,898	Klein 983	Ennis 634	S. Thompson .... .335	V. Hayes 202
F. Williams 217	Ashburn 2,764	S. Thompson 958	Magee 539	Klein .... .326	Ashburn 199
R. Allen 204	F. Williams 2,539	Magee 889	Callison 534	V. Davis .... .321	Maddox 189
Callison 185	Magee 2,463	Luzinski 811	F. Williams 503	Allen .... .312	Schmidt 174
W. Jones 180	Callison 2,426	F. Williams 796	Luzinski 497	Leach .... .312	Taylor 169
V. Hayes 124	Luzinski 2,263	W. Jones 753	R. Allen 472	Ashburn .... .311	Dykstra 166
Daulton 123	S. Thompson 2,248	Whitney 734	S. Thompson 456	Kruk .... .309	R. Thomas 164
Seminick 123				Whitney .... .307	

PIRATES

HOME RUNS	TOTAL BASES	RUNS BATTED IN	EXTRA BASE HITS	BATTING AVG.	STOLEN BASES
Stargell 475	Clemente 4,492	Stargell 1,540	Stargell 953	P. Waner .... .340	Carey 678
Kiner 301	Wagner 4,234	Wagner 1,475	Wagner 869	Cuyler .... .336	Wagner 639
Clemente 240	Stargell 4,190	Clemente 1,305	P. Waner 850	E.E. Smith .... .328	Moreno 412
Bonds 176	P. Waner 4,120	Traynor 1,273	Clemente 846	Wagner .... .328	Clarke 261
Parker 166	Traynor 3,289	P. Waner 1,177	Traynor 593	M. Alou .... .327	Bonds 251
F. Thomas 163	Carey 3,285	Mazeroski 853	Carey 589	Vaughan .... .324	Leach 249
Mazeroski 138	L. Waner 2,898	Kiner 801	Parker 524	Beaumont .... .321	Taveras 206
Oliver 135	Mazeroski 2,848	Suhr 789	Mazeroski 494	Traynor .... .320	Beaumont 200
Hebner 128	Vaughan 2,484	Vaughan 764	Vaughan 491	L. Waner .... .319	Bigbee 182
Stuart 117	Parker 2,397	Parker 758	Kiner 486	Clemente .... .317	Traynor 158
Van Slyke 117					

CARDINALS

HOME RUNS	TOTAL BASES	RUNS BATTED IN	EXTRA BASE HITS	BATTING AVG.	STOLEN BASES
Musial 475	Musial 6,134	Musial 1,951	Musial 1,377	Hornsby .... .359	Brock 888
K. Boyer 255	Brock 3,776	Slaughter 1,148	Hornsby 703	Mize .... .336	Coleman 549
Hornsby 193	Hornsby 3,342	Bottomley 1,105	Brock 684	Medwick .... .335	O. Smith 426
Bottomley 181	Slaughter 3,138	Hornsby 1,067	Slaughter 647	Musial .... .331	McGee 274
Simmons 172	K. Boyer 3,011	K. Boyer 1,001	Bottomley 644	Hafey .... .326	Frisch 195
Mize 158	Bottomley 2,852	Simmons 929	Medwick 610	Bottomley .... .325	J. Smith 192
Medwick 152	Schoendienst 2,657	Medwick 923	K. Boyer 585	Frisch .... .312	Huggins 174
Slaughter 146	Simmons 2,626	Brock 814	Simmons 541	Watkins .... .309	L. Smith 173
White 140	Medwick 2,585	Frisch 720	Schoendienst 482	Torre .... .308	Herr 152
Brock 129	Flood 2,464	Mize 653	Mize 442	J. Collins .... .307	Konetchy 151

PADRES

HOME RUNS	TOTAL BASES	RUNS BATTED IN	EXTRA BASE HITS	BATTING AVG.	STOLEN BASES
Colbert 163	Gwynn 3,206	Gwynn 804	Gwynn 551	Gwynn .... .336	Gwynn 285
Winfield 154	Winfield 1,853	Winfield 626	Winfield 372	B. Roberts .... .298	Richards 242
Gwynn 87	Templeton 1,531	Colbert 481	Colbert 315	Richards .... .291	Wiggins 171
Santiago 85	Colbert 1,443	Templeton 427	Templeton 274	Grubb .... .286	B. Roberts 148
McGriff 84	Richards 1,321	Kennedy 424	Kennedy 241	Winfield .... .284	O. Smith 147
Martinez 82	Kennedy 1,217	Santiago 375	Santiago 224	Garvey .... .275	Winfield 133
Gaston 77	Santiago 1,167	Martinez 337	Richards 212	Kennedy .... .274	Hernandez 129
Kennedy 76	Gaston 1,054	Garvey 316	Martinez 200	Salazar .... .267	Templeton 101
Tenace 68	Martinez 948	Gaston 316	Gaston 199	Santiago .... .264	Salazar 93
McReynolds 65	Garvey 937	McReynolds 260	Garvey 176	Turner .... .259	R. Alomar 90

GIANTS

HOME RUNS	TOTAL BASES	RUNS BATTED IN	EXTRA BASE HITS	BATTING AVG.	STOLEN BASES
Mays 646	Mays 5,907	Ott 1,860	Mays 1,289	Terry .... .341	Mays 336
Ott 511	Ott 5,041	Mays 1,859	Ott 1,071	G.S. Davis .... .335	G. Burns 334
McCovey 469	McCovey 3,779	McCovey 1,388	McCovey 822	Connor .... .334	L. Doyle 271
Cepeda 226	Terry 3,253	Terry 1,078	Terry 640	Van Haltren .... .323	Devlin 264
Williams 225	Tiernan 2,765	Jackson 929	Tiernan 515	Youngs .... .322	Bo. Bonds 263
Thomson 189	Jackson 2,636	Tiernan 852	Jackson 512	Frisch .... .321	Murray 231
Bo. Bonds 186	L. Doyle 2,461	G.S. Davis 805	Cepeda 474	Lindstrom .... .318	Frisch 224
W. Clark 176	Cepeda 2,234	Cepeda 767	W. Clark 462	Tiernan .... .317	Merkle 192
J. Clark 163	Lockman 2,216	Kelly 761	Doyle 459	Ewing .... .315	Snodgrass 190
Hart 157	J. Moore 2,216	L. Doyle 728	Connor 445	E. Meusel .... .314	Van Haltren 156
Mize 157					

61

ALL-TIME HOME RUN LEADERS, SEASON—AT EACH POSITION

Team	CATCHER	HR	Year	FIRST BASEMAN	HR	Year	SECOND BASEMAN	HR	Year	SHORTSTOP	HR	Year
BOSTON	Walker Cooper	18	1951	Earl Torgeson	24	1951	Rogers Hornsby	21	1928	Eddie Miller	14	1940
MILWAUKEE	Joe Torre	27	1965	Joe Adcock	38	1956	Frank Bolling	15	1961	Denis Menke	20	1964
ATLANTA	Joe Torre	36	1966	Hank Aaron	47	1971	Dave Johnson	43	1973	Denis Menke	15	1966
										Jeff Blauser	15	1993
CHICAGO	Gabby Hartnett	37	1930	Ernie Banks	37	1962	Rogers Hornsby	40	1929	Ernie Banks	47	1958
							Ryne Sandberg	40	1990			
CINCINNATI	Johnny Bench	45	1970	Ted Kluszewski	49	1954	Joe Morgan	27	1976	Leo Cardenas	20	1966
										Barry Larkin	20	1991
COLORADO	Joe Girardi	8	1995	Andres Galarraga	31	1994	Jason Bates	8	1995	Vinny Castilla	9	1993
					31	1995						
FLORIDA	Benito Santiago	13	1993	Greg Colbrunn	23	1995	Bret Barberie	5	1993	Kurt Abbott	17	1995
								5	1994			
							Quilvio Veras	5	1995			
HOUSTON	John Bateman	17	1966	Jeff Bagwell	39	1994	Craig Biggio	22	1995	Dickie Thon	20	1983
BROOKLYN	Roy Campanella	41	1953	Gil Hodges	42	1954	Jackie Robinson	19	1951	Glenn Wright	22	1930
								19	1952			
LOS ANGELES	Mike Piazza	35	1993	Steve Garvey	33	1977	Dave Lopes	28	1979	Don Zimmer	17	1958
MONTREAL	Gary Carter	31	1977	Andres Galarraga	29	1988	Pete Mackanin	12	1975	Wil Cordero	15	1994
							Vance Law	12	1987			
NEW YORK Mets	Gary Carter	32	1985	Dave Kingman	37	1982	Jeff Kent	21	1993	Ed Bressoud	10	1966
										Kevin Elster	10	1989
PHILADELPHIA	Stan Lopata	32	1956	Deron Johnson	34	1971	Juan Samuel	28	1987	Granny Hamner	17	1952
PITTSBURGH	Jim Pagliaroni	17	1965	Dick Stuart	35	1961	Bill Mazeroski	19	1958	Arky Vaughan	19	1935
ST. LOUIS	Ted Simmons	26	1979	Johnny Mize	43	1940	Rogers Hornsby	42	1922	Solly Hemus	15	1952
SAN DIEGO	Terry Kennedy	21	1982	Nate Colbert	38	1970	Dave Campbell	12	1970	Steve Huntz	11	1970
					38	1972						
NEW YORK Giants	Walker Cooper	35	1947	Johnny Mize	51	1947	Rogers Hornsby	26	1927	Alvin Dark	23	1953
SAN FRANCISCO	Tom Haller	27	1966	Orlando Cepeda	46	1961	Robby Thompson	19	1991	Daryl Spencer	17	1958
							Robby Thompson	19	1993			

ALL-TIME RUNS-BATTED-IN LEADERS, SEASON—AT EACH POSITION

Team	CATCHER	RBI	Year	FIRST BASEMAN	RBI	Year	SECOND BASEMAN	RBI	Year	SHORTSTOP	RBI	Year
BOSTON	Phil Masi	62	1946	Stuffy McInnis	95	1923	Rogers Hornsby	94	1928	Eddie Miller	79	1940
MILWAUKEE	Joe Torre	109	1964	Joe Adcock	108	1961	Jack Dittmer	63	1953	Johnny Logan	83	1955
ATLANTA	Joe Torre	101	1966	Hank Aaron	118	1971	Dave Johnson	99	1973	Jeff Blauser	73	1993
CHICAGO	Gabby Hartnett	122	1930	Ernie Banks	106	1965	Rogers Hornsby	149	1929	Ernie Banks	143	1959
					106	1969						
CINCINNATI	Johnny Bench	148	1970	Ted Kluszewski	141	1954	Joe Morgan	111	1976	Eddie Miller	87	1947
COLORADO	Joe Girardi	55	1995	Andres Galarraga	106	1995	Jason Bates	46	1995	Walt Weiss	32	1994
FLORIDA	Benito Santiago	50	1993	Greg Colbrunn	89	1995	Bret Barberie	33	1993	Kurt Abbott	60	1995
HOUSTON	John Bateman	70	1966	Jeff Bagwell	116	1994	Phil Garner	83	1982	Denis Menke	92	1970
BROOKLYN	Roy Campanella	142	1953	Jack Fournier	130	1925	Jackie Robinson	124	1949	Glenn Wright	126	1930
				Gil Hodges	130	1954						
LOS ANGELES	Mike Piazza	112	1993	Steve Garvey	115	1977	Charlie Neal	83	1959	Bill Russell	65	1974
											65	1976
MONTREAL	Gary Carter	106	1984	Al Oliver	109	1982	Mike Lansing	62	1995	Hubie Brooks	100	1985
NEW YORK Mets	Gary Carter	105	1986	Eddie Murray	100	1993	Jeff Kent	80	1993	Jose Vizcaino	56	1995
PHILADELPHIA	Darren Daulton	109	1992	Don Hurst	143	1932	Juan Samuel	100	1987	Granny Hamner	87	1952
PITTSBURGH	Al Todd	86	1937	Gus Suhr	118	1936	George Grantham	99	1930	Glenn Wright	121	1925
ST. LOUIS	Ted Simmons	103	1974	Jim Bottomley	137	1929	Rogers Hornsby	152	1922	Doc Lavan	82	1921
				Johnny Mize	137	1940						
SAN DIEGO	Terry Kennedy	98	1983	Nate Colbert	111	1972	Roberto Alomar	60	1990	Garry Templeton	64	1982
NEW YORK Giants	Walker Cooper	122	1947	Johnny Mize	138	1947	Rogers Hornsby	125	1927	Travis Jackson	101	1934
SAN FRANCISCO	Dick Dietz	107	1970	Orlando Cepeda	142	1961	Robby Thompson	65	1993	Daryl Spencer	74	1958

NOTE—For purposes of this table, players who performed at more than one position are considered for the position they played most often that particular year and are credited with their entire season's home run and RBI totals.

ALL-TIME HOME RUN LEADERS, SEASON—AT EACH POSITION

	THIRD BASEMAN	HR	Year	LEFT FIELDER	HR	Year	CENTER FIELDER	HR	Year	RIGHT FIELDER	HR	Year
BOSTON	Chuck Workman	25	1945	Wally Berger	38	1930	Wally Berger	34	1935	Tommy Holmes	28	1945
	Ed Mathews	25	1952					34	1936			
MILWAUKEE	Ed Mathews	47	1953	Frank Thomas	25	1961	Hank Aaron	45	1962	Hank Aaron	44	1957
											44	1963
ATLANTA	Darrell Evans	41	1973	Ron Gant	36	1993	Dale Murphy	37	1985	Hank Aaron	44	1966
											44	1969
										Dale Murphy	44	1987
CHICAGO	Ron Santo	33	1965	Dave Kingman	48	1979	Hack Wilson	56	1930	Andre Dawson	49	1987
CINCINNATI	Tony Perez	40	1970	George Foster	52	1977	Eric Davis	37	1987	Wally Post	40	1955
COLORADO	Vinny Castilla	32	1995	Dante Bichette	40	1995	Ellis Burks	14	1995	Larry Walker	36	1995
FLORIDA	Terry Pendleton	14	1995	Jeff Conine	18	1994	Chuck Carr	4	1993	Gary Sheffield	27	1994
HOUSTON	Doug Rader	25	1970	Jim Wynn	26	1968	Jim Wynn	37	1967	Roman Mejias	24	1962
										Jim Wynn	24	1972
BROOKLYN	Harvey Hendrick	11	1928	Andy Pafko	19	1952	Duke Snider	43	1956	Babe Herman	35	1930
LOS ANGELES	Pedro Guerrero	32	1983	Pedro Guerrero	33	1985	Jim Wynn	32	1974	Reggie Smith	32	1977
										Pedro Guerrero	32	1982
MONTREAL	Larry Parrish	30	1979	Mack Jones	22	1969	Andre Dawson	32	1983	Rusty Staub	30	1970
				Moises Alou	22	1994						
NEW YORK Mets	Howard Johnson	38	1991	Dave Kingman	36	1975	Tommie Agee	26	1969	Darryl Strawberry	39	1987
											39	1988
PHILADELPHIA	Mike Schmidt	48	1980	Greg Luzinski	39	1977	Cy Williams	41	1923	Chuck Klein	43	1929
PITTSBURGH	Frank Thomas	35	1958	Ralph Kiner	54	1949	Frank Thomas	30	1953	Bobby Bonilla	32	1990
ST. LOUIS	Ken Boyer	32	1960	Stan Musial	32	1951	Ray Lankford	25	1995	Stan Musial	39	1948
SAN DIEGO	Gary Sheffield	33	1992	Phil Plantier	34	1993	Clarence Gaston	29	1970	Dave Winfield	34	1979
NEW YORK Giants	Mel Ott	36	1938	Monte Irvin	24	1951	Willie Mays	51	1955	Mel Ott	42	1929
SAN FRANCISCO	Matt Williams	43	1994	Kevin Mitchell	47	1989	Willie Mays	52	1965	Bobby Bonds	39	1973

ALL-TIME RUNS-BATTED-IN LEADERS, SEASON—AT EACH POSITION

	THIRD BASEMAN	RBI	Year	LEFT FIELDER	RBI	Year	CENTER FIELDER	RBI	Year	RIGHT FIELDER	RBI	Year
BOSTON	Bob Elliott	113	1947	Wally Berger	119	1930	Wally Berger	130	1935	Tommy Holmes	117	1945
MILWAUKEE	Ed Mathews	135	1953	Rico Carty	88	1964	Hank Aaron	128	1962	Hank Aaron	132	1957
ATLANTA	Terry Pendleton	105	1992	Ron Gant	117	1993	Dale Murphy	121	1983	Hank Aaron	127	1966
CHICAGO	Ron Santo	123	1969	Billy Williams	129	1970	Hack Wilson	190	1930	Andre Dawson	137	1987
CINCINNATI	Deron Johnson	130	1965	George Foster	149	1977	Cy Seymour	119	1905	Frank Robinson	136	1962
COLORADO	Charlie Hayes	98	1993	Dante Bichette	128	1995	Ellis Burks	49	1995	Larry Walker	101	1995
FLORIDA	Terry Pendleton	78	1995	Jeff Conine	105	1995	Chuck Carr	41	1993	Gary Sheffield	78	1994
HOUSTON	Doug Rader	90	1972	Jose Cruz	95	1984	Jim Wynn	107	1967	Jim Wynn	90	1972
BROOKLYN	Cookie Lavagetto	87	1939	Zack Wheat	112	1922	Duke Snider	136	1955	Babe Herman	130	1930
LOS ANGELES	Ron Cey	110	1977	Tommy Davis	153	1962	Jim Wynn	108	1974	Frank Howard	119	1962
MONTREAL	Tim Wallach	123	1987	Moises Alou	85	1993	Andre Dawson	113	1983	Ken Singleton	103	1973
NEW YORK Mets	Howard Johnson	117	1991	Kevin McReynolds	99	1988	Lee Mazzilli	79	1979	Darryl Strawberry	108	1990
PHILADELPHIA	Pinky Whitney	124	1932	Greg Luzinski	130	1977	Cy Williams	114	1923	Chuck Klein	170	1930
PITTSBURGH	Pie Traynor	124	1928	Ralph Kiner	127	1947	Frank Thomas	102	1953	Paul Waner	131	1927
					127	1949						
ST. LOUIS	Joe Torre	137	1971	Joe Medwick	154	1937	Willie McGee	105	1987	Stan Musial	131	1948
SAN DIEGO	Gary Sheffield	100	1992	Phil Plantier	100	1993	Joe Carter	115	1990	Dave Winfield	118	1979
NEW YORK Giants	Mel Ott	116	1938	Irish Meusel	132	1922	Willie Mays	127	1955	Mel Ott	151	1929
SAN FRANCISCO	Matt Williams	122	1990	Kevin Mitchell	125	1989	Willie Mays	141	1962	Jack Clark	103	1982

NOTE—For purposes of this table, players who performed at more than one position are considered for the position they played most often that particular year and are credited with their entire season's home run and RBI totals.

CLUBS' YEARLY RUNS-BATTED-IN LEADERS SINCE 1920

Year	BRAVES	CUBS	REDS	ROCKIES	MARLINS	ASTROS	DODGERS	Year
1920	Holke..........64	Robertson..........75	Roush..........90				Myers..........80	1920
1921	Boeckel..........84	Grimes..........79	Roush..........71				Wheat..........85	1921
1922	Ford..........60	Grimes..........99	Duncan..........94				Wheat..........112	1922
1923	McInnis..........95	Friberg-Miller..........88	Roush..........88				Fournier..........102	1923
1924	McInnis..........59	Friberg..........82	Roush..........72				Fournier..........116	1924
1925	Burrus..........87	Grimm..........76	Roush..........83				Fournier..........130	1925
1926	Brown*..........84	Wilson..........109	Pipp..........99				F. Herman..........73	1926
1927	Brown*..........75	Wilson..........129	C. Walker..........80				F. Herman..........73	1927
1928	Hornsby..........94	Wilson..........120	C. Walker..........73				Bissonette..........106	1928
1929	Sisler..........79	Wilson..........159	Kelly..........103				F. Herman..........113	1929
1930	Berger..........119	**Wilson..........190**	Heilmann..........91				F. Herman..........130	1930
1931	Berger..........84	Hornsby..........90	Cuccinello..........93				F. Herman..........97	1931
1932	Berger..........73	Stephenson..........85	F. Herman..........87				Wilson..........123	1932
1933	Berger..........106	F. Herman..........93	Bottomley..........83				Cuccinello*..........65	1933
1934	Berger..........121	Hartnett..........90	Bottomley..........78				Leslie..........102	1934
1935	Berger..........130	Hartnett..........91	Goodman..........72				Leslie..........93	1935
1936	Berger..........91	Demaree..........96	Cuyler..........74				Hassett..........82	1936
1937	Cuccinello..........80	Demaree..........115	Kampouris..........71				Manush..........73	1937
1938	Cuccinello..........76	Galan..........69	F. McCormick..........106				Camilli..........100	1938
1939	West..........82	Leiber..........88	F. McCormick..........128				Camilli..........104	1939
1940	Ross..........89	Nicholson..........98	F. McCormick..........127				Camilli..........96	1940
1941	West-Miller..........68	Nicholson..........98	F. McCormick..........97				Camilli..........120	1941
1942	West..........56	Nicholson..........78	F. McCormick..........89				Camilli..........109	1942
1943	Workman..........67	Nicholson..........128	Miller..........71				W. Herman..........100	1943
1944	Holmes..........73	Nicholson..........122	F. McCormick..........102				Galan..........93	1944
1945	Holmes..........117	Pafko..........110	F. McCormick..........81				Walker..........124	1945
1946	Holmes..........79	Cavarretta..........78	Hatton..........69				Walker..........116	1946
1947	R. Elliott..........113	Nicholson..........75	Miller..........87				Walker..........94	1947
1948	R. Elliott..........100	Pafko..........101	Sauer..........97				Robinson..........85	1948
1949	R. Elliott..........76	Sauer*..........83	Hatton..........69				Robinson..........124	1949
1950	R. Elliott..........107	Sauer..........103	Kluszewski..........111				Hodges..........113	1950
1951	Gordon..........109	Sauer..........89	Kluszewski..........77				Campanella..........108	1951
1952	Gordon..........75	Sauer..........121	Kluszewski..........86				Hodges..........102	1952
1953	**Mathews..........135**	Kiner*..........87	Kluszewski..........108				Campanella..........142	1953
1954	Mathews..........103	Sauer..........103	Kluszewski..........141				Hodges-Snider..........130	1954
1955	H. Aaron..........106	Banks..........117	Kluszewski..........113				Snider..........136	1955
1956	Adcock..........103	Banks..........85	Kluszewski..........102				Snider..........101	1956
1957	H. Aaron..........132	Banks..........102	Crowe..........92				Hodges..........98	1957
1958	H. Aaron..........95	Banks..........129	Robinson..........83				Furillo..........83	1958
1959	H. Aaron..........123	Banks..........143	Robinson..........125				Snider..........88	1959
1960	H. Aaron..........126	Banks..........117	Robinson..........83				Larker..........78	1960
1961	H. Aaron..........120	Altman..........96	Robinson..........124			Mejias..........75	Moon..........88	1961
1962	H. Aaron..........128	Banks..........104	Robinson..........136			Bateman..........59	**T. Davis..........153**	1962
1963	H. Aaron..........130	Santo..........99	Pinson..........106			Bond..........85	T. Davis..........88	1963
1964	Torre..........109	Santo..........114	Robinson..........96			Wynn..........73	T. Davis..........86	1964
1965	Mathews..........95	B. Williams..........108	Johnson..........130			Staub..........81	Fairly..........70	1965
1966	H. Aaron..........127	Santo..........94	Cardenas-Johnson..........81			Wynn..........107	Lefebvre..........74	1966
1967	H. Aaron..........109	Santo..........98	Perez..........102			Staub..........72	Fairly..........55	1967
1968	H. Aaron..........86	Santo-B. Williams..........98	Perez..........92			Menke..........90	Haller..........53	1968
1969	H. Aaron..........97	Santo..........123	Perez..........122			Menke..........92	Kosco..........74	1969
1970	H. Aaron..........118	B. Williams..........129	Bench..........148			Cedeno..........81	Parker..........111	1970
1971	H. Aaron..........118	B. Williams..........93	May..........98			May..........98	Allen..........90	1971
1972	E. Williams..........87	B. Williams..........122	Bench..........125			May..........105	W. Davis..........79	1972
1973	Evans..........104	B. Williams..........86	Bench..........104			Cedeno..........102	Ferguson..........88	1973
1974	Evans..........79	Morales..........82	Bench..........129			Watson..........85	Garvey..........111	1974
1975	Evans..........73	Morales..........91	Bench..........110			Watson..........102	Cey..........101	1975
1976	Wynn..........66	Madlock..........84	Foster..........121			Watson..........110	Cey-Garvey..........80	1976
1977	Burroughs..........114	Murcer..........89	**Foster..........149**			J. Cruz..........83	Garvey..........115	1977
1978	Murphy..........79	Kingman..........79	Foster..........120			J. Cruz..........72	Garvey..........113	1978
1979	Horner..........98	Kingman..........115	Foster..........98			J. Cruz..........91	Garvey..........110	1979
1980	Horner-Murphy..........89	Martin..........73	Foster..........93			J. Cruz..........55	Garvey..........106	1980
1981	Chambliss..........51	Buckner..........75	Foster..........90			Garner..........83	Garvey..........64	1981
1982	Murphy..........109	Buckner..........105	Cedeno-Driessen..........57			J. Cruz..........92	Guerrero..........100	1982
1983	Murphy..........121	Cey..........90	Oester..........58			J. Cruz..........95	Guerrero..........103	1983
1984	Murphy..........100	Cey..........97	Parker..........94			J. Cruz..........79	Guerrero..........72	1984
1985	Murphy..........111	Moreland..........106	Parker..........125			G. Davis..........101	Marshall..........95	1985
1986	Horner..........87	Moreland..........79	Parker..........116			G. Davis..........93	Madlock..........60	1986
1987	Murphy..........105	Dawson..........137	E. Davis..........100			G. Davis..........99	Guerrero..........89	1987
1988	Murphy..........77	Dawson..........79	E. Davis..........93			G. Davis..........89	Marshall..........82	1988
1989	Murphy..........84	Grace..........79	E. Davis..........101			Stubbs..........71	Murray..........88	1989
1990	Gant..........84	Dawson-Sandberg..........100	E. Davis..........86			Bagwell..........82	Murray..........95	1990
1991	Gant..........105	Dawson..........104	O'Neill..........91			Bagwell..........96	Strawberry..........99	1991
1992	Pendleton..........105	Dawson..........90	Larkin..........78			Bagwell..........88	Karros..........88	1992
1993	Justice..........120	Grace..........98	Sanders..........83	Galarraga-Hayes..........98	Destrade..........87	**Bagwell..........116**	Piazza..........112	1993
1994	McGriff..........94	Sosa..........70	Morris..........78	Bichette..........95	Conine..........82	Bagwell..........116	Piazza..........92	1994
1995	McGriff..........93	Sosa..........119	R. Sanders..........99	**Bichette..........128**	**Conine..........105**	Bagwell..........87	Karros..........105	1995

(*)—1927, Brown topped by Eddie Farrell (92) who began season with New York; 1933, Cuccinello topped by Sam Leslie (73) who began season with New York; 1934, Moore's season total (98), balance made with Cincinnati; 1936, Camilli topped by Chuck Klein (104) who began season with Chicago; 1939, Fletcher's season total (77), balance made with Boston; 1940, Rizzo's season total (72), balance made with Pittsburgh and Cincinnati; 1943, Gordon topped by Medwick (70) who began season with Brooklyn; 1945, Kurowski topped by Adams (109) who began season with Philadelphia; 1949, Sauer's season total (99), balance made with Cincinnati; 1953, Kiner's season total (116), balance made with Pittsburgh; 1961, Demeter's season total (70), balance made with Los Angeles; 1990, V. Hayes topped by Dale Murphy (83), who began season with Atlanta.

Bold face type indicates team leader

Rockies: JOINED LEAGUE AS ACTIVE PARTICIPANT IN 1993
Marlins: JOINED LEAGUE AS ACTIVE PARTICIPANT IN 1993
Astros: JOINED LEAGUE AS ACTIVE PARTICIPANT IN 1962

CLUBS' YEARLY RUNS-BATTED-IN LEADERS SINCE 1920

Year	EXPOS	METS	PHILLIES	PIRATES	CARDINALS	PADRES	GIANTS	Year
1920			Williams ... 72	Whitted ... 74	Hornsby ... 94		Kelly ... 94	1920
1921			Williams ... 75	Grimm ... 71	Hornsby ... 126		Kelly ... 122	1921
1922			Williams ... 92	Bigbee ... 99	Hornsby ... 152		E. Meusel ... 132	1922
1923			Williams ... 114	Traynor ... 101	Stock ... 96		E. Meusel ... 125	1923
1924			Williams ... 93	Wright ... 111	Bottomley ... 111		Kelly ... 136	1924
1925			Harper ... 97	Wright ... 121	Hornsby ... 143		E. Meusel ... 111	1925
1926			Leach ... 71	Cuyler-Traynor ... 92	Bottomley ... 120		Kelly ... 80	1926
1927			Williams ... 98	P. Waner ... **131**	Bottomley ... 124		Hornsby ... 125	1927
1928			Whitney ... 103	Traynor ... 124	Bottomley ... 136		Lindstrom ... 107	1928
1929			Klein ... 145	Traynor ... 108	Bottomley ... 137		Ott ... **151**	1929
1930			**Klein ... 170**	Comorosky-Traynor ... 119	Frisch ... 114		Terry ... 129	1930
1931			Klein ... 121	Traynor ... 103	Hafey ... 95		Ott ... 115	1931
1932	JOINED LEAGUE AS ACTIVE PARTICIPANT IN 1969	JOINED LEAGUE AS ACTIVE PARTICIPANT IN 1962	Hurst ... 143	Piet ... 85	J. Collins ... 91	JOINED LEAGUE AS ACTIVE PARTICIPANT IN 1969	Ott ... 123	1932
1933			Klein ... 120	Vaughan ... 97	Medwick ... 98		Ott ... 103	1933
1934			J. Moore* ... 93	Suhr ... 103	J. Collins ... 128		Ott ... 135	1934
1935			J. Moore ... 93	Vaughan ... 99	Medwick ... 126		Ott ... 114	1935
1936			Camilli* ... 102	Suhr ... 118	Medwick ... 138		Ott ... 135	1936
1937			Camilli ... 80	Suhr ... 97	**Medwick ... 154**		Ott ... 95	1937
1938			Arnovich ... 72	Rizzo ... 111	Medwick ... 122		Ott ... 116	1938
1939			Arnovich ... 67	Fletcher* ... 71	Medwick ... 117		Bonura ... 85	1939
1940			Rizzo* ... 53	Van Robays ... 116	Mize ... 137		Young ... 101	1940
1941			Etten ... 79	Di Maggio ... 100	Mize ... 100		Young ... 104	1941
1942			Litwhiler ... 56	Elliott ... 89	Slaughter ... 98		Mize ... 110	1942
1943			Northey ... 68	Elliott ... 101	Musial-Cooper ... 81		S. Gordon* ... 63	1943
1944			Northey ... 104	Elliott ... 108	Sanders ... 102		Medwick ... 85	1944
1945			DiMaggio ... 84	Elliott ... 108	Kurowski* ... 102		Ott ... 79	1945
1946			Ennis ... 73	Kiner ... 81	Slaughter ... 130		Mize ... 70	1946
1947			Ennis ... 81	Kiner ... 127	Kurowski ... 104		Mize ... 138	1947
1948			Ennis ... 95	Kiner ... 123	Musial ... 131		Mize ... 125	1948
1949			Ennis ... 110	Kiner ... 127	Musial ... 123		Thomson ... 109	1949
1950			Ennis ... 126	Kiner ... 118	Musial ... 109		Thompson ... 91	1950
1951			Jones ... 81	Kiner ... 109	Musial ... 108		Irvin ... 121	1951
1952			Ennis ... 107	Kiner ... 87	Slaughter ... 101		Thomson ... 108	1952
1953			Ennis ... 125	Thomas ... 102	Musial ... 113		Thomson ... 106	1953
1954			Ennis ... 119	Thomas ... 94	Musial ... 126		Mays ... 110	1954
1955			Ennis ... 120	Long ... 79	Musial ... 108		Mays ... 127	1955
1956			Ennis-Lopata ... 95	Long ... 91	Musial ... 109		Mays ... 84	1956
1957			Bouchee ... 76	Thomas ... 89	Ennis ... 105		Mays ... 97	1957
1958			Anderson ... 97	Thomas ... 109	Boyer ... 90		Cepeda-Mays ... 96	1958
1959			Post ... 94	Stuart ... 78	Boyer ... 94		Cepeda ... 105	1959
1960			Herrera ... 71	Clemente ... 94	Boyer ... 97		Mays ... 103	1960
1961			Demeter* ... 68	Stuart ... 117	Boyer ... 95		Cepeda ... 142	1961
1962		Thomas ... 94	Demeter ... 107	Mazeroski ... 81	White ... 102		Mays ... 141	1962
1963		Thomas ... 60	Demeter ... 83	Clemente ... 76	Boyer ... 111		Mays ... 103	1963
1964		Christopher ... 76	Callison ... 104	Clemente ... 87	Boyer ... 119		Mays ... 111	1964
1965		Smith ... 62	Callison ... 101	Stargell ... 107	Flood ... 83		Mays ... 112	1965
1966		Boyer ... 61	Allen ... 110	Clemente ... 119	Flood ... 78		Mays ... 103	1966
1967		Davis ... 73	Allen ... 77	Clemente ... 110	Cepeda ... 111		Hart ... 99	1967
1968		Swoboda ... 59	Allen ... 90	Clendenon ... 87	Shannon ... 79		McCovey ... 105	1968
1969	Laboy ... 83	Agee ... 76	Allen ... 89	Stargell ... 92	Torre ... 101	Colbert ... 66	McCovey ... 126	1969
1970	Staub ... 94	Clendenon ... 97	Johnson ... 93	Stargell ... 85	Allen ... 101	Gaston ... 93	McCovey ... 126	1970
1971	Staub ... 97	Jones ... 69	Montanez ... 99	Stargell ... 125	Torre ... 137	Colbert ... 84	Bonds ... 102	1971
1972	Fairly ... 68	Jones ... 52	Luzinski ... 68	Stargell ... 112	Simmons ... 96	Colbert ... 111	Kingman ... 83	1972
1973	Singleton ... 103	Staub ... 76	Luzinski ... 97	Stargell ... 119	Simmons ... 91	Colbert ... 80	Bonds ... 96	1973
1974	W. Davis ... 89	Staub ... 78	Schmidt ... 116	Zisk ... 100	Simmons ... 103	Winfield ... 75	Matthews ... 82	1974
1975	Carter ... 68	Staub ... 105	Luzinski ... 120	Parker ... 101	Simmons ... 100	Winfield ... 76	Murcer ... 91	1975
1976	Parrish ... 61	Kingman ... 86	Schmidt ... 107	Parker ... 90	Simmons ... 75	Ivie ... 70	Murcer ... 90	1976
1977	Perez ... 91	Henderson ... 65	Luzinski ... 130	Robinson ... 104	Simmons ... 95	Winfield ... 92	McCovey ... 86	1977
1978	Perez ... 78	Montanez ... 96	Luzinski ... 101	Parker ... 117	Simmons ... 80	Winfield ... 97	J. Clark ... 98	1978
1979	Dawson ... 92	Hebner-Mazzilli ... 79	Schmidt ... 114	Parker ... 94	Hernandez ... 105	**Winfield ... 118**	Ivie ... 89	1979
1980	Carter ... 101	Mazzilli ... 76	Schmidt ... 121	Parker ... 79	Hendrick ... 109	Winfield ... 87	J. Clark ... 82	1980
1981	Carter ... 68	Kingman ... 59	Schmidt ... 91	Parker ... 48	Hendrick ... 61	Richards ... 42	J. Clark ... 53	1981
1982	Oliver ... 109	Kingman ... 99	Schmidt ... 87	Thompson ... 101	Hendrick ... 104	Kennedy ... 97	J. Clark ... 103	1982
1983	Dawson ... 113	Foster ... 90	Schmidt ... 109	Thompson ... 76	Hendrick ... 97	Kennedy ... 98	Leonard ... 87	1983
1984	Carter ... 106	Strawberry ... 97	Schimdt ... 106	Pena ... 78	Hendrick ... 69	Garvey ... 86	Leonard ... 86	1984
1985	Brooks ... 100	Carter ... 100	Wilson ... 102	Ray ... 70	Herr ... 110	Garvey ... 81	Leonard ... 62	1985
1986	Dawson ... 78	Carter ... 105	Schmidt ... 119	Morrison ... 88	Herr-Van Slyke ... 61	McReynolds ... 96	Maldonado ... 85	1986
1987	**Wallach ... 123**	Strawberry ... 104	Schmidt ... 113	Van Slyke ... 82	J. Clark ... 106	Kruk ... 91	W. Clark ... 91	1987
1988	Galarraga ... 92	Strawberry ... 101	Samuel ... 67	Bonilla-Van Slyke ... 100	Brunansky ... 79	Gwynn ... 70	W. Clark ... 109	1988
1989	Galarraga ... 85	H. Johnson ... 101	V. Hayes ... 78	Bonilla ... 86	Guerrero ... 117	Ja. Clark ... 94	Mitchell ... 125	1989
1990	Wallach ... 98	Strawberry ... 108	V. Hayes* ... 73	Bonilla ... 120	Guerrero ... 80	Carter ... 115	Williams ... 122	1990
1991	Calderon ... 75	**Johnson ... 117**	Kruk ... 92	Bonds ... 116	Zeile ... 81	McGriff ... 106	W. Clark ... 116	1991
1992	Walker ... 93	Murray ... 93	Daulton ... 109	Bonds ... 103	Lankford ... 86	McGriff ... 104	W. Clark ... 73	1992
1993	Grissom ... 95	Murray ... 100	Daulton ... 105	King ... 98	Zeile ... 103	Plantier ... 100	Bonds ... 123	1993
1994	Walker ... 86	Kent ... 68	Daulton ... 56	Merced ... 51	Zeile ... 75	Gwynn ... 64	Williams ... 96	1994
1995	Lansing ... 62	Brogna ... 76	Hayes ... 85	King ... 87	Lankford ... 82	Caminiti ... 94	Bonds ... 104	1995

(*)—1927, Brown topped by Eddie Farrell (92) who began season with New York; 1933, Cuccinello topped by Sam Leslie (73) who began season with New York; 1934, Moore's season total (98), balance made with Cincinnati; 1936, Camilli topped by Chuck Klein (104) who began season with Chicago; 1939, Fletcher's season total (77), balance made with Boston; 1940, Rizzo's season total (72), balance made with Pittsburgh and Cincinnati; 1943, Gordon topped by Medwick (70) who began season with Brooklyn; 1945, Kurowski topped by Adams (109) who began season with Philadelphia; 1949, Sauer's season total (99), balance made with Cincinnati; 1953, Kiner's season total (116), balance made with Pittsburgh; 1961, Demeter's season total (70), balance made with Los Angeles; 1990, V. Hayes topped by Dale Murphy (83), who began season with Atlanta.

Bold face type indicates team leader

1995 PITCHING RECORDS AGAINST OPPOSING CLUBS

ATLANTA (90-54)

Pitcher	Chi. W-L-S	Cin. W-L-S	Col. W-L-S	Fla. W-L-S	Hou. W-L-S	L.A. W-L-S	Mon. W-L-S	N.Y. W-L-S	Phi. W-L-S	Pit. W-L-S	St.L. W-L-S	S.D. W-L-S	S.F. W-L-S	Totals W	L	S	Pct.
Avery	0-3-0	0-0-0	2-1-0	1-2-0	1-0-0	0-2-0	0-2-0	1-0-0	1-1-0	0-0-0	0-2-0	0-0-0	1-0-0	7	13	0	.350
Bedrosian	1-0-0	0-1-0	0-0-0	0-0-0	0-0-0	0-0-0	0-0-0	0-0-0	0-1-0	0-0-0	0-0-0	0-0-0	0-0-0	1	2	0	.333
Borbon	0-0-0	0-1-1	0-0-1	0-1-0	0-0-0	0-0-0	1-0-0	0-0-0	1-0-0	0-0-0	0-0-0	0-0-0	0-0-0	2	2	2	.500
Clontz	0-0-0	0-1-0	0-0-0	1-0-1	0-0-0	1-0-1	1-0-0	0-0-1	0-0-0	3-0-0	0-0-0	1-0-0	1-0-1	8	1	4	.889
Glavine	2-1-0	2-1-0	1-0-0	2-0-0	1-1-0	0-0-0	3-0-0	0-1-0	1-1-0	0-0-0	2-1-0	1-0-0	1-1-0	16	7	0	.696
Maddux	1-0-0	2-1-0	0-1-0	1-0-0	2-0-0	0-0-0	2-0-0	2-0-0	2-0-0	1-0-0	3-0-0	1-0-0	2-0-0	19	2	0	.905
McMichael	0-0-0	0-0-1	1-0-0	2-0-1	0-0-0	2-0-0	0-1-0	1-0-0	0-0-0	0-0-0	1-0-0	0-1-0	0-0-0	7	2	2	.778
Mercker	1-0-0	0-0-0	2-1-0	0-0-0	2-0-0	0-2-0	1-1-0	0-1-0	1-1-0	0-0-0	0-1-0	0-1-0	0-0-0	7	8	0	.467
Murray	0-0-0	0-0-0	0-0-0	0-0-0	0-1-0	0-0-0	0-0-0	0-0-0	0-0-0	0-0-0	0-1-0	0-0-0	0-0-0	0	2	0	.000
Schmidt	1-0-0	0-0-0	1-0-0	0-0-0	0-0-0	0-0-0	0-0-0	0-2-0	0-0-0	0-0-0	0-0-0	0-0-0	0-0-0	2	2	0	.500
Smoltz	2-0-0	3-0-0	1-0-0	1-0-0	0-2-0	1-0-0	1-0-0	1-2-0	1-2-0	0-1-0	0-0-0	1-0-0	0-0-0	12	7	0	.632
Stanton	0-0-0	0-0-0	0-0-0	0-0-0	0-1-0	0-0-0	0-0-0	0-0-0	0-0-0	0-0-1	0-0-0	0-0-0	1-0-0	1	1	1	.500
Wade	0-0-0	0-0-0	0-0-0	0-0-0	0-0-0	0-0-0	0-0-0	0-1-0	0-0-0	0-0-0	0-0-0	0-0-0	0-0-0	0	1	0	.000
Wohlers	0-0-4	1-0-2	1-0-1	1-0-3	0-1-2	1-0-1	0-0-3	0-1-3	0-0-2	0-1-2	1-0-0	1-0-2	1-0-0	7	3	25	.700
Woodall	0-0-0	0-0-0	0-1-0	1-0-0	0-0-0	0-0-0	0-0-0	0-0-0	0-0-0	0-0-0	0-0-0	0-0-0	0-0-0	1	1	0	.500
TOTALS	8-4-4	8-5-4	9-4-2	10-3-5	6-6-2	5-4-2	9-4-3	5-8-4	7-6-2	4-2-3	7-5-0	5-2-2	7-1-1	90	54	34	.625

NO DECISIONS OR SAVES: Clark, May, Nichols, Pena, Thobe.

CHICAGO (73-71)

Pitcher	Atl. W-L-S	Cin. W-L-S	Col. W-L-S	Fla. W-L-S	Hou. W-L-S	L.A. W-L-S	Mon. W-L-S	N.Y. W-L-S	Phi. W-L-S	Pit. W-L-S	St.L. W-L-S	S.D. W-L-S	S.F. W-L-S	Totals W	L	S	Pct.
Adams	0-0-0	0-0-0	0-0-0	0-0-0	0-1-0	1-0-1	0-0-0	0-0-0	0-0-0	0-0-0	0-0-0	0-0-0	0-0-0	1	1	1	.500
Banks	0-0-0	0-0-0	0-0-0	0-0-0	0-0-0	0-0-0	0-0-0	0-0-0	0-0-0	0-1-0	0-0-0	0-0-0	0-0-0	0	1	0	.000
Bullinger	1-1-0	1-0-0	0-1-0	0-1-0	1-1-0	1-2-0	0-1-0	1-0-0	2-0-0	1-1-0	3-0-0	0-0-0	1-0-0	12	8	0	.600
Casian	0-0-0	0-0-0	0-0-0	0-0-0	0-0-0	0-0-0	0-0-0	0-0-0	0-0-0	1-0-0	0-0-0	0-0-0	0-0-0	1	0	0	1.000
Castillo	0-2-0	0-0-0	3-0-0	1-1-0	0-2-0	1-0-0	0-2-0	0-0-0	1-0-0	0-0-0	1-1-0	3-1-0	1-1-0	11	10	0	.524
Edens	0-0-0	1-0-0	0-0-0	0-0-0	0-0-0	0-0-0	0-0-0	0-0-0	0-0-0	0-0-0	0-0-0	0-0-0	0-0-0	1	0	0	1.000
Foster	0-1-0	1-1-0	1-1-0	3-0-0	1-0-0	1-0-0	1-1-0	1-0-0	0-0-0	2-0-0	1-2-0	0-3-0	0-2-0	12	11	0	.522
Hickerson	0-1-0	0-0-0	0-0-0	0-1-0	0-0-0	1-0-0	0-0-0	0-1-0	0-0-1	1-0-0	0-0-0	0-0-0	0-0-0	2	3	1	.400
Morgan	1-0-0	0-1-0	1-0-0	0-0-0	0-0-0	0-0-0	0-0-0	0-0-0	0-0-0	0-0-0	0-0-0	0-0-0	0-0-0	2	1	0	.667
Myers	0-0-4	0-1-2	0-1-4	0-0-3	0-0-2	1-0-2	0-0-2	0-0-3	0-0-2	0-0-3	0-0-8	0-0-1	0-0-2	1	2	38	.333
Nabholz	0-0-0	0-0-0	0-0-0	0-0-0	0-0-0	0-0-0	0-0-0	0-0-0	0-0-0	0-0-0	0-1-0	0-0-0	0-0-0	0	1	0	.000
Navarro	2-0-0	0-1-0	0-1-0	2-0-0	1-0-0	0-1-0	2-1-0	1-0-0	1-0-0	2-0-0	0-0-0	1-0-0	2-2-0	14	6	0	.700
Perez	0-1-0	0-1-1	0-1-0	0-1-1	1-1-0	0-0-0	0-0-0	0-0-0	0-0-0	0-0-0	1-0-0	0-1-0	0-0-0	2	6	2	.250
Trachsel	0-2-0	0-1-0	0-1-0	1-0-0	0-1-0	0-1-0	0-0-0	1-1-0	0-1-0	0-2-0	3-0-0	1-2-0	1-1-0	7	13	0	.350
Walker	0-0-0	0-0-0	0-0-0	0-0-0	0-2-0	1-0-0	0-0-0	0-1-1	0-0-0	0-0-0	0-0-0	0-0-0	0-0-0	1	3	1	.250
Wendell	0-0-0	0-0-0	0-1-0	1-0-0	0-0-0	0-0-0	0-0-0	0-0-0	1-0-0	1-0-0	0-0-0	0-0-0	0-0-0	3	1	0	.750
Young	0-0-0	0-1-0	1-0-0	0-0-0	1-0-1	0-1-0	0-0-1	0-0-0	1-0-0	0-1-0	0-0-0	0-0-0	0-1-0	3	4	2	.429
TOTALS	4-8-4	3-7-3	6-7-4	8-4-4	5-8-3	7-5-3	3-5-3	4-3-4	6-1-3	8-5-3	9-4-8	5-7-1	5-7-2	73	71	45	.507

NO DECISIONS OR SAVES: Garces, Rivera, Sturtze, Swartzbaugh.

CINCINNATI (85-59)

Pitcher	Atl. W-L-S	Chi. W-L-S	Col. W-L-S	Fla. W-L-S	Hou. W-L-S	L.A. W-L-S	Mon. W-L-S	N.Y. W-L-S	Phi. W-L-S	Pit. W-L-S	St.L. W-L-S	S.D. W-L-S	S.F. W-L-S	Totals W	L	S	Pct.
Brantley	1-0-3	0-0-4	0-0-1	0-0-0	2-0-3	0-0-1	0-0-3	0-0-4	0-0-5	0-1-3	0-0-0	0-0-1	0-1-0	3	2	28	.600
Burba	1-0-0	0-0-0	1-0-0	0-0-0	1-0-0	0-0-0	0-0-0	0-1-0	1-0-0	0-1-0	1-0-0	0-0-0	1-0-0	6	2	0	.750
Carrasco	1-1-0	0-0-0	0-2-0	0-0-1	0-0-2	0-0-0	1-0-1	0-0-0	0-1-0	0-0-0	0-1-1	0-2-0	0-0-0	2	7	5	.222
Hernandez	1-0-0	1-0-1	0-0-0	0-0-1	2-0-0	0-0-0	0-0-0	1-0-0	1-1-1	1-0-0	0-0-0	0-0-0	0-1-0	7	2	3	.778
Jackson	0-0-0	2-0-0	0-0-0	1-0-0	0-0-0	0-0-1	1-0-1	0-0-0	1-0-0	0-0-0	0-1-0	1-0-0	0-0-0	6	1	2	.857
Jarvis	0-0-0	0-0-0	1-1-0	1-1-0	0-0-0	0-0-0	0-1-0	0-0-0	0-0-0	0-1-0	1-0-0	0-0-0	0-0-0	3	4	0	.429
McElroy	0-2-0	0-1-0	0-0-0	0-0-0	0-0-0	0-0-0	0-0-0	1-1-0	0-0-0	1-0-0	0-0-0	1-0-0	0-0-0	3	4	0	.429
Nitkowski	0-1-0	0-0-0	0-0-0	0-0-0	0-0-0	0-1-0	0-0-0	0-0-0	1-0-0	0-0-0	0-0-0	0-1-0	0-0-0	1	3	0	.250
Portugal	0-1-0	0-0-0	1-0-0	0-1-0	2-0-0	0-1-0	2-0-0	0-0-0	0-0-0	1-0-0	0-1-0	0-1-0	0-0-0	6	5	0	.545
Pugh	0-0-0	0-1-0	0-1-0	1-0-0	1-0-0	0-1-0	1-0-0	1-1-0	0-0-0	0-0-0	2-0-0	0-1-0	0-0-0	6	5	0	.545
Rijo	0-0-0	1-1-0	0-0-0	0-1-0	0-0-0	0-0-0	1-0-0	1-0-0	0-1-0	0-1-0	1-0-0	0-0-0	1-0-0	5	4	0	.556
Schourek	0-1-0	2-0-0	1-1-0	2-1-0	1-0-0	2-0-0	2-0-0	1-1-0	2-0-0	3-0-0	1-1-0	0-1-0	1-1-0	18	7	0	.720
Smiley	1-1-0	1-0-0	0-1-0	1-1-0	2-0-0	2-0-0	0-1-0	1-1-0	2-0-0	2-0-0	0-0-0	0-0-0	0-0-0	12	5	0	.706
Smith	0-1-0	0-0-0	1-0-0	0-0-0	0-0-0	0-0-0	0-0-0	0-0-0	0-0-0	0-0-0	0-1-0	0-0-0	0-0-0	1	2	0	.333
Viola	0-0-0	0-0-0	0-0-0	0-0-0	0-1-0	0-0-0	0-0-0	0-0-0	0-0-0	0-0-0	0-0-0	0-0-0	0-0-0	0	1	0	.000
Wells	0-0-0	0-0-0	0-1-0	0-1-0	1-0-0	0-0-0	0-2-0	1-0-0	1-0-0	0-1-0	2-0-0	1-0-0	0-0-0	6	5	0	.545
TOTALS	5-8-3	7-3-5	5-7-1	6-6-2	12-1-5	4-3-2	8-4-5	7-5-4	9-3-6	8-5-3	8-5-1	3-6-1	3-3-0	85	59	38	.590

NO DECISIONS OR SAVES: Courtright, Grott, Pennington, Reed, Remlinger, Roper, Ruffin, Sullivan.

COLORADO (77-67)

Pitcher	Atl. W-L-S	Chi. W-L-S	Cin. W-L-S	Fla. W-L-S	Hou. W-L-S	L.A. W-L-S	Mon. W-L-S	N.Y. W-L-S	Phi. W-L-S	Pit. W-L-S	St.L. W-L-S	S.D. W-L-S	S.F. W-L-S	Totals W	L	S	Pct.
Acevedo	0-2-0	0-1-0	1-0-0	0-0-0	0-0-0	0-1-0	1-0-0	0-0-0	0-0-0	0-1-0	1-1-0	0-0-0	1-0-0	4	6	0	.400
Bailey	0-1-0	1-1-0	0-1-0	0-1-0	1-0-0	0-1-0	0-0-0	0-0-0	0-0-0	2-0-0	1-1-0	2-0-0	0-0-0	7	6	0	.538
Freeman	0-1-0	0-1-0	0-1-0	0-1-0	0-0-0	0-1-0	1-1-0	0-0-0	0-0-0	1-0-0	1-0-0	0-1-0	0-0-0	3	7	0	.300
Grahe	0-0-0	0-0-0	1-0-0	0-1-0	0-0-0	0-0-0	1-0-0	0-0-0	0-0-0	1-0-0	0-1-0	1-0-0	0-1-0	4	3	0	.571
Hickerson	1-0-0	0-0-0	0-0-0	0-0-0	0-0-0	0-0-0	0-0-0	0-0-0	0-0-0	0-0-0	0-0-0	0-0-0	0-0-0	1	0	0	1.000
Holmes	1-1-0	1-0-0	0-0-1	0-0-0	0-0-2	0-0-0	0-0-3	0-0-3	0-0-2	1-0-1	1-0-1	1-0-1	1-0-0	6	1	14	.857
Leskanic	1-0-0	1-0-1	1-0-2	0-0-1	1-1-0	0-0-0	0-0-1	1-0-0	0-0-0	0-0-3	1-1-0	0-0-0	0-1-2	6	3	10	.667
Munoz	0-1-0	1-0-1	0-0-0	0-0-0	0-1-0	0-0-1	0-0-0	0-0-0	1-1-0	0-0-0	0-0-0	0-0-0	0-1-0	2	4	2	.333
Olivares	0-1-0	0-0-0	0-0-0	0-0-0	1-1-0	0-1-0	0-0-0	0-0-0	0-0-0	0-0-0	0-0-0	0-0-0	0-0-0	1	3	0	.250
Painter	1-0-0	0-0-0	0-0-1	0-0-0	0-0-0	0-0-0	0-0-0	0-0-0	0-0-0	1-0-0	0-0-0	0-0-0	1-0-0	3	0	1	1.000
Reed	0-0-0	0-0-1	1-0-0	2-1-1	0-0-0	0-1-0	0-0-0	1-0-0	0-0-0	0-0-0	0-0-0	1-0-0	0-0-1	5	2	3	.714
Rekar	0-0-0	0-1-0	0-1-0	0-1-0	0-0-0	0-0-0	1-0-0	0-0-0	2-0-0	1-0-0	0-1-0	0-0-0	0-2-0	4	6	0	.400
Reynoso	0-1-0	1-0-0	1-0-0	0-0-0	0-1-0	0-0-0	2-0-0	0-2-0	0-0-0	0-1-0	0-1-0	2-1-0	1-0-0	7	7	0	.500
Ritz	0-0-1	1-1-0	1-2-1	1-2-0	1-0-0	1-2-0	1-0-0	1-1-0	0-1-0	1-1-0	0-0-0	1-1-0	2-0-0	11	11	2	.500
Ruffin	0-0-1	0-0-0	0-0-0	0-0-3	0-0-2	0-0-0	0-0-0	0-0-0	0-0-0	0-0-1	0-1-1	0-0-3	0-0-0	0	1	11	.000
Saberhagen	0-0-0	0-1-0	0-0-0	0-0-0	0-0-0	2-0-0	0-0-0	0-0-0	0-0-0	0-0-0	0-0-0	0-0-0	0-0-0	2	1	0	.667
Swift	0-1-0	0-0-0	1-0-0	2-0-0	0-0-0	1-1-0	0-0-0	1-0-0	1-0-0	0-1-0	0-0-0	1-0-0	2-0-0	9	3	0	.750
Thompson	0-0-0	1-0-0	0-0-0	0-0-0	0-0-0	0-1-0	0-0-0	1-1-0	0-0-0	0-0-0	0-0-0	0-1-0	0-0-0	2	3	0	.400
TOTALS	4-9-2	7-6-3	7-5-5	5-7-5	4-4-4	4-9-1	7-1-4	5-4-3	4-2-2	8-4-5	5-7-2	9-4-4	8-5-3	77	67	43	.535

NO DECISIONS OR SAVES: Nied, Sager.

FLORIDA (67-76)

Pitcher	Atl. W-L-S	Chi. W-L-S	Cin. W-L-S	Col. W-L-S	Hou. W-L-S	L.A. W-L-S	Mon. W-L-S	N.Y. W-L-S	Phi. W-L-S	Pit. W-L-S	St.L. W-L-S	S.D. W-L-S	S.F. W-L-S	Totals W	L	S	Pct.
Banks	0-1-0	0-1-0	0-0-0	0-0-0	1-0-0	0-0-0	0-0-0	0-0-0	0-1-0	1-0-0	0-0-0	0-0-0	0-0-0	2	3	0	.400
Bowen	0-0-0	0-0-0	0-0-0	0-0-0	0-0-0	0-0-0	0-0-0	1-0-0	1-0-0	0-0-0	0-0-0	0-0-0	0-0-0	2	0	0	1.000
Burkett	0-1-0	1-2-0	1-1-0	1-1-0	2-0-0	0-2-0	1-1-0	1-2-0	2-1-0	1-1-0	1-1-0	1-0-0	2-1-0	14	14	0	.500
Dunbar	0-0-0	0-0-0	0-1-0	0-0-0	0-0-0	0-0-0	0-0-0	0-0-0	0-0-0	0-0-0	0-0-0	0-0-0	0-0-0	0	1	0	.000
Garces	0-0-0	0-0-0	0-1-0	0-0-0	0-1-0	0-0-0	0-0-0	0-0-0	0-0-0	0-0-0	0-0-0	0-0-0	0-0-0	0	2	0	.000
Gardner	0-1-0	0-0-0	1-0-0	0-1-0	1-0-1	0-1-0	0-1-0	0-0-0	0-0-0	0-1-0	1-0-0	2-0-0	0-0-0	5	5	1	.500
Groom	0-0-0	0-0-0	0-0-0	1-0-0	0-0-0	0-0-0	0-0-0	0-0-0	0-0-0	0-2-0	0-0-0	0-0-0	0-0-0	1	2	0	.333
Hammond	0-0-0	0-3-0	0-2-0	1-0-0	0-0-0	1-1-0	1-0-0	2-0-0	1-0-0	2-0-0	1-0-0	0-0-0	0-0-0	9	6	0	.600
Lewis	0-0-0	0-0-0	0-0-0	0-0-0	0-0-0	0-0-0	0-0-0	0-0-0	0-1-0	0-0-0	0-0-0	0-0-0	0-0-0	0	1	0	.000
Mantei	0-0-0	0-0-0	0-0-0	0-0-0	0-0-0	0-0-0	0-0-0	0-0-0	0-0-0	0-0-0	0-1-0	0-0-0	0-0-0	0	1	0	.000
Mathews	1-0-0	0-0-0	0-0-1	1-1-0	0-0-0	0-1-0	0-1-1	0-1-0	0-0-0	1-0-0	0-0-0	0-0-1	1-0-0	4	4	3	.500
Murphy	0-0-0	0-0-0	0-0-0	0-0-0	0-0-0	0-0-0	0-0-0	0-1-0	0-0-0	0-0-0	0-0-0	0-0-0	1-0-0	1	1	0	.500
Nen	0-3-1	0-0-2	0-0-2	0-0-1	0-1-4	0-0-2	0-1-2	0-0-3	0-1-2	0-1-1	0-0-2	0-0-0	0-0-1	0	7	23	.000
Pena	0-0-0	0-0-0	0-0-0	1-0-0	0-0-0	0-0-0	1-0-0	0-0-0	0-0-0	0-0-0	0-0-0	0-0-0	0-0-0	2	0	0	1.000
Perez	0-2-0	0-0-0	0-0-0	0-0-0	0-1-0	0-0-0	0-1-0	0-0-0	1-1-0	0-0-1	1-0-0	0-1-0	0-0-0	2	6	1	.250
Rapp	2-0-0	2-0-0	2-1-0	1-2-0	1-0-0	1-1-0	2-1-0	2-1-0	1-0-0	0-0-0	0-0-0	0-0-0	0-1-0	14	7	0	.667
Small	0-0-0	0-0-0	0-0-0	0-0-0	1-0-0	0-0-0	0-0-0	0-0-0	0-0-0	0-0-0	0-0-0	0-0-0	0-0-0	1	0	0	1.000
Veres	0-1-0	1-0-0	0-0-0	0-0-0	1-0-1	1-0-0	0-0-0	1-1-0	0-1-0	0-1-0	0-0-0	0-0-0	0-0-0	4	4	1	.500
Weathers	0-0-0	0-2-0	2-0-0	0-0-0	1-0-0	0-0-0	1-1-0	0-0-0	0-1-0	0-0-0	0-0-0	0-1-0	0-0-0	4	5	0	.444
Witt	0-1-0	0-0-0	0-0-0	1-0-0	0-1-0	0-1-0	0-0-0	0-0-0	0-0-0	0-2-0	0-1-0	0-0-0	1-1-0	2	7	0	.222
TOTALS	3-10-1	4-8-2	6-6-3	7-5-1	8-4-6	3-7-2	6-7-3	7-6-3	6-7-2	5-8-2	4-3-2	3-2-1	5-3-1	67	76	29	.469

NO DECISIONS OR SAVES: Harvey, Hernandez, Johnstone, Myers, Powell, Scheid, Valdes.

HOUSTON (76-68)

Pitcher	Atl. W-L-S	Chi. W-L-S	Cin. W-L-S	Col. W-L-S	Fla. W-L-S	L.A. W-L-S	Mon. W-L-S	N.Y. W-L-S	Phi. W-L-S	Pit. W-L-S	St.L. W-L-S	S.D. W-L-S	S.F. W-L-S	Totals W	L	S	Pct.
Brocail	0-1-0	0-1-0	0-0-0	1-0-0	0-1-0	0-0-0	1-0-0	0-0-1	0-0-0	2-0-0	0-0-0	1-0-0	1-1-0	6	4	1	.600
Dougherty	0-0-0	1-0-0	0-0-0	0-1-0	3-1-0	0-1-0	0-0-0	1-0-0	0-0-0	0-0-0	0-0-0	1-0-0	2-1-0	8	4	0	.667
Drabek	1-1-0	0-1-0	1-0-0	0-0-0	0-2-0	1-0-0	1-1-0	1-1-0	1-1-0	0-0-0	1-2-0	2-0-0	1-0-0	10	9	0	.526
Hampton	0-1-0	0-1-0	0-1-0	1-1-0	0-0-0	1-0-0	0-0-0	1-2-0	1-1-0	0-1-0	3-0-0	1-0-0	1-0-0	9	8	0	.529
Hartgraves	0-0-0	0-0-0	0-0-0	0-0-0	0-0-0	0-0-0	0-0-0	0-0-0	1-0-0	0-0-0	1-0-0	0-0-0	0-0-0	2	0	0	1.000
Henneman	0-0-0	0-0-1	0-0-0	0-0-0	0-0-1	0-0-0	0-0-1	0-0-3	0-1-1	0-0-1	0-0-0	0-0-0	0-0-0	0	1	8	.000
Hudek	1-0-1	0-0-0	0-0-0	0-0-1	0-1-1	0-0-0	1-0-1	0-0-0	0-1-1	0-0-1	0-0-1	0-0-0	0-0-0	2	2	7	.500
Jones	1-0-1	1-1-3	0-1-0	1-0-1	0-0-0	0-0-1	0-0-2	0-1-0	0-1-1	1-1-3	1-0-1	1-0-1	0-0-1	6	5	15	.545
Kile	0-1-0	1-1-0	0-2-0	1-2-0	0-0-0	0-0-0	1-0-0	0-0-0	1-1-0	0-2-0	0-0-0	0-2-0	0-1-0	4	12	0	.250
McMurtry	0-1-0	0-0-0	0-0-0	0-0-0	0-0-0	0-0-0	0-0-0	0-0-0	0-0-0	0-0-0	0-0-0	0-0-0	0-0-0	0	1	0	.000
Reynolds	2-0-0	2-0-0	0-4-0	0-0-0	0-2-0	1-0-0	1-1-0	1-2-0	0-0-0	2-0-0	1-0-0	0-2-0	0-0-0	10	11	0	.476
Swindell	1-1-0	1-0-0	0-2-0	0-0-0	0-1-0	0-1-0	2-1-0	1-0-0	0-1-0	3-0-0	1-2-0	1-0-0	0-0-0	10	9	0	.526
Tabaka	0-0-0	0-0-0	0-0-0	0-0-0	0-0-0	0-0-0	1-0-0	0-0-0	0-0-0	0-0-0	0-0-0	0-0-0	0-0-0	1	0	0	1.000
Veres	0-0-0	1-0-0	0-1-0	0-0-0	1-0-0	0-0-0	1-0-0	0-0-0	1-0-0	1-0-0	0-0-0	0-0-0	0-0-1	5	1	1	.833
Wall	0-0-0	1-0-0	0-1-0	0-0-0	0-0-0	0-0-0	0-0-0	1-0-0	0-0-0	0-0-0	1-0-0	0-0-0	0-0-0	3	1	0	.750
TOTALS	6-6-2	8-5-4	1-12-0	4-4-2	4-8-2	3-2-1	9-3-4	6-6-4	5-7-3	9-4-5	9-4-2	7-4-1	5-3-2	76	68	32	.528

NO DECISIONS OR SAVES: Cangelosi, Martinez, Powell, Wagner.

LOS ANGELES (78-66)

Pitcher	Atl. W-L-S	Chi. W-L-S	Cin. W-L-S	Col. W-L-S	Fla. W-L-S	Hou. W-L-S	Mon. W-L-S	N.Y. W-L-S	Phi. W-L-S	Pit. W-L-S	St.L. W-L-S	S.D. W-L-S	S.F. W-L-S	Totals W	L	S	Pct.
Astacio	0-1-0	0-0-0	0-0-0	0-0-0	1-1-0	1-0-0	0-0-0	1-1-0	0-2-0	1-1-0	2-2-0	1-0-0	0-0-0	7	8	0	.467
Banks	0-0-0	0-0-0	0-1-0	0-0-0	0-0-0	0-1-0	0-0-0	0-0-0	0-0-0	0-0-0	0-0-0	0-0-0	0-0-0	0	2	0	.000
Bruske	0-0-0	0-0-0	0-0-0	0-0-0	0-0-0	0-0-0	0-0-0	0-0-0	0-0-0	0-0-0	0-0-0	0-0-1	0-0-0	0	0	1	.000
Candiotti	0-0-0	0-1-0	0-1-0	0-2-0	2-1-0	0-1-0	0-0-0	1-2-0	1-2-0	0-0-0	2-0-0	0-2-0	1-2-0	7	14	0	.333
Cummings	1-0-0	0-0-0	0-0-0	0-0-0	0-0-0	0-0-0	0-0-0	0-1-0	1-0-0	1-0-0	0-0-0	0-0-0	0-0-0	3	1	0	.750
Daal	1-0-0	0-0-0	0-0-0	1-0-0	0-0-0	0-0-0	0-0-0	1-0-0	0-0-0	0-0-0	0-0-0	1-0-0	0-0-0	4	0	0	1.000
Guthrie	0-0-0	0-2-0	0-0-0	0-0-0	0-0-0	0-0-0	0-0-0	0-0-0	0-0-0	0-0-0	0-0-0	0-0-0	0-0-0	0	2	0	.000
Hansell	0-0-0	0-0-0	0-0-0	0-0-0	0-0-0	0-0-0	0-0-0	0-0-0	0-0-0	0-0-0	0-0-0	0-0-0	0-1-0	0	1	0	.000
Martinez	0-1-0	1-1-0	2-0-0	2-2-0	2-0-0	1-0-0	3-1-0	0-0-0	1-1-0	3-0-0	0-0-0	1-1-0	1-0-0	17	7	0	.708
Murphy	0-1-0	0-0-0	0-0-0	0-0-0	0-0-0	0-0-0	0-0-0	0-0-0	0-0-0	0-0-0	0-0-0	0-0-0	0-0-0	0	1	0	.000
Nomo	0-0-0	2-0-0	1-0-0	1-0-0	1-0-0	0-1-0	1-1-0	1-1-0	0-1-0	1-0-0	1-1-0	2-0-0	2-1-0	13	6	0	.684
Osuna	0-0-0	0-0-0	0-0-0	0-0-0	0-0-0	0-0-0	0-0-0	0-0-0	0-0-0	0-0-0	0-2-0	0-2-0	2-0-0	2	4	0	.333
F. Rodriguez	0-0-0	0-1-0	0-0-0	0-0-0	0-0-0	0-0-0	0-0-0	1-0-0	0-0-0	0-0-0	0-0-0	0-0-0	0-0-0	1	1	0	.500
Seanez	0-1-0	0-1-0	0-0-0	0-0-1	0-0-2	0-0-0	0-0-0	0-0-0	0-1-0	0-0-0	0-0-0	0-0-0	1-0-0	1	3	3	.250
Tapani	0-0-0	0-0-0	0-1-0	2-0-0	0-0-0	0-0-0	0-1-0	0-0-0	1-0-0	1-0-0	0-0-0	0-0-0	0-0-0	4	2	0	.667
Valdes	2-1-0	2-1-0	0-1-0	1-0-1	1-1-0	0-0-0	2-2-0	0-0-0	0-2-0	2-1-0	1-0-0	1-1-0	1-1-0	13	11	1	.542
T. Williams	0-0-0	0-0-0	0-0-0	1-0-0	0-0-0	0-0-0	0-0-0	0-0-0	0-0-0	0-2-0	1-0-0	0-0-0	0-0-0	2	2	0	.500
Worrell	0-0-1	0-0-1	0-0-1	1-0-3	0-0-3	0-0-1	1-0-2	1-1-3	0-0-1	0-0-5	0-0-4	1-0-2	0-0-5	4	1	32	.800
TOTALS	4-5-1	5-7-1	3-4-1	9-4-5	7-3-5	2-3-1	7-5-2	6-6-3	4-9-1	9-4-5	7-5-4	7-6-3	8-5-5	78	66	37	.542

NO DECISIONS OR SAVES: Eischen, Park, Parra.

1995 PITCHING RECORDS AGAINST OPPOSING CLUBS

MONTREAL (66-78)

Pitcher	Atl.	Chi.	Cin.	Col.	Fla.	Hou.	L.A.	N.Y.	Phi.	Pit.	St.L.	S.D.	S.F.	Totals			
	W-L-S	W-L-S	W-L-S	W-L-S	W-L-S	W-L-S	W-L-S	W-L-S	W-L-S	W-L-S	W-L-S	W-L-S	W-L-S	W	L	S	Pct.
Alvarez	0-0-0	0-0-0	0-2-0	0-0-0	0-0-0	0-0-0	0-1-0	0-0-0	0-1-0	0-0-0	0-0-0	0-0-0	1-1-0	1	5	0	.167
Aquino	0-1-0	0-0-0	0-1-0	0-0-0	0-0-0	0-0-0	0-0-0	0-0-1	0-0-0	0-0-0	0-0-0	0-0-1	0-0-0	0	2	2	.000
DeLeon	0-0-0	0-0-0	0-0-0	0-0-0	0-0-0	0-0-0	0-0-0	0-0-0	0-0-0	0-0-0	0-0-0	0-0-0	0-1-0	0	1	0	.000
Fassero	0-2-0	0-0-0	0-3-0	0-2-0	2-0-0	0-1-0	1-3-0	2-1-0	1-1-0	2-1-0	1-0-0	4-0-0	0-0-0	13	14	0	.481
Fraser	0-0-0	0-0-0	0-0-0	0-0-0	1-0-0	0-0-1	0-1-0	0-0-0	0-0-0	0-0-0	0-0-0	1-0-1	0-0-0	2	1	2	.667
Harris	0-0-0	0-0-0	0-0-0	0-0-0	1-0-0	0-1-0	1-0-0	0-0-0	0-0-0	0-1-0	0-0-0	0-1-0	0-0-0	2	3	0	.400
Henry	1-1-0	2-1-0	1-0-0	0-2-0	0-0-0	1-1-0	0-0-0	0-0-0	1-1-0	0-0-0	0-1-0	0-2-0	1-0-0	7	9	0	.438
Heredia	0-0-0	1-0-0	0-0-0	0-1-0	0-1-1	1-1-0	1-1-0	0-0-0	1-1-0	0-0-0	0-0-0	0-1-0	1-0-0	5	6	1	.455
Leiper	0-1-0	0-0-0	0-0-0	0-0-0	0-0-0	0-0-1	0-0-0	0-0-0	0-0-1	0-0-0	0-0-0	0-0-0	0-1-0	0	2	2	.000
Martinez	1-2-0	1-1-0	0-1-0	1-1-0	0-0-0	1-3-0	0-0-0	3-0-0	2-0-0	1-1-0	1-0-0	1-1-0	2-0-0	14	10	0	.583
Perez	2-1-0	0-0-0	1-0-0	0-0-0	1-2-0	0-1-0	1-1-0	0-2-0	2-1-0	1-0-0	2-0-0	0-0-0	0-0-0	10	8	0	.556
Rojas	0-1-2	0-0-3	0-0-2	0-0-0	1-0-4	0-0-0	0-0-3	0-0-4	0-0-4	0-0-1	0-1-2	0-0-4	0-2-1	1	4	30	.200
Rueter	0-0-0	0-1-0	2-0-0	0-0-0	1-1-0	0-0-0	1-0-0	0-1-0	0-0-0	0-0-0	0-0-0	0-0-0	1-0-0	5	3	0	.625
Scott	0-0-0	0-0-0	0-0-0	0-0-0	0-0-0	0-0-0	0-0-2	1-0-0	1-0-0	0-0-0	0-0-0	0-0-0	0-0-0	2	0	2	1.000
Shaw	0-0-0	0-0-1	0-0-0	0-0-0	0-1-0	0-1-0	0-0-0	0-2-0	0-0-0	0-0-0	0-1-1	1-0-0	0-1-1	1	6	3	.143
Urbina	0-0-0	1-0-0	0-0-0	0-1-0	0-0-0	0-0-0	0-0-0	1-0-0	0-0-0	0-1-0	0-0-0	0-0-0	0-0-0	2	2	0	.500
G. White	0-0-0	0-0-0	0-1-0	0-0-0	0-1-0	0-0-0	0-0-0	0-0-0	0-0-0	0-0-0	0-0-0	0-0-0	1-0-0	1	2	0	.333
TOTALS	4-9-2	5-3-4	4-8-2	1-7-0	7-6-5	3-9-2	5-7-5	7-6-5	8-5-5	4-4-1	4-3-3	7-5-6	7-6-2	66	78	42	.458

NO DECISIONS OR SAVES: Cornelius, Eversgerd, Schmidt, Thobe.

NEW YORK (69-75)

Pitcher	Atl.	Chi.	Cin.	Col.	Fla.	Hou.	L.A.	Mon.	Phi.	Pit.	St.L.	S.D.	S.F.	Totals			
	W-L-S	W-L-S	W-L-S	W-L-S	W-L-S	W-L-S	W-L-S	W-L-S	W-L-S	W-L-S	W-L-S	W-L-S	W-L-S	W	L	S	Pct.
Birkbeck	0-0-0	0-0-0	0-0-0	0-0-0	0-0-0	0-0-0	0-1-0	0-0-0	0-0-0	0-0-0	0-0-0	0-0-0	0-0-0	0	1	0	.000
Byrd	0-0-0	0-0-0	0-0-0	0-0-0	0-0-0	0-0-0	0-0-0	1-0-0	0-0-0	0-0-0	0-0-0	0-0-0	1-0-0	2	0	0	1.000
Cornelius	0-0-0	0-0-0	1-1-0	0-0-0	0-1-0	0-2-0	0-0-0	0-0-0	2-0-0	0-0-0	0-0-0	0-1-0	0-2-0	3	7	0	.300
DiPoto	0-0-0	1-0-0	0-0-0	0-0-0	0-0-0	0-0-0	1-2-0	0-1-0	0-0-1	1-0-0	1-1-0	0-2-0	0-0-1	4	6	2	.400
Florence	0-0-0	0-0-0	0-0-0	0-0-0	0-0-0	0-0-0	0-0-0	0-0-0	1-0-0	0-0-0	0-0-0	1-0-0	1-0-0	3	0	0	1.000
Franco	0-0-5	1-0-0	0-0-3	1-0-1	0-0-2	0-0-2	0-0-4	1-0-3	0-0-3	1-1-2	0-0-2	1-0-2	0-2-0	5	3	29	.625
Gunderson	0-0-0	0-0-0	0-0-0	0-0-0	0-0-0	0-1-0	0-0-0	0-0-0	1-0-0	0-0-0	0-0-0	0-0-0	0-0-0	1	1	0	.500
Harnisch	0-1-0	0-1-0	0-2-0	1-0-0	0-0-0	0-0-0	0-1-0	0-0-0	0-2-0	0-0-0	0-0-0	1-1-0	0-0-0	2	8	0	.200
Henry	1-0-0	0-0-0	0-1-1	0-1-0	0-0-0	1-0-1	1-1-1	0-0-0	0-0-0	0-0-0	0-1-0	0-1-0	0-1-1	3	6	4	.333
Isringhausen	1-0-0	0-0-0	1-0-0	0-0-0	0-1-0	0-0-0	1-0-0	1-1-0	2-0-0	1-0-0	0-0-0	2-0-0	0-0-0	9	2	0	.818
Jacome	0-0-0	0-0-0	0-1-0	0-0-0	0-0-0	0-1-0	0-0-0	0-2-0	0-0-0	0-0-0	0-0-0	0-0-0	0-0-0	0	4	0	.000
B. Jones	2-1-0	1-0-0	1-2-0	1-1-0	1-2-0	2-0-0	0-0-0	1-0-0	0-2-0	0-0-0	0-1-0	0-1-0	1-0-0	10	10	0	.500
Lomon	0-0-0	0-0-0	0-0-0	0-1-0	0-0-0	0-0-0	0-0-0	0-0-0	0-0-0	0-0-0	0-0-0	0-0-0	0-0-0	0	1	0	.000
Manzanillo	0-1-0	0-0-0	0-0-0	0-0-0	0-0-0	0-0-0	0-0-0	1-1-0	0-0-0	0-0-0	0-0-0	0-0-0	0-0-0	1	2	0	.333
Minor	1-0-0	0-0-0	1-0-0	0-0-0	1-0-0	0-0-0	0-0-0	0-0-0	0-0-0	0-0-0	1-0-0	0-1-1	0-1-0	4	2	1	.667
Mlicki	1-1-0	0-0-0	0-0-0	0-0-0	1-2-0	2-1-0	3-0-0	0-0-0	0-1-0	0-0-0	1-1-0	0-0-0	1-1-0	9	7	0	.563
Person	0-0-0	0-0-0	1-0-0	0-0-0	0-0-0	0-0-0	0-0-0	0-0-0	0-0-0	0-0-0	0-0-0	0-0-0	0-0-0	1	0	0	1.000
Pulsipher	0-0-0	0-2-0	0-0-0	1-0-0	1-1-0	0-1-0	0-0-0	1-1-0	0-1-0	1-1-0	0-0-0	1-0-0	0-0-0	5	7	0	.417
Remlinger	0-0-0	0-0-0	0-0-0	0-1-0	0-0-0	0-0-0	0-0-0	0-0-0	0-0-0	0-0-0	0-0-0	0-0-0	0-0-0	0	1	0	.000
Saberhagen	1-0-0	0-1-0	0-0-0	0-1-0	2-0-0	1-0-0	0-1-0	0-1-0	0-0-0	0-1-0	0-0-0	0-0-0	1-0-0	5	5	0	.500
Telgheder	0-1-0	0-0-0	0-0-0	0-0-0	0-0-0	0-0-0	0-0-0	0-0-0	1-0-0	0-0-0	0-0-0	0-0-0	0-1-0	1	2	0	.333
Walker	1-0-0	0-0-0	0-0-0	0-0-0	0-0-0	0-0-0	0-0-0	0-0-0	0-0-0	0-0-0	0-0-0	0-0-0	0-0-0	1	0	0	1.000
TOTALS	8-5-5	3-4-0	5-7-4	4-5-1	6-7-2	6-6-3	6-6-5	6-7-3	7-6-4	4-3-2	3-4-2	6-7-3	5-8-2	69	75	36	.479

PHILADELPHIA (69-75)

Pitcher	Atl.	Chi.	Cin.	Col.	Fla.	Hou.	L.A.	Mon.	N.Y.	Pit.	St.L.	S.D.	S.F.	Totals			
	W-L-S	W-L-S	W-L-S	W-L-S	W-L-S	W-L-S	W-L-S	W-L-S	W-L-S	W-L-S	W-L-S	W-L-S	W-L-S	W	L	S	Pct.
Abbott	1-0-0	0-0-0	0-0-0	0-0-0	0-0-0	0-0-0	0-0-0	0-0-0	0-0-0	0-0-0	0-0-0	1-0-0	0-0-0	2	0	0	1.000
Borland	0-0-1	0-0-0	0-1-0	0-0-0	0-1-0	0-0-1	0-1-0	0-0-1	0-0-0	1-0-0	0-0-2	0-0-1	0-0-0	1	3	6	.250
Bottalico	0-0-0	0-0-0	0-0-0	0-1-0	2-0-0	2-0-0	0-1-0	0-1-0	0-0-1	0-0-0	0-0-0	0-0-0	1-0-0	5	3	1	.625
Charlton	0-0-0	1-0-0	0-1-0	0-0-0	0-0-0	0-1-0	0-0-0	0-0-0	0-0-0	0-1-0	0-1-0	0-1-0	1-0-0	2	5	0	.286
Deshaies	0-0-0	0-1-0	0-0-0	0-0-0	0-0-0	0-0-0	0-0-0	0-0-0	0-0-0	0-0-0	0-0-0	0-0-0	0-0-0	0	1	0	.000
Fernandez	1-0-0	0-0-0	0-0-0	0-0-0	0-0-0	0-0-0	1-0-0	1-1-0	0-0-0	0-0-0	1-0-0	1-0-0	1-0-0	6	1	0	.857
Fletcher	0-0-0	0-0-0	0-0-0	0-0-0	0-0-0	1-0-0	0-0-0	0-0-0	0-0-0	0-0-0	0-0-0	0-0-0	0-0-0	1	0	0	1.000
Frey	0-0-0	0-0-0	0-0-0	0-0-0	0-0-1	0-0-0	0-0-0	0-0-0	0-0-0	0-0-0	0-0-0	0-0-0	0-0-0	0	0	1	.000
Grace	0-0-0	0-0-0	0-0-0	0-0-0	0-0-0	0-0-0	1-0-0	0-0-0	0-0-0	0-0-0	0-0-0	0-1-0	0-0-0	1	1	0	.500
Green	2-0-0	0-0-0	0-0-0	0-2-0	0-1-0	0-1-0	2-0-0	1-1-0	2-1-0	0-1-0	1-0-0	0-0-0	0-2-0	8	9	0	.471
Greene	0-0-0	0-0-0	0-1-0	0-0-0	0-0-0	0-0-0	0-1-0	0-1-0	0-1-0	0-0-0	0-0-0	0-1-0	0-0-0	0	5	0	.000
Harris	0-0-0	0-0-0	1-0-0	0-0-0	0-0-0	0-0-0	0-0-0	0-0-0	0-0-0	0-0-0	0-0-0	0-1-0	1-1-0	2	2	0	.500
Juden	0-0-0	0-0-0	0-1-0	0-0-0	0-0-0	1-1-0	1-1-0	0-0-0	0-0-0	0-0-0	0-0-0	0-0-0	0-1-0	2	4	0	.333
Mimbs	1-2-0	0-1-0	0-1-0	0-0-0	2-0-0	0-0-0	1-0-0	0-1-0	2-1-0	1-0-0	0-1-0	1-0-1	1-0-0	9	7	1	.563
Munoz	0-1-0	0-1-0	0-0-0	0-0-0	0-0-0	0-0-0	0-0-0	0-0-0	0-0-0	0-0-0	0-0-0	0-0-0	0-0-0	0	2	0	.000
Olivares	0-0-0	0-0-0	0-0-0	0-0-0	0-0-0	0-0-0	0-0-0	0-0-0	0-0-0	0-0-0	0-1-0	0-0-0	0-0-0	0	1	0	.000
Quantrill	0-1-0	0-0-0	0-1-0	0-1-0	0-2-0	1-0-0	2-0-0	1-2-0	1-2-0	3-1-0	2-0-0	1-0-0	0-2-0	11	12	0	.478
Ricci	0-0-0	0-0-0	1-0-0	0-0-0	0-0-0	0-0-0	0-0-0	0-0-0	0-0-0	0-0-0	0-0-0	0-0-0	0-0-0	1	0	0	1.000
Schilling	1-1-0	0-1-0	1-1-0	1-0-0	1-0-0	1-1-0	0-0-0	1-0-0	0-0-0	0-0-0	0-1-0	1-0-0	0-0-0	7	5	0	.583
Slocumb	0-1-5	0-1-1	0-1-1	1-0-1	1-0-4	1-1-4	1-0-3	0-0-2	0-1-3	0-0-3	0-0-2	0-1-1	1-0-2	5	6	32	.455
D. Springer	0-0-0	0-0-0	0-1-0	0-0-0	0-1-0	0-0-0	0-0-0	0-1-0	0-0-0	0-0-0	0-0-0	0-0-0	0-0-0	0	3	0	.000
West	0-1-0	0-0-0	0-0-0	0-0-0	0-1-0	0-0-0	0-0-0	0-0-0	1-0-0	1-0-0	1-0-0	0-0-0	0-0-0	3	2	0	.600
Williams	0-0-0	0-1-0	0-0-0	0-0-0	1-0-0	0-0-0	0-0-0	1-0-0	0-1-0	0-0-0	0-0-0	1-1-0	0-0-0	3	3	0	.500
TOTALS	6-7-6	1-6-1	3-9-1	2-4-1	7-6-5	7-5-5	9-4-3	5-8-3	6-7-4	6-3-3	5-4-4	6-6-3	6-6-2	69	75	41	.479

NO DECISIONS OR SAVES: Carter, Karp, R. Springer.

PITTSBURGH (58-86)

Pitcher	Atl.	Chi.	Cin.	Col.	Fla.	Hou.	L.A.	Mon.	N.Y.	Phi.	St.L.	S.D.	S.F.	Totals			
	W-L-S	W-L-S	W-L-S	W-L-S	W-L-S	W-L-S	W-L-S	W-L-S	W-L-S	W-L-S	W-L-S	W-L-S	W-L-S	W	L	S	Pct.
Christiansen	0-0-0	0-0-0	0-0-0	0-0-0	0-0-0	0-1-0	1-0-0	0-0-0	0-0-0	0-0-0	0-0-0	0-1-0	0-1-0	1	3	0	.250
Dyer	1-0-0	0-2-0	0-0-0	0-0-0	1-0-0	0-0-0	0-1-0	0-0-0	0-0-0	0-1-0	2-0-0	0-0-0	0-1-0	4	5	0	.444
Ericks	0-0-0	0-2-0	0-0-0	0-1-0	0-0-0	1-0-0	0-1-0	0-2-0	1-0-0	1-1-0	0-0-0	0-2-0	0-0-0	3	9	0	.250
Gott	0-1-0	0-1-0	0-0-0	0-0-0	0-0-0	0-1-0	0-0-1	1-0-0	1-0-0	0-0-1	0-0-1	0-1-0	0-0-0	2	4	3	.333
Lieber	0-0-0	0-1-0	1-1-0	0-1-0	0-0-0	0-1-0	0-1-0	0-1-0	0-0-0	0-0-0	0-0-0	2-1-0	1-0-0	4	7	0	.364
Loaiza	0-1-0	0-0-0	0-2-0	1-0-0	1-1-0	2-0-0	0-1-0	1-0-0	1-0-0	1-0-0	0-3-0	0-1-0	1-0-0	8	9	0	.471
Maddux	0-0-0	1-0-0	0-0-0	0-0-0	0-0-0	0-0-0	0-0-0	0-0-0	0-0-0	0-0-0	0-0-0	0-0-0	0-0-0	1	0	0	1.000
McCurry	0-0-0	0-0-0	0-0-0	0-1-0	1-0-0	0-0-1	0-1-0	0-0-0	0-0-0	0-0-0	0-0-0	0-0-0	0-2-0	1	4	1	.200
Miceli	0-0-2	1-1-3	0-1-3	0-0-1	2-0-2	1-0-2	0-0-2	0-0-1	0-1-0	0-0-0	0-0-2	0-0-2	0-1-1	4	4	21	.500
Morel	0-0-0	0-0-0	0-0-0	0-0-0	0-0-0	0-0-0	0-0-0	0-0-0	0-0-0	0-0-0	0-1-0	0-0-0	0-0-0	0	1	0	.000
Neagle	0-0-0	2-0-0	1-1-0	1-1-0	0-2-0	0-2-0	2-1-0	1-0-0	0-0-0	0-1-0	1-0-0	1-0-0	4-0-0	13	8	0	.619
Parris	1-0-0	1-0-0	0-1-0	0-0-0	1-1-0	0-2-0	0-0-0	1-0-0	0-1-0	0-1-0	1-0-0	1-0-0	0-0-0	6	6	0	.500
Plesac	0-2-0	0-0-1	1-0-1	0-0-0	1-0-0	0-0-0	1-0-0	0-0-0	0-0-0	1-1-0	0-0-0	0-1-0	0-0-1	4	4	3	.500
Powell	0-0-0	0-0-0	0-0-0	0-1-0	0-0-0	0-0-0	0-0-0	0-0-0	0-1-0	0-0-0	0-0-0	0-0-0	0-0-0	0	2	0	.000
Wagner	0-0-0	0-1-0	1-2-0	2-2-0	1-1-1	0-1-0	0-3-0	0-1-0	0-1-0	0-1-0	1-2-0	0-1-0	0-0-0	5	16	1	.238
White	0-0-0	0-0-0	1-0-0	0-1-0	0-0-0	0-1-0	0-0-0	0-0-0	0-0-0	0-0-0	1-1-0	0-0-0	0-0-0	2	3	0	.400
Wilson	0-0-0	0-0-0	0-0-0	0-0-0	0-0-0	0-0-0	0-0-0	0-0-0	0-0-0	0-0-0	0-0-0	0-0-0	0-1-0	0	1	0	.000
TOTALS	2-4-2	5-8-4	5-8-4	4-8-1	8-5-3	4-9-3	4-9-3	4-4-1	3-4-0	3-6-1	6-7-3	4-8-2	6-6-2	58	86	29	.403

NO DECISIONS OR SAVES: Hancock, Hope, Konuszewski, Manzanillo.

ST. LOUIS (62-81)

Pitcher	Atl.	Chi.	Cin.	Col.	Fla.	Hou.	L.A.	Mon.	N.Y.	Phi.	Pit.	S.D.	S.F.	Totals			
	W-L-S	W-L-S	W-L-S	W-L-S	W-L-S	W-L-S	W-L-S	W-L-S	W-L-S	W-L-S	W-L-S	W-L-S	W-L-S	W	L	S	Pct.
Arocha	0-1-0	0-0-0	0-1-0	0-0-0	0-1-0	0-0-0	1-0-0	0-0-0	0-1-0	1-0-0	0-0-0	0-0-0	1-1-0	3	5	0	.375
Barber	0-0-0	0-0-0	1-0-0	1-0-0	0-0-0	0-0-0	0-0-0	0-0-0	0-0-0	0-0-0	0-1-0	0-0-0	0-0-0	2	1	0	.667
Benes	0-0-0	0-1-0	0-0-0	0-0-0	0-0-0	0-0-0	0-0-0	0-0-0	0-0-0	0-0-0	1-1-0	0-0-0	0-0-0	1	2	0	.333
DeLucia	1-0-0	0-1-0	1-1-0	1-0-0	0-0-0	0-2-0	0-0-0	2-0-0	0-1-0	1-0-0	0-0-0	0-2-0	2-0-0	8	7	0	.533
Fossas	0-0-0	0-0-0	0-0-0	1-0-0	0-0-0	0-0-0	0-0-0	0-0-0	1-0-0	0-0-0	0-0-0	1-0-0	0-0-0	3	0	0	1.000
Frascatore	0-1-0	0-0-0	0-0-0	0-0-0	0-0-0	0-0-0	1-0-0	0-0-0	0-0-0	0-0-0	0-0-0	0-0-0	0-0-0	1	1	0	.500
Habyan	1-0-0	0-1-0	0-0-0	1-0-0	1-0-0	0-0-0	0-0-0	0-0-0	0-0-0	0-0-0	0-0-0	0-0-0	0-1-0	3	2	0	.600
Henke	0-0-4	0-0-1	0-0-3	0-0-3	0-0-1	0-0-4	1-1-3	0-0-1	0-0-2	0-0-2	0-0-4	0-0-5	0-0-3	1	1	36	.500
Hill	1-0-0	2-0-0	0-1-0	1-0-0	0-1-0	0-0-0	0-1-0	0-1-0	0-0-0	0-2-0	2-0-0	0-1-0	0-0-0	6	7	0	.462
Jackson	0-1-0	0-1-0	0-1-0	0-1-0	1-0-0	0-2-0	0-1-0	0-1-0	0-0-0	1-1-0	0-1-0	0-2-0	0-0-0	2	12	0	.143
Mathews	0-0-0	0-0-0	1-0-0	0-0-1	0-0-0	0-0-0	0-0-0	0-0-0	0-0-0	0-0-0	0-0-1	0-1-0	0-0-0	1	1	2	.500
Morgan	0-1-0	0-1-0	1-0-0	1-0-0	0-0-0	0-1-0	0-1-0	1-0-0	0-0-0	1-0-0	1-0-0	0-0-0	0-2-0	5	6	0	.455
Osborne	0-0-0	0-1-0	0-1-0	0-0-0	0-0-0	0-1-0	0-0-0	0-0-0	0-0-0	0-1-0	2-1-0	1-0-0	1-1-0	4	6	0	.400
Palacios	0-0-0	0-0-0	0-1-0	0-0-0	0-0-0	1-0-0	0-1-0	0-0-0	0-1-0	0-0-0	0-0-0	0-0-0	1-0-0	2	3	0	.400
Parrett	0-1-0	1-1-0	1-0-0	0-2-0	0-0-0	1-0-0	0-1-0	0-0-0	0-0-0	0-0-0	0-1-0	1-1-0	0-0-0	4	7	0	.364
Petkovsek	0-1-0	0-0-0	0-0-0	1-1-0	0-1-0	0-2-0	2-0-0	0-0-0	1-0-0	0-0-0	0-0-0	1-0-0	1-1-0	6	6	0	.500
Urbani	1-1-0	1-0-0	0-0-0	0-0-0	0-0-0	0-1-0	0-0-0	0-1-0	1-0-0	0-1-0	0-0-0	0-0-0	0-1-0	3	5	0	.375
Watson	1-0-0	0-2-0	0-2-0	0-1-0	1-1-0	2-0-0	0-1-0	0-1-0	1-0-0	0-0-0	1-1-0	1-0-0	0-0-0	7	9	0	.438
TOTALS	5-7-4	4-9-1	5-8-3	7-5-4	3-4-1	4-9-4	5-7-3	3-4-1	4-3-2	4-5-2	7-6-5	5-7-5	6-7-3	62	81	38	.434

NO DECISIONS OR SAVES: Bailey, Creek, Rodriguez.

SAN DIEGO (70-74)

Pitcher	Atl.	Chi.	Cin.	Col.	Fla.	Hou.	L.A.	Mon.	N.Y.	Phi.	Pit.	St.L.	S.F.	Totals			
	W-L-S	W-L-S	W-L-S	W-L-S	W-L-S	W-L-S	W-L-S	W-L-S	W-L-S	W-L-S	W-L-S	W-L-S	W-L-S	W	L	S	Pct.
Ashby	0-0-0	1-1-0	0-0-0	1-1-0	0-1-0	3-0-0	2-0-0	0-1-0	0-2-0	0-2-0	2-1-0	2-0-0	1-1-0	12	10	0	.545
Benes	0-1-0	1-1-0	1-0-0	0-0-0	0-0-0	0-2-0	0-0-0	0-0-0	0-0-0	0-1-0	1-1-0	0-0-0	1-1-0	4	7	0	.364
Berumen	0-0-0	1-0-0	1-0-0	0-1-0	0-0-0	0-0-0	0-0-0	0-2-0	0-0-0	0-0-0	0-0-0	0-0-1	0-0-0	2	3	1	.400
Blair	0-1-0	1-0-0	1-1-0	1-0-0	1-0-0	0-0-0	0-1-0	1-0-0	1-1-0	0-0-0	0-1-0	0-0-0	1-0-0	7	5	0	.583
Bochtler	1-0-0	0-1-0	0-0-0	0-0-0	0-0-0	0-0-0	0-2-0	0-0-0	1-0-0	0-0-0	1-0-1	1-1-0	0-0-0	4	4	1	.500
Dishman	1-0-0	0-0-0	0-0-0	1-2-0	0-2-0	0-0-0	1-0-0	0-1-0	0-0-0	0-1-0	0-0-0	1-1-0	0-1-0	4	8	0	.333
Florie	0-1-0	0-0-0	0-0-0	0-0-0	1-0-0	0-0-0	0-1-0	0-0-0	0-0-0	0-0-0	1-0-0	0-0-1	0-0-0	2	2	1	.500
Hamilton	0-2-0	1-0-0	0-1-0	1-2-0	0-0-0	1-0-0	0-0-0	1-1-0	1-0-0	0-1-0	0-1-0	1-1-0	0-0-0	6	9	0	.400
Hermanson	0-0-0	1-0-0	0-0-0	0-0-0	0-0-0	0-0-0	1-0-0	0-0-0	0-0-0	0-1-0	0-0-0	1-0-0	0-0-0	3	1	0	.750
Hoffman	0-0-2	0-0-4	1-1-3	0-0-1	0-0-1	0-0-1	0-0-3	1-0-2	1-2-2	3-0-3	0-0-3	1-0-2	0-1-4	7	4	31	.636
Kroon	0-0-0	0-0-0	0-0-0	0-0-0	0-0-0	0-1-0	0-0-0	0-0-0	0-0-0	0-0-0	0-0-0	0-0-0	0-0-0	0	1	0	.000
Mauser	0-0-0	0-0-0	0-0-0	0-1-0	0-0-0	0-0-0	0-0-0	0-0-0	0-0-0	0-0-0	0-0-0	0-0-0	0-0-0	0	1	0	.000
Sanders	0-0-0	0-1-0	1-0-0	0-1-0	0-0-0	0-0-0	1-0-0	2-0-0	1-1-0	0-0-0	0-0-0	0-1-0	0-1-0	5	5	0	.500
Valenzuela	0-0-0	1-0-0	0-0-0	0-0-0	0-0-0	0-1-0	0-1-0	0-0-0	1-0-0	3-0-0	2-0-0	0-0-0	1-1-0	8	3	0	.727
Villone	0-0-0	0-0-0	0-0-0	0-0-0	0-0-0	0-0-0	0-0-0	0-1-0	0-0-1	0-0-0	1-0-0	0-0-0	1-0-0	2	1	1	.667
B. Williams	0-0-0	0-1-0	1-0-0	0-1-0	0-0-0	0-3-0	0-2-0	0-1-0	1-0-0	0-0-0	0-0-0	0-1-0	1-1-0	3	10	0	.231
Worrell	0-0-0	0-0-0	0-0-0	0-0-0	0-0-0	0-0-0	1-0-0	0-0-0	0-0-0	0-0-0	0-0-0	0-0-0	0-0-0	1	0	0	1.000
TOTALS	2-5-2	7-5-4	6-3-3	4-9-1	2-3-1	4-7-1	6-7-3	5-7-2	7-6-3	6-6-3	8-4-4	7-5-4	6-7-4	70	74	35	.486

NO DECISIONS OR SAVES: Elliott, Krueger, Tabaka.

SAN FRANCISCO (67-77)

Pitcher	Atl.	Chi.	Cin.	Col.	Fla.	Hou.	L.A.	Mon.	N.Y.	Phi.	Pit.	St.L.	S.D.	Totals			
	W-L-S	W-L-S	W-L-S	W-L-S	W-L-S	W-L-S	W-L-S	W-L-S	W-L-S	W-L-S	W-L-S	W-L-S	W-L-S	W	L	S	Pct.
Aquino	0-0-0	0-0-0	0-1-0	0-0-0	0-0-0	0-0-0	0-0-0	0-0-0	0-0-0	0-0-0	0-0-0	0-0-0	0-0-0	0	1	0	.000
Barton	0-0-0	0-0-0	1-0-0	1-0-0	0-0-0	0-0-0	0-0-1	1-0-0	1-0-0	0-0-0	0-0-0	0-0-0	0-1-0	4	1	1	.800
Bautista	0-0-0	0-1-0	0-0-0	0-2-0	0-1-0	0-0-0	0-1-0	2-1-0	0-1-0	0-1-0	0-0-0	1-0-0	0-0-0	3	8	0	.273
Beck	0-2-1	0-0-5	0-0-2	0-0-3	0-1-1	0-0-1	0-1-0	0-0-4	0-1-2	1-1-3	2-0-4	2-0-3	0-0-4	5	6	33	.455
Brewington	1-0-0	0-0-0	0-0-0	2-0-0	1-0-0	0-0-0	0-1-0	1-0-0	0-0-0	0-1-0	0-1-0	1-1-0	0-0-0	6	4	0	.600
Burba	0-1-0	0-0-0	1-0-0	0-0-0	0-0-0	0-0-0	0-1-0	1-0-0	1-0-0	0-0-0	1-0-0	0-0-0	0-0-0	4	2	0	.667
Dewey	0-0-0	0-0-0	0-0-0	0-0-0	0-0-0	0-0-0	0-0-0	0-0-0	1-0-0	0-0-0	0-0-0	0-0-0	0-0-0	1	0	0	1.000
Estes	0-0-0	0-0-0	0-0-0	0-1-0	0-0-0	0-0-0	0-0-0	0-0-0	0-0-0	0-0-0	0-1-0	0-0-0	0-1-0	0	3	0	.000
Frey	0-0-0	0-0-0	0-0-0	0-0-0	0-0-0	0-0-0	0-0-0	0-0-0	0-0-0	0-0-0	0-0-0	0-1-0	0-0-0	0	1	0	.000
Greer	0-1-0	0-0-0	0-0-0	0-0-0	0-0-0	0-1-0	0-0-0	0-0-0	0-0-0	0-0-0	0-0-0	0-0-0	0-0-0	0	2	0	.000
Hook	0-0-0	0-0-0	0-0-0	0-0-0	0-0-0	2-0-0	1-0-0	0-0-0	1-0-0	0-1-0	0-0-0	0-0-0	1-0-0	5	1	0	.833
Leiter	0-0-0	0-3-0	1-1-0	0-2-0	1-0-0	1-0-0	2-1-0	0-3-0	1-0-0	2-0-0	0-1-0	1-1-0	1-0-0	10	12	0	.455
Mintz	0-0-0	1-0-0	0-0-0	0-0-0	0-0-0	0-0-0	0-0-0	0-1-0	0-0-0	0-0-0	0-1-0	0-0-0	0-0-0	1	2	0	.333
Mulholland	0-2-0	1-1-0	0-1-0	0-2-0	0-1-0	0-1-0	1-1-0	0-1-0	1-1-0	1-0-0	0-0-0	0-1-0	1-1-0	5	13	0	.278
Portugal	0-1-0	2-0-0	0-0-0	0-0-0	0-1-0	0-1-0	0-1-0	0-0-0	1-0-0	0-0-0	0-1-0	1-0-0	1-0-0	5	5	0	.500
Rosselli	0-0-0	0-0-0	0-0-0	0-0-0	0-0-0	0-0-0	0-0-0	0-0-0	0-0-0	0-0-0	1-0-0	0-0-0	1-1-0	2	1	0	.667
Service	0-0-0	0-0-0	0-0-0	1-0-0	0-0-0	0-1-0	0-0-0	1-0-0	0-0-0	0-0-0	1-0-0	0-0-0	0-0-0	3	1	0	.750
Torres	0-0-0	0-0-0	0-0-0	0-0-0	0-1-0	0-0-0	0-0-0	0-0-0	0-0-0	0-0-0	0-0-0	0-0-0	0-0-0	0	1	0	.000
C. Valdez	0-0-0	0-0-0	0-0-0	0-0-0	0-0-0	0-0-0	0-0-0	0-0-0	0-1-0	0-0-0	0-0-0	0-0-0	0-0-0	0	1	0	.000
S. Valdez	0-0-0	2-0-0	0-0-0	1-0-0	0-0-0	0-0-0	0-0-0	0-0-0	1-0-0	0-1-0	0-1-0	0-1-0	0-2-0	4	5	0	.444
VanLandingham	0-0-0	1-0-0	0-0-0	0-0-0	0-0-0	0-0-0	1-1-0	0-1-0	0-0-0	1-0-0	1-0-0	1-1-0	1-0-0	6	3	0	.667
Wilson	0-0-0	0-0-0	0-0-0	0-1-0	1-0-0	0-1-0	0-0-0	0-0-0	0-1-0	1-1-0	0-0-0	0-0-0	1-0-0	3	4	0	.429
TOTALS	1-7-1	7-5-5	3-3-2	5-8-3	3-5-1	3-5-1	5-8-1	6-7-4	8-5-2	6-6-3	6-6-4	7-6-3	7-6-4	67	77	34	.465

NO DECISIONS OR SAVES: Burgos, Gomez, Roper.

PITCHERS' LIFETIME RECORDS AGAINST OPPOSING CLUBS

A.L. Records in Parentheses   20 OR MORE DECISIONS—PITCHERS ACTIVE IN 1995 SEASON OR ARE ON 1996 N.L. ROSTERS

	W	L	Pct.	Braves W-L	Cubs W-L	Reds W-L	Rockies W-L	Marlins W-L	Astros W-L	Dodgers W-L	Expos W-L	Mets W-L	Phillies W-L	Pirates W-L	Cardinals W-L	Padres W-L	Giants W-L
Aguilera, Rick (22-29)	37	27	.578	5-3	5-4	4-1	—	—	0-1	3-1	4-5	—	5-4	6-2	2-4	2-1	1-1
Aquino, Luis (23-20)	8	12	.400	1-3	1-2	0-2	3-0	0-0	0-1	0-0	0-0	0-0	1-0	0-1	0-1	1-1	0-1
Arocha, Rene	18	17	.514	0-1	1-3	1-2	1-1	2-1	1-2	2-1	0-0	1-2	1-0	2-0	—	2-0	0-2
Ashby, Andy	23	39	.371	0-2	3-1	0-6	1-2	0-2	6-3	3-3	0-3	1-4	0-5	4-3	3-3	0-0	2-4
Assenmacher, Paul (9-6)	39	30	.565	2-1	0-0	4-3	0-0	0-1	3-3	3-5	4-1	6-6	4-3	6-1	3-3	3-0	1-3
Astacio, Pedro	32	30	.516	0-6	0-4	4-1	3-1	3-1	5-1	—	2-3	3-3	2-3	3-3	3-4	2-0	2-1
Avery, Steve	65	52	.556	—	4-3	7-5	4-1	2-4	8-3	8-4	2-7	5-3	5-5	6-3	5-4	4-4	5-5
Ayala, Bobby (10-8)	9	11	.450	0-2	0-0	—	0-1	1-1	1-1	1-0	0-1	2-0	0-1	1-1	0-2	2-1	1-1
Banks, Willie (16-17)	10	18	.357	0-2	0-1	0-3	0-1	1-0	1-2	2-0	0-1	1-1	1-1	2-3	0-1	1-2	0-0
Bautista, Jose (10-20)	17	16	.515	0-0	0-1	1-1	2-2	2-2	2-1	1-2	3-3	2-1	0-2	2-2	0-3	1-0	0-2
Beck, Rod	14	15	.483	0-3	0-1	0-2	0-0	0-1	1-0	3-1	0-0	1-2	1-2	3-1	3-1	1-1	—
Bedrosian, Steve (5-3)	71	76	.483	6-2	7-3	8-7	0-0	0-1	6-9	6-9	3-9	5-7	4-4	6-9	10-2	4-9	6-5
Belcher, Tim (20-32)	74	58	.561	9-5	7-6	5-7	1-1	—	9-3	2-3	3-4	2-5	7-5	10-4	3-4	8-6	8-5
Belinda, Stan (11-4)	19	15	.559	2-1	3-5	1-1	0-0	0-0	2-0	0-3	2-1	3-2	0-4	—	3-1	0-1	1-1
Benes, Andy (7-2)	69	75	.479	3-9	8-6	7-8	3-2	2-2	8-9	5-6	3-11	7-3	9-3	5-6	2-4	—	7-6
Bielecki, Mike (8-11)	55	52	.514	5-3	0-1	5-8	0-0	0-0	5-2	4-2	8-4	2-5	5-8	4-6	4-3	4-9	6-3
Black, Bud (87-84)	34	32	.515	4-6	0-0	2-2	1-1	6-2	4-0	2-4	2-0	5-0	5-2	4-3	2-1	2-3	—
Blair, Willie (5-8)	18	27	.400	2-2	2-1	3-1	1-0	2-2	0-0	1-5	0-0	2-2	2-2	1-3	0-0	2-4	3-1
Boever, Joe (20-12)	14	31	.311	0-0	1-1	3-4	—	—	1-3	2-6	1-1	1-1	1-0	0-4	2-3	2-5	3-1
Boskie, Shawn (7-8)	23	35	.397	1-1	2-0	1-2	0-0	1-1	2-3	0-4	2-2	1-2	2-1	1-9	4-2	4-1	2-0
Bowen, Ryan	17	28	.378	0-4	1-1	2-3	2-1	—	0-1	1-0	1-1	1-1	1-2	3-3	1-3	3-2	2-1
Brantley, Jeff	38	28	.576	5-3	5-3	1-3	0-0	0-1	6-5	4-3	4-0	2-1	1-1	2-4	2-0	4-3	2-1
Brocail, Doug	10	17	.370	1-2	1-2	1-0	1-1	0-2	0-1	1-0	0-2	1-0	1-0	3-0	0-1	1-1	0-2
Browning, Tom (0-2)	123	88	.583	14-5	10-10	—	0-0	0-0	15-11	13-10	7-5	8-6	9-9	10-8	8-7	14-8	11-8
Bullinger, Jim	21	18	.538	2-2	—	2-0	1-1	1-1	1-2	1-2	0-2	2-1	2-2	1-2	4-1	0-1	1-1
Burba, Dave (2-2)	25	20	.556	2-0	2-4	2-3	1-0	1-0	2-1	1-2	1-2	3-3	2-3	4-2	1-2	1-0	1-0
Burkett, John	81	56	.591	6-6	6-2	9-6	5-2	1-1	11-5	5-7	5-5	2-2	8-5	7-4	6-6	7-4	2-2
Candiotti, Tom (84-78)	33	46	.418	2-3	1-2	0-0	0-3	3-2	2-3	—	2-3	3-4	5-5	5-2	4-4	4-3	2-2
Carrasco, Hector	7	13	.350	1-1	0-0	—	0-3	0-3	0-2	0-0	0-2	1-0	0-0	1-1	2-1	2-0	0-0
Castillo, Frank	34	37	.479	0-6	—	2-3	2-0	2-4	3-3	4-2	2-5	1-4	2-1	0-2	6-3	6-2	3-2
Charlton, Norm (3-4)	33	29	.532	6-3	4-2	0-1	—	0-0	2-3	1-4	1-1	3-3	1-1	4-3	2-2	4-5	5-1
Cone, David (49-30)	80	48	.625	9-3	5-8	6-2	—	—	6-4	6-6	8-6	—	7-3	7-2	11-5	8-5	7-4
Cook, Dennis (13-15)	19	13	.594	2-2	0-0	2-0	—	—	1-1	1-2	1-1	1-1	0-2	3-1	5-2	1-2	2-0
Cooke, Steve	16	21	.432	1-3	0-2	1-1	—	3-0	1-2	2-1	0-2	2-1	2-4	—	1-1	1-2	2-2
Cormier, Rheal (7-5)	24	23	.511	0-2	2-0	1-1	0-0	1-1	1-2	3-0	4-5	2-4	4-1	2-2	—	0-3	4-2
Cox, Danny (9-10)	65	65	.500	3-5	11-7	6-4	—	—	4-5	4-10	6-5	5-8	7-5	5-11	8-0	4-2	5-5
Darling, Ron (37-44)	99	72	.579	13-3	8-9	10-5	—	—	6-5	8-4	12-10	—	11-9	11-6	8-7	6-7	6-7
Darwin, Danny (104-117)	44	33	.571	7-1	3-6	4-4	—	—	—	3-2	6-2	3-3	5-1	1-2	3-3	2-2	5-5
DeLeon, Jose (23-22)	63	97	.394	7-7	11-14	6-10	—	0-0	7-6	2-9	9-7	4-12	6-4	0-6	4-7	5-9	2-6
Deshaies, Jim (17-26)	67	69	.493	10-8	2-7	7-8	0-0	0-0	2-0	11-6	3-2	6-5	5-5	6-9	5-3	3-11	7-5
Dibble, Rob (1-2)	26	23	.531	1-4	3-1	—	0-0	0-0	3-2	2-3	2-0	3-1	2-1	4-5	5-6	4-3	2-2
Drabek, Doug (7-8)	123	95	.564	10-9	15-10	9-6	4-1	0-2	4-4	4-8	14-12	11-8	15-8	2-2	10-13	9-7	12-5
Eckersley, Dennis (165-133)	27	26	.509	0-3	—	4-2	—	—	2-1	3-2	4-3	3-1	6-2	5-2	2-4	1-2	2-2
Fassero, Jeff	43	37	.538	3-4	4-1	1-3	1-3	2-2	2-3	4-4	—	5-4	2-3	4-2	5-2	7-7	2-3
Fernandez, Sid (6-10)	104	80	.565	6-5	10-6	7-8	2-0	0-0	9-7	8-7	8-9	—	15-10	12-8	11-7	7-7	8-4
Foster, Kevin	15	16	.484	0-1	—	1-1	1-1	3-0	1-1	2-1	1-0	1-1	0-1	3-1	1-2	0-4	1-2
Franco, John	68	54	.557	5-4	5-8	2-0	1-0	1-0	7-5	6-9	4-3	—	2-3	5-7	5-6	6-6	10-2
Freeman, Marvin	28	19	.596	1-1	4-1	2-2	—	1-0	2-2	2-4	2-2	2-2	1-1	2-1	0-0	4-0	3-2
Gardner, Mark (4-6)	37	42	.468	3-4	4-5	2-4	0-1	—	6-1	4-5	1-3	3-4	2-2	3-3	4-6	4-2	2-2
Glavine, Tom	124	82	.602	—	9-6	18-6	3-2	4-2	6-10	11-11	9-11	7-3	13-5	13-7	8-4	14-5	9-9
Gott, Jim (21-30)	35	44	.443	1-5	3-5	1-4	0-1	1-0	4-4	1-0	6-3	5-5	4-1	4-3	0-4	3-8	2-1
Greene, Tommy	38	24	.613	2-1	4-1	4-2	2-0	1-1	1-1	4-3	6-2	3-2	—	4-1	0-4	3-0	3-1
Gross, Kevin (9-15)	120	134	.472	8-11	10-16	10-12	1-1	1-1	10-13	11-8	13-8	14-12	3-6	14-10	5-17	10-11	10-8
Guzman, Jose (66-62)	14	12	.538	1-2	—	2-0	1-0	0-1	0-2	2-0	1-2	1-2	2-1	1-0	0-2	2-1	0-0
Hamilton, Joey	15	15	.500	0-2	1-2	1-1	2-2	0-0	0-1	1-1	1-1	2-1	0-1	1-2	1-0	—	5-0
Hammaker, Atlee (1-3)	58	64	.475	6-5	5-7	8-6	—	—	9-10	1-5	5-5	4-2	9-5	3-2	4-4	4-9	—
Hammond, Chris	38	41	.481	2-0	3-4	1-5	1-2	2-4	1-0	3-3	3-1	5-2	7-2	4-3	3-3	2-5	1-3
Hampton, Mike (1-3)	11	9	.550	0-0	1-0	0-1	1-1	1-0	—	1-0	0-0	1-1	1-1	1-0	3-2	1-2	1-1
Harkey, Mike (8-9)	27	27	.500	2-2	0-0	1-3	3-0	1-3	4-2	1-2	2-2	3-3	1-1	2-0	0-5	1-1	5-1
Harnisch, Pete (16-22)	47	41	.534	6-7	6-3	4-7	2-1	1-2	—	4-3	2-4	3-1	3-5	3-2	3-4	5-1	3-3
Harris, Greg A. (59-66)	15	24	.385	1-2	0-2	0-2	0-0	1-0	1-2	1-3	0-3	4-1	2-3	0-1	1-1	2-2	2-0
Harris, Greg W. (0-5)	45	59	.433	3-5	2-2	6-10	2-0	0-0	8-3	4-6	6-5	3-6	0-5	5-4	4-1	—	2-6
Harris, Gene (2-6)	10	12	.455	1-0	0-1	1-1	1-1	1-1	0-0	1-0	0-3	3-1	0-0	0-1	0-0	1-1	1-1
Hartley, Mike (1-2)	17	11	.607	3-1	4-0	1-1	—	—	1-1	0-0	1-3	0-0	0-1	1-2	0-0	3-0	3-0
Henry, Butch	24	30	.444	2-2	4-2	2-1	0-2	3-0	2-1	1-2	2-2	2-2	1-1	3-3	0-3	2-5	0-4
Heredia, Gil	17	16	.515	2-0	2-0	0-4	1-2	1-1	2-1	2-3	2-1	—	1-2	2-2	0-2	2-0	0-0
Hernandez, Xavier (5-4)	24	16	.600	3-3	3-3	3-1	0-4	0-0	2-0	1-2	0-0	1-1	1-1	2-0	1-0	2-1	5-1
Hershiser, Orel (16-6)	134	102	.568	20-9	8-7	14-9	3-0	1-0	15-12	—	10-8	7-8	5-9	11-9	7-8	13-11	20-9
Hibbard, Greg (42-39)	15	11	.577	1-1	—	0-0	3-2	0-1	1-0	2-0	1-0	2-1	0-1	2-3	1-0	1-1	1-1
Hickerson, Bryan	21	21	.500	1-0	0-4	2-0	2-1	1-1	2-0	1-6	2-0	3-0	3-0	1-2	1-1	0-3	2-2
Hill, Ken (4-1)	70	60	.538	5-7	6-7	2-6	2-0	1-2	7-3	5-4	3-2	5-4	5-1	6-7	7-3	8-3	5-5
Hoffman, Trevor	15	14	.517	0-1	1-0	1-4	2-0	1-1	1-0	2-1	0-2	3-0	1-2	4-2	0-0	—	0-1
Honeycutt, Rick (74-97)	33	45	.423	3-3	3-5	2-2	—	—	5-2	—	3-6	3-0	3-4	3-5	4-1	4-6	2-5
Howe, Steve (23-15)	24	25	.490	2-3	3-0	0-3	—	—	5-3	—	3-1	1-3	1-2	2-5	3-1	2-1	1-4
Jackson, Danny (37-49)	72	72	.500	6-9	5-4	2-3	1-0	3-0	7-9	4-5	6-6	6-2	7-5	6-2	6-6	11-7	6-4
Jackson, Mike R. (22-25)	24	25	.490	3-2	5-3	3-3	0-0	1-0	1-1	3-7	0-1	4-4	2-2	1-1	3-0	1-3	1-2
Jones, Doug (26-36)	17	22	.436	1-0	2-1	2-1	1-0	0-3	3-0	0-0	1-3	0-2	1-2	2-0	1-3	2-1	1-6
Jones, Bobby J.	24	21	.533	2-3	1-2	2-2	1-2	1-3	3-0	0-0	3-1	—	3-3	2-0	1-1	3-2	3-2
Jones, Todd	12	9	.571	0-1	1-1	2-1	2-0	1-0	—	—	0-0	2-0	1-2	0-2	1-2	0-0	0-0
Kile, Darryl	40	47	.460	2-2	5-2	2-4	2-4	3-0	—	0-3	2-6	3-2	2-6	4-6	4-2	4-2	5-2
Langston, Mark (154-132)	12	9	.571	0-0	3-1	1-0	1-0	1-1	1-0	1-0	2-1	0-2	1-2	3-0	1-1	0-0	0-1
Leiter, Mark (28-26)	10	12	.455	—	0-3	1-0	0-2	1-1	0-2	1-0	0-3	1-0	1-1	3-0	1-1	1-0	1-1
Lieber, Jon	10	14	.417	0-1	1-2	0-2	1-1	1-0	2-1	1-2	0-1	1-0	0-2	—	1-2	0-0	2-0
Lilliquist, Derek (12-11)	13	23	.361	0-3	2-2	1-1	—	—	2-3	2-0	0-2	2-0	1-0	2-4	1-3	1-2	1-1

68

PITCHERS' LIFETIME RECORDS AGAINST OPPOSING CLUBS

A.L. Records in Parentheses   20 OR MORE DECISIONS—PITCHERS ACTIVE IN 1995 SEASON OR ARE ON 1996 N.L. ROSTERS

Pitcher	W	L	Pct.	Braves W-L	Cubs W-L	Reds W-L	Rockies W-L	Marlins W-L	Astros W-L	Dodgers W-L	Expos W-L	Mets W-L	Phillies W-L	Pirates W-L	Cardinals W-L	Padres W-L	Giants W-L
Maddux, Greg	150	93	.617	7-3	3-0	9-10	4-1	5-1	15-6	6-3	13-10	19-10	18-7	11-13	14-13	14-7	12-9
Maddux, Mike (4-1)	25	27	.481	0-4	6-5	5-0	0-0	0-0	1-4	1-3	2-1	0-0	0-1	5-1	3-3	0-2	2-3
Martinez, Dennis (131-104)	100	72	.581	9-5	11-7	10-6	2-2	1-0	8-6	6-8	—	11-10	9-4	10-7	9-5	8-5	6-7
Martinez, Pedro J.	35	21	.625	3-3	3-2	1-2	1-2	1-1	1-5	1-5	1-0	7-0	3-0	4-1	2-2	2-1	4-1
Martinez, Ramon	91	63	.591	10-7	6-2	10-5	5-4	4-1	7-3	—	8-7	5-7	6-8	6-4	6-3	8-4	10-8
McDowell, Roger (7-4)	62	65	.488	5-3	10-6	7-8	2-0	0-0	2-7	3-4	3-3	4-5	2-3	5-5	9-9	5-3	5-7
McElroy, Chuck	16	18	.471	2-2	0-2	0-3	0-1	0-0	0-3	1-1	3-1	1-2	1-1	3-0	1-0	3-0	1-1
McMichael, Greg	13	11	.542	—	0-0	1-2	3-0	2-0	0-1	2-0	0-1	1-1	0-2	0-2	1-0	2-2	1-0
McMurtry, Craig (3-6)	25	36	.410	0-1	0-3	5-3	0-0	0-0	3-0	2-6	4-2	3-3	3-4	1-1	1-4	2-6	0-3
Mercker, Kent	31	25	.554	—	3-1	1-1	5-1	1-0	3-4	2-2	4-2	1-2	1-2	1-1	2-3	4-2	3-2
Minor, Blas	12	9	.571	3-0	0-1	2-1	0-1	0-0	0-0	0-0	0-1	1-1	0-1	0-0	0-2	1-1	1-1
Morgan, Mike (34-68)	68	76	.472	5-10	6-3	8-6	3-3	1-0	8-9	2-2	3-8	5-8	8-4	4-13	4-3	5-4	7-6
Moyer, Jamie (31-37)	28	39	.418	1-4	0-0	2-3	—	—	3-3	1-2	5-4	3-1	4-8	4-6	2-1	2-3	1-3
Mulholland, Terry (6-7)	62	71	.466	5-8	8-8	8-2	1-3	1-2	4-6	7-5	9-2	2-8	1-0	3-4	7-4	4-6	6-5
Murphy, Rob (5-14)	27	24	.529	3-6	0-3	1-2	2-0	1-0	1-0	3-1	2-2	2-0	3-4	1-2	0-1	3-1	3-1
Myers, Randy	34	49	.410	2-3	3-1	3-3	0-3	0-1	3-6	5-3	2-2	0-0	4-3	3-7	3-3	3-2	1-4
Nabholz, Chris (3-5)	34	30	.531	1-3	4-3	2-1	0-0	1-0	2-0	1-2	—	5-3	4-6	6-1	2-1	2-4	3-2
Navarro, Jaime (62-59)	14	6	.700	2-0	—	0-1	0-1	2-0	1-0	0-0	2-1	1-1	1-0	2-0	0-1	1-0	7-1
Neagle, Denny (0-1)	29	29	.500	2-1	3-1	3-2	2-2	1-2	1-4	4-3	1-4	3-2	1-1	1-0	2-2	0-4	2-0
Nied, David	17	16	.515	0-3	1-3	0-2	—	1-1	3-1	1-2	2-2	6-3	5-1	1-4	1-2	0-1	1-2
Olivares, Omar	30	28	.517	3-4	1-6	2-1	1-1	2-0	1-1	2-3	2-1	2-2	1-1	1-2	—	5-3	4-2
Orosco, Jesse (21-19)	50	49	.505	1-6	4-7	7-0	—	—	2-3	2-3	8-6	0-0	5-3	8-3	3-11	—	3-3
Osborne, Donovan	25	22	.532	1-1	1-3	1-1	1-1	1-0	1-1	2-1	3-2	1-0	4-4	1-2	—	5-1	3-2
Palacios, Vicente	17	19	.472	1-3	2-1	2-1	0-0	0-2	2-2	1-1	2-2	2-1	0-2	2-2	0-1	1-1	2-0
Parrett, Jeff (9-1)	44	39	.530	6-3	6-6	3-2	0-0	0-0	6-3	4-2	1-3	1-1	3-2	7-4	5-3	2-8	0-0
Patterson, Bob (9-9)	25	21	.543	1-1	5-0	1-2	0-0	0-0	0-3	2-3	0-0	1-6	6-3	—	5-1	2-1	2-1
Pena, Alejandro (1-1)	55	50	.524	7-3	6-4	4-7	1-0	1-0	8-8	1-1	6-6	5-3	4-3	4-4	6-3	3-6	4-3
Perez, Mike	21	16	.568	2-3	0-4	0-1	2-1	2-1	1-2	2-0	2-0	1-4	2-1	2-2	1-0	2-2	3-0
Portugal, Mark (11-19)	73	48	.603	4-6	7-4	6-2	—	2-0	3-2	2-4	7-6	8-3	5-1	1-4	4-6	3-8	11-3
Pugh, Tim	23	25	.479	0-2	2-2	—	2-2	2-2	2-2	2-2	2-0	3-4	1-2	2-0	3-1	0-1	0-1
Quantrill, Paul (9-16)	13	14	.481	0-1	1-0	0-1	0-1	0-1	0-3	1-0	0-2	1-2	2-0	—	3-1	1-2	1-0
Rapp, Pat	25	23	.521	2-0	2-1	3-3	4-3	—	1-1	2-5	1-7	1-1	4-3	4-0	0-0	1-1	1-0
Rasmussen, Dennis (44-28)	47	49	.490	4-7	8-4	5-4	—	—	0-0	0-1	1-1	2-1	1-3	0-0	6-2	1-1	1-0
Reed, Steve	18	9	.667	0-2	1-1	5-0	0-0	0-0	0-3	2-0	3-0	1-0	1-2	1-0	0-0	3-0	1-1
Reynolds, Shane	19	19	.500	2-0	4-1	1-0	2-1	2-0	—	3-1	3-2	1-2	1-0	4-1	1-2	2-2	4-2
Reynoso, Armando	25	23	.521	0-5	5-1	2-1	—	2-0	2-0	3-1	3-1	1-1	1-1	0-4	1-3	3-2	2-3
Righetti, Dave (77-64)	5	15	.250	0-1	0-0	1-1	0-0	0-1	0-3	2-2	0-2	1-1	1-2	0-1	0-1	0-3	8-10
Rijo, Jose (19-30)	92	57	.617	7-6	6-3	—	3-1	2-0	12-6	7-7	6-2	9-5	4-3	6-3	8-9	7-2	1-1
Ritz, Kevin (6-18)	16	17	.485	1-1	2-1	1-3	—	1-2	2-1	1-1	1-3	2-1	1-0	1-1	2-1	1-1	1-0
Rodriguez, Rich	15	14	.517	1-1	0-0	0-0	0-2	0-0	4-4	0-0	2-4	2-0	1-1	2-0	1-1	1-0	0-1
Rojas, Mel	22	19	.537	2-2	2-2	0-1	4-1	3-0	0-0	1-3	2-1	—	3-2	1-1	2-0	0-4	1-1
Rueter, Kirk	20	6	.769	1-0	0-2	1-0	2-0	1-0	1-1	3-0	2-0	—	0-0	1-1	2-1	3-0	2-1
Ruffin, Bruce (1-6)	52	69	.430	7-7	5-7	4-5	—	—	0-0	9-5	3-4	3-6	5-7	1-1	6-7	3-7	2-8
Russell, Jeff (43-47)	10	23	.303	1-3	1-3	—	—	—	—	0-3	0-1	1-1	0-1	1-4	4-2	2-1	2-2
Saberhagen, Bret (110-78)	31	22	.585	1-1	0-2	1-1	1-2	5-1	1-1	1-1	1-0	2-1	0-1	1-1	1-0	1-2	1-1
Sanders, Scott	12	16	.429	1-1	1-1	1-1	1-2	1-0	2-0	0-2	0-0	1-2	2-1	2-0	1-4	—	1-2
Sanderson, Scott (61-50)	102	91	.528	8-8	10-4	8-3	0-0	0-0	2-1	5-7	8-6	3-4	10-12	9-12	13-11	10-11	8-4
Scanlan, Bob (6-13)	14	19	.424	0-3	—	0-0	0-0	0-2	0-0	2-1	1-2	4-3	3-1	0-3	3-1	0-2	1-0
Schilling, Curt (1-6)	42	36	.538	3-5	4-3	3-2	3-1	3-0	4-2	2-1	6-2	8-1	0-0	1-3	2-3	2-5	4-2
Schourek, Pete	41	33	.554	2-3	4-3	1-2	5-1	5-2	2-1	3-3	4-1	1-1	3-3	1-4	3-0	4-0	2-1
Scott, Tim	18	5	.783	1-0	0-0	0-0	2-1	1-0	0-0	0-0	0-0	1-0	4-1	2-1	1-0	2-0	2-0
Shaw, Jeff (3-10)	8	15	.348	0-2	2-1	0-0	1-0	0-0	2-1	1-2	—	0-2	1-0	0-1	1-1	0-0	0-1
Slocumb, Heathcliff (3-1)	13	11	.542	1-1	1-0	2-2	3-0	1-1	1-0	2-1	1-0	1-0	—	0-0	0-2	1-1	0-1
Smiley, John (16-9)	86	66	.566	6-8	7-7	5-0	2-3	3-1	10-6	6-5	7-11	12-7	8-4	4-4	2-6	5-4	1-1
Smith, Lee (13-16)	55	71	.437	5-4	1-2	2-4	1-1	1-0	6-4	1-3	5-3	9-12	8-14	3-10	2-5	4-2	3-5
Smith, Pete J.	35	60	.368	1-1	1-4	4-7	2-0	2-0	1-2	7-4	1-3	3-7	4-3	8-10	7-7	2-5	1-6
Smith, Zane (8-8)	88	101	.466	3-5	7-6	8-7	5-0	2-0	12-11	8-11	6-10	9-9	7-7	4-8	8-7	7-7	9-9
Smoltz, John	90	82	.523	—	13-6	9-10	5-0	3-1	9-5	3-3	8-5	11-3	13-6	3-2	5-5	4-3	3-2
Stanton, Mike (1-0)	18	21	.462	—	1-1	4-2	3-2	1-0	—	—	2-1	1-0	2-1	1-1	1-1	1-0	1-3
Stewart, Dave (150-116)	18	13	.581	3-3	3-0	5-2	—	—	—	—	1-1	2-1	1-1	0-1	1-2	0-1	1-2
Swift, Bill (30-40)	48	22	.686	1-4	3-1	5-1	4-0	3-0	2-2	3-2	5-1	5-0	1-2	6-1	3-1	1-1	3-5
Swindell, Greg (60-55)	42	39	.519	2-5	5-1	1-1	5-0	3-4	1-2	0-2	1-1	2-1	0-4	2-4	5-1	3-4	5-4
Tewksbury, Bob (18-16)	67	50	.573	3-5	10-3	8-4	2-4	2-3	5-1	1-2	6-0	8-5	4-5	5-8	—	8-3	5-3
Trachsel, Steve	16	22	.421	1-2	—	2-2	1-0	0-2	2-3	1-2	0-1	1-0	1-1	0-1	0-3	3-1	4-1
Urbani, Tom	7	15	.318	2-1	1-2	1-0	0-0	0-0	0-1	1-0	0-1	0-1	3-1	0-3	—	0-2	0-1
Valdes, Ismael	16	12	.571	2-1	1-0	1-1	0-1	1-0	1-1	—	1-0	2-0	2-0	2-1	1-0	1-2	1-2
Valenzuela, Fernando (8-12)	150	121	.554	19-8	10-9	10-13	0-0	—	16-12	—	13-7	10-10	15-7	11-7	13-12	15-12	17-22
Viola, Frank (137-114)	38	33	.535	2-3	2-7	2-1	—	—	3-3	3-4	8-1	4-2	—	5-2	5-3	2-5	1-4
Wagner, Paul	22	32	.407	3-1	2-4	1-6	2-4	2-4	1-0	0-1	2-0	3-2	0-1	—	1-4	1-0	1-3
Wakefield, Tim (16-8)	14	12	.538	2-1	1-1	2-1	—	—	0-1	1-0	0-1	2-0	2-0	—	2-1	1-1	1-1
Watson, Allen	19	21	.475	2-0	3-3	2-1	1-1	0-2	2-0	1-1	1-0	1-2	1-2	1-0	—	2-3	0-1
Weathers, Dave (1-0)	14	20	.412	1-2	1-3	3-0	3-0	2-0	0-0	—	0-3	0-1	1-2	1-2	0-0	0-0	1-1
West, David	14	18	.438	0-3	1-0	1-2	2-0	2-0	2-2	2-0	2-1	1-0	—	0-2	1-1	0-1	0-3
Wetteland, John (1-5)	25	25	.500	1-2	2-2	4-2	0-0	0-0	0-5	2-1	—	0-5	0-1	0-3	5-1	7-1	2-1
Williams, Brian	20	26	.435	2-1	2-1	2-3	0-1	0-0	0-6	0-3	3-2	2-2	5-1	1-1	0-3	1-0	0-3
Williams, Mitch (19-21)	26	36	.419	5-5	5-5	3-2	2-0	2-1	1-4	1-3	1-2	4-6	1-3	0-1	0-8	4-6	0-0
Wilson, Trevor	41	46	.471	3-4	3-5	1-2	1-0	3-0	5-5	2-3	5-3	3-1	4-6	0-4	3-5	2-0	—
Wohlers, Mark	24	10	.706	—	0-1	1-1	1-1	3-0	4-1	0-0	2-0	3-1	1-1	3-1	2-0	4-1	0-1
Worrell, Todd	44	40	.524	4-2	1-2	2-2	2-1	1-0	2-0	4-3	4-3	6-6	10-4	2-4	1-1	5-3	0-3
Young, Anthony	12	45	.211	1-2	1-4	2-4	0-5	1-1	0-3	2-0	0-4	1-6	0-1	1-3	0-4	1-4	2-4

NATIONAL LEAGUE ACTIVE PITCHERS—LIFETIME MAJOR LEAGUE TOTALS—20+ DECISIONS

Pitcher	W	L	PCT.	ERA	G	SV	IP	H	R	ER	BB	SO
Abbott, Kyle	4	16	.200	4.86	54	0	181.1	197	103	98	74	121
Aquino, Luis	31	32	.492	3.68	222	5	678.1	698	311	277	224	318
Arocha, Rene	18	17	.514	3.87	118	11	320.2	346	155	138	70	183
Ashby, Andy	23	39	.371	4.46	105	1	559.0	576	313	277	201	398
Astacio, Pedro	32	30	.516	3.66	113	0	521.1	490	233	212	164	353
Avery, Steve	65	52	.556	3.75	179	0	1091.1	1034	507	455	331	729
Banks, Willie	26	35	.426	5.03	100	0	488.2	532	311	273	241	344
Bautista, Jose	27	36	.429	4.59	243	3	563.1	596	302	287	142	277
Beck, Rod	14	15	.483	2.80	280	127	331.0	281	110	103	75	292
Benes, Andy	76	77	.497	3.68	199	0	1298.0	1200	581	531	435	1081
Blair, Willie	23	35	.397	4.75	200	3	521.0	592	314	275	189	339
Bowen, Ryan	17	28	.378	5.30	64	0	326.0	350	208	192	184	216
Brantley, Jeff	38	28	.576	3.12	405	85	641.0	556	242	222	267	509
Brocail, Doug	10	17	.370	4.64	75	1	236.2	268	138	122	74	135
Brown, Kevin	88	73	.547	3.78	213	0	1451.0	1477	702	610	476	859
Bullinger, Jim	21	18	.538	4.12	111	10	351.2	329	181	161	162	211
Burba, Dave	27	22	.551	4.28	214	1	391.1	366	203	186	180	335
Burkett, John	81	56	.591	3.90	193	1	1185.2	1233	562	514	302	717
Candiotti, Tom	117	124	.485	3.47	331	0	2165.1	2054	960	834	707	1428
Carrasco, Hector	7	13	.350	3.38	109	11	143.2	128	62	54	76	105
Castillo, Frank	34	37	.479	3.86	113	0	669.1	652	318	287	192	446
Cooke, Steve	16	21	.432	4.28	68	1	368.0	386	189	175	109	216
Cormier, Rheal	31	28	.525	4.11	135	0	553.2	602	282	253	106	325
DeLeon, Jose	86	119	.420	3.76	415	6	1897.1	1556	877	793	841	1594
DeLucia, Rich	27	34	.443	4.53	161	1	437.1	424	239	220	186	323
Drabek, Doug	130	103	.558	3.32	314	0	2081.2	1932	840	767	546	1317
Dyer, Mike	9	13	.409	4.70	85	4	161.0	170	95	84	79	103
Eiland, Dave	6	15	.286	5.28	53	0	235.1	284	163	138	70	82
Fassero, Jeff	43	37	.538	3.16	228	10	618.1	565	258	217	219	528
Fernandez, Sid	110	90	.550	3.35	295	1	1798.2	1367	722	670	687	1663
Fossas, Tony	14	10	.583	3.84	385	5	293.1	293	141	125	116	224
Foster, Kevin	15	16	.484	4.27	45	0	255.1	232	132	121	107	227
Franco, John	68	54	.557	2.62	661	295	822.0	752	290	239	315	600
Fraser, Willie	38	40	.487	4.47	239	7	657.0	640	354	326	238	328
Frey, Steve	18	14	.563	3.64	283	28	269.2	259	130	109	136	145
Gardner, Mark	41	48	.461	4.38	170	1	813.1	771	425	396	316	593
Glavine, Tom	124	82	.602	3.52	262	0	1721.0	1649	751	673	579	1031
Gott, Jim	56	74	.431	3.87	554	91	1120.0	1081	546	481	466	837
Greene, Tommy	38	24	.613	4.10	117	0	619.0	581	303	282	236	450
Guthrie, Mark	29	29	.500	4.17	264	8	509.1	546	263	236	183	407
Guzman, Jose	80	74	.519	4.05	193	0	1224.1	1193	616	551	482	889
Hamilton, Joey	15	15	.500	3.05	47	0	313.0	287	129	106	85	184
Hammond, Chris	38	41	.481	4.13	121	0	683.2	697	344	314	251	407
Hampton, Mike	12	12	.500	3.92	81	1	209.0	215	112	91	82	147
Harnisch, Pete	63	63	.500	3.72	186	0	1151.0	1032	520	476	448	867
Harris, Greg A.	74	90	.451	3.69	703	54	1467.1	1329	689	601	652	1141
Henry, Doug	12	18	.400	3.72	230	65	254.1	227	115	105	111	200
Hernandez, Xavier	29	20	.592	3.76	312	28	485.2	450	225	203	186	404
Hernandez, Jeremy	10	14	.417	3.64	133	20	193.0	191	88	78	67	122
Hoffman, Trevor	15	14	.517	3.52	169	56	199.1	167	84	78	73	199
Holmes, Darren	14	16	.467	4.11	254	51	297.2	290	147	136	121	263
Jackson, Danny	109	121	.474	3.88	323	1	1968.2	1979	979	848	772	1166
Jackson, Mike	46	50	.479	3.30	550	38	738.0	578	301	271	322	651
Jones, Doug	43	58	.426	3.12	526	239	721.1	730	291	250	159	579
Jones, Bobby	24	21	.533	3.71	63	0	417.1	427	217	172	131	242
Jones, Todd	12	9	.571	2.96	143	22	209.2	169	75	69	93	184
Kile, Darryl	40	47	.460	4.09	140	0	725.1	687	380	330	371	549
Leiter, Al	33	32	.508	4.36	113	2	522.0	490	272	253	309	439
Leiter, Mark	38	38	.500	4.35	178	3	670.2	669	351	324	236	469
Lieber, Jon	10	14	.417	4.76	38	0	181.1	219	118	96	39	116
Maddux, Greg	150	93	.617	2.88	301	0	2120.2	1877	783	679	561	1471
Martinez, Pedro J.	35	21	.625	3.25	121	3	454.1	355	173	164	169	443
Martinez, Ramon	91	63	.591	3.48	201	0	1327.2	1166	582	513	509	970

NATIONAL LEAGUE ACTIVE PITCHERS— LIFETIME MAJOR LEAGUE TOTALS—20+ DECISIONS

Pitcher	W	L	PCT.	ERA	G	SV	IP	H	R	ER	BB	SO
Mathews, Terry	12	9	.571	3.91	155	4	225.1	217	101	98	85	170
McElroy, Chuck	16	18	.471	3.43	315	14	354.2	331	162	135	177	295
McMichael, Greg	13	11	.542	2.77	192	42	231.0	198	78	71	80	210
McMurtry, Craig	28	42	.400	4.08	212	4	667.2	650	341	303	336	349
Minor, Blas	12	9	.571	4.44	118	4	162.0	168	83	80	48	144
Morgan, Mike	102	144	.415	3.98	366	3	2045.0	2101	1001	904	689	1012
Mulholland, Terry	68	78	.466	4.24	230	0	1318.1	1385	684	621	330	706
Munoz, Mike	9	11	.450	5.06	232	5	176.0	185	107	99	108	117
Munoz, Bobby	10	10	.500	3.69	62	1	165.2	164	80	68	70	98
Nabholz, Chris	37	35	.514	3.94	141	0	611.2	542	289	268	278	405
Navarro, Jaime	76	65	.539	4.13	212	1	1243.1	1319	630	571	374	652
Neagle, Denny	29	30	.492	4.35	167	3	534.1	547	275	258	181	436
Nen, Robb	7	13	.350	4.26	130	38	179.2	171	91	85	86	167
Nichols, Rod	11	31	.262	4.43	100	1	412.2	460	234	203	121	214
Nied, David	17	16	.515	4.87	46	0	236.1	257	136	128	97	142
Olivares, Omar	30	28	.517	4.21	157	3	647.2	655	320	303	255	346
Osborne, Donovan	25	22	.532	3.78	79	0	448.0	458	222	188	119	269
Palacios, Vicente	17	19	.472	4.36	127	7	361.1	336	180	175	153	262
Parrett, Jeff	53	40	.570	3.84	440	22	658.1	608	311	281	314	552
Pena, Alejandro	56	51	.523	3.10	499	74	1053.1	955	422	363	330	834
Perez, Mike	21	16	.568	3.47	273	22	298.2	290	126	115	99	185
Plesac, Dan	37	45	.451	3.49	534	137	702.0	648	300	272	247	605
Portugal, Mark	84	67	.556	3.81	259	5	1340.0	1285	623	567	487	856
Rapp, Pat	25	23	.521	3.80	71	0	404.2	399	196	171	190	237
Reed, Steve	18	9	.667	3.41	214	9	248.0	233	109	94	80	192
Reynolds, Shane	19	19	.500	3.50	76	0	349.2	377	159	136	70	305
Reynoso, Armando	25	23	.521	4.61	68	1	365.1	413	214	187	133	194
Rijo, Jose	111	87	.561	3.16	332	3	1786.0	1602	718	628	634	1556
Ritz, Kevin	22	35	.386	5.14	96	2	424.0	453	267	242	224	298
Rodriguez, Rich	15	14	.517	3.20	284	4	356.2	330	144	127	148	212
Rojas, Mel	22	19	.537	3.00	311	73	428.2	367	161	143	151	326
Rueter, Kirk	20	6	.769	3.83	43	0	225.1	229	110	96	50	109
Ruffin, Bruce	53	75	.414	4.19	375	32	1176.1	1272	627	547	518	738
Saberhagen, Bret	141	100	.585	3.26	337	1	2227.2	2100	880	807	421	1510
Sanders, Scott	12	16	.429	4.48	49	1	253.1	236	141	126	102	234
Schilling, Curt	43	42	.506	3.56	206	13	805.0	731	348	318	241	618
Schourek, Pete	41	33	.554	4.14	149	2	622.1	635	310	286	206	428
Scott, Tim	18	5	.783	3.61	194	4	227.0	213	101	91	96	190
Shaw, Jeff	11	25	.306	4.50	203	5	363.2	380	200	182	125	207
Slocumb, Heathcliff	16	12	.571	3.64	225	34	274.1	279	133	111	134	204
Smiley, John	102	75	.576	3.67	300	4	1536.0	1451	689	627	401	993
Smith, Pete	35	60	.368	4.40	157	0	819.1	821	437	401	318	507
Smoltz, John	90	82	.523	3.53	231	0	1550.2	1346	668	609	572	1252
Stottlemyre, Todd	83	77	.519	4.41	237	1	1348.2	1410	714	661	494	867
Swift, Bill	78	62	.557	3.62	353	25	1371.1	1397	629	551	425	656
Swindell, Greg	102	94	.520	3.80	272	0	1748.1	1839	823	739	372	1188
Tapani, Kevin	79	65	.549	4.10	197	0	1235.2	1305	605	563	273	769
Tewksbury, Bob	85	66	.563	3.72	214	1	1283.1	1445	603	530	198	534
Trachsel, Steve	16	22	.421	4.25	55	0	326.1	323	171	154	133	239
Urbani, Tom	7	15	.318	4.48	62	0	225.0	270	132	112	68	128
Valdes, Ismael	16	12	.571	3.07	54	1	226.0	189	86	77	61	178
Valdez, Sergio	12	20	.375	5.06	116	0	302.2	332	194	170	109	190
Valenzuela, Fernando	158	133	.543	3.49	402	2	2669.1	2435	1164	1036	1038	1918
Wagner, Paul	22	32	.407	4.45	112	3	439.0	462	238	217	169	325
Watson, Allen	19	21	.475	5.07	59	0	316.0	346	194	178	122	172
Weathers, Dave	15	20	.429	5.48	83	0	289.0	347	193	176	143	182
West, David	29	36	.446	4.58	191	3	539.0	487	298	274	293	411
Wilson, Trevor	41	46	.471	3.87	154	0	720.1	657	342	310	300	425
Wohlers, Mark	24	10	.706	3.38	211	32	218.2	184	94	82	106	223
Worrell, Todd	44	40	.524	2.86	480	177	568.2	478	197	181	209	501
Young, Anthony	12	45	.211	3.84	153	20	426.2	435	225	182	145	226

20-GAME WINNERS 1901—1995

1901
Bill Donovan, Dodgers	25-15
Deacon Phillippe, Pirates	22-12
Noodles Hahn, Reds	22-19
Jack Chesbro, Pirates	21- 9
John Powell, Pirates	21-20
Charles Harper, Cardinals	20-12
Al Orth, Phillies	20-12
Frank Donahue, Phillies	20-13
Charles Nichols, Braves	20-14
Christy Mathewson, Giants	20-17

1902
Jack Chesbro, Pirates	28- 6
Charles Pittinger, Braves	27-14
Vic Willis, Braves	27-19
Noodles Hahn, Reds	22-12
Jack Taylor, Cubs	22-10
*Joe McGinnity, Balt.-Giants	21-18
Jess Tannehill, Pirates	20- 6
Deacon Phillippe, Pirates	20- 9

1903
Joe McGinnity, Giants	31-20
Christy Mathewson, Giants	30-13
Sam Leever, Pirates	25- 7
Deacon Phillippe, Pirates	25- 9
Noodles Hahn, Reds	22-12
Henry Schmidt, Dodgers	22-13
Jack Taylor, Cubs	21-14
Jake Weimer, Cubs	20- 8
Bob Wicker, Cubs	20- 9

1904
Joe McGinnity, Giants	35- 8
Christy Mathewson, Giants	33-12
Charles Harper, Reds	23- 9
Charles Nichols, Cardinals	21-13
Luther Taylor, Giants	21-15
Jake Weimer, Cubs	20-14
Jack Taylor, Cardinals	20-19

1905
Christy Mathewson, Giants	31- 9
Charles Pittinger, Phillies	23-14
Leon Ames, Giants	22- 8
Joe McGinnity, Giants	21-15
Sam Leever, Pirates	20- 5
Bob Ewing, Reds	20-11
Deacon Phillippe, Pirates	20-13
Irving Young, Braves	20-21

1906
Joe McGinnity, Giants	27-12
Mordecai Brown, Cubs	26- 6
Vic Willis, Pirates	23-13
Sam Leever, Pirates	22- 7
Christy Mathewson, Giants	22-12
John Pfiester, Cubs	20- 8
Jack Taylor, Cards-Cubs	20-12
Jake Weimer, Reds	20-14

1907
Christy Mathewson, Giants	24-12
Orval Overall, Cubs	23- 8
Frank Sparks, Phillies	22- 8
Vic Willis, Pirates	21-11
Mordecai Brown, Cubs	20- 6
Al Leifield, Pirates	20-16

1908
Christy Mathewson, Giants	37-11
Mordecai Brown, Cubs	29- 9
Ed Reulbach, Cubs	24- 7
Nick Maddox, Pirates	23- 8
Vic Willis, Pirates	23-11
George Wiltse, Giants	23-14
George McQuillan, Phillies	23-17

1909
Mordecai Brown, Cubs	27- 9
Christy Mathewson, Giants	25- 6
Howard Camnitz, Pirates	25- 6
Vic Willis, Pirates	22-11
Orval Overall, Cubs	20-11
George Wiltse, Giants	20-11

1910
Christy Mathewson, Giants	27- 9
Mordecai Brown, Cubs	25-14
Earl Moore, Phillies	22-15
Leonard Cole, Cubs	20- 4
George Suggs, Reds	20-12

1911
Grover Alexander, Phillies	28-13
Christy Mathewson, Giants	26-13
Rube Marquard, Giants	24- 7
Bob Harmon, Cardinals	23-16
Babe Adams, Pirates	22-12
Nap Rucker, Dodgers	22-18
Mordecai Brown, Cubs	21-11
Howard Camnitz, Pirates	20-15

1912
Larry Cheney, Cubs	26-10
Rube Marquard, Giants	26-11
Claude Hendrix, Pirates	24- 9
Christy Mathewson, Giants	23-12
Howard Camnitz, Pirates	22-12

1913
Tom Seaton, Phillies	27-12
Christy Mathewson, Giants	25-11
Rube Marquard, Giants	23-10
Grover Alexander, Phillies	22- 8
Jeff Tesreau, Giants	22-13
Babe Adams, Pirates	21-10
Larry Cheney, Cubs	21-14

1914
Dick Rudolph, Braves	27-10
Grover Alexander, Phillies	27-15
Bill James, Braves	26- 7
Jeff Tesreau, Giants	26-10
Christy Mathewson, Giants	24-13
Ed Pfeffer, Dodgers	23-12
Jim Vaughn, Cubs	21-13
Erskine Mayer, Phillies	21-19
Larry Cheney, Cubs	20-18

1915
Grover Alexander, Phillies	31-10
Dick Rudolph, Braves	22-19
Al Mamaux, Pirates	21- 8
Erskine Mayer, Phillies	21-15
Jim Vaughn, Cubs	20-12

1916
Grover Alexander, Phillies	33-12
Ed Pfeffer, Dodgers	25-11
Eppa Rixey, Phillies	22-10
Al Mamaux, Pirates	21-15

1917
Grover Alexander, Phillies	30-13
Fred Toney, Reds	24-16
Jim Vaughn, Cubs	23-13
Ferdie Schupp, Giants	21- 7
Pete Schneider, Reds	20-19

1918
Jim Vaughn, Cubs	22-10
Claude Hendrix, Cubs	20- 7

1919
Jess Barnes, Giants	25- 9
Slim Sallee, Reds	21- 7
Jim Vaughn, Cubs	21-14

1920
Grover Alexander, Cubs	27-14
Wilbur Cooper, Pirates	24-15
Burleigh Grimes, Dodgers	23-11
Fred Toney, Giants	21-11
Art Nehf, Giants	21-12
Jess Barnes, Giants	20-15
Bill Doak, Cardinals	20-12

1921
Burleigh Grimes, Dodgers	22-13
Wilbur Cooper, Pirates	22-14
Art Nehf, Giants	20-10
Joe Oeschger, Braves	20-14

1922
Eppa Rixey, Reds	25-13
Wilbur Cooper, Pirates	23-14
Dutch Ruether, Dodgers	21-12

1923
Adolfo Luque, Reds	27- 8
John Morrison, Pirates	25-13
Grover Alexander, Cubs	22-12
Pete Donohue, Reds	21-15
Burleigh Grimes, Dodgers	21-18
Jesse Haines, Cardinals	20-13
Eppa Rixey, Reds	20-15

1924
Dazzy Vance, Dodgers	28- 6
Burleigh Grimes, Dodgers	22-13
Carl Mays, Reds	20- 9
Wilbur Cooper, Pirates	20-14

1925
Dazzy Vance, Dodgers	22- 9
Eppa Rixey, Reds	21-11
Pete Donohue, Reds	21-14

1926
Remy Kremer, Pirates	20- 6
Flint Rhem, Cardinals	20- 7
Lee Meadows, Pirates	20- 9
Pete Donohue, Reds	20-14

1927
Charles Root, Cubs	26-15
Jesse Haines, Cardinals	24-10
Carmen Hill, Pirates	22-11
Grover Alexander, Cardinals	21-10

1928
Larry Benton, Giants	25- 9
Burleigh Grimes, Pirates	25-14
Dazzy Vance, Dodgers	22-10
Bill Sherdel, Cardinals	21-10
Jesse Haines, Cardinals	20- 8
Fred Fitzsimmons, Giants	20- 9

1929
Pat Malone, Cubs	22-10

1930
Pat Malone, Cubs	20- 9
Remy Kremer, Pirates	20-12

1931
—None—

1932
Lon Warneke, Cubs	22- 6
Watson Clark, Dodgers	20-12

1933
Carl Hubbell, Giants	23-12
Guy Bush, Cubs	20-12
Ben Cantwell, Braves	20-10
Dizzy Dean, Cardinals	20-18

1934
Dizzy Dean, Cardinals	30- 7
Hal Schumacher, Giants	23-10
Lon Warneke, Cubs	22-10
Carl Hubbell, Giants	21-12

1935
Dizzy Dean, Cardinals	28-12
Carl Hubbell, Giants	23-12
Paul Derringer, Reds	22-13
Bill Lee, Cubs	20- 6
Lon Warneke, Cubs	20-13

1936
Carl Hubbell, Giants	26- 6
Dizzy Dean, Cardinals	24-13

1937
Carl Hubbell, Giants	22- 8
Cliff Melton, Giants	20- 9
Lou Fette, Braves	20-10
Jim Turner, Braves	20-11

1938
Bill Lee, Cubs	22- 9
Paul Derringer, Reds	21-14

1939
Bucky Walters, Reds	27-11
Paul Derringer, Reds	25- 7
Curt Davis, Cardinals	22- 9
Luke Hamlin, Dodgers	20-13

1940
Bucky Walters, Reds	22-10
Paul Derringer, Reds	20-12
Claude Passeau, Cubs	20-13

1941
J. Whitlow Wyatt, Dodgers	22-10
Kirby Higbe, Dodgers	22- 9

20-GAME WINNERS 1901—1995 (Continued)

1942
Mort Cooper, Cardinals .... 22 - 7
John Beazley, Cardinals .... 21 - 6

1943
Mort Cooper, Cardinals .... 21 - 8
Truett Sewell, Pirates .... 21 - 9
Elmer Riddle, Reds .... 21 - 11

1944
Bucky Walters, Reds .... 23 - 8
Mort Cooper, Cardinals .... 22 - 7
Truett Sewell, Pirates .... 21 - 12
Bill Voiselle, Giants .... 21 - 16

1945
Chas. Barrett, Braves-Cards .... 23 - 12
Hank Wyse, Cubs .... 22 - 10
†Hank Borowy, Yanks-Cubs .... 21 - 7

1946
**Howard Pollet, Cardinals .... 21 - 10
Johnny Sain, Braves .... 20 - 14

1947
Ewell Blackwell, Reds .... 22 - 8
Warren Spahn, Braves .... 21 - 10
Johnny Sain, Braves .... 21 - 12
Ralph Branca, Dodgers .... 21 - 12
Larry Jansen, Giants .... 21 - 5

1948
Johnny Sain, Braves .... 24 - 15
Harry Brecheen, Cardinals .... 20 - 7

1949
Warren Spahn, Braves .... 21 - 14
Howard Pollet, Cardinals .... 20 - 9

1950
Warren Spahn, Braves .... 21 - 17
Robin Roberts, Phillies .... 20 - 11
Johnny Sain, Braves .... 20 - 13

1951
**Larry Jansen, Giants .... 23 - 11
Sal Maglie, Giants .... 23 - 6
Preacher Roe, Dodgers .... 22 - 3
Warren Spahn, Braves .... 22 - 14
Robin Roberts, Phillies .... 21 - 15
Don Newcombe, Dodgers .... 20 - 9
Murry Dickson, Pirates .... 20 - 16

1952
Robin Roberts, Phillies .... 28 - 7

1953
Warren Spahn, Braves .... 23 - 7
Robin Roberts, Phillies .... 23 - 16
Carl Erskine, Dodgers .... 20 - 6
Harvey Haddix, Cardinals .... 20 - 9

1954
Robin Roberts, Phillies .... 23 - 15
John Antonelli, Giants .... 21 - 7
Warren Spahn, Braves .... 21 - 12

1955
Robin Roberts, Phillies .... 23 - 14
Don Newcombe, Dodgers .... 20 - 5

1956
Don Newcombe, Dodgers .... 27 - 7
Warren Spahn, Braves .... 20 - 11
John Antonelli, Giants .... 20 - 13

1957
Warren Spahn, Braves .... 21 - 11

1958
Warren Spahn, Braves .... 22 - 11
Bob Friend, Pirates .... 22 - 14
Lew Burdette, Braves .... 20 - 10

1959
Lew Burdette, Braves .... 21 - 15
Sam Jones, Giants .... 21 - 15
Warren Spahn, Braves .... 21 - 15

1960
Ernie Broglio, Cardinals .... 21 - 9
Warren Spahn, Braves .... 21 - 10
Vernon Law, Pirates .... 20 - 9

1961
Joey Jay, Reds .... 21 - 10
Warren Spahn, Braves .... 21 - 13

1962
Don Drysdale, Dodgers .... 25 - 9
Jack Sanford, Giants .... 24 - 7
Bob Purkey, Reds .... 23 - 5
Joey Jay, Reds .... 21 - 14

1963
Sandy Koufax, Dodgers .... 25 - 5
Juan Marichal, Giants .... 25 - 8
Warren Spahn, Braves .... 23 - 7
Jim Maloney, Reds .... 23 - 7
Dick Ellsworth, Cubs .... 22 - 10

1964
Larry Jackson, Cubs .... 24 - 11
Juan Marichal, Giants .... 21 - 8
Ray Sadecki, Cardinals .... 20 - 11

1965
Sandy Koufax, Dodgers .... 26 - 8
Tony Cloninger, Braves .... 24 - 11
Don Drysdale, Dodgers .... 23 - 12
Sammy Ellis, Reds .... 22 - 10
Juan Marichal, Giants .... 22 - 13
Jim Maloney, Reds .... 20 - 9
Bob Gibson, Cardinals .... 20 - 12

1966
Sandy Koufax, Dodgers .... 27 - 9
Juan Marichal, Giants .... 25 - 6
Gaylord Perry, Giants .... 21 - 8
Bob Gibson, Cardinals .... 21 - 12
Chris Short, Phillies .... 20 - 10

1967
Mike McCormick, Giants .... 22 - 10
Fergie Jenkins, Cubs .... 20 - 13

1968
Juan Marichal, Giants .... 26 - 9
Bob Gibson, Cardinals .... 22 - 9
Fergie Jenkins, Cubs .... 20 - 15

1969
Tom Seaver, Mets .... 25 - 7
Phil Niekro, Braves .... 23 - 13
Juan Marichal, Giants .... 21 - 11
Fergie Jenkins, Cubs .... 21 - 15
Bill Singer, Dodgers .... 20 - 12
Bob Gibson, Cardinals .... 20 - 13
Larry Dierker, Astros .... 20 - 13
Bill Hands, Cubs .... 20 - 14
Claude Osteen, Dodgers .... 20 - 15

1970
Bob Gibson, Cardinals .... 23 - 7
Gaylord Perry, Giants .... 23 - 13
Fergie Jenkins, Cubs .... 22 - 16
Jim Merritt, Reds .... 20 - 12

1971
Fergie Jenkins, Cubs .... 24 - 13
Steve Carlton, Cardinals .... 20 - 9
Al Downing, Dodgers .... 20 - 9
Tom Seaver, Mets .... 20 - 10

1972
Steve Carlton, Phillies .... 27 - 10
Tom Seaver, Mets .... 21 - 12
Claude Osteen, Dodgers .... 20 - 11
Fergie Jenkins, Cubs .... 20 - 12

1973
Ron Bryant, Giants .... 24 - 12

1974
Andy Messersmith, Dodgers .... 20 - 6
Phil Niekro, Braves .... 20 - 13

1975
Tom Seaver, Mets .... 22 - 9
Randy Jones, Padres .... 20 - 12

1976
Randy Jones, Padres .... 22 - 14
Jerry Koosman, Mets .... 21 - 10
Don Sutton, Dodgers .... 21 - 10
Steve Carlton, Phillies .... 20 - 7
J.R. Richard, Astros .... 20 - 15

1977
Steve Carlton, Phillies .... 23 - 10
Tom Seaver, Mets-Reds .... 21 - 6
John Candelaria, Pirates .... 20 - 5
Bob Forsch, Cardinals .... 20 - 7
Tommy John, Dodgers .... 20 - 7
Rick Reuschel, Cubs .... 20 - 10

1978
Gaylord Perry, Padres .... 21 - 6
Ross Grimsley, Expos .... 20 - 11

1979
Joe Niekro, Astros .... 21 - 11
Phil Niekro, Braves .... 21 - 20

1980
Steve Carlton, Phillies .... 24 - 9
**Joe Niekro, Astros .... 20 - 12

1981
—None—

1982
Steve Carlton, Phillies .... 23 - 11

1983
—None—

1984
Joaquin Andujar, Cardinals .... 20 - 14
#Rick Sutcliffe, Indians-Cubs .... 20 - 6

1985
Dwight Gooden, Mets .... 24 - 4
Joaquin Andujar, Cardinals .... 21 - 12
John Tudor, Cardinals .... 21 - 8
Tom Browning, Reds .... 20 - 9

1986
Fernando Valenzuela, Dodgers .... 21 - 11
Mike Krukow, Giants .... 20 - 9

1987
—None—

1988
Orel Hershiser, Dodgers .... 23 - 8
Danny Jackson, Reds .... 23 - 8
David Cone, Mets .... 20 - 3

1989
Mike Scott, Astros .... 20 - 10

1990
Doug Drabek, Pirates .... 22 - 6
Ramon Martinez, Dodgers .... 20 - 6
Frank Viola, Mets .... 20 - 12

1991
Tom Glavine, Braves .... 20 - 11
John Smiley, Pirates .... 20 - 8

1992
Tom Glavine, Braves .... 20 - 8
Greg Maddux, Cubs .... 20 - 11

1993
Tom Glavine, Braves .... 22 - 6
John Burkett, Giants .... 22 - 7
Bill Swift, Giants .... 21 - 8
Greg Maddux, Braves .... 20 - 10

1994
—None—

1995
—None—

*—Won 13 in A.L., 8 in N.L. (1902)
†—Won 10 in A.L., 11 in N.L. (1945)
#—Won 4 in A.L., 16 in N.L. (1984)
**—Includes playoff victory (1946, 1951, 1980)

30-GAME WINNERS
(since 1900)

W	Pitcher	Year
41	Jack Chesbro, New York (AL)	1904
40	Ed Walsh, Chicago (AL)	1908
37	Christy Mathewson, New York (NL)	1908
36	Walter Johnson, Washington	1913
35	Joe McGinnity, New York (NL)	1904
34	Joe Wood, Boston (AL)	1912
33	Cy Young, Boston (AL)	1901
33	Grover Alexander, Philadelphia (NL)	1916
33	Christy Mathewson, New York (NL)	1904
32	Cy Young, Boston (AL)	1901
32	Cy Young, Boston (AL)	1902
31	Joe McGinnity, New York (NL)	1903
31	Christy Mathewson, New York (NL)	1905
31	Jack Coombs, Philadelphia (AL)	1910
31	Grover Alexander, Philadelphia (NL)	1915
31	Jim Bagby, Cleveland	1920
31	Lefty Grove, Philadelphia (AL)	1931
31	Denny McLain, Detroit	1968
30	Christy Mathewson, New York (NL)	1903
30	Grover Alexander, Philadelphia	1917
30	Dizzy Dean, St. Louis (NL)	1934

CLUBS' ALL-TIME LEADERS IN PITCHING CATEGORIES

WINS

BRAVES
- Warren Spahn ... 356
- Kid Nichols ... 328
- Phil Niekro ... 268
- Lew Burdette ... 179
- Tommy Bond ... 149
- Vic Willis ... 149

CUBS
- Charles Root ... 201
- Mordecai Brown ... 188
- Bill Hutchinson ... 181
- Larry Corcoran ... 175
- Ferguson Jenkins ... 167

REDS
- Eppa Rixey ... 179
- Paul Derringer ... 161
- Bucky Walters ... 160
- Dolf Luque ... 154
- Jim Maloney ... 134

ROCKIES
- Armando Reynoso ... 22
- Steve Reed ... 17
- Kevin Ritz ... 16
- David Nied ... 14
- Marvin Freeman ... 13

MARLINS
- Pat Rapp ... 25
- Chris Hammond ... 24
- John Burkett ... 14
- Charlie Hough ... 14
- Dave Weathers ... 14

ASTROS
- Joe Niekro ... 144
- Larry Dierker ... 137
- Mike Scott ... 110
- J.R. Richard ... 107
- Nolan Ryan ... 106

DODGERS
- Don Sutton ... 233
- Don Drysdale ... 209
- Dazzy Vance ... 190
- Brickyard Kennedy ... 176
- Sandy Koufax ... 165

EXPOS
- Steve Rogers ... 158
- Dennis Martinez ... 100
- Bryn Smith ... 81
- Bill Gullickson ... 72
- Steve Renko ... 68

METS
- Tom Seaver ... 198
- Dwight Gooden ... 157
- Jerry Koosman ... 140
- Ron Darling ... 99
- Sid Fernandez ... 98

PHILLIES
- Steve Carlton ... 241
- Robin Roberts ... 234
- Grover Alexander ... 190
- Chris Short ... 132
- Curt Simmons ... 115

PIRATES
- Wilbur Cooper ... 202
- Sam Leever ... 194
- Babe Adams ... 194
- Bob Friend ... 191
- Deacon Phillippe ... 165

CARDINALS
- Bob Gibson ... 251
- Jesse Haines ... 210
- Bob Forsch ... 163
- Bill Sherdel ... 153
- Bill Doak ... 145

PADRES
- Eric Show ... 100
- Randy Jones ... 92
- Ed Whitson ... 77
- Andy Benes ... 69
- Andy Hawkins ... 60

GIANTS
- Christy Mathewson ... 372
- Carl Hubbell ... 253
- Mickey Welch ... 243
- Juan Marichal ... 238
- Amos Rusie ... 230

GAMES

BRAVES
- Phil Niekro ... 740
- Warren Spahn ... 714
- Gene Garber ... 557
- Kid Nichols ... 543
- Lew Burdette ... 468

CUBS
- Charles Root ... 605
- Lee Smith ... 458
- Don Elston ... 449
- Guy Bush ... 428
- Ferguson Jenkins ... 401

REDS
- Pedro Borbon ... 531
- Clay Carroll ... 486
- Joe Nuxhall ... 484
- Tom Hume ... 457
- Eppa Rixey ... 440

ROCKIES
- Steve Reed ... 196
- Darren Holmes ... 159
- Bruce Ruffin ... 152
- Mike Munoz ... 142
- Curtis Leskanic ... 102

MARLINS
- Richie Lewis ... 123
- Robb Nen ... 121
- Yorkis Perez ... 113
- Terry Mathews ... 81
- Bryan Harvey ... 72

ASTROS
- Dave Smith ... 563
- Ken Forsch ... 421
- Joe Niekro ... 397
- Joe Sambito ... 353
- Larry Dierker ... 345

DODGERS
- Don Sutton ... 550
- Don Drysdale ... 518
- Jim Brewer ... 474
- Ron Perranoski ... 457
- Clem Labine ... 425

EXPOS
- Tim Burke ... 425
- Steve Rogers ... 399
- Jeff Reardon ... 359
- Mel Rojas ... 311
- Woodie Fryman ... 297

METS
- Tom Seaver ... 401
- Jerry Koosman ... 376
- Jesse Orosco ... 372
- Tug McGraw ... 361
- Dwight Gooden ... 305

PHILLIES
- Robin Roberts ... 529
- Steve Carlton ... 499
- Tug McGraw ... 463
- Chris Short ... 459
- Ron Reed ... 458

PIRATES
- Roy Face ... 802
- Kent Tekulve ... 722
- Bob Friend ... 568
- Vernon Law ... 483
- Babe Adams ... 481

CARDINALS
- Jesse Haines ... 554
- Bob Gibson ... 528
- Bill Sherdel ... 465
- Bob Forsch ... 455
- Al Brazle ... 441

PADRES
- Craig Lefferts ... 375
- Eric Show ... 309
- Rollie Fingers ... 265
- Randy Jones ... 264
- Dave Tomlin ... 239

GIANTS
- Gary Lavelle ... 647
- Christy Mathewson ... 634
- Greg Minton ... 552
- Carl Hubbell ... 535
- Randy Moffitt ... 459

SHUTOUTS

BRAVES
- Warren Spahn ... 63
- Kid Nichols ... 44
- Phil Niekro ... 43
- Tommy Bond ... 30
- Lew Burdette ... 30

CUBS
- Mordecai Brown ... 50
- James Vaughn ... 35
- Ed Reulbach ... 31
- Ferguson Jenkins ... 29
- Orval Overall ... 28

REDS
- Bucky Walters ... 32
- Jim Maloney ... 30
- Johnny Vander Meer ... 30
- Ken Raffensberger ... 25
- 3 tied ... 24

ROCKIES
- David Nied ... 1

MARLINS
- Chris Hammond ... 3
- Pat Rapp ... 3
- Ryan Bowen ... 1
- Mark Gardner ... 1
- Charlie Hough ... 1

ASTROS
- Larry Dierker ... 25
- Joe Niekro ... 21
- Mike Scott ... 21
- Don Wilson ... 20
- J.R. Richard ... 19

DODGERS
- Don Sutton ... 52
- Don Drysdale ... 49
- Sandy Koufax ... 40
- Nap Rucker ... 38
- Claude Osteen ... 34

EXPOS
- Steve Rogers ... 37
- Bill Stoneman ... 15
- Dennis Martinez ... 13
- Woodie Fryman ... 8
- Charlie Lea ... 8
- Scott Sanderson ... 8
- Bryn Smith ... 8

METS
- Tom Seaver ... 44
- Jerry Koosman ... 26
- Jon Matlack ... 26
- Dwight Gooden ... 23
- David Cone ... 15

PHILLIES
- Grover Alexander ... 61
- Steve Carlton ... 39
- Robin Roberts ... 35
- Chris Short ... 24
- Jim Bunning ... 23

PIRATES
- Babe Adams ... 47
- Sam Leever ... 39
- Bob Friend ... 35
- Vernon Law ... 33
- Lefty Leifield ... 28

CARDINALS
- Bob Gibson ... 56
- Bill Doak ... 32
- Mort Cooper ... 28
- Harry Brecheen ... 25
- Jesse Haines ... 24

PADRES
- Randy Jones ... 18
- Steve Arlin ... 11
- Eric Show ... 11
- Bruce Hurst ... 10
- Andy Benes ... 8

GIANTS
- Christy Mathewson ... 83
- Juan Marichal ... 52
- Carl Hubbell ... 36
- Amos Rusie ... 29
- Hal Schumacher ... 29
- Hooks Wiltse ... 29

SAVES

BRAVES
- Gene Garber ... 141
- Cecil Upshaw ... 78
- Rick Camp ... 57
- Mike Stanton ... 55
- Don McMahon ... 50

CUBS
- Lee Smith ... 180
- Bruce Sutter ... 133
- Randy Myers ... 112
- Don Elston ... 63
- Phil Regan ... 60

REDS
- John Franco ... 148
- Clay Carroll ... 119
- Rob Dibble ... 88
- Tom Hume ... 88
- Pedro Borbon ... 76

ROCKIES
- Darren Holmes ... 42
- Bruce Ruffin ... 29
- Curtis Leskanic ... 10
- Steve Reed ... 9
- Willie Blair ... 9
- Mike Munoz ... 3

MARLINS
- Bryan Harvey ... 51
- Robb Nen ... 38
- Jeremy Hernandez ... 9
- Terry Mathews ... 3
- Trevor Hoffman ... 2

ASTROS
- Dave Smith ... 199
- Fred Gladding ... 76
- Joe Sambito ... 72
- Doug Jones ... 62
- Ken Forsch ... 50

DODGERS
- Jim Brewer ... 125
- Ron Perranoski ... 101
- Jay Howell ... 85
- Clem Labine ... 83
- Tom Niedenfuer ... 64

EXPOS
- Jeff Reardon ... 152
- John Wetteland ... 105
- Tim Burke ... 101
- Mike Marshall ... 75
- Mel Rojas ... 73

METS
- John Franco ... 147
- Jesse Orosco ... 107
- Tug McGraw ... 86
- Roger McDowell ... 84
- Neil Allen ... 69

PHILLIES
- Steve Bedrosian ... 103
- Mitch Williams ... 102
- Tug McGraw ... 94
- Ron Reed ... 90
- Dick Farrell ... 65

PIRATES
- Roy Face ... 188
- Kent Tekulve ... 158
- Dave Giusti ... 133
- Stan Belinda ... 61
- Al McBean ... 59

CARDINALS
- Lee Smith ... 160
- Todd Worrell ... 129
- Bruce Sutter ... 127
- Lindy McDaniel ... 64
- Al Brazle ... 60
- Joe Hoerner ... 60

PADRES
- Rollie Fingers ... 108
- Rich Gossage ... 83
- Mark Davis ... 78
- Craig Lefferts ... 64
- Trevor Hoffman ... 54

GIANTS
- Rod Beck ... 127
- Gary Lavelle ... 127
- Greg Minton ... 125
- Randy Moffitt ... 83
- Frank Linzy ... 78

INNINGS PITCHED

BRAVES
- Warren Spahn ... 5048.0
- Phil Niekro ... 4622.0
- Kid Nichols ... 4570.0
- Lew Burdette ... 2638.0
- Vic Willis ... 2575.0

CUBS
- Charles Root ... 3138.0
- Bill Hutchinson ... 3026.0
- Ferguson Jenkins ... 2672.2
- Larry Corcoran ... 2337.2
- Mordecai Brown ... 2329.0

REDS
- Eppa Rixey ... 2890.0
- Dolf Luque ... 2669.0
- Paul Derringer ... 2616.0
- Bucky Walters ... 2355.0
- Joe Nuxhall ... 2171.0

ROCKIES
- Armando Reynoso ... 334.1
- Kevin Ritz ... 247.0
- Steve Reed ... 232.1
- Bruce Ruffin ... 229.1
- Willie Blair ... 223.2

MARLINS
- Chris Hammond ... 425.1
- Pat Rapp ... 394.2
- Charlie Hough ... 318.0
- Dave Weathers ... 271.0
- Ryan Bowen ... 220.2

ASTROS
- Larry Dierker ... 2295.0
- Joe Niekro ... 2270.0
- Nolan Ryan ... 1855.0
- Don Wilson ... 1749.0
- Bob Knepper ... 1738.1

DODGERS
- Don Sutton ... 3815.1
- Don Drysdale ... 3432.0
- Brickyard Kennedy ... 2857.0
- Dazzy Vance ... 2758.0
- Burleigh Grimes ... 2426.0

EXPOS
- Steve Rogers ... 2839.1
- Dennis Martinez ... 1609.0
- Bryn Smith ... 1400.1
- Steve Renko ... 1360.0
- Bill Gullickson ... 1186.0

METS
- Tom Seaver ... 3045.1
- Jerry Koosman ... 2545.0
- Dwight Gooden ... 2169.2
- Ron Darling ... 1620.0
- Sid Fernandez ... 1584.2

PHILLIES
- Robin Roberts ... 3739.1
- Steve Carlton ... 3696.1
- Grover Alexander ... 2513.1
- Chris Short ... 2253.0
- Curt Simmons ... 1939.2

PIRATES
- Bob Friend ... 3481.0
- Wilbur Cooper ... 3201.0
- Babe Adams ... 2991.0
- Vernon Law ... 2673.0
- Sam Leever ... 2645.0

CARDINALS
- Bob Gibson ... 3885.0
- Jesse Haines ... 3203.0
- Bob Forsch ... 2695.0
- Bill Sherdel ... 2459.0
- Bill Doak ... 2387.0

PADRES
- Randy Jones ... 1765.0
- Eric Show ... 1603.1
- Ed Whitson ... 1354.1
- Andy Benes ... 1235.0
- Clay Kirby ... 1129.0

GIANTS
- Christy Mathewson ... 4772.0
- Carl Hubbell ... 3591.0
- Mickey Welch ... 3579.0
- Amos Rusie ... 3523.0
- Juan Marichal ... 3443.0

STRIKEOUTS

BRAVES
- Phil Niekro ... 2912
- Warren Spahn ... 2493
- Kid Nichols ... 1684
- John Smoltz ... 1252
- Vic Willis ... 1161

CUBS
- Ferguson Jenkins ... 2038
- Charles Root ... 1432
- Rick Reuschel ... 1367
- Bill Hutchinson ... 1226
- James Vaughn ... 1138

REDS
- Jim Maloney ... 1592
- Mario Soto ... 1449
- Joe Nuxhall ... 1289
- Johnny Vander Meer ... 1251
- Jose Rijo ... 1201

ROCKIES
- Bruce Ruffin ... 214
- Armando Reynoso ... 182
- Steve Reed ... 181
- Kevin Ritz ... 173
- Darren Holmes ... 154
- Curtis Leskanic ... 154

MARLINS
- Chris Hammond ... 274
- Pat Rapp ... 204
- Charlie Hough ... 191
- Dave Weathers ... 166
- Robb Nen ... 155

ASTROS
- Nolan Ryan ... 1866
- J.R. Richard ... 1493
- Larry Dierker ... 1487
- Mike Scott ... 1318
- Don Wilson ... 1283

DODGERS
- Don Sutton ... 2696
- Don Drysdale ... 2486
- Sandy Koufax ... 2396
- Dazzy Vance ... 1918
- Fernando Valenzuela ... 1759

EXPOS
- Steve Rogers ... 1621
- Dennis Martinez ... 973
- Bryn Smith ... 838
- Bill Stoneman ... 831
- Steve Renko ... 810

METS
- Tom Seaver ... 2541
- Dwight Gooden ... 1875
- Jerry Koosman ... 1799
- Sid Fernandez ... 1449
- David Cone ... 1159

PHILLIES
- Steve Carlton ... 3031
- Robin Roberts ... 1871
- Chris Short ... 1585
- Grover Alexander ... 1410
- Jim Bunning ... 1197

PIRATES
- Bob Friend ... 1682
- Bob Veale ... 1652
- Wilbur Cooper ... 1191
- John Candelaria ... 1142
- Vernon Law ... 1092

CARDINALS
- Bob Gibson ... 3117
- Dizzy Dean ... 1087
- Bob Forsch ... 1079
- Jesse Haines ... 979
- Steve Carlton ... 951

PADRES
- Andy Benes ... 1036
- Eric Show ... 951
- Clay Kirby ... 802
- Ed Whitson ... 767
- Randy Jones ... 677

GIANTS
- Christy Mathewson ... 2502
- Juan Marichal ... 2281
- Amos Rusie ... 1838
- Carl Hubbell ... 1677
- Gaylord Perry ... 1606

74

LEAGUE LEADER WON AND LOST PERCENTAGE
(15 or More Decisions)

Year	Pitcher	W-L	PCT
1901	Sam Leever, Pittsburgh	14-5	.774
1902	Jack Chesbro, Pittsburgh	28-6	.824
1903	Sam Leever, Pittsburgh	25-7	.781
1904	Joe McGinnity, New York	35-8	.814
1905	Sam Leever, Pittsburgh	20-5	.800
1906	Ed Ruelbach, Chicago	19-4	.826
1907	Ed Ruelbach, Chicago	17-4	.810
1908	Ed Ruelbach, Chicago	24-7	.774
1909	Howie Camnitz, Pittsburgh	25-6	.806
	Christy Mathewson, New York	25-6	.806
1910	Deacon Phillippe, Pittsburgh	14-2	.875
1911	Rube Marquard, New York	24-7	.774
1912	Claude Hendrix, Pittsburgh	24-9	.727
1913	Bert Humphries, Chicago	16-4	.800
1914	Bill James, Boston	26-7	.788
1915	Grover Alexander, Philadelphia	31-10	.756
1916	Tom Hughes, Boston	16-3	.842
1917	Ferdie Schupp, New York	21-7	.750
1918	Claude Hendrix, Chicago	20-7	.741
1919	Dutch Ruether, Cincinnati	19-6	.760
1920	Burleigh Grimes, Brooklyn	23-11	.676
1921	Babe Adams, Pittsburgh	14-5	.737
	Whitey Glazner, Pittsburgh	14-5	.737
1922	Phil Douglas, New York	11-4	.733
1923	Dolf Luque, Cincinnati	27-8	.771
1924	Emil Yde, Pittsburgh	16-3	.842
1925	Bill Sherdel, St. Louis	15-6	.714
1926	Ray Kremer, Pittsburgh	20-6	.769
1927	Larry Benton, New York	17-7	.708
1928	Larry Benton, New York	25-9	.735
1929	Charlie Root, Chicago	19-6	.760
1930	Freddie Fitzsimmons, New York	19-7	.731
1931	Jesse Haines, St. Louis	12-3	.800
1932	Lon Warneke, Chicago	22-6	.786
1933	Bud Tinning, Chicago	13-6	.684
1934	Dizzy Dean, St. Louis	30-7	.811
1935	Bill Lee, Chicago	20-6	.769
1936	Carl Hubbell, New York	26-6	.813
1937	Carl Hubbell, New York	22-8	.733
1938	Bill Lee, Chicago	22-9	.710
1939	Paul Derringer, Cincinnati	25-7	.781
1940	Freddie Fitzsimmons, Brooklyn	16-2	.889
1941	Elmer Riddle, Cincinnati	19-4	.826
1942	Howie Krist, St. Louis	13-3	.813
1943	Clyde Shoun, Cincinnati	14-5	.737
	Whit Wyatt, Brooklyn	14-5	.737
1944	Ted Wilks, St. Louis	17-4	.810
1945	Harry Brecheen, St. Louis	15-4	.789
1946	Schoolboy Rowe, Philadelphia	11-4	.733
1947	Larry Jansen, New York	21-5	.808
1948	Rip Sewell, Pittsburgh	13-3	.813
1949	Ralph Branca, Brooklyn	13-5	.722
1950	Sal Maglie, New York	18-4	.818
1951	Preacher Roe, Brooklyn	22-3	.880
1952	Hoyt Wilhelm, New York	15-3	.833
1953	Carl Erskine, Brooklyn	20-6	.769
1954	John Antonelli, New York	21-7	.750
	Hoyt Wilhelm, New York	12-4	.750
1955	Don Newcombe, Brooklyn	20-5	.800
1956	Don Newcombe, Brooklyn	27-7	.794
1957	Bob Buhl, Milwaukee	18-7	.720
1958	Warren Spahn, Milwaukee	20-10	.667
	Lew Burdette, Milwaukee	20-10	.667
1959	ElRoy Face, Pittsburgh	18-1	.947
1960	Lindy McDaniel, St. Louis	12-4	.750
1961	John Podres, Los Angeles	18-5	.783
1962	Bob Purkey, Cincinnati	23-5	.821
1963	Ron Perranoski, Los Angeles	16-3	.842
1964	Sandy Koufax, Los Angeles	19-5	.792
1965	Sandy Koufax, Los Angeles	26-8	.765
1966	Phil Regan, Los Angeles	14-1	.933
1967	Nelson Briles, St. Louis	14-5	.737
1968	Steve Blass, Pittsburgh	18-6	.750
1969	Bob Moose, Pittsburgh	14-3	.824
1970	Wayne Simpson, Cincinnati	14-3	.824
1971	Tug McGraw, New York	11-4	.733
1972	Gary Nolan, Cincinnati	15-5	.750
1973	George Stone, New York	12-3	.800
1974	Tommy John, Los Angeles	13-3	.813
1975	Al Hrabosky, St. Louis	13-3	.813
1976	Rick Rhoden, Los Angeles	12-3	.800
1977	John Candelaria, Pittsburgh	20-5	.800
1978	Gaylord Perry, San Diego	21-6	.778
1979	Jim Bibby, Pittsburgh	12-4	.750
1980	Jim Bibby, Pittsburgh	19-6	.760
1981	Tom Seaver, Cincinnati	14-2	.875
1982	Phil Niekro, Atlanta	17-4	.810
1983	John Denny, Philadelphia	19-6	.760
1984	Rick Sutcliffe, Chicago	16-1	.941
1985	Orel Hershiser, Los Angeles	19-3	.864
1986	Bob Ojeda, New York	18-5	.783
1987	Dennis Martinez, Montreal	11-4	.733
1988	David Cone, New York	20-3	.870
1989	Sid Fernandez, New York	14-5	.737
	Scott Garrelts, San Francisco	14-5	.737
1990	Doug Drabek, Pittsburgh	22-6	.786
1991	John Smiley, Pittsburgh	20-8	.714
	Jose Rijo, Cincinnati	15-6	.714
1992	Bob Tewksbury, St. Louis	16-5	.762
1993	Mark Portugal, Houston	18-4	.818
1994	Marvin Freeman, Colorado*	10-2	.833
1995	Greg Maddux, Atlanta	19-2	.905

*Based on 10 or more decisions due to strike-shortened season.

1995 SHUTOUTS BY PITCHING STAFF

Club	Shutouts
Chicago	12
Atlanta	11
Los Angeles	11
Cincinnati	10
San Diego	10
Montreal	9
New York	9
Houston	8
Philadelphia	8
Florida	7
Pittsburgh	7
St. Louis	6
San Francisco	5
Colorado	1

1995 LOW-RUN COMPLETE GAMES

Pitcher and Club	Shutouts	1-Run	2-Run	Total
Maddux, Greg, Atlanta	3	5	2	10
Leiter, Mark, San Francisco	1	6	0	7
Valdes, Ismael, Los Angeles	2	2	1	5
Nomo, Hideo, Los Angeles	3	1	0	4
Neagle, Denny, Pittsburgh	1	1	2	4
Burkett, John, Florida	0	3	1	4
Rapp, Pat, Florida	2	1	0	3
Martinez, Ramon, Los Angeles	2	0	1	3
Hammond, Chris, Florida	2	0	1	3
Green, Tyler, Philadelphia	2	0	1	3
Wagner, Paul, Pittsburgh	1	1	1	3
Wells, David, Cincinnati	0	2	1	3
Reynolds, Shane, Houston	2	0	0	2
Martinez, Pedro, Montreal	2	0	0	2
Hamilton, Joey, San Diego	2	0	0	2
Castillo, Frank, Chicago	2	0	0	2
Ashby, Andy, San Diego	2	0	0	2
Glavine, Tom, Atlanta	1	1	0	2
Avery, Steve, Atlanta	1	1	0	2
Perez, Carlos, Montreal	1	0	1	2
Mimbs, Michael, Philadelphia	1	0	1	2
Jones, Bobby, New York	1	0	1	2
Jackson, Danny, St. Louis	1	0	1	2
Drabek, Doug, Houston	1	0	1	2
Trachsel, Steve, Chicago	0	2	0	2
Schourek, Pete, Cincinnati	0	1	1	2
Mulholland, Terry, San Francisco	0	0	2	2
Swindell, Greg, Houston	1	0	0	1
Smoltz, John, Atlanta	1	0	0	1
Rueter, Kirk, Montreal	1	0	0	1
Petkovsek, Mark, St. Louis	1	0	0	1
Parris, Steve, Pittsburgh	1	0	0	1
Navarro, Jaime, Chicago	1	0	0	1
Jarvis, Kevin, Cincinnati	1	0	0	1
Henry, Butch, Montreal	1	0	0	1
Gardner, Mark, Florida	1	0	0	1
Candiotti, Tom, Los Angeles	1	0	0	1
Burba, Dave, Cincinnati	1	0	0	1
Bullinger, Jim, Chicago	1	0	0	1
Benes, Andy, San Diego	1	0	0	1
Astacio, Pedro, Los Angeles	1	0	0	1
Smiley, John, Cincinnati	0	1	0	1
Schilling, Curt, Philadelphia	0	1	0	1
Pulsipher, Bill, New York	0	1	0	1
Portugal, Mark, San Francisco	0	1	0	1
Morgan, Mike, St. Louis	0	1	0	1
Isringhausen, Jason, New York	0	1	0	1
Sanders, Scott, San Diego	0	0	1	1
Fassero, Jeff, Montreal	0	0	1	1
Ericks, John, Pittsburgh	0	0	1	1

1995 LOW-RUN GAMES BY PITCHING STAFF

Pitcher and Club	Shutouts	1-Run	2-Run	Total
Atlanta	11	25	19	55
Los Angeles	11	19	25	55
Cincinnati	10	18	23	51
Montreal	9	17	22	48
Philadelphia	8	13	20	41
Chicago	12	11	16	39
San Diego	10	10	18	38
Houston	8	11	17	36
New York	9	13	13	35
Florida	7	13	15	35
San Francisco	5	20	9	34
Pittsburgh	7	7	19	33
St. Louis	6	13	14	33
Colorado	1	13	16	30

LIFETIME SHUTOUTS

Active N.L. pitchers for 1996 and those pitching N.L. shutouts in 1995
(A.L. shutouts in parentheses)

Pitcher	Team	SHO
Fernando Valenzuela	Padres (2)	31
Doug Drabek	Astros	21
Greg Maddux	Braves	20
Ramon Martinez	Dodgers	18
Bret Saberhagen	Rockies (14)	16
Danny Jackson	Cardinals (6)	15
Tom Glavine	Braves	13
Greg Swindell	Astros (7)	12
Tom Candiotti	Dodgers (8)	11
Mike Morgan	Cardinals (3)	10
Terry Mulholland	FREE AGENT	10
Sid Fernandez	Phillies	9
Pedro Astacio	Dodgers	8
Andy Benes	Cardinals	8
Kevin Brown	Marlins (7)	7
Jose DeLeon	FREE AGENT	7
Jaime Navarro	Cubs (6)	7
John Smoltz	Braves	7
Steve Avery	Braves	6
Pete Harnisch	Mets	6
Curt Schilling	Phillies	6
John Smiley	Reds (2)	6
Kevin Tapani	FREE AGENT (6)	6
Tommy Greene	Phillies	5
Bob Tewksbury	Padres (1)	5
Mark Gardner	Marlins	4
Jose Guzman	Cubs (3)	4
Jose Rijo	Reds	4
Pete Smith	Padres	4
Todd Stottlemyre	Cardinals (4)	4
Bill Swift	Rockies (1)	4
Trevor Wilson	FREE AGENT	4
Luis Aquino	Giants (3)	3
John Burkett	Marlins	3
Jim Gott	FREE AGENT (3)	3
Joey Hamilton	Padres	3
Chris Hammond	Marlins	3
Pedro J. Martinez	Expos	3
Craig McMurtry	Astros	3
Hideo Nomo	Dodgers	3
Mark Portugal	Reds	3
Pat Rapp	Marlins	3
Shane Reynolds	Astros	3
Bruce Ruffin	Rockies	3
Andy Ashby	Padres	2
Frank Castillo	Cubs	2
Tyler Green	Phillies	2
Butch Henry	Red Sox	2
Bobby Jones	Mets	2
Darryl Kile	Astros	2
Al Leiter	Marlins (2)	2
Chris Nabholz	Mets	2
Vicente Palacios	FREE AGENT	2
Ismael Valdes	Dodgers	2
Paul Wagner	Pirates	2
Rene Arocha	Cardinals	1
Willie Banks	Phillies	1
Ryan Bowen	Marlins	1
Jim Bullinger	Cubs	1
Dave Burba	Reds	1
Steve Cooke	Pirates	1
Willie Fraser	FREE AGENT (1)	1
Mark Guthrie	Dodgers (1)	1
Kevin Jarvis	Reds	1
Mark Leiter	Giants	1
Michael Mimbs	Phillies	1
Denny Neagle	Pirates	1
Rod Nichols	Braves (1)	1
David Nied	Rockies	1
Steve Parris	Pirates	1
Carlos Perez	Expos	1
Mark Petkovsek	Cardinals	1
Kirk Rueter	Expos	1
Pete Schourek	Reds	1

TWO OR MORE NO-HIT GAMES

- **7** Nolan Ryan, California (AL), 1973 (2), 1974, 1975; Houston (NL), 1981; Texas (AL), 1990, 1991
- **4** Sandy Koufax, Los Angeles (NL), 1962, 1963, 1964, 1965
- **3** Larry Corcoran, Chicago (NL), 1880, 1882, 1884
  Bob Feller, Cleveland (AL), 1940, 1946, 1951
  Cy Young, Cleveland (NL), 1897; Boston (AL), 1904, 1908
- **2** Al Atkinson, Philadelphia (AA), 1884, 1886
  Ted Breitenstein, St. Louis (AA), 1891; Cincinnati (NL), 1898
  Jim Bunning, Detroit (AL), 1958; Philadelphia (NL), 1964
  Steve Busby, Kansas City (AL), 1973, 1974
  Carl Erskine, Brooklyn (NL), 1952, 1956
  Bob Forsch, St. Louis (NL), 1978, 1983
  Pud Galvin, Buffalo (NL), 1880, 1884
  Ken Holtzman, Chicago (NL), 1969, 1971
  Addie Joss, Cleveland (AL), 1908, 1910
  Dutch Leonard, Boston (AL), 1916, 1918
  Jim Maloney, Cincinnati (NL), 1965, 1969
  Christy Mathewson, New York (NL), 1901, 1905
  Allie Reynolds, New York (AL), 1951 (2)
  Frank Smith, Chicago (AL), 1905, 1908
  Warren Spahn, Milwaukee (NL), 1960, 1961
  Bill Stoneman, Montreal (NL), 1969, 1972
  Adonis Terry, Brooklyn (AA), 1886, 1888
  Virgil Trucks, Detroit (AL), 1952 (2)
  Johnny Vander Meer, Cincinnati (NL), 1938 (2)
  Don Wilson, Houston (NL), 1967, 1969

1995 NATIONAL LEAGUE SHUTOUTS

Individual

Pitcher	SHO
Greg Maddux, Braves	3
Hideo Nomo, Dodgers	3
Andy Ashby, Padres	2
Frank Castillo, Cubs	2
Tyler Green, Phillies	2
Joey Hamilton, Padres	2
Chris Hammond, Marlins	2
Pedro Martinez, Expos	2
Ramon Martinez, Dodgers	2
Pat Rapp, Marlins	2
Shane Reynolds, Astros	2
Ismael Valdes, Dodgers	2
Pedro Astacio, Dodgers	1
Steve Avery, Braves	1
Andy Benes, Padres	1
Jim Bullinger, Cubs	1
Dave Burba, Reds	1
Tom Candiotti, Dodgers	1
Doug Drabek, Astros	1
Mark Gardner, Marlins	1
Tom Glavine, Braves	1
Butch Henry, Expos	1
Danny Jackson, Cardinals	1
Kevin Jarvis, Reds	1
Bobby Jones, Mets	1
Mark Leiter, Giants	1
Mike Mimbs, Phillies	1
Jaime Navarro, Cubs	1
Denny Neagle, Pirates	1
Steve Parris, Pirates	1
Carlos Perez, Expos	1
Mark Petkovsek, Cardinals	1
Kirk Rueter, Expos	1
John Smoltz, Braves	1
Greg Swindell, Astros	1
Paul Wagner, Pirates	1

Combined

Combination	SHO
Schourek-Brantley, Reds	2
Pulsipher-Franco, Mets	2
Maddux-McMichael, Braves	1
Maddux-McMichael-Schmidt, Braves	1
Maddux-Wohlers, Braves	1
Mercker-Borbon-Wohlers, Braves	1
Schmidt-Wohlers, Braves	1
Bullinger-Casian-Wendell-Nabholz-Myers, Cubs	1
Castillo-Hickerson-Myers, Cubs	1
Castillo-Perez, Cubs	1
Foster-Myers, Cubs	1
Morgan-Myers, Cubs	1
Navarro-Myers, Cubs	1
Trachsel-Nabholz-Perez-Myers, Cubs	1
Trachsel-Perez-Hickerson, Cubs	1
Burba-Jackson-Brantley, Reds	1
Nitkowski-Brantley, Reds	1
Rijo-Carrasco-Jackson-Pennington, Reds	1
Schourek-Carrasco-Brantley, Reds	1
Schourek-Jackson, Reds	1
Smiley-Carrasco-McElroy-Brantley, Reds	1
Rekar-Reed, Rockies	1
Burkett-Nen, Marlins	1
Hammond-Veres-Nen, Marlins	1
Hampton-Jones-Hartgraves, Astros	1
Hampton-Martinez, Astros	1
Reynolds-Tabaka-Jones, Astros	1
Swindell-Jones-Veres-Henneman, Astros	1
Martinez-Seanez-Worrell, Dodgers	1
Valdes-Worrell, Dodgers	1
Henry-Rojas, Expos	1
Heredia-Scott-Shaw-Rojas, Expos	1
Martinez-Rojas, Expos	1
Rueter-Heredia, Expos	1
Harnisch-Henry, Mets	1
Isringhausen-Florence-Franco, Mets	1
Isringhausen-Henry, Mets	1
Isringhausen-Henry-Walker, Mets	1
Jones-Franco, Mets	1
Jones-Henry, Mets	1
Fernandez-Borland, Phillies	1
Fernandez-Bottalico-Slocumb, Phillies	1
Grace-Bottalico-Slocumb, Phillies	1
Quantrill-Slocumb, Phillies	1
Schilling-Harris, Phillies	1
Ericks-Christiansen-Miceli, Pirates	1
Loaiza-Christiansen-Miceli, Pirates	1
Neagle-Gott-Miceli, Pirates	1
Parris-Plesac-Miceli, Pirates	1
Hill-Habyan, Cardinals	1
Morgan-Parrett, Cardinals	1
Urbani-DeLucia-Henke, Cardinals	1
Watson-Henke, Cardinals	1
Ashby-Hoffman, Padres	1
Benes-Hoffman, Padres	1
Blair-Florie-Hoffman, Padres	1
Blair-Hoffman, Padres	1
Valenzuela-Florie, Padres	1
Williams-Hoffman, Padres	1
Brewington-Service-Barton-Beck, Giants	1
Leiter-Dewey-Bautista-Beck, Giants	1
Mulholland-Burba-Bautista, Giants	1
Wilson-Dewey-Beck, Giants	1

NO-HIT AND ONE-HIT PITCHERS

The following pitchers (on N.L. rosters) have recorded no-hit or one-hit games in N.L. competition:

NO-HIT GAMES

Tommy Greene, Phi. at Mtl., May 23, 1991.
Darryl Kile, Hou. vs. N.Y., Sept. 8, 1993.
Ramon Martinez, L.A. vs. Fla., July 14, 1995.
Terry Mulholland, Phi. vs. S.F., Aug. 15, 1990.
Fernando Valenzuela, L.A. vs. St.L., June 29, 1990.

ONE-HIT GAMES

Braves: Greg Maddux, Atl. at Hou., May, 28, 1995.

Cubs: Jim Bullinger, Chi. vs. S.F., Aug. 30, 1992.
Frank Castillo, Chi. vs. St.L., Sept. 25, 1995.
Jose Guzman, Chi. vs. Atl., Apr. 6, 1993.

Reds: Tim Pugh, Cin. at S.D., Sept. 29, 1993.
Jose Rijo, Cin. at Col., Sept. 25, 1993.
Pete Schourek, N.Y. vs. Mtl., Sept. 10, 1991.
John Smiley (2), Pit. vs. Mtl., June 3, 1988; Pit. vs. N.Y., Apr. 17, 1991.

Marlins: Pat Rapp, Fla. at Col. Sept. 17, 1995.

Astros: Doug Drabek (2), Pit. at Phil., Aug. 3, 1990; Pit. at St.L., May 27, 1991.

Dodgers: Hideo Nomo, L.A. at S.F., Aug. 5, 1995.

Expos: Kirk Rueter, Mtl. vs. S.F., Aug. 27, 1995.

Mets: Pete Harnisch (2), Hou. at Chi., July 10, 1993; Hou. vs. S.D., Sept. 17, 1993.
Chris Nabholz, Mtl. at N.Y., Sept. 20, 1990.

Phillies: Curt Schilling, Phil. vs. N.Y., Sept. 9, 1992.

Pirates: Paul Wagner, Pit. vs. Col., Aug. 29, 1995.

Cardinals: Andy Benes, S.D. vs. N.Y., July 3, 1994.
Rick Honeycutt, L.A. at S.D., Apr. 27, 1984.

Padres: Bob Tewksbury, St.L. vs. Hou., Aug. 17, 1990.

CLUBS' TOP MARKS SINCE 1900 (Individual Leaders)

BATTING	BRAVES		CUBS		REDS		ROCKIES		MARLINS	
Batting	Rogers Hornsby (1928)	.387	Rogers Hornsby (1929)	.380	Cy Seymour (1905)	.377	Andres Galarraga (1993)	.370	Jeff Conine (1995) / Jeff Conine (1994***)	.302 / .319
Hitting Streak	Tommy Holmes (1945)	37	Jerome Walton (1989)	30	Pete Rose (1978)	44	Dante Bichette (1995)	23	Greg Colbrunn (1995)	17
Home Runs	Eddie Mathews (1953) / Hank Aaron (1971)	47 / 47	Hack Wilson (1930)	56	George Foster (1977)	52	Dante Bichette (1995)	40	Gary Sheffield (1994)	27
Runs Batted In	Eddie Mathews (1953)	135	Hack Wilson (1930)	190	George Foster (1977)	149	Dante Bichette (1995)	128	Jeff Conine (1995)	105
Hits	Tommy Holmes (1945)	224	Rogers Hornsby (1929)	229	Pete Rose (1973)	230	Dante Bichette (1995)	197	Jeff Conine (1993)	174
Runs	Dale Murphy (1983)	131	Rogers Hornsby (1929)	156	Frank Robinson (1962)	134	Dante Bichette (1995)	102	Quilvio Veras (1995)	86
Extra Base Hits	Hank Aaron (1959)	92	Hack Wilson (1930)	97	Frank Robinson (1962)	92	Dante Bichette (1995)	80	Jeff Conine (1993)	53
One Base Hits	Ralph Garr (1971)	180	Earl Adams (1927)	165	Pete Rose (1973)	181	Dante Bichette (1995)	117	Jeff Conine (1993)	135
Two Base Hits	Tommy Holmes (1945)	47	Billy Herman (1935, 1936)	57	Frank Robinson (1962) / Pete Rose (1978)	51 / 51	Charlie Hayes (1993)	45	Terry Pendleton (1995)	32
Three Base Hits	Ray Powell (1921)	18	Frank Schulte (1911) / Victor Saier (1913)	21 / 21	Sam Crawford (1902)	23	Eric Young (1995)	9	Kurt Abbott (1995) / Quilvio Veras (1995)	7 / 7
Total Bases	Hank Aaron (1959)	400	Hack Wilson (1930)	423	George Foster (1977)	388	Dante Bichette (1995)	359	Jeff Conine (1995)	251
Stolen Bases	Otis Nixon (1991)	72	Frank Chance (1903)	67	Bob Bescher (1911)	81	Eric Young (1993)	42	Chuck Carr (1993)	58
At Bats	Ralph Garr (1973)	668	Billy Herman (1935)	666	Pete Rose (1973)	680	Dante Bichette (1995)	579	Jeff Conine (1993)	595
Bases on Balls	Bob Elliott (1948)	131	Jimmy Sheckard (1911)	147	Joe Morgan (1975)	132	Walt Weiss (1995)	98	Quilvio Veras (1995)	80
Strikeouts (most)	Dale Murphy (1978)	145	Byron Browne (1966)	143	Lee May (1969)	142	Andres Galarraga (1995)	146	Jeff Conine (1993)	135
Strikeouts (fewest)*	Stuffy McInnis (1924)	6	Charles Hollocher (1922)	5	Edd Roush (1921)	8	Eric Young (1993)	41	Quilvio Veras (1995)	68
Games	Felix Millan (1969) / Dale Murphy (1982, 1983, 1984, 1985)	162 / 162	Ron Santo (1965) / Billy Williams (1965)	164 / 164	Leo Cardenas (1964) / Pete Rose (1974)	163 / 163	Charlie Hayes (1993)	157	Jeff Conine (1993)	162
Grounded into Double Play (most)	Sid Gordon (1951)	28	Ron Santo (1973)	27	Ernie Lombardi (1938)	30	Charlie Hayes (1993)	25	Orestes Destrade (1993)	17
Grounded into Double Play (fewest)*	David Justice (1992)	1	Augie Galan (1935)	0	Lonnie Frey (1938)	1	Walt Weiss (1994)	6	Walt Weiss (1993) / Chuck Carr (1994)	5 / 5

PITCHING	BRAVES		CUBS		REDS		ROCKIES		MARLINS	
Percentage**	Greg Maddux (1995) 19-2	.905	Rick Sutcliffe (1984) 16-1	.941	Tom Seaver (1981) 14-2	.875	David Nied (1994) 9-7	.563	Pat Rapp (1995) 14-7	.667
Games (Appearances)	Rick Camp (1980)	77	Ted Abernathy (1965) / Dick Tidrow (1980)	84 / 84	Wayne Granger (1969)	90	Curt Leskanic (1995)	76	Yorkis Perez (1995)	69
Complete Games	Vic Willis (1902)	45	John Taylor (1903) / Grover Alexander (1920)	33 / 33	Noodles Hahn (1901)	41	Armando Reynoso (1993)	4	John Burkett (1995)	4
Innings Pitched	Vic Willis (1902)	402	Grover Alexander (1920)	363	Noodles Hahn (1901)	375	Armando Reynoso (1993)	189	Charlie Hough (1993)	204
Games Won	Vic Willis (1902); Chas. Pittinger (1902); Dick Rudolph (1914)	27	Mordecai Brown (1908)	29	Adolfo Luque (1923) / Bucky Walters (1939)	27 / 27	Armando Reynoso (1993)	12	John Burkett (1995) / Pat Rapp (1995)	14 / 14
Games Lost	Vic Willis (1905)	29	Tom Hughes (1901) / Dick Elsworth (1966) / Bill Bonham (1974)	22 / 22 / 22	Paul Derringer (1933)	25	Greg W. Harris (1994)	12	Jack Armstrong (1993)	17
Games Started	Vic Willis (1902)	45	Fergie Jenkins (1969)	42	Noodles Hahn (1901)	42	Armando Reynoso (1993)	30	Charlie Hough (1993)	34
Games Finished	Gene Garber (1982)	56	Randy Myers (1993)	69	Tom Hume (1980)	62	Darren Holmes (1993)	51	Bryan Harvey (1993) / Robb Nen (1995)	54 / 54
Bases on Balls	Phil Niekro (1977)	164	Sam Jones (1955)	185	John VanderMeer (1943)	162	Bruce Ruffin (1993)	69	Ryan Bowen (1993)	87
Strikeouts	Phil Niekro (1977)	262	Fergie Jenkins (1970)	274	Mario Soto (1982)	274	Bruce Ruffin (1993)	126	Charlie Hough (1993) / John Burkett (1995) / Chris Hammond (1995)	126 / 126 / 126
Shutouts	Charles Pittinger (1902) / Irv Young (1905) / Warren Spahn (1947, 1951, 1963)	7 / 7 / 7	Mordecai Brown (1906, 1908) / Orval Overall (1907, 1909) / Grover Alexander (1919) / Bill Lee (1938)	9 / 9 / 9 / 9	Jake Weimer (1906) / Fred Toney (1917) / Hod Eller (1919) / Jack Billingham (1973)	7 / 7 / 7 / 7	David Nied (1994)	1	Chris Hammond (1995) / Pat Rapp (1995)	2 / 2

*Based on 400 or more at bats **Based on 15 or more decisions ***Incomplete season

CLUBS' TOP MARKS SINCE 1900 (Individual Leaders)

BATTING

	ASTROS	DODGERS	EXPOS	METS	PHILLIES
Batting	Derek Bell (1995) .334 / Jeff Bagwell (1994***) .368	Babe Herman (1930) .393	Tim Raines (1986) .334 / Moises Alou (1994***) .339	Cleon Jones (1969) .340	Frank O'Doul (1929) .398
Hitting Streak	Art Howe (1981) 23	Willie Davis (1969) 31	Delino DeShields (1993) 21	Hubie Brooks (1984) 24	Chuck Klein (1930-twice) 26
Home Runs	Jeff Bagwell (1994) 39	Duke Snider (1956) 43	Andre Dawson (1983) 32	Darryl Strawberry (1987, 1988) 39	Mike Schmidt (1980) 48
Runs Batted In	Jeff Bagwell (1994) 116	Tommy Davis (1962) 153	Tim Wallach (1987) 123	Howard Johnson (1991) 117	Chuck Klein (1930) 170
Hits	Enos Cabell (1978) 195	Babe Herman (1930) 241	Al Oliver (1982) 204	Felix Millan (1975) 191	Frank O'Doul (1929) 254
Runs	Craig Biggio (1995) 123	Babe Herman (1930) 143	Tim Raines (1983) 133	Darryl Strawberry (1987) 108 / Howard Johnson (1991) 108	Chuck Klein (1930) 158
Extra Base Hits	Jeff Bagwell (1994) 73	Babe Herman (1930) 94	Andres Galarraga (1988) 79	Howard Johnson (1989) 80	Chuck Klein (1930) 107
One Base Hits	Sonny Jackson (1966) 160	Willie Keeler (1900) 179 / Maury Wills (1964) 179	Tim Raines (1986) 140 / Marquis Grissom (1993) 140	Felix Millan (1973) 155	Frank O'Doul (1929) 181 / Richie Ashburn (1951) 181
Two Base Hits	Rusty Staub (1967) 44 / Craig Biggio (1994) 44	John Frederick (1929) 52	Warren Cromartie (1979) 46	Howard Johnson (1989) 41	Chuck Klein (1930) 59
Three Base Hits	Roger Metzger (1973) 14	Harry "Hi" Myers (1920) 22	Rodney Scott (1980) 13 / Tim Raines (1985) 13 / Mitch Webster (1986) 13	Mookie Wilson (1984) 10	Juan Samuel (1984) 19
Total Bases	Cesar Cedeno (1972) 300 / Jeff Bagwell (1994) 300	Babe Herman (1930) 416	Andre Dawson (1983) 341	Howard Johnson (1989) 319	Chuck Klein (1930) 445
Stolen Bases	Gerald Young (1988) 65	Maury Wills (1962) 104	Ron LeFlore (1980) 97	Mookie Wilson (1982) 58	Juan Samuel (1984) 72
At Bats	Enos Cabell (1978) 660	Maury Wills (1962) 695	Warren Cromartie (1979) 659	Felix Millan (1975) 676	Juan Samuel (1984) 701
Bases on Balls	Jim Wynn (1969) 148	Eddie Stanky (1945) 148	Ken Singleton (1973) 123	Keith Hernandez (1984) 97 / Darryl Strawberry (1987) 97	Lenny Dykstra (1993) 129
Strikeouts (most)	Lee May (1972) 145	Billy Grabarkewitz (1970) 149	Andres Galarraga (1990) 169	Tommie Agee (1970) 156 / Dave Kingman (1982) 156	Mike Schmidt (1975) 180
Strikeouts (fewest)*	Bob Lillis (1965) 10	Ivy Olson (1922) 10	Ron Hunt (1974) 17	Felix Millan (1974) 14	Emil Verban (1947) 8
Games	Enos Cabell (1978) 162 / Bill Doran (1987) 162 / Jeff Bagwell (1992) 162 / Craig Biggio (1992) 162 / Steve Finley (1992) 162	Maury Wills (1962) 165	Rusty Staub (1971) 162 / Ken Singleton (1973) 162 / Warren Cromartie (1980) 162	Felix Millan (1975) 162	Pete Rose (1979) 163
Grounded into Double Play (most)	Doug Rader (1970) 23	Carl Furillo (1956) 27	John Bateman (1971) 27 / Ken Singleton (1973) 27	Cleon Jones (1970) 26	Del Ennis (1950) 25 / Ted Sizemore (1977) 25
Grounded into Double Play (fewest)*	Al Spangler (1962) 1	Brett Butler (1994) 2	Ron Hunt (1971) 1	Lenny Dykstra (1987) 1	Richie Ashburn (1948) 1

PITCHING

	ASTROS	DODGERS	EXPOS	METS	PHILLIES
Percentage**	Mark Portugal (1993) 18-4 .818	Phil Regan (1966) 14-1 .933	Bryn Smith (1985) 18-5 .783	David Cone (1988) 20-3 .870	Robin Roberts (1952) 28-7 .800 / Tommy Greene (1993) 16-4 .800
Games (Appearances)	Juan Agosto (1990) 82	Mike Marshall (1974) 106	Mike Marshall (1973) 92	Jeff Innis (1992) 76	Kent Tekulve (1987) 90
Complete Games	Larry Dierker (1969) 20	Oscar Jones (1904) 38	Bill Stoneman (1971) 20	Tom Seaver (1971) 21	Grover Alexander (1916) 38
Innings Pitched	Larry Dierker (1969) 305	Oscar Jones (1904) 378	Steve Rogers (1977) 302	Tom Seaver (1970) 291	Grover Alexander (1916) 389
Games Won	Joe Niekro (1979) 21	Joe McGinnity (1900) 29	Ross Grimsley (1978) 20	Tom Seaver (1969) 25	Grover Alexander (1916) 33
Games Lost	Dick Farrell (1962) 20	George Bell (1910) 27	Steve Rogers (1974) 22	Roger Craig (1962) 24 / Jack Fisher (1965) 24	Charles Fraser (1904) 24
Games Started	Jerry Reuss (1973) 40	Don Drysdale (1963, 1965) 42	Steve Rogers (1977) 40	Jack Fisher (1965) 36 / Tom Seaver (1970, 1973, 1975) 36	Grover Alexander (1916) 45
Games Finished	Doug Jones (1992) 70	Mike Marshall (1974) 83	Mike Marshall (1973) 73	Jesse Orosco (1984) 52 / Roger McDowell (1986) 52	Jim Konstanty (1950) 62
Bases on Balls	J.R. Richard (1976) 151	Bill Donovan (1901) 151	Bill Stoneman (1971) 146	Nolan Ryan (1971) 116	Earl Moore (1911) 164
Strikeouts	J.R. Richard (1979) 313	Sandy Koufax (1965) 382	Bill Stoneman (1971) 251	Tom Seaver (1971) 289	Steve Carlton (1972) 310
Shutouts	Dave Roberts (1973) 6	Sandy Koufax (1963) 11	Bill Stoneman (1969) 5 / Steve Rogers (1979, 1983) 5 / Dennis Martinez (1991) 5	Dwight Gooden (1985) 8	Grover Alexander (1916) 16

*Based on 400 or more at bats   **Based on 15 or more decisions   ***Incomplete season

(Continued on next page)

CLUBS' TOP MARKS SINCE 1900 (Individual Leaders)

BATTING	PIRATES	CARDINALS	PADRES	GIANTS
Batting	Arky Vaughan (1935) .385	Rogers Hornsby (1924) .424	Tony Gwynn (1987) .370 / Tony Gwynn (1994***) .394	Bill Terry (1930) .401
Hitting Streak	Danny O'Connell (1953) 26	Rogers Hornsby (1922) 33	Benito Santiago (1987) 34	Jack Clark (1978) 26
Home Runs	Ralph Kiner (1949) 54	Johnny Mize (1940) 43	Nate Colbert (1970, 1972) 38	Willie Mays (1965) 52
Runs Batted In	Paul Waner (1927) 131	Joe Medwick (1937) 154	Dave Winfield (1979) 118	Mel Ott (1929) 151
Hits	Paul Waner (1927) 237	Rogers Hornsby (1922) 250	Tony Gwynn (1987) 218	Bill Terry (1930) 254
Runs	Kiki Cuyler (1925) 144	Rogers Hornsby (1922) 141	Tony Gwynn (1987) 119	Bill Terry (1930) 139
Extra Base Hits	Willie Stargell (1973) 90	Stan Musial (1948) 103	Dave Winfield (1979) 71	Willie Mays (1962) 90
One Base Hits	Lloyd Waner (1927) 198	Jesse Burkett (1901) 180	Tony Gwynn (1984) 177	Bill Terry (1930) 177
Two Base Hits	Paul Waner (1932) 62	Joe Medwick (1936) 64	Terry Kennedy (1982) 42	Jack Clark (1978) 46
Three Base Hits	J. Owen Wilson (1912) 36	Tom Long (1915) 25	Tony Gwynn (1987) 13	Larry Doyle (1911) 25
Total Bases	Kiki Cuyler (1925) 366	Rogers Hornsby (1922) 450	Dave Winfield (1979) 333	Bill Terry (1930) 392
Stolen Bases	Omar Moreno (1979) 77	Lou Brock (1974) 118	Alan Wiggins (1984) 70	George Burns (1914) 62
At Bats	Matty Alou (1969) 698	Lou Brock (1967) 689	Steve Garvey (1985) 654	Joe Moore (1935) 681
Bases on Balls	Ralph Kiner (1951) 137	Jack Clark (1987) 136	Jack Clark (1989) 132	Eddie Stanky (1950) 144
Strikeouts (most)	Donn Clendenon (1968) 163	Ray Lankford (1992) 147	Nate Colbert (1970) 150	Bobby Bonds (1970) 189
Strikeouts (fewest)*	Lloyd Waner (1936) 5	Frank Frisch (1927) 10	Tony Gwynn (1995) 15	Don Mueller (1956) 7
Games	Bill Mazeroski (1967) 163 / Bobby Bonilla (1989) 163	Jose Oquendo (1989) 163	Steve Garvey (1985) 162 / Joe Carter (1990) 162	Jose Pagan (1962) 164
Grounded into Double Play (most)	Al Todd (1938) 25	Ted Simmons (1973) 29	Steve Garvey (1984, 1985) 25	Bill Jurges (1939) 26 / Sid Gordan (1943) 26
Grounded into Double Play (fewest)*	Omar Moreno (1981) 1	Ray Lankford (1994) 0	Alan Wiggins (1984) 2	Gus Mancuso (1936) 1
PITCHING				
Percentage**	ElRoy Face (1959) 18-1 .947	Howie Krist (1949) 13-3 .813 / Al Hrabosky (1975) 13-3 .813	Gaylord Perry (1978) 21-6 .778 / Dennis Rasmussen (1988) 14-4 .778	Hoyt Wilhelm (1952) 15-3 .833
Games (Appearances)	Kent Tekulve (1979) 94	Mike Perez (1992) 77	Craig Lefferts (1986) 83	Mike Jackson (1993) 81
Complete Games	Vic Willis (1906) 32	John Taylor (1904) 39	Randy Jones (1976) 25	Joe McGinnity (1903) 44
Innings Pitched	Burleigh Grimes (1928) 331	Grant McGlynn (1907) 352	Randy Jones (1976) 315	Joe McGinnity (1903) 434
Games Won	Jack Chesbro (1902) 28	Dizzy Dean (1934) 30	Randy Jones (1976) 22	Christy Mathewson (1908) 37
Games Lost	Murry Dickson (1952) 21	Grant McGlynn (1907) 25 / Arthur Raymond (1908) 25	Randy Jones (1974) 22	Luther Taylor (1901) 27
Games Started	Bob Friend (1956) 42	John Taylor (1904) 39	Randy Jones (1976) 40	Joe McGinnity (1903) 48
Games Finished	Kent Tekulve (1979) 67	Bruce Sutter (1984) 63	Rollie Fingers (1977) 69	Rod Beck (1993) 71
Bases on Balls	Marty O'Toole (1912) 159	Bob Harmon (1911) 181	Steve Arlin (1972) 122	Jeff Tesreau (1914) 128
Strikeouts	Bob Veale (1965) 276	Bob Gibson (1970) 274	Clay Kirby (1971) 231	Christy Mathewson (1903) 267
Shutouts	Jack Chesbro (1902), Al Leifield (1906), Al Mamaux (1915) & Charles Adams (1920) 8	Bob Gibson (1968) 13	Fred Norman (1972) 6 / Randy Jones (1975) 6	Christy Mathewson (1908) 12

*Based on 400 or more at bats   **Based on 15 or more decisions   ***Incomplete season

NATIONAL LEAGUE WORLD SERIES APPEARANCES

Dodgers (18)
1916, 1920, 1941, 1947, 1949, 1952, 1953, 1955, 1956, 1959, 1963, 1965, 1966, 1974, 1977, 1978, 1981, 1988

Giants (16)
1905, 1911, 1912, 1913, 1917, 1921, 1922, 1923, 1924, 1933, 1936, 1937, 1951, 1954, 1962, 1989

Cardinals (15)
1926, 1928, 1930, 1931, 1934, 1942, 1943, 1944, 1946, 1964, 1967, 1968, 1982, 1985, 1987

Cubs (10)
1906, 1907, 1908, 1910, 1918, 1929, 1932, 1935, 1938, 1945

Reds (9)
1919, 1939, 1940, 1961, 1970, 1972, 1975, 1976, 1990

Braves (7)
1914, 1948, 1957, 1958, 1991, 1992, 1995

Pirates (7)
1903, 1909, 1925, 1927, 1960, 1971, 1979

Phillies (5)
1915, 1950, 1980, 1983, 1993

Mets (3)
1969, 1973, 1986

Padres (1)
1984

HOW THEY FINISHED 1900-1968 INCLUSIVE

Year	Braves Fin.	Braves Won—Lost	Braves Pct.	Cubs Fin.	Cubs Won—Lost	Cubs Pct.	Reds Fin.	Reds Won—Lost	Reds Pct.	Astros Fin.	Astros Won—Lost	Astros Pct.	Dodgers Fin.	Dodgers Won—Lost	Dodgers Pct.	Expos Fin.	Expos Won—Lost	Expos Pct.	Year
1900	4	66— 72	.478	5†	65— 75	.464	7	62— 77	.446				1	82— 54	.603				1900
1901	5	69— 69	.500	6	53— 86	.381	8	52— 87	.374				3	79— 57	.581				1901
1902	3	73— 64	.533	5	68— 69	.496	4	70— 70	.500				2	75— 63	.543				1902
1903	6	58— 80	.420	3	82— 56	.594	4	74— 65	.532				5	70— 66	.515				1903
1904	7	55— 98	.359	2	93— 60	.608	3	88— 65	.575				6	56— 97	.366				1904
1905	7	51—103	.331	3	92— 61	.601	5	79— 74	.516				8	48—104	.316				1905
1906	8	49—102	.325	1	116— 36	.763	6	64— 87	.424				5	66— 86	.434				1906
1907	7	58— 90	.392	1*	107— 45	.704	6	66— 87	.431				5	65— 83	.439				1907
1908	6	63— 91	.409	1*	99— 55	.643	5	73— 81	.474				7	53—101	.344				1908
1909	8	45—108	.294	2	104— 49	.680	4	77— 76	.503				6	55— 98	.359				1909
1910	8	53—100	.346	1	104— 50	.675	5	75— 79	.487				6	64— 90	.416				1910
1911	8	44—107	.291	2	92— 62	.597	6	70— 83	.458				7	64— 86	.427				1911
1912	8	52—101	.340	3	91— 59	.607	4	75— 78	.490				7	58— 95	.379				1912
1913	5	69— 82	.457	3	88— 65	.575	7	64— 89	.418				6	65— 84	.436				1913
1914	1*	94— 59	.614	4	78— 76	.506	8	60— 94	.390				5	75— 79	.487				1914
1915	2	83— 69	.546	4	73— 80	.477	7	71— 83	.461				3	80— 72	.526				1915
1916	3	89— 63	.586	5	67— 86	.438	7†	60— 93	.392				1	94— 60	.610				1916
1917	6	72— 81	.471	5	74— 80	.481	4	78— 76	.506				7	70— 81	.464				1917
1918	7	53— 71	.427	1	84— 45	.651	3	68— 60	.531				5	57— 69	.452				1918
1919	6	57— 82	.410	3	75— 65	.536	1*	96— 44	.686				5	69— 71	.493				1919
1920	7	62— 90	.408	5†	75— 79	.487	3	82— 71	.536				1	93— 61	.604				1920
1921	4	79— 74	.516	7	64— 89	.418	6	70— 83	.458				5	77— 75	.507				1921
1922	8	53—100	.346	5	80— 74	.519	2	86— 68	.558				6	76— 78	.494				1922
1923	7	54—100	.351	4	83— 71	.539	2	91— 63	.591				6	76— 78	.494				1923
1924	8	53—100	.346	5	81— 72	.529	4	83— 70	.542				2	92— 62	.597				1924
1925	5	70— 83	.458	8	68— 86	.442	3	80— 73	.523				6†	68— 85	.444				1925
1926	7	66— 86	.434	4	82— 72	.532	2	87— 67	.565				6	71— 82	.464				1926
1927	7	60— 94	.390	4	85— 68	.556	5	75— 78	.490				6	65— 88	.425				1927
1928	7	50—103	.327	3	91— 63	.591	5	78— 74	.513				6	77— 76	.503				1928
1929	8	56— 98	.364	1	98— 54	.645	7	66— 88	.429				6	70— 83	.458				1929
1930	6	70— 84	.455	2	90— 64	.584	7	59— 95	.383				4	86— 68	.558				1930
1931	7	64— 90	.416	3	84— 70	.545	8	58— 96	.377				4	79— 73	.520				1931
1932	5	77— 77	.500	1	90— 64	.584	8	60— 94	.390				3	81— 73	.526				1932
1933	4	83— 71	.539	3	86— 68	.558	8	58— 94	.382				6	65— 88	.425				1933
1934	4	78— 73	.517	3	86— 65	.570	8	52— 99	.344				6	71— 81	.467				1934
1935	8	38—115	.248	1	100— 54	.649	6	68— 85	.444				5	70— 83	.458				1935
1936	6	71— 83	.461	2†	87— 67	.565	5	74— 80	.481				7	67— 87	.435				1936
1937	5	79— 73	.520	2	93— 61	.604	8	56— 98	.364				6	62— 91	.405				1937
1938	5	77— 75	.507	1	89— 63	.586	4	82— 68	.547				7	69— 80	.463				1938
1939	7	63— 88	.417	4	84— 70	.545	1*	97— 57	.630				3	84— 69	.549				1939
1940	7	65— 87	.428	5	75— 79	.487	1*	100— 53	.654				2	88— 65	.575				1940
1941	7	62— 92	.403	6	70— 84	.455	3	88— 66	.571				1	100— 54	.649				1941
1942	7	59— 89	.399	6	68— 86	.442	4	76— 76	.500				2	104— 50	.675				1942
1943	6	68— 85	.444	5	74— 79	.484	2	87— 67	.565				3	81— 72	.529				1943
1944	6	65— 89	.422	4	75— 79	.487	3	89— 65	.578				7	63— 91	.409				1944
1945	6	67— 85	.441	1	98— 56	.636	7	61— 93	.396				3	87— 67	.565				1945
1946	4	81— 72	.529	3	82— 71	.536	6	67— 87	.435				2**	96— 60	.615				1946
1947	3	86— 68	.558	6	69— 85	.448	5	73— 81	.474				1	94— 60	.610				1947
1948	1	91— 62	.595	8	64— 90	.416	7	64— 89	.418				3	84— 70	.545				1948
1949	4	75— 79	.487	8	61— 93	.396	7	62— 92	.403				1	97— 57	.630				1949
1950	4	83— 71	.539	7	64— 89	.418	6	66— 87	.431				2	89— 65	.578				1950
1951	4	76— 78	.494	8	62— 92	.403	6	68— 86	.442				2**	97— 60	.618				1951
1952	7	64— 89	.418	5	77— 77	.500	6	69— 85	.448				1	96— 57	.627				1952
1953	2	92— 62	.597	7	65— 89	.422	6	68— 86	.442				1	105— 49	.682				1953
1954	3	89— 65	.578	7	64— 90	.416	5	74— 80	.481				2	92— 62	.597				1954
1955	2	85— 69	.552	6	72— 81	.471	5	75— 79	.487				1*	98— 55	.641				1955
1956	2	92— 62	.597	8	60— 94	.390	3	91— 63	.591				1	93— 61	.604				1956
1957	1*	95— 59	.617	7†	62— 92	.403	4	80— 74	.519				3	84— 70	.545				1957
1958	1	92— 62	.597	5†	72— 82	.468	4	76— 78	.494				7	71— 83	.461				1958
1959	2**	86— 70	.551	5†	74— 80	.481	5†	74— 80	.481				1†*	88— 68	.564				1959
1960	2	88— 66	.571	7	60— 94	.390	6	67— 87	.435				4	82— 72	.532				1960
1961	4	83— 71	.539	7	64— 90	.416	1	93— 61	.604				2	89— 65	.578				1961
1962	5	86— 76	.531	9	59—103	.364	3	98— 64	.605	8	64— 96	.400	2**	102— 63	.618				1962
1963	6	84— 78	.519	7	82— 80	.506	5	86— 76	.531	9	66— 96	.407	1*	99— 63	.611				1963
1964	5	88— 74	.543	8	76— 86	.469	2†	92— 70	.568	9	66— 96	.407	6†	80— 82	.494				1964
1965	5	86— 76	.531	8	72— 90	.444	4	89— 73	.549	9	65— 97	.401	1	97— 65	.599				1965
1966	5	85— 77	.525	10	59—103	.364	7	76— 84	.475	8	72— 90	.444	1	95— 67	.586				1966
1967	7	77— 85	.475	3	87— 74	.540	4	87— 75	.537	9	69— 93	.426	8	73— 89	.451				1967
1968	5	81— 81	.500	3	84— 78	.519	4	83— 79	.512	10	72— 90	.444	7†	76— 86	.469				1968

ASTROS: JOINED LEAGUE AS ACTIVE PARTICIPANT IN 1962

EXPOS: JOINED LEAGUE AS ACTIVE PARTICIPANT IN 1969

HOW THEY FINISHED 1900-1968 INCLUSIVE

Year	METS Fin.	Won—Lost	Pct.	PHILLIES Fin.	Won—Lost	Pct.	PIRATES Fin.	Won—Lost	Pct.	CARDINALS Fin.	Won—Lost	Pct.	PADRES Fin.	Won—Lost	Pct.	GIANTS§ Fin.	Won—Lost	Pct.	Year
1900				3	75— 63	.543	2	79— 60	.568	5†	65— 75	.464				8	60— 78	.435	1900
1901				2	83— 57	.593	1	90— 49	.647	4	76— 64	.543				7	52— 85	.380	1901
1902				7	56— 81	.409	1	103— 36	.741	6	56— 78	.418				8	48— 88	.353	1902
1903				7	49— 86	.363	1	91— 49	.650	8	43— 94	.314				2	84— 55	.604	1903
1904				8	52—100	.342	4	87— 66	.569	5	75— 79	.487				1	106— 47	.693	1904
1905				4	83— 69	.546	2	96— 57	.627	6	58— 96	.377				1*	105— 48	.686	1905
1906				4	71— 82	.464	3	93— 60	.608	7	52— 98	.347				2	96— 56	.632	1906
1907				3	83— 64	.565	2	91— 63	.591	8	52—101	.340				4	82— 71	.536	1907
1908				4	83— 71	.539	2†	98— 56	.636	8	49—105	.318				2†	98— 56	.636	1908
1909				5	74— 79	.484	1*	110— 42	.724	7	54— 98	.355				3	92— 61	.601	1909
1910				4	78— 75	.510	3	86— 57	.562	7	63— 90	.412				2	91— 63	.591	1910
1911				4	79— 73	.520	3	85— 69	.552	5	75— 74	.503				1	99— 54	.647	1911
1912				5	73— 79	.480	2	93— 58	.616	6	63— 90	.412				1	103— 48	.682	1912
1913				2	88— 63	.583	4	78— 71	.523	8	51— 99	.340				1	101— 51	.664	1913
1914				6	74— 80	.481	7	69— 85	.448	3	81— 72	.529				2	84— 70	.545	1914
1915				1	90— 62	.592	5	73— 81	.474	6	72— 81	.471				8	69— 83	.454	1915
1916				2	91— 62	.595	6	65— 89	.422	7†	60— 93	.392				4	86— 66	.566	1916
1917				2	87— 65	.572	8	51—103	.331	3	82— 70	.539				1	98— 56	.636	1917
1918				6	55— 68	.447	4	65— 60	.520	8	51— 78	.395				2	71— 53	.573	1918
1919				8	47— 90	.343	4	71— 68	.511	7	54— 83	.394				2	87— 53	.621	1919
1920				8	62— 91	.405	4	79— 75	.513	5†	75— 79	.487				2	86— 68	.558	1920
1921				8	51—103	.331	2	90— 63	.588	3	87— 66	.569				1*	94— 59	.614	1921
1922				7	57— 96	.373	3†	85— 69	.552	3†	85— 69	.552				1*	93— 61	.604	1922
1923				8	50—104	.325	3	87— 67	.565	5	79— 74	.516				1	95— 58	.621	1923
1924				7	55— 96	.364	3	90— 63	.588	6	65— 89	.422				1	93— 60	.608	1924
1925				6†	68— 85	.444	1*	95— 58	.621	4	77— 76	.503				2	86— 66	.566	1925
1926				8	58— 93	.384	3	84— 69	.549	1*	89— 65	.578				5	74— 77	.490	1926
1927				8	51—103	.331	1	94— 60	.610	2	92— 61	.601				3	92— 62	.597	1927
1928				8	43—109	.283	4	85— 67	.559	1	95— 59	.617				2	93— 61	.604	1928
1929				5	71— 82	.464	2	88— 65	.575	4	78— 74	.513				3	84— 67	.556	1929
1930				8	52—102	.338	5	80— 74	.519	1	92— 62	.597				3	87— 67	.565	1930
1931				6	66— 88	.429	5	75— 79	.487	1*	101— 53	.656				2	87— 65	.572	1931
1932				4	78— 76	.506	2	86— 68	.558	6†	72— 82	.468				6†	72— 82	.468	1932
1933				7	60— 92	.395	2	87— 67	.565	5	82— 71	.536				1*	91— 61	.599	1933
1934				7	56— 93	.376	5	74— 76	.493	1*	95— 58	.621				2	93— 60	.608	1934
1935				7	64— 89	.418	4	86— 67	.562	2	96— 58	.623				3	91— 62	.595	1935
1936				8	54—100	.351	4	84— 70	.545	2†	87— 67	.565				1	92— 62	.597	1936
1937				7	61— 92	.399	3	86— 68	.558	4	81— 73	.526				1	95— 57	.625	1937
1938				8	45—105	.300	2	86— 64	.573	6	71— 80	.470				3	83— 67	.553	1938
1939				8	45—106	.298	6	68— 85	.444	2	92— 61	.601				5	77— 74	.510	1939
1940				8	50—103	.327	4	78— 76	.506	3	84— 69	.549				6	72— 80	.474	1940
1941				8	43—111	.279	4	81— 73	.526	2	97— 56	.634				5	74— 79	.484	1941
1942				8	42—109	.278	5	66— 81	.449	1*	106— 48	.688				3	85— 67	.559	1942
1943				7	64— 90	.416	4	80— 74	.519	1	105— 49	.682				8	55— 98	.359	1943
1944				8	61— 92	.399	2	90— 63	.588	1*	105— 49	.682				5	67— 87	.435	1944
1945				8	46—108	.299	4	82— 72	.532	2	95— 59	.617				5	78— 74	.513	1945
1946				5	69— 85	.448	7	63— 91	.409	1‡*	98— 58	.628				8	61— 93	.396	1946
1947				7†	62— 92	.403	7	62— 92	.403	2	89— 65	.578				4	81— 73	.526	1947
1948				6	66— 88	.429	2	83— 71	.539	2	85— 69	.552				5	78— 76	.506	1948
1949				3	81— 73	.526	6	71— 83	.461	2	96— 58	.623				5	73— 81	.474	1949
1950				1	91— 63	.591	8	57— 96	.373	5	78— 75	.510				3	86— 68	.558	1950
1951				5	73— 81	.474	7	64— 90	.416	3	81— 73	.526				1‡	98— 59	.624	1951
1952				4	87— 67	.565	8	42—112	.273	3	88— 66	.571				2	92— 62	.597	1952
1953				3†	83— 71	.539	8	50—104	.325	3†	83— 71	.539				5	70— 84	.455	1953
1954				4	75— 79	.487	8	53—101	.344	6	72— 82	.468				1*	97— 57	.630	1954
1955				4	77— 77	.500	8	60— 94	.390	7	68— 86	.442				3	80— 74	.519	1955
1956				5	71— 83	.461	7	66— 88	.429	4	76— 78	.494				6	67— 87	.435	1956
1957				5	77— 77	.500	7†	62— 92	.403	2	87— 67	.565				6	69— 85	.448	1957
1958				8	69— 85	.448	2	84— 70	.545	5†	72— 82	.468				3	80— 74	.519	1958
1959				8	64— 90	.416	4	78— 76	.506	7	71— 83	.461				3	83— 71	.539	1959
1960				8	59— 95	.383	1*	95— 59	.617	3	86— 68	.558				5	79— 75	.513	1960
1961				8	47—107	.305	6	75— 79	.487	5	80— 74	.519				3	85— 69	.552	1961
1962	10	40—120	.250	7	81— 80	.503	4	93— 68	.578	6	84— 78	.519				1‡	103— 62	.624	1962
1963	10	51—111	.315	4	87— 75	.537	8	74— 88	.457	2	93— 69	.574				3	88— 74	.543	1963
1964	10	53—109	.327	2†	92— 70	.568	6†	80— 82	.494	1*	93— 69	.574				4	90— 72	.556	1964
1965	10	50—112	.309	6	85— 76	.528	3	90— 72	.556	7	80— 81	.497				2	95— 67	.586	1965
1966	9	66— 95	.410	4	87— 75	.537	3	92— 70	.568	6	83— 79	.512				2	93— 68	.578	1966
1967	10	61—101	.377	5	82— 80	.506	6	81— 81	.500	1*	101— 60	.627				2	91— 71	.562	1967
1968	9	73— 89	.451	7†	76— 86	.469	6	80— 82	.494	1	97— 65	.599				2	88— 74	.543	1968

METS: JOINED LEAGUE AS ACTIVE PARTICIPANT IN 1962

PADRES: JOINED LEAGUE AS ACTIVE PARTICIPANT IN 1969

81

HOW THEY FINISHED 1969-1995 INCLUSIVE

Year	BRAVES* Fin.	Won—Lost	Pct.	CUBS Fin.	Won—Lost	Pct.	REDS Fin.	Won—Lost	Pct.	ROCKIES Fin.	Won—Lost	Pct.	MARLINS Fin.	Won—Lost	Pct.	ASTROS Fin.	Won—Lost	Pct.	DODGERS# Fin.	Won—Lost	Pct.	Year
1969	1W	93— 69	.574	2E	92— 70	.568	3W	89— 73	.549							5W	81— 81	.500	4W	85— 77	.525	1969
1970	5W	76— 86	.469	2E	84— 78	.519	1W	102— 60	.630							4W	79— 83	.540	2W	87— 74	.540	1970
1971	3W	82— 80	.506	3E†	83— 79	.512	4W†	79— 83	.488							4W†	79— 83	.488	2W	89— 73	.549	1971
1972	4W	70— 84	.455	2E	85— 70	.548	1W	95— 59	.617							2W	84— 69	.549	3W	85— 70	.548	1972
1973	5W	76— 85	.472	5E	77— 84	.478	1W	99— 63	.611							4W	82— 80	.506	2W	95— 66	.590	1973
1974	3W	88— 74	.543	6E	66— 96	.407	2W	98— 64	.605							4W	81— 81	.500	1W	102— 60	.630	1974
1975	5W	67— 94	.416	5E†	75— 87	.463	1W*	108— 54	.667							6W	64— 97	.398	2W	88— 74	.543	1975
1976	6W	70— 92	.432	4E	75— 87	.463	1W*	102— 60	.630							3W	80— 82	.494	2W	92— 70	.568	1976
1977	6W	61—101	.377	4E	81— 81	.500	2W	88— 74	.543							3W	81— 81	.500	1W	98— 64	.605	1977
1978	6W	69— 93	.426	3E	79— 83	.488	2W	92— 69	.571							5W	74— 88	.457	1W	95— 67	.586	1978
1979	6W	66— 94	.413	5E	80— 82	.494	1W	90— 71	.559							2W	89— 73	.549	3W	79— 83	.488	1979
1980	4W	81— 80	.503	6E	64— 98	.395	3W	89— 73	.549							1‡	93— 70	.571	2W**	92— 71	.564	1980
1981 (1H)	4W	25— 29	.463	6E	15— 37	.288	2W	35— 21	.625							3W	28— 29	.491	1W*	36— 21	.632	(1H) 1981
1981 (2H)	5W	25— 27	.481	5E	23— 28	.451	2W	31— 21	.596							1W	33— 20	.623	4W	27— 26	.509	(2H) 1981
1982	1W	89— 73	.549	5E	73— 89	.451	6W	61—101	.377							5W	77— 85	.475	2W	88— 74	.543	1982
1983	2W	88— 74	.543	5E	71— 91	.438	6W	74— 88	.457							3W	85— 77	.525	1W	91— 71	.562	1983
1984	2W†	80— 82	.494	1E	96— 65	.596	5W	70— 92	.432							2W†	80— 82	.494	4W	79— 83	.488	1984
1985	5W	66— 96	.407	4E	77— 84	.478	2W	89— 72	.553							3W†	83— 79	.512	1W	95— 67	.586	1985
1986	6W	72— 89	.447	5E	70— 90	.438	2W	86— 76	.531							1W	96— 66	.593	5W	73— 89	.451	1986
1987	5W	69— 92	.429	6E	76— 85	.472	2W	84— 78	.519							3W	76— 86	.469	4W	73— 89	.451	1987
1988	6W	54—106	.338	4E	77— 85	.475	2W	87— 74	.540							5W	82— 80	.506	1W*	94— 67	.584	1988
1989	6W	63— 97	.394	1E	93— 69	.574	5W	75— 87	.463							3W	86— 76	.531	4W	77— 83	.481	1989
1990	6W	65— 97	.401	4E†	77— 85	.475	1W*	91— 71	.562							4W†	75— 87	.463	2W	86— 76	.531	1990
1991	1W	94— 68	.580	4E	77— 83	.481	5W	74— 88	.457							6W	65— 97	.401	2W	93— 69	.574	1991
1992	1W	98— 64	.605	4E	78— 84	.481	2W	90— 72	.556							4W	81— 81	.500	6W	63— 99	.389	1992
1993	1W	104— 58	.642	4E	84— 78	.519	5W	73— 89	.451	6W	67— 95	.414	6E	64— 98	.395	3W	85— 77	.525	4W	81— 81	.500	1993
1994	2E	68— 46	.596	5C	49— 64	.434	1C	66— 48	.579	3W	53— 64	.453	5E	51— 64	.443	2C	66— 49	.574	1W	58— 56	.509	1994
1995	1E*	90— 54	.625	3C	73— 71	.507	1C	85— 59	.590	2W	77— 67	.535	4E	67— 76	.469	2C	76— 68	.528	1W	78— 66	.542	1995
Total		6936—7812	.470		7502—7283	.507		7465—7325	.505		197—226	.466		182—238	.433		2615—2765	.486		7723—7051	.523	

*Boston, 1990-1952, Incl.   Milwaukee, 1953-65, Incl.   *World Champions   †Tie for Place   **Lost Playoff   #Brooklyn, 1900-1957, Incl.   (E) East   (C) Central   (W) West

AVERAGE TIME OF 9-INNING GAMES, 1995

	AT ATL	AT CHI	AT CIN	AT COL	AT FLA	AT HOU	AT LA	AT MON	AT NY	AT PHI	AT PIT	AT STL	AT SD	AT SF	AVG. GAMES
Atlanta	---	2:38	2:39	2:39	2:55	2:48	2:48	2:44	2:41	2:34	2:34	2:29	2:34	2:19	2:40
Chicago	2:40	---	2:42	2:55	2:42	3:06	2:43	2:49	2:48	2:46	2:55	2:47	2:45	2:29	2:47
Cincinnati	2:39	2:50	---	2:45	2:34	2:43	2:22	2:49	2:43	2:50	2:51	2:44	2:53	2:58	2:45
Colorado	2:36	2:42	2:42	---	2:46	2:45	2:40	2:47	2:48	2:35	2:39	2:45	2:36	2:37	2:41
Florida	2:43	2:47	2:35	2:45	---	3:01	2:34	2:52	2:38	2:34	2:41	2:25	---	2:51	2:42
Houston	2:38	3:22	2:55	3:00	2:55	---	3:04	3:03	2:49	2:56	2:50	2:52	2:47	3:22	2:56
Los Angeles	2:30	2:56	2:40	3:13	3:01	2:39	---	2:45	2:47	2:44	2:49	2:39	2:44	2:49	2:48
Montreal	2:22	2:44	2:47	2:38	2:48	2:49	2:59	---	2:46	2:52	2:48	2:25	2:46	2:51	2:46
New York	2:30	2:56	2:47	2:55	2:38	2:39	2:57	2:46	---	2:50	2:36	2:50	2:34	2:50	2:45
Philadelphia	2:48	2:42	2:35	2:43	2:41	2:59	2:38	2:45	2:45	---	2:40	2:49	2:38	2:42	2:44
Pittsburgh	2:25	2:51	2:51	2:51	2:42	2:49	2:55	2:20	2:33	2:40	---	2:28	2:39	2:39	2:42
St. Louis	2:33	2:49	2:39	2:49	2:23	2:32	2:48	2:41	3:00	2:35	2:36	---	2:33	2:39	2:40
San Diego	2:45	2:50	2:47	3:05	2:39	2:41	3:00	2:41	2:35	2:40	2:38	2:23	---	2:38	2:43
San Francisco	2:37	2:49	3:13	3:01	2:33	3:00	2:51	2:39	2:43	2:45	2:52	2:33	2:51	---	2:48
Avg. Home Games	2:36	2:50	2:45	2:53	2:44	2:49	2:48	2:45	2:43	2:44	2:44	2:38	2:42	2:43	2:45
Avg. Home & Road	2:38	2:48	2:45	2:47	2:43	2:52	2:48	2:46	2:44	2:44	2:43	2:39	2:43	2:46	2:45

NATIONAL LEAGUE RECORDS

FIRST PLACE
Most—17, New York (1888-89, 1904-05, 1911-13, 1917, 1921-24, 1933, 1936-37, 1951, 1954)
Consecutive—4, New York (1921-24)
Earliest Date to Clinch—September 7, Cincinnati 1975
Days in First Place
  Most—181, Philadelphia 1993
  Fewest—3, New York 1951 (before playoff)

LAST PLACE
Most—25, Philadelphia (1883, 1904, 1919-21, 1923, 1926-28, 1930, 1936, 1938-42, 1944-45, 1947, 1958-61, 1972, 1992)
Consecutive—5, Philadelphia (1938-42)

PLAYOFF WINNERS
1 Game—Houston (Los Angeles) 1980
2 Games—St. Louis (Brooklyn) 1946
        Los Angeles (Milwaukee) 1959
3 Games—New York (Brooklyn) 1951
        San Francisco (Los Angeles) 1962

HOW THEY FINISHED 1969-1995 INCLUSIVE

Year	EXPOS Fin.	Won—Lost	Pct.	METS Fin.	Won—Lost	Pct.	PHILLIES Fin.	Won—Lost	Pct.	PIRATES Fin.	Won—Lost	Pct.	CARDINALS Fin.	Won—Lost	Pct.	PADRES Fin.	Won—Lost	Pct.	GIANTS§ Fin.	Won—Lost	Pct.	Year
1969	6E	52—110	.321	1E*	100— 62	.617	5E	63— 99	.389	3E	88— 74	.543	4E	87— 75	.537	6W	52—110	.321	2W	90— 72	.556	1969
1970	6E	73— 89	.451	3E†	83— 79	.512	5E	73— 88	.453	1E	89— 73	.549	4E	76— 86	.469	6W	63— 99	.389	3W	86— 76	.531	1970
1971	5E	71— 90	.441	3E†	83— 79	.512	6E	67— 95	.414	1E*	97— 65	.599	2E	90— 72	.556	6W	61—100	.379	1W	90— 72	.556	1971
1972	5E	70— 86	.449	3E	83— 73	.532	6E	59— 97	.378	1E	96— 59	.619	4E	75— 81	.481	6W	58— 95	.379	5W	69— 86	.445	1972
1973	4E	79— 83	.488	1E	82— 79	.509	6E	71— 91	.438	3E	80— 82	.494	2E	81— 81	.500	6W	60—102	.370	3W	88— 74	.543	1973
1974	4E	79— 82	.491	5E	71— 91	.438	3E	80— 82	.494	1E	88— 74	.543	2E	86— 75	.534	6W	60—102	.370	5W	72— 90	.444	1974
1975	5E†	75— 87	.463	3E†	82— 80	.506	2E	86— 76	.531	1E	92— 69	.571	3E†	82— 80	.506	4W	71— 91	.438	3W	80— 81	.497	1975
1976	6E	55—107	.340	3E	86— 76	.531	1E	101— 61	.623	2E	92— 70	.568	5E	72— 90	.444	5W	73— 89	.451	4W	74— 88	.457	1976
1977	5E	75— 87	.463	6E	64— 98	.395	1E	101— 61	.623	2E	96— 66	.593	3E	83— 79	.512	5W	69— 93	.426	4W	75— 87	.463	1977
1978	4E	76— 86	.469	6E	66— 96	.407	1E	90— 72	.556	2E	88— 73	.547	5E	69— 93	.426	4W	84— 78	.519	3W	89— 73	.549	1978
1979	2E	95— 65	.594	6E	63— 99	.389	4E	84— 78	.519	1E*	98— 64	.605	3E	86— 76	.531	5W	68— 93	.422	4W	71— 91	.438	1979
1980	2E	90— 72	.556	5E	67— 95	.414	1E*	91— 71	.562	3E	83— 79	.512	4E	74— 88	.457	6W	73— 89	.451	5W	75— 86	.466	1980
1981 (1H)	3E	30— 25	.545	5E	17— 34	.333	1E	34— 21	.618	4E	25— 23	.521	2E	30— 20	.600	6W	23— 33	.411	5W	27— 32	.458	(1H) 1981
1981 (2H)	1E	30— 23	.566	4E	24— 28	.462	3E	25— 27	.481	6E	21— 33	.389	2E	29— 23	.558	6W	18— 36	.333	3W	29— 23	.558	(2H) 1981
1982	3E	86— 76	.531	6E	65— 97	.401	2E	89— 73	.549	4E	84— 78	.519	1E*	92— 70	.568	4W	81— 81	.500	3W	87— 75	.537	1982
1983	3E	82— 80	.506	6E	68— 94	.420	1E	90— 72	.556	2E	84— 78	.519	4E	79— 83	.488	4W	81— 81	.500	5W	79— 83	.488	1983
1984	5E	78— 83	.484	2E	90— 72	.556	4E	81— 81	.500	6E	75— 87	.463	3E	84— 78	.519	1W	92— 70	.568	6W	66— 96	.407	1984
1985	3E	84— 77	.522	2E	98— 64	.605	5E	75— 87	.463	6E	57—104	.354	1E	101— 61	.623	3W†	83— 79	.512	6W	62—100	.383	1985
1986	4E	78— 83	.484	1E*	108— 54	.667	2E	86— 75	.534	6E	64— 98	.395	3E	79— 82	.491	4W	74— 88	.457	3W	83— 79	.512	1986
1987	3E	91— 71	.562	2E	92— 70	.568	4E†	80— 82	.494	4E†	80— 82	.494	1E	95— 67	.586	6W	65— 97	.401	1W	90— 72	.556	1987
1988	3E	81— 81	.500	1E	100— 60	.625	6E	65— 96	.404	2E	85— 75	.531	5E	76— 86	.469	3W	83— 78	.516	4W	83— 79	.512	1988
1989	4E	81— 81	.500	2E	87— 75	.537	6E	67— 95	.414	5E	74— 88	.457	3E	86— 76	.531	2W	89— 73	.549	1W	92— 70	.568	1989
1990	3E	85— 77	.525	2E	91— 71	.562	4E†	77— 85	.475	1E	95— 67	.586	6E	70— 92	.432	4W†	75— 87	.463	3W	85— 77	.525	1990
1991	6E	71— 90	.441	5E	77— 84	.478	3E	78— 84	.481	1E	98— 64	.605	2E	84— 78	.519	3W	84— 78	.519	4W	75— 87	.463	1991
1992	2E	87— 75	.537	5E	72— 90	.444	6E	70— 92	.432	1E	96— 66	.593	3E	83— 79	.512	3W	82— 80	.506	5W	72— 90	.444	1992
1993	2E	94— 68	.580	7E	59—103	.364	1E	97— 65	.599	5E	75— 87	.463	3E	87— 75	.537	7W	61—101	.377	2W	103— 59	.636	1993
1994	1E	74— 40	.649	3E	55— 58	.487	4E	54— 61	.470	3C†	53— 61	.465	3C†	53— 61	.465	4W	47— 70	.402	2W	55— 60	.478	1994
1995	5E	66— 78	.458	2E†	69— 75	.479	2E†	69— 75	.479	5C	58— 86	.403	4C	62— 81	.434	3W	70— 74	.486	4W	67— 77	.465	1995
Total		2088—2152	.492		2496—2873	.465		6768—7984	.459		7706—7068	.522		7607—7169	.515		1900—2347	.447		7942—6834	.537	

*World Champions †Tie for Place ‡Won Playoff §New York, 1900-1957, Incl. (E) East (C) Central (W) West

INTER-CLUB TOTALS 1900 TO 1995, INCLUSIVE

	Giants W-L	Dodgers W-L	Pirates W-L	Cards W-L	Cubs W-L	Reds W-L	Expos W-L	Astros W-L	Braves W-L	Rockies W-L	Mets W-L	Phillies W-L	Padres W-L	Marlins W-L	W	L	Pct.
N.Y.-San Francisco	—	980- 955	961- 828	920- 858	935- 859	1062- 862	167- 153	296-290	1053-857	22- 14	245-200	1042-735	244-212	15-11	7942	6834	.537
Brk.-Los Angeles	955- 980	—	923- 860	889- 894	887- 897	976- 952	181-138	322-258	1054-861	21- 15	249-194	1000-779	249-212	17-11	7723	7051	.523
Pittsburgh	828- 961	860- 923	—	1016- 914	1023- 912	918- 870	243-214	253-191	976-799	11- 18	311-263	1057-864	189-127	21-12	7706	7068	.522
St. Louis	858- 920	894- 889	914-1016	—	936- 990	947- 840	228-229	235-210	975-812	18- 18	310-268	1093-830	180-136	19-11	7607	7169	.515
Chicago	859- 935	897- 887	912-1023	990- 936	—	907- 880	213-234	208-238	985-798	20- 17	290-286	1021-900	182-153	18-16	7502	7283	.507
Cincinnati	862-1062	952- 976	870- 918	840- 947	880- 907	—	171-144	323-264	1028-900	18- 15	251-189	990-790	260-197	20-16	7465	7325	.505
Montreal	153- 167	138- 181	214- 243	229- 228	234- 213	144- 171	—	140-173	169-148	12- 14	228-231	228-230	177-140	22-13	2088	2152	.492
Houston	290- 296	258- 322	191- 253	210- 235	238- 208	264- 323	173-140	—	273-306	11-20	246-193	202-240	242-216	17-13	2615	2765	.486
Bos.-Mil.-Atlanta	857-1053	861-1054	799- 976	812- 975	798- 985	900-1028	148-169	306-273	—	30- 6	233-209	917-867	250-205	25-12	6936	7812	.470
Colorado	14- 22	15- 21	18- 11	18- 18	17- 20	15- 18	14- 12	20- 11	6- 30	—	16- 11	9- 15	20- 16	15-21	197	226	.466
New York	200- 245	194- 249	263- 311	268- 310	286- 290	189- 251	231-228	193-246	209-233	11-16	—	267-323	166-154	19-17	2496	2873	.465
Philadelphia	735-1042	779-1000	864-1057	830-1093	900-1021	790- 990	230-228	240-202	867-917	15- 9	323-267	—	173-144	22-14	6768	7984	.459
San Diego	212- 244	212- 249	127- 189	136- 180	133- 182	197- 260	140-177	216-242	205-250	16-20	154-166	144-173	—	8-15	1900	2347	.447
Florida	11- 15	11- 17	12- 21	11- 19	16- 18	16- 20	13- 22	13- 17	12- 25	21-15	17- 19	14- 22	15- 8	—	182	238	.433

NATIONAL LEAGUE CLUB RECORDS SINCE DIVISIONAL PLAY (1969-1995)

EAST DIVISION

CLUB	TOTAL GAMES	W	L	Pct.
New York	4238	2102	2136	.496
Philadelphia	4245	2103	2142	.495
Montreal	4240	2088	2152	.492
Atlanta	4233	2049	2184	.484
Florida	420	182	238	.433

CENTRAL DIVISION

CLUB	TOTAL GAMES	W	L	Pct.
Cincinnati	4242	2302	1940	.543
Pittsburgh	4240	2211	2029	.521
St. Louis	4239	2151	2088	.507
Houston	4248	2141	2107	.504
Chicago	4233	2050	2183	.484

WEST DIVISION

CLUB	TOTAL GAMES	W	L	Pct.
Los Angeles	4245	2279	1966	.537
San Francisco	4249	2114	2135	.498
Colorado	423	191	232	.452
San Diego	4247	1900	2347	.447

IN LEADERS 1920-1995

Year	Player	RBI
	...sby, St. Louis	94
	...Kelly, New York	94
	...gers Hornsby, St. Louis	126
	Rogers Hornsby, St. Louis	155
1923	Emil Meusel, New York	125
1924	George Kelly, New York	136
1925	Rogers Hornsby, St. Louis	143
1926	Jim Bottomley, St. Louis	120
1927	Paul Waner, Pittsburgh	131
1928	Jim Bottomley, St. Louis	136
1929	Hack Wilson, Chicago	159
1930	Hack Wilson, Chicago	190
1931	Chuck Klein, Philadelphia	121
1932	Frank Hurst, Philadelphia	143
1933	Chuck Klein, Philadelphia	120
1934	Mel Ott, New York	135
1935	Wally Berger, Boston	130
1936	Joe Medwick, St. Louis	138
1937	Joe Medwick, St. Louis	154
1938	Joe Medwick, St. Louis	122
1939	Frank McCormick, Cincinnati	128
1940	Johnny Mize, St. Louis	137
1941	Dolf Camilli, Brooklyn	120
1942	Johnny Mize, New York	110
1943	Bill Nicholson, Chicago	128
1944	Bill Nicholson, Chicago	122
1945	Dixie Walker, Brooklyn	124
1946	Enos Slaughter, St. Louis	130
1947	Johnny Mize, New York	138
1948	Stan Musial, St. Louis	131
1949	Ralph Kiner, Pittsburgh	127
1950	Del Ennis, Philadelphia	126
1951	Monte Irvin, New York	121
1952	Hank Sauer, Chicago	121
1953	Roy Campanella, Brooklyn	142
1954	Ted Kluszewski, Cincinnati	141
1955	Duke Snider, Brooklyn	136
1956	Stan Musial, St. Louis	109
1957	Hank Aaron, Milwaukee	132
1958	Ernie Banks, Chicago	129
1959	Ernie Banks, Chicago	143
1960	Hank Aaron, Milwaukee	126
1961	Orlando Cepeda, San Francisco	142
1962	Tommy Davis, Los Angeles	153
1963	Hank Aaron, Milwaukee	130
1964	Ken Boyer, St. Louis	119
1965	Deron Johnson, Cincinnati	130
1966	Hank Aaron, Atlanta	127
1967	Orlando Cepeda, St. Louis	111
1968	Willie McCovey, San Francisco	105
1969	Willie McCovey, San Francisco	126
1970	Johnny Bench, Cincinnati	148
1971	Joe Torre, St. Louis	137
1972	Johnny Bench, Cincinnati	125
1973	Willie Stargell, Pittsburgh	119
1974	Johnny Bench, Cincinnati	129
1975	Greg Luzinski, Philadelphia	120
1976	George Foster, Cincinnati	121
1977	George Foster, Cincinnati	149
1978	George Foster, Cincinnati	120
1979	Dave Winfield, San Diego	118
1980	Mike Schmidt, Philadelphia	121
1981	Mike Schmidt, Philadelphia	91
1982	Dale Murphy, Atlanta	109
	Al Oliver, Montreal	109
1983	Dale Murphy, Atlanta	121
1984	Gary Carter, Montreal	106
	Mike Schmidt, Philadelphia	106
1985	Dave Parker, Cincinnati	125
1986	Mike Schmidt, Philadelphia	119
1987	Andre Dawson, Chicago	137
1988	Will Clark, San Francisco	109
1989	Kevin Mitchell, San Francisco	125
1990	Matt Williams, San Francisco	122
1991	Howard Johnson, New York	117
1992	Darren Daulton, Philadelphia	109
1993	Barry Bonds, San Francisco	123
1994	Jeff Bagwell, Houston	116
1995	Dante Bichette, Colorado	128

MVP

BARRY LARKIN
CINCINNATI REDS

Barry Larkin of the Cincinnati Reds was voted the 1995 National League MVP, garnering 11 of 28 first place votes. Larkin is the first Reds player to be named MVP since George Foster in 1977 and the 11th Reds player to win the award.

Larkin was among the league leaders in six offensive categories. He was sixth in batting with a .319 average, 10th in hits with 158, fifth in runs scored with 98, ninth in multi-hit games with 48, second in stolen bases with 51, and ninth in on-base percentage, .394. For the year, the Reds' shortstop hit 15 home runs with 66 RBI and excelled defensively, finishing second among shortstops with a .980 fielding percentage.

Larkin became the first shortstop to be named MVP since Maury Wills of the Dodgers won the award in 1962. He won his second Rawlings Gold Glove Award for fielding excellence and was selected to his seventh All-Star team.

1995 MVP VOTING

Player—Club	1	2	3	4	5	6	7	8	9	10	Pts.
Larkin, Cincinnati	11	5	7	2	1	1	—	—	—	1	281
Bichette, Colorado	6	6	6	6	3	1	—	—	—	—	251
Maddux, Atlanta	7	8	5	3	—	2	1	1	—	1	249
Piazza, Los Angeles	3	7	6	4	3	—	2	1	2	—	214
Karros, Los Angeles	—	2	3	3	7	3	1	1	4	—	135
R. Sanders, Cincinnati	—	—	—	3	7	3	5	6	1	2	120
Walker, Colorado	—	—	1	1	—	8	3	6	1	1	88
Sosa, Chicago	—	—	—	—	2	1	6	2	2	7	3	81
Gwynn, San Diego	—	—	—	2	4	1	2	3	3	6	72
Biggio, Houston	—	—	—	2	1	1	5	2	2	3	58
Gant, Cincinnati	1	—	—	—	—	1	1	2	—	2	31
Bonds, San Francisco	—	—	—	—	—	—	3	1	2	2	21
Grace, Chicago	—	—	—	—	1	—	—	1	1	3	14
Bell, Houston	—	—	—	—	—	—	1	1	1	—	12
Bagwell, Houston	—	—	—	—	—	—	1	—	—	1	5
Hayes, Philadelphia	—	—	—	—	—	—	—	1	—	—	4
Galarraga, Colorado	—	—	—	—	—	—	—	2	—	—	4
Jones, Atlanta	—	—	—	—	—	—	1	—	—	—	3
Castilla, Colorado	—	—	—	—	—	—	—	—	1	1	3
McGriff, Atlanta	—	—	—	—	—	—	—	—	1	—	2
Schourek, Cincinnati	—	—	—	—	—	—	—	—	1	—	2
Conine, Florida	—	—	—	—	—	—	—	—	1	—	1
Henke, St. Louis	—	—	—	—	—	—	—	—	—	1	1

MOST VALUABLE PLAYER AWARD WINNERS

Year	Winner	Year	Winner
1931	Frank Frisch, Cardinals	1964	Ken Boyer, Cardinals
1932	Chuck Klein, Phillies	1965	Willie Mays, Giants
1933	Carl Hubbell, Giants	1966	Roberto Clemente, Pirates
1934	Dizzy Dean, Cardinals	1967	Orlando Cepeda, Cardinals
1935	Gabby Hartnett, Cubs	1968	Bob Gibson, Cardinals
1936	Carl Hubbell, Giants	1969	Willie McCovey, Giants
1937	Joe Medwick, Cardinals	1970	Johnny Bench, Reds
1938	Ernie Lombardi, Reds	1971	Joe Torre, Cardinals
1939	Bucky Walters, Reds	1972	Johnny Bench, Reds
1940	Frank McCormick, Reds	1973	Pete Rose, Reds
1941	Dolph Camilli, Dodgers	1974	Steve Garvey, Dodgers
1942	Mort Cooper, Cardinals	1975	Joe Morgan, Reds
1943	Stan Musial, Cardinals	1976	Joe Morgan, Reds
1944	Marty Marion, Cardinals	1977	George Foster, Reds
1945	Phil Cavarretta, Cubs	1978	Dave Parker, Pirates
1946	Stan Musial, Cardinals	1979	Keith Hernandez, Cardinals
1947	Bob Elliott, Braves		Willie Stargell, Pirates
1948	Stan Musial, Cardinals	1980	Mike Schmidt, Phillies
1949	Jackie Robinson, Dodgers	1981	Mike Schmidt, Phillies
1950	Jim Konstanty, Phillies	1982	Dale Murphy, Braves
1951	Roy Campanella, Dodgers	1983	Dale Murphy, Braves
1952	Hank Sauer, Cubs	1984	Ryne Sandberg, Cubs
1953	Roy Campanella, Dodgers	1985	Willie McGee, Cardinals
1954	Willie Mays, Giants	1986	Mike Schmidt, Phillies
1955	Roy Campanella, Dodgers	1987	Andre Dawson, Cubs
1956	Don Newcombe, Dodgers	1988	Kirk Gibson, Dodgers
1957	Hank Aaron, Braves	1989	Kevin Mitchell, Giants
1958	Ernie Banks, Cubs	1990	Barry Bonds, Pirates
1959	Ernie Banks, Cubs	1991	Terry Pendleton, Braves
1960	Dick Groat, Pirates	1992	Barry Bonds, Pirates
1961	Frank Robinson, Reds	1993	Barry Bonds, Giants
1962	Maury Wills, Dodgers	1994	Jeff Bagwell, Astros
1963	Sandy Koufax, Dodgers	1995	Barry Larkin, Reds

Prior to 1931, the League had awards that reflected what the MVP is today. Those early winners included:
- 1924 Vance, Arthur C., Brk. (P)
- 1925 Hornsby, Rogers, St.L. (2B)
- 1926 O'Farrell, Robert A., St.L. (C)
- 1927 Waner, Paul G., Pit. (OF)
- 1928 Bottomley, James L., St.L. (1B)
- 1929 Hornsby, Rogers, Chi. (2B)

Even earlier than 1924, the Chalmers Award carried the prestige of the MVP. Those winners included:
- 1911 Schulte, Frank, Chi. (OF)
- 1912 Doyle, Lawrence J., N.Y. (2B)
- 1913 Daubert, Jacob E., Brk. (1B)
- 1914 Evers, John J., Bos. (2B)

RAWLINGS GOLD GLOVE AWARD

The Rawlings Gold Glove is awarded for fielding excellence. The award has been given since 1957 when one team was selected. Since 1958 the award has been presented to a player at each position from both leagues.

Position	Player, Club	Years Won
P	Greg Maddux, Braves	6
C	Charles Johnson, Marlins	1
1B	Mark Grace, Cubs	3
2B	Craig Biggio, Astros	2
3B	Ken Caminiti, Padres	1
SS	Barry Larkin, Reds	2
OF	Steve Finley, Padres	1
	Marquis Grissom, Braves	3
	Raul Mondesi, Dodgers	1

84

NATIONAL LEAGUE HOME RUN CHAMPIONS 1900-1995

Year	Player	HR
1900	Herman Long, Boston	12
1901	Sam Crawford, Cincinnati	16
1902	Tom Leach, Pittsburgh	6
1903	Jim Sheckard, Brooklyn	9
1904	Harry Lumley, Brooklyn	9
1905	Fred Odwell, Cincinnati	9
1906	Tim Jordan, Brooklyn	12
1907	Dave Brain, Boston	10
1908	Tim Jordan, Brooklyn	12
1909	Red Murray, New York	7
1910	Fred Beck, Boston	10
	Frank Schulte, Chicago	10
1911	Frank Schulte, Chicago	21
1912	Heinie Zimmerman, Chicago	14
1913	Gavvy Cravath, Philadelphia	19
1914	Gavvy Cravath, Philadelphia	19
1915	Gavvy Cravath, Philadelphia	24
1916	Dave Robertson, New York	12
	Cy Williams, Chicago	12
1917	Gavvy Cravath, Philadelphia	12
	Dave Robertson, New York	12
1918	Gavvy Cravath, Philadelphia	8
1919	Gavvy Cravath, Philadelphia	12
1920	Cy Williams, Philadelphia	15
1921	George Kelly, New York	23
1922	Rogers Hornsby, St. Louis	42
1923	Cy Williams, Philadelphia	41
1924	Jack Fournier, Brooklyn	27
1925	Rogers Hornsby, St. Louis	39
1926	Hack Wilson, Chicago	21
1927	Cy Williams, Pittsburgh	30
	Hack Wilson, Chicago	30
1928	Jim Bottomley, St. Louis	31
	Hack Wilson, Chicago	31
1929	Chuck Klein, Philadelphia	43
1930	Hack Wilson, Chicago	56
1931	Chuck Klein, Philadelphia	31
1932	Chuck Klein, Philadelphia	38
	Mel Ott, New York	38
1933	Chuck Klein, Philadelphia	28
1934	Rip Collins, St. Louis	35
	Mel Ott, New York	35
1935	Wally Berger, Boston	34
1936	Mel Ott, New York	33
1937	Joe Medwick, St. Louis	31
	Mel Ott, New York	31
1938	Mel Ott, New York	36
1939	Johnny Mize, St. Louis	28
1940	Johnny Mize, St. Louis	43
1941	Dolf Camilli, Brooklyn	34
1942	Mel Ott, New York	30
1943	Bill Nicholson, Chicago	29
1944	Bill Nicholson, Chicago	33
1945	Tom Holmes, Boston	28
1946	Ralph Kiner, Pittsburgh	23
1947	Ralph Kiner, Pittsburgh	51
	Johnny Mize, New York	51
1948	Ralph Kiner, Pittsburgh	40
	Johnny Mize, New York	40
1949	Ralph Kiner, Pittsburgh	54
1950	Ralph Kiner, Pittsburgh	47
1951	Ralph Kiner, Pittsburgh	42
1952	Ralph Kiner, Pittsburgh	37
	Hank Sauer, Chicago	37
1953	Eddie Mathews, Milwaukee	47
1954	Ted Kluszewski, Cincinnati	49
1955	Willie Mays, New York	51
1956	Duke Snider, Brooklyn	43
1957	Hank Aaron, Milwaukee	44
1958	Ernie Banks, Chicago	47
1959	Eddie Mathews, Milwaukee	46
1960	Ernie Banks, Chicago	41
1961	Orlando Cepeda, San Francisco	46
1962	Willie Mays, San Francisco	49
1963	Hank Aaron, Milwaukee	44
	Willie McCovey, San Francisco	44
1964	Willie Mays, San Francisco	47
1965	Willie Mays, San Francisco	52
1966	Hank Aaron, Atlanta	44
1967	Hank Aaron, Atlanta	39
1968	Willie McCovey, San Francisco	36
1969	Willie McCovey, San Francisco	45
1970	Johnny Bench, Cincinnati	45
1971	Willie Stargell, Pittsburgh	48
1972	Johnny Bench, Cincinnati	40
1973	Willie Stargell, Pittsburgh	44
1974	Mike Schmidt, Philadelphia	36
1975	Mike Schmidt, Philadelphia	38
1976	Mike Schmidt, Philadelphia	38
1977	George Foster, Cincinnati	52
1978	George Foster, Cincinnati	40
1979	Dave Kingman, Chicago	48
1980	Mike Schmidt, Philadelphia	48
1981	Mike Schmidt, Philadelphia	31
1982	Dave Kingman, New York	37
1983	Mike Schmidt, Philadelphia	40
1984	Dale Murphy, Atlanta	36
	Mike Schmidt, Philadelphia	36
1985	Dale Murphy, Atlanta	37
1986	Mike Schmidt, Philadelphia	37
1987	Andre Dawson, Chicago	49
1988	Darryl Strawberry, New York	39
1989	Kevin Mitchell, San Francisco	47
1990	Ryne Sandberg, Chicago	40
1991	Howard Johnson, New York	38
1992	Fred McGriff, San Diego	35
1993	Barry Bonds, San Francisco	46
1994	Matt Williams, San Francisco	43
1995	Dante Bichette, Colorado	40

MEL OTT AWARD

DANTE BICHETTE
COLORADO ROCKIES

Dante Bichette of the Colorado Rockies hit 40 home runs, winning the 1995 Mel Ott Award as the National League home run champion. Bichette becomes the first Rockies player to win the award. It is Bichette's first home run title.

Bichette finished in the top 10 in 10 offensive categories. He led the N.L. in runs batted in (128), hits (197), total bases (359), slugging percentage (.431), extra-base hits (80), and had a 23-game hitting streak, the longest in the N.L. The left fielder finished second in multi-hit games (58), third in batting average (.340) and third in doubles (38).

Bichette excelled at Coors Field, where he hit 31 home runs. He also played in his second All-Star Game in 1995.

JACKIE ROBINSON
ROOKIE OF THE YEAR

HIDEO NOMO
LOS ANGELES DODGERS

Hideo Nomo of the Los Angeles Dodgers garnered 18 of 28 first place votes narrowly defeating the Braves' Chipper Jones to win the Jackie Robinson National League Rookie of the Year Award for 1995.

Nomo is the 15th Dodger player to win the award and became the fourth consecutive Dodger to win the award (Eric Karros, 1992; Mike Piazza, 1993 and Raul Mondesi, 1994).

The Japanese native was 13-6 with a 2.34 ERA during the season. He led the National League in strikeouts with 236 and opponents batting average against with a .182 average. Nomo tied for the league lead in shutouts (4), finished second in ERA, fifth in complete games (4), and finished eighth in winning percentage (.684).

NATIONAL LEAGUE ROOKIE OF THE YEAR

*1947	Jackie Robinson, Dodgers
*1948	Alvin Dark, Braves
1949	Don Newcombe, Dodgers
1950	Sam Jethroe, Braves
1951	Willie Mays, Giants
1952	Joe Black, Dodgers
1953	Junior Gilliam, Dodgers
1954	Wally Moon, Cardinals
1955	Bill Virdon, Cardinals
1956	Frank Robinson, Reds
1957	Jack Sanford, Phillies
1958	Orlando Cepeda, Giants
1959	Willie McCovey, Giants
1960	Frank Howard, Dodgers
1961	Billy Williams, Cubs
1962	Ken Hubbs, Cubs
1963	Pete Rose, Reds
1964	Richie Allen, Phillies
1965	Jim Lefebvre, Dodgers
1966	Tommy Helms, Reds
1967	Tom Seaver, Mets
1968	Johnny Bench, Reds
1969	Ted Sizemore, Dodgers
1970	Carl Morton, Expos
1971	Earl Williams, Braves
1972	Jon Matlack, Mets
1973	Gary Matthews, Giants
1974	Bake McBride, Cardinals
1975	John Montefusco, Giants
1976	Pat Zachry, Reds
	Butch Metzger, Padres
1977	Andre Dawson, Expos
1978	Bob Horner, Braves
1979	Rick Sutcliffe, Dodgers
1980	Steve Howe, Dodgers
1981	Fernando Valenzuela, Dodgers
1982	Steve Sax, Dodgers
1983	Darryl Strawberry, Mets
1984	Dwight Gooden, Mets
1985	Vince Coleman, Cardinals
1986	Todd Worrell, Cardinals
1987	Benito Santiago, Padres
1988	Chris Sabo, Reds
1989	Jerome Walton, Cubs
1990	Dave Justice, Braves
1991	Jeff Bagwell, Astros
1992	Eric Karros, Dodgers
1993	Mike Piazza, Dodgers
1994	Raul Mondesi, Dodgers
1995	Hideo Nomo, Dodgers

*One player selected as Major League Rookie of the Year in 1947 and 1948. Policy of naming a player from each league was inaugurated in 1949.

SILVER SLUGGER AWARD

The Silver Slugger Award honors the top offensive players at each position. The award has been given since 1980.

Pos.	Player, Club	Years Won
P	Tom Glavine, Braves	2
C	Mike Piazza, Dodgers	3
1B	Eric Karros, Dodgers	1
2B	Craig Biggio, Astros	2
3B	Vinny Castilla, Rockies	1
SS	Barry Larkin, Reds	6
OF	Dante Bichette, Rockies	1
OF	Tony Gwynn, Padres	6
OF	Sammy Sosa, Cubs	1

1995 NATIONAL LEAGUE ROOKIE OF THE YEAR VOTING

	1	2	3	Pts.
Hideo Nomo, L.A.	18	9	1	118
Chipper Jones, Atl.	10	18	0	104
Quilvio Veras, Fla.	0	1	11	14
Jason Isringhausen, N.Y.	0	0	4	4
John Mabry, St.L.	0	0	4	4
Carlos Perez, Mon.	0	0	4	4
Chad Fonville, Mon.-L.A.	0	0	1	1
Brian Hunter, Hou.	0	0	1	1
Charles Johnson, Fla.	0	0	1	1
Ismael Valdez, L.A.	0	0	1	1

CY YOUNG AWARD ERA LEADER

**GREG MADDUX
ATLANTA BRAVES**

Greg Maddux of the Atlanta Braves, for the second consecutive season, was the unanimous winner of the 1995 National League Cy Young Award. He becomes the first pitcher in Major League history to win an unprecedented four consecutive Cy Young Awards.

Maddux led the N.L. in earned run average for the third consecutive year, posting a 1.63 ERA, and led the N.L. in four other categories—wins (19), complete games (10), winning percentage (.905), and he had a 10-game winning streak. He tied for the league lead in shutouts with three. The righthander finished second in innings pitched with 209.2, second in opponents batting average against (.197), and third in strikeouts with 181. Maddux won his sixth Rawlings Gold Glove Award for fielding excellence in 1995.

CY YOUNG AWARD WINNERS

1956—Don Newcombe, Dodgers	1976—Randy Jones, Padres
1957—Warren Spahn, Braves	1977—Steve Carlton, Phillies
1958—Bob Turley, Yankees	1978—Gaylord Perry, Padres
1959—Early Wynn, White Sox	1979—Bruce Sutter, Cubs
1960—Vernon Law, Pirates	1980—Steve Carlton, Phillies
1961—Whitey Ford, Yankees	1981—Fernando Valenzuela, Dodgers
1962—Don Drysdale, Dodgers	1982—Steve Carlton, Phillies
1963—Sandy Koufax, Dodgers	1983—John Denny, Phillies
1964—Dean Chance, Angels	1984—Rick Sutcliffe, Cubs
1965—Sandy Koufax, Dodgers	1985—Dwight Gooden, Mets
1966—Sandy Koufax, Dodgers	1986—Mike Scott, Astros
1967—Mike McCormick, Giants	1987—Steve Bedrosian, Phillies
1968—Bob Gibson, Cardinals	1988—Orel Hershiser, Dodgers
1969—Tom Seaver, Mets	1989—Mark Davis, Padres
1970—Bob Gibson, Cardinals	1990—Doug Drabek, Pirates
1971—Ferguson Jenkins, Cubs	1991—Tom Glavine, Braves
1972—Steve Carlton, Phillies	1992—Greg Maddux, Cubs
1973—Tom Seaver, Mets	1993—Greg Maddux, Braves
1974—Mike Marshall, Dodgers	1994—Greg Maddux, Braves
1975—Tom Seaver, Mets	1995—Greg Maddux, Braves

Note: From 1956-1966 there was only one Cy Young Award Winner for the Major Leagues. Beginning in 1967 a winner was selected for each league.

EARNED RUN AVERAGE LEADERS 1912-1995

Year	Player	ERA
1912	Jeff Tesreau, New York	1.96
1913	Christy Mathewson, New York	2.06
1914	Bill Doak, St. Louis	1.72
1915	Grover Alexander, Philadelphia	1.22
1916	Grover Alexander, Philadelphia	1.55
1917	Grover Alexander, Philadelphia	1.85
1918	Hippo Vaughn, Chicago	1.74
1919	Grover Alexander, Chicago	1.72
1920	Grover Alexander, Chicago	1.91
1921	Bill Doak, St. Louis	2.58
1922	Rosy Ryan, New York	3.00
1923	Dolf Luque, Cincinnati	1.93
1924	Dazzy Vance, Brooklyn	2.16
1925	Dolf Luque, Cincinnati	2.63
1926	Ray Kremer, Pittsburgh	2.61
1927	Ray Kremer, Pittsburgh	2.47
1928	Dazzy Vance, Brooklyn	2.09
1929	Bill Walker, New York	3.08
1930	Dazzy Vance, Brooklyn	2.61
1931	Bill Walker, New York	2.26
1932	Lon Warneke, Chicago	2.37
1933	Carl Hubbell, New York	1.66
1934	Carl Hubbell, New York	2.30
1935	Cy Blanton, Pittsburgh	2.59
1936	Carl Hubbell, New York	2.31
1937	Jim Turner, Boston	2.38
1938	Bill Lee, Chicago	2.66
1939	Bucky Walters, Cincinnati	2.29
1940	Bucky Walters, Cincinnati	2.48
1941	Elmer Riddle, Cincinnati	2.24
1942	Mort Cooper, St. Louis	1.77
1943	Howie Pollet, St. Louis	1.75
1944	Ed Heusser, Cincinnati	2.38
1945	Hank Borowy, Chicago	2.14
1946	Howie Pollet, St. Louis	2.10
1947	Warren Spahn, Boston	2.33
1948	Harry Brecheen, St. Louis	2.24
1949	Dave Koslo, New York	2.50
1950	Jim Hearn, St. Louis-New York	2.49
1951	Chet Nichols, Boston	2.88
1952	Hoyt Wilhelm, New York	2.43
1953	Warren Spahn, Milwaukee	2.10
1954	John Antonelli, New York	2.29
1955	Bob Friend, Pittsburgh	2.84
1956	Lew Burdette, Milwaukee	2.71
1957	John Podres, Brooklyn	2.66
1958	Stu Miller, San Francisco	2.47
1959	Sam Jones, San Francisco	2.82
1960	Mike McCormick, San Francisco	2.70
1961	Warren Spahn, Milwaukee	3.01
1962	Sandy Koufax, Los Angeles	2.54
1963	Sandy Koufax, Los Angeles	1.88
1964	Sandy Koufax, Los Angeles	1.74
1965	Sandy Koufax, Los Angeles	2.04
1966	Sandy Koufax, Los Angeles	1.73
1967	Philip Niekro, Atlanta	1.87
1968	Bob Gibson, St. Louis	1.12
1969	Juan Marichal, San Francisco	2.10
1970	Tom Seaver, New York	2.81
1971	Tom Seaver, New York	1.76
1972	Steve Carlton, Philadelphia	1.98
1973	Tom Seaver, New York	2.08
1974	Buzz Capra, Atlanta	2.28
1975	Randy Jones, San Diego	2.24
1976	John Denny, St. Louis	2.52
1977	John Candelaria, Pittsburgh	2.34
1978	Craig Swan, New York	2.43
1979	J.R. Richard, Houston	2.71
1980	Don Sutton, Los Angeles	2.21
1981	Nolan Ryan, Houston	1.69
1982	Steve Rogers, Montreal	2.40
1983	Atlee Hammaker, San Francisco	2.25
1984	Alejandro Pena, Los Angeles	2.48
1985	Dwight Gooden, New York	1.53
1986	Mike Scott, Houston	2.22
1987	Nolan Ryan, Houston	2.76
1988	Joe Magrane, St. Louis	2.18
1989	Scott Garrelts, San Francisco	2.28
1990	Danny Darwin, Houston	2.21
1991	Dennis Martinez, Montreal	2.39
1992	Bill Swift, San Francisco	2.08
1993	Greg Maddux, Atlanta	2.36
1994	Greg Maddux, Atlanta	1.56
1995	Greg Maddux, Atlanta	1.63

1995 NATIONAL LEAGUE CY YOUNG AWARD VOTING

	1	2	3	Pts.
Greg Maddux, Atlanta	28	-	-	140
Pete Schourek, Cincinnati	-	16	7	55
Tom Glavine, Atlanta	-	6	12	30
Hideo Nomo, Los Angeles	-	5	4	19
Ramon Martinez, Los Angeles	-	1	5	8

MANAGER OF THE YEAR

**DON BAYLOR
COLORADO ROCKIES**

Don Baylor of the Colorado Rockies won the 1995 N.L. Manager of the Year Award, leading the Rockies to their first ever postseason appearance in only their third season as an expansion franchise. The Rockies earned the N.L. Wild-Card berth, finishing one game behind the Dodgers in the N.L. Western Division.

Baylor garnered 19 of 28 first place votes. Davey Johnson of the Cincinnati Reds finished second in the voting for the second consecutive season.

1995 MANAGER OF THE YEAR VOTING

	1	2	3	Pts.
Don Baylor, Rockies	19	9	0	122
Davey Johnson, Reds	8	15	4	89
Bobby Cox, Braves	1	1	12	20
Terry Collins, Astros	0	2	5	11
Jim Riggleman, Cubs	0	1	3	6
Dallas Green, Mets	0	0	3	3
Bruce Bochy, Padres	0	0	1	1

MANAGERS OF THE YEAR

1983	Tom Lasorda, Los Angeles Dodgers
1984	Jim Frey, Chicago Cubs
1985	Whitey Herzog, St. Louis Cardinals
1986	Hal Lanier, Houston Astros
1987	Buck Rodgers, Montreal Expos
1988	Tom Lasorda, Los Angeles Dodgers
1989	Don Zimmer, Chicago Cubs
1990	Jim Leyland, Pittsburgh Pirates
1991	Bobby Cox, Atlanta Braves
1992	Jim Leyland, Pittsburgh Pirates
1993	Dusty Baker, San Francisco Giants
1994	Felipe Alou, Montreal Expos
1995	Don Baylor, Colorado Rockies

BATTING CHAMPION

**TONY GWYNN
SAN DIEGO PADRES**

Tony Gwynn of the San Diego Padres, batting .368 in 1995, won his second consecutive batting title and his sixth overall. Gwynn led the N.L. in multi-hit games (65), finished second in hits (197) and third in on-base percentage (.404).

Gwynn's closest rival was Mike Piazza of the Dodgers, who batted .346.

NATIONAL LEAGUE BATTING CHAMPIONS

Year	Player	AVG
1876	Roscoe Barnes, Chicago	.403
1877	James White, Boston	.385
1878	Abner Dalrymple, Milwaukee	.356
1879	Cap Anson, Chicago	.407
1880	George Gore, Chicago	.365
1881	Cap Anson, Chicago	.399
1882	Dan Brouthers, Buffalo	.367
1883	Dan Brouthers, Buffalo	.371
1884	Jim O'Rourke, Buffalo	.350
1885	Roger Connor, New York	.371
1886	Mike Kelly, Chicago	.388
1887	Cap Anson, Chicago	.421
1888	Cap Anson, Chicago	.343
1889	Dan Brouthers, Boston	.373
1890	Jack Glasscock, New York	.336
1891	Billy Hamilton, Philadelphia	.338
1892	"Cupid" Childs, Cleveland	.335
1892	Dan Brouthers, Brooklyn	.335
1893	Hugh Duffy, Boston	.378
1894	Hugh Duffy, Boston	.438
1895	Jesse Burkett, Cleveland	.423
1896	Jesse Burkett, Cleveland	.410
1897	Willie Keeler, Baltimore	.432
1898	Willie Keeler, Baltimore	.379
1899	Ed Delahanty, Philadelphia	.408
1900	Honus Wagner, Pittsburgh	.380
1901	Jesse Burkett, St. Louis	.382
1902	C.H. Beaumont, Pittsburgh	.357
1903	Honus Wagner, Pittsburgh	.355
1904	Honus Wagner, Pittsburgh	.349
1905	J. Bentley Seymour, Cincinnati	.377
1906	Honus Wagner, Pittsburgh	.339
1907	Honus Wagner, Pittsburgh	.350
1908	Honus Wagner, Pittsburgh	.354
1909	Honus Wagner, Pittsburgh	.339
1910	Sherwood Magee, Philadelphia	.331
1911	Honus Wagner, Pittsburgh	.334
1912	Heinie Zimmerman, Chicago	.372
1913	Jake Daubert, Brooklyn	.350
1914	Jake Daubert, Brooklyn	.329
1915	Larry Doyle, New York	.320
1916	Hal Chase, Cincinnati	.339
1917	Edd Roush, Cincinnati	.341
1918	Zack Wheat, Brooklyn	.335
1919	Edd Roush, Cincinnati	.321
1920	Rogers Hornsby, St. Louis	.370
1921	Rogers Hornsby, St. Louis	.397
1922	Rogers Hornsby, St. Louis	.401
1923	Rogers Hornsby, St. Louis	.384
1924	Rogers Hornsby, St. Louis	.424
1925	Rogers Hornsby, St. Louis	.403
1926	Bubbles Hargrave, Cincinnati	.353
1927	Paul Waner, Pittsburgh	.380
1928	Rogers Hornsby, Boston	.387
1929	Lefty O'Doul, Philadelphia	.398
1930	Bill Terry, New York	.401
1931	Chick Hafey, St. Louis*	.349
1932	Lefty O'Doul, Brooklyn	.368
1933	Chuck Klein, Philadelphia	.368
1934	Paul Waner, Pittsburgh	.362
1935	Arky Vaughan, Pittsburgh	.385
1936	Paul Waner, Pittsburgh	.373
1937	Joe Medwick, St. Louis	.374
1938	Ernie Lombardi, Cincinnati	.342
1939	Johnny Mize, St. Louis	.349
1940	Debs Garms, Pittsburgh	.355
1941	Pete Reiser, Brooklyn	.343
1942	Ernie Lombardi, Boston	.330
1943	Stan Musial, St. Louis	.357
1944	Dixie Walker, Brooklyn	.357
1945	Phil Cavarretta, Chicago	.355
1946	Stan Musial, St. Louis	.365
1947	Harry Walker, St.L.-Phi.	.363
1948	Stan Musial, St. Louis	.376
1949	Jackie Robinson, Brooklyn	.342
1950	Stan Musial, St. Louis	.346
1951	Stan Musial, St. Louis	.355
1952	Stan Musial, St. Louis	.336
1953	Carl Furillo, Brooklyn	.344
1954	Willie Mays, New York	.345
1955	Richie Ashburn, Philadelphia	.338
1956	Hank Aaron, Milwaukee	.328
1957	Stan Musial, St. Louis	.351
1958	Richie Ashburn, Philadelphia	.350
1959	Hank Aaron, Milwaukee	.355
1960	Dick Groat, Pittsburgh	.325
1961	Roberto Clemente, Pittsburgh	.351
1962	Tommy Davis, Los Angeles	.346
1963	Tommy Davis, Los Angeles	.326
1964	Roberto Clemente, Pittsburgh	.339
1965	Roberto Clemente, Pittsburgh	.329
1966	Matty Alou, Pittsburgh	.342
1967	Roberto Clemente, Pittsburgh	.357
1968	Pete Rose, Cincinnati	.335
1969	Pete Rose, Cincinnati	.348
1970	Rico Carty, Atlanta	.366
1971	Joe Torre, St. Louis	.363
1972	Billy Williams, Chicago	.333
1973	Pete Rose, Cincinnati	.338
1974	Ralph Garr, Atlanta	.353
1975	Bill Madlock, Chicago	.354
1976	Bill Madlock, Chicago	.339
1977	Dave Parker, Pittsburgh	.338
1978	Dave Parker, Pittsburgh	.334
1979	Keith Hernandez, St. Louis	.344
1980	Bill Buckner, Chicago	.324
1981	Bill Madlock, Pittsburgh	.341
1982	Al Oliver, Montreal	.331
1983	Bill Madlock, Pittsburgh	.323
1984	Tony Gwynn, San Diego	.351
1985	Willie McGee, St. Louis	.353
1986	Tim Raines, Montreal	.334
1987	Tony Gwynn, San Diego	.370
1988	Tony Gwynn, San Diego	.313
1989	Tony Gwynn, San Diego	.336
1990	Willie McGee, St. Louis	.335
1991	Terry Pendleton, Atlanta	.319
1992	Gary Sheffield, San Diego	.330
1993	Andres Galarraga, Colorado	.370
1994	Tony Gwynn, San Diego	.394
1995	Tony Gwynn, San Diego	.368

*Hafey led with .3489, Bill Terry, New York, second with .3486, Jim Bottomley, St. Louis, third with .3482.

1995 PLAYERS OF THE MONTH

May — **Matt Williams**, San Francisco
(.405, 45/111, 7 2B, 12 HR, 31 RBI, 23 R, .451 OBP, .811 SLG)

June — **Jeff Conine**, Florida
(.340, 34/100, 6 2B, 9 HR, 24 RBI, 22 R, .670 SLG)

July — **Dante Bichette**, Colorado
(.296, 32/108, 4 2B, 21 R, 11 HR, 35 RBI, .639 SLG, .313 OBP)

Aug. — **Mike Piazza**, Los Angeles
(.400, 46/115, 9 HR, 25 RBI, 24 R, 9 BB, 7 2B, .440 OBP, .696 SLG)

Sept. — **Dante Bichette**, Colorado
(.365, 42/115, 8 HR, 28 RBI, 10 2B, 23 R, .392 OBP, .661 SLG)

1995 PITCHERS OF THE MONTH

May — **Heathcliff Slocumb**, Philadelphia
(12 SV, 14 G, 15.1 IP, 12 SO, 8 H, 1 HR, 1-0, 1.76 ERA)

June — **Hideo Nomo**, Los Angeles
(6-0, 6 GS, 50.1 IP, 60 SO, 25 H, 2 HR, 16 BB, 0.89 ERA)

July — **Greg Maddux**, Atlanta
(4-0, 1.27 ERA, 3 CG, 49.2 IP, 49 SO, 5 BB, 33 H, 1 HR)

Aug. — **Sid Fernandez**, Philadelphia
(5-0, 2.68 ERA, 7 GS, 43.2 IP, 54 SO, 15 BB, 31 H, 6 HR)

Sept. — **Greg Maddux**, Atlanta
(4-0, 0.29 ERA, 1 CG, 1 SHO, 31 IP, 29 SO, 3 BB, 21 H)

1995 PLAYERS OF THE WEEK

April 25-30 — **Raul Mondesi**, Los Angeles
(.536, 10/19, 3 HR, 3 2B, 7 RBI, 9 R, .591 OBP, 1.158 SLG)

May 1-7 — **Mike Piazza**, Los Angeles
(.520, 13/25, 3 HR, 11 RBI, 3 2B, .520 OBP, 1.000 SLG)

May 8-14 — **Vinny Castilla**, Colorado
(.609, 14/23, 2 2B, 1 3B, 4 HR, 6 R, 30 TB, 1.304 SLG)

May 15-21 — **Craig Biggio**, Houston
(.429, 9/21, 4 HR, 1 HR, 5 R, 5 RBI, .538 OBP, .762 SLG)

May 22-28 — **Greg Maddux**, Atlanta
(.2-0, 1.00 ERA, 2 CG, 15 SO, 6 H, 2 R, 1.02 vs. opp. batters)

May 29-June 4 — **Reggie Sanders**, Cincinnati
(.435, 10/23, 6 R, 11 RBI, 3 SB, 2 2B, 2 HR, 20 TB, .870 SLG)

June 5-11 — **Rondell White**, Montreal
(.520, 13/25, 2 2B, 2 HR, 7 RBI, 1 3B, 10 R, 1.050 SLG)

June 12-18 — **Mike Benjamin**, San Francisco
(set modern ML record with 14 H in 3 consec. games. Tied modern ML record for most hits in 2 straight games with 10. For week: .600, 18/30, 1 2B, 1 HR, 6 RBI, 6 R)

June 19-25 — **Hideo Nomo**, Los Angeles
(1-0, 1 SHO, 5 H, 2 R, 1 ER, 6 BB, 21 SO, 6 BB, 17.1 IP)

June 26-July 2 — **Derek Bell**, Houston
(.409, 9/22, 2 HR, 8 H, 4 BB, reached base 15 out of 16 times)

Ken Caminiti, San Diego
(.400, 8/20, 3 HR, 6 R, 2nd career grand slam 6/27)

July 3-9 — **Andres Galarraga**, Colorado
(.429, 12/28, 3 2B, 4 HR, 9 RBI, 11 R, 24 TB incl. 13 on 7/3, .964 SLG, set club record with 6 H on 7/3)

July 12-16 — **Ramon Martinez**, Los Angeles
(No-hitter on 7/14 vs. FLA, 1 BB, 8 SO)

July 17-23 — **Brett Butler**, New York
(.576, 19/33, 2 3B, 12 R, .611 OBP, 2 SB, 4th NL player this century to have 3 consec. 4-hit games)

July 24-30 — **Doug Drabek**, Houston
(2-0, 1 CG, 9 H, 1 ER, 0 BB, 10 SO, 15 IP)

Eric Karros, Los Angeles
(.417, 10/24, 2 HR, 6 RBI, 8 R, .462 OBP, .792 SLG)

July 31-Aug. 6 — **Dante Bichette**, Colorado
(.433, 13/30, 6 HR, 5 in 5 consec. games, 14 RBI, 10 R, 13 TB, 1.100 SLG)

Aug. 7-13 — **Eric Karros**, Los Angeles
(.385, 10/26, 4 HR, 5 R, .448 OBP, .846 SLG)

Aug. 14-20 — **Sammy Sosa**, Chicago
(.400, 12/30, 14 RBI, 9 R, .933 SLG, 8/14 hit 10,000th HR in franchise history)

Aug. 21-17 — **Mike Piazza**, Los Angeles
(.467, 14/30, 8 HR, 14 RBI, 2 2B, 13 R, .500 OBP, 1.367 SLG)

Aug. 28-Sept. 4 — **Sammy Sosa**, Chicago
(.357, 10/28, 5 HR, 10 RBI, 2 2B, 10 R, .438 OBP, .964 SLG)

Sept. 5-10 — **Ray Lankford**, St. Louis
(.619, 13/21, 3 HR, 8 RBI, 3 2B, 8 R, .640 OBP, 1.296 SLG)

Sept. 11-17 — **Ken Caminiti**, San Diego
(.542, 13/24, 4 HR, 8 RBI, 8 R, 2 2B, 1.125 SLG, 1st NL player to HR from both sides of plate in consec. games)

Sept. 18-24 — **Gary Sheffield**, Florida
(.471, 8/17, 3 HR, 10 RBI, .714 on-base)

Sept. 25-Oct. 1 — **Mark Grace**, Chicago
(.516, 16/31, 2 HR, 9 RBI, 9 R, 3 2B, .871 SLG, his 51 2B made him 1st NL player since P. Rose in '78 to hit 50)

LOU BROCK AWARD

QUILVIO VERAS
FLORIDA MARLINS

Quilvio Veras of the Florida Marlins led the National League with 56 stolen bases to be named the Lou Brock Base-Stealing Champion for the 1995 season. The Marlins' rookie second baseman becomes the second Marlins player to win the award (Chuck Carr, 1993) in their third year as an expansion franchise.

Barry Larkin of the Reds finished second in the N.L. with 51 stolen bases.

NATIONAL LEAGUE CAREER STOLEN BASE LEADERS
(1898-1995)

Lou Brock*	938
Max Carey*	738
Honus Wagner*	703
Joe Morgan*	681
Vince Coleman	648
Tim Raines	634
Maury Wills	586
OZZIE SMITH	573
Cesar Cedeno	550
Davey Lopes	495

*IN HALL OF FAME
ALL CAPS — Active N.L. Players

STOLEN BASE LEADERS 1900-1995

Year	Player	SB
1900	Jim Barrett, Cincinnati	46
1901	Honus Wagner, Pittsburgh	48
1902	Honus Wagner, Pittsburgh	43
1903	Frank Chance, Chicago	67
	Jim Sheckard, Brooklyn	67
1904	Honus Wagner, Pittsburgh	53
1905	Art Devlin, New York	59
	Bill Maloney, Chicago	59
1906	Frank Chance, Chicago	57
1907	Honus Wagner, Pittsburgh	61
1908	Honus Wagner, Pittsburgh	53
1909	Bob Bescher, Cincinnati	54
1910	Bob Bescher, Cincinnati	70
1911	Bob Bescher, Cincinnati	81
1912	Bob Bescher, Cincinnati	67
1913	Max Carey, Pittsburgh	61
1914	George Burns, New York	62
1915	Max Carey, Pittsburgh	36
1916	Max Carey, Pittsburgh	63
1917	Max Carey, Pittsburgh	46
1918	Max Carey, Pittsburgh	58
1919	George Burns, New York	40
1920	Max Carey, Pittsburgh	52
1921	Frank Frisch, New York	49
1922	Max Carey, Pittsburgh	51
1923	Max Carey, Pittsburgh	51
1924	Max Carey, Pittsburgh	49
1925	Max Carey, Pittsburgh	46
1926	Kiki Cuyler, Pittsburgh	35
1927	Frank Frisch, St. Louis	48
1928	Kiki Cuyler, Chicago	37
1929	Kiki Cuyler, Chicago	43
1930	Kiki Cuyler, Chicago	37
1931	Frank Frisch, St. Louis	28
1932	Chuck Klein, Philadelphia	20
1933	Pepper Martin, St. Louis	26
1934	Pepper Martin, St. Louis	23
1935	Augie Galan, Chicago	22
1936	Pepper Martin, St. Louis	23
1937	Augie Galan, Chicago	23
1938	Stan Hack, Chicago	16
1939	Stan Hack, Chicago	17
	Lee Handley, Pittsburgh	17
1940	Lonny Frey, Cincinnati	22
1941	Dan Murtaugh, Philadelphia	18
1942	Pete Reiser, Brooklyn	20
1943	Arky Vaughan, Brooklyn	20
1944	John Barrett, Pittsburgh	28
1945	Red Schoendienst, St. Louis	26
1946	Pete Reiser, Brooklyn	34
1947	Jackie Robinson, Brooklyn	29
1948	Richie Ashburn, Philadelphia	32
1949	Jackie Robinson, Brooklyn	37
1950	Sam Jethroe, Boston	35
1951	Sam Jethroe, Boston	35
1952	Pee Wee Reese, Brooklyn	30
1953	Bill Bruton, Milwaukee	26
1954	Bill Bruton, Milwaukee	34
1955	Bill Bruton, Milwaukee	25
1956	Willie Mays, New York	40
1957	Willie Mays, New York	38
1958	Willie Mays, San Francisco	31
1959	Willie Mays, San Francisco	27
1960	Maury Wills, Los Angeles	50
1961	Maury Wills, Los Angeles	35
1962	Maury Wills, Los Angeles	104
1963	Maury Wills, Los Angeles	40
1964	Maury Wills, Los Angeles	53
1965	Maury Wills, Los Angeles	94
1966	Lou Brock, St. Louis	74
1967	Lou Brock, St. Louis	52
1968	Lou Brock, St. Louis	62
1969	Lou Brock, St. Louis	53
1970	Bob Tolan, Cincinnati	57
1971	Lou Brock, St. Louis	64
1972	Lou Brock, St. Louis	63
1973	Lou Brock, St. Louis	70
1974	Lou Brock, St. Louis	118
1975	Dave Lopes, Los Angeles	77
1976	Dave Lopes, Los Angeles	63
1977	Frank Taveras, Pittsburgh	70
1978	Omar Moreno, Pittsburgh	71
1979	Omar Moreno, Pittsburgh	77
1980	Ron LeFlore, Montreal	97
1981	Tim Raines, Montreal	71
1982	Tim Raines, Montreal	78
1983	Tim Raines, Montreal	90
1984	Tim Raines, Montreal	75
1985	Vince Coleman, St. Louis	110
1986	Vince Coleman, St. Louis	107
1987	Vince Coleman, St. Louis	109
1988	Vince Coleman, St. Louis	81
1989	Vince Coleman, St. Louis	65
1990	Vince Coleman, St. Louis	77
1991	Marquis Grissom, Montreal	76
1992	Marquis Grissom, Montreal	78
1993	Chuck Carr, Florida	58
1994	Craig Biggio, Houston	39
1995	Quilvio Veras, Florida	56

NATIONAL LEAGUE CLUB STOLEN BASES—1995

Club	SB	CS	Pct.
Cincinnati	190	68	.736
Houston	176	60	.746
San Francisco	138	46	.750
Florida	131	53	.712
Los Angeles	127	45	.738
Colorado	125	59	.679
San Diego	124	46	.729
Montreal	120	49	.710
Chicago	105	37	.739
Pittsburgh	84	55	.604
St. Louis	79	46	.632
Atlanta	73	43	.629
Philadelphia	72	25	.742
New York	58	39	.598

BASIC AGREEMENT ARTICLE XX MAJOR LEAGUE FREE AGENTS

(Unsigned at press time; Players are listed with last 1995 club)

PITCHERS (10)

Mike Bielecki, California
Danny Darwin, Texas
Tom Henke, St. Louis
Terry Mulholland, San Francisco
Dave Righetti, Chicago AL
Jeff Russell, Texas
Zane Smith, Boston
Frank Viola, Cincinnati
Bill Wegman, Milwaukee
Trevor Wilson, San Francisco

CATCHERS (4)

Pat Borders, Houston
Brian Harper, Oakland
Joe Oliver, Milwaukee
Don Slaught, Pittsburgh

INFIELDERS (5)

Scott Fletcher, Detroit
Don Mattingly, New York AL
Spike Owen, California
Franklin Stubbs, Detroit
Lou Whitaker, Detroit

OUTFIELDERS (6)

Kevin Bass, Baltimore
Dave Gallagher, California
Howard Johnson, Chicago NL
Candy Maldonado, Texas
Darryl Strawberry, New York AL
Andy Van Slyke, Philadelphia

YEARLY STRIKEOUT LEADERS

Year	Player	K
1900	George (Rube) Waddell, Pittsburgh	133
1901	Frank (Noodles) Hahn, Cincinnati	233
1902	Victor Willis, Boston	226
1903	Christopher Mathewson, New York	267
1904	Christopher Mathewson, New York	212
1905	Christopher Mathewson, New York	206
1906	Frederick Beebe, Chicago-St. Louis	171
1907	Christopher Mathewson, New York	178
1908	Christopher Mathewson, New York	259
1909	Orval Overall, Chicago	205
1910	Christopher Mathewson, New York	190
1911	Richard (Rube) Marquard, New York	237
1912	Grover Alexander, Philadelphia	195
1913	Thomas Seaton, Philadelphia	168
1914	Grover Alexander, Philadelphia	214
1915	Grover Alexander, Philadelphia	241
1916	Grover Alexander, Philadelphia	167
1917	Grover Alexander, Philadelphia	200
1918	James (Hippo) Vaughn, Chicago	148
1919	James (Hippo) Vaughn, Chicago	141
1920	Grover Alexander, Chicago	173
1921	Burleigh Grimes, Brooklyn	136
1922	Arthur (Dazzy) Vance, Brooklyn	134
1923	Arthur (Dazzy) Vance, Brooklyn	197
1924	Arthur (Dazzy) Vance, Brooklyn	262
1925	Arthur (Dazzy) Vance, Brooklyn	221
1926	Arthur (Dazzy) Vance, Brooklyn	140
1927	Arthur (Dazzy) Vance, Brooklyn	184
1928	Arthur (Dazzy) Vance, Brooklyn	200
1929	Perce (Pat) Malone, Chicago	166
1930	William Hallahan, St. Louis	177
1931	William Hallahan, St. Louis	159
1932	Jerome (Dizzy) Dean, St. Louis	191
1933	Jerome (Dizzy) Dean, St. Louis	199
1934	Jerome (Dizzy) Dean, St. Louis	195
1935	Jerome (Dizzy) Dean, St. Louis	182
1936	Van Lingle Mungo, Brooklyn	238
1937	Carl Hubbell, New York	159
1938	Claiborne Bryant, Chicago	135
1939	Claude Passeau, Phila.-Chi.	137
	William (Bucky) Walters, Cincinnati	137
1940	W. Kirby Higbe, Philadelphia	137
1941	John Vander Meer, Cincinnati	202
1942	John Vander Meer, Cincinnati	186
1943	John Vander Meer, Cincinnati	174
1944	William Voiselle, New York	161
1945	Elwin (Preacher) Roe, Pittsburgh	148
1946	John Schmitz, Chicago	135
1947	Ewell Blackwell, Cincinnati	193
1948	Harry Brecheen, St. Louis	149
1949	Warren Spahn, Boston	151
1950	Warren Spahn, Boston	191
1951	Warren Spahn, Boston	164
	Donald Newcombe, Brooklyn	164
1952	Warren Spahn, Boston	183
1953	Robin Roberts, Philadelphia	198
1954	Robin Roberts, Philadelphia	185
1955	Samuel Jones, Chicago	198
1956	Samuel Jones, Chicago	176
1957	John Sanford, Philadelphia	188
1958	Samuel Jones, St. Louis	225
1959	Donald Drysdale, Los Angeles	242
1960	Donald Drysdale, Los Angeles	246
1961	Sanford Koufax, Los Angeles	269
1962	Donald Drysdale, Los Angeles	232
1963	Sanford Koufax, Los Angeles	306
1964	Robert Veale, Pittsburgh	250
1965	Sanford Koufax, Los Angeles	382
1966	Sanford Koufax, Los Angeles	317
1967	James Bunning, Philadelphia	253
1968	Robert Gibson, St. Louis	268
1969	Ferguson Jenkins, Chicago	273
1970	G. Thomas Seaver, New York	283
1971	G. Thomas Seaver, New York	289
1972	Steven Carlton, Philadelphia	310
1973	G. Thomas Seaver, New York	251
1974	Steven Carlton, Philadelphia	240
1975	G. Thomas Seaver, New York	243
1976	G. Thomas Seaver, New York	235
1977	Philip Niekro, Atlanta	262
1978	James R. Richard, Houston	303
1979	James R. Richard, Houston	313
1980	Steven Carlton, Philadelphia	286
1981	Fernando Valenzuela, Los Angeles	180
1982	Steven Carlton, Philadelphia	286
1983	Steven Carlton, Philadelphia	275
1984	Dwight Gooden, New York	276
1985	Dwight Gooden, New York	268
1986	Michael Scott, Houston	306
1987	L. Nolan Ryan, Houston	270
1988	L. Nolan Ryan, Houston	228
1989	Jose DeLeon, St. Louis	201
1990	David Cone, New York	233
1991	David Cone, New York	241
1992	John Smoltz, Atlanta	215
1993	Jose Rijo, Cincinnati	227
1994	Andy Benes, San Diego	189
1995	Hideo Nomo, Los Angeles	236

★ ★ ★ ★ ★ ★ ★

CLUB ATTENDANCE HIGHS SINCE 1969

ATLANTA
53,575 (n)	4/ 8/74	vs. LA
50,597 (tn)	7/ 4/72	vs. Chi.
50,595 (n)	7/ 4/77	vs. Cin.
50,419 (tn)	7/24/76	vs. Cin.
49,559 (n)	7/14/94	vs. Fla.

CHICAGO
45,777	4/14/78	vs. Pit.
44,818	4/13/76	vs. NY
43,066 (dh)	8/ 8/71	vs. SF
42,497 (dh)	7/ 1/73	vs. NY
41,052 (dh)	7/22/79	vs. Cin.

CINCINNATI
55,456	4/ 5/93	vs. Mon.
55,438	4/ 4/88	vs. St.L.
55,385	4/ 3/89	vs. LA
55,356	4/ 6/92	vs. SD
55,205	4/ 8/91	vs. Hou.

COLORADO
80,227	4/ 9/93	vs. Mon.
73,957 (n)	6/24/94	vs. SF
73,171	6/26/94	vs. SF
72,470	4/ 4/94	vs. Phi.
72,431	8/ 1/93	vs. SF

FLORIDA
45,900	10/ 3/93	vs. NY
45,796 (n)	8/27/93	vs. SF
45,278 (n)	8/29/93	vs. SF
45,037 (n)	7/ 3/94	vs. Atl.
44,689 (n)	8/ 7/93	vs. Phi.

HOUSTON
50,016 (n)	4/30/94	vs. St.L.
49,075 (n)	6/19/93	vs. SF
48,945 (n)	8/ 6/94	vs. SF
48,176 (n)	4/21/79	vs. Pit.
47,501 (n)	7/30/93	vs. Atl.

LOS ANGELES
55,185 (n)	7/28/73	vs. SF
55,110 (n)	6/26/70	vs. SD
54,859 (n)	7/ 4/94	vs. Mon.
54,709 (n)	5/25/94	vs. Chi.
54,667 (n)	6/30/93	vs. SF

MONTREAL
59,282 (dh)	9/16/79	vs. St.L.
59,260 (tn)	7/27/79	vs. Pit.
57,694	8/15/82	vs. Phi.
57,592	4/15/77	vs. Phi.
57,121 (n)	10/ 3/80	vs. Phi.

NEW YORK
59,083 (n)	7/ 9/69	vs. Chi.
58,874	9/20/69	vs. Pit.
55,901 (dh)	9/21/69	vs. Pit.
55,862 (dh)	6/22/69	vs. St.L.
55,391	7/27/69	vs. Cin.

PHILADELPHIA
63,816 (n)	7/ 3/84	vs. Cin.
63,501 (n)	7/ 5/82	vs. SF
63,346 (tn)	8/10/79	vs. Pit.
63,283 (n)	7/ 4/77	vs. NY
61,475 (n)	7/ 3/86	vs. Cin.

PITTSBURGH
54,274 (n)	4/ 8/91	vs. Mon.
54,098 (n)	4/11/88	vs. Phi.
52,119 (n)	4/10/87	vs. St.L.
51,726	6/ 6/76	vs. SD
51,695	4/ 6/73	vs. St.L.

ST. LOUIS
53,415 (n)	7/30/94	vs. Chi.
53,146 (n)	7/10/93	vs. Col.
52,657 (tn)	7/22/94	vs. Atl.
52,298	8/ 8/93	vs. Chi.
52,052	7/23/94	vs. Atl.

SAN DIEGO
54,841 (n)	5/10/91	vs. Mon.
54,732	6/ 7/86	vs. Atl.
54,517 (n)	6/ 1/91	vs. Hou.
54,490 (n)	4/15/85	vs. SF
54,395 (n)	5/11/85	vs. Chi.

SAN FRANCISCO
58,077	4/ 4/94	vs. Pit.
56,689	4/12/93	vs. Fla.
56,678	5/ 9/93	vs. LA
56,196	4/10/79	vs. SD
56,103	5/28/78	vs. LA

NATIONAL BASEBALL HALL OF FAME

For the first time in 25 years, the Baseball Writers' Association of America failed to elect a player to the Hall of Fame in 1996. But despite the lack of players elected by the writers in 1971, eight baseball greats did gain election. Dave Bancroft, Jake Beckley, Chick Hafey, Harry Hooper, Joe Kelley, Rube Marquard and George Weiss were named to the hall by the Committee on Veterans; while Satchel Paige was named by the Special Committee on Negro Leagues. The Veterans' Committee will hold its meeting and selection of candidates for induction on March 5, 1996.

The Hall of Fame logo (left) was unveiled on Memorial Day, 1995 in Cooperstown. It features five stars which represent the Hall of Fame's original 1936 electees: Ty Cobb, Walter Johnson, Christy Mathewson, Babe Ruth and Honus Wagner.

NATIONAL BASEBALL HALL OF FAME AND MUSEUM
25 Main Street, Box 590
Cooperstown, NY 13326
(607) 547-7200
FAX: (607) 547-2044

1996 HALL OF FAME WEEKEND
Induction—Sunday, August 4
Game—Monday, August 5
California Angels vs. Montreal Expos
Doubleday Field
Cooperstown, New York

There are 54 pitchers, 11 catchers, 15 first basemen, 13 second basemen, 8 third basemen, 17 shortstops, 18 left fielders, 15 center fielders, 21 right fielders, 12 Negro League players, 11 managers, 22 pioneers/executives and 7 umpires in the Hall of Fame.

★ ★ ★ ★ ★

NATIONAL LEAGUE MEMBERS OF THE HALL OF FAME

Hank Aaron, Braves
Grover Cleveland Alexander, Phillies, Cubs, Cards
Walter Alston, Cardinals, Dodgers
Adrian C. "Cap" Anson, Cubs
Richie Ashburn, Phillies, Cubs, Mets
Earl Averill, Braves
Dave Bancroft, Phillies, Giants, Braves, Dodgers
Ernie Banks, Cubs
Al Barlick, Umpire
Jake Beckley, Pirates, Giants, Reds, Cardinals
Johnny Bench, Reds
Yogi Berra, Mets
James Bottomley, Cardinals, Reds
Roger Bresnahan, Giants, Cardinals, Cubs
Lou Brock, Cubs, Cardinals
Dennis "Dan" Brouthers, Braves, Dodgers, Phillies
Mordecai P. Brown, Cardinals, Cubs, Reds
Jesse C. Burkett, Cleveland (NL), Cardinals
Roy Campanella, Dodgers
Max Carey, Pirates, Dodgers
Steve Carlton, Cardinals, Phillies, Giants
Frank Chance, Cubs
Jack Chesbro, Pirates
Fred Clarke, Pirates
John Clarkson, Cubs, Braves, Cleveland (NL)
Roberto Clemente, Pirates
James J. Collins, Braves
Charles Comiskey, Reds
John "Jocko" Conlan, Umpire
Roger Connor, Giants, Phillies, Cardinals
Samuel Crawford, Reds
Joe Cronin, Pirates
*W.A. "Candy" Cummings
Hazen "Kiki" Cuyler, Pirates, Cubs, Reds, Dodgers
Dizzy Dean, Cardinals, Cubs
Ed Delahanty, Phillies
Don Drysdale, Dodgers
Hugh Duffy, Cubs, Braves, Phillies
Leo Durocher, Reds, Cardinals, Dodgers, Giants
 Cubs, Astros

Johnny Evers, Cubs, Braves, Phillies
William "Buck" Ewing, Giants, Reds
Rollie Fingers, Padres
Elmer Flick, Phillies
*Ford Frick
Frankie Frisch, Giants, Cardinals
James "Pud" Galvin, Cardinals, Buffalo (NL), Pirates
Bob Gibson, Cardinals
Warren Giles, Reds, League President
Hank Greenberg, Pirates
Clark C. Griffith, Cubs, Reds
Burleigh Grimes, Pirates, Dodgers, Giants, Braves, Cardinals, Cubs
Charles "Chick" Hafey, Cardinals, Reds
Jesse "Pop" Haines, Reds, Cardinals
William "Billy" Hamilton, Phillies, Braves
Stanley "Bucky" Harris, Phillies (Mgr. only)
Charles "Gabby" Hartnett, Cubs, Giants
Billy Herman, Cubs, Dodgers, Braves, Pirates
Rogers Hornsby, Cardinals, Giants, Braves, Cubs
Waite Hoyt, Giants, Dodgers, Pirates
Carl Hubbell, Giants
Miller Huggins, Reds, Cardinals
*William Hulbert
Monte Irvin, Giants, Cubs
Travis Jackson, Giants
Ferguson Jenkins, Phillies, Cubs
Hugh Jennings, Dodgers, Phillies
Tim Keefe, Giants, Phillies
Willie Keeler, Giants, Dodgers
Joseph Kelley, Braves, Pirates, Baltimore (NL), Dodgers, Reds
George Kelly, Giants, Pirates, Reds, Cubs, Dodgers
Mike "King" Kelly, Reds, Cubs, Braves, Giants
Ralph Kiner, Pirates, Cubs
Chuck Klein, Phillies, Cubs
Bill Klem, Umpire
Sandy Koufax, Dodgers
Nap Lajoie, Phillies
Fred Lindstrom, Giants, Pirates, Cubs, Dodgers

Ernie Lombardi, Dodgers, Reds, Braves, Giants
Al Lopez, Dodgers, Braves, Pirates
Connie Mack, Pirates
*Larry MacPhail, Reds, Dodgers
Heinie Manush, Dodgers, Pirates
Rabbit Maranville, Braves, Pirates, Cubs, Dodgers, Cardinals
Juan Marichal, Giants, Dodgers
Richard "Rube" Marquard, Giants, Dodgers, Reds, Braves
Eddie Mathews, Braves, Astros
Christy Mathewson, Giants, Reds
Willie Mays, Giants, Mets
Joseph McCarthy, Cubs (Mgr. only)
Thomas F. McCarthy, Braves, Phillies, Dodgers
Willie McCovey, Giants, Padres
Joseph J. McGinnity, Dodgers, Giants
John J. McGraw, Cardinals, Giants
Bill McKechnie, Pirates, Cards, Giants, Braves, Reds
Joseph "Ducky" Medwick, Cardinals, Dodgers, Giants, Braves
Johnny Mize, Cardinals, Giants
Joe Morgan, Astros, Reds, Giants, Phillies
Stan Musial, Cardinals
Charles "Kid" Nichols, Braves, Cards, Phillies
James H. O'Rourke, Braves, Giants
Mel Ott, Giants
Gaylord Perry, Giants, Padres, Braves
Charles Radbourne, Braves, Reds
Harold "Pee Wee" Reese, Dodgers
*Branch Rickey, Cardinals, Dodgers, Pirates
Eppa Rixey, Phillies, Reds
Robin Roberts, Phillies, Astros, Cubs
Frank Robinson, Reds, Dodgers
Jackie Robinson, Dodgers
Wilbert Robinson, Baltimore (NL), Dodgers, Giants
Edd Roush, Giants, Reds
Amos Rusie, Giants, Reds
Mike Schmidt, Phillies
Red Schoendienst, Cardinals, Giants, Braves

Tom Seaver, Mets, Reds
George Sisler, Braves
Enos Slaughter, Cardinals, Braves
Duke Snider, Dodgers, Mets, Giants
Warren Spahn, Braves, Mets, Giants
*Albert Spalding
Willie Stargell, Pirates
Casey Stengel, Dodgers, Pirates, Phillies, Giants, Braves
Bill Terry, Giants
Sam Thompson, Detroit (NL), Phillies
Joe Tinker, Cubs, Reds
Harold "Pie" Traynor, Pirates
Arthur "Dazzy" Vance, Pirates, Giants, Dodgers, Cards, Reds
Arky Vaughn, Pirates, Dodgers
Honus Wagner, Pirates
Lloyd Waner, Pirates, Braves, Reds, Phillies, Dodgers
Paul Waner, Pirates, Dodgers, Braves
John Montgomery Ward, Giants, Dodgers
*George M. Weiss, Mets
Mickey Welch, Troy (NL), Giants
Zachary "Zack" Wheat, Dodgers
Hoyt Wilhelm, Giants, Cardinals, Braves, Cubs, Dodgers
Billy Williams, Cubs
Vic Willis, Braves, Pirates, Cardinals
Hack Wilson, Cubs, Dodgers, Phillies, Giants
George Wright, Red Stockings, Braves, Providence
Wm. Henry "Harry" Wright, Red Stockings, Braves, Providence, Phillies
Denton "Cy" Young, Cleveland (NL), Cards, Braves
Ross Youngs, Giants

*Selected for meritorious service to baseball

CLUB AND PLAYER STREAKS, ETC. DURING 1995 SEASON

EASTERN DIVISION

	BRAVES	MARLINS	EXPOS	METS	PHILLIES
Winning Streak	9 games	8 games	4 games (4 times)	6 games (twice)	7 games
Losing Streak	5 games	6 games (twice)	6 games (twice)	6 games (twice)	8 games
Runs, Game	17 (June 6)	17 (Sept. 17)	13 (May 11)	13 (July 14)	17 (Aug. 25)
Hits, Game	20 (May 16; June 6)	21 (Sept. 17)	20 (June 11)	20 (July 14)	19 (June 22)
Home Runs, Game	5 (June 6)	4 (4 times)	5 (May 11)	4 (July 25; Sept. 13)	4 (Aug. 18)
Runs, Inning	8 (4th inn., June 6)	8 (8th inn., July 17; 5th inn., Sept. 17)	6 (5 times)	8 (8th inn., July 21)	8 (4th inn., Aug. 26)
Errors, Game	4 (Aug. 22)	4 (July 27, 2nd game)	5 (May 5)	4 (May 12; July 6)	3 (3 times)
Stolen Bases, Game	3 (7 times)	6 (Sept. 18)	5 (June 9)	4 (Aug. 10)	3 (May 6; July 13)
Double Plays, Game	4 (Sept. 13)	4 (3 times)	4 (Sept. 26)	4 (Sept. 5)	4 (Sept. 8)
Triple Plays, Game	None	None	None	None	None
Winning Streak, Pitcher	10 Maddux	9 Rapp	5 Perez	7 Isringhausen	6 Fernandez
Losing Streak, Pitcher	4 Avery	7 Nen	5 Perez	5 Cornelius	5 (3 times)
Batting Streak	15 Lemke	17 Colbrunn	18 Segui	13 Bonilla	13 Jefferies

CENTRAL DIVISION

	CUBS	REDS	ASTROS	PIRATES	CARDINALS
Winning Streak	8 games	9 games	5 games (twice)	6 games	6 games
Losing Streak	7 games	6 games	11 games	6 games (3 times)	6 games (twice)
Runs, Game	26 (Aug. 18)	19 (Aug. 25)	19 (June 25)	13 (Aug. 18, 1st game)	13 (Sept. 11)
Hits, Game	27 (Aug. 18)	19 (Aug. 25; Aug. 26)	19 (June 25; Aug. 29)	22 (Aug. 12)	18 (Aug. 27)
Home Runs, Game	5 (Aug. 23)	4 (8 times)	5 (Aug. 29)	4 (July 15; Aug. 8)	3 (4 times)
Runs, Inning	7 (1st inn., Aug. 18)	7 (2nd inn., Sept. 29)	9 (8th inn., June 25)	9 (2nd inn., Aug. 8)	6 (2nd inn., Sept. 11)
Errors, Game	4 (July 17; Aug. 2)	3 (4 times)	4 (Sept. 13)	5 (July 23; Aug. 27)	7 (May 12)
Stolen Bases, Game	4 (June 30)	5 (5 times)	7 (Sept. 16; Sept. 28)	4 (Sept. 2)	4 (July 17)
Double Plays, Game	3 (5 times)	3 (6 times)	3 (8 times)	4 (May 26; Sept. 19)	4 (May 17; Aug. 11, 2nd game)
Triple Plays, Game	None	1 (July 17; Sept. 12)	None	None	None
Winning Streak, Pitcher	5 Navarro	6 Schourek, Smiley	6 Hampton	5 Neagle	4 Hill, Osborne
Losing Streak, Pitcher	5 Trachsel	4 Carrasco, Pugh	5 Kile, Swindell	6 Wagner	9 Jackson
Batting Streak	15 Grace	13 Larkin, R. Sanders	12 (3 times)	21 Garcia	16 Lankford

WESTERN DIVISION

	ROCKIES	DODGERS	PADRES	GIANTS
Winning Streak	6 games	6 games	4 games (5 times)	4 games (twice)
Losing Streak	5 games (twice)	6 games	7 games	5 games
Runs, Game	16 (Aug. 12)	17 (May 6)	16 (Aug. 6)	15 (Aug. 4)
Hits, Game	21 (July 3)	21 (May 6)	21 (Apr. 27)	15 (May 6; Sept. 28)
Home Runs, Game	5 (July 3)	5 (June 17; June 22)	5 (Sept. 17)	5 (July 18; Aug. 18)
Runs, Inning	7 (3 times)	7 (2th inn., June 21)	11 (8th inn., Aug. 2)	6 (4th inn., May 6; 9th inn., May 29)
Errors, Game	4 (Aug. 22)	7 (Sept. 1)	4 (May 3)	5 (June 5)
Stolen Bases, Game	4 (Aug. 25; Sept. 22)	5 (Aug. 20)	6 (Aug. 12)	5 (July 3; July 16)
Double Plays, Game	3 (9 times)	3 (7 times)	4 (June 24)	4 (June 8)
Triple Plays, Game	None	None	None	None
Winning Streak, Pitcher	7 Swift	7 Nomo	6 Valenzuela	5 Hook
Losing Streak, Pitcher	5 Ritz	6 Astacio	5 Benes	9 Mulholland
Batting Streak	19 Bichette, Young	17 Karros	15 Gwynn	12 Williams

1995 NATIONAL LEAGUE HIGHS AND LOWS

CLUB

Most Runs, Game—
26, Chicago at Colorado, August 18
Most Runs, Game, Both Clubs—
33, Chicago (26) at Colorado (7), August 18
Most Runs, Inning—
11, San Diego vs. San Francisco, August 2 (8th)
Most Hits, Game—
27, Chicago at Colorado, August 18
Most Hits, Game, Both Clubs—
39, Pittsburgh (22) at Los Angeles (17), August 12 (11 inn.)
38, Los Angeles (21) at Colorado (17), May 6
Most Total Bases, Game—
45, Chicago at Colorado, August 18
Most Doubles, Game—
8, Chicago vs. Los Angeles, September 11
Most Triples, Game—
4, Florida vs. San Francisco, July 25
Most Home Runs, Game—
5, Montreal at Philadelphia, May 11
Atlanta vs. Chicago, June 6
Los Angeles at Chicago, June 17
Los Angeles vs. San Francisco, June 22
Colorado vs. Houston, July 3
San Francisco at Philadelphia, August 18
Chicago vs. Florida, August 23
San Diego vs. Chicago, September 17
San Francisco vs. Florida, July 18 (14 inn.)
Houston at Atlanta, August 29 (13 inn.)
Most Home Runs, Game, Both Clubs—
9, San Francisco (5) at Philadelphia (4), August 18
Most Home Runs, Doubleheader—
5, Pittsburgh vs. Florida, August 18 (13 inn.)
4, Florida at Pittsburgh, August 18 (13 inn.)
3, Pittsburgh at Philadelphia, July 26
Most Extra Base Hits, Game—
11, Chicago at Colorado, August 18
Most Walks, Game—
12, Cincinnati vs. Colorado, May 20 (10 inn.)
Most Walks, Game, Both Clubs—
22, Florida (12) at San Francisco (10), July 17
Most Strikeouts, Game—
18, Los Angeles at San Francisco, May 2 (15 inn.)
San Diego at Houston, July 8 (17 inn., 1g)
17, Pittsburgh vs. Los Angeles, June 14
San Diego at Houston, July 6 (12 inn.)
Florida vs. Philadelphia, May 17 (13 inn.)
Chicago vs. San Francisco, June 14 (13 inn.)
Houston at San Francisco, July 16 (14 inn.)
Most Strikeouts, Game, Both Clubs—
33, Los Angeles (18) at San Francisco (15), May 2 (15 inn.)
32, San Diego (17) at Houston (15), July 6 (12 inn.)
Houston (17) at San Francisco (15), July 16 (14 inn.)
31, San Diego (18) at Houston (13), July 8 (17 inn., 1g)
29, Cincinnati (14) at Philadelphia (15), September 23 (13 inn.)
26, Atlanta (13) at Houston (13), May 27 (10 inn.)
San Francisco (9) at Chicago (17), June 14 (13 inn.)
25, Los Angeles (15) at Atlanta (10), July 5
Los Angeles (11) at New York (14), August 20
Cincinnati (11) at Philadelphia (14), September 22
St. Louis (13) at Chicago (12), September 25
Most Stolen Bases, Game—
7, Houston at Montreal, September 16

Most Stolen Bases, Game, Both Clubs—
10, San Francisco (5) at Cincinnati (5), July 3
Most Double Plays, Game—
4, Occurred 12 times
Most Double Plays, Game, Both Clubs—
6, Houston (3) at Cincinnati (3), May 23
Colorado (2) at Pittsburgh (4), May 26
Florida (3) at Philadelphia (3), June 16
Colorado (2) at San Diego (4), June 24
St. Louis (4) at San Diego (2), August 11 (2g)
Atlanta (4) at Colorado (2), September 13
Most Errors, Game—
7, St. Louis at Los Angeles, May 12
Los Angeles vs. Montreal, September 1
Most Errors, Game, Both Clubs—
12, St. Louis (7) at Los Angeles (5), May 12
Most Left On Base, Game—
18, Florida at Pittsburgh, August 18 (13 inn., 2g)
Florida vs. Atlanta, September 10 (11 inn.)
17, Chicago vs. Los Angeles, September 13 (13 inn.)
16, Philadelphia vs. San Diego, August 22
Most Left On Base, Game, Both Clubs—
29, Florida (18) at Pittsburgh (11), August 18 (13 inn., 2g)
San Francisco (16) at Philadelphia (13), August 20 (10 inn.)
Atlanta (11) at Florida (18), September 10 (11 inn.)
28, Montreal (14) at San Francisco (14), June 11 (13 inn.)
Colorado (13) at San Francisco (15), June 28 (11 inn.)
Atlanta (13) at Pittsburgh (15), July 25 (10 inn.)
26, San Diego (10) at Philadelphia (16), August 22
Most Innings, Game—
17, Houston vs. San Diego, July 8 (1g)
Longest Time, Game—
5:16, San Francisco vs. Los Angeles, May 2 (15 inn.)
4:54, San Francisco vs. Houston, July 16 (14 inn.)
4:53, New York vs. Houston, June 16 (16 inn.)
4:51, Chicago vs. Houston, September 28 (11 inn.)
4:47, Colorado vs. New York, April 26 (14 inn.)
3:55, Florida vs. Houston, May 29
Shortest Time, Game—
1:50, St. Louis vs. Atlanta, August 20
Highest Attendance, Game—
59,203, Philadelphia vs. Atlanta, July 3
Longest Winning Streak—
9, Cincinnati, May 22-31
9, Atlanta, July 1-9
Longest Losing Streak—
11, Houston, August 17-28

INDIVIDUAL BATTING

Longest Hitting Streak—
23, Bichette, Colorado, May 22-June 18
Most Runs, Game—
5, Biggio, Houston at Colorado, July 4
Weiss, Colorado at San Diego, September 20
White, Montreal at San Francisco, June 11 (13 inn.)
Biggio, Houston at Chicago, September 28 (11 inn.)
Most Hits, Game—
6, Galarraga, Colorado vs. Houston, July 3
White, Montreal at San Francisco, June 11 (13 inn.)
Benjamin, San Francisco at Chicago, June 14 (13 inn.)
Most Total Bases, Game—
13, Galarraga, Colorado vs. Houston, July 3
White, Montreal at San Francisco, June 11 (13 inn.)

Most Doubles, Game—
3, Williams, San Francisco vs. St. Louis, May 21
Clayton, San Francisco at St. Louis, June 18
Thompson, Houston vs. Pittsburgh, June 30
Bonilla, New York at Colorado, July 21
Young, Colorado at Atlanta, August 12
Livingstone, San Diego at Philadelphia, August 22
Grace, Chicago vs. Los Angeles, September 11
Bichette, Colorado vs. Atlanta, September 13
Johnson, Florida at Houston, June 6 (11 inn.)
Walker, Colorado vs. New York, April 26 (14 inn.)
Most Triples, Game—
2, Alfonso, New York at Philadelphia, August 9
Tavarez, Florida vs. Houston, August 28
Walker, Colorado vs. Florida, September 15
Butler, New York at St. Louis, July 19 (10 inn.)
Most Home Runs, Game—
3, Galarraga, Colorado at San Diego, June 25
R. Sanders, Cincinnati vs. Colorado, August 15
Most Extra Bases, Game—
4, Piazza, Los Angeles at Philadelphia, August 27
White, Montreal at San Francisco, June 11 (13 inn.)
Most Runs Batted In, Game—
8, Caminiti, San Diego vs. Colorado, September 19
Most Stolen Bases, Game—
4, Finley, San Diego vs. St. Louis, August 12
Biggio, Houston at Montreal, September 16
Hunter, Houston at Chicago, September 28 (11 inn.)

INDIVIDUAL PITCHING

Most Strikeouts, Game (Starter)—
16, Nomo, Los Angeles at Pittsburgh, June 14
Most Strikeouts, Game (Reliever)—
7, Williams, Philadelphia vs. Montreal, May 11
Dewey, San Francisco vs. New York, June 8
Most Innings, Game (Starter)—
10.0, Jones, New York vs. Houston, June 16 (16 inn.)
Most Innings, Game (Reliever)—
6.2, Watson, St. Louis at San Diego, August 11 (1g)
Bautista, San Francisco vs. Chicago, August 12
Most Home Runs Allowed, Game—
4, Bautista, San Francisco at Los Angeles, June 22
Harnisch, New York vs. Cincinnati, July 1
Foster, Chicago vs. Cincinnati, July 16
Jones, New York at Colorado, July 23
Weathers, Florida at Chicago, August 23
No-Hitters, Complete Game—
Martinez, Los Angeles vs. Florida, July 14
One-Hitters, Complete Game—
Maddux, Atlanta at Houston, May 28
Nomo, Los Angeles at San Francisco, August 5
Rueter, Montreal vs. San Francisco, August 27
Wagner, Pittsburgh vs. Colorado, August 29
Rapp, Florida at Colorado, September 17
Castillo, Chicago vs. St. Louis, September 25
Longest Winning Streak—
10, Maddux, Atlanta, May 23-August 4
Longest Losing Streak—
9, Jackson, St. Louis, April 27-July 2
Mulholland, San Francisco, May 11-July 29
Most Consecutive Scoreless Innings—
24.0, Bullinger, Chicago, July 24-August 11

1995 NATIONAL LEAGUE LEADERS

BATTING

ON-BASE PCT.
Barry Bonds, San Francisco	.431
Craig Biggio, Houston	.406
Tony Gwynn, San Diego	.404
Walt Weiss, Colorado	.403
Mike Piazza, Los Angeles	.400
Jeff Bagwell, Houston	.399
Reggie Sanders, Cincinnati	.397
Mark Grace, Chicago	.395
Barry Larkin, Cincinnati	.394
Jose Offerman, Los Angeles	.389

BATTING AVERAGE
Tony Gwynn, San Diego	.368	Barry Larkin, Cincinnati	.319
Mike Piazza, Los Angeles	.346	Vinny Castilla, Colorado	.309
Dante Bichette, Colorado	.340	David Segui, N.Y.-Mon.	.309
Derek Bell, Houston	.334	Gregg Jefferies, Philadelphia	.306
Mark Grace, Chicago	.326	Reggie Sanders, Cincinnati	.306

SLUGGING PCT.
Dante Bichette, Colorado	.620
Larry Walker, Colorado	.607
Mike Piazza, Los Angeles	.606
Reggie Sanders, Cincinnati	.579
Barry Bonds, San Francisco	.577
Vinny Castilla, Colorado	.564
Ron Gant, Cincinnati	.554
Eric Karros, Los Angeles	.535
Jeff Conine, Florida	.520
Mark Grace, Chicago	.516

DOUBLES
Mark Grace, Chicago	51
Dante Bichette, Colorado	38
Brian McRae, Chicago	38
Reggie Sanders, Cincinnati	36
Wil Cordero, Montreal	35
Ray Lankford, St. Louis	35
Bret Boone, Cincinnati	34
Vinny Castilla, Colorado	34
Mickey Morandini, Philadelphia	34
Four players tied with	33

RUNS SCORED
Craig Biggio, Houston	123
Barry Bonds, San Francisco	109
Steve Finley, San Diego	104
Dante Bichette, Colorado	102
Barry Larkin, Cincinnati	98
Mark Grace, Chicago	97
Larry Walker, Colorado	96
Brian McRae, Chicago	92
Raul Mondesi, Los Angeles	91
Reggie Sanders, Cincinnati	91

HITS
Dante Bichette, Colorado	197
Tony Gwynn, San Diego	197
Mark Grace, Chicago	180
Craig Biggio, Houston	167
Steve Finley, San Diego	167
Brian McRae, Chicago	167
Eric Karros, Los Angeles	164
Vinny Castilla, Colorado	163
Ken Caminiti, San Diego	159
Barry Larkin, Cincinnati	158

RUNS BATTED IN
Dante Bichette, Colorado	128
Sammy Sosa, Chicago	119
Andres Galarraga, Colorado	106
Eric Karros, Los Angeles	105
Barry Bonds, San Francisco	104
Larry Walker, Colorado	101
Reggie Sanders, Cincinnati	99
Ken Caminiti, San Diego	94
Two players tied with	93

HITTING STREAKS
Dante Bichette, Colorado	23
(May 22-June 18)	
Carlos Garcia, Pittsburgh	22
(June 5-27)	
Eric Young, Colorado	19
(July 18-Aug. 10)	
Dante Bichette, Colorado	19
(July 19-Aug. 8)	

TRIPLES
Brett Butler, N.Y.-L.A.	9
Eric Young, Colorado	9
Steve Finley, San Diego	8
Luis Gonzalez, Hou.-Chi.	8
Deion Sanders, Cin.-S.F.	8
Six players tied with	7

HOME RUNS
Dante Bichette, Colorado	40
Sammy Sosa, Chicago	36
Larry Walker, Colorado	36
Barry Bonds, San Francisco	33
Vinny Castilla, Colorado	32
Eric Karros, Los Angeles	32
Mike Piazza, Los Angeles	32
Andres Galarraga, Colorado	31
Ron Gant, Cincinnati	29
Reggie Sanders, Cincinnati	28

TOTAL BASES
Dante Bichette, Colorado	359
Larry Walker, Colorado	300
Vinny Castilla, Colorado	297
Eric Karros, Los Angeles	295
Barry Bonds, San Francisco	292
Mark Grace, Chicago	285
Andres Galarraga, Colorado	283
Sammy Sosa, Chicago	282
Reggie Sanders, Cincinnati	280
Ken Caminiti, San Diego	270

PITCHING

OPP. BATTING AVG. AGAINST
Hideo Nomo, Los Angeles	.182
Greg Maddux, Atlanta	.197
Pedro Martinez, Montreal	.227
Ismael Valdes, Los Angeles	.228
Pete Schourek, Cincinnati	.228
Ramon Martinez, Los Angeles	.231
John Smoltz, Atlanta	.232
Kevin Foster, Chicago	.240
Tom Glavine, Atlanta	.246
Joey Hamilton, San Diego	.246

WINS
Greg Maddux, Atlanta	19
Pete Schourek, Cincinnati	18
Ramon Martinez, Los Angeles	17
Tom Glavine, Atlanta	16
John Burkett, Florida	14
Pedro Martinez, Montreal	14
Jaime Navarro, Chicago	14
Pat Rapp, Florida	14
Four pitchers tied with	14

EARNED RUN AVERAGE
Greg Maddux, Atlanta	1.63	Joey Hamilton, San Diego	3.08
Hideo Nomo, Los Angeles	2.54	John Smoltz, Atlanta	3.18
Andy Ashby, San Diego	2.94	Frank Castillo, Chicago	3.21
Ismael Valdes, Los Angeles	3.05	Pete Schourek, Cincinnati	3.22
Tom Glavine, Atlanta	3.08	Jaime Navarro, Chicago	3.28

INNINGS PITCHED
Greg Maddux, Atlanta	209.2
Denny Neagle, Pittsburgh	209.2
Ramon Martinez, Los Angeles	206.1
Joey Hamilton, San Diego	204.1
Jaime Navarro, Chicago	200.1
Tom Glavine, Atlanta	198.2
Ismael Valdes, Los Angeles	197.2
Bobby Jones, New York	195.2
Mark Leiter, San Francisco	195.2
Pedro Martinez, Montreal	194.2

WINNING PCT. (15 Decisions)
Greg Maddux, Atlanta	.905
Pete Schourek, Cincinnati	.720
Dave Burba, San Francisco	.714
Ramon Martinez, Los Angeles	.708
John Smiley, Cincinnati	.706
Jaime Navarro, Chicago	.700
Tom Glavine, Atlanta	.696
Hideo Nomo, Los Angeles	.684
Pat Rapp, Florida	.667
John Smoltz, Atlanta	.632

GAMES
Curt Leskanic, Colorado	76
Dave Veres, Houston	72
Steve Reed, Colorado	71
Yorkis Perez, Florida	69
Todd Jones, Houston	68
Darren Holmes, Colorado	68
Mike Perez, Chicago	68
Greg McMichael, Atlanta	67
Mark Wohlers, Atlanta	65
Two pitchers tied with	54

COMPLETE GAMES
Greg Maddux, Atlanta	10
Mark Leiter, San Francisco	7
Ismael Valdes, Los Angeles	6
Denny Neagle, Pittsburgh	5
John Burkett, Florida	4
Tyler Green, Philadelphia	4
Ramon Martinez, Los Angeles	4
Hideo Nomo, Los Angeles	4
Three pitchers tied with	3

SAVES
Randy Myers, Chicago	38
Tom Henke, St. Louis	36
Rod Beck, San Francisco	33
Heathcliff Slocumb, Philadelphia	32
Todd Worrell, Los Angeles	32
Trevor Hoffman, San Diego	31
Mel Rojas, Montreal	30
John Franco, New York	29
Jeff Brantley, Cincinnati	28
Mark Wohlers, Atlanta	25

STRIKEOUTS
Hideo Nomo, Los Angeles	236
John Smoltz, Atlanta	193
Greg Maddux, Atlanta	181
Shane Reynolds, Houston	175
Pedro Martinez, Montreal	174
Jeff Fassero, Montreal	164
Pete Schourek, Cincinnati	160
Andy Ashby, San Diego	150
Denny Neagle, Pittsburgh	150
Ismael Valdes, Los Angeles	150

SHUTOUTS
Greg Maddux, Atlanta	3
Hideo Nomo, Los Angeles	3
Ten pitchers tied with	2

INDIVIDUAL BATTING—1995

ALL PLAYERS LISTED ALPHABETICALLY

BATTER	TEAM	B	AVG	G	AB	R	H	TB	2B	3B	HR	RBI	SH	SF	HP	BB	IBB	SO	SB	CS	GIDP	SLG	OBP	E
Abbott, K	FLA	R	.255	120	420	60	107	190	18	7	17	60	2	5	5	36	4	110	4	3	6	.452	.318	19
Abbott, K	PHI	L	.500	18	2	1	1	1	0	0	0	0	0	0	0	0	0	1	0	0	0	.500	.500	1
Acevedo, J	COL	R	.056	17	18	0	1	1	0	0	0	0	0	0	0	1	0	6	0	0	2	.056	.105	1
Alfonzo, E	NY	R	.278	101	335	26	93	128	13	5	4	41	4	4	1	12	1	37	1	1	7	.382	.301	7
Alou, M	MON	R	.273	93	344	48	94	158	22	0	14	58	0	4	9	29	6	56	4	3	9	.459	.342	3
Alvarez, C	MON	R	.000	8	12	1	0	0	0	0	0	0	2	0	0	0	0	4	0	0	0	.000	.000	1
Andrews, S	MON	R	.214	84	220	27	47	83	10	1	8	31	1	2	1	17	2	68	1	1	4	.377	.271	7
Anthony, E	CIN	L	.269	47	134	19	36	57	6	0	5	23	0	3	0	13	2	30	2	1	1	.425	.327	4
Aquino, L	MON-SF	R	.250	34	4	0	1	1	0	0	0	0	0	0	0	1	0	2	0	0	0	.250	.400	0
Arias, A	FLA	R	.269	94	216	22	58	80	9	2	3	26	3	3	2	22	1	20	1	0	8	.370	.337	9
Arocha, R	STL	R	.000	41	1	0	0	0	0	0	0	0	0	0	0	0	0	1	0	0	0	.000	.000	0
Ashby, A	SD	R	.163	31	49	2	8	9	1	0	0	3	17	0	0	1	0	24	1	0	0	.184	.180	1
Ashley, B	LA	R	.237	81	215	17	51	80	5	0	8	27	0	2	2	25	4	88	0	0	8	.372	.320	3
Astacio, P	LA	R	.125	48	24	0	3	4	1	0	0	0	2	0	0	1	0	9	0	0	1	.167	.160	0
Aude, R	PIT	R	.248	42	109	10	27	41	8	0	2	19	0	0	0	6	0	20	1	2	4	.376	.287	1
Aurilia, R	SF	R	.474	9	19	4	9	18	3	0	2	4	1	1	0	1	0	2	1	0	1	.947	.476	0
Ausmus, B	SD	R	.293	103	328	44	96	135	16	4	5	34	4	4	2	31	3	56	16	5	6	.412	.353	6
Avery, S	ATL	L	.208	29	53	4	11	20	1	1	2	4	8	1	0	1	0	17	0	0	0	.377	.218	2
Bagwell, J	HOU	R	.290	114	448	88	130	222	29	0	21	87	0	6	6	79	12	102	12	5	9	.496	.399	7
Bailey, R	COL	R	.125	39	16	2	2	2	0	0	0	1	3	0	0	1	0	3	0	0	0	.125	.176	2
Banks, W	CHI-LA-FLA	R	.269	28	26	2	7	8	1	0	0	1	1	0	1	1	0	9	0	0	0	.308	.321	1
Barber, B	STL	R	.125	9	8	0	1	1	0	0	0	0	0	0	0	1	0	2	0	0	0	.125	.222	0
Barry, J	NY	S	.133	15	15	2	2	3	1	0	0	0	0	0	0	1	0	8	0	0	0	.200	.188	0
Barton, S	SF	R	.000	52	0	0	0	0	0	0	0	0	1	0	0	0	0	0	0	0	0	.000	.000	0
Bates, J	COL	S	.267	116	322	42	86	135	17	4	8	46	2	0	2	42	3	70	3	6	4	.419	.355	5
Battle, A	STL	R	.271	61	118	13	32	37	5	0	0	2	3	0	1	15	0	26	3	3	0	.314	.358	1
Bautista, J	SF	R	.000	52	18	0	0	0	0	0	0	0	1	0	0	1	0	9	0	0	0	.000	.053	1
Bean, B	SD	L	.000	4	7	1	0	0	0	0	0	0	0	0	0	1	0	4	0	0	0	.000	.125	1
Beck, R	SF	R	.333	60	3	0	1	1	0	0	0	0	0	0	0	0	0	1	0	0	0	.333	.333	0
Bell, D	STL	R	.250	39	144	13	36	53	7	2	2	19	0	1	2	4	0	25	1	2	0	.368	.278	7
Bell, D	HOU	R	.334	112	452	63	151	200	21	2	8	86	0	6	8	33	2	71	27	9	10	.442	.385	8
Bell, J	PIT	R	.262	138	530	79	139	214	28	4	13	55	3	1	4	55	1	110	2	5	13	.404	.336	14
Belliard, R	ATL	R	.222	75	180	12	40	44	2	1	0	7	4	0	2	6	2	28	2	2	4	.244	.255	1
Benard, M	SF	L	.382	13	34	5	13	18	2	0	1	4	0	0	0	1	0	7	1	0	1	.529	.400	0
Benes, A	SD	R	.150	19	40	2	6	7	1	0	0	3	3	0	0	1	0	18	0	0	1	.175	.171	1
Benes, A	STL	R	.000	3	6	0	0	0	0	0	0	0	0	0	0	0	0	3	0	0	0	.000	.000	0
Benitez, Y	MON	R	.385	14	39	8	15	25	2	1	2	7	0	0	0	1	0	7	0	2	1	.641	.400	1
Benjamin, M	SF	R	.220	68	186	19	41	56	6	0	3	12	7	0	1	8	3	51	11	1	3	.301	.256	4
Bennett, G	PHI	R	.000	1	1	0	0	0	0	0	0	0	0	0	0	0	0	1	0	0	0	.000	.000	0
Benzinger, T	SF	S	.200	9	10	2	2	5	0	0	1	2	0	1	0	2	1	3	0	0	0	.500	.308	0
Berry, S	MON	R	.318	103	314	38	100	166	22	1	14	55	2	5	2	25	1	53	3	8	5	.529	.367	12
Berryhill, D	CIN	S	.183	34	82	6	15	24	3	0	2	11	1	4	0	10	2	19	0	0	3	.293	.260	2
Berumen, A	SD	R	.000	37	1	0	0	0	0	0	0	0	0	0	0	0	0	1	0	0	0	.000	.000	1
Bichette, D	COL	R	.340	139	579	102	197	359	38	2	40	128	0	7	4	22	5	96	13	9	16	.620	.364	3
Biggio, C	HOU	R	.302	141	553	123	167	267	30	2	22	77	11	7	22	80	1	85	33	8	6	.483	.406	10
Birkbeck, M	NY	R	.333	4	6	1	2	2	0	0	0	0	1	0	1	1	0	1	0	0	0	.333	.500	0
Blair, W	SD	R	.000	40	24	2	0	0	0	0	0	1	4	0	0	1	0	17	0	0	0	.000	.040	2
Blauser, J	ATL	R	.211	115	431	60	91	147	16	2	12	31	2	2	12	57	2	107	8	5	6	.341	.319	15
Bochtler, D	SD	R	.000	34	2	0	0	0	0	0	0	0	0	0	0	0	0	0	0	0	0	.000	.000	0
Bogar, T	NY	R	.290	78	145	17	42	52	7	0	1	21	2	1	0	9	0	25	1	0	2	.359	.329	6
Bonds, B	SF	L	.294	144	506	109	149	292	30	7	33	104	0	4	5	120	22	83	31	10	12	.577	.431	6
Bonilla, B	NY	S	.325	80	317	49	103	190	25	4	18	53	0	2	1	31	10	48	0	3	11	.599	.385	14
Boone, B	CIN	R	.267	138	513	63	137	220	34	2	15	68	5	5	6	41	0	84	5	1	14	.429	.326	4
Borbon, P	ATL	R	.000	41	1	0	0	0	0	0	0	0	0	0	0	0	0	0	0	0	0	.000	.000	0
Borders, P	HOU	R	.114	11	35	1	4	4	0	0	0	0	0	0	0	2	1	7	0	0	2	.114	.162	1
Borland, T	PHI	R	.200	50	5	1	1	1	0	0	0	1	0	1	0	0	0	1	0	0	0	.200	.167	2
Bottalico, R	PHI	L	.000	62	5	0	0	0	0	0	0	0	1	0	0	0	0	4	0	0	0	.000	.000	0
Bowen, R	FLA	R	.333	4	6	1	2	2	0	0	0	0	0	0	0	0	0	3	0	0	0	.333	.333	0
Bradshaw, T	STL	L	.227	19	44	6	10	13	1	1	0	2	0	0	0	2	0	10	1	2	0	.295	.261	1
Branson, J	CIN	L	.260	122	331	43	86	144	18	2	12	45	1	6	2	44	14	69	2	1	9	.435	.345	9
Brantley, J	CIN	R	.000	56	3	0	0	0	0	0	0	0	0	0	0	0	0	1	0	0	0	.000	.000	0
Brewington, J	SF	R	.217	14	23	3	5	5	0	0	0	1	4	0	0	0	0	7	0	0	0	.217	.217	0
Brito, J	COL	R	.216	18	51	5	11	14	3	0	0	7	1	0	1	2	0	17	1	0	1	.275	.259	1
Brocail, D	HOU	L	.250	37	16	3	4	6	0	1	0	1	4	0	0	0	0	5	0	0	0	.375	.250	0
Brogna, R	NY	L	.289	134	495	72	143	240	27	2	22	76	2	2	2	39	7	111	0	0	10	.485	.342	3
Browne, J	FLA	S	.255	77	184	21	47	54	4	0	1	17	9	1	1	25	0	20	1	1	7	.293	.346	3
Brumfield, J	PIT	R	.271	116	402	64	109	148	23	2	4	26	0	1	5	37	0	71	22	12	3	.368	.339	8
Brumley, M	HOU	S	.056	18	18	1	1	4	0	0	1	2	0	0	0	0	0	6	1	0	0	.222	.056	1
Buechele, S	CHI	R	.189	32	106	10	20	25	2	0	1	9	1	0	0	11	0	19	0	0	1	.236	.265	5
Buford, D	NY	R	.235	44	136	24	32	49	5	0	4	12	0	2	5	19	0	28	7	7	3	.360	.346	2
Bullett, S	CHI	L	.273	104	150	19	41	69	5	7	3	22	1	0	1	12	2	30	8	3	4	.460	.331	2
Bullinger, J	CHI	R	.128	25	47	1	6	9	3	0	0	5	8	2	0	5	0	16	0	0	1	.191	.204	0
Burba, D	SF-CIN	R	.067	52	15	2	1	1	0	0	0	0	4	0	0	3	0	9	0	0	0	.067	.222	0
Burkett, J	FLA	R	.106	31	66	3	7	8	1	0	0	3	4	0	1	2	0	23	0	0	1	.121	.145	0
Burks, E	COL	R	.266	103	278	41	74	138	10	6	14	49	1	1	2	39	0	72	7	3	7	.496	.359	5
Busch, M	LA	R	.235	13	17	3	4	13	0	0	3	6	0	0	0	0	0	7	0	0	0	.765	.235	1
Butler, B	NY-LA	L	.300	129	513	78	154	193	18	9	1	38	10	6	0	67	2	51	32	8	5	.376	.377	2
Byrd, P	NY	R	1.000	17	1	0	1	1	0	0	0	0	0	0	0	0	0	0	0	0	0	1.000	1.000	1
Caminiti, K	SD	S	.302	143	526	74	159	270	33	0	26	94	0	6	1	69	8	94	12	5	11	.513	.380	27
Candiotti, T	LA	R	.109	30	55	2	6	6	0	0	0	2	5	0	0	3	0	16	0	0	1	.109	.155	1
Cangelosi, J	HOU	S	.318	90	201	46	64	79	5	2	2	18	2	1	4	48	2	42	21	5	3	.393	.457	5
Caraballo, R	STL	S	.202	34	99	10	20	32	4	1	2	3	2	0	3	6	0	33	3	2	1	.323	.269	6
Carr, C	FLA	R	.227	105	308	54	70	96	20	0	2	20	7	2	2	46	1	49	25	11	2	.312	.330	3
Carrasco, H	CIN	R	.000	64	7	0	0	0	0	0	0	0	0	0	0	0	0	4	0	0	0	.000	.000	2
Carreon, M	SF	R	.301	117	396	53	119	194	24	0	17	65	0	3	4	23	1	37	0	1	7	.490	.343	7
Carter, A	PHI	L	1.000	4	1	0	1	1	0	0	0	0	0	0	0	0	0	0	0	0	0	1.000	1.000	0
Casian, L	CHI	R	.000	42	2	0	0	0	0	0	0	0	0	0	0	0	0	1	0	0	0	.000	.000	0
Castellano, P	COL	R	.000	4	5	0	0	0	0	0	0	0	0	0	0	2	0	3	0	0	0	.000	.286	0
Castilla, V	COL	R	.309	139	527	82	163	297	34	2	32	90	4	6	4	30	2	87	2	8	15	.564	.347	15
Castillo, A	NY	R	.103	13	29	2	3	3	0	0	0	0	0	0	1	3	0	9	1	0	0	.103	.212	2
Castillo, F	CHI	R	.102	29	59	1	6	6	0	0	0	1	7	0	0	3	0	25	0	0	0	.102	.145	2
Castro, J	LA	R	.250	11	4	0	1	1	0	0	0	0	0	0	0	1	0	1	0	0	0	.250	.400	0
Cedeno, A	SD	R	.210	120	390	42	82	120	16	2	6	31	0	1	5	28	7	92	5	3	12	.308	.271	17
Cedeno, R	LA	S	.238	40	42	4	10	12	2	0	0	3	0	1	0	3	0	10	1	0	1	.286	.283	1
Charlton, N	PHI	S	1.000	25	1	0	1	2	1	0	0	1	0	0	0	0	0	0	0	0	0	2.000	1.000	0
Christiansen, J	PIT	R	.000	63	1	0	0	0	0	0	0	0	0	0	0	0	0	1	0	0	0	.000	.000	2
Cianfrocco, A	SD	R	.263	51	118	22	31	53	7	0	5	31	0	1	2	11	1	28	0	2	3	.449	.333	3
Clark, D	PIT	L	.281	77	196	30	55	73	6	0	4	24	0	2	1	24	1	38	3	3	9	.372	.359	4
Clark, P	SD	R	.216	75	97	12	21	30	3	0	2	7	0	2	1	8	1	18	0	2	3	.309	.278	0
Clayton, R	SF	R	.244	138	509	56	124	174	29	3	5	58	4	3	3	38	1	109	24	9	7	.342	.298	20
Clontz, B	ATL	R	.000	59	2	0	0	0	0	0	0	0	0	0	0	0	0	0	0	0	0	.000	.000	0
Colbrunn, G	FLA	R	.277	138	528	70	146	239	22	1	23	89	0	4	6	22	4	69	11	3	15	.453	.311	5
Coles, D	STL	R	.225	63	138	13	31	47	7	0	3	16	0	1	3	16	1	20	0	0	1	.341	.316	3
Conine, J	FLA	R	.302	133	483	72	146	251	26	2	25	105	0	12	1	66	5	94	2	0	13	.520	.379	6
Cooper, S	STL	L	.230	118	374	29	86	117	18	2	3	40	0	4	3	49	3	85	0	3	9	.313	.321	18
Cordero, W	MON	R	.286	131	514	64	147	216	35	2	10	49	1	4	9	36	4	88	9	5	11	.420	.341	22
Cornelius, R	MON-NY	R	.100	18	20	0	2	2	0	0	0	0	0	0	0	0	0	7	0	0	0	.100	.100	1
Counsell, C	COL	L	.000	3	1	0	0	0	0	0	0	0	0	0	0	1	0	0	0	0	0	.000	.500	0
Cromer, T	STL	R	.226	105	345	36	78	112	19	0	5	18	1	5	4	14	2	66	0	0	14	.325	.261	17
Cummings, J	LA	L	.000	35	3	0	0	0	0	0	0	0	0	0	0	0	0	1	0	0	0	.000	.000	0
Cummings, M	PIT	L	.243	59	152	13	37	52	7	1	2	15	0	0	0	13	3	30	1	0	1	.342	.303	1
Daulton, D	PHI	L	.249	98	342	44	85	137	19	3	9	55	0	2	5	55	2	52	3	0	4	.401	.359	4
Dawson, A	FLA	R	.257	79	226	30	58	98	10	3	8	37	0	3	8	9	1	45	0	0	7	.434	.305	8
Decker, S	FLA	R	.226	51	133	12	30	43	2	1	3	13	0	2	0	19	1	22	1	0	1	.323	.318	5
DeLeon, J	MON	R	.000	7	0	0	0	0	0	0	0	0	1	0	0	1	0	0	0	0	0	.000	1.000	0
DeLucia, R	STL	R	.200	56	10	1	2	2	0	0	0	0	1	0	0	1	0	3	0	0	1	.200	.273	2
Deshaies, J	PHI	L	.000	2	1	0	0	0	0	0	0	0	0	0	0	0	0	1	0	0	0	.000	.000	0
DeShields, D	LA	L	.256	127	425	66	109	157	18	3	8	37	3	1	1	63	4	83	39	14	6	.369	.353	11
Devereaux, M	ATL	R	.255	29	55	7	14	20	3	0	1	8	0	0	0	2	0	11	2	0	1	.364	.281	0
Dewey, M	SF	R	.000	27	1	0	0	0	0	0	0	0	0	0	0	0	0	1	0	0	0	.000	.000	1
Diaz, M	FLA	R	.230	49	87	5	20	26	3	0	1	6	1	0	0	1	0	12	0	0	4	.299	.239	2
DiPoto, J	NY	R	.000	58	5	0	0	0	0	0	0	0	1	0	0	0	0	3	0	0	0	.000	.000	3
Dishman, G	SD	R	.200	19	30	4	6	6	0	0	0	4	2	1	1	0	0	13	0	0	0	.200	.219	0
Donnels, C	HOU	L	.300	19	30	4	9	9	0	0	0	2	0	0	0	3	2	6	0	0	1	.300	.364	2
Dougherty, J	HOU	R	.125	56	8	1	1	1	0	0	0	0	1	0	0	0	0	2	0	0	0	.125	.125	0
Drabek, D	HOU	R	.233	33	60	4	14	17	3	0	0	8	8	0	0	2	0	17	0	0	0	.283	.258	2
Duncan, M	PHI-CIN	R	.287	81	265	36	76	112	14	2	6	36	1	5	1	5	0	62	1	3	7	.423	.297	11
Dunston, S	CHI	R	.296	127	477	58	141	225	30	6	14	69	7	3	6	10	3	75	10	5	8	.472	.317	17
Dyer, M	PIT	R	.571	55	7	1	4	4	0	0	0	1	1	0	0	0	0	2	0	0	0	.571	.571	0
Dykstra, L	PHI	L	.264	62	254	37	67	90	15	1	2	18	0	2	3	33	2	28	10	5	1	.354	.353	2
Eischen, J	LA	L	.000	17	1	0	0	0	0	0	0	0	0	0	0	0	0	1	0	0	0	.000	.000	0
Eisenreich, J	PHI	L	.316	129	377	46	119	175	22	2	10	55	2	5	1	38	4	44	10	0	7	.464	.375	0
Elster, K	PHI	R	.208	26	53	10	11	20	4	1	1	9	2	2	1	7	1	14	0	0	1	.377	.302	1
Encarnacion, A	PIT	R	.226	58	159	18	36	53	7	2	2	10	3	0	0	13	5	28	1	1	3	.333	.285	7
Ericks, J	PIT	R	.097	19	31	2	3	4	1	0	0	1	6	0	0	0	0	12	0	0	0	.129	.097	3
Estes, S	SF	R	.000	3	5	0	0	0	0	0	0	0	0	0	0	0	0	2	0	0	1	.000	.000	0
Eusebio, T	HOU	R	.299	113	368	46	110	151	21	1	6	58	1	5	3	31	1	59	0	2	12	.410	.354	5
Everett, C	NY	S	.260	79	289	48	75	126	13	1	12	54	1	0	2	39	2	67	2	5	11	.436	.352	3
Eversgerd, B	MON	R	.000	25	1	0	0	0	0	0	0	0	0	0	0	0	0	0	0	0	0	.000	.000	1
Faneyte, R	SF	R	.198	46	86	7	17	23	4	1	0	4	1	0	0	11	0	27	1	0	2	.267	.289	1
Fassero, J	MON	L	.070	30	57	6	4	4	0	0	0	1	8	0	0	5	0	29	0	0	0	.070	.145	4
Fernandez, S	PHI	L	.043	11	23	1	1	1	0	0	0	1	1	0	0	1	0	15	0	0	0	.043	.083	1
Finley, S	SD	L	.297	139	562	104	167	236	23	8	10	44	4	2	3	59	5	62	36	12	8	.420	.366	7
Fletcher, D	MON	L	.286	110	350	42	100	156	21	1	11	45	1	2	4	32	1	23	0	1	15	.446	.351	4
Flora, K	PHI	R	.213	24	75	12	16	25	3	0	2	7	2	0	0	4	0	22	1	0	0	.333	.253	0
Florence, D	NY	R	.000	14	1	0	0	0	0	0	0	0	0	0	0	0	0	1	0	0	0	.000	.000	0
Florie, B	SD	R	.000	47	2	0	0	0	0	0	0	0	0	0	0	0	0	2	0	0	0	.000	.000	1
Floyd, C	MON	L	.130	29	69	6	9	13	1	0	1	8	0	0	1	7	0	22	3	0	1	.188	.221	3
Foley, T	MON	L	.208	11	24	2	5	7	2	0	0	2	0	0	0	2	0	4	1	0	2	.292	.269	0
Fonville, C	MON-LA	S	.278	102	320	43	89	97	6	1	0	16	6	0	1	23	1	42	20	7	3	.303	.328	11
Fordyce, B	NY	R	.500	4	2	1	1	2	1	0	0	0	0	0	0	1	0	0	0	0	0	1.000	.667	0
Foster, K	CHI	R	.250	33	60	7	15	21	1	1	1	9	5	0	0	3	0	16	2	0	0	.350	.286	0
Franco, M	CHI	L	.294	16	17	3	5	6	1	0	0	1	0	0	0	0	0	4	0	0	0	.353	.294	0
Frascatore, J	STL	R	.000	14	7	0	0	0	0	0	0	0	1	0	0	1	0	6	0	0	0	.000	.125	0
Fraser, W	MON	R	.000	22	2	0	0	0	0	0	0	0	0	0	0	0	0	0	0	0	0	.000	.000	0
Frazier, L	MON	S	.190	35	63	6	12	14	2	0	0	3	0	1	2	8	0	12	4	0	1	.222	.297	1
Freeman, M	COL	R	.087	22	23	2	2	5	0	0	1	4	6	0	0	1	0	16	0	0	0	.217	.125	3
Frey, S	SF-PHI	L	.000	18	1	0	0	0	0	0	0	0	0	0	0	0	0	1	0	0	0	.000	.000	1
Galarraga, A	COL	R	.280	143	554	89	155	283	29	3	31	106	0	5	13	32	6	146	12	2	14	.511	.331	13
Gallagher, D	PHI	R	.318	62	157	12	50	65	12	0	1	12	2	1	0	16	0	20	0	0	5	.414	.379	0
Gant, R	CIN	R	.276	119	410	79	113	227	19	4	29	88	1	5	3	74	5	108	23	8	11	.554	.386	3
Garces, R	CHI-FLA	R	.000	18	1	0	0	0	0	0	0	0	0	0	0	0	0	0	0	0	0	.000	.000	0
Garcia, F	PIT	R	.140	42	57	5	8	11	1	1	0	1	1	0	0	8	0	17	0	1	0	.193	.246	1
Garcia, C	PIT	R	.294	104	367	41	108	154	24	2	6	50	5	3	2	25	5	55	8	4	4	.420	.340	15
Garcia, K	LA	L	.200	13	20	1	4	4	0	0	0	0	0	0	0	0	0	4	0	0	0	.200	.200	0
Gardner, M	FLA	R	.190	39	21	1	4	4	0	0	0	1	4	0	0	0	0	6	0	0	0	.190	.190	2
Giannelli, R	STL	L	.091	9	11	0	1	1	0	0	0	0	0	0	0	3	0	4	0	0	0	.091	.286	0
Gibralter, S	CIN	R	.333	4	3	0	1	1	0	0	0	0	0	0	0	0	0	0	0	0	0	.333	.333	0

INDIVIDUAL BATTING—1995

BATTER	TEAM	B	AVG	G	AB	R	H	TB	2B	3B	HR	RBI	SH	SF	HP	BB	IBB	SO	SB	CS	GIDP	SLG	OBP	E
Gilkey, B.	STL	R	.298	121	480	73	143	235	33	4	17	69	1	3	5	42	3	70	12	6	17	.490	.358	3
Giovanola, E.	ATL	L	.071	13	14	2	1	1	0	0	0	0	0	0	0	3	0	5	0	0	1	.071	.235	0
Girardi, J.	COL	R	.262	125	462	63	121	166	17	2	8	55	12	1	2	29	0	76	3	3	15	.359	.308	10
Glavine, T.	ATL	L	.222	29	63	6	14	18	1	0	1	8	8	0	1	2	0	15	0	0	0	.286	.258	1
Goff, J.	HOU	L	.154	12	26	2	4	9	2	0	1	3	0	0	0	4	0	13	0	0	1	.346	.267	0
Gomez, P.	SF	L	.000	18	1	0	0	0	0	0	0	0	0	0	0	0	0	1	0	0	0	.000	.000	0
Gonzalez, L.	HOU-CHI	L	.276	133	471	69	130	214	29	8	13	69	1	6	6	57	8	63	6	8	16	.454	.357	6
Gott, J.	PIT	R	.000	25	1	0	0	0	0	0	0	0	0	0	0	0	0	1	0	0	0	.000	.000	1
Grace, M.	PHI	R	.000	2	2	0	0	0	0	0	0	0	2	0	0	0	0	2	0	0	0	.000	.000	0
Grace, M.	CHI	L	.326	143	552	97	180	285	51	3	16	92	1	7	2	65	9	46	6	2	10	.516	.395	7
Grahe, J.	COL	R	.417	17	12	1	5	6	1	0	0	2	6	0	0	0	0	3	0	0	0	.500	.417	1
Green, T.	PHI	R	.182	27	44	2	8	16	5	0	1	5	8	0	0	0	0	16	0	1	0	.364	.182	1
Greene, T.	PHI	R	.000	11	8	0	0	0	0	0	0	0	1	0	0	2	0	3	0	0	0	.000	.200	0
Greene, W.	CIN	L	.105	8	19	1	2	2	0	0	0	0	0	0	0	3	0	7	0	0	1	.105	.227	0
Greer, K.	SF	R	.000	8	1	0	0	0	0	0	0	0	0	0	0	0	0	1	0	0	0	.000	.000	1
Gregg, T.	FLA	L	.237	72	156	20	37	60	5	0	6	20	0	2	2	16	1	33	3	1	3	.385	.313	1
Grissom, M.	ATL	R	.258	139	551	80	142	207	23	3	12	42	1	4	3	47	4	61	29	9	8	.376	.317	2
Grudzielanek, M.	MON	R	.245	78	269	27	66	85	12	2	1	20	3	0	7	14	4	47	8	3	7	.316	.300	10
Gunderson, E.	NY	R	.000	30	0	1	0	0	0	0	0	0	0	0	1	0	0	0	0	0	0	.000	1.000	0
Guthrie, M.	LA	S	.000	24	1	0	0	0	0	0	0	0	0	0	0	0	0	0	0	0	0	.000	.000	0
Gutierrez, R.	HOU	R	.276	52	156	22	43	49	6	0	0	12	1	1	1	10	3	33	5	0	4	.314	.321	8
Gwynn, C.	LA	L	.214	67	84	8	18	28	3	2	1	10	0	1	1	6	1	23	0	0	5	.333	.272	0
Gwynn, T.	SD	L	.368	135	535	82	197	259	33	1	9	90	0	6	1	35	10	15	17	5	20	.484	.404	2
Habyan, J.	STL	R	.000	31	2	0	0	0	0	0	0	0	0	0	0	0	0	1	0	0	0	.000	.000	0
Hajek, D.	HOU	R	.000	5	2	0	0	0	0	0	0	0	2	0	0	1	0	1	1	0	0	.000	.333	0
Hamilton, J.	SD	R	.108	31	65	4	7	9	2	0	0	3	5	1	0	2	0	38	0	0	1	.138	.132	6
Hammond, C.	FLA	L	.271	25	48	7	13	18	2	0	1	4	5	0	0	7	0	16	0	0	1	.375	.364	1
Hampton, M.	HOU	R	.146	24	48	7	7	7	0	0	0	0	4	0	1	4	0	14	0	0	0	.146	.226	3
Haney, T.	CHI	R	.411	25	73	11	30	44	8	0	2	6	1	0	0	7	0	11	0	0	0	.603	.463	2
Hansen, D.	LA	L	.287	100	181	19	52	65	10	0	1	14	0	1	1	28	4	28	0	0	4	.359	.384	7
Harnisch, P.	NY	R	.091	18	33	0	3	3	0	0	0	0	3	0	0	0	0	6	0	0	0	.091	.091	2
Harris, G.	MON	S	.333	45	3	0	1	2	1	0	0	0	0	0	0	0	0	1	0	0	0	.667	.333	2
Harris, L.	CIN	L	.208	101	197	32	41	61	8	3	2	16	3	1	0	14	0	20	10	1	6	.310	.259	4
Hartgraves, D.	HOU	R	.000	40	2	0	0	0	0	0	0	0	1	0	0	0	0	1	0	0	0	.000	.000	0
Hayes, C.	PHI	R	.276	141	529	58	146	215	30	3	11	85	0	6	4	50	2	88	5	1	22	.406	.340	14
Hemond, S.	STL	R	.144	57	118	11	17	27	1	0	3	9	1	1	2	12	0	31	0	0	8	.229	.233	3
Henke, T.	STL	R	.000	52	1	0	0	0	0	0	0	0	0	0	0	0	0	0	0	0	0	.000	.000	0
Henry, B.	MON	L	.048	21	42	1	2	2	0	0	0	1	5	0	0	0	0	11	0	0	0	.048	.048	0
Henry, D.	NY	R	1.000	51	1	1	1	1	0	0	0	0	1	0	0	0	0	0	0	0	0	1.000	1.000	1
Heredia, G.	MON	R	.182	40	33	1	6	6	0	0	0	2	5	0	0	1	0	3	0	0	0	.182	.206	0
Hernandez, C.	LA	R	.149	45	94	3	14	21	1	0	2	8	1	0	1	7	0	25	0	0	5	.223	.216	4
Hernandez, J.	FLA	R	.000	7	1	0	0	0	0	0	0	0	0	0	0	0	0	0	0	0	0	.000	.000	0
Hernandez, J.	CHI	R	.245	93	245	37	60	118	11	4	13	40	8	2	0	13	3	69	1	0	8	.482	.281	9
Hernandez, X.	CIN	L	.000	59	8	0	0	0	0	0	0	0	0	0	0	0	0	4	0	0	0	.000	.000	0
Hickerson, B.	CHI-COL	L	.667	56	3	1	2	4	0	1	0	3	1	0	0	1	0	0	0	0	0	1.333	.750	0
Hill, G.	SF	R	.264	132	497	71	131	240	29	4	24	86	0	2	1	39	4	98	25	5	11	.483	.317	10
Hill, K.	STL	R	.194	18	31	1	6	6	0	0	0	3	5	1	0	2	0	10	0	0	0	.194	.235	1
Hoffman, T.	SD	R	.500	55	2	1	1	2	1	0	0	2	0	0	0	0	0	1	0	0	0	1.000	.500	0
Holbert, R.	SD	R	.178	63	73	11	13	23	2	1	2	5	3	0	2	8	1	20	4	0	3	.315	.277	5
Hollandsworth, T.	LA	L	.233	41	103	16	24	41	2	0	5	13	0	1	1	10	2	29	2	1	1	.398	.304	4
Hollins, D.	PHI	S	.229	65	205	46	47	84	12	2	7	25	0	4	5	53	4	38	1	1	4	.410	.393	7
Holmes, D.	COL	R	.000	68	1	0	0	0	0	0	0	0	3	0	0	0	0	0	0	0	0	.000	.000	1
Hook, C.	SF	R	.000	45	3	0	0	0	0	0	0	0	0	0	0	0	0	2	0	0	0	.000	.000	0
Howard, T.	CIN	S	.302	113	281	42	85	113	15	2	3	26	1	1	1	20	0	37	17	8	3	.402	.350	2
Hubbard, M.	CHI	R	.174	15	23	2	4	4	0	0	0	1	0	0	0	2	0	2	0	0	1	.174	.240	1
Hubbard, T.	COL	R	.310	24	58	13	18	31	4	0	3	9	1	0	0	8	0	6	2	1	2	.534	.394	0
Hudek, J.	HOU	S	1.000	19	1	0	1	1	0	0	0	2	0	0	0	0	0	0	0	0	0	1.000	1.000	0
Hulett, T.	STL	R	.182	4	11	0	2	2	0	0	0	0	0	0	0	0	0	3	0	0	0	.182	.182	2
Hundley, T.	NY	S	.280	90	275	39	77	133	11	0	15	51	1	3	5	42	5	64	1	0	4	.484	.382	7
Hunter, B.	HOU	R	.302	78	321	52	97	127	14	5	2	28	2	3	2	21	0	52	24	7	2	.396	.346	9
Hunter, B.	CIN	R	.215	40	79	9	17	26	6	0	1	9	0	2	1	11	1	21	2	1	2	.329	.312	3
Huskey, B.	NY	R	.189	28	90	8	17	27	1	0	3	11	1	1	0	10	0	16	1	0	3	.300	.267	6
Hyers, T.	SD	L	.000	6	5	0	0	0	0	0	0	0	0	0	0	0	0	1	0	0	1	.000	.000	0
Ingram, G.	LA	R	.200	44	55	5	11	13	2	0	0	3	2	0	0	9	0	8	3	0	0	.236	.313	8
Isringhausen, J.	NY	R	.148	14	27	2	4	5	1	0	0	0	4	0	1	2	0	10	0	0	0	.185	.233	2
Jackson, D.	STL	R	.161	19	31	1	5	7	2	0	0	2	4	0	0	1	0	16	0	0	0	.226	.188	3
Jackson, M.	CIN	R	.250	40	4	0	1	1	0	0	0	0	0	0	0	0	0	0	0	0	0	.250	.250	0
Jacome, J.	NY	L	.000	5	7	0	0	0	0	0	0	0	1	0	0	0	0	6	0	0	0	.000	.000	1
Jarvis, K.	CIN	R	.143	19	21	2	3	4	1	0	0	0	1	0	1	0	0	8	0	0	0	.190	.182	2
Jefferies, G.	PHI	S	.306	114	480	69	147	215	31	2	11	56	0	6	0	35	5	26	9	5	15	.448	.349	3
Johnson, B.	SD	R	.251	68	207	20	52	70	9	0	3	29	1	4	1	11	2	39	0	0	2	.338	.287	4
Johnson, C.	FLA	R	.251	97	315	40	79	129	15	1	11	39	4	2	4	46	2	71	0	2	11	.410	.351	6
Johnson, H.	CHI	S	.195	87	169	26	33	60	4	1	7	22	0	2	1	34	0	46	1	1	2	.355	.330	7
Johnson, M.	PIT	L	.208	79	221	32	46	93	6	1	13	28	0	1	2	37	2	66	5	2	2	.421	.326	8
Jones, B.	NY	R	.161	30	56	3	9	9	0	0	0	2	18	0	0	1	0	25	0	0	0	.161	.175	6
Jones, C.	ATL	S	.265	140	524	87	139	236	22	3	23	86	1	4	0	73	1	99	8	4	10	.450	.353	25
Jones, C.	NY	R	.280	79	182	33	51	85	6	2	8	31	2	3	1	13	1	45	2	1	2	.467	.327	2
Jones, T.	HOU	L	.200	68	5	1	1	2	1	0	0	0	0	0	0	0	0	1	0	0	0	.400	.200	1
Jordan, B.	STL	R	.296	131	490	83	145	239	20	4	22	81	0	2	11	22	4	79	24	9	5	.488	.339	1
Jordan, K.	PHI	R	.185	24	54	6	10	17	1	0	2	6	0	0	1	2	1	9	0	0	0	.315	.228	1
Juden, J.	PHI	R	.056	13	18	1	1	4	0	0	1	4	3	0	0	0	0	12	0	0	0	.222	.056	0
Justice, D.	ATL	L	.253	120	411	73	104	197	17	2	24	78	0	5	2	73	5	68	4	2	5	.479	.365	4
Karros, E.	LA	R	.298	143	551	83	164	295	29	3	32	105	0	4	4	61	4	115	4	4	14	.535	.369	7
Kelly, M.	ATL	R	.190	97	137	26	26	43	6	1	3	17	2	1	2	11	0	49	7	3	2	.314	.258	4
Kelly, R.	MON-LA	R	.278	136	504	58	140	188	23	2	7	57	0	7	6	22	6	79	19	10	14	.373	.312	6
Kent, J.	NY	R	.278	125	472	65	131	219	22	3	20	65	1	4	8	29	3	89	3	3	9	.464	.327	10
Kile, D.	HOU	R	.111	25	36	1	4	5	1	0	0	6	5	0	0	4	0	20	0	0	1	.139	.200	3
King, J.	PIT	R	.265	122	445	61	118	203	27	2	18	87	0	8	1	55	5	63	7	4	10	.456	.342	17
Kingery, M.	COL	L	.269	119	350	66	94	144	18	4	8	37	6	1	0	45	1	40	13	5	7	.411	.351	5
Klesko, R.	ATL	L	.310	107	329	48	102	200	25	2	23	70	0	3	2	47	10	72	5	4	8	.608	.396	8
Kmak, J.	CHI	R	.245	19	53	7	13	19	3	0	1	6	0	1	1	6	0	12	0	0	2	.358	.328	0
Kowitz, B.	ATL	L	.167	10	24	3	4	5	1	0	0	3	1	0	1	2	0	5	0	1	0	.208	.259	0
Laker, T.	MON	R	.234	64	141	17	33	52	8	1	3	20	1	1	1	14	4	38	0	1	5	.369	.306	7
Lampkin, T.	SF	L	.276	65	76	8	21	26	2	0	1	9	0	0	1	9	1	8	2	0	1	.342	.360	0
Lankford, R.	STL	L	.277	132	483	81	134	248	35	2	25	82	0	5	2	63	6	110	24	8	10	.513	.360	3
Lansing, M.	MON	R	.255	127	467	47	119	183	30	2	10	62	1	3	3	28	2	65	27	4	14	.392	.299	6
Larkin, B.	CIN	R	.319	131	496	98	158	244	29	6	15	66	3	4	3	61	2	49	51	5	6	.492	.394	11
Ledesma, A.	NY	R	.242	21	33	4	8	8	0	0	0	3	0	0	0	6	1	7	0	0	2	.242	.359	2
Lee, M.	STL	S	1.000	1	1	1	1	1	0	0	0	0	0	0	0	0	0	0	0	0	0	1.000	1.000	1
Leiper, D.	MON	L	.000	26	1	0	0	0	0	0	0	0	0	0	0	0	0	0	0	0	0	.000	.000	0
Leiter, M.	SF	R	.098	30	61	2	6	6	0	0	0	5	9	0	0	4	0	33	0	0	2	.098	.154	4
Lemke, M.	ATL	S	.253	116	399	42	101	142	16	5	5	38	7	3	0	44	4	40	2	2	17	.356	.325	5
Leonard, M.	SF	L	.190	14	21	4	4	8	1	0	1	4	0	0	0	5	1	2	0	0	1	.381	.346	0
Leskanic, C.	COL	R	.143	76	7	1	1	1	0	0	0	0	2	0	0	0	0	1	0	0	0	.143	.143	0
Lewis, D.	SF-CIN	R	.250	132	472	66	118	140	13	3	1	24	12	1	8	34	0	57	32	18	9	.297	.311	2
Lewis, M.	CIN	R	.339	81	171	25	58	82	13	1	3	30	0	2	0	21	2	33	0	3	1	.480	.407	4
Lewis, R.	FLA	R	.000	21	1	0	0	0	0	0	0	0	0	0	0	1	0	1	0	0	0	.000	.500	2
Lieber, J.	PIT	L	.048	21	21	0	1	1	0	0	0	0	0	0	0	0	0	14	0	0	1	.048	.048	1
Lieberthal, M.	PHI	R	.255	16	47	1	12	14	2	0	0	4	2	0	0	5	0	5	0	0	1	.298	.327	1
Liriano, N.	PIT	S	.286	107	259	29	74	103	12	1	5	38	1	3	2	24	3	34	2	2	2	.398	.347	5
Livingstone, S.	SD	L	.337	99	196	26	66	96	15	0	5	32	0	2	0	15	1	22	2	1	3	.490	.380	3
Loaiza, E.	PIT	R	.192	33	52	4	10	13	1	1	0	2	7	1	0	1	0	11	0	0	1	.250	.204	0
Lomon, K.	NY	R	.000	6	0	0	0	0	0	0	0	0	1	0	0	0	0	0	0	0	0	.000	.000	1
Longmire, T.	PHI	L	.356	59	104	21	37	53	7	0	3	19	0	1	1	11	1	19	1	1	1	.510	.419	0
Lopez, J.	ATL	R	.315	100	333	37	105	166	11	4	14	51	0	3	2	14	0	57	0	1	13	.498	.344	8
Mabry, J.	STL	L	.307	129	388	35	119	157	21	1	5	41	0	4	2	24	5	45	0	3	6	.405	.347	4
Maddux, G.	ATL	R	.153	28	72	8	11	13	2	0	0	1	6	0	0	3	0	22	0	0	0	.181	.187	0
Magadan, D.	HOU	L	.313	127	348	44	109	139	24	0	2	51	1	2	0	71	9	56	2	1	9	.399	.428	18
Manwaring, K.	SF	R	.251	118	379	21	95	126	15	2	4	36	4	4	10	27	6	72	1	0	8	.332	.314	7
Manzanillo, R.	PIT	L	.000	5	1	0	0	0	0	0	0	0	0	0	0	0	0	1	0	0	0	.000	.000	0
Marsh, T.	PHI	R	.294	43	109	13	32	46	3	1	3	15	0	1	0	4	0	25	0	1	1	.422	.316	3
Martin, A.	PIT	L	.282	124	439	70	124	194	25	3	13	41	1	0	2	44	6	92	20	11	5	.442	.351	5
Martinez, P.	HOU	L	.000	25	0	1	0	0	0	0	0	0	0	0	0	1	0	0	0	0	0	.000	1.000	0
Martinez, P.	MON	R	.111	30	63	2	7	7	0	0	0	2	5	2	2	0	0	30	0	0	1	.111	.134	2
Martinez, R.	LA	R	.172	30	64	2	11	15	4	0	0	4	13	0	0	1	0	19	0	0	0	.234	.185	3
Mathews, T.	FLA	L	.462	57	13	2	6	8	2	0	0	3	0	0	0	0	0	4	0	0	1	.615	.462	0
Mathews, T.	STL	R	.000	23	2	0	0	0	0	0	0	0	0	0	0	0	0	1	0	0	0	.000	.000	1
Mauser, T.	SD	R	.000	5	1	0	0	0	0	0	0	0	0	0	0	0	0	1	0	0	0	.000	.000	0
May, D.	HOU	L	.301	78	206	29	62	103	15	1	8	41	0	3	1	19	0	24	5	0	4	.500	.358	2
McCarty, D.	SF	R	.250	12	20	1	5	6	1	0	0	2	0	0	0	2	0	4	1	0	0	.300	.318	1
McCracken, Q.	COL	S	.000	3	1	0	0	0	0	0	0	0	0	0	0	0	0	1	0	0	0	.000	.000	0
McCurry, J.	PIT	R	.000	55	3	0	0	0	0	0	0	0	0	0	0	0	0	1	0	0	0	.000	.000	0
McDavid, R.	SD	L	.176	11	17	2	3	3	0	0	0	0	0	0	0	2	0	6	1	1	1	.176	.263	0
McElroy, C.	CIN	L	.000	44	3	0	0	0	0	0	0	0	0	0	0	0	0	0	0	0	0	.000	.000	0
McGriff, F.	ATL	L	.280	144	528	85	148	258	27	1	27	93	0	6	5	65	6	99	3	6	19	.489	.361	5
McMichael, G.	ATL	R	.000	67	6	0	0	0	0	0	0	0	0	0	0	1	0	4	0	0	0	.000	.143	1
McMurtry, C.	HOU	R	.000	11	1	0	0	0	0	0	0	0	0	0	0	0	0	1	0	0	0	.000	.000	0
McRae, B.	CHI	S	.288	137	580	92	167	255	38	7	12	48	3	1	7	47	1	92	27	8	12	.440	.348	3
Mejia, R.	COL	R	.154	23	52	5	8	12	1	0	1	4	0	1	1	0	0	17	0	1	1	.231	.167	2
Merced, O.	PIT	L	.300	132	487	75	146	228	29	4	15	83	0	5	1	52	9	74	7	2	9	.468	.365	6
Mercker, K.	ATL	L	.104	29	48	1	5	8	3	0	0	5	6	0	0	0	0	17	0	0	0	.167	.104	1
Miceli, D.	PIT	R	.000	58	1	0	0	0	0	0	0	0	0	0	0	0	0	1	0	0	0	.000	.000	0
Miller, O.	HOU	R	.262	92	324	36	85	122	20	1	5	36	4	0	5	22	8	71	3	4	7	.377	.319	15
Mimbs, M.	PHI	L	.143	35	35	2	5	6	1	0	0	2	8	0	0	0	0	12	0	0	1	.171	.143	1
Minor, B.	NY	R	.000	35	2	0	0	0	0	0	0	0	0	0	0	0	0	0	0	0	0	.000	.000	0
Mintz, S.	SF	L	.000	14	3	0	0	0	0	0	0	0	0	0	0	0	0	3	0	0	0	.000	.000	0
Mlicki, D.	NY	R	.051	29	39	2	2	2	0	0	0	2	12	0	0	8	0	12	0	0	0	.051	.213	1
Mondesi, R.	LA	R	.285	139	536	91	153	266	23	6	26	88	0	7	4	33	4	96	27	4	7	.496	.328	6
Morandini, M.	PHI	L	.283	127	494	65	140	206	34	7	6	49	4	1	9	42	3	80	9	6	11	.417	.350	7
Mordecai, M.	ATL	R	.280	69	75	10	21	36	6	0	3	11	2	1	0	9	0	16	0	0	1	.480	.353	0
Morgan, M.	CHI-STL	R	.053	21	38	2	2	2	0	0	0	0	4	0	0	3	0	20	0	0	0	.053	.122	1
Morman, R.	FLA	R	.278	34	72	9	20	33	7	0	2	7	0	0	1	3	0	12	0	0	5	.458	.316	1
Morris, H.	CIN	L	.279	101	359	53	100	162	25	2	11	51	1	1	1	29	7	58	1	1	10	.451	.333	5
Mouton, J.	HOU	R	.262	104	298	42	78	112	18	2	4	27	3	1	4	25	1	59	25	8	5	.376	.326	0
Mulholland, T.	SF	R	.102	30	49	3	5	11	1	1	1	3	3	1	0	1	0	22	0	0	1	.224	.118	3
Munoz, B.	PHI	R	.000	3	5	0	0	0	0	0	0	0	0	0	0	0	0	2	0	0	0	.000	.000	1
Munoz, M.	COL	L	.500	64	2	1	1	2	1	0	0	1	0	0	0	0	0	1	0	0	0	1.000	.750	0
Munoz, N.	LA	R	.000	2	1	0	0	0	0	0	0	0	0	0	0	0	0	0	0	0	0	.000	.000	0
Murphy, R.	LA-FLA	L	1.000	14	1	0	1	1	0	0	0	0	0	0	0	0	0	0	0	0	0	1.000	1.000	0
Murray, M.	ATL	R	.500	4	2	0	1	1	0	0	0	0	0	0	0	0	0	1	0	0	0	.500	.500	0
Myers, R.	CHI	L	.000	57	0	0	0	0	0	0	0	0	1	0	0	1	0	0	0	0	0	.000	1.000	0
Nabholz, C.	CHI	L	.000	34	1	0	0	0	0	0	0	0	0	0	0	0	0	0	0	0	0	.000	.000	0
Natal, R.	FLA	R	.233	16	43	2	10	20	2	1	2	6	1	1	0	1	0	9	0	0	0	.465	.244	1
Navarro, J.	CHI	R	.185	29	65	0	12	17	5	0	0	7	8	0	0	1	0	25	0	0	0	.262	.197	1
Neagle, D.	PIT	L	.122	32	74	5	9	15	3	0	1	8	5	0	0	4	0	26	0	0	0	.203	.167	1
Nevin, P.	HOU	R	.117	18	60	4	7	8	1	0	0	1	1	0	1	7	1	13	1	0	2	.133	.221	3
Newfield, M.	SD	R	.309	21	55	6	17	27	5	1	1	7	0	0	0	2	0	8	0	0	3	.491	.333	0
Nieves, M.	SD	S	.205	98	234	32	48	98	6	1	14	38	1	3	5	19	0	88	2	3	9	.419	.276	2

INDIVIDUAL BATTING—1995

BATTER	TEAM	B	AVG	G	AB	R	H	TB	2B	3B	HR	RBI	SH	SF	HP	BB	IBB	SO	SB	CS	GI DP	SLG	OBP	E
Nitkowski, C	CIN	L	.200	9	10	1	2	2	0	0	0	1	0	0	0	0	0	6	0	0	0	.200	.200	1
Nokes, M	COL	L	.182	10	11	1	2	3	1	0	0	0	0	0	0	1	1	4	0	0	1	.273	.250	1
Nomo, H	LA	R	.091	28	66	2	6	6	0	0	0	4	5	1	0	0	0	33	0	0	1	.091	.090	3
O'Brien, C	ATL	R	.227	67	198	18	45	79	7	0	9	23	0	0	6	29	2	40	0	1	8	.399	.343	4
Ochoa, A	NY	R	.297	11	37	7	11	12	1	0	0	0	0	0	0	2	0	10	1	0	1	.324	.333	0
Offerman, J	LA	S	.287	119	429	69	123	161	14	6	4	33	10	0	3	69	0	67	2	7	5	.375	.389	35
Oliva, J	ATL-STL	R	.142	70	183	15	26	52	5	0	7	20	0	1	2	12	0	46	0	0	5	.284	.202	7
Olivares, O	COL-PHI	R	.222	17	9	1	2	6	1	0	1	2	1	0	0	1	0	4	0	0	0	.667	.300	0
Oquendo, J	STL	S	.209	88	220	31	46	66	8	3	2	17	4	1	0	35	3	21	1	1	1	.300	.316	6
Orsulak, J	NY	L	.283	108	290	41	82	108	19	2	1	37	1	6	1	19	2	35	1	3	3	.372	.323	4
Osborne, D	STL	L	.161	19	31	1	5	8	3	0	0	4	3	0	1	3	0	15	0	0	0	.258	.257	0
Osuna, P	LA	R	.000	39	2	0	0	0	0	0	0	0	0	0	0	0	0	0	0	0	0	.000	.000	0
Otero, R	NY	S	.137	35	51	5	7	9	2	0	0	1	1	0	0	3	0	10	2	1	1	.176	.185	0
Owens, E	CIN	R	1.000	2	2	0	2	2	0	0	0	1	1	0	0	0	0	0	0	0	0	1.000	1.000	0
Owens, J	COL	R	.244	18	45	7	11	25	2	0	4	12	0	1	1	2	0	15	0	0	0	.556	.286	1
Pagnozzi, T	STL	R	.215	62	219	17	47	69	14	1	2	15	0	1	1	11	0	31	0	1	9	.315	.254	2
Painter, L	COL	L	.111	33	9	0	1	2	1	0	0	0	1	0	0	1	0	4	0	0	0	.222	.200	0
Palacios, V	STL	R	.167	20	6	1	1	1	0	0	0	0	1	0	0	0	0	4	0	0	0	.167	.167	0
Parent, M	PIT-CHI	R	.234	81	265	30	62	127	11	0	18	38	1	0	0	26	2	69	0	0	6	.479	.302	4
Park, C	LA	R	.000	2	1	0	0	0	0	0	0	0	0	0	0	0	0	1	0	0	0	.000	.000	0
Parker, R	LA	R	.276	27	29	3	8	8	0	0	0	4	2	0	0	2	0	4	1	1	1	.276	.323	0
Parra, J	LA	R	.000	8	0	0	0	0	0	0	0	0	2	0	0	0	0	0	0	0	0	.000	.000	0
Parrett, J	STL	R	.500	59	2	0	1	1	0	0	0	0	0	0	0	0	0	1	0	0	0	.500	.500	2
Parris, S	PIT	R	.250	15	28	2	7	9	2	0	0	4	1	0	0	0	0	10	0	0	0	.321	.250	0
Patterson, J	SF	S	.205	95	205	27	42	56	5	3	1	14	6	0	12	14	1	41	4	2	7	.273	.294	4
Pegues, S	PIT	R	.246	82	171	17	42	68	8	0	6	16	0	3	1	4	0	36	1	2	3	.398	.263	4
Pena, A	FLA-ATL	R	.000	27	1	0	0	0	0	0	0	0	0	0	0	0	0	1	0	0	0	.000	.000	0
Pena, G	STL	S	.267	32	101	20	27	38	6	1	1	8	4	2	1	16	1	30	3	2	2	.376	.367	3
Pendleton, T	FLA	S	.290	133	513	70	149	225	32	1	14	78	0	4	2	38	7	84	1	2	7	.439	.339	18
Pennington, B	CIN	L	.000	6	2	0	0	0	0	0	0	0	0	0	0	0	0	1	0	0	0	.000	.000	1
Perez, C	MON	L	.133	28	45	1	6	12	1	1	1	5	4	0	0	4	0	21	0	0	0	.267	.204	2
Perez, E	ATL	R	.308	7	13	1	4	8	1	0	1	4	0	0	0	0	0	2	0	0	0	.615	.308	0
Perez, M	CHI	R	.000	68	4	1	0	0	0	0	0	0	1	0	0	2	0	4	0	0	0	.000	.333	1
Perez, Y	FLA	S	.000	69	2	0	0	0	0	0	0	0	0	0	0	0	0	1	0	0	0	.000	.000	0
Perry, G	STL	L	.165	65	79	4	13	17	4	0	0	5	0	0	0	6	0	12	0	0	2	.215	.224	0
Person, R	NY	R	.667	3	3	1	2	2	0	0	0	0	0	0	0	0	0	0	0	0	0	.667	.667	0
Petagine, R	SD	L	.234	89	124	15	29	46	8	0	3	17	2	0	0	26	2	41	0	0	2	.371	.367	1
Petkovsek, M	STL	R	.081	26	37	4	3	3	0	0	0	2	3	1	0	5	0	11	0	0	0	.081	.186	0
Phillips, J	SF	L	.195	92	231	27	45	81	9	0	9	28	2	0	0	19	2	69	1	1	3	.351	.256	4
Piazza, M	LA	R	.346	112	434	82	150	263	17	0	32	93	0	1	1	39	10	80	1	0	10	.606	.400	9
Plantier, P	HOU-SD	L	.255	76	216	33	55	88	6	0	9	34	0	3	1	28	3	48	1	1	3	.407	.339	4
Plesac, D	PIT	L	.250	58	4	0	1	1	0	0	0	0	0	0	0	0	0	3	0	0	0	.250	.250	0
Polonia, L	ATL	L	.264	28	53	6	14	21	7	0	0	2	1	0	0	3	0	9	3	0	0	.396	.304	0
Portugal, M	SF-CIN	R	.138	31	58	5	8	13	5	0	0	5	8	0	0	5	0	13	0	0	1	.224	.206	1
Powell, R	HOU-PIT	L	.000	27	3	0	0	0	0	0	0	0	1	0	0	0	0	1	0	0	0	.000	.000	0
Pratt, T	CHI	R	.133	25	60	3	8	10	2	0	0	4	0	1	0	6	1	21	0	0	1	.167	.209	3
Pride, C	MON	L	.175	48	63	10	11	12	1	0	0	2	1	0	0	5	0	16	3	2	2	.190	.235	2
Prince, T	LA	R	.200	18	40	3	8	15	2	1	1	4	0	0	0	4	0	10	0	0	0	.375	.273	1
Pugh, T	CIN	R	.143	29	28	2	4	6	2	0	0	1	4	0	0	1	0	12	0	0	1	.214	.172	1
Pulliam, H	COL	R	.400	5	5	1	2	6	1	0	1	3	0	0	0	0	0	2	0	0	0	1.200	.400	0
Pulsipher, W	NY	L	.105	17	38	4	4	6	2	0	0	4	4	2	0	5	0	19	0	0	0	.158	.200	0
Pye, E	LA	R	.000	7	8	0	0	0	0	0	0	0	0	0	0	0	0	4	0	0	0	.000	.000	0
Quantrill, P	PHI	L	.105	33	57	5	6	6	0	0	0	0	7	0	0	3	0	24	0	0	1	.105	.150	1
Rapp, P	FLA	R	.107	28	56	1	6	7	1	0	0	5	9	0	0	0	0	25	0	0	1	.125	.107	1
Ready, R	PHI	R	.138	23	29	3	4	4	0	0	0	0	1	0	0	3	0	6	0	1	2	.138	.219	1
Reed, J	SF	L	.265	66	113	12	30	32	2	0	0	9	1	0	0	20	3	17	0	0	3	.283	.376	1
Reed, J	SD	R	.256	131	445	58	114	146	18	1	4	40	3	3	5	59	1	38	6	4	9	.328	.348	4
Reed, R	CIN	R	.000	4	3	0	0	0	0	0	0	0	2	0	0	0	0	0	0	0	0	.000	.000	0
Reed, S	COL	R	.333	71	3	0	1	1	0	0	0	0	0	0	0	0	0	1	0	0	0	.333	.333	1
Rekar, B	COL	R	.038	15	26	1	1	1	0	0	0	0	4	0	0	3	0	15	0	1	2	.038	.138	1
Remlinger, M	NY-CIN	L	.000	7	1	0	0	0	0	0	0	0	0	0	0	0	0	0	0	0	0	.000	.000	0
Reynolds, S	HOU	R	.127	31	63	4	8	9	1	0	0	1	10	0	0	1	0	30	0	0	2	.143	.141	1
Reynoso, A	COL	R	.133	20	30	1	4	4	0	0	0	0	2	0	0	1	0	11	0	0	2	.133	.161	2
Rhodes, K	CHI	L	.125	13	16	2	2	2	0	0	0	2	0	1	0	0	0	4	0	0	1	.125	.118	1
Rijo, J	CIN	R	.136	14	22	1	3	4	1	0	0	3	2	0	0	0	0	3	0	0	0	.182	.136	0
Ritz, K	COL	R	.188	31	48	3	9	10	1	0	0	2	11	0	2	2	0	20	1	1	1	.208	.250	0
Roberson, K	CHI	S	.184	32	38	5	7	20	1	0	4	6	0	0	1	6	0	14	0	1	1	.526	.311	0
Roberts, B	SD	S	.304	73	296	40	90	110	14	0	2	25	1	0	2	17	1	36	20	2	2	.372	.346	4
Rodriguez, H	LA-MON	L	.239	45	138	13	33	45	4	1	2	15	0	1	0	11	2	28	0	1	5	.326	.293	1
Rojas, M	MON	R	.000	59	6	0	0	0	0	0	0	0	2	0	0	0	0	4	0	0	0	.000	.000	0
Roper, J	CIN-SF	R	.000	3	1	0	0	0	0	0	0	0	1	0	0	0	0	0	0	0	0	.000	.000	0
Rosselli, J	SF	R	.200	9	10	1	2	2	0	0	0	1	1	0	0	0	0	3	0	0	0	.200	.200	0
Rueter, K	MON	L	.000	9	16	0	0	0	0	0	0	1	2	0	0	0	0	6	0	0	0	.000	.000	0
Ruffin, B	COL	S	.000	37	2	0	0	0	0	0	0	0	0	0	0	0	0	2	0	0	0	.000	.000	0
Ruffin, J	CIN	R	.000	10	2	0	0	0	0	0	0	0	0	0	0	0	0	0	0	0	0	.000	.000	0
Saberhagen, B	NY-COL	R	.102	25	49	3	5	6	1	0	0	0	5	0	0	2	0	12	0	0	0	.122	.137	1
Sabo, C	STL	R	.154	5	13	0	2	3	1	0	0	3	0	0	0	1	0	2	1	0	1	.231	.214	1
Sager, A	COL	R	.000	10	3	0	0	0	0	0	0	0	0	0	0	0	0	1	0	0	0	.000	.000	0
Sanchez, R	CHI	R	.278	114	428	57	119	154	22	2	3	27	8	2	1	14	2	48	6	4	9	.360	.301	7
Sanders, D	CIN-SF	L	.268	85	343	48	92	137	11	8	6	28	3	2	4	27	0	60	24	9	1	.399	.327	5
Sanders, R	CIN	R	.306	133	484	91	148	280	36	6	28	99	0	6	8	69	4	122	36	12	9	.579	.397	5
Sanders, S	SD	R	.296	17	27	2	8	9	1	0	0	4	3	0	0	1	0	3	1	0	0	.333	.321	0
Santangelo, F	MON	S	.296	35	98	11	29	39	5	1	1	9	1	0	2	12	0	9	1	1	0	.398	.384	1
Santiago, B	CIN	R	.286	81	266	40	76	129	20	0	11	44	0	2	4	24	1	48	2	2	7	.485	.351	2
Sasser, M	PIT	L	.154	14	26	1	4	5	1	0	0	0	0	0	0	0	0	0	0	0	0	.192	.154	0
Scarsone, S	SF	R	.266	80	233	33	62	111	10	3	11	29	3	1	6	18	0	82	3	2	2	.476	.333	11
Schall, G	PHI	R	.231	24	65	2	15	17	2	0	0	5	0	0	1	6	1	16	0	0	1	.262	.306	2
Scheid, R	FLA	L	.000	6	1	0	0	0	0	0	0	0	0	0	0	0	0	0	0	0	0	.000	.000	0
Schilling, C	PHI	R	.175	17	40	3	7	9	2	0	0	3	5	0	0	0	0	15	0	0	1	.225	.175	1
Schmidt, J	ATL	R	.200	9	5	0	1	1	0	0	0	0	1	0	0	1	0	2	0	0	0	.200	.333	0
Schofield, D	LA	R	.100	9	10	0	1	1	0	0	0	0	0	0	0	1	0	3	0	0	0	.100	.182	0
Schourek, P	CIN	L	.220	29	59	7	13	15	2	0	0	4	12	0	0	0	0	12	0	0	1	.254	.220	1
Scott, T	MON	R	.250	62	4	0	1	1	0	0	0	0	0	0	0	0	0	2	0	0	0	.250	.250	0
Seanez, R	LA	R	.000	37	1	0	0	0	0	0	0	0	0	0	0	0	0	1	0	0	0	.000	.000	1
Sefcik, K	PHI	R	.000	5	4	1	0	0	0	0	0	0	0	0	0	0	0	2	0	0	0	.000	.000	0
Segui, D	NY-MON	S	.309	130	456	68	141	210	25	4	12	68	8	3	3	40	5	47	2	7	10	.461	.367	3
Servais, S	HOU-CHI	R	.265	80	264	38	70	131	22	0	13	47	2	3	3	32	8	52	2	2	9	.496	.348	12
Service, S	SF	R	.000	28	1	0	0	0	0	0	0	0	0	0	0	0	0	1	0	0	0	.000	.000	0
Sharperson, M	ATL	R	.143	7	7	1	1	2	1	0	0	2	0	0	0	0	0	2	0	0	0	.286	.143	0
Shaw, J	MON	R	.000	50	6	2	0	0	0	0	0	0	0	0	0	2	0	4	0	0	0	.000	.250	0
Sheaffer, D	STL	R	.231	76	208	24	48	75	10	1	5	30	0	1	0	23	2	38	0	0	8	.361	.306	3
Sheffield, G	FLA	R	.324	63	213	46	69	125	8	0	16	46	0	2	4	55	8	45	19	4	3	.587	.467	7
Shipley, C	HOU	R	.263	92	232	23	61	80	8	1	3	24	1	2	2	8	3	28	6	1	13	.345	.291	3
Siddall, J	MON	L	.300	7	10	4	3	3	0	0	0	1	0	0	1	3	0	3	0	0	0	.300	.500	2
Silvestri, D	MON	R	.264	39	72	12	19	31	6	0	2	7	1	1	0	9	0	27	2	0	2	.431	.341	1
Simms, M	HOU	R	.256	50	121	14	31	62	4	0	9	24	0	1	3	13	0	28	1	2	3	.512	.341	1
Slaught, D	PIT	R	.304	35	112	13	34	40	6	0	0	13	1	0	1	9	2	8	0	0	5	.357	.361	1
Slocumb, H	PHI	R	.000	61	1	0	0	0	0	0	0	0	0	0	0	0	0	0	0	0	0	.000	.000	1
Smiley, J	CIN	L	.164	28	55	6	9	16	1	0	2	5	6	1	0	4	0	26	0	0	1	.291	.217	0
Smith, D	ATL	L	.252	103	131	16	33	54	8	2	3	21	0	1	2	13	1	35	0	3	2	.412	.327	2
Smith, O	STL	S	.199	44	156	16	31	38	5	1	0	11	5	2	2	17	0	12	4	3	6	.244	.282	7
Smith, P	CIN	R	.000	11	3	0	0	0	0	0	0	0	0	0	0	2	0	2	0	0	0	.000	.400	0
Smoltz, J	ATL	R	.107	29	56	5	6	6	0	0	0	1	6	0	0	7	0	25	0	0	0	.107	.206	2
Sosa, S	CHI	R	.268	144	564	89	151	282	17	3	36	119	0	2	5	58	11	134	34	7	8	.500	.340	13
Spehr, T	MON	R	.257	41	35	4	9	17	5	0	1	3	3	0	0	6	0	7	0	0	0	.486	.366	1
Spiers, B	NY	L	.208	63	72	5	15	19	2	1	0	11	1	2	0	12	1	15	0	1	0	.264	.314	7
Springer, D	PHI	R	.125	4	8	0	1	1	0	0	0	0	0	0	0	0	0	3	0	0	0	.125	.125	1
Springer, R	PHI	R	.000	14	1	0	0	0	0	0	0	0	1	0	0	0	0	1	0	0	0	.000	.000	0
Stankiewicz, A	HOU	R	.115	43	52	6	6	7	1	0	0	7	1	0	0	12	2	19	4	2	1	.135	.281	1
Stinnett, K	NY	R	.219	77	196	23	43	65	8	1	4	18	0	0	6	29	3	65	2	0	3	.332	.338	7
Stocker, K	PHI	S	.218	125	412	42	90	113	14	3	1	32	10	3	9	43	9	75	6	1	7	.274	.304	17
Sullivan, S	CIN	R	.000	3	1	0	0	0	0	0	0	0	0	0	0	0	0	1	0	0	0	.000	.000	0
Sweeney, M	STL	L	.273	37	77	5	21	29	2	0	2	13	1	2	0	10	0	15	1	1	3	.377	.348	2
Swift, B	COL	R	.194	19	36	5	7	11	1	0	1	4	5	0	0	2	0	5	1	0	0	.306	.237	1
Swindell, G	HOU	R	.240	34	50	4	12	15	3	0	0	5	6	0	0	3	0	9	0	0	1	.300	.283	1
Tabaka, J	SD-HOU	R	.000	34	1	0	0	0	0	0	0	0	1	0	0	0	0	0	0	0	0	.000	.000	0
Tapani, K	LA	R	.176	13	17	0	3	4	1	0	0	2	3	0	0	0	0	7	0	0	0	.235	.176	1
Tarasco, T	MON	L	.249	126	438	64	109	177	18	4	14	40	3	1	2	51	12	78	24	3	2	.404	.329	5
Tatum, J	COL	R	.235	34	34	4	8	11	1	1	0	4	0	0	0	1	0	7	0	0	1	.324	.257	0
Taubensee, E	CIN	L	.284	80	218	32	62	107	14	2	9	44	1	1	2	22	2	52	2	2	2	.491	.354	6
Tavarez, J	FLA	S	.289	63	190	31	55	71	6	2	2	13	3	1	1	16	1	27	7	5	1	.374	.346	0
Telgheder, D	NY	R	.333	7	6	1	2	2	0	0	0	1	1	0	0	0	0	3	0	0	0	.333	.333	0
Thompson, M	HOU	L	.220	92	132	14	29	44	9	0	2	19	2	1	1	14	3	37	4	2	3	.333	.297	1
Thompson, M	COL	R	.385	21	13	2	5	5	0	0	0	0	1	0	0	0	0	7	0	0	0	.385	.385	0
Thompson, R	SF	R	.223	95	336	51	75	114	15	0	8	23	9	0	4	42	1	76	1	2	3	.339	.317	3
Thompson, R	NY	R	.251	75	267	39	67	101	13	0	7	31	0	4	4	19	1	77	3	1	12	.378	.306	3
Timmons, O	CHI	R	.263	77	171	30	45	81	10	1	8	28	0	1	0	13	2	32	3	0	8	.474	.314	2
Torres, S	SF	R	.000	4	1	0	0	0	0	0	0	0	0	0	0	0	0	0	0	0	0	.000	.000	0
Trachsel, S	CHI	R	.265	30	49	3	13	15	2	0	0	4	6	1	0	2	0	17	0	0	0	.306	.288	1
Treadway, J	LA-MON	L	.209	58	67	6	14	18	2	1	0	13	0	0	0	5	1	4	0	1	0	.269	.264	0
Tucker, S	HOU	R	.286	5	7	1	2	5	0	0	1	1	0	0	0	0	0	0	0	0	0	.714	.286	0
Urbani, T	STL	L	.316	24	19	3	6	10	1	0	1	3	2	0	0	3	0	6	0	0	0	.526	.409	0
Urbina, U	MON	R	.333	7	6	0	2	2	0	0	0	0	0	0	0	0	0	4	0	0	0	.333	.333	0
Valdes, I	LA	R	.097	33	62	2	6	6	0	0	0	1	7	0	0	1	0	26	1	0	0	.097	.111	1
Valdes, M	FLA	R	.000	3	2	0	0	0	0	0	0	0	0	0	0	0	0	0	0	0	0	.000	.000	0
Valdez, C	SF	R	.000	11	1	0	0	0	0	0	0	0	0	0	0	0	0	1	0	0	0	.000	.000	0
Valdez, S	SF	R	.095	13	21	1	2	2	0	0	0	1	3	0	0	0	0	9	0	0	0	.095	.095	2
Valenzuela, F	SD	L	.250	29	32	3	8	15	1	0	2	8	3	0	0	0	0	6	0	0	0	.469	.250	0
Vander Wal, J	COL	L	.347	105	101	15	35	60	8	1	5	21	0	1	0	16	5	23	1	1	2	.594	.432	2
VanLandingham, W	SF	R	.152	18	46	1	7	12	2	0	1	3	1	0	0	0	0	24	0	0	1	.261	.152	1
Van Slyke, A	PHI	L	.243	63	214	26	52	75	10	2	3	16	0	2	2	28	1	41	7	0	6	.350	.333	2
Varsho, G	PHI	L	.252	72	103	7	26	29	1	1	0	11	0	1	2	7	1	17	2	0	1	.282	.310	2
Veras, Q	FLA	S	.261	124	440	86	115	164	20	7	5	32	7	2	9	80	0	68	56	21	7	.373	.384	9
Veres, D	HOU	R	.000	72	5	0	0	0	0	0	0	0	1	0	0	0	0	4	0	0	0	.000	.000	1
Veres, R	FLA	R	.000	47	3	0	0	0	0	0	0	0	0	0	0	0	0	0	0	0	0	.000	.000	1
Villone, R	SD	L	.000	19	1	0	0	0	0	0	0	0	0	0	0	0	0	0	0	0	0	.000	.000	0
Viola, F	CIN	L	.167	3	6	0	1	2	1	0	0	0	0	0	0	0	0	1	0	0	0	.333	.167	0
Vizcaino, J	NY	S	.287	135	509	66	146	186	21	5	3	56	13	3	1	35	4	76	8	3	14	.365	.332	10
Wagner, P	PIT	R	.214	34	42	5	9	10	1	0	0	4	6	0	0	4	0	11	0	0	1	.238	.283	0
Walker, L	COL	L	.306	131	494	96	151	300	31	5	36	101	0	5	14	49	13	72	16	3	13	.607	.381	3
Walker, M	CHI	R	.000	42	3	0	0	0	0	0	0	0	0	0	0	0	0	1	0	0	0	.000	.000	1
Wall, D	HOU	R	.000	6	5	0	0	0	0	0	0	0	3	0	0	0	0	2	0	0	0	.000	.000	1
Wallach, T	LA	R	.266	97	327	24	87	140	22	2	9	38	0	4	4	27	4	69	0	0	11	.428	.326	5
Walton, J	CIN	R	.290	102	162	32	47	85	12	1	8	22	3	2	4	17	0	25	10	7	0	.525	.368	2
Watson, A	STL	L	.417	21	36	5	15	19	4	0	0	5	3	0	0	2	0	7	0	0	1	.528	.447	0
Weathers, D	FLA	R	.154	28	26	1	4	4	0	0	0	1	5	0	0	0	0	17	0	0	0	.154	.154	2
Webster, L	PHI	R	.267	49	150	18	40	61	9	0	4	14	1	0	0	16	0	27	0	0	4	.407	.337	3
Webster, M	LA	S	.179	54	56	6	10	16	1	1	1	3	2	0	1	4	1	14	0	0	1	.286	.246	0

INDIVIDUAL BATTING—1995

BATTER	TEAM	B	AVG	G	AB	R	H	TB	2B	3B	HR	RBI	SH	SF	HP	BB	IBB	SO	SB	CS	GIDP	SLG	OBP	E
Wehner, J	PIT	R	.308	52	107	13	33	39	0	3	0	5	4	2	0	10	1	17	3	1	2	.364	.361	0
Weiss, W	COL	S	.260	137	427	65	111	137	17	3	1	25	6	1	5	98	8	57	15	3	7	.321	.403	16
Wells, D	CIN	L	.143	11	28	2	4	4	0	0	0	0	1	0	0	0	0	5	0	0	0	.143	.143	0
Wendell, T	CHI	L	.000	43	7	0	0	0	0	0	0	0	1	0	0	0	0	5	0	0	0	.000	.125	0
West, D	PHI	L	.125	8	8	1	1	4	0	0	1	3	6	0	0	1	0	4	0	0	1	.500	.222	1
White, G	MON	L	.000	19	3	0	0	0	0	0	0	1	0	0	0	0	0	3	0	0	0	.000	.000	0
White, R	PIT	R	.067	15	15	1	1	2	1	0	0	1	2	0	0	0	0	3	0	0	0	.133	.067	1
White, R	MON	R	.295	130	474	87	140	220	33	4	13	57	0	4	6	41	1	87	25	5	11	.464	.356	4
Whiten, M	PHI	S	.269	60	212	38	57	102	10	1	11	37	0	0	1	31	1	63	7	0	4	.481	.365	4
Whitmore, D	FLA	L	.190	27	58	6	11	16	2	0	1	2	1	1	0	5	0	15	0	0	1	.276	.250	1
Wilkins, R	CHI-HOU	L	.203	65	202	30	41	65	3	0	7	19	0	2	1	46	2	61	0	0	9	.322	.351	4
Williams, B	SD	R	.071	44	14	1	1	2	1	0	0	0	0	0	0	0	0	4	0	0	1	.143	.071	0
Williams, E	SD	R	.260	97	296	35	77	126	11	1	12	47	0	2	4	23	0	47	0	0	21	.426	.320	7
Williams, M	SF	R	.336	76	283	53	95	183	17	1	23	65	0	3	2	30	8	58	2	0	8	.647	.399	10
Williams, M	PHI	R	.125	33	16	0	2	3	1	0	0	1	7	0	0	2	0	5	0	0	1	.188	.176	1
Williams, M	LA	S	.091	15	11	2	1	1	0	0	0	1	0	0	2	0	0	3	0	0	0	.091	.231	0
Williams, T	LA	R	.500	16	2	0	1	1	0	0	0	0	0	0	0	0	0	0	0	0	0	.500	.500	0
Wilson, G	PIT	R	.000	10	0	0	0	0	0	0	0	1	0	0	0	0	0	0	0	0	0	.000	.000	0
Wilson, N	CIN	L	.000	5	7	0	0	0	0	0	0	0	0	0	0	0	0	4	0	0	0	.000	.000	0
Wilson, T	SF	L	.233	19	30	1	7	8	1	0	0	3	3	0	0	0	0	8	0	0	0	.267	.233	1
Witt, B	FLA	R	.063	21	32	0	2	3	1	0	0	2	4	1	0	1	0	10	0	0	0	.094	.088	0
Wohlers, M	ATL	R	.000	65	3	0	0	0	0	0	0	0	0	0	0	0	0	3	0	0	0	.000	.000	0
Woodall, B	ATL	S	1.000	9	1	0	1	1	0	0	0	1	0	0	0	0	0	0	0	0	0	1.000	1.000	0
Worrell, T	SD	R	.000	9	1	0	0	0	0	0	0	0	0	0	0	0	0	0	0	0	0	.000	.000	0
Worrell, T	LA	R	.000	59	2	0	0	0	0	0	0	0	0	0	0	0	0	2	0	0	0	.000	.000	0
Worthington, C	CIN	R	.278	10	18	1	5	9	1	0	1	2	0	0	0	2	0	1	0	0	0	.500	.350	0
Young, A	CHI	R	.667	32	3	2	2	2	0	0	0	0	2	0	0	0	0	0	0	0	0	.667	.667	2
Young, E	COL	R	.317	120	366	68	116	173	21	9	6	36	3	1	5	49	3	29	35	12	4	.473	.404	11
Young, K	PIT	R	.232	56	181	13	42	69	9	0	6	22	1	3	2	8	0	53	1	3	5	.381	.268	12
Zeile, T	STL-CHI	R	.246	113	426	50	105	169	22	0	14	52	4	5	4	34	1	76	1	0	13	.397	.305	19
Zosky, E	FLA	R	.200	6	5	0	1	1	0	0	0	0	0	0	0	0	0	0	0	0	0	.200	.200	1

BATSMEN AWARDED FIRST BASE ON INTERFERENCE OR OBSTRUCTION:
Phi. (2): Van Slyke (Piazza, L.A.); Whiten (Piazza, L.A.); Cin. (1): Boone (Castillo, N.Y.); L.A. (1): Kelly (Taubensee, Cin.); Mon. (1): Segui (Johnson, S.D.); S.D. (1): Cianfrocco (Encarnacion, Pit.).

1995 CLUB BATTING

CLUB	AVG	G	AB	R	OR	H	TB	2B	3B	HR	GS	RBI	SH	SF	HP	BB	IBB	SO	SB	CS	GIDP	LOB	SHO	SLG	OB
COLORADO	.282	144	4994	785	783	1406	2351	259	43	200	3	749	82	31	56	484	47	943	125	59	118	1017	11	.471	.350
HOUSTON	.275	144	5097	747	674	1403	2034	260	22	109	3	694	78	47	69	566	58	992	176	60	114	1153	4	.399	.353
SAN DIEGO	.272	144	4950	668	672	1345	1964	231	20	116	9	618	56	38	35	447	45	872	124	46	125	998	6	.397	.334
CINCINNATI	.270	144	4903	747	623	1326	2156	277	35	161	1	694	62	50	40	519	42	946	190	68	92	1001	3	.440	.342
NEW YORK	.267	144	4958	657	618	1323	1984	218	34	125	4	617	92	43	42	446	44	994	58	39	105	1041	8	.400	.330
CHICAGO	.265	144	4963	693	671	1315	2134	267	39	158	2	648	71	35	34	440	46	953	105	37	110	956	5	.430	.327
LOS ANGELES	.264	144	4942	634	609	1303	1976	191	31	140	4	593	68	35	30	468	46	1023	127	45	99	1049	12	.400	.329
PHILADELPHIA	.262	144	4950	615	658	1296	1901	263	30	94	2	576	77	41	46	497	38	884	72	25	107	1114	9	.384	.332
FLORIDA	.262	143	4886	673	673	1278	1982	214	29	144	7	636	69	48	49	517	36	916	131	53	105	1028	9	.406	.335
PITTSBURGH	.259	144	4937	629	736	1281	1955	245	27	125	3	587	51	33	24	456	49	972	84	55	88	1010	8	.396	.323
MONTREAL	.259	144	4905	621	638	1268	1935	265	24	118	5	572	58	32	56	400	43	901	120	49	107	970	8	.394	.320
SAN FRANCISCO	.253	144	4971	652	776	1256	2007	229	33	152	2	610	79	24	57	472	55	1060	138	46	92	1046	8	.404	.323
ATLANTA	.250	144	4814	645	540	1202	1970	210	27	168	2	618	56	34	40	520	37	933	73	43	106	988	4	.409	.326
ST. LOUIS	.247	143	4779	563	658	1182	1789	238	24	107	1	533	48	40	46	436	31	920	79	46	110	957	19	.374	.314
TOTALS	.263	1007	69049	9329	9329	18184	28138	3367	418	1917	48	8745	947	531	624	6668	613	13309	1602	671	1478	14328	114	.408	.331

1995 CLUB FIELDING

CLUB	PCT	G	PO	A	E	TC	DP	TP	PB
CINCINNATI	.986	144	3868	1507	79	5454	140	2	11
PHILADELPHIA	.982	144	3871	1520	97	5488	139	0	19
ATLANTA	.982	144	3875	1569	100	5544	113	0	8
COLORADO	.981	144	3865	1665	107	5637	146	0	10
SAN FRANCISCO	.980	144	3881	1548	108	5537	142	0	7
SAN DIEGO	.980	144	3854	1538	108	5500	130	0	8
MONTREAL	.980	144	3851	1558	109	5518	119	0	6
ST. LOUIS	.980	143	3797	1622	113	5532	156	0	9
NEW YORK	.979	144	3873	1603	115	5591	125	0	14
CHICAGO	.979	144	3903	1563	115	5581	115	0	19
FLORIDA	.979	143	3858	1466	115	5439	143	0	8
HOUSTON	.979	144	3961	1639	121	5721	120	0	14
PITTSBURGH	.978	144	3826	1588	122	5536	138	0	12
LOS ANGELES	.976	144	3885	1490	130	5505	120	0	19
TOTALS	.980	1007	54168	21876	1539	77583	1846	2	164

INDIVIDUAL FIELDING—1995

FIRST BASEMEN

PLAYER	TEAM	T	PCT	G	PO	A	E	TC	DP
Andrews, S	MON	R	.977	29	160	11	4	175	11
Anthony, E	CIN	L	.966	17	102	10	4	116	11
Aude, R	PIT	R	.996	32	223	11	1	235	28
Ausmus, B	SD	R	.000	1	0	0	0	0	0
Bagwell, J	HOU	R	.994	114	1004	129	7	1140	81
Benzinger, T	SF	R	1.000	5	15	0	0	15	3
Berry, S	MON	R	1.000	3	22	4	0	26	0
Berryhill, D	CIN	R	1.000	1	1	0	0	1	0
Bogar, T	NY	R	1.000	10	47	5	0	52	6
Bonilla, B	NY	R	1.000	10	85	3	0	88	5
Branson, J	CIN	R	.000	1	0	0	0	0	0
Brogna, R	NY	L	.998	131	1112	93	3	1208	95
Brumley, M	HOU	R	1.000	1	1	1	0	2	0
Busch, M	LA	R	1.000	2	8	1	0	9	2
Carreon, M	SF	L	.993	81	703	44	5	752	65
Cianfrocco, A	SD	R	1.000	30	76	7	0	83	7
Clark, P	SD	R	1.000	2	7	0	0	7	1
Colbrunn, G	FLA	R	.996	134	1067	89	5	1161	108
Coles, D	STL	R	.992	18	122	7	1	130	7
Conine, J	FLA	R	.991	14	97	11	1	109	10
Decker, S	FLA	R	1.000	2	3	0	0	3	0
Duncan, M	PHI-CIN	R	.985	18	122	6	2	130	11
Elster, K	PHI	R	1.000	4	17	0	0	17	1
Floyd, C	MON	R	.987	18	143	12	2	157	13
Foley, T	MON	R	1.000	4	21	2	0	23	1
Franco, M	CHI	R	1.000	1	2	0	0	2	0
Galarraga, A	COL	R	.991	142	1299	120	13	1432	129
Giannelli, R	STL	R	1.000	2	8	0	0	8	1
Grace, M	CHI	L	.995	143	1211	114	7	1332	93
Gregg, T	FLA	L	1.000	2	17	1	0	18	2
Gwynn, C	LA	L	1.000	2	5	1	0	6	2
Harris, L	CIN	R	1.000	23	127	13	0	140	10
Hollins, D	PHI	R	.988	61	532	30	7	569	53
Hunter, B	CIN	L	.983	23	164	12	3	179	20
Hyers, T	SD	L	1.000	1	1	1	0	2	0
Jefferies, G	PHI	R	.994	59	492	33	3	528	53
Johnson, B	SD	R	.900	2	9	0	1	10	0
Johnson, H	CHI	R	1.000	3	15	1	0	16	3
Johnson, M	PIT	L	.986	70	527	36	8	571	53
Jones, C	NY	R	1.000	5	43	3	0	46	3
Karros, E	LA	R	.995	143	1234	109	7	1350	101
King, J	PIT	R	.994	35	296	27	2	325	22
Kingery, M	COL	L	.963	5	25	1	1	27	0
Klesko, R	ATL	L	.957	4	20	2	1	23	0
Ledesma, A	NY	R	1.000	2	3	0	0	3	0
Livingstone, S	SD	R	.991	43	297	17	3	317	25
Mabry, J	STL	R	.994	73	595	53	4	652	63
Magadan, D	HOU	R	1.000	11	66	4	0	70	5
May, D	HOU	R	.000	1	0	0	0	0	0
McCarty, D	SF	L	1.000	2	14	0	0	14	0
McGriff, F	ATL	L	.996	144	1285	96	5	1386	103
Merced, O	PIT	R	.995	35	175	15	1	191	22
Mordecai, M	ATL	R	1.000	9	24	2	0	26	3
Morman, R	FLA	R	1.000	3	10	2	0	12	1
Morris, H	CIN	L	.994	99	757	73	5	835	78
Nieves, M	SD	R	.917	2	11	0	1	12	1
Oliva, J	ATL-STL	R	1.000	3	16	1	0	17	2
Orsulak, J	NY	L	1.000	1	3	1	0	4	0
Perez, E	ATL	R	1.000	1	3	0	0	3	1
Perry, G	STL	R	1.000	11	69	3	0	72	4
Petagine, R	SD	L	.996	51	262	22	1	285	21
Phillips, J	SF	L	.993	79	535	37	4	576	47
Ready, R	PHI	R	.967	3	28	1	1	30	3
Rodriguez, H	LA-MON	L	1.000	11	83	7	0	90	8
Sabo, C	STL	R	.929	2	11	2	1	14	1
Santiago, B	CIN	R	1.000	8	19	2	0	21	2
Scarsone, S	SF	R	1.000	11	79	6	0	85	12
Schall, G	PHI	R	.984	14	112	10	2	124	9
Segui, D	NY-MON	L	.997	104	881	73	3	957	72
Sheaffer, D	STL	R	1.000	3	31	4	0	35	1
Shipley, C	HOU	R	1.000	1	1	0	0	1	0
Silvestri, D	MON	R	1.000	4	22	1	0	23	4
Simms, M	HOU	R	.995	25	204	17	1	222	17
Sweeney, M	STL	L	.994	19	153	11	1	165	20
Taubensee, E	CIN	R	1.000	3	12	1	0	13	2
Vander Wal, J	COL	L	.957	10	42	3	2	47	3
Wallach, T	LA	R	1.000	1	11	0	0	11	0
Walton, J	CIN	R	1.000	3	3	0	0	3	0
Wilkins, R	HOU	R	1.000	2	6	2	0	8	1
Williams, E	SD	R	.989	81	571	49	7	627	53
Worthington, C	CIN	R	1.000	4	24	2	0	26	3
Young, K	PIT	R	1.000	6	30	2	0	32	2
Zeile, T	STL-CHI	R	.981	35	327	30	7	364	34

SECOND BASEMEN

PLAYER	TEAM	T	PCT	G	PO	A	E	TC	DP
Alfonzo, E	NY	R	.989	29	36	51	1	88	7
Arias, A	FLA	R	1.000	6	9	19	0	28	3
Bates, J	COL	R	.991	82	136	188	3	327	50
Bell, D	STL	R	.967	37	75	103	6	184	27
Belliard, R	ATL	R	1.000	32	41	91	0	132	11
Benjamin, M	SF	R	1.000	8	7	14	0	21	0
Biggio, C	HOU	R	.986	141	299	419	10	728	78
Bogar, T	NY	R	.929	7	6	20	2	28	6
Boone, B	CIN	R	.994	138	311	362	4	677	106
Branson, J	CIN	R	1.000	6	1	1	0	2	0
Browne, J	FLA	R	.992	27	62	66	1	129	13
Caraballo, R	STL	R	.956	24	56	73	6	135	20
Cianfrocco, A	SD	R	1.000	3	7	6	0	13	1
Cromer, T	STL	R	.969	11	15	16	1	32	4
DeShields, D	LA	R	.980	113	204	330	11	545	55
Diaz, M	FLA	R	.944	9	15	19	2	36	8
Donnels, C	HOU	R	1.000	1	0	1	0	1	0
Duncan, M	PHI-CIN	R	.958	31	63	73	6	142	20
Foley, T	MON	R	1.000	3	2	5	0	7	2
Fonville, C	MON-LA	R	.966	38	71	98	6	175	14
Franco, M	CHI	R	1.000	3	0	2	0	2	0
Frazier, L	MON	R	1.000	1	0	1	0	1	0
Garcia, C	PIT	R	.982	92	217	264	9	490	70
Giovanola, E	ATL	R	1.000	7	9	5	0	14	1
Grudzielanek, M	MON	R	.963	13	26	26	2	54	5
Haney, T	CHI	R	.978	17	31	57	2	90	12
Harris, L	CIN	R	1.000	1	2	0	0	2	0
Hemond, S	STL	R	1.000	6	4	7	0	11	0
Hernandez, J	CHI	R	.971	29	56	76	4	136	18
Holbert, R	SD	R	1.000	7	3	3	0	6	1
Hulett, T	STL	R	.941	2	5	11	1	17	3
Ingram, G	LA	R	1.000	7	7	11	0	18	3
Johnson, H	CHI	R	.889	8	7	9	2	18	2
Jordan, K	PHI	R	.984	9	28	33	1	62	8
Kent, J	NY	R	.984	122	245	353	10	608	69
King, J	PIT	R	1.000	8	8	14	0	22	4
Lansing, M	MON	R	.991	127	306	373	6	685	77
Lee, M	STL	R	.800	1	2	2	1	5	0
Lemke, M	ATL	R	.990	115	205	305	5	515	61
Lewis, M	CIN	R	1.000	2	0	3	0	3	0
Liriano, N	PIT	R	.981	67	130	132	5	267	31
Livingstone, S	SD	R	1.000	4	2	3	0	5	1
Mejia, R	COL	R	.971	16	36	30	2	68	4
Morandini, M	PHI	R	.989	122	269	337	7	613	74
Mordecai, M	ATL	R	1.000	21	14	19	0	33	8
Oquendo, J	STL	R	.981	62	114	148	5	267	37
Patterson, J	SF	R	.983	53	114	112	4	230	34
Pena, G	STL	R	.976	25	50	73	3	126	18
Ready, R	PHI	R	1.000	1	1	1	0	2	0
Reed, J	SD	R	.994	130	303	362	4	669	79
Roberts, B	SD	R	.981	25	37	68	2	107	11
Sanchez, R	CHI	R	.987	111	194	342	7	543	58
Santangelo, F	MON	R	1.000	5	1	0	0	1	0
Scarsone, S	SF	R	.954	13	26	36	3	65	12
Shipley, C	HOU	R	1.000	4	5	10	0	15	1
Silvestri, D	MON	R	1.000	3	3	2	0	5	0
Spiers, B	NY	R	1.000	6	4	12	0	16	1
Stankiewicz, A	HOU	R	1.000	6	3	7	0	10	0
Thompson, R	SF	R	.993	91	181	238	3	422	51
Treadway, J	LA-MON	R	1.000	12	12	16	0	28	3
Veras, Q	FLA	R	.986	122	297	315	9	621	85
Vizcaino, J	NY	R	1.000	1	0	1	0	1	0
Young, E	COL	R	.973	77	165	228	11	404	55
Zosky, E	FLA	R	1.000	1	0	1	0	1	1

THIRD BASEMEN

PLAYER	TEAM	T	PCT	G	PO	A	E	TC	DP
Alfonzo, E	NY	R	.962	58	40	111	6	157	9
Andrews, S	MON	R	.973	51	22	86	3	111	2
Arias, A	FLA	R	.939	21	8	23	2	33	3
Bates, J	COL	R	.973	15	10	26	1	37	1
Bell, D	STL	R	.875	3	2	5	1	8	0
Bell, J	PIT	R	1.000	3	1	6	0	7	1
Benjamin, M	SF	R	.964	43	29	77	4	110	3
Berry, S	MON	R	.947	83	54	162	12	228	19
Bogar, T	NY	R	.950	25	9	29	2	40	4
Bonilla, B	NY	R	.882	46	24	73	13	110	8
Branson, J	CIN	R	.971	98	52	179	7	238	23
Browne, J	FLA	R	1.000	7	1	10	0	11	0
Brumley, M	HOU	R	.000	1	0	0	1	1	0
Buechele, S	CHI	R	.942	32	26	55	5	86	3
Busch, M	LA	R	.875	10	2	5	1	8	0

THIRD BASEMEN (Continued)

PLAYER	TEAM	T	PCT	G	PO	A	E	TC	DP
Caminiti, K	SD	R	.936	143	102	295	27	424	28
Castellano, P	COL	R	1.000	3	1	0	0	1	0
Castilla, V	COL	R	.958	137	84	256	15	355	21
Castro, J	LA	R	1.000	7	2	3	0	5	0
Cedeno, A	SD	R	.500	1	0	1	1	2	0
Cianfrocco, A	SD	R	.000	3	0	0	0	0	0
Coles, D	STL	R	.951	22	13	26	2	41	1
Cooper, S	STL	R	.945	110	65	243	18	326	24
Diaz, M	FLA	R	1.000	3	1	0	0	1	0
Donnels, C	HOU	R	.818	9	3	6	2	11	2
Duncan, M	CIN	R	1.000	1	2	2	0	4	0
Elster, K	PHI	R	1.000	2	2	2	0	4	0
Franco, M	CHI	R	.000	1	0	0	0	0	0
Garcia, F	PIT	R	.955	8	6	15	1	22	4
Giovanola, E	ATL	R	.000	3	0	0	0	0	0
Greene, W	CIN	R	1.000	7	1	13	0	14	1
Grudzielanek, M	MON	R	.935	31	18	68	6	92	2
Gutierrez, R	HOU	R	.000	2	0	0	0	0	0
Haney, T	CHI	R	1.000	4	3	4	0	7	0
Hansen, D	LA	R	.933	58	27	70	7	104	6
Harris, L	CIN	R	.939	24	9	53	4	66	3
Hayes, C	PHI	R	.963	141	104	264	14	382	27
Hernandez, J	CHI	R	1.000	20	12	36	0	48	1
Huskey, B	NY	R	.925	27	14	60	6	80	2
Ingram, G	LA	R	.750	12	9	15	8	32	0
Johnson, H	CHI	R	.926	34	10	53	5	68	4
Jones, C	ATL	R	.931	123	81	254	25	360	19
Jordan, K	PHI	R	1.000	1	1	2	0	3	0
King, J	PIT	R	.942	84	48	164	13	225	14
Kmak, J	CHI	R	1.000	1	0	1	0	1	0
Ledesma, A	NY	R	.875	10	2	12	2	16	0
Lewis, M	CIN	R	.968	72	19	103	4	126	4
Liriano, N	PIT	R	1.000	5	0	5	0	5	0
Livingstone, S	SD	R	1.000	13	1	13	0	14	0
Magadan, D	HOU	R	.922	100	55	159	18	232	9
Mordecai, M	ATL	R	1.000	6	0	5	0	5	0
Nevin, P	HOU	R	.933	16	10	32	3	45	4
Oliva, J	ATL-STL	R	.933	43	25	72	7	104	7
Oquendo, J	STL	R	.000	2	0	0	0	0	0
Owens, E	CIN	R	.000	2	0	0	0	0	0
Parker, R	LA	R	.000	2	0	0	0	0	0
Pendleton, T	FLA	R	.952	129	104	250	18	372	24
Pye, E	LA	R	.000	2	0	0	0	0	0
Sabo, C	STL	R	1.000	1	0	1	0	1	0
Scarsone, S	SF	R	.927	50	30	71	8	109	8
Schofield, D	LA	R	.000	1	0	0	0	0	0
Sefcik, K	PHI	R	1.000	2	0	1	0	1	1
Sharperson, M	ATL	R	.000	1	0	0	0	0	0
Sheaffer, D	STL	R	1.000	1	0	2	0	2	0
Shipley, C	HOU	R	.982	65	27	82	2	111	5
Silvestri, D	MON	R	.938	8	2	13	1	16	0
Spiers, B	NY	R	.794	11	9	18	7	34	2
Stankiewicz, A	HOU	R	1.000	3	2	1	0	3	0
Treadway, J	LA-MON	R	1.000	3	0	1	0	1	0
Wallach, T	LA	R	.976	96	50	156	5	211	10
Wehner, J	PIT	R	1.000	19	11	26	0	37	1
Williams, M	SF	R	.958	74	49	178	10	237	10
Worthington, C	CIN	R	1.000	2	2	2	0	4	0
Young, K	PIT	R	.919	48	28	108	12	148	7
Zeile, T	CHI	R	.939	75	35	134	11	180	13

SHORTSTOPS

PLAYER	TEAM	T	PCT	G	PO	A	E	TC	DP
Abbott, K	FLA	R	.959	115	149	290	19	458	66
Alfonzo, E	NY	R	1.000	6	5	9	0	14	3
Arias, A	FLA	R	.947	36	40	85	7	132	15
Aurilia, R	SF	R	1.000	6	8	16	0	24	4
Bates, J	COL	R	.985	20	24	41	1	66	5
Bell, J	PIT	R	.978	136	205	409	14	628	88
Belliard, R	ATL	R	.992	40	33	90	1	124	11
Benjamin, M	SF	R	1.000	16	15	30	0	45	6
Blauser, J	ATL	R	.970	115	151	337	15	503	62
Bogar, T	NY	R	.971	27	20	46	2	68	5
Branson, J	CIN	R	.980	32	31	65	2	98	15
Brumley, M	HOU	R	1.000	3	0	1	0	1	0
Castilla, V	COL	R	1.000	5	2	8	0	10	1
Castro, J	LA	R	1.000	4	1	4	0	5	2
Cedeno, A	SD	R	.965	116	139	304	16	459	58
Cianfrocco, A	SD	R	.945	15	17	35	3	55	7
Clayton, R	SF	R	.969	136	223	411	20	654	93
Cordero, W	MON	R	.960	105	124	280	17	421	47
Counsell, C	COL	R	1.000	3	1	1	0	2	1

INDIVIDUAL FIELDING—1995

SHORTSTOPS (Continued)

PLAYER	TEAM	T	PCT	G	PO	A	E	TC	DP
Cromer, T	STL	R	.960	95	111	276	16	403	57
Diaz, M	FLA	R	1.000	5	6	11	0	17	4
Duncan, M	PHI-CIN	R	.966	20	22	64	3	89	11
Dunston, S	CHI	R	.969	125	187	336	17	540	51
Elster, K	PHI	R	.982	19	18	36	1	55	11
Fonville, C	LA	R	.971	38	38	95	4	137	13
Garcia, C	PIT	R	.895	15	17	34	6	57	6
Giovanola, E	ATL	R	1.000	1	0	2	0	2	0
Grudzielanek, M	MON	R	.987	34	50	103	2	155	17
Gutierrez, R	HOU	R	.956	44	64	108	8	180	17
Hernandez, J	CHI	R	.961	43	45	77	5	127	18
Holbert, R	SD	R	.940	30	24	55	5	84	12
Hulett, T	STL	R	.750	1	1	2	1	4	0
Johnson, H	CHI	R	1.000	1	1	2	0	3	1
King, J	PIT	R	.333	2	0	1	2	3	0
Lansing, M	MON	R	1.000	2	0	1	0	1	0
Larkin, B	CIN	R	.980	130	192	341	11	544	72
Ledesma, A	NY	R	.000	2	0	0	0	0	0
Lewis, M	CIN	R	1.000	2	0	1	0	1	0
Liriano, N	PIT	R	.000	1	0	0	0	0	0
Miller, O	HOU	R	.964	89	131	270	15	416	52
Mordecai, M	ATL	R	1.000	6	1	5	0	6	1
Offerman, J	LA	R	.932	115	165	312	35	512	61
Oquendo, J	STL	R	.988	24	20	61	1	82	14
Parker, R	LA	R	.000	2	0	0	0	0	0
Reed, J	SD	R	1.000	5	1	3	0	4	1
Roberts, B	SD	R	.960	7	6	18	1	25	4
Sanchez, R	CHI	R	1.000	4	1	9	0	10	2
Schofield, D	LA	R	1.000	3	3	9	0	12	3
Shipley, C	HOU	R	.971	11	10	24	1	35	2
Silvestri, D	MON	R	1.000	9	8	20	0	28	1
Smith, O	STL	R	.964	41	60	129	7	196	28
Stankiewicz, A	HOU	R	.985	14	15	51	1	67	6
Stocker, K	PHI	R	.969	125	147	383	17	547	72
Vizcaino, J	NY	R	.984	134	189	411	10	610	80
Wehner, J	PIT	R	1.000	1	0	2	0	2	0
Weiss, W	COL	R	.974	136	201	406	16	623	99
Zosky, E	FLA	R	.667	4	1	1	1	3	0

OUTFIELDERS

PLAYER	TEAM	T	PCT	G	PO	A	E	TC	DP
Alou, M	MON	R	.981	92	147	5	3	155	2
Anthony, E	CIN	L	1.000	24	39	2	0	41	0
Ashley, B	LA	R	.972	69	102	2	3	107	0
Barry, J	NY	R	1.000	2	2	0	0	2	0
Battle, A	STL	R	.984	32	61	0	1	62	0
Bean, B	SD	L	.750	4	3	0	1	4	0
Bell, D	HOU	R	.963	110	201	10	8	219	2
Benard, M	SF	L	1.000	7	19	0	0	19	0
Benitez, Y	MON	R	.950	14	18	1	1	20	0
Bichette, D	COL	R	.986	136	208	9	3	220	0
Bogar, T	NY	R	.000	1	0	0	0	0	0
Bonds, B	SF	L	.980	143	279	12	6	297	2
Bonilla, B	NY	R	.983	31	55	4	1	60	0
Bradshaw, T	STL	R	.952	10	19	1	1	21	0
Browne, J	FLA	R	.959	29	45	2	2	49	2
Brumfield, J	PIT	R	.969	104	241	8	8	257	1
Brumley, M	HOU	R	1.000	3	2	0	0	2	0
Buford, D	NY	R	.972	39	67	2	2	71	0
Bullett, S	CHI	L	.968	64	59	1	2	62	0
Burks, E	COL	R	.970	80	158	3	5	166	0
Butler, B	NY-LA	L	.993	128	282	6	2	290	1
Cangelosi, J	HOU	L	.950	59	92	3	5	100	0
Carr, C	FLA	R	.987	103	217	8	3	228	1
Carreon, M	SF	L	.938	22	29	1	2	32	0
Cedeno, R	LA	R	.977	36	43	0	1	44	0
Cianfrocco, A	SD	R	1.000	7	11	2	0	13	0
Clark, D	PIT	R	.961	61	98	1	4	103	0
Clark, P	SD	R	1.000	34	25	0	0	25	0
Coles, D	STL	R	1.000	1	1	0	0	1	0
Conine, J	FLA	R	.976	118	195	7	5	207	2
Cordero, W	MON	R	.902	26	45	1	5	51	0
Cummings, M	PIT	R	.988	41	79	2	1	82	0
Dawson, A	FLA	R	.908	59	76	3	8	87	2
Devereaux, M	ATL	R	1.000	27	41	0	0	41	0
Duncan, M	CIN	R	1.000	3	6	0	0	6	0
Dykstra, L	PHI	L	.987	61	153	2	2	157	1
Eisenreich, J	PHI	L	1.000	111	205	2	0	207	1
Everett, C	NY	R	.981	77	147	9	3	159	3
Faneyte, R	SF	R	.981	34	49	3	1	53	0
Finley, S	SD	L	.977	138	291	8	7	306	0
Flora, K	PHI	R	1.000	20	33	1	0	34	1

OUTFIELDERS (Continued)

PLAYER	TEAM	T	PCT	G	PO	A	E	TC	DP
Floyd, C	MON	R	.750	4	3	0	1	4	0
Fonville, C	LA	R	.947	11	16	2	1	19	1
Frazier, L	MON	R	.973	25	36	0	1	37	0
Gallagher, D	PHI	R	1.000	55	89	1	0	90	0
Gant, R	CIN	R	.985	117	191	7	3	201	0
Garcia, F	PIT	R	1.000	10	13	0	0	13	0
Garcia, K	LA	L	1.000	5	5	2	0	7	1
Giannelli, R	STL	R	1.000	2	2	0	0	2	0
Gibralter, S	CIN	R	1.000	2	1	0	0	1	0
Gilkey, B	STL	R	.986	118	206	10	3	219	4
Gonzalez, L	HOU-CHI	R	.978	131	266	7	6	279	1
Gregg, T	FLA	L	.984	38	63	0	1	64	0
Grissom, M	ATL	R	.994	136	309	9	2	320	1
Gwynn, C	LA	L	1.000	17	21	0	0	21	0
Gwynn, T	SD	L	.992	133	245	8	2	255	1
Harris, L	CIN	R	1.000	8	9	2	0	11	0
Hill, G	SF	R	.959	125	226	10	10	246	1
Holbert, R	SD	R	.000	1	0	0	0	0	0
Hollandsworth, T	LA	L	.938	37	60	1	4	65	0
Howard, T	CIN	R	.985	82	126	2	2	130	1
Hubbard, T	COL	R	1.000	16	16	1	0	17	0
Hunter, B	HOU	R	.955	74	182	8	9	199	2
Hunter, B	CIN	L	1.000	4	7	1	0	8	0
Huskey, B	NY	R	1.000	1	2	0	0	2	0
Ingram, G	LA	R	1.000	4	1	0	0	1	0
Jefferies, G	PHI	R	1.000	55	87	3	0	90	1
Johnson, H	CHI	R	1.000	13	12	0	0	12	0
Jones, C	ATL	R	1.000	20	22	1	0	23	0
Jones, C	NY	R	.976	52	79	3	2	84	1
Jordan, B	STL	R	.996	126	267	4	1	272	2
Justice, D	ATL	L	.984	120	233	8	4	245	0
Kelly, M	ATL	R	.940	83	63	0	4	67	0
Kelly, R	MON-LA	R	.974	134	225	3	6	234	1
Kingery, M	COL	L	.979	108	180	4	4	188	0
Klesko, R	ATL	L	.942	102	111	2	7	120	0
Kowitz, B	ATL	L	1.000	8	6	0	0	6	0
Lampkin, T	SF	R	1.000	6	3	0	0	3	0
Lankford, R	STL	L	.990	129	300	7	3	310	2
Leonard, M	SF	R	1.000	6	9	0	0	9	0
Lewis, D	SF-CIN	R	.994	130	321	5	2	328	1
Longmire, T	PHI	R	1.000	23	33	2	0	35	0
Mabry, J	STL	R	1.000	39	57	5	0	62	2
Marsh, T	PHI	R	.939	29	44	2	3	49	0
Martin, A	PIT	L	.977	121	206	8	5	219	2
May, D	HOU	R	.974	55	74	0	2	76	0
McCarty, D	SF	L	.833	4	5	0	1	6	0
McCracken, Q	COL	R	.000	1	0	0	0	0	0
McDavid, R	SD	R	1.000	7	5	0	0	5	0
McRae, B	CHI	R	.991	137	345	4	3	352	0
Merced, O	PIT	R	.976	107	199	8	5	212	2
Mondesi, R	LA	R	.980	138	282	16	6	304	3
Mordecai, M	ATL	R	.000	1	0	0	0	0	0
Morman, R	FLA	R	.955	18	21	0	1	22	0
Mouton, J	HOU	R	1.000	94	136	4	0	140	0
Newfield, M	SD	R	1.000	19	24	1	0	25	0
Nieves, M	SD	R	.990	79	95	5	1	101	1
Ochoa, A	NY	R	1.000	10	20	1	0	21	0
Oquendo, J	STL	R	.000	1	0	0	0	0	0
Orsulak, J	NY	L	.965	86	108	3	4	115	0
Otero, R	NY	L	1.000	23	31	1	0	32	0
Parker, R	LA	R	1.000	21	20	1	0	21	1
Pegues, S	PIT	R	.954	53	81	2	4	87	1
Petagine, R	SD	L	1.000	2	1	0	0	1	0
Phillips, J	SF	L	1.000	1	1	0	0	1	0
Plantier, P	HOU-SD	R	.959	59	89	5	4	98	1
Polonia, L	ATL	L	1.000	15	9	0	0	9	0
Pride, C	MON	R	.920	24	23	0	2	25	0
Pulliam, H	COL	R	.000	1	0	0	0	0	0
Rhodes, K	CHI	L	.889	11	8	0	1	9	0
Roberson, K	CHI	R	1.000	11	8	0	0	8	0
Roberts, B	SD	R	.989	50	92	2	1	95	0
Rodriguez, H	LA-MON	L	.977	28	42	0	1	43	0
Sanders, D	CIN-SF	L	.977	85	215	2	5	222	1
Sanders, R	CIN	R	.983	130	269	12	5	286	2
Santangelo, F	MON	R	.979	25	46	0	1	47	0
Schall, G	PHI	R	1.000	4	3	0	0	3	0
Segui, D	NY-MON	L	1.000	20	15	2	0	17	0
Sheffield, G	FLA	R	.942	61	109	5	7	121	1
Silvestri, D	MON	R	.000	3	0	0	0	0	0
Simms, M	HOU	R	1.000	12	17	0	0	17	0

OUTFIELDERS (Continued)

PLAYER	TEAM	T	PCT	G	PO	A	E	TC	DP
Smith, D	ATL	R	.923	25	24	0	2	26	0
Sosa, S	CHI	R	.962	143	320	13	13	346	4
Sweeney, M	STL	L	.000	1	0	0	1	1	0
Tarasco, T	MON	R	.979	116	230	7	5	242	3
Tatum, J	COL	R	1.000	2	1	0	0	1	0
Tavarez, J	FLA	R	1.000	61	118	1	0	119	1
Thompson, M	HOU	R	.979	34	45	2	1	48	1
Thompson, R	NY	R	.985	74	193	4	3	200	2
Timmons, O	CHI	R	.970	55	63	1	2	66	1
Vander Wal, J	COL	L	1.000	10	9	1	0	10	0
Van Slyke, A	PHI	R	.984	56	117	5	2	124	1
Varsho, G	PHI	R	.939	25	31	0	2	33	0
Veras, Q	FLA	R	1.000	2	2	0	0	2	0
Walker, L	COL	R	.988	129	225	13	3	241	1
Walton, J	CIN	R	.982	89	107	2	2	111	0
Webster, M	LA	L	1.000	25	12	0	0	12	0
Wehner, J	PIT	R	1.000	23	22	1	0	23	1
White, R	MON	R	.986	119	269	5	4	278	2
Whiten, M	PHI	R	.965	55	105	4	4	113	0
Whitmore, D	FLA	R	.960	16	24	0	1	25	0
Williams, R	LA	R	1.000	14	6	0	0	6	0
Wilson, N	CIN	L	1.000	2	2	0	0	2	0
Young, E	COL	R	1.000	19	15	3	0	18	0
Zeile, T	CHI	R	.000	2	0	0	1	1	0

CATCHERS

PLAYER	TEAM	T	PCT	G	PO	A	E	TC	DP	PB
Ausmus, B	SD	R	.992	100	656	63	6	725	14	3
Berryhill, D	CIN	R	.988	29	152	12	2	166	1	1
Borders, P	HOU	R	.987	11	70	5	1	76	2	2
Brito, J	COL	R	.991	18	109	6	1	116	0	4
Castillo, A	NY	R	.974	12	66	9	2	77	0	2
Daulton, D	PHI	R	.994	95	631	45	4	680	5	9
Decker, S	FLA	R	.985	46	296	24	5	325	3	3
Encarnacion, A	PIT	R	.979	55	278	43	7	328	2	4
Eusebio, T	HOU	R	.993	103	645	49	5	699	9	11
Fletcher, D	MON	R	.994	98	612	45	4	661	8	0
Girardi, J	COL	R	.988	122	730	61	10	801	7	5
Goff, J	HOU	R	1.000	11	80	6	0	86	1	1
Hemond, S	STL	R	.985	38	185	15	3	203	1	7
Hernandez, C	LA	R	.983	41	210	25	4	239	4	5
Hubbard, M	CHI	R	.971	9	33	0	1	34	0	0
Hundley, T	NY	R	.987	89	488	29	7	524	8	6
Johnson, B	SD	R	.993	55	394	32	3	429	2	5
Johnson, C	FLA	R	.992	97	641	63	6	710	9	5
Kmak, J	CHI	R	1.000	18	93	8	0	101	0	1
Laker, T	MON	R	.977	61	265	27	7	299	1	4
Lampkin, T	SF	R	1.000	17	59	5	0	64	1	1
Lieberthal, M	PHI	R	.991	14	95	10	1	106	1	7
Lopez, J	ATL	R	.988	93	625	50	8	683	5	8
Manwaring, K	SF	R	.990	118	607	55	7	669	10	5
Munoz, N	LA	R	1.000	2	6	0	0	6	0	0
Natal, R	FLA	R	.988	13	80	3	1	84	1	0
Nokes, M	COL	R	.909	3	10	0	1	11	0	0
O'Brien, C	ATL	R	.992	64	446	23	4	473	4	0
Owens, J	COL	R	.988	16	79	6	1	86	2	1
Pagnozzi, T	STL	R	.995	61	336	38	2	376	4	1
Parent, M	PIT-CHI	R	.992	77	430	44	4	478	1	9
Perez, E	ATL	R	1.000	5	31	2	0	33	2	0
Piazza, M	LA	R	.990	112	805	52	9	866	8	12
Pratt, T	CHI	R	.981	25	149	9	3	161	1	1
Prince, T	LA	R	.988	17	71	8	1	80	2	2
Reed, J	SF	R	.995	42	175	21	1	197	2	1
Santiago, B	CIN	R	.996	75	461	33	2	496	4	6
Sasser, M	PIT	R	1.000	11	35	3	0	38	0	0
Servais, S	HOU-CHI	R	.980	80	526	50	12	588	6	9
Sheaffer, D	STL	R	.993	67	360	37	3	400	9	1
Siddall, J	MON	R	.882	7	14	1	2	17	0	2
Slaught, D	PIT	R	.996	33	220	9	1	230	2	1
Spehr, T	MON	R	.990	38	92	12	1	105	3	0
Stinnett, K	NY	R	.983	67	380	22	7	409	1	6
Tatum, J	COL	R	1.000	1	3	0	0	3	0	0
Taubensee, E	CIN	R	.983	65	326	21	6	353	0	4
Tucker, S	HOU	R	1.000	3	7	1	0	8	0	0
Webster, L	PHI	R	.990	43	274	18	3	295	1	3
Wehner, J	PIT	R	1.000	1	2	0	0	2	0	0
Wilkins, R	CHI-HOU	R	.990	62	375	33	4	412	7	6

INDIVIDUAL PITCHING RECORDS—1995

ALL PITCHERS LISTED ALPHABETICALLY

PITCHER	TEAM	T	W	L	ERA	G	GS	CG	SHO	GF	SV	IP	H	TBF	R	ER	HR	SH	SF	HB	BB	IBB	SO	WP	BK	OPP AVG
Abbott, K	PHI	L	2	0	3.81	18	0	0	0	3	0	28.1	28	122	12	12	3	0	1	0	16	0	21	2	1	.267
Acevedo, J	COL	R	4	6	6.44	17	11	0	0	0	0	65.2	82	291	53	47	15	4	2	6	20	2	40	2	1	.317
Adams, T	CHI	R	1	1	6.50	18	0	0	0	7	1	18.0	22	86	15	13	0	0	0	0	10	1	15	1	0	.289
Alvarez, C	MON	R	1	5	6.75	8	8	0	0	0	0	37.1	46	173	30	28	2	1	0	3	14	0	17	1	0	.297
Aquino, L	MON-SF	R	0	3	5.10	34	0	0	0	9	2	42.1	57	199	34	24	6	1	1	3	13	2	26	3	0	.315
Arocha, R	STL	R	3	5	3.99	41	0	0	0	13	0	49.2	55	216	24	22	6	8	2	3	18	4	25	2	0	.297
Ashby, A	SD	R	12	10	2.94	31	31	2	2	0	0	192.2	180	800	79	63	17	10	4	11	62	3	150	7	0	.253
Astacio, P	LA	R	7	8	4.24	48	11	1	1	7	0	104.0	103	436	53	49	12	5	3	4	29	5	80	5	0	.261
Avery, S	ATL	L	7	13	4.67	29	29	3	1	0	0	173.1	165	724	92	90	22	6	4	6	52	4	141	3	0	.252
Bailey, P	STL	R	0	0	7.36	3	0	0	0	0	0	3.2	2	15	3	3	0	0	0	0	2	1	5	1	0	.154
Bailey, R	COL	R	7	6	4.98	39	6	0	0	9	0	81.1	88	360	49	45	9	7	2	1	39	3	33	7	1	.283
Banks, W	CHI-LA-FLA	R	2	6	5.66	25	15	0	0	2	0	90.2	106	430	71	57	14	6	3	2	58	7	62	9	1	.294
Barber, B	STL	R	2	1	5.22	9	4	0	0	2	0	29.1	31	130	17	17	4	0	3	0	16	0	27	3	0	.279
Barton, S	SF	L	4	1	4.26	52	0	0	0	11	1	44.1	37	181	22	21	3	1	3	2	19	1	22	0	1	.237
Bautista, J	SF	R	3	8	6.44	52	6	0	0	19	0	100.2	120	451	77	72	24	8	5	5	26	3	45	1	2	.295
Beck, R	SF	R	5	6	4.45	60	0	0	0	52	33	58.2	60	255	31	29	7	4	3	2	21	3	42	2	0	.267
Bedrosian, S	ATL	R	1	2	6.11	29	0	0	0	7	0	28.0	40	129	21	19	6	1	2	1	12	2	22	0	0	.354
Benes, A	STL	R	1	2	8.44	3	3	0	0	0	0	16.0	24	76	15	15	2	1	0	1	4	0	20	3	0	.343
Benes, A	SD	R	4	7	4.17	19	19	1	1	0	0	118.2	121	518	65	55	10	3	4	4	45	3	126	3	0	.262
Berumen, A	SD	R	2	3	5.68	37	0	0	0	17	1	44.1	37	207	29	28	3	1	3	3	36	3	42	6	0	.226
Birkbeck, M	NY	R	0	1	1.63	4	4	0	0	0	0	27.2	22	104	5	5	2	2	0	0	2	0	14	3	1	.220
Blair, W	SD	R	7	5	4.34	40	12	0	0	11	0	114.0	112	485	60	55	11	8	2	2	45	3	83	4	0	.262
Bochtler, D	SD	R	4	4	3.57	34	0	0	0	11	1	45.1	38	181	18	18	5	2	1	0	19	0	45	1	0	.239
Borbon, P	ATL	L	2	2	3.09	41	0	0	0	19	2	32.0	29	143	12	11	2	3	1	1	17	4	33	0	1	.240
Borland, T	PHI	R	1	3	3.77	50	0	0	0	18	6	74.0	81	339	37	31	3	3	2	5	37	7	59	12	0	.277
Bottalico, R	PHI	R	5	3	2.46	62	0	0	0	20	1	87.2	50	350	25	24	7	3	1	4	42	3	87	1	0	.167
Bowen, R	FLA	R	2	0	3.78	4	3	0	0	0	0	16.2	23	85	11	7	3	1	2	0	12	2	15	0	0	.329
Brantley, J	CIN	R	3	2	2.82	56	0	0	0	49	28	70.1	53	283	22	22	11	2	3	1	20	3	62	2	2	.206
Brewington, J	SF	R	6	4	4.54	13	13	0	0	0	0	75.1	68	334	38	38	8	4	4	4	45	6	45	3	0	.245
Brocail, D	HOU	R	6	4	4.19	36	7	0	0	12	1	77.1	87	339	40	36	10	1	1	4	22	2	39	1	1	.280
Bruske, J	LA	R	0	0	4.50	9	0	0	0	3	1	10.0	12	45	7	5	0	0	0	1	4	0	5	1	0	.300
Bullinger, J	CHI	R	12	8	4.14	24	24	1	1	0	0	150.0	152	665	80	69	14	12	5	9	65	7	93	5	1	.265
Burba, D	SF-CIN	R	10	4	3.97	52	9	1	1	7	0	106.2	90	451	50	47	9	4	1	0	51	3	96	5	0	.228
Burgos, E	SF	L	0	0	8.64	5	0	0	0	2	0	8.1	14	44	8	8	1	0	0	1	6	0	12	2	0	.378
Burkett, J	FLA	R	14	14	4.30	30	30	4	0	0	0	188.1	208	810	95	90	22	10	0	6	57	5	126	2	1	.282
Byrd, P	NY	R	2	0	2.05	17	0	0	0	6	0	22.0	18	91	6	5	1	0	2	1	7	1	26	1	2	.222
Candiotti, T	LA	R	7	14	3.50	30	30	1	1	0	0	190.1	187	812	93	74	18	7	5	9	58	2	141	7	0	.255
Cangelosi, J	HOU	L	0	0	0.00	1	0	0	0	1	0	1.0	0	4	0	0	0	0	0	0	1	0	0	0	0	.000
Carrasco, H	CIN	R	2	7	4.12	64	0	0	0	28	5	87.1	86	391	45	40	1	2	6	2	46	5	64	15	0	.257
Carter, A	PHI	L	0	0	6.14	4	0	0	0	1	0	7.1	4	28	5	5	3	0	1	1	2	1	6	0	0	.167
Casian, L	CHI	L	1	0	1.93	42	0	0	0	5	0	23.1	23	107	6	5	1	1	2	0	15	6	11	2	0	.258
Castillo, F	CHI	R	11	10	3.21	29	29	2	2	0	0	188.0	179	795	75	67	22	11	3	6	52	4	135	3	1	.248
Charlton, N	PHI	L	2	5	7.36	25	0	0	0	5	0	22.0	23	102	19	18	2	1	1	3	15	3	12	1	0	.280
Christiansen, J	PIT	L	1	3	4.15	63	0	0	0	13	0	56.1	49	255	28	26	5	6	3	3	34	9	53	4	1	.234
Clark, T	ATL	R	0	0	4.91	3	0	0	0	1	0	3.2	3	18	2	2	0	0	0	0	5	0	2	1	0	.231
Clontz, B	ATL	R	8	1	3.65	59	0	0	0	14	4	69.0	71	295	29	28	5	3	2	4	22	4	55	0	0	.269
Cornelius, R	MON-NY	R	3	7	5.54	18	10	0	0	1	0	66.2	75	301	44	41	11	4	3	3	30	5	39	2	1	.288
Courtright, J	CIN	L	0	0	9.00	1	0	0	0	0	0	1.0	2	5	1	1	0	1	0	0	0	0	0	0	0	.500
Creek, P	STL	L	0	0	0.00	6	0	0	0	1	0	6.2	2	24	0	0	0	0	0	0	3	0	10	0	0	.095
Cummings, J	LA	L	3	1	3.00	35	0	0	0	11	0	39.0	38	165	16	13	3	2	1	0	10	4	21	1	0	.250
Daal, O	LA	L	4	0	7.20	28	0	0	0	0	0	20.0	29	100	16	16	1	1	1	1	15	4	11	0	1	.354
DeLeon, J	MON	R	0	1	7.56	7	0	0	0	1	0	8.1	7	40	7	7	2	0	2	1	7	0	12	0	0	.233
DeLucia, R	STL	R	8	7	3.39	56	1	0	0	8	0	82.1	63	342	38	31	9	5	2	3	36	2	76	5	0	.213
Deshaies, J	PHI	L	0	1	20.25	2	2	0	0	0	0	5.1	15	32	12	12	3	0	0	0	1	0	6	0	0	.484
Dewey, M	SF	R	1	0	3.13	27	0	0	0	5	0	31.2	30	137	12	11	2	1	1	0	17	6	32	1	0	.254
DiPoto, J	NY	R	4	6	3.78	58	0	0	0	26	2	78.2	77	330	41	33	2	6	3	4	29	8	49	3	1	.267
Dishman, G	SD	L	4	8	5.01	19	16	0	0	1	0	97.0	104	421	60	54	11	6	3	4	34	1	43	3	1	.278
Dougherty, J	HOU	R	8	4	4.92	56	0	0	0	11	0	67.2	76	294	37	37	7	3	3	3	25	1	49	1	0	.292
Drabek, D	HOU	R	10	9	4.77	31	31	2	1	0	0	185.0	205	797	104	98	18	4	3	8	54	4	143	8	1	.282
Dunbar, M	FLA	L	0	1	11.57	8	0	0	0	1	0	7.0	12	45	9	9	0	2	0	1	11	3	5	1	0	.387
Dyer, M	PIT	R	4	5	4.34	55	0	0	0	15	0	74.2	81	327	40	36	9	3	1	5	30	3	53	4	1	.281
Edens, T	CHI	R	1	0	6.00	5	0	0	0	1	0	3.0	6	18	3	2	0	0	0	0	3	0	2	0	0	.400
Eischen, J	LA	L	0	0	3.10	17	0	0	0	8	0	20.1	19	95	9	7	1	0	0	2	11	1	15	1	0	.232
Elliott, D	SD	R	0	0	0.00	1	0	0	0	1	0	2.0	2	9	0	0	0	0	0	0	1	0	3	0	0	.250
Ericks, J	PIT	R	3	9	4.58	19	18	1	0	0	0	106.0	108	472	59	54	7	5	5	2	50	4	80	11	1	.263
Estes, S	SF	L	0	3	6.75	3	3	0	0	0	0	17.1	16	76	14	13	2	0	0	1	5	0	14	4	0	.229
Eversgerd, B	MON	L	0	0	5.14	25	0	0	0	5	0	21.0	22	95	13	12	2	1	2	1	9	2	8	1	0	.268
Fassero, J	MON	L	13	14	4.33	30	30	1	0	0	0	189.0	207	833	102	91	15	19	7	2	74	3	164	7	1	.283
Fernandez, S	PHI	L	6	1	3.34	11	11	0	0	0	0	64.2	48	263	25	24	11	1	0	1	21	0	79	0	1	.200
Fletcher, P	PHI	R	1	0	5.40	10	0	0	0	1	0	13.1	15	64	8	8	2	1	1	1	9	2	10	2	0	.288
Florence, D	NY	L	3	0	1.50	14	0	0	0	3	0	12.0	17	57	3	2	0	1	0	0	6	0	5	0	0	.340
Florie, B	SD	R	2	2	3.01	47	0	0	0	10	1	68.2	49	290	30	23	8	5	1	4	38	3	68	7	2	.202
Fossas, T	STL	L	3	0	1.47	58	0	0	0	20	0	36.2	28	145	6	6	1	2	1	1	10	3	40	1	0	.214
Foster, K	CHI	R	12	11	4.51	30	28	0	0	1	0	167.2	149	703	90	84	32	4	6	6	65	4	146	2	2	.240
Franco, J	NY	L	5	3	2.44	48	0	0	0	41	29	51.2	48	213	17	14	4	4	1	0	17	2	41	0	0	.251
Frascatore, J	STL	R	1	1	4.41	14	4	0	0	3	0	32.2	39	151	19	16	3	1	1	2	16	1	21	0	0	.298
Fraser, W	MON	R	2	1	5.61	22	0	0	0	6	2	25.2	25	114	17	16	6	1	0	3	9	1	12	2	0	.248
Freeman, M	COL	R	3	7	5.89	22	18	0	0	0	0	94.2	122	437	64	62	15	7	3	2	41	1	61	5	1	.318
Frey, S	SF-PHI	L	0	1	2.12	18	0	0	0	4	1	17.0	10	65	7	4	2	2	1	0	4	1	7	0	0	.172
Garces, R	CHI-FLA	R	0	2	4.44	18	0	0	0	7	0	24.1	25	108	15	12	1	1	0	0	11	2	22	0	0	.260
Gardner, M	FLA	R	5	5	4.49	39	11	1	1	7	1	102.1	109	456	60	51	14	7	0	5	43	5	87	3	1	.272
Glavine, T	ATL	L	16	7	3.08	29	29	3	1	0	0	198.2	182	822	76	68	9	7	5	5	66	0	127	3	0	.246
Gomez, P	SF	L	0	0	5.14	18	0	0	0	3	0	14.0	16	70	8	8	2	0	0	0	12	1	15	0	1	.276
Gott, J	PIT	R	2	4	6.03	25	0	0	0	12	3	31.1	38	147	26	21	2	1	1	1	12	2	19	3	0	.288

MAJOR LEAGUE RECORDS SET

Most hits by pinch-hitter, season—28, John Vander Wal, Colorado

Most hits in three consecutive games—14, Mike Benjamin, San Francisco, June 11 (13 innings), 13, 14 (13 innings) (set modern major league record)

Most games hitting home runs from both sides of plate, season—3, Ken Caminiti, San Diego

Most consecutive games hitting home runs from both sides of plate—2, Ken Caminiti, San Diego, September 16, 17

Most home runs by pinch-hitters, season—75

Most home runs at home, club, season—134, Colorado

Most relief appearances, club, season—456, Colorado

Most assists, shortstop, lifetime—8,213, Ozzie Smith, St. Louis*

Most double plays, shortstop, lifetime—1,554, Ozzie Smith, St. Louis

MAJOR LEAGUE RECORDS TIED

Most pitchers used by both clubs, extra-inning game—18, Houston 10, Chicago 8, September 28 (11 innings)

Most doubles, inning—2, Bobby Bonilla, New York, July 21, eighth inning

Most home runs, inning—2, Jeff King, Pittsburgh, August 8, second inning

Most home runs by pinch-hitters, club, inning—2, Cincinnati vs. Atlanta, June 22, eighth inning (Anthony and Taubensee)

Most players with 30 or more home runs, club, season—4, Colorado

Most strikeouts, three consecutive games—10, Andujar Cedeno, San Diego, July 5 (2; 10 innings), 6 (5; 12 innings), 7 (3)

Most strikeouts by batters, club, inning—4, Chicago vs. Atlanta, June 7, ninth inning; San Diego vs. Colorado, September 19, sixth inning

Most strikeouts by pitcher, inning—4, Mark Wohlers, Atlanta, June 7, ninth inning

Most pitchers used, club, season—27, Florida

NATIONAL LEAGUE RECORDS SET

Most players used, season—588

Most years leading league in singles—6, Tony Gwynn, San Diego*

Most home runs, switch-hitter, lifetime—209, Howard Johnson, Chicago*

Most games hitting home runs from both sides of plate, lifetime—6, Bobby Bonilla, New York*

Most hit batsmen, season—624

Most pitchers used, season—290

Most games, shortstop, lifetime—2,459, Ozzie Smith, St. Louis*

NATIONAL LEAGUE RECORDS TIED

Most runs, club, 10th inning—9, San Diego vs. Philadelphia, May 28 (tied modern N.L. record)

Most grand slams, club, season—9, San Diego

Most years leading league in intentional walks—4, Barry Bonds, San Francisco

Most consecutive years leading league in intentional walks—4, Barry Bonds, San Francisco

Most sacrifice flies, club, game—4, Houston vs. Pittsburgh, May 9; Houston vs. Philadelphia, September 8

Most sacrifice flies by both clubs, game—5, San Francisco 3, Colorado 2, October 1

Most consecutive home runs allowed, inning—3, Gabe White, Montreal, July 7, second inning

*Extended own record

INDIVIDUAL PITCHING RECORDS—1995

PITCHER	TEAM	T	W	L	ERA	G	GS	CG	SHO	GF	SV	IP	H	TBF	R	ER	HR	SH	SF	HB	BB	IBB	SO	WP	BK	OPP AVG
Grace, M	PHI	R	1	1	3.18	2	2	0	0	0	0	11.1	10	47	4	4	0	1	0	0	4	0	7	0	0	.238
Grahe, J	COL	R	4	3	5.08	17	9	0	0	0	0	56.2	69	265	42	32	6	3	3	3	27	2	27	3	2	.301
Green, T	PHI	R	8	9	5.31	26	25	4	2	0	0	140.2	157	623	86	83	15	5	6	4	66	3	85	9	2	.290
Greene, T	PHI	R	0	5	8.29	11	6	0	0	3	0	33.2	45	167	32	31	6	2	1	3	20	0	24	3	1	.319
Greer, K	SF	R	0	2	5.25	8	0	0	0	1	0	12.0	15	61	12	7	3	2	1	1	5	2	7	0	0	.288
Groom, B	FLA	L	1	2	7.20	14	0	0	0	5	0	15.0	26	71	12	12	2	0	0	0	6	0	12	0	0	.400
Grott, M	CIN	L	0	0	21.60	2	0	0	0	0	0	1.2	6	11	4	4	1	0	0	0	0	0	2	0	0	.545
Gunderson, E	NY	L	1	1	3.70	30	0	0	0	7	0	24.1	25	103	10	10	2	0	1	1	8	3	19	1	0	.269
Guthrie, M	LA	L	0	2	3.66	24	0	0	0	7	0	19.2	19	91	11	8	1	2	0	1	9	2	19	2	0	.241
Habyan, J	STL	R	3	2	2.88	31	0	0	0	9	0	40.2	32	165	18	13	0	4	1	1	15	4	35	2	3	.222
Hamilton, J	SD	R	6	9	3.08	31	30	2	2	1	0	204.1	189	850	89	70	17	12	4	11	56	5	123	2	0	.246
Hammond, C	FLA	L	9	6	3.80	25	24	3	2	0	0	161.0	157	683	73	68	17	7	7	9	47	2	126	3	1	.256
Hampton, M	HOU	L	9	8	3.35	24	24	0	0	0	0	150.2	141	641	73	56	13	11	5	4	49	3	115	3	1	.247
Hancock, L	PIT	L	0	0	1.93	11	0	0	0	3	0	14.0	10	54	3	3	0	0	0	0	2	0	6	2	0	.196
Hansell, G	LA	R	0	1	7.45	20	0	0	0	7	0	19.1	29	93	17	16	5	1	1	2	6	1	13	0	0	.349
Harnisch, P	NY	R	2	8	3.68	18	18	0	0	0	0	110.0	111	462	55	45	13	4	6	3	24	4	82	0	1	.261
Harris, G	PHI	R	2	2	4.26	21	0	0	0	5	0	19.0	19	82	9	9	2	1	0	0	8	0	9	0	0	.260
Harris, G	MON	R	2	3	2.61	45	0	0	0	12	0	48.1	45	204	18	14	6	3	0	1	16	1	47	3	0	.245
Hartgraves, D	HOU	L	2	0	3.22	40	0	0	0	11	0	36.1	30	150	14	13	2	1	1	0	16	2	24	1	0	.227
Harvey, B	FLA	R	0	0	....	1	0	0	0	0	0	0.0	2	3	3	3	1	0	0	0	1	0	0	0	0	.000
Henke, T	STL	R	1	1	1.82	52	0	0	0	47	36	54.1	42	221	11	11	2	2	0	0	18	0	48	1	0	.209
Henneman, M	HOU	R	0	1	3.00	21	0	0	0	18	8	21.0	21	87	7	7	1	0	2	2	4	1	19	3	0	.266
Henry, B	MON	L	7	9	2.84	21	21	1	1	0	0	126.2	133	524	47	40	11	7	3	2	28	3	60	0	1	.275
Henry, D	NY	R	3	6	2.96	51	0	0	0	20	4	67.0	48	273	23	22	7	3	2	1	25	6	62	6	1	.198
Heredia, G	MON	R	5	6	4.31	40	18	0	0	5	1	119.0	137	509	60	57	7	9	4	5	21	1	74	1	0	.291
Hermanson, D	SD	R	3	1	6.82	26	0	0	0	6	0	31.2	35	151	26	24	8	3	0	1	22	1	19	3	0	.280
Hernandez, J	FLA	R	0	0	11.57	7	0	0	0	3	0	7.0	12	36	9	9	2	1	1	1	3	1	5	0	0	.400
Hernandez, X	CIN	R	7	2	4.60	59	0	0	0	19	3	90.0	95	391	47	46	8	6	2	4	31	1	84	7	0	.273
Hickerson, B	CHI-COL	L	3	3	8.57	56	0	0	0	13	1	48.1	69	239	52	46	8	2	0	1	28	5	40	5	1	.332
Hill, K	STL	R	6	7	5.06	18	18	0	0	0	0	110.1	125	493	71	62	16	9	2	0	45	4	50	3	0	.286
Hoffman, T	SD	R	7	4	3.88	55	0	0	0	51	31	53.1	48	218	25	23	10	0	0	0	14	3	52	1	0	.235
Holmes, D	COL	R	6	1	3.24	68	0	0	0	33	14	66.2	59	286	26	24	3	5	3	1	28	3	61	7	1	.237
Hook, C	SF	R	5	1	5.50	45	0	0	0	14	0	52.1	55	239	33	32	7	3	3	3	29	3	40	2	0	.274
Hope, J	PIT	R	0	0	30.86	3	0	0	0	0	0	2.1	8	21	8	8	0	0	1	3	4	0	2	0	0	.615
Hudek, J	HOU	R	2	2	5.40	19	0	0	0	16	7	20.0	19	83	12	12	3	1	0	0	5	0	29	2	0	.247
Isringhausen, J	NY	R	9	2	2.81	14	14	1	0	0	0	93.0	88	385	29	29	6	3	3	2	31	2	55	4	1	.254
Jackson, D	STL	L	2	12	5.90	19	19	2	1	0	0	100.2	120	467	82	66	10	10	7	6	48	1	52	6	0	.303
Jackson, M	CIN	R	6	1	2.39	40	0	0	0	10	2	49.0	38	200	13	13	5	1	1	1	19	1	41	1	1	.213
Jacome, J	NY	L	0	4	10.29	5	5	0	0	0	0	21.0	33	110	24	24	3	1	1	1	15	0	11	1	0	.359
Jarvis, K	CIN	R	3	4	5.70	19	11	1	1	2	0	79.0	91	354	56	50	13	2	5	3	32	2	33	2	0	.292
Johnstone, J	FLA	R	0	0	3.86	4	0	0	0	0	0	4.2	7	23	2	2	1	0	0	0	2	1	3	0	0	.333
Jones, B	NY	R	10	10	4.19	30	30	3	1	0	0	195.2	209	839	107	91	20	11	6	7	53	6	127	2	1	.274
Jones, T	HOU	R	6	5	3.07	68	0	0	0	40	15	99.2	89	442	38	34	8	5	4	6	52	17	96	5	0	.237
Juden, J	PHI	R	2	4	4.02	13	10	1	0	0	0	62.2	53	271	31	28	6	5	4	5	31	0	47	4	1	.235
Karp, R	PHI	L	0	0	4.50	1	0	0	0	0	0	2.0	1	10	1	1	0	0	0	0	3	0	2	1	0	.143
Kile, D	HOU	R	4	12	4.96	25	21	0	0	1	0	127.0	114	570	81	70	5	7	3	12	73	2	113	11	1	.240
Konuszewski, D	PIT	R	0	0	54.00	1	0	0	0	0	0	0.1	3	5	2	2	0	1	0	0	1	0	0	0	0	.000
Kroon, M	SD	R	0	1	10.80	2	0	0	0	1	0	1.2	1	7	2	2	0	0	0	0	2	0	2	0	0	.200
Krueger, B	SD	L	0	0	7.04	6	0	0	0	0	0	7.2	13	41	6	6	1	2	0	0	4	1	6	2	0	.371
Leiper, D	MON	L	0	2	2.86	26	0	0	0	7	2	22.0	16	88	8	7	2	2	0	0	6	0	12	0	1	.200
Leiter, M	SF	R	10	12	3.82	30	29	7	1	0	0	195.2	185	817	91	83	19	10	6	17	55	4	129	9	3	.254
Leskanic, C	COL	R	6	3	3.40	76	0	0	0	27	10	98.0	83	406	38	37	7	3	2	0	33	1	107	6	1	.226
Lewis, R	FLA	R	0	1	3.75	21	1	0	0	6	0	36.0	30	152	15	15	9	2	0	1	15	5	32	1	2	.224
Lieber, J	PIT	R	4	7	6.32	21	12	0	0	3	0	72.2	103	327	56	51	7	5	6	4	14	0	45	3	0	.346
Loaiza, E	PIT	R	8	9	5.16	32	31	1	0	0	0	172.2	205	762	115	99	21	10	9	5	55	3	85	6	1	.300
Lomon, K	NY	R	0	1	6.75	6	0	0	0	1	0	9.1	17	47	8	7	0	0	0	0	5	1	6	0	0	.405
Maddux, G	ATL	R	19	2	1.63	28	28	10	3	0	0	209.2	147	785	39	38	8	9	1	4	23	3	181	1	0	.197
Maddux, M	PIT	R	1	0	9.00	8	0	0	0	1	0	9.0	14	42	9	9	0	0	0	0	3	1	4	1	0	.359
Mantei, M	FLA	R	0	1	4.73	12	0	0	0	3	0	13.1	12	64	8	7	1	1	1	0	13	0	15	1	0	.245
Manzanillo, J	NY	R	1	2	7.88	12	0	0	0	4	0	16.0	18	73	15	14	3	0	1	0	6	2	14	5	0	.273
Manzanillo, R	PIT	L	0	0	4.91	5	0	0	0	0	0	3.2	3	16	3	2	0	0	0	1	2	0	1	0	0	.231
Martinez, P	MON	R	14	10	3.51	30	30	2	2	0	0	194.2	158	784	79	76	21	7	3	11	66	1	174	5	2	.227
Martinez, P	HOU	L	0	0	7.40	25	0	0	0	3	0	20.2	29	109	18	17	3	2	1	2	16	1	17	0	1	.330
Martinez, R	LA	R	17	7	3.66	30	30	4	2	0	0	206.1	176	859	95	84	19	7	5	5	81	5	138	3	0	.231
Mathews, T	STL	R	1	1	1.52	23	0	0	0	12	2	29.2	21	120	7	5	1	4	0	0	11	1	28	2	0	.200
Mathews, T	FLA	R	4	4	3.38	57	0	0	0	14	3	82.2	70	332	32	31	9	5	1	1	27	4	72	3	0	.235
Mauser, T	SD	R	0	1	9.53	5	0	0	0	1	0	5.2	4	30	6	6	0	0	0	0	9	0	9	0	0	.190
May, D	ATL	L	0	0	11.25	2	0	0	0	1	0	4.0	10	21	5	5	0	0	1	0	0	0	1	0	0	.500
McCurry, J	PIT	R	1	4	5.02	55	0	0	0	10	1	61.0	82	282	38	34	9	4	0	5	30	4	27	2	0	.337
McElroy, C	CIN	L	3	4	6.02	44	0	0	0	11	0	40.1	46	178	29	27	5	1	3	1	15	3	27	1	0	.291
McMichael, G	ATL	R	7	2	2.79	67	0	0	0	16	2	80.2	64	337	27	25	8	5	0	0	32	9	74	3	0	.213
McMurtry, C	HOU	R	0	1	7.84	11	0	0	0	3	0	10.1	15	56	11	9	0	2	2	1	9	1	4	2	0	.357
Mercker, K	ATL	L	7	8	4.15	29	26	0	0	1	0	143.0	140	622	73	66	16	8	7	3	61	2	102	6	2	.258
Miceli, D	PIT	R	4	4	4.66	58	0	0	0	51	21	58.0	61	264	30	30	7	2	4	4	28	5	56	4	0	.270
Mimbs, M	PHI	L	9	7	4.15	35	19	2	1	6	1	136.2	127	603	70	63	10	6	8	6	75	2	93	9	0	.250
Minor, B	NY	R	4	2	3.66	35	0	0	0	10	1	46.2	44	192	21	19	6	4	0	1	13	1	43	3	0	.253
Mintz, S	SF	R	1	2	7.45	14	0	0	0	3	0	19.1	26	96	16	16	4	2	1	2	12	3	7	0	0	.329
Mlicki, D	NY	R	9	7	4.26	29	25	0	0	1	0	160.2	160	696	82	76	23	8	5	4	54	2	123	5	1	.256
Morel, R	PIT	R	0	1	2.84	5	0	0	0	0	0	6.1	6	23	2	2	0	1	0	0	2	1	3	0	0	.300
Morgan, M	CHI-STL	R	7	7	3.56	21	21	1	0	0	0	131.1	133	548	56	52	12	12	5	6	34	2	61	6	0	.271
Mulholland, T	SF	L	5	13	5.80	29	24	2	0	2	0	149.0	190	666	112	96	25	11	6	4	38	1	65	4	0	.313
Munoz, B	PHI	R	0	2	5.74	3	3	0	0	0	0	15.2	15	70	13	10	2	0	2	3	9	0	6	0	0	.268
Munoz, M	COL	L	2	4	7.42	64	0	0	0	19	2	43.2	54	208	38	36	9	2	2	1	27	0	37	5	0	.307
Murphy, R	LA-FLA	L	1	2	10.95	14	0	0	0	1	0	12.1	14	58	16	15	3	2	0	0	8	1	7	1	0	.292

THE FOLLOWING PITCHERS APPEARED AS PINCH-HITTERS/PINCH-RUNNERS:

PITCHER	TEAM	TOTAL GAMES	
Banks, W	FLA	12	2 GAMES AS PINCH-RUNNER 1 GAME AS PINCH-HITTER
Brewington, J	SF	14	1 GAME AS PINCH-RUNNER
Brocail, D	HOU	37	1 GAME AS PINCH-HITTER
Bullinger, J	CHI	25	1 GAME AS PINCH-HITTER
Burkett, J	FLA	31	1 GAME AS PINCH-HITTER
Drabek, D	HOU	33	2 GAMES AS PINCH-RUNNER
Foster, K	CHI	33	3 GAMES AS PINCH-RUNNER
Green, T	PHI	27	1 GAME AS PINCH-RUNNER
Hickerson, B	COL	18	1 GAME AS PINCH-HITTER
Loaiza, E	PIT	33	1 GAME AS PINCH-HITTER
Mathews, T	FLA	57	1 GAME AS PINCH-HITTER
Mulholland, T	SF	30	1 GAME AS PINCH-RUNNER
Neagle, D	PIT	32	1 GAME AS PINCH-RUNNER
Olivares, O	COL	12	1 GAME AS PINCH-RUNNER
Olivares, O	PHI	5	1 GAME AS PINCH-HITTER
Painter, L	COL	33	1 GAME AS PINCH-HITTER
Pugh, T	CIN	29	1 GAME AS PINCH-HITTER
Reynolds, S	HOU	31	1 GAME AS PINCH-RUNNER
Schmidt, J	ATL	9	1 GAME AS PINCH-HITTER
Swindell, G	HOU	34	1 GAME AS PINCH-HITTER
Wagner, P	PIT	34	1 GAME AS PINCH-HITTER
Wilson, T	SF	19	1 GAME AS PINCH-RUNNER 1 GAME AS PINCH-HITTER
Witt, B	FLA	21	2 GAMES AS PINCH-RUNNER

THE FOLLOWING POSITION PLAYERS HAD PITCHING APPEARANCES AS INDICATED:

PITCHER	TEAM	TOTAL GAMES	
Cangelosi, J	HOU	90	1 GAME PITCHED

STRIKEOUTS PER 9 INNINGS

11.1	Hideo Nomo	L.A.
9.0	John Smoltz	Atl.
8.3	Shane Reynolds	Hou.
8.0	Pedro Martinez	Mon.
7.8	Kevin Foster	Chi.
7.8	Jeff Fassero	Mon.
7.8	Greg Maddux	Atl.
7.6	Pete Schourek	Cin.
7.3	Steve Avery	Atl.
7.0	Chris Hammond	Fla.

OPPONENTS BATTING AVERAGE AGAINST

.182	Hideo Nomo	L.A.
.197	Greg Maddux	Atl.
.227	Pedro Martinez	Mon.
.228	Ismael Valdez	L.A.
.228	Pete Schourek	Cin.
.231	Ramon Martinez	L.A.
.232	John Smoltz	Atl.
.240	Kevin Foster	Chi.
.246	Tom Glavine	Atl.
.246	Joey Hamilton	S.D.

1995 statistics compiled by MLB Baseball Information System. Other statistics were compiled by the Elias Sports Bureau, the official statistician for the National League.

INDIVIDUAL PITCHING RECORDS—1995

PITCHER	TEAM	T	W	L	ERA	G	GS	CG	SHO	GF	SV	IP	H	TBF	R	ER	HR	SH	SF	HB	BB	IBB	SO	WP	BK	OPP AVG
Murray, M	ATL	R	0	2	6.75	4	1	0	0	1	0	10.2	10	46	8	8	3	1	0	1	5	0	3	0	0	.256
Myers, M	FLA	L	0	0	0.00	2	0	0	0	2	0	2.0	1	9	0	0	0	0	0	0	3	0	0	0	0	.167
Myers, R	CHI	L	1	2	3.88	57	0	0	0	47	38	55.2	49	240	25	24	7	2	3	0	28	1	59	0	0	.237
Nabholz, C	CHI	L	0	1	5.40	34	0	0	0	4	0	23.1	22	104	15	14	4	1	2	0	14	3	21	2	0	.253
Navarro, J	CHI	R	14	6	3.28	29	29	1	1	0	0	200.1	194	837	79	73	19	2	3	3	56	7	128	1	0	.251
Neagle, D	PIT	L	13	8	3.43	31	31	5	1	0	0	209.2	221	876	91	80	20	13	6	3	45	3	150	6	0	.273
Nen, R	FLA	R	0	7	3.29	62	0	0	0	54	23	65.2	62	279	26	24	6	0	1	1	23	3	68	2	0	.244
Nichols, R	ATL	R	0	0	5.40	5	0	0	0	0	0	6.2	14	38	11	4	3	0	0	0	5	1	3	0	0	.424
Nied, D	COL	R	0	0	20.77	2	0	0	0	0	0	4.1	11	27	10	10	2	0	0	0	3	0	3	0	0	.458
Nitkowski, C	CIN	L	1	3	6.12	9	7	0	0	0	0	32.1	41	154	25	22	4	2	1	2	15	1	18	1	2	.306
Nomo, H	LA	R	13	6	2.54	28	28	4	3	0	0	191.1	124	780	63	54	14	11	4	5	78	2	236	19	5	.182
Olivares, O	COL-PHI	R	1	4	6.91	16	6	0	0	4	0	41.2	55	195	34	32	5	2	2	3	23	0	22	4	0	.333
Osborne, D	STL	L	4	6	3.81	19	19	0	0	0	0	113.1	112	477	58	48	17	8	3	2	34	2	82	0	0	.260
Osuna, P	LA	R	2	4	4.43	39	0	0	0	8	0	44.2	39	186	22	22	5	2	1	1	20	2	46	1	0	.241
Painter, L	COL	L	3	0	4.37	33	1	0	0	7	1	45.1	55	198	23	22	9	0	0	2	10	0	36	4	1	.296
Palacios, V	STL	R	2	3	5.80	20	5	0	0	3	0	40.1	48	184	29	26	7	2	1	2	19	1	34	1	0	.300
Park, C	LA	R	0	0	4.50	2	1	0	0	0	0	4.0	2	16	2	2	1	0	0	0	2	0	7	0	1	.143
Parra, J	LA	R	0	0	4.35	8	0	0	0	0	0	10.1	10	47	8	5	2	0	1	1	6	1	7	0	1	.256
Parrett, J	STL	R	4	7	3.64	59	0	0	0	17	0	76.2	71	328	33	31	8	5	2	1	28	5	71	7	0	.243
Parris, S	PIT	R	6	6	5.38	15	15	1	1	0	0	82.0	89	360	49	49	12	3	2	7	33	1	61	4	0	.283
Pena, A	FLA-ATL	R	2	0	2.61	27	0	0	0	6	0	31.0	22	121	9	9	3	0	0	0	7	1	39	0	0	.193
Pennington, B	CIN	L	0	0	5.59	6	0	0	0	2	0	9.2	9	47	8	6	0	0	2	1	11	0	7	3	0	.273
Perez, C	MON	L	10	8	3.69	28	23	2	1	2	0	141.1	142	592	61	58	18	6	1	5	28	2	106	8	4	.257
Perez, M	CHI	R	2	6	3.66	68	0	0	0	18	2	71.1	72	308	30	29	8	5	3	4	27	8	49	4	0	.268
Perez, Y	FLA	L	2	6	5.21	69	0	0	0	11	1	46.2	35	205	29	27	6	2	1	2	28	4	47	2	0	.203
Person, R	NY	R	1	0	0.75	3	1	0	0	0	0	12.0	5	44	1	1	1	0	0	0	2	0	10	0	0	.119
Petkovsek, M	STL	R	6	6	4.00	26	21	1	1	1	0	137.1	136	569	71	61	11	4	4	6	35	3	71	1	1	.262
Plesac, D	PIT	L	4	4	3.58	58	0	0	0	16	3	60.1	53	259	26	24	3	4	3	1	27	7	57	1	0	.237
Portugal, M	SF-CIN	R	11	10	4.01	31	31	1	0	0	0	181.2	185	775	91	81	17	9	1	4	56	2	96	7	0	.262
Powell, J	FLA	R	0	0	1.08	9	0	0	0	1	0	8.1	7	38	2	1	0	1	0	2	6	1	4	0	0	.241
Powell, R	HOU-PIT	L	0	2	6.98	27	3	0	0	6	0	29.2	36	148	26	23	6	3	1	2	21	4	20	4	0	.298
Pugh, T	CIN	R	6	5	3.84	28	12	0	0	4	0	98.1	100	413	46	42	13	2	2	1	32	2	38	3	1	.267
Pulsipher, W	NY	L	5	7	3.98	17	17	2	0	0	0	126.2	122	530	58	56	11	2	1	4	45	0	81	2	1	.255
Quantrill, P	PHI	R	11	12	4.67	33	29	0	0	1	0	179.1	212	784	102	93	20	9	6	6	44	3	103	0	3	.295
Rapp, P	FLA	R	14	7	3.44	28	28	3	2	0	0	167.1	158	716	72	64	10	8	0	7	76	2	102	7	0	.253
Reed, R	CIN	R	0	0	5.82	4	3	0	0	1	0	17.0	18	70	12	11	5	1	0	0	3	0	10	0	0	.273
Reed, S	COL	R	5	2	2.14	71	0	0	0	15	3	84.0	61	327	24	20	8	3	1	1	21	3	79	0	2	.203
Rekar, B	COL	R	4	6	4.98	15	14	1	0	0	0	85.0	95	375	51	47	11	7	4	3	24	2	60	3	2	.282
Remlinger, M	NY-CIN	L	0	1	6.75	7	0	0	0	4	0	6.2	9	34	6	5	1	1	0	0	5	0	7	0	0	.321
Reynolds, S	HOU	R	10	11	3.47	30	30	3	2	0	0	189.1	196	792	87	73	15	8	0	2	37	6	175	7	1	.263
Reynoso, A	COL	R	7	7	5.32	20	18	0	0	0	0	93.0	116	418	61	55	12	8	2	5	36	3	40	2	0	.316
Ricci, C	PHI	R	1	0	1.80	7	0	0	0	3	0	10.0	9	40	2	2	0	1	2	1	3	0	9	0	0	.273
Rijo, J	CIN	R	5	4	4.17	14	14	0	0	0	0	69.0	76	295	33	32	6	3	3	0	22	1	62	3	0	.285
Ritz, K	COL	R	11	11	4.21	31	28	0	0	3	2	173.1	171	743	91	81	16	8	5	6	65	3	120	6	0	.259
Rivera, R	CHI	L	0	0	5.40	7	0	0	0	2	0	5.0	8	23	3	3	1	0	0	0	2	0	2	0	0	.381
Rodriguez, F	LA	R	1	1	2.53	11	0	0	0	5	0	10.2	11	45	3	3	2	0	0	0	5	0	5	0	0	.275
Rodriguez, R	STL	L	0	0	0.00	1	0	0	0	0	0	1.2	0	4	0	0	0	0	0	0	0	0	0	0	0	.000
Rojas, M	MON	R	1	4	4.12	59	0	0	0	48	30	67.2	69	302	32	31	2	2	1	7	29	4	61	6	0	.262
Roper, J	CIN-SF	R	0	0	12.38	3	2	0	0	0	0	8.0	15	44	12	11	3	1	1	0	6	0	6	0	1	.417
Rosselli, J	SF	L	2	1	8.70	9	5	0	0	0	0	30.0	39	140	29	29	5	2	4	0	20	2	7	0	1	.342
Rueter, K	MON	L	5	3	3.23	9	9	1	1	0	0	47.1	38	184	17	17	3	4	0	1	9	0	28	0	0	.224
Ruffin, B	COL	L	0	1	2.12	37	0	0	0	19	11	34.0	26	140	8	8	1	4	0	0	19	1	23	1	0	.222
Ruffin, J	CIN	R	0	0	1.35	10	0	0	0	6	0	13.1	4	54	3	2	0	0	0	0	11	0	11	3	0	.093
Saberhagen, B	NY-COL	R	7	6	4.18	25	25	3	0	0	0	153.0	165	658	78	71	21	7	3	10	33	3	100	3	0	.273
Sager, A	COL	R	0	0	7.36	10	0	0	0	2	0	14.2	19	70	16	12	1	2	0	0	7	1	10	0	0	.311
Sanders, S	SD	R	5	5	4.30	17	15	1	0	0	0	90.0	79	383	46	43	14	2	2	2	31	4	88	6	1	.228
Scheid, R	FLA	L	0	0	6.10	6	0	0	0	1	0	10.1	14	50	7	7	1	1	1	0	7	0	10	1	0	.341
Schilling, C	PHI	R	7	5	3.57	17	17	1	0	0	0	116.0	96	473	52	46	12	5	2	3	26	2	114	0	1	.220
Schmidt, C	MON	R	0	0	6.97	11	0	0	0	0	0	10.1	15	54	8	8	1	1	0	2	9	0	7	0	0	.357
Schmidt, J	ATL	R	2	2	5.76	9	2	0	0	1	0	25.0	27	119	17	16	2	2	4	1	18	3	19	1	0	.287
Schourek, P	CIN	L	18	7	3.22	29	29	2	0	0	0	190.1	158	754	72	68	17	4	4	8	45	3	160	1	1	.228
Scott, T	MON	R	2	0	3.98	62	0	0	0	15	2	63.1	52	268	30	28	6	4	1	6	23	2	57	4	0	.222
Seanez, R	LA	R	1	3	6.75	37	0	0	0	12	3	34.2	39	159	27	26	5	3	0	1	18	3	29	0	0	.285
Service, S	SF	R	3	1	3.19	28	0	0	0	6	0	31.0	18	129	11	11	4	3	2	2	20	4	30	3	0	.176
Shaw, J	MON	R	1	6	4.62	50	0	0	0	17	3	62.1	58	268	35	32	4	6	1	3	26	4	45	0	0	.250
Slocumb, H	PHI	R	5	6	2.89	61	0	0	0	54	32	65.1	64	289	26	21	2	4	0	1	35	3	63	3	0	.257
Small, A	FLA	R	1	0	1.42	7	0	0	0	1	0	6.1	7	32	2	1	1	0	0	0	6	0	5	0	0	.269
Smiley, J	CIN	L	12	5	3.46	28	27	1	0	0	0	176.2	173	724	72	68	11	17	5	4	39	3	124	5	1	.263
Smith, P	CIN	R	1	2	6.66	11	2	0	0	3	0	24.1	30	106	19	18	8	1	3	1	7	1	14	1	0	.319
Smoltz, J	ATL	R	12	7	3.18	29	29	2	1	0	0	192.2	166	808	76	68	15	13	5	4	72	8	193	13	0	.232
Springer, D	PHI	R	0	3	4.84	4	4	0	0	0	0	22.1	21	94	15	12	3	2	0	1	9	1	15	1	0	.256
Springer, R	PHI	R	0	0	3.71	14	0	0	0	3	0	26.2	22	112	11	11	5	1	2	2	10	3	32	1	0	.227
Stanton, M	ATL	L	1	1	5.59	26	0	0	0	10	1	19.1	31	94	14	12	3	2	1	1	6	2	13	1	1	.369
Sturtze, T	CHI	R	0	0	9.00	2	0	0	0	0	0	2.0	2	9	2	2	1	0	0	0	1	0	0	0	0	.250
Sullivan, S	CIN	R	0	0	4.91	3	0	0	0	1	0	3.2	4	17	2	2	0	1	0	0	2	0	2	0	0	.286
Swartzbaugh, D	CHI	R	0	0	0.00	7	0	0	0	2	0	7.1	5	27	2	0	0	0	0	0	3	1	5	0	0	.208
Swift, B	COL	R	9	3	4.94	19	19	0	0	0	0	105.2	122	463	62	58	12	6	1	1	43	2	68	2	0	.296
Swindell, G	HOU	L	10	9	4.47	33	26	1	1	3	0	153.0	180	659	86	76	21	4	8	2	39	2	96	3	0	.297
Tabaka, J	SD-HOU	L	1	0	3.23	34	0	0	0	6	0	30.2	27	128	11	11	2	0	0	0	17	1	25	1	0	.243
Tapani, K	LA	R	4	2	5.05	13	11	0	0	0	0	57.0	72	255	37	32	8	3	2	1	14	2	43	1	0	.306
Telgheder, D	NY	R	1	2	5.61	7	4	0	0	2	0	25.2	34	118	18	16	4	3	1	0	7	3	16	0	1	.318
Thobe, J	MON	R	0	0	9.00	4	0	0	0	2	0	4.0	6	21	4	4	0	0	0	0	3	0	0	1	0	.333
Thobe, T	ATL	L	0	0	10.80	3	0	0	0	1	0	3.1	7	17	4	4	0	0	0	0	0	0	2	0	0	.412
Thompson, M	COL	R	2	3	6.53	21	5	0	0	3	0	51.0	73	240	42	37	7	4	4	1	22	2	30	2	0	.349

1996 IMPORTANT DATES TO REMEMBER

Jan. 5-16 Period in which player may make submission to binding arbitration.

Jan. 8 Last day for former clubs to re-sign players who refused arbitration.

Feb. 15 First date pitchers, catchers and injured players can **voluntarily** work out at spring training.

Feb. 20 First date all others can **voluntarily** work out at spring training.

Feb. 27 Earliest mandatory date for first spring training workout.

Mar. 2 First date to renew contracts. Ten-day renewal period ends on March 11th.

Mar. 6 Earliest date to request major league and special waivers on players chosen in the 1995 Major League Rule 5 draft meeting or draft-excluded players acquired after August 15, 1995.

Mar. 11 First date players chosen in the 1995 Major League Rule 5 draft meeting or draft-excluded players acquired after August 15, 1995 may be assigned to a National Association club.

Mar. 31 Official opening of the 1996 Championship Season.

Apr. 29 Waivers secured on or after November 11th expire at 5:00 P.M. (EDT).

Apr. 30 New waiver period. Waivers secured on or after this date are good through 5:00 P.M. (EDT) July 31st. Beginning today, outright assignments to National Association may be made only with outright waivers in effect.

May 1 First day former clubs may re-sign free agent players who refused binding arbitration and were unsigned after January 8th.

May 15 Earliest date Clubs may re-sign players whom they unconditionally released after midnight, August 31, 1995.

May 28 Start of amateur free agent closed period re summer draft—12:01 A.M. (EDT).

June 4-6 Summer free agent draft.

July 9 All-Star Game at Veterans Stadium, Philadelphia.

July 31 Waivers secured on or after April 30, 1996 expire 5:00 P.M. (EDT). Players may be traded between Major League Clubs until MIDNIGHT (EDT) tonight without any waivers in effect.

Players recalled not to report after midnight tonight for the purpose of securing outright waivers for assignment to the National Association can ONLY be outrighted to the N.A. Club they were recalled from.

Aug. 1 New waiver period begins. Beginning this date and ending on the day following the close of the championship season, players may be assigned between Major League clubs only after Major League waivers have been secured during the current waiver period.

Aug. 5 Hall of Fame Game at Cooperstown (California Angels vs. Montreal Expos).

Aug. 15 Last date to bring player up for "full trial" (to avoid draft excluded status).

Aug. 31 Any player released after midnight tonight may not be re-signed to a Major League contract by the Club that released him until May 15th of the following season.

Aug. 31 Post-season rosters are established at midnight. To be eligible, a player must be a bona fide member of a qualifying club on August 31st and must remain a bona fide member until the end of the season.

Sept. 1 Active player limit increased from 25 to 40 beginning today, until 30 days of the 1997 season have expired, outright assignments to National Association may be made only with special waivers in effect.

Sept. 29 Official closing of the 1996 Championship Season.

Sept. 30 Beginning today, players may be traded between Major League Clubs without waivers in effect.

Oct. 1 All players on optional assignment MUST be recalled.

Oct. 9 Last date for requesting major league waivers until November 11.

Oct. 15 Last day (5:00 PM EDT) to assign a potential minor league free agent outright to the N.A.

Close of World Series Commencement of 15-day period during which eligible players may elect free agency.

Nov. 10 Waivers secured on or after August 1, 1996, expire 5:00 P.M. (EST).

Nov. 11 New waiver period begins. Major League waiver requests may be withdrawn by a club on any player only once in each waiver period; subsequent Major League waiver requests in that period are irrevocable.

Nov. TBA Last date to file Rookie, A, AA and AAA reserve lists with National Association and Commissioner. Also, last date to file Major League reserve lists with League and Commissioner.

Nov. TBA No contract of a major league player shall be assigned to a club of lower classification during the period from 5:00 P.M. (EST) of the Monday preceding the Major League draft meeting until draft meeting has been concluded.

Dec. 20 Last date to tender contracts.

Note: A new collective bargaining agreement will take precedence over the dates listed above. These dates, therefore, are subject to change.

INDIVIDUAL PITCHING RECORDS—1995

PITCHER	TEAM	T	W	L	ERA	G	GS	CG	SHO	GF	SV	IP	H	TBF	R	ER	HR	SH	SF	HB	BB	IBB	SO	WP	BK	OPP AVG
Torres, S	SF	R	0	1	9.00	4	1	0	0	2	0	8.0	13	40	8	8	4	0	0	0	7	0	2	0	0	.394
Trachsel, S	CHI	R	7	13	5.15	30	29	2	0	0	0	160.2	174	722	104	92	25	12	5	0	76	8	117	2	1	.277
Urbani, T	STL	L	3	5	3.70	24	13	0	0	2	0	82.2	99	354	40	34	11	6	0	2	21	4	52	5	0	.305
Urbina, U	MON	R	2	2	6.17	7	4	0	0	0	0	23.1	26	109	17	16	6	0	0	0	14	1	15	2	0	.280
Valdes, I	LA	R	13	11	3.05	33	27	6	2	1	1	197.2	168	804	76	67	17	10	5	1	51	5	150	1	3	.228
Valdes, M	FLA	R	0	0	14.14	3	3	0	0	1	0	7.0	17	49	13	11	1	1	1	1	9	0	2	1	0	.459
Valdez, C	SF	R	0	1	6.14	11	0	0	0	3	0	14.2	19	69	10	10	1	0	1	1	8	1	7	1	1	.322
Valdez, S	SF	R	4	5	4.75	13	11	0	0	0	0	66.1	78	290	43	35	12	5	3	3	17	3	29	2	1	.298
Valenzuela, F	SD	L	8	3	4.98	29	15	0	0	5	0	90.1	101	395	53	50	16	10	2	0	34	2	57	4	0	.289
VanLandingham, W	SF	R	6	3	3.67	18	18	1	0	0	0	122.2	124	523	58	50	14	6	5	2	40	2	95	5	4	.264
Veres, D	HOU	R	5	1	2.26	72	0	0	0	15	0	103.1	89	418	29	26	5	6	8	4	30	6	94	4	0	.241
Veres, R	FLA	R	4	4	3.88	47	0	0	0	15	1	48.2	46	215	25	21	6	5	4	1	22	7	31	2	0	.251
Villone, R	SD	L	2	1	4.21	19	0	0	0	8	0	25.2	24	111	12	12	5	0	1	0	11	0	37	2	0	.242
Viola, F	CIN	L	0	1	6.28	3	3	0	0	0	0	14.1	20	64	11	10	3	0	1	0	3	1	4	1	0	.333
Wade, T	ATL	L	0	1	4.50	3	0	0	0	1	0	4.0	3	18	2	2	1	2	0	0	4	0	3	1	0	.214
Wagner, B	HOU	L	0	0	0.00	1	0	0	0	1	0	0.1	0	1	0	0	0	0	0	0	0	0	0	0	0	.000
Wagner, P	PIT	R	5	16	4.80	33	25	3	1	1	0	165.0	174	725	96	88	18	7	2	7	72	7	120	8	0	.273
Walker, M	CHI	R	1	3	3.22	42	0	0	0	12	1	44.2	45	206	22	16	2	4	4	0	24	3	20	3	1	.259
Walker, P	NY	R	0	1	4.58	13	0	0	0	10	0	17.2	24	79	9	9	3	0	1	0	5	0	5	0	0	.329
Wall, D	HOU	R	3	1	5.55	6	5	0	0	0	0	24.1	33	110	19	15	5	0	2	0	5	0	16	1	0	.320
Watson, A	STL	L	7	9	4.96	21	19	0	0	0	0	114.1	126	491	68	63	17	2	1	5	41	0	49	2	2	.285
Weathers, D	FLA	R	4	5	5.98	28	15	0	0	4	0	90.1	104	419	68	60	8	7	3	5	52	3	60	3	0	.295
Wells, D	CIN	L	6	5	3.59	11	11	0	0	0	0	72.2	74	300	34	29	6	4	1	0	16	4	50	1	1	.265
Wendell, T	CHI	R	3	1	4.92	43	0	0	0	17	0	60.1	71	270	35	33	11	3	3	2	24	4	50	1	0	.298
West, D	PHI	L	3	2	3.79	8	8	0	0	0	0	38.0	33	163	17	16	5	2	0	1	19	0	25	1	0	.241
White, G	MON	L	1	2	7.01	19	1	0	0	8	0	25.2	26	115	21	20	7	2	3	0	9	0	25	0	0	.260
White, R	PIT	R	2	3	4.75	15	9	0	0	2	0	55.0	66	247	33	29	3	3	3	2	18	0	29	2	0	.299
Williams, B	SD	R	3	10	6.00	44	6	0	0	7	0	72.0	79	337	54	48	3	7	1	3	38	4	75	7	1	.279
Williams, M	PHI	R	3	3	3.29	33	8	0	0	7	0	87.2	78	367	37	32	10	5	3	3	29	2	57	7	0	.239
Williams, T	LA	R	2	2	5.12	16	0	0	0	5	0	19.1	19	83	11	11	3	1	0	1	7	2	8	0	0	.264
Wilson, G	PIT	R	0	1	5.02	10	0	0	0	1	0	14.1	13	61	8	8	2	0	2	0	5	0	8	1	0	.241
Wilson, T	SF	L	3	4	3.92	17	17	0	0	0	0	82.2	82	354	42	36	8	5	2	4	38	1	38	0	1	.269
Witt, B	FLA	R	2	7	3.90	19	19	1	0	0	0	110.2	104	472	52	48	9	8	5	3	47	1	95	2	0	.251
Wohlers, M	ATL	R	7	3	2.09	65	0	0	0	49	25	64.2	51	269	16	15	2	2	2	0	24	3	90	4	0	.211
Woodall, B	ATL	R	1	1	6.10	9	0	0	0	3	0	10.1	8	52	10	7	1	0	0	0	8	1	5	1	0	.310
Worrell, T	SD	R	4	4	4.73	9	0	0	0	4	0	13.1	16	63	7	7	2	1	0	1	6	0	13	1	0	.291
Worrell, T	LA	R	4	1	2.02	59	0	0	0	53	32	62.1	50	249	15	14	4	1	2	1	19	2	61	2	0	.221
Young, A	CHI	R	3	4	3.70	32	1	0	0	8	2	41.1	47	181	20	17	5	1	0	3	14	2	15	6	0	.288

1995 CLUB PITCHING

CLUB	W	L	ERA	G	CG	SHO	REL	SV	IP	H	R	ER	HR	HB	BB	IBB	SO	WP	BK	OPP AVG
ATLANTA	90	54	3.44	144	18	11	339	34	1291.2	1184	540	494	107	32	436	46	1087	38	4	.244
LOS ANGELES	78	66	3.66	144	16	11	355	37	1295.0	1188	609	526	125	37	462	45	1060	49	12	.243
NEW YORK	69	75	3.88	144	9	9	298	36	1291.0	1296	618	556	133	35	401	48	901	39	12	.262
CINCINNATI	85	59	4.03	144	8	10	330	38	1289.1	1270	623	578	131	31	424	32	903	58	10	.260
HOUSTON	76	68	4.06	144	6	8	394	32	1320.1	1357	674	596	118	50	460	52	1056	53	6	.266
ST. LOUIS	62	81	4.09	143	4	6	377	38	1265.2	1290	658	575	135	40	445	24	842	51	6	.268
MONTREAL	66	78	4.11	144	7	9	396	42	1283.2	1286	638	586	128	59	416	26	950	45	9	.262
CHICAGO	73	71	4.13	144	6	12	414	45	1301.0	1313	671	597	162	34	518	68	926	38	6	.262
SAN DIEGO	70	74	4.13	144	6	10	337	35	1284.2	1242	672	590	142	51	512	37	1047	60	5	.255
PHILADELPHIA	69	75	4.21	144	8	8	341	41	1290.1	1241	658	603	134	55	538	36	980	57	10	.254
FLORIDA	67	76	4.27	143	12	7	400	29	1286.0	1299	673	610	139	46	562	54	994	36	5	.264
PITTSBURGH	58	86	4.70	144	11	7	391	29	1275.1	1407	736	666	130	57	477	50	871	65	4	.283
SAN FRANCISCO	67	77	4.86	144	12	5	381	34	1293.0	1368	776	699	173	56	505	51	801	43	15	.275
COLORADO	77	67	4.97	144	1	1	456	43	1288.1	1443	783	711	160	41	512	31	891	62	13	.286
TOTALS	1007	1007	4.18	1007	124	114	5209	513	18056.0	18184	9329	8387	1917	624	6668	613	13309	694	117	.263

TEN TOUGHEST TO FAN

(minimum: 446 plate appearances)

Player and Club	Games	PA	SO	SO Rate*
Gwynn, S.D.	135	577	15	38.5
Jefferies, Phi.	114	521	26	20.0
Grace, Chi.	143	627	46	13.6
Reed, S.D.	131	515	38	13.6
Butler, N.Y.-L.A.	129	596	51	11.7
Larkin, Cin.	131	567	49	11.6
Lemke, Atl.	116	453	40	11.3
Segui, N.Y.-Mon.	130	511	47	10.9
Finley, S.D.	139	630	62	10.2
Grissom, Atl.	139	606	61	9.9

*Average plate appearances per strikeout.

TEN TOUGHEST TO DOUBLE

(minimum: 446 plate appearances)

Player and Club	Games	PA	GIDP	DP Rate*
Tarasco, Mon.	126	495	2	219.0
Butler, N.Y.-L.A.	129	596	5	102.6
Jordan, St.L.	131	525	5	98.0
Biggio, Hou.	141	673	6	92.2
Martin, Pit.	124	486	5	87.8
Offerman, L.A.	119	511	5	85.8
Larkin, Cin.	131	567	6	82.7
Justice, Atl.	120	491	4	82.2
Mondesi, L.A.	139	580	7	76.6
Pendleton, Fla.	133	557	7	73.3

*Average at bats per grounded into double play.

TOP TEN CONTROL ARTISTS

(minimum: 144 innings)

Pitcher and Club	Games	IP	BB	BB/9 INN
Maddux, Atl.	28	209.2	23	0.99
Reynolds, Hou.	30	189.1	37	1.76
Neagle, Pit.	31	209.2	45	1.93
Saberhagen, N.Y.-Col.	25	153.0	33	1.94
Smiley, Cin.	28	176.2	39	1.99
Schourek, Cin.	29	190.1	45	2.13
Quantrill, Phi.	33	179.1	44	2.21
Swindell, Hou.	33	153.0	39	2.29
Mulholland, S.F.	29	149.0	38	2.30
Valdes, L.A.	33	197.2	51	2.32

NATIONAL LEAGUE ANNUAL ATTENDANCE FIGURES—1901-1995

1901— 1,920,031	1921— 3,986,984	1941— 4,777,647	1961— 8,731,502	1981—12,478,390
1902— 1,683,012	1922— 3,941,820	1942— 4,353,353	1962—11,360,159	1982—21,507,425
1903— 2,390,362	1923— 4,069,817	1943— 3,769,342	1963—11,382,227	1983—21,549,285
1904— 2,664,271	1924— 4,340,644	1944— 3,974,588	1964—12,045,190	1984—20,781,436
1905— 2,734,310	1925— 4,353,704	1945— 5,260,703	1965—13,581,136	1985—22,292,154
1906— 2,781,213	1926— 4,920,399	1946— 8,902,107	1966—15,051,471	1986—22,333,471
1907— 2,640,220	1927— 5,309,917	1947—10,388,470	1967—12,971,430	1987—24,734,155
1908— 3,512,108	1928— 4,881,097	1948— 9,770,743	1968—11,758,358	1988—24,499,268
1909— 3,496,420	1929— 4,925,713	1949— 9,484,718	1969—15,094,946	1989—25,323,834
1910— 3,494,544	1930— 5,446,532	1950— 8,320,616	1970—16,662,198	1990—24,491,508
1911— 3,231,768	1931— 4,583,815	1951— 7,244,002	1971—17,324,857	1991—24,696,172
1912— 2,735,759	1932— 3,841,334	1952— 6,339,148	1972—15,529,730	1992—24,112,770
1913— 2,831,531	1933— 3,162,821	1953— 7,419,721	1973—16,675,322	1993—36,923,856*
1914— 1,707,397	1934— 3,200,105	1954— 8,013,519	1974—16,978,314	1994—25,807,819
1915— 2,430,142	1935— 3,657,309	1955— 7,674,412	1975—16,600,490	1995—25,110,248
1916— 3,051,634	1936— 3,903,691	1956— 8,994,525	1976—16,660,529	
1917— 2,361,136	1937— 4,204,228	1957— 8,819,601	1977—19,070,228	Total—960,867,043
1918— 1,372,127	1938— 4,560,837	1958—10,164,596	1978—20,106,921	
1919— 2,878,203	1939— 4,707,177	1959— 9,994,525	1979—21,178,419	
1920— 4,036,575	1940— 4,389,693	1960—10,684,963	1980—21,124,084	

*National League Record.

ATTENDANCE—1995-1994

CLUB	1995 Openings	HOME 1995	HOME 1994	ROAD 1995	ROAD 1994
Atlanta	72	2,561,831	2,539,240	2,024,693	2,201,468
Chicago	71	1,918,265	1,845,208	1,951,435	1,860,891
Cincinnati	71	1,837,649	1,897,681	1,781,065	1,599,126
Colorado	72	3,390,037	3,281,511	1,794,948	1,758,853
Florida	70	1,700,466	1,937,467	1,718,138	1,796,836
Houston	71	1,363,801	1,561,136	1,650,552	1,701,925
Los Angeles	72	2,766,251	2,279,355	1,917,341	2,068,070
Montreal	72	1,309,618	1,276,250	1,740,321	1,900,467
New York	71	1,273,183	1,151,471	1,827,201	1,821,608
Philadelphia	71	2,043,598	2,290,971	1,660,641	1,716,129
Pittsburgh	70	905,517	1,222,520	1,742,370	1,798,714
St. Louis	72	1,756,727	1,866,544	1,747,948	2,040,295
San Diego	71	1,041,805	953,857	1,725,753	1,704,300
San Francisco	72	1,241,500	1,704,608	1,827,842	1,839,137
TOTALS	998	25,110,248	25,807,819	25,110,248	25,807,819

1996 NATIONAL LEAGUE TICKET PRICES*

*Prices subject to change

ATLANTA
- Dugout Level $25.00
- Club $20.00
- Field Level $17.00
- Lower Pavilion $12.00
- Upper Level $10.00
- Upper Pavilion $5.00

CHICAGO#
- Club Box $19.00
- Field Box $19.00
- Terrace Box $15.00
- Upper Deck Box $15.00
- Family Section $15.00
- Terrace Reserved $12.00
- Upper Deck Reserved
  - Adult (14 & Over) $9.00
  - Child (13 & Under) $6.00
- Bleacher $10.00
- Senior Citizen (Weds.) $4.00
- Handicapped $12.00
- Standing Room Only $6.00
- Family Section $11.00

CINCINNATI
- Blue Level Box Seats $11.50
- Green & Yellow Level Box Seats $10.00
- Red Level Box Seats $9.00
- Green Level Reserved $8.00
- Red Level Reserved $6.50
- "Top Six" Reserved $3.50

COLORADO
- Infield Box $20.00
- Outfield Box $16.00
- Club Level $26.00
- Lower Reserved $12.00
- Upper Reserved $10.00
- Rightfield Box $10.00
- Rightfield Mezzanine $8.00
- Lower Rightfield Reserved $6.00
- Upper Rightfield Reserved $5.00
- Pavilion $5.00
- Centerfield Bleachers $4.00
- Rockpile $1.00

FLORIDA
- Club Seats—Zone A $30.00
- Club Seats—Zone B $20.00
- Club Seats—Zone C $13.00
- Terrace Box $13.00
- Mezzanine Box $11.00
- Mezzanine Reserved $7.00
- Outfield Reserved—Adults $8.00
- Outfield Reserved—Kids $3.50
- General Admission—Adults $4.00
- General Admission—Kids (12 and under) $1.50

HOUSTON
- Star Deck $19.00
- Field Box $16.00
- Mezzanine $14.00
- Loge $11.00
- Upper Box $7.00
- Upper Reserved $5.00

HOUSTON (Cont.)
- Pavilion (General Admission) $4.00
- Pavilion (Children) $1.00

LOS ANGELES
- Box Seats (Inner) $14.00
- Box Seats (Middle) $12.00
- Box Seats (Outer) $11.00
- Reserved Seats (Between Dugouts) $9.00
- Reserved Seats $8.00
- General Admission $6.00
- Children General Admission (at game time) $3.00

MONTREAL*
- VIP Box $28.00
- Box Seats $19.00
- Terrace $11.00
- General Admission, Bleachers $7.00

*Figures are Canadian dollars.

NEW YORK
- Box Seats $17.00
- Upper Level Box $12.00
- Loge & Mezzanine Reserved $13.00
- Back Rows, Loge & Mezzanine Reserved $6.50
- Upper Level Reserved $6.50
- Picnic Area (Groups of 100 or more) $13.00
- Senior Citizen (Day of Game Only) $1.00

PHILADELPHIA
- Field Boxes $16.00
- Terrace & Loge Boxes $14.00
- Reserved .... $5.00 & $10.00

PITTSBURGH
- Club Boxes $15.00
- Family Boxes, Terrace Boxes $10.00
- Reserve (Upper & Outfield) $8.00
- General Admission $5.00
- Youth General Admission (14 and under) $1.00

ST. LOUIS
- Loge Box (Rows 1-4) $14.00
- Loge Box (Rows 5-7) $12.00
- Loge Reserved $10.50
- Terrace Boxes $12.00
- Terrace Reserved $9.50
- Youth Terrace Reserved (15 and under) $6.00
- General Admission $5.50
- Youth General Admission (15 and under) $2.00

SAN DIEGO
- Sky Boxes, Field Level/Infield $14.00
- Field Level/Outfield, Plaza Level/Infield $13.00
- Plaza Level/Outfield $12.00
- Loge Level $11.00
- Press Level $10.00
- Left Field Grandstand $7.00
- High Fives, Bleachers $5.00

SAN FRANCISCO
- Low Box MVP $20.00
- Lower Box, Upper Box MVP $15.50
- Lower Reserve, Upper Box $12.50
- Upper Reserve $7.50
- Pavilion, Senior Lower Reserve $6.50
- Child Upper Reserve $5.50
- Senior Upper Reserve $4.00
- Child Pavilion, Senior Pavilion $3.50

#Prices are less for weekday afternoon games in April, May and September.

CLUB	SEASON AT HOME	SEASON ON ROAD	SINGLE DAY GAMES	NIGHT GAMES	DOUBLEHEADERS (DAY)
Atlanta	3,884,725 in 1993	2,944,157 in 1993	51,275 vs. Los Angeles—6/26/66	53,775 vs. Los Angeles—4/8/74	46,489 vs. San Francisco—7/18/71
Chicago	2,653,763 in 1993	2,592,790 in 1993	46,572 vs. Brooklyn—5/18/47	39,002 vs. Pittsburgh—8/7/89	46,965 vs. Pittsburgh—5/31/48
Cincinnati	2,629,708 in 1976	2,532,257 in 1993	55,456 vs. Montreal—4/5/93	53,790 vs. Houston—9/17/83	52,147 vs. Atlanta—6/23/74
Colorado	4,483,350 in 1993	2,695,071 in 1993	80,227 vs. Montreal—4/9/93	73,957 vs. San Francisco—6/24/94	60,613 vs. New York—8/21/93
Florida	3,064,847 in 1993	2,701,068 in 1993	45,900 vs. New York—10/3/93	45,796 vs. San Francisco—8/27/93	35,019 vs. San Francisco—6/1/93
Houston	2,278,217 in 1980	2,421,566 in 1993	49,442 vs. Los Angeles—9/5/65	50,908 vs. Los Angeles—6/22/66	45,115 vs. Atlanta—8/4/79
Los Angeles	3,608,881 in 1982	2,663,828 in 1993	78,672 vs. San Francisco—4/18/58	72,140 vs. Cincinnati—8/16/61 (tn)	53,856 vs. Cincinnati—7/7/63
Montreal	2,320,651 in 1983	2,620,064 in 1993	57,592 vs. Philadelphia—4/15/77	57,121 vs. Philadelphia—10/3/80	59,282 vs. St. Louis—9/16/79
New York	3,055,445 in 1988	2,660,426 in 1993	56,738 vs. Los Angeles—6/23/68	56,658 vs. San Francisco—5/13/66	57,175 vs. Los Angeles—6/13/65
Philadelphia	3,137,674 in 1993	2,666,219 in 1993	60,985 vs. Chicago—4/9/93	63,816 vs. Cincinnati—7/3/84	40,720 vs. Brooklyn—5/11/47
Pittsburgh	2,065,302 in 1991	2,507,346 in 1993	51,726 vs. San Diego—6/6/76	54,274 vs. Montreal—4/8/91	49,341 vs. Houston—7/16/72
St. Louis	3,080,980 in 1989	2,612,017 in 1993	52,298 vs. Chicago—8/8/93	53,415 vs. Chicago—7/30/94	49,743 vs. Atlanta—6/23/68
San Diego	2,210,352 in 1985	2,534,072 in 1993	53,375 vs. San Francisco—6/22/85	54,841 vs. Montreal—5/10/91	43,473 vs. Philadelphia—6/13/76
San Francisco	2,606,354 in 1993	2,772,975 in 1993	58,077 vs. Pittsburgh—4/4/94	55,920 vs. Cincinnati—6/20/78	53,179 vs. Los Angeles—7/31/83